Florida For Dummies, 1st Edition

Cheat Sheet

Greater Miami

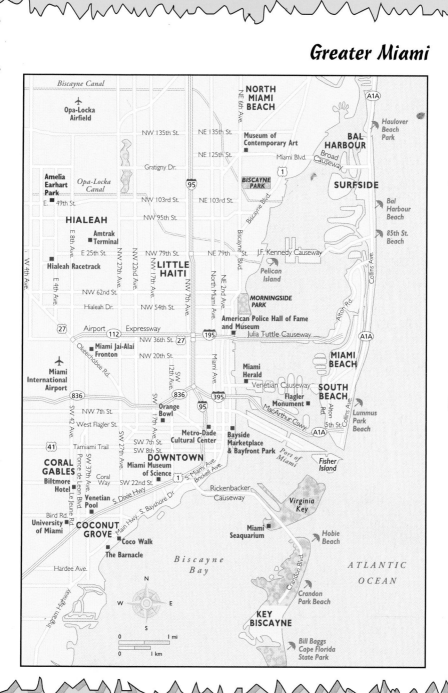

For Dummies®: Bestselling Book Series for Beginners

Florida For Dummies,
1st Edition

Cheat Sheet

Sarasota & Bradenton

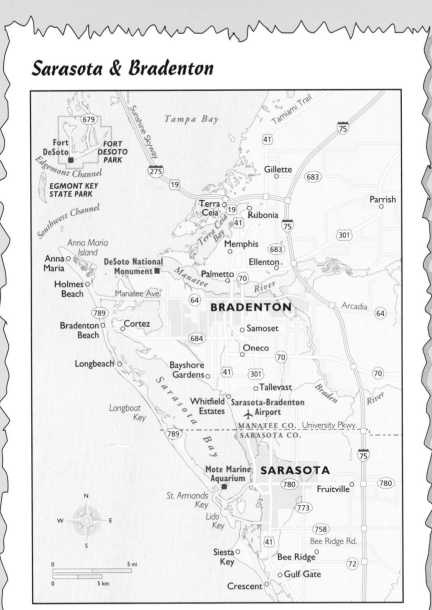

Hungry Minds™

For Dummies®: Bestselling Book Series for Beginners

Katsoulis

Katsoulis

Florida

FOR

DUMMIES®

1ST EDITION

by Jim and Cynthia Tunstall

Hungry Minds™

HUNGRY MINDS, INC.

New York, NY ◆ Cleveland, OH ◆ Indianapolis, IN

Florida For Dummies®

Published by:
Hungry Minds, Inc.
909 Third Avenue
New York, NY 10022
www.hungryminds.com
www.dummies.com

Library of Congress Control Number: 00-112175

ISBN: 0-7645-6361-0

ISSN: 1531-7617

Printed in the United States of America

10 9 8 7 6 5 4 3 2 1

1B/RX/QV/QR/IN

Distributed in the United States by Hungry Minds, Inc.

Distributed by CDG Books Canada Inc. for Canada; by Transworld Publishers Limited in the United Kingdom; by IDG Norge Books for Norway; by IDG Sweden Books for Sweden; by IDG Books Australia Publishing Corporation Pty. Ltd. for Australia and New Zealand; by TransQuest Publishers Pte Ltd. for Singapore, Malaysia, Thailand, Indonesia, and Hong Kong; by Gotop Information Inc. for Taiwan; by ICG Muse, Inc. for Japan; by Intersoft for South Africa; by Eyrolles for France; by International Thomson Publishing for Germany, Austria and Switzerland; by Distribuidora Cuspide for Argentina; by LR International for Brazil; by Galileo Libros for Chile; by Ediciones ZETA S.C.R. Ltda. for Peru; by WS Computer Publishing Corporation, Inc., for the Philippines; by Contemporanea de Ediciones for Venezuela; by Express Computer Distributors for the Caribbean and West Indies; by Micronesia Media Distributor, Inc. for Micronesia; by Chips Computadoras S.A. de C.V. for Mexico; by Editorial Norma de Panama S.A. for Panama; by American Bookshops for Finland.

For general information on Hungry Minds' products and services please contact our Customer Care department; within the U.S. at 800-762-2974, outside the U.S. at 317-572-3993 or fax 317-572-4002.

For sales inquiries and resellers information, including discounts, premium and bulk quantity sales and foreign language translations please contact our Customer Care department at 800-434-3422, fax 317-572-4002 or write to Hungry Minds, Inc., Attn: Customer Care department, 10475 Crosspoint Boulevard, Indianapolis, IN 46256.

For information on licensing foreign or domestic rights, please contact our Sub-Rights Customer Care department at 650-653-7098.

For information on using Hungry Minds' products and services in the classroom or for ordering examination copies, please contact our Educational Sales department at 800-434-2086 or fax 317-572-4005.

Please contact our Public Relations department at 212-884-5174 for press review copies or 212-884-5000 for author interviews and other publicity information or fax 212-884-5400.

For authorization to photocopy items for corporate, personal, or educational use, please contact Copyright Clearance Center, 222 Rosewood Drive, Danvers, MA 01923, or fax 978-750-4470.

Hungry Minds™ is a trademark of Hungry Minds, Inc.

About the Authors

Jim and Cynthia Tunstall are the dummies behind this guide.

Jim has been an editor and writer for The Tampa Tribune since 1978. Cynthia is a freelance writer and photographer whose work has appeared in *Better Homes & Gardens, Elegant Bride,* and the *Atlanta Journal-Constitution*, among others. Together, they've authored six travel guides, including *Frommer's Walt Disney World & Orlando 2001* and *Walt Disney World & Orlando For Dummies 2001.*

The Tunstalls are native Floridians who live in Lecanto, Florida — a radar blip that's 70 miles west of the Magic Mickey. They currently share space with two horses, two dogs, two cats, a parrot, and a lot of cranky wildlife, including a gopher tortoise named Ike.

Authors' Acknowledgments

Now we know why those folks babble on so much at the Academy Awards.

Angie Ranck at the Orlando/Orange County Convention & Visitors Bureau and Sandra Robert at Walt Disney World make sure that we survive our time in the trenches. Kudos as well to Rhonda Murphy and Marga Senzig at Universal Orlando, and to Michelle Abram at the Miami Convention and Visitors Bureau.

We would also like to thank the many Society of American Travel Writers associate members who helped us compile this book.

And Naomi Kraus, lord high czarina and our editor at Hungryminds.com, has soft hands. She keeps our style intact, while saving us, in a literary sense, from wearing the emperor's clothes.

Publisher's Acknowledgments

We're proud of this book; please send us your comments through our Online Registration Form located at www.dummies.com.

Some of the people who helped bring this book to market include the following:

Editorial

Editors: Sherri Fugit, Naomi Kraus

Copy Editors: Mike Baker, Esmeralda St. Clair

Cartographer: Elizabeth Puhl

Editorial Manager: Jennifer Ehrlich

Editorial Assistant: Jennifer Young

Senior Photo Editor: Richard Fox

Assistant Photo Editor: Michael Ross

Production

Project Coordinator: Maridee Ennis

Layout and Graphics: Amy Adrian, LeAndra Johnson, Kristin Pickett, Heather Pope, Julie Trippetti

Proofreaders: Dave Faust, Carl Pierce, TECHBOOKS Production Services

Indexer: TECHBOOKS Production Services

Special Help: Tonya Maddox

General and Administrative

Hungry Minds, Inc.: John Kilcullen, CEO; Bill Barry, President and COO; John Ball, Executive VP, Operations & Administration; John Harris, CFO

Hungry Minds Consumer Reference Group

Business: Kathleen A. Welton, Vice President and Publisher; Kevin Thornton, Acquisitions Manager

Cooking/Gardening: Jennifer Feldman, Associate Vice President and Publisher

Education/Reference: Diane Graves Steele, Vice President and Publisher; Greg Tubach, Publishing Director

Lifestyles: Kathleen Nebenhaus, Vice President and Publisher; Tracy Boggier, Managing Editor

Pets: Dominique De Vito, Associate Vice President and Publisher; Tracy Boggier, Managing Editor

Travel: Michael Spring, Vice President and Publisher; Suzanne Jannetta, Editorial Director; Brice Gosnell, Managing Editor

Hungry Minds Consumer Editorial Services: Kathleen Nebenhaus, Vice President and Publisher; Kristin A. Cocks, Editorial Director; Cindy Kitchel, Editorial Director

Hungry Minds Consumer Production: Debbie Stailey, Production Director

♦

The publisher would like to give special thanks to Patrick J. McGovern, without whom this book would not have been possible.

♦

Contents at a Glance

Introduction *1*

Part I: Getting Started *7*

Chapter 1: Discovering the Best of Florida 9
Chapter 2: Deciding When and Where to Go 17
Chapter 3: Planning Your Budget 35
Chapter 4: Planning for Travelers with Special Needs 43

Part II: Ironing Out the Details *51*

Chapter 5: Getting to Florida 53
Chapter 6: Getting Around 67
Chapter 7: Booking Your Accommodations 75
Chapter 8: Managing Your Money 83
Chapter 9: Tying Up Last-Minute Loose Ends 87

Part III: South Florida *97*

Chapter 10: Settling into Miami 99
Chapter 11: Exploring Miami 129
Chapter 12: Unlocking the Keys 149
Chapter 13: The Everglades 185
Chapter 14: The Gold Coast 201

Part IV: The Gulf Coast *233*

Chapter 15: Tampa 235
Chapter 16: St. Petersburg, Clearwater, and Beaches 261
Chapter 17: Sarasota, Fort Myers, and Naples 287

Part V: Visiting Central Florida: Mickey Mania *317*

Chapter 18: Settling into Walt Disney World and Orlando 319
Chapter 19: The Theme Parks 349
Chapter 20: Exploring the Rest of Orlando 385

Part VI: The Great North *405*

Chapter 21: Daytona Beach 407
Chapter 22: Northeast Florida 427
Chapter 23: The Panhandle 455

Part VII: The Part of Tens *481*

Chapter 24: The Top Ten Florida Beaches 483
Chapter 25: Ten or More of Florida's Favorite Foods 487

Appendix: Quick Concierge *491*

Worksheets *499*

Index *507*

Back of Book Registration .... *Back of Book*

Cartoons at a Glance

By Rich Tennant

page 481

page 7

page 233

page 51

page 97

page 405

page 317

Cartoon Information:
Fax: 978-546-7747
E-Mail: richtennant@the5thwave.com
World Wide Web: www.the5thwave.com

Maps at a Glance

Florida 10
Florida Driving Times and Distances 68
Miami at a Glance 104
South Beach Accommodations 110
Miami Beach Accommodations 114
Accommodations Elsewhere in Miami 118
South Beach Dining 123
Miami Beach Dining 125
Dining Elsewhere in Miami..127
Central Miami Attractions 130
Attractions in South Miami-Dade County 137
The Florida Keys 151
Key West..173
The Everglades 186
Fort Lauderdale 206
Palm Beach and Boca Raton 220
Tampa Accommodations and Dining 240
Tampa Attractions 264
Downtown St. Petersburg..264
St. Pete & Clearwater Beaches 274
Sarasota and Bradenton 290
Fort Myers, Sanibel & Naples 301
Orlando Neighborhoods 325
Accommodations & Dining in Walt Disney World &
    Lake Buena Vista 330
Other Orlando Area Accommodations & Dining 335
Accommodations & Dining on International Drive....................................338
Walt Disney World 350
Other Disney Attractions 386
Yet More Attractions in Orlando 391
Daytona Beach..409
St. Augustine..429
Jacksonville..441
Amelia Island and Fernandina Beach 443
The Panhandle 456
Pensacola 458

Table of Contents

Introduction *1*

    About This Book 1

    Foolish Assumptions 2

    Conventions Used in This Book 3

    How This Book Is Organized 4

        Part I: Getting Started 4

        Part II: Ironing Out the Details 4

        Part III: South Florida 4

        Part IV: The Gulf Coast 4

        Part V: Visiting Central Florida: Mickey Mania 5

        Part VI: The Great North 5

        Part VII: The Part of Tens 5

    Icons Used in This Book 6

    Where to Go from Here 6

Part 1: Getting Started *7*

    Chapter 1: Discovering the Best of Florida **9**

        Whetting Your Appetite 9

        Finding the Best Romantic Hideaways 13

        First-Rate Family Attractions 13

        Super Chills and Thrills 14

        Tip-Top Places to Get Tipsy 15

        Party On 15

        Cool Places to Cast Your Reel 16

    Chapter 2: Deciding When and Where to Go **17**

        Diving into Florida's Regions 17

            South Florida 18

            The Gulf Coast 19

            Central Florida 19

            The Great North 20

        The Secret of the Seasons 21

            Springtime in Florida 22

            Heating up the scene in summer 22

            Falling into the tropics 23

            Heading south for the winter 23

        Wising Up about the Weather 24

        Weather Warnings 25

            Making hurricane waves 25

            Tumbling tornadoes 26

            Lightning up the sky 26

            Forgoing some sun 26

            Raining down 27

Florida's Calendar of Events 27
January 28
February 29
March 30
April 30
May 31
June 31
July 31
August 32
September 32
October 32
November 33
December 33

Chapter 3: Planning Your Budget 35
Adding Up the Elements 35
Hitting the road 36
Shacking up 36
Feeding your face 37
Keeping yourself entertained 37
Hitting the stores 38
Boogieing the night away 38
Keeping a Lid on Hidden Expenses 40
Cutting Costs 41

Chapter 4: Planning for Travelers with Special Needs 43
Making Family Travel Fun 43
Planning Tips for the Senior Set 45
Traveling Without Barriers 46
Planning Advice for Gay and Lesbian Travelers 48

Part 11: Ironing Out the Details 51

Chapter 5: Getting to Florida 53
Friend or Foe? Hiring a Travel Agent 53
Packaging Your Travel 55
Buying package tours 55
Taking an escorted tour 56
Finding packagers 57
Making Your Own Arrangements 59
Flying there 59
Finding affordable airfare 60
Booking great deals online 61
Getting There Wingless 63
By car 63
By train 64

Chapter 6: Getting Around 67
Driving Around Florida 67
Minding the road rules 68
Renting some wheels 69

Ringing up the cost of renting a car 70
Booking a rental on the Internet 71
Winging It 71
Riding the Tracks 72
Bussing It 73

Chapter 7: Booking Your Accommodations 75

Avoiding Rack Rates (And Why You Don't Have to Pay Them) 75
Getting the Best Room at the Best Rate 76
Lining Up the Lodgings 77
Pricing our picks 78
The view: To do or not to do 79
Finding the right room 80
Surfing the Web for Hotel Deals 80
Arriving without a Reservation 82

Chapter 8: Managing Your Money 83

Paper, Plastic, or Pocket Change 83
Carrying the cards: Charge! 84
Finding an ATM ASAP 84
Toting traveler's checks 85
Keeping Your Money Safe (And What to Do If It's Stolen) 85

Chapter 9: Tying Up Last-Minute Loose Ends 87

Buying Travel Insurance: Good Idea or Bad? 87
Combating Illness Away from Home 88
Beating the Crowd: Reservations and Tickets 90
Reserving a table 90
Reserving a ticket and getting event information 90
Reserving a green 91
Gearing Up: Practical Packing Advice 91
Packing criteria 92
Packing pointers 92
Dragging along Fido and Fluffy 94

Part III: South Florida *97*

Chapter 10: Settling into Miami 99

Getting There 99
By plane 100
By car 101
By train 101
Orienting Yourself 101
Making Miami by Neighborhood 102
Coconut Grove 102
Coral Gables 103
Downtown Miami 103
Greater Miami 103
Little Havana 104
Miami Beach 105

North Miami Beach 105
South Beach 105
Showing Street Smarts: Where to Get Information
After Arrival 105
Getting Around Miami 106
By car 106
By taxi 106
By bus 107
By rail 107
Staying in Style 107
Miami's Best Hotels 108
Runner-up Accommodations 116
Dining in Miami 119
Miami's Best Restaurants 119
Runner-up Restaurants 126

Chapter 11: Exploring Miami 129

Seeing the Top Sights 129
More Cool Things to See and Enjoy 135
Visiting museums, gardens, parks, and more 135
Golfing 136
Watching the big-league teams 138
Fishing 139
Laying down some bets 139
Seeing Miami by Guided Tour 140
A bus tour 140
Walking tours 140
A bike tour 140
Sightseeing Itineraries 140
Miami in 3 Days 141
Miami in 4 Days 141
Shopping 141
Burning some bucks 142
Crawling through the malls 143
Lighting Up the Night 143
Toasting the town 144
Clubbing 144
Splashes of culture 145
Fast Facts 146
Gathering More Information 147

Chapter 12: Unlocking the Keys 149

Getting a Clue about the Keys 149
Choosing Your Transportation 150
Marking every mile 152
Seeing the Keys in 5 Days 153
Laying Back in Key Largo 153
Key Largo's Best Hotels 154
Key Largo's Best Restaurants 155
Frolicking with fauna 156
Touring the waters 157

Shopping 158
Lacking karaoke 158
Enjoying Islamorada Is Easier than Pronouncing It 158
Islamorada's Best Hotels 159
Islamorada's Best Restaurants 160
Exploring Islamorada 161
Pursuing outdoor delights 162
Lighting up the night 162
Meandering Through Marathon 163
Marathon's Best Hotels 163
Marathon's Best Restaurants 164
Exploring Marathon 165
Outdoor pursuits 166
Escaping to the Lower Keys 167
The Lower Keys' Best Hotels 167
The Lower Keys' Best Restaurants 168
Exploring the Lower Keys 169
Taking it to the water 170
Going Key West, Young Man 171
Key West's Best Hotels 171
Key West's Best Restaurants 174
Exploring Key West's Major Attractions 176
Seeing Key West by guided tour 178
Outdoor adventures 179
Seeing Key West in 3 Days 180
Keeping a bit of the Keys for yourself 181
If you like the nightlife . . . if you like to boogie 181
Coming out to enjoy the gay scene 182
Fast Facts 183

Chapter 13: The Everglades 185
Introducing the Everglades 185
Getting There 188
Getting Around 189
The Everglades' Best Hotels 189
The Everglades' Best Restaurants 190
Exploring the Everglades 191
Everglades National Park 192
Big Cypress National Preserve 194
Fakahatchee Strand State Park 195
Collier-Seminole State Park 196
Outdoors in the Everglades 197
Organized Tours 198
Fast Facts 198

Chapter 14: The Gold Coast 201
Finding the Gold Coast's Attractions 201
Fort Lauderdale, Hollywood, and Beyond 202
Getting there 202
Getting around 203
Staying in the Fort Lauderdale Area 205

Dining out in the Fort Lauderdale Area 209
Exploring Fort Lauderdale, Hollywood, and Beyond 211
Shopping 215
Living the Nightlife 215
Fort Lauderdale and Hollywood in 2 Days 216
Fast Facts 217
Palm Beach, West Palm Beach, and Boca Raton 218
Getting there 218
Getting around 219
Staying in Palm Beach County 219
Dining out in Palm Beach County 223
Exploring Palm Beach, West Palm Beach,
and Boca Raton 225
Shopping 228
Living the Nightlife 229
Palm Beach County in 3 Days 230
Fast Facts 230

Part IV: The Gulf Coast 233

Chapter 15: Tampa 235

Getting to Tampa 235
By plane 236
By car 236
By train 236
Orienting Yourself to Tampa 236
Tampa by neighborhood 237
Street smarts: Getting information after arriving 237
Getting Around Tampa 237
By car 238
By taxi 238
By bus 238
Staying in Tampa 238
Tampa's best hotels 239
Runner-up accommodations 244
Dining Out in Tampa 244
Tampa's best restaurants 244
Runner-up restaurants 247
Exploring Tampa 247
Going into the bush: Busch Gardens 250
Seeing other top sights 251
Seeing and doing more cool things 253
Seeing Tampa by guided tour 255
Shopping 255
Tampa's best shopping areas 256
Hitting the malls 256
Living the Nightlife 256
Bars 257
Clubs 257
Cultural centers 257

Sightseeing Itineraries 257
    Tampa in 2 Days 257
    Tampa in 3 Days 258
Fast Facts 258

Chapter 16: St. Petersburg, Clearwater, and Beaches 261

Searching the Suncoast: What's Where? 262
St. Petersburg and Beaches 262
    Getting there 263
    Getting around 263
    The Suncoast's best hotels..................................265
    Staying on the Suncoast 265
    Dining out on the Suncoast 268
    Exploring St. Petersburg 270
    Seeing the shore by guided tour 272
    Shopping 272
    Living the nightlife 272
North Pinellas and Beaches 273
    Getting there 273
    Getting around 273
    Staying in North Pinellas County 275
    Dining out in North Pinellas County 277
    Exploring Clearwater 279
    Seeing the area by guided tour 281
    Shopping 281
    Living the nightlife 282
Suggested Itineraries 282
    The Suncoast in 3 Days 282
    The Suncoast and Tampa in 4 Days 283
Day Tripping to Weeki Wachee, Homosassa Springs,
    and Crystal River 283
Fast Facts 284

Chapter 17: Sarasota, Fort Myers, and Naples 287

Southwest Florida: What's Where? 288
Sarasota and Bradenton 288
    Getting there 288
    Getting around 289
    Staying the night 291
    Dining out in the Sarasota region 293
    Exploring Sarasota and Bradenton 295
    Shopping 298
    Living the nightlife 298
    Seeing Sarasota and Bradenton in 3 Days 299
Fort Myers, Sanibel, Naples, and Marco Island 299
    Getting there 300
    Getting around 300
    Staying in Sanibel, Naples, Fort Myers, and Captiva 302
    Dining out in Sanibel, Naples, Fort Myers,
        and Marco Island 305

Exploring Fort Myers, Sanibel, Naples,
and Marco Island 307
Seeing the area by guided tour 310
Shopping 311
Living the nightlife 312
Suggested itineraries 313
Fast Facts 313

Part V: Visiting Central Florida: Mickey Mania 317

Chapter 18: Settling into Walt Disney World and Orlando 319

Getting There 319
By plane 320
By car 321
By train 321
Orienting Yourself in Orlando 322
Ordering Orlando by Neighborhood 322
Showing Street Smarts: Getting Information on Arrival 323
Getting Around Orlando 324
Disney transportation system 324
By car 324
By bus 326
By trolley 326
By shuttle 326
By taxi 326
Staying the Night in Orlando 326
Accommodations in Orlando and Walt Disney World 327
The area's best hotels 327
Runner-up accommodations 337
Dining out in Orlando 339
Orlando's Best Restaurants 339
Runner-up restaurants 344
Disney character dining 345
Dinner shows 347

Chapter 19: The Theme Parks 349

Walt Disney World 349
Pricing theme parks 350
Getting the most out of Walt Disney World 351
The Magic Kingdom 352
Main Street, U.S.A. 352
Tomorrowland 352
Mickey's Toontown Fair 354
Fantasyland 354
Liberty Square 355
Frontierland 356
Adventureland 357
Parades and fireworks 358

Entering Epcot 358
    Future World 359
    World Showcase 361
    Fireworks and more 364
Disney-MGM Studios 364
    Checking out the best of Disney-MGM 364
    Parades and fireworks 367
Animal Kingdom 367
    The Oasis 368
    Safari Village 368
    Camp Minnie-Mickey 369
    Africa 369
    Asia 370
    Dinoland, U.S.A. 370
Universal Orlando 371
Universal Studios Florida 372
    Hollywood 372
    New York 373
    Production Central 373
    San Francisco 374
    Woody Woodpecker's KidZone 374
    World Expo 375
Islands of Adventure 376
    Port of Entry 376
    Suess Landing 376
    Marvel Super Hero Island 377
    Toon Lagoon 378
    Jurassic Park 378
    The Lost Continent 379
SeaWorld 380
    SeaWorld attractions 381
    More SeaWorld fun 383
Discovery Cove 383

Chapter 20: Exploring the Rest of Orlando 385

Seeing the Top Smaller Attractions 385
    The never-ending world of Disney 385
    Beyond Disney 389
Seeing and Doing More Cool Stuff 392
Shopping 393
    Orlando's best shopping areas 393
    Searching for shopping hot spots 395
Enjoying the Nightlife 396
    Disney after dark 396
    Universal after dark 398
    Other nighttime venues 400
    Side-Tripping to John F. Kennedy Space Center 400
    Side-Tripping to Cypress Gardens 401
Fast Facts 403

Part VI: The Great North 405

Chapter 21: Daytona Beach 407

Getting There 408
  By plane 408
  By car 408
  By train 408
Orienting Yourself in Daytona Beach 408
  Daytona Beach by neighborhoods 410
  Street smarts: Where to get information after arriving 410
Getting Around 410
  By bus 411
  By car 411
  By taxi 411
Staying in Daytona Beach 411
  Daytona Beach's best hotels 412
  Runner-up accommodations 415
Dining Out in Daytona Beach 416
  Daytona Beach's best restaurants 416
  Runner-up restaurants 418
Exploring Daytona Beach 419
  Touring the top sights 419
  Seeing and doing more cool things 421
Seeing Daytona Beach in 3 Days 422
Shopping 423
Enjoying the Nightlife 424
  Bars 424
  Clubs 424
  Performing arts 424
Fast Facts 425

Chapter 22: Northeast Florida 427

Visiting Northeast Florida and Its Attractions 428
St. Augustine 428
  Getting there 430
  Getting around 430
Staying in St. Augustine 431
  St. Augustine's best hotels 431
  Runner-up accommodations 432
Dining Out in St. Augustine 433
  St. Augustine's best restaurants 433
  Runner-up restaurants 435
Exploring St. Augustine 436
  Touring the top sights 436
  Doing more cool stuff 438
  Seeing St. Augustine by guided tour 439
  Shopping 439
  Enjoying the nightlife 440
  Seeing St. Augustine in 2 Days 440

Jacksonville, Amelia Island, and Fernandina Beach 440
  Getting there 440
  Getting around 442
Staying in the Jacksonville Area 444
  The area's best hotels 444
  Runner-up accommodations 446
Dining Out in the Jacksonville Area 446
  The area's best restaurants 447
  Runner-up restaurants 448
Exploring the Jacksonville Area 449
  Touring the top sights..449
  Shopping 452
  Enjoying the nightlife 453
  Seeing Jacksonville and Fernandina in 2 Days 453
Fast Facts 454

Chapter 23: The Panhandle 455
Visiting the Panhandle and Its Attractions 457
Pensacola 457
  Getting there 457
  Getting around 459
  Staying in Pensacola 459
  Dining out in Pensacola 462
  Exploring Pensacola 464
  Shopping 467
  Living the nightlife 467
  Seeing Pensacola in 2 Days 468
Panama City, Fort Walton Beach, Destin, and Seaside 468
  Getting there 468
  Getting around 469
  Staying in the beach communities 469
  Dining out at the beaches 472
  Exploring Panama City, Fort Walton Beach,
    Destin, and Seaside 475
  Shopping 478
  Living the Nightlife 478
  Seeing Panama City, Fort Walton Beach,
    and Destin in 2 days 479
Fast Facts 479

Part VII: The Part of Tens *481*

Chapter 24: The Top Ten Florida Beaches 483

Chapter 25: Ten or More of Florida's Favorite Foods 487
Ambrosia 488
Citrus Fruits 488
Conch 488
Cuban Cuisine 488
Divinity 489

Florida Lobster 489
Grits 489
Key Lime Pie 489
Mullet 489
Seafood 490
Stone Crab Claws 490

Appendix: Quick Concierge *491*
Florida A to Z: Facts at Your Fingertips 491
Toll-Free Numbers and Web Sites 494
Where to Get More Information 496
Online sources 496
Official state welcome centers 497
Other sources of information 497

Worksheets *499*

Index *507*

Book Registration Information ....*Back of Book*

Introduction

*P*once de Leon didn't get a Welcome Wagon reception when he landed in Florida in 1513. Mosquitoes sucked his blood, alligators ate his men, and the natives sent their regards via Flaming Arrow Express. Thankfully, the state has changed, and visitors now get the royal treatment when they visit Florida. Whether your passion involves water sports, beach bathing, theme-park hopping, or wining and dining, this state offers a wealth of opportunities for you to experience at your leisure. Florida has come a long way from the old days when your ancestors had to settle for the activities of the day — the wild-boar duck-and-dodge, and no-cleavage sunbathing.

You don't need to fret about being stuck in yesterday, although you may actually enjoy looking back at the past, if you head off to St. Augustine. Florida theme parks, especially those clustered in and around Orlando, are constantly trying to out-duel each other with high-tech animatronics, virtual experiences, and all-too-real thrill rides where you strap yourself in and pray your bladder doesn't become a stranger with a mind of its own. Miami's sizzling South Beach offers some of the hottest nightlife on American soil. Daytona Beach is world-renowned — or infamous, depending on your point of view — for its spring-break spunk. And, Destin and Fort Walton offer miles of sand for you to stretch out on.

Florida's a big place. Navigating your way through all the fun and sun without exhausting yourself should be your biggest priority — after all, you are on vacation. All you need to ensure a great trip to Florida is some patience, some advance planning, and some suntan lotion — now how hard is that?

About This Book

With a little help from us, you won't have to

- ✔ Do it their way
- ✔ Pay full price
- ✔ Read the fine print

There's no need for any of that. You chose this book because you know the *For Dummies* label and probably already have made your first decision — you're thinking hard about a trip to Ponce de Leon's favorite flatland, Florida. You probably also know what you want to spend, the pace you want to keep, and how much planning you can stomach. Most of y'all (forgive our Southern slang) also don't want to tend to every little detail. Yet you don't trust just anyone to do it for you. That's why you hired us.

Our job is to boil down what, honestly, is a very long spit of real estate — 931 miles from Key West to Jacksonville, then leftward to Pensacola. At current count, Florida has about 15 million residents and five times that many tourists per year — all more or less crowded into about 20 percent of the land. The rest of the state is pasture, swamp, and closed public lands that most folks never see. Because your time and money are valuable, we have narrowed down the cities and regions in Florida that deserve your attention. This book doesn't cover Florida comprehensively; it covers the best that Florida has to offer. We won't worry you with the secondary stuff that while perfectly fine, isn't up to snuff for your vacation.

How can anyone sort through that kind of mess, you ask? It takes experience. After three decades of stomping through the state, we know where to find the best deals (of the non-rip-off variety). In this book, we guide you through Florida in a clear, easy-to-understand way, allowing you to find the best hotels, restaurants, and attractions without having to read this book like a novel — cover to cover. Although you can read this book from cover to cover if you choose, you can also flip to only those sections that interest you. We also promise not to overwhelm you with choices. We simply deliver the best, most essential ingredients for a great vacation.

Foolish Assumptions

As we wrote this book, we made some assumptions about you and what your needs may be as a traveler:

- You may be an inexperienced traveler trying to determine whether or not to take a trip to Florida or are looking for guidance to determine when and how to make this trip.

- You may be an experienced traveler, but you don't have much time to devote to trip planning or you don't have much time to spend in Florida when you get there. You want expert advice on how to maximize your time and enjoy a hassle-free trip.

✔ You're not looking for a book that provides all the information available on Florida or one that lists every hotel, restaurant, or attraction available to you. Instead, you want a book that focuses on places that give you the best or most unique experiences in the Sunshine State.

If you fit any of these criteria, *Florida For Dummies* gives you the information you're looking for!

Conventions Used in This Book

To make this book an easier reference guide for you, (because Florida does its best to make you max them out) we use the following abbreviations for commonly accepted credit cards:

AE: American Express

CB: Carte Blanche

DC: Diners Club

DISC: Discover

JCB: Japan Credit Bank

MC: MasterCard

V: Visa

We also include some general pricing information to help you as you decide where to unpack your bags or dine on the local cuisine. We've used a system of dollar signs to show a range of costs for one night in a hotel or a meal at a restaurant. (Included in the cost of each meal is the main course; allow for the 6 to 7 percent sales tax, as well as any appetizers, drinks, or other extras you desire.) Check out the following table to decipher the dollar signs:

Cost	Hotel	Restaurant
$	$50–$100	$15 and under
$$	$100–$200	$15–$25
$$$	$200–$250	$25–$40
$$$$	$250 and up	$40 and up

How This Book Is Organized

Florida For Dummies is divided into seven parts. The chapters in each part lay out the specific details of that part's topic. Each chapter, and part, is written so you don't have to read what came before or after, though we sometimes refer you to other areas for more information. Here is a brief look at the parts:

Part 1: Getting Started

Think of this part as the hors d'oeuvres. In this part, we tempt you with the best experiences, hotels, eateries, and attractions in Florida. We throw in a weather forecast, look at special events, and then help you plan a budget. We also provide special tips for families, seniors, travelers with disabilities, and gay and lesbian travelers.

Part II: Ironing Out the Details

Should you use a travel agent? How about buying a package tour? Where can you find the best airfare? We answer those questions, and then talk about booking tips and online sources in this part. We also get into money matters, discussing whether it's best to use credit cards, ATMs, traveler's checks or cash. Before moving on, we tie up some last-minute details and talk about travel insurance, renting a car, and packing tips.

Part III: South Florida

This part of the book deals with Miami, the Keys, the Everglades, Fort Lauderdale, Palm Beach, and the 'burbs. We introduce the neighborhoods, and then explore some of the *modus transporto* (local buses, trolleys, taxis, shuttles, and other vehicles to get you from hither to yon). We also help you decide where to stay, where to eat, and which attractions to see. Finally, we profile the best shopping areas, present the best clubs, and offer some suggested itineraries.

Part IV: The Gulf Coast

Florida's left coast has pockets of development, particularly around the Tampa Bay area, but this area is not nearly as cramped as the Atlantic side. In this part, we introduce you to Tampa, St. Petersburg, and the Gulf beaches, and then venture south to Sarasota, Fort Myers, and Naples. We include the region's best accommodations, restaurants, attractions, shops, and clubs, as well as sightseeing itineraries.

Part V: Visiting Central Florida: Mickey Mania

There's so much shoehorned into Orlando and the Walt Disney World area that this section of Florida deserves its own part — three meaty chapters. First off, we help you get there, profile the neighborhoods, and present the best accommodations and eateries in town. Then, we devote a chapter to the major theme parks operated by Disney, Universal, and SeaWorld. Last but not least, we present some of the smaller (and cheaper) attractions, explore shopping and partying venues, and then take side trips to the Kennedy Space Center and Cypress Gardens.

Part VI: The Great North

Except for a few development clusters — most notably along the upper Atlantic Coast — North Florida is pretty wide-open. Most of the places here are oriented more toward backpackers and cow tippers than typical tourists. In Northeast Florida, we offer you a front-row seat in the oldest city in the United States, St. Augustine, and explore Daytona Beach, Amelia Island, Fernandina Beach, and Jacksonville. Before ending our grand tour of Florida, we take a spin into the Panhandle, visiting Pensacola, Fort Walton Beach, Destin, and Panama City.

Part VII: The Part of Tens

Every *For Dummies* book has "The Part of Tens." The appearance of this part is as certain as annual rate increases at Florida's theme parks. Here, we give you some parting advice about the state's best beaches, foods, and tourist traps.

You can also find two other elements near the back of this book. First, we include an *Appendix* — your "Quick Concierge." The Appendix contains lots of handy information you may need when traveling in Florida, like phone numbers and addresses for emergency personnel or area hospitals and pharmacies, protocol for sending mail, and more. Check out the Appendix when searching for the answers to lots of little questions that may come up as you travel.

Second, we include a bunch of *worksheets* to make your travel planning easier — among other things, you can determine your travel budget, create specific itineraries, and keep a log of your favorite restaurants, so you can hit them again next time you're in town. You can find these worksheets easily, because they're printed on yellow paper.

Icons Used in This Book

Several icons (those little pictures in the margins) are scattered throughout this guide. Consider them your road map for finding the information you need.

This icon tells you how to save time (including ways to beat the lines) and provides other handy facts.

Watch for this icon to identify annoying or potentially dangerous situations, such as tourist traps, unsafe neighborhoods, budget breakers, and other things to beware.

We use this icon to identify particularly family-friendly hotels, restaurants, and other places, although most of Orlando is receptive to small fry.

Keep an eye out for this icon as you seek out money-saving tips and/or great deals.

This icon highlights particularly noteworthy beaches, parks, preserves, and other natural attractions in Florida, a state known for its natural beauty.

Where to Go from Here

Okay. You know what to expect from this book and how to use it to plan a sun-filled and fun-filled vacation to Florida. So, start reading. There's much to do before you arrive, from arranging a place to park yourself each night to exploring the best beaches, attractions, and nightlife that Florida has to offer. Like the Boy Scouts, the successful Florida traveler needs to be prepared; follow the advice in this book, and you will be. And, last but not least, have fun — this state was designed to bring sunshine into its visitors' lives, so you might as well enjoy it.

Part I
Getting Started

The 5th Wave   By Rich Tennant

"Welcome to Jackhammer Key! Just ahead are some local musicians to greet your arrival."

In this part . . .

Deciding on a vacation destination shouldn't cause angst, but making a few decisions now — before the landing gear lowers — will help you get the most out of your vacation. Our goal in this part is to help you cut through the first wave of options that you encounter when deciding on a Florida destination.

But before you do, you get to do a little dreaming about the premier experiences Florida offers, and the grand excursions you can embark upon when you get there.

Chapter 1

Discovering the Best of Florida

● ●

In This Chapter

▶ Dining in the top restaurants

▶ Landing in the most intimate spots

▶ Playing like an all-star

▶ Partying with the best of them

● ●

*W*hether you prefer diving with dolphins, working on your suntan, or gorging on great food, Florida's wealth of activities, dining opportunities, and entertainment will impress even the most jaded traveler. Millions of visitors flock here each year, drawn by the promise of warm winters, a bounty of beaches, and fabulous attractions of both the man-made and natural variety. But before we dive into the details, we review some of Florida's best places to stay, eat, and have fun. In these first pages, we tell you about some of the things that convince snowbirds, families, honeymooners, and outdoor enthusiasts to come here every year and in the process, help you find a few things to fill your own dance card.

Of course, selecting the *best* from such a large, visitor-friendly state is no easy job, and the choices we list here are simply some of the highlights. You can discover hundreds of other hotels, restaurants, activities, and attractions in the following chapters. And, dare we say, you'll probably find a few of your own, after you arrive at ground zero. (See the "Florida" map.)

We're going to keep an ace in the hole and save our favorite Florida beaches for Chapter 24, but for now, here are the hors d'oeuvres.

Whetting Your Appetite

When it comes to Florida dining, there are basically two categories: seafood and not seafood. Fish is a fixture on Floridian menus. Even if you usually don't favor marine cuisine, you should sample the fresh

Florida

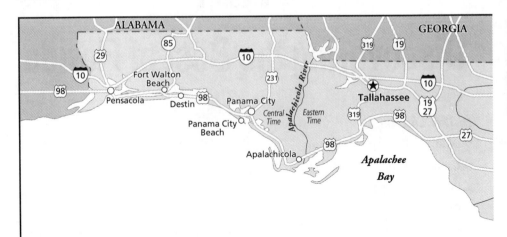

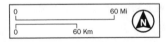

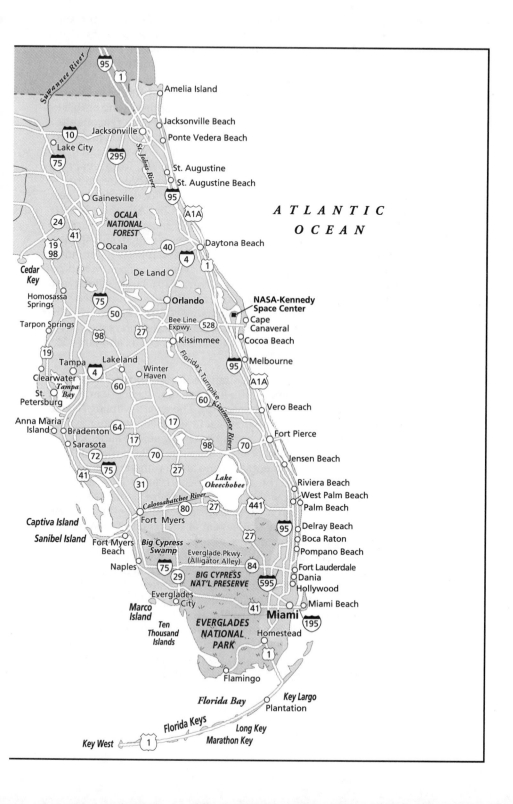

and well-prepared seafood dishes — from soft-shell crabs in the south to oysters in the north — served regularly at most restaurants. If you prefer to travel the other-than-seafood circuit, you won't go hungry either. Here are our culinary top draft picks, from south to north:

- ✔ **South Florida: Monty's Stone Crab & Seafood House** in Miami's South Beach wins the Great Crab War by serving stone crab, she-crab soup, and grouper in white wine at somewhat reasonable prices (see Chapter 10). **Atlantic's Edge** in Islamorada makes a mean Thai-spiced snapper, or you can bring your own catch, and the staff will prepare it for you (see Chapter 12). **Testa's** in Palm Beach continues its 75-year family tradition with seared tuna, almond-crusted prawns, and an amazing seafood marinara (see Chapter 14). In the nonseafood category, **Chef Allen's** in North Miami Beach boasts a show kitchen and a menu that features goat-cheese encrusted lamb chops and mesquite-grilled, soft-shell crabs (see Chapter 10). **Norman's** in Coral Gables is a perennial award winner thanks to such treats as venison *au poivre* and pork tenderloin with Haitian grits (see Chapter 10). **Louie's Backyard** in Key West serves up grilled yellowfin tuna and spice-rubbed venison, while you watch a spectacular sunset (see Chapter 12). **Burt & Jack's,** on the waterfront in Fort Lauderdale, offers a pricey but palate-pleasing rack of lamb, as well as veal chops and large Maine lobsters (see Chapter 14).

- ✔ **Central Florida:** Ybor City's **Columbia Restaurant,** a Tampa area fixture since 1905, offers a Latin-flavored dining experience and a fabulous floor show (see Chapter 15). The award-winning **Beach Bistro** on Holmes Beach near Sarasota serves up grouper in a coconut-and-cashew crust, an impressive wine list, and spectacular views of the Gulf (see Chapter 17). **Euphemia Haye** on Longboat Key offers unique continental cuisine and a romantic atmosphere (see Chapter 17). **Dux,** the signature restaurant at The Peabody Orlando, wows guests with a posh atmosphere, a long wine list, and exquisitely prepared haute cuisine (see Chapter 18). **Emeril's,** TV Chef Emeril Lagasse's main event at Universal's CityWalk, beckons with creative Creole dishes, a cigar room, and a delightful atmosphere (see Chapter 18). **Ted Peters' Famous Smoked Fish** is a St. Petersburg institution — life doesn't get much better than sipping a cold beer while diving into red-oak smoked mullet, mackerel, or salmon at this open-air restaurant (see Chapter 16). If you're hanging out near Clearwater Beach, **Seafood & Sunsets at Julie's** offers magnificent sunset views, right off the beach, and Key West-inspired seafood (see Chapter 16). **Fulton's Crab House** at Downtown Disney in Orlando serves Mississippi Delta-style seafood that has a spicy kick (see Chapter 18).

✔ **North Florida:** Destin's **Back Porch** has a reputation for being the birthplace of just about the finest char-grilled amberjack on the planet. The almost 20-year-old **Marina Café,** also in Destin, features a progressive menu of new American cuisine and an incredible view of Destin Harbor (see Chapter 23). The **Beech Street Grill** in Jacksonville is housed in an historic two-story home. This perennial award winner serves tasty, upscale cuisine (see Chapter 22).

Finding the Best Romantic Hideaways

Florida is loaded with places for starry-eyed sweethearts to get away from it all. Islamorada's **Cheeca Lodge** is a world-class resort with a laid-back style. This destination offers you a chance to share private moments, or hobnob with celebrities and royalty (see Chapter 12). **Little Palm Island,** a resort on a five-acre isle near Little Torch Key, is only accessible by boat. Kids under 16 are prohibited, and the rooms don't have phones, TVs, or alarm clocks (see Chapter 12). The 40 rooms in Key West's **Marquesa Hotel** have the charm of a romantic bed-and-breakfast, to go along with four-poster beds, marble baths, and private porches (see Chapter 12). The **Renaissance Vinoy Hotel** in St. Petersburg has a pampering spa and an ambiance straight out of an F. Scott Fitzgerald novel (see Chapter 16). The **Sanibel Inn** uses rattan furnishings, and hummingbird and butterfly gardens to blend into a back-to-nature setting (see Chapter 17). The sophistication of **The Peabody Orlando** ranges from its famous marching mallards to candlelit dinners at its restaurant (see Chapter 18). The **Casa Monica Hotel** in St. Augustine, built in 1888, has the charm and Spanish architecture common to the oldest city in the United States (see Chapter 22), while **Seaside,** near Destin, is a gulf-front, Victorian-style community that has become very popular with honeymooners (see Chapter 23).

First-Rate Family Attractions

The **Miami MetroZoo,** after loosing a little of its luster during Hurricane Andrew, is still a popular attraction thanks to a petting zoo and 700 critters, including white tigers, black rhinos, and Komodo dragons (see Chapter 11). The **Dolphin Research Center** in Marathon is arguably the best of Florida's swim-with-the-dolphin programs (see Chapter 12). **Lion Country Safari** in Loxahatchee, near West Palm Beach, lets you drive through and walk grounds that not only harbor lions, but also elephants, rhinos, and wildebeests (see Chapter 14). **Busch Gardens** in Tampa offers close-up views of African animals, as well as guided tours, shows, flume and raft rides, and five roller coasters (see Chapter 15). Our personal fab four **(Disney's Magic Kingdom, Disney-MGM Studios, Universal Studios Florida,** and **Islands of Adventure)** are the best of Orlando's eight theme parks (see Chapter 19). The **Kennedy Space Center** offers a ton of fun that centers on the past, present, and future of space travel (see Chapter 20). Finally, **Daytona USA** is a state-of-the-art, interactive attraction that's even popular with non-race fans (see Chapter 21).

Super Chills and Thrills

When it comes to thrill-a-minute (or second) experiences, there are only two major players in Florida, Tampa and Orlando. As we mentioned earlier, Tampa's **Busch Gardens** has, a whopping, five roller coasters. The newest is **Gwazi,** a wooden coaster whose 50 mph thrills include weightlessness. **Kumba** and **Montu** are 10 mph faster. **The Python** offers a double corkscrew and a 70-foot plunge, while **The Scorpion** has a 60-foot dive and a 360-degree loop (see Chapter 15).

Moving on to Orlando (see Chapters 18, 19, and 20):

- ✔ **Summit Plummet** at Disney's Blizzard Beach starts slow but finishes with a 120-foot, wedgie-inducing freefall. You know that this one must be good, because there are viewing stands to watch suckers — er, riders — make the journey.

- ✔ **The Amazing Adventures of Spider-Man** at Islands of Adventure is a 3-D simulator that dips and twists through comic-book action. Watch out for the simulated, but very realistic feeling, 400-foot drop.

- ✔ **The Incredible Hulk Coaster** at Islands of Adventure launches you from 0 to 40 mph in 2 seconds and then does seven rollovers and two deep drops — you'll feel weightless, and possibly nauseous.

- ✔ **Dueling Dragons,** also at Islands of Adventure, catapults frail bodies on dueling coasters through five inversions at 55 to 60 mph, and get this — you'll come within 12 inches of the other coaster on three separate occasions.

- ✔ **Rock 'n Roller Coaster** at Disney-MGM Studios rips from 0 to 60 mph in 2.8 seconds and goes right into an inversion, as the 120 speakers in your stretch limo blast Aerosmith. And as if that isn't enough, all this takes place in the dark.

- ✔ **Twilight Zone Tower of Terror,** also at Disney-MGM, is a free-fall experience that leaves your stomach hanging at several levels — Rod Serling would have loved it.

Tip-Top Places to Get Tipsy

After some occasionally mind-altering research, we have found four places in Florida that are head-and-shoulders above the rest, when it comes to having fun — of the liquid variety or otherwise:

- ✔ **Woody's Saloon and Restaurant** in Islamorada features Big Dick and the Extenders. The leader of the band is a frequently profound and almost as frequently profane Native American who loves to pick on his audience (see Chapter 12).

- ✔ Some believe that **Capt. Tony's** in Key West was the original Sloppy Joe's frequented by Ernest Hemingway. Undergarments left hanging from the ceiling pretty much set the tone of this dive (see Chapter 12).

- ✔ **Stan's Idle Hour Restaurant** in Goodland has gained fame as the home of some odd events, including the Goodland Mullet Festival, the Buzzard Lope Queens, and Polish Octoberfest (see Chapter 17).

- ✔ Last but certainly not least, the **Flora-Bama Lounge** on Perdido Key bills itself as "The Last Great American Roadhouse," and it emphasizes the point with April's big event — the Interstate Mullet Toss and Beach Party, which you have to see to believe (see Chapter 23).

Party On

Floridians love to have a good time, so it's no surprise that most of the major cities have happening places where the locals and tourists can party all night. **South Beach,** the two southernmost miles of Miami Beach, is an art-deco district with clubs and bars featuring everything from rock to rumba (see Chapter 11). **Duval Street** in Key West is another great place to cruise the bars and take in the Sunset Celebration at Mallory Square (see Chapter 12). **Las Olas Boulevard** in Fort Lauderdale and **Clematis Street** in West Palm Beach offer lively action in pubs and clubs (see Chapter 14). Likewise, **Ybor City** near Tampa really gets lively with salsa-fied fun after the sun goes down (see Chapter 15). Orlando may be the fairest of them all when it comes to party spots. The city has a three-pack of entertainment districts. Disney's **Pleasure Island,** Universal's **CityWalk,** and Downtown's **Church Street Station** let you party well into the wee hours (see Chapter 20).

Cool Places to Cast Your Reel

Florida has numerous rivers and streams, plus approximately 30,000 lakes — oh yeah, and an ocean. Fishing isn't just a fun activity, it may be the state's most popular sport; you'll find Floridians fishing everywhere. **Miami** and **Fort Lauderdale** are good launching points for anglers looking for redfish, trout, snook, Spanish and king mackerel, sailfish, snapper, and grouper (see Chapters 11 and 14, respectively). **The Keys** are heaven for game fishermen (blue and white marlin, bonefish, tarpon, and permit), as well as anglers looking to put something on the dinner table (see Chapter 12). **Treasure Island** is a good place to launch if you're hankering for grouper, amberjack, sea bass, and snapper (see Chapter 16). The fishing off **Boca Grande** is wonderful, and things really heat up in July when The World's Richest Tarpon Tournament is staged (see Chapter 17). Finally, **Destin** earns its reputation as the World's Luckiest Fishing Village by supporting a charter fleet of more than 140 boats (see Chapter 23).

Chapter 2

Deciding When and Where to Go

In This Chapter

▶ Knowing what to expect

▶ Greeting the seasons

▶ Wising up to weather warnings

▶ Checking out the calendar

*F*lorida is a year-round destination — it has only a few rain dates — but some places are best sampled in the so-called off-season. Unless you're into togetherness, two of our most popular destinations are best avoided during certain times of the year. **Walt Disney World** and Orlando's other major theme parks amount to instant insanity any time kids are out of school, such as summer and holidays. The more popular **Florida beaches** (Miami, Daytona, and St. Petersburg) also do a feverish business in summer, as well as during the annual snowbird season (winter) and spring break.

We give you the ammunition to help you decide when to go, but it's quite likely that personal factors will end up cementing your decision. Some of you, for example, plan a vacation to avoid wicked weather back home. Others take advantage of seasonal savings that are too good to pass up. And many of you have to travel when the school calendar allows. The good news is that there's a season for everyone.

Where you go will depend on your interests and budget. Do you want to soak in the sun? Avoid another human life form for a while? Hook a tuna? Explore the oldest city in the United States? This guide offers all of these possibilities and more.

Diving into Florida's Regions

Many of you want to come to Florida but don't know much about it, which means you're in good company. Natives live their whole lives here, and are lucky if they get to know all their own backyards.

This is a big state. Some of you may try to see, or at least think about seeing, the whole thing. But it's futile to bite off more than a fraction of the state in one visit. So we separate the state into manageable chunks that you can study, before deciding what you want to tackle this year (and perhaps, in the many years to come).

For starters, here are thumbnail sketches of the cities and regions to get you thinking about a wish list. Do you want nightlife? Are the kids making the decisions for you? Do you like the beach? Hate the forest? Don't be bashful. It doesn't cost a thing to dream, and you'll have time later to whittle your list down to size. We give you all the tools necessary to make the decision that's right for you.

South Florida

The unofficial capital of the South Florida region, **Miami,** is sophisticated and picturesque, an exceptional city that has a pulsating nightlife. **South Beach** offers a glimpse of what Havana might have been if not for Castro. **Villa Vizcaya** and **Coral Castle** are two of the region's finest architectural marvels, while attractions such as the **Miami MetroZoo** and **Miami Seaquarium** have been tickling tourists for decades. The sports scene includes pro football, baseball, basketball, and hockey franchises. But Miami is a moderately expensive destination, and it has many of the other problems associated with a metropolis, including crime, congestion, and pollution. (See Chapters 10 and 11 for details about Miami.) Things thin and chill out a bit in the **Keys,** where the mood and the magic are a little off-center, but that's just the Conch Republic's way of life. Only a single road stretches over the 110 miles from the mainland to Key West and **Seven-Mile Bridge,** which leads from Marathon to Key West. This single road can make the drive seem like an endless journey when accidents close one or both lanes. The Keys are best for those who want to kick back and forget about following a schedule. Water sports rule through most of the Keys, especially at such gems as **Bahia Honda State Recreation Area** on Big Pine Key and **John Pennekamp Coral Reef State Park** in Key Largo. For those who appreciate the arts and history, Key West was a favorite stomping ground (and watering hole) for several of the most notable literary and artistic figures of the twentieth century. Its attractions include the **Audubon House** and the **Ernest Hemingway Home & Museum** (see Chapter 12).

South Florida is also the gateway to Florida's greatest natural treasure, **The Everglades** (see Chapter 13). And Palm Beach is the winter home of some of America's rich and famous. Even if you're not one of them, it's fun to window shop along **Worth Avenue,** known as the Rodeo Drive of the South.

Fort Lauderdale has several of Florida's best **golf courses,** and the **International Museum of Cartoon Art** in Boca Raton is one of the region's most popular new tourist draws. While these areas are a bit less cluttered and congested than Miami, a big slice of what's here is geared toward retirees, so the pace may be a bit too slow for active travelers or those packing kids. (See Chapter 14 for more on Fort Lauderdale and Boca Raton.)

The Gulf Coast

With very few exceptions, this coast hasn't experienced the explosive growth that the Atlantic side has. The water is part of the reason. The Atlantic is alive with crashing waves, as good as the surf gets in Florida. Across the way, the Gulf of Mexico is calm and tepid, like a soothing tub.

Tampa's Latin influence adds a welcome touch to the region's food, culture, and architecture. The city has a moderately good arts calendar, a dandy nightclub scene in Ybor City, and in **Busch Gardens,** a theme park that rivals Orlando's offerings. The **Florida Aquarium, Lowry Park Zoo,** and the **Museum of Science and Industry** are other popular attractions. St. Petersburg's signature attractions include its **Gulf Beaches,** the **Salvador Dalí Museum,** and the **Florida International Museum.**

The two cities have a top-rate sports calendar that includes big-league baseball, football, and hockey teams. But tourism is an afterthought on Tampa's side of the bay, and St. Petersburg is nearly as overbuilt as Miami. (See Chapters 15 and 16 for more on Tampa and St. Petersburg.)

Sarasota's **Asolo Theatre** and the **Ringling Museum of Art** give the cultural community plenty of reason to crow. Gulf-view towns, such as Naples and Fort Myers, are far quieter than most of Florida's other beachfront cities. This stretch of the coast has more than 10,000 islands including **Sanibel, Captiva, Gasparilla,** and **Boca Grande.**

On the downside, this area is spread far and wide. There are few day-filling activities, and you'll have to drive a while to get to your next stop. (See Chapter 17 for information on Sarasota, Naples, and Fort Myers.)

Central Florida

If Orlando were a rock group, it would be called "Mickey Mania and the Wannabes." In Central Florida, Walt Disney World is the lead vocalist, **Universal** and **SeaWorld** play the guitar and keyboards, and dozens of smaller attractions are found on the drums. Their music can create sweet dreams — or nightmares. This area truly is fantasyland, but the crowds, cost, and confusion can turn your trip into a frightful experience.

As late as 1970, Orlando was a small town surrounded by cow patties, orange blossoms, and palmetto stands. A year later, Disney changed that forever. Uncle Walt's legacy spawned four theme parks **(Magic Kingdom, Epcot, Disney-MGM Studios,** and **Animal Kingdom)** and nearly a dozen minor attractions, plus a supporting cast of resorts, restaurants, and stores — enough to be its own city. Orlando is also home to the ever-expanding world of Universal Orlando **(Universal Studios Florida, Islands of Adventure,** and more), as well as **SeaWorld** and its new water park, **Discovery Cove.** (Check out Chapter 19 for information on all of the Disney, Universal, and SeaWorld attractions.)

If ever there was a destination that virtually had it all, Orlando is it, which is why some of you will love it. (If you are 55-years-old or younger and grew up with Disney, it's tough not to feel like a kid again.) It's a reasonably convenient place to park yourself — much of the hoopla is in two areas, Lake Buena Vista and International Drive, and most of its neighborhoods have just about everything you need for a fantastic vacation.

On the flip side, traffic and crowds can be brutal, and the theme parks are expensive. (Most visits cost a family of four $170, just for admission.)

The Great North

Daytona Beach's calling cards are bikinis, bikers, and fast cars. The city bills itself as "the world's most famous beach." This title is disputable, but Daytona is a wide stretch of ghost-white sand, bathed in frothy Atlantic waters. Driving your vehicle on some stretches of Daytona Beach is permitted, but those areas are shrinking because of environmental outcries. Aside from the beach, Daytona's most popular tourist attractions are the **Daytona International Speedway** and **Daytona USA,** a pretty high-tech, interactive, jump-and-shout exhibit in front of the speedway (see Chapter 21). But if you're not into sun, sand, and speed, Daytona may feel like you woke up in *Wayne's World* with a Southern twang. And if you arrive in March and aren't a member of the spring break squad, you're likely to feel claustrophobic on the beach.

The oldest city in the United States, **St. Augustine** (founded in 1565), is located a little farther north of Daytona on the Atlantic coast. If the idea of castles and other musty mysteries appeals to you, here's a chance to go back to the days of the earliest colonization. **Castillo de San Marcos** is a precious link to the past, as are several storefronts that stake a claim to being the oldest something or other (jail, school, store, and so on). Although the city has its share of tourist trappings (a pseudo **Fountain of Youth,** for example), it also has some compelling places to visit, such as the **St. Augustine Alligator Farm,** a throwback attraction, and the **Bridge of Lions** (see Chapter 22).

Continuing north, **Jacksonville** is a Navy town that has traded paper mills for sprawl and interstate clutter. The **Jacksonville Zoo** and the natural beaches, such as the one at **Little Talbot Island State Park,** are pluses, but most tourists find themselves having to scatter to find things to do in the Jacksonville area. One of northeast Florida's nicer resorts, **Amelia Island Plantation,** is 30 miles north. This resort blends environmental consciousness with top-flight golf, tennis, and beach activities. At the other end of the island, **Fort Clinch State Park,** near **Fernandina Beach,** offers living-history presentations that are a joy to see.

The Panhandle is the most spread out of all Florida tourist areas. The heart of this area is the coastline that stretches from Pensacola to Tallahassee. If you have the luxury of traveling by car, we recommend driving U.S. 98 and Highway 30-A, where you can pass through beautiful coastal villages, such as Grayton Beach, Seaside, Mexico Beach, Cape San Blas, Apalachicola, and Carrabelle. Many of these villages remain as they were in the 1950s. They're seldom crowded, and since this part of the coast stretches from east to west, you get wonderful views of sunrises *and* sunsets along the beach.

Pensacola's historic area is a blend of Spanish, French, and British cultures. The city also is the home of the **National Museum of Naval Aviation** and the **Flora-Bama Lounge,** where you may get to witness the world championship mullet toss. But like Jacksonville, Pensacola isn't an especially popular choice among visitors.

The **Redneck Riviera** — basically, Fort Walton Beach, Destin, and Panama City — got its name because of its popularity among tourists from Georgia and Alabama. Expect beautiful beaches and great fishing, combined with honky-tonks, glitter, and spring breakers — a combination that often makes the Redneck Riviera loud and rowdy.

The state capital, **Tallahassee,** is noted for moss-draped live oaks and antebellum mansions. The **Old Capitol** and **Mission San Luis** are a couple of the featured attractions, and south of town, **Wakulla Springs State Park** is a favorite among folks who like the outdoors. But this is another area not noted for tourism.

The Secret of the Seasons

Seasons? You bet Florida has them.

Of course, they're far less pronounced than in places like Europe, Canada, and North Dakota. Sometimes it's hard to even tell if we have an autumn or spring. Summer's heat and humidity often last six months or more. As a tradeoff, winters are generally mild. Florida skies are unusually sunny, except for a short spring rainy season and the daily thunderstorms that come and go quickly in summer. Temperatures in Florida are more moderate along the coasts, particularly on the Atlantic side, which has a decent sea breeze; the center of the state tends to be a bit colder in winter and hotter in summer.

Most of us enjoy our vacations more when crowds are thin and the weather is mild — spring and fall in Florida. Except for in Orlando, rooms and (in some cases) other expenses are cheaper during these seasons.

If you have youngsters, think about pulling them out of school for a few days during the off-season to avoid crowds and lines at theme parks and other attractions. Ask their teachers for schoolwork to take with you. You can also suggest that your kids write a report on some educational element of the vacation. If you're a senior who can travel when you please, think about avoiding the peak of the winter snowbird season, as well as the summer and holiday family times.

Here's our seasonal score sheet.

Springtime in Florida

Spring is a popular vacation time for most travelers, and Florida is no different. Some of the best reasons to go to Florida in the springtime follow:

- The weather is mild.
- Think flower power. Spring is when Florida really blooms.
- Accommodations that give discounts give them now.
- The lines at attractions are relatively thin.

However, keep in mind the following springtime pitfalls:

- Without a winter, a long spring is rare. Temps can get warm and sticky in April (heat + humidity = Hades).
- The pollen drives hay-fever sufferers crazy.
- Spring break cometh. Avoid it unless you're a breaker.

Heating up the scene in summer

Florida bustles during the summer season, in spite of the sizzling temperatures. Here are some points to consider:

- Wow — picturesque 6 a.m. sunrises and 9 p.m. sunsets.
- August means back-to-school sales at malls and outlets.
- Air conditioning is alive and well. Savvy travelers spend the middle of the day indoors, whether it's in a cool attraction or their accommodations.

But, again, keep in mind the following:

- ✔ The heat and humidity are oppressive.

- ✔ Let's just say that the smell of sweaty crowds doesn't resemble a rose garden.

- ✔ Summer thunderstorms cool things off a little, but they pass quickly, allowing the sun to turn concrete and asphalt walks into frying pans. (Despite the more than 400 miles between them, things don't feel a great deal different in Jacksonville and Key West.) Summer is also the heart of hurricane season (see the "Weather Warnings" section in this chapter).

- ✔ Discounts? Ha! Why cut prices with these crowds?

Falling into the tropics

Fall is a beautiful time of year to visit Florida. Here are some of the state's autumn bonuses:

- ✔ Ah, fall foliage. Florida has the same fiery reds and brilliant oranges and yellows as New England. The difference is that ours lasts about 17 minutes.

- ✔ Accommodations that give discounts do so in the fall, too.

- ✔ Lines and crowds begin to shrink.

Some things to look out for, however:

- ✔ It's cooler, but temps aren't as mild as those in spring until Thanksgiving or later.

- ✔ The hurricane season lasts through November and activity can run high in September and October.

Heading south for the winter

Winter brings visions of softly falling snowflakes (and slick roads and salt trucks) to most travelers, but that's not the case in Florida. You should consider the following pluses when planning a winter vacation in Florida:

- ✔ There really isn't a true winter, just a few days at or near freezing, followed by mild, sunny weather. So leave those winter blues back home.

- ✔ Lines are short in many tourist areas during most of the winter season.

Winter does have its downside, however. Consider the following:

✔ International and snowbird visitors keep room rates reasonably high along the coasts and in Orlando.

✔ The mid-December to early January holidays are nearly as crowded as the dead of summer.

✔ There's no northern holiday spirit. It's common for temperatures to be in the 90s during Hanukkah, Christmas, and Kwanzaa.

✔ After mid-December arrives, prices rise.

Wising Up about the Weather

You can check out Table 2-1 for the average 24-hour temperatures for selected Florida cities. Beyond these averages and the seasonal information we provide in this chapter, there's no way to get a true-blue, long-term forecast. But there are a few places to find short-term forecasts (presuming you trust meteorologists).

✔ **The Weather Channel:** The cable channel is on 24 hours a day; it features Florida on a regular basis; and it offers ongoing coverage when big weather news happens. You also can get information on the Internet at www.weatherchannel.com, which has local (city and state) forecasts, Doppler radar, road conditions, and more.

✔ **The Weather Center:** Also known as Tampa Bay Online, this is a service of *The Tampa Tribune,* with an assist from WFLA-TV. The Weather Center (www.weathercenter.com) is another good statewide site that lets you link to specific cities. Its features include data on tides, lake levels, rainfall, and temperatures, severe weather warnings, live radar, heat indexes, and a link to the National Weather Service. Speaking of the service, you can jump to its site at www.nws.noaa.gov for more information.

Table 2-1   Average 24-Hour Temperatures for Sample Cities (°F)

Miami

Jan	Feb	Mar	Apr	May	June	July	Aug	Sept	Oct	Nov	Dec
64.7	65.1	69.3	74.5	78.8	81.9	83.5	84.1	81.9	76.4	70.4	66.6

Tampa

Jan	Feb	Mar	Apr	May	June	July	Aug	Sept	Oct	Nov	Dec
60.1	60.5	66.8	72.5	76.4	80.1	82.4	82.6	81.3	74.8	67.5	63.1

Orlando											
Jan	Feb	Mar	Apr	May	June	July	Aug	Sept	Oct	Nov	Dec
60.2	61.5	66.8	71.5	77.3	80.9	82.4	82.5	81.1	74.9	67.4	62.1

Jacksonville											
Jan	Feb	Mar	Apr	May	June	July	Aug	Sept	Oct	Nov	Dec
57.2	58.3	63.6	68.6	76.5	79.7	81.4	81.6	79.1	73.4	65.2	61.1

Fort Walton Beach/Destin											
Jan	Feb	Mar	Apr	May	June	July	Aug	Sept	Oct	Nov	Dec
58.3	60.0	65.3	70.1	77.2	80.9	82.7	81.9	80.8	74.2	66.3	61.6

Weather Warnings

There's no need for paranoia, but knowing a little about Florida's climatic temper tantrums can reduce the odds of one or all of them ruining your vacation.

Making hurricane waves

Should you worry? No, but it helps to be aware of them. The hurricane season runs from June 1 to November 30. In an average year, ten hurricanes are born somewhere in the Gulf and Atlantic waters, and also on average, one or two may affect some portions of Florida, especially in the coastal areas. If you're unlucky enough to be in Florida when a hurricane is threatening, modern tracking gives you plenty of warning. (If the thought of a hurricane really bothers you, consider steering clear of the most active months, which are usually July to mid-October, which are also the months when Florida is at its hottest and most crowded.)

It's a week before your much-anticipated vacation, and Hurricane Harry plows right through your destination. How can you tell whether Miami's Fountainbleau hotel or Disney-MGM Studios's Twilight Zone Tower of Terror has toppled? You could ask a reservationist or someone at the local chamber of commerce. But if you're a Doubting Danielle, you may want to turn to a third party. The state **Division of Emergency Management** in Tallahassee (☎ 850-413-9900) is the agency in charge of putting Florida back together again. You should get a fair, impartial report on damage to specific areas. You can also find information on the agency's Web site at www.dca.state.fl.us/fdem/.

Tumbling tornadoes

Tornadoes are fairly uncommon, but they're a fringe benefit of summer thunderstorms. You're more likely to run into one at Universal Studios' "Twister" attraction, but don't take any chances. When there are warnings, go indoors and stay clear of windows. April, May, and June are considered peak periods — though some nasty ones have dropped into the Florida Panhandle in February and March.

Lightning up the sky

Lightning should not be taken lightly. Here are a few quick facts:

- ✔ Lightning is 50,000 degrees, five times hotter than the sun.
- ✔ Lightning can reach out from the sky and zap you from 10 miles away.
- ✔ Lightning travels fast — a radar gun clocked its speed at 186,000 miles per second.

But you have to be pretty unlucky to be standing in the wrong place (under an oak tree, wading in water, or trying to hit a golf ball while wearing metal cleats and holding a metal club) at the wrong time (again, usually during a summer thunderstorm). Lightning will more than likely entertain you: the pyrotechnics really light up the sky. But keep your distance. The fireworks are better and safer at Walt Disney World.

Much of central Florida is considered the Lightning Capital of the United States. Tampa and St. Petersburg are among the most common targets, with 88 days of lightning activity and some 50 strikes per square mile a year. An average house in this part of the universe gets hit every 20 or 30 years. If you were as big as a house and never moved, well, then that gives you an idea of the likelihood of a run-in with lightning.

Forgoing some sun

Floridians are as proud of that big orange thing in the sky as Bubba is of his prize blue-tick hound. We even nicknamed ourselves the Sunshine State. The sun certainly is a friend of Florida tourism, but it isn't always a friend of Florida tourists, especially the ones who arrive unprepared for its sucker punches. One of these blows from the sun, sunburn, is a bad hombre, but its evil twin, sun poisoning, can ruin your vacation. Most burns can be eased with over-the-counter creams or aloe. But sun poisoning — sunburn to the fourth or fifth power — is far more dangerous. It can result in fever, chills, headaches, dizziness, nausea, and in the worst cases, sunstroke.

Prevention is simple. Lather your skin with a sun block that has an SPF (sun protection factor) rating of 25 or higher. (*Do not* use tanning oil. That's like slathering yourself with bacon grease before jumping into a low-burning skillet.) Many of you think the ultimate souvenir is a Florida tan. But the tans are not all they're cracked up to be. Ask any native about the skin-cancer scare. If nothing worse happens, your Florida tan will start to peel by the time you get back on the block.

Some of you, of course, won't listen. You'll skip the prevention advice and go straight to the I'm-on-fire-and-I-feel-a-bit-woozy phase. If that happens, helping hands are on standby at **Poison Control** (☎ 800-282-3171).

Remember to bring a wide-brimmed hat and don't forget a native's favorite fashion statement — sunglasses.

Raining down

Rain doesn't hurt anyone, but it can dampen a beach vacation or outdoor activities. Much of the Panhandle and the Atlantic Coast in Miami-Dade, Broward, and Palm Beach Counties get more than 60 inches of rain a year, 7 more inches than the state average. The Keys customarily get about 40 inches. Summers bring brief but daily rains to much of the state. You can often wait out a rainstorm if some shelter, or your car, is nearby; don't automatically pack up for the day, unless it looks like there's no end in sight.

Florida's Calendar of Events

Keep in mind that although many of Florida's calendar events are fun-filled, some are especially rowdy and crowded. Here are a few of the more notorious:

✔ **February:** Hundreds of boats and hundreds of thousands of revelers fill the bay and downtown Tampa for the **Gasparilla,** a festival capped by a pirate invasion. A barge masquerading as a ship, mostly filled with city bigwigs, invades and captures Tampa on behalf of the mythical pirate, Jose Gaspar. Most of the bigwigs have 80-proof blood when this happens (even though it's 10 a.m.), but contrary to what some think, they're not Bike Week rejects. In all, there are two weeks of events, including foot races, street parties, and parades. It's a smaller version of Mardi Gras, but one that should be experienced in limited doses, if at all. If you want a dose, call ☎ 813-251-4500.

✔ **February to mid-March:** The **Bike Week** events are to be avoided at all costs, unless you like motorcycles and bikers in all sizes, shapes, and levels of sobriety. Daytona Beach doesn't exaggerate when it says that more than 500,000 two-wheel enthusiasts show up for the events, which include parades, races, shows, entertainment, and a fair share of falling down on the beach. If you're a glutton for noise and crowds, call ☎ **800-854-1234** (U.S. only) or 904-255-0981.

✔ **March to April: Spring Break** — *Arrggghhhh!!!* — brings an annual invasion of partying college kids to beach hot spots including Panama City, Daytona, Miami, and Fort Lauderdale. Orlando gets its share of mayhem, too.

✔ **October:** If Bike Week tickles your fancy, the Daytona Beach **Biketoberfest** blowout probably will, too. Races, touring rides, parades, costumed bikers, and other activities — such as biker tipping — fill the final weeks of October. Give them a loud shout at ☎ **800-854-1234** (U.S. only) or 904-255-0415.

At the risk of sounding like we're picking on Daytona and Tampa, the **Guavaween** festival held in Tampa's Ybor City is a Latin-style Halloween celebration that, sadly, has become seedier over the years. Still, some of you will be curious enough to call ☎ **813-248-3712** or 813-621-7121 to get more information.

January

Art Deco Weekend: Held on Miami's South Beach, the weekend features bands, vittles, antiques vendors, artists, tours, and other festivities in a celebration of the whimsical architecture that's made this restored area one of America's most unique neighborhoods. Call ☎ **305-672-2014.**

Epiphany: This daylong Greek holy celebration, held in Tarpon Springs (north of St. Petersburg), progresses from young boys diving for the cross and the promise of a year's good luck to food, music, and dancing. For more information, call ☎ **727-937-3540.**

Goodland Mullet Festival: You've never been to a party until you've been to a mullet fest. This one, held just south of Naples and Marco Island on the lower Gulf Coast, honors a fish that is most frequently served smoked, fried in cornmeal, or as a dip. A fashion show gives this mullet festival a little more class than some, but the fish-cleaning contest provides an equalizer. If that rings your fun chime, call ☎ **941-394-3041.**

Zora Neale Hurston Festival: The 4-day festival is held just north of Orlando in Eatonville, the first incorporated African-American town in America, and it highlights the life and work of author Zora Neale Hurston. It's usually the last weekend in January. Call ☎ **800-352-3865** or 407-647-3307 for exact details.

February

Everglades Seafood Festival: Held in Everglades City, this is a stomp in the swamp, where Seminole arts and crafts compliment 3,000 pounds of local seafood. Those who drink enough beer might even see one of our infamous skunk apes. Call ☎ **941-695-4100.**

Florida State Fair: Dusty midways, hopeless games, and greasy food join hands with livestock exhibits, arts and crafts, and big-name country entertainers at this fair. This two-week event is held on the east side of Tampa. Give the state fair folks a call at ☎ **800-345-3247** (Florida only) or 813-621-7821.

Florida Strawberry Festival: Plant City, which is just east of Tampa and the state fair, hosts this 11-day affair, which features rides, entertainment, and the area's most famous crop of strawberries served on shortcakes, in jams, or deliciously naked. For more information, dial ☎ **813-752-9194.**

Mardi Gras at Universal Studios: Authentic parade floats from New Orleans, stilt walkers, and traditional doubloons and beads thrown to the crowd signify this festive event. Special entertainment adds to the fun. It's in mid-February. Call ☎ **800-837-2273** or 407-363-8000, or visit www.uescape.com.

Miami International Boat Show: Mega-yachts, dinghies, and everything in between are featured at this show, which draws hundreds of thousands of boat enthusiasts to the Miami Beach Convention Center. Call ☎ **305-531-8410.**

Sarasota Medieval Fair: On the grounds of the charming Ringling Museum of Art, this fair offers a bridge to the past that ends with a festival that includes jousting, human chest games, and loads of bawdy fun. For fair information, call ☎ **941-957-1877.**

Silver Spurs Rodeo: Kissimmee puts on what arguably is the largest rodeo east of the Mississippi River, as top cowboys and cowgirls compete for prizes and yippee-i-o rights. Rustle up your phone and dial ☎ **407-847-4052.**

Spring Training: Twenty of Major League Baseball's teams use Florida for their Spring Training camps. Pitchers and catchers land in mid-February; exhibition games are played from early March to the beginning of April. Florida's Grapefruit League teams include the Atlanta Braves, Baltimore Orioles, Boston Red Sox, Cincinnati Reds, Cleveland Indians, Detroit Tigers, Florida Marlins, Houston Astros, Kansas City Royals, Los Angeles Dodgers, Minnesota Twins, Montreal Expos, New York Mets, New York Yankees, Philadelphia Phillies, Pittsburgh Pirates, St. Louis

Cardinals, Tampa Bay Devil Rays, Texas Rangers, and Toronto Blue Jays. You can get information through your hometown Ticketmaster, or you can look online at www.majorleaguebaseball.com.

March

Carnival Miami/Calle Ocho: If you need proof that Miami's predominantly Hispanic community knows how to throw a party, head for this 9-day ethnic celebration. The largest of its kind in the country, the party comes to a pounding finale with the 23-block Calle Ocho street festival. Call ☎ **305-644-8888.**

Havana Music Fest: The town of Havana, located 45 minutes east of the state capital, Tallahassee, uses the festival to show off its artsy antiques shops, some of which are converted tobacco warehouses. There are plenty of wonderful sounds — jazz, rhythm and blues, swing, country, and gospel. For details, call ☎ **850-539-6040.**

Spring Flower Festival: Cypress Gardens comes alive with hundreds of annual blossoms at this event, which runs into May. For more information, call ☎ **800-282-2123,** or visit Cypress Gardens online at www.cypressgardens.com.

April

Festival of States: This parade has been a St. Petersburg regular since 1921. It's combined with concerts, band competitions, and sports. Dial ☎ **727-898-3654** for more information.

Orlando International Fringe Festival: More than 100 acts from around the world participate in the eclectic event, held for 10 days in April and May at various locations in downtown Orlando. Entertainers perform drama, comedy, political satire, experimental theater, and a 7-minute version of Hamlet, all on an outdoor stage. Ticket prices vary, but most performances are under $12. For exact details, call ☎ **407-648-0077.**

Sun 'N Fun Fly-In: Calling this one of the Southeast's largest aviation conventions is no idle boast. Lakeland's Fly-In is a great place for private pilots to converge for some fun, food, music, and war stories. It's also a good place for groupies to get an eyeful of vintage and aerobatic airplanes. Give the organizers a buzz at ☎ **863-644-2431.**

Suwannee River Jam: If country music is your thing, this event attracts some of the top stars in the business for an annual blowout at the Spirit of the Suwannee Park in Live Oak, which is nearly midway between Jacksonville and Tallahassee. Y'all should call ☎ **904-364-1683** for details.

May

Coconuts Dolphin Tournament: Key Largo hosts the largest fishing tournament in the Keys, enticing anglers with a $26,000 prize fund, including $7,000 for the winner. Call ☎ **305-451-4107.**

Destin Mayfest: Destin and Fort Walton Beach join hands in the spirit of the bayou at this festival, where saxophones and clarinets literally smoke the harbor area. For more information, call ☎ **850-837-6241.**

Fernandina Beach Shrimp Festival: This festival in the northeast corner of the state is held in Florida's oldest port and the birthplace of a still succulently strong shrimp industry. Call ☎ **800-226-3542** (U.S. only) or 904-277-0717.

SunFest: Accurately billed as Florida's largest music, art, and waterfront festival, SunFest features forty bands, including national acts, which perform on three stages. There's also an art show, fireworks, youth activities, and more. For information on this year's festival, call ☎ **800-786-3378** or 561-659-5980 or check out www.sunfest.org.

June

Coconut Grove Goombay Festival: Not to be outdone by Carnival Miami/Calle Ocho, this extravaganza is billed as the largest black-heritage festival in the United States. Info abounds at ☎ **800-283-2707** or 305-372-9966 and on the Web at www.tropicoolmiami.com.

Gay Weekend: The first weekend in June draws tens of thousands of gay and lesbian travelers to Central Florida. This event grew out of Gay Day, an unofficial event at Disney World dating to the early 1990s, when it drew 50,000 people. Universal and SeaWorld also roll out the red carpet for gays and lesbians over this weekend. Check www.gayday.com for a detailed listing of activities.

The International Hemingway Festival: Held on Sanibel Island, this festival should be approached with caution because it's relatively new, evolving after a dispute between the late author's family and the organizer of the Key West event (see "Hemingway Days" in July), which dates to the early 1980s. This newbie can be fun, with literary and artistic workshops, contests, and sports events honoring Hemingway, who had firm roots in Key West. The question is: Will it survive? For answers to this question, call ☎ **800-916-9727** (U.S. only) or 941-275-1272.

July

Hemingway Days: A long-running celebration of the legendary author's literary influence, lifestyle, looks, and thirst, Hemingway Days is Key

West's signature festival, but its road became rocky in the mid-1990s when the organizer and the family got into a dispute that led to a separate event in June on Sanibel Island (see "The International Hemingway Festival" in June). Will either or both survive? Call ☎ **305-294-4440** for more information.

Underwater Music Festival: This festival, held at the Looe Key National Marine Sanctuary on Big Pine Key, gives divers a chance to listen to an underwater symphony. Give ☎ **800-872-3722** a ring for more information.

World's Richest Tarpon Tournament: Held on Boca Grande, the tournament offers approximately $200,000 in prize money for anglers working the tarpon-rich waters off Southwest Florida. This is a mid-week event in the second week of July. For details on this year's tournament, call ☎ **800-237-6444.**

August

Shark's Tooth & Seafood Festival: The west-coast city of Venice hosts this event, which lets kids scramble for mako molars while grownups gorge on fruits of the sea, browse through arts and crafts, and enjoy ice sculptures. Call ☎ **941-488-2236.**

September

Days in Spain: This bash celebrates the birthday of the oldest city in the United States, St. Augustine, which was founded in 1565. Dial ☎ **904-829-1711** for more info.

Night of Joy: One weekend each September, the Magic Kingdom is home to a contemporary Christian music festival featuring top artists. This is a very popular event; if it's on your dance card, get tickets ($25 to $30) early. For more details, call ☎ **407-824-4321.**

October

Destin Fishing Rodeo: If you want to start your own seafood festival from scratch, this month-long rodeo is held in an area that's billed as the "World's Luckiest Fishing Village." That may be a stretch, but it is a hot spot for anglers. Get on the line and call ☎ **850-837-6734.**

Halloween Horror Nights: Universal Studios transforms its grounds for 19 fright-filled evenings, featuring haunted attractions with live bands, a psychopath's maze, special shows, and hundreds of ghouls and goblins roaming the streets. The studio closes at dusk and then reopens in a new, macabre form at 7 p.m. Special admission is charged for this event, where liquor flows freely. Guests aren't allowed to wear costumes so that Universal employees can spot their peers, who dress the part. Call ☎ **800-837-2273** or 407-363-8000 or visit its Web site at www.uescape.com.

John's Pass Seafood Festival: Held on Madeira Beach, west of St. Petersburg, this festival may not be the best of its kind in Florida, but if you're in the bay area and not adverse to crowds, you can enjoy lots of fresh fish, shrimp, crab, and other local seafood. Call ☎ **727-391-7373.**

November

Chrysanthemum Festival: Cypress Gardens gets decked out with, get this, 3 million blooms that use a cascading waterfall for a centerpiece. Call ☎ **800-282-2123** or surf over to www.cypressgardens.com.

St. Petersburg Fall Boat Show: Held at the Bayfront Center, this event has grown into one of the largest shows in the Southeast — a good place to go for both shoppers and dreamers. Call ☎ **727-892-5767** for details about this year's show.

The Walt Disney World Festival of the Masters: One of the largest art shows in the South takes place at Downtown Disney Marketplace for three days, including the second weekend in November. The exhibition features top artists, photographers, and craftspeople, all winners of juried shows throughout the country. Admission is free. Call ☎ **407-824-4321** or visit the Mouse at http://disney.go.com/DisneyWorld/intro.html.

December

British Night Watch and Grand Illumination: Re-enactors in period costumes lead a torch-lit procession through St. Augustine's historic district during this stirring welcome to the holiday season. Daytime events include living-history displays. Discover more by calling ☎ **800-653-2489** (U.S. only) or 904-829-1711.

Disney Christmas: During the Disney Christmas festivities, Main Street in the Magic Kingdom is lavishly decked out with lights and holly, and carolers greet visitors. Thousands of colored lights illuminate an 80-foot tree. Epcot, Disney-MGM Studios, and Animal Kingdom also offer special embellishments and entertainment throughout the holiday season, as do all Disney resorts. Some holiday highlights include

 ✔ **Mickey's Very Merry Christmas Party,** an after-dark ticketed event. This event takes place weekends at the Magic Kingdom and offers a traditional Christmas parade and fireworks display. Admission is usually under $40, and it includes cookies, cocoa, and a souvenir photo. The best part? Shorter lines for the rides.

✔ The **Candlelight Procession** at Epcot features hundreds of candle-holding carolers, a celebrity narrator telling the Christmas story, and a 450-voice choir. It's very moving.

✔ **The Osborne Family Christmas Lights** came to Disney-MGM Studios in 1995, when an Arkansas family ran into trouble with hometown authorities over their multimillion-light display. In a twinkle, Disney moved the whole shebang to Florida. Call ☎ 407-824-4321 or visit the Disney Web site at http://disney.go.com/DisneyWorld/intro.html.

Christmas in the Park: Winter Park's signature holiday celebration uses the Morse Museum's Tiffany glass collection as a setting for the Bach Festival Choir program. Call ☎ 407-645-5311 for more information about the festivities hosted by this small town outside of Orlando.

Victorian Seaside Christmas: Amelia Island, located between Jacksonville and Fernandina Beach, puts on a month-long celebration that includes tours of bed-and-breakfasts, teddy bear teas, and sleigh rides on the beach. For more information, dial ☎ 800-226-3542 (U.S. only) or 904-277-0717.

Chapter 3

Planning Your Budget

. . . .

In This Chapter

▶ Managing your dollars and cents

▶ Avoiding surprise expenses

▶ Cutting costs and other frugal tidbits

. . . .

*D*eveloping a realistic budget is an important key to enjoying your vacation. The last thing that you want to experience when you get to Florida is sticker shock, and the state has been known to exact a pound of flesh from even the most cost-conscious travelers. From hotel rooms to restaurant tabs to admission fees, you can ring up a high tally if you don't do your homework in advance. The good news is that we can help you make sure that you don't bust your bankroll.

Adding Up the Elements

Budgeting a Florida vacation is easy. You can get a pretty accurate estimate of your total vacation cost, if you use the worksheets in the back of this book. The hard part is sticking to the budget. Call it the feeling-good phenomenon: Sometimes tourist attractions, souvenir stands, beaches, and 80-proof fun make people so giddy that they get separated from both their common sense and their finances. They end up in shock — especially when those credit-card bills begin arriving in the mail. But if you avoid too much impulse bingeing — er, buying — and draft an honest budget, you're home free.

Make sure to include everything in your vacation budget. Add in the cost of getting to the airport, airport parking (if you drive yourself), airline tickets (you can find tips for getting the best airfare in Chapter 5), transportation from your destination airport to your room or the rental car charge, the room rate, meals, attractions admissions (multiplied by the number of days you'll visit them), the cost of any sightseeing tours, souvenirs, and entertainment expenses. Tack on another 15 to 20 percent as a safety net.

Later in this chapter, we offer you a few ways to beat the high cost of Florida travel. (Also, check out the destination chapters, Chapters 10

to 23, for more money-saving travel tips.) But first, here are some
things to expect in the way of prices when you get to Florida.

Hitting the road

If you're going to stay put in one of Florida's big cities, you can get by
without a rental car. You can get around Miami (see Chapter 10),
Orlando (see Chapter 18), and to a lesser degree, Fort Lauderdale (see
Chapter 14), St. Petersburg (see Chapter 16), and Daytona Beach (see
Chapter 21) by hotel or private shuttles and tour services, especially if
you pick a room that's near the places you want to visit. You can also
get by without a car in St. Augustine and Key West, because most of
their hot spots are concentrated in reasonably small areas.

That said, you'll be at the mercy of the aforementioned services, you
may waste a good deal of time getting around using public and private
transportation, and in some cities (Miami for one), relying on taxis will
cost you a bundle. If you don't want the hassle or you're visiting a
smaller destination, rentals are advisable, if not a necessity. Rates start
at about $35 a day and $110 a week. Don't forget to add in the hotel and
attractions' parking fees, noted in the destination chapters (Chapters
10 to 23), as well as the 20 percent state taxes that are assessed on
rental cars in Florida.

Shacking up

Florida is a big state that wears several different faces, so don't pay
attention to hotel price information that mentions a statewide average —
averages don't exist here. A $50-a-night room in Crystal River (see
Chapter 16) may be a little above average, while a similarly priced room
in Miami will put you in an area that you definitely don't want to be in.
Due to these differences in rates, we give you a range in the destination
chapters (Chapters 10 to 23) that goes from low to high like this: $50 to
$100 inexpensive, $100 to $200 moderate, $200 to $250 expensive, and
$250 into the ionosphere. Those of you who insist on an average (don't
hold us to it) room rate, should expect to spend

- ✔ $30 to $60 in towns that are not-yet-discovered escapes

- ✔ $60 to $90 in the mid-Atlantic coastal region, north of Palm Beach
  and south of Cocoa Beach/Titusville, and on the Gulf Coast, north of
  the St. Pete/Tampa area and south of Sarasota (excluding Naples)

- ✔ $90 to $140 for the mainstream hotels in Miami and Orlando; the
  beaches of Daytona, Fort Lauderdale, and Naples; and the corporate zones in Tampa and Fort Lauderdale

- ✔ $150 to $250 for the expensive (but not top-notch) accommodations around Miami, Orlando, and Palm Beach; the state's golf and
  spa resorts; and the upper-end corporate and business zones in
  Fort Lauderdale, Jacksonville, Miami, Orlando, Tampa, and so on

> ✔ $250 and higher at the high-end resorts and corporate retreats found in Miami, Naples/Marco Island, Orlando, Palm Beach, and the Jacksonville area

Feeding your face

In most Florida cities, you can buy three squares for about $35 per person, per day (excluding tax, tip, and the 80-proof fun we mentioned a little earlier). You won't eat at gourmet restaurants for that amount, but you won't be condemned to Uncle Mel's No-Frills Grille, either. Allowing for $35 per person per day gets you into C+ to B+ eateries. Major tourist cities, such as Miami and Orlando, as well as business destinations, such as Jacksonville and Tampa, are going to be a pinch pricier. And if you're going to doom yourself to the theme parks, expect to pay 20 percent more for the same or lesser quality food.

We promise to give you four price levels in the dining areas of the destination chapters — $15 and under, $15 to $25, $25 to $40, and $40 and up — although we cater more to those of you on moderate budgets.

Keeping yourself entertained

When it comes to a day's entertainment, the amount you spend depends on what city you visit and what attractions and activities interest you the most. Orlando will unquestionably cost you more than any other Florida city. SeaWorld's new theme park, **Discovery Cove** (see Chapter 19) has raised the bar on attraction prices in Florida. Tickets are $199 for a day-long adventure in Discovery Cove that includes a 30-minute swim with the dolphins, seven days' admission to SeaWorld, lunch, and a few other wet-and-wild goodies. (It's $79, if you can skip the dolphin swim.)

Walt Disney World's four theme parks, **Universal's** two, and **SeaWorld** are at the next tier: $48 daily for adults and $38 for kids between the ages of 3 and 11. If you're going to be a regular, buy one of the multi-day, multi-park passes outlined in Chapter 19. **Busch Gardens** in Tampa (see Chapter 15) also falls in this tier.

The fees for Florida's other attractions range downward from those that you would pay at theme parks to free or next to nothing, for an endless string of museums. Table 3-1 has a cross section.

Table 3-1   A Sampling of Florida's Entertainment Options

Attraction	What It's Going to Cost You
Cypress Gardens (see Chapter 20)	$32 adults, $15 kids 6 to 17
Kennedy Space Center (see Chapter 20)	$24 adults, $15 kids 3 to 11

(continued)

Table 3-1   *(continued)*

Attraction	What It's Going to Cost You
Miami Seaquarium (see Chapter 11)	$22 adults, $17 kids 3 to 9
Key West Conch Train (see Chapter 12)	$18 adults, $9 kids 4 to 12
Daytona USA (see Chapter 21)	$12 adults, $6 kids 6 to 12
Salvador Dalí Museum (see Chapter 16)	$9 adults, free for kids under 10
Miami MetroZoo (see Chapter 11)	$8 adults, $4 kids 3 to 12

Hitting the stores

You won't find many bargains here. You also won't find much that's patently Florida, except overpriced seashells, stuffed Mickeys, and T-shirts from tourist-courting bars. Our best advice: Avoid the shops in the vacation zones. If you must buy, scout local newspapers for ads aimed at the townies and shop where they do. Also, be wary of the so-called factory outlets that promise deep discounts. Most of them don't deliver. (Knowing the suggested retail prices coming in is a good idea, so you can smell a rat, if there's one lurking.) Miami, being an international city, features the most diverse shopping anywhere in the state.

We have many of the same retailers found in other U.S. states: **Sears, Lord & Taylor, Burdines,** and **Dillard's.** Their sales will probably appeal to travelers coming from another country, but Americans can find the same prices at home. Ditto for the discount chains, such as **Service Merchandise,** computer sellers, such as **CompUSA,** and electronics marts, including **Circuit City** and **Radio Shack.**

Boogieing the night away

Here's a good rule of thumb when it comes to Florida nightlife: If a destination has a beach, it has a bar that hops from mid-morning into the wee hours. Miami, specifically **South Beach,** arguably has the hottest nightclub scene, thanks to its Latin culture. Disney's **Pleasure Island** and Universal's **CityWalk** have given Orlando reason to shine after dark. (Table 3-2 lists examples of expenses you'll likely encounter during an Orlando stay.) To a smaller degree, that's also the case in **Ybor City** near Tampa, where the music also has Latin spice.

Most bars are free, and cover charges vary according to city. Covers generally run from free to $20, depending on the city; Miami and Orlando clubs generally charge the highest covers in the state. The most expensive clubs are located in the hot spots mentioned, where drinks tend to be pricey ($5 and up), so try to hit a happy hour — getting loaded won't cost you a load of cash. Clubbing, assuming that you can find a club in some of the quieter spots, usually costs much less in the smaller cities. (Table 3-3 lists expense examples similar to those you'll encounter during a stay in Naples.)

Table 3-2   What Things Cost in Orlando

Item	U.S.$	U.K.£ (At press time, $1.48=1£)
Taxi from airport to Walt Disney World	42.00	28.42
Shuttle from airport to Walt) Disney World (adult fare	14.00	9.47
Double room at Disney's Grand Floridian Resort & Spa	304.00–1,995.00	205.72–1,350.02
Double room at Portofino Bay Hotel	235.00–770.00	152.70–534.75
Double room at Disney's Port Orleans Resort	124.00–189.00	83.91–127.90
Double room at Disney's All-Star Movie Resort	74.00–104.00	50.08–70.38
All-you-can-eat buffet dinner at Akershus in Epcot, not including tip or wine	18.50	12.52
Dinner entrees at Dux	19.00–45.00	13.15–31.25
Bottle of beer (restaurant)	2.50	1.69
Coca-Cola (restaurant)	1.25	.85
Roll of Kodak film, 36 exposures, purchased at Walt Disney World	9.45	6.39
Adult 1-day, 1-park admission to Walt Disney World, Universal, or SeaWorld	48.00	32.05
Child 1-day, 1-park admission to Walt Disney World, Universal, or SeaWorld	38.00	25.68

Table 3-3   What Things Cost in Naples

Item	U.S.$	U.K.£ (At press time, $1.48=1£)
Shuttle for 3 from Southwest Florida International Airport	38.00–56.00	25.68–37.84
Double room at The Inn on Fifth (winter/peak)	209.00–369.00	141.21–249.32

(continued)

Table 3-3 *(continued)*

Item	U.S.$	U.K.£ *(At press time, $1.48=1£)*
Double room at The Naples Beach Hotel & Golf Club (summer/value)	95.00–200.00	64.19–135.14
Dinner entrees at Marek's Collier House Restaurant (Marco Island)	18.00–32.50	12.16–21.96
Dinner entrees at The Dock at Crayton Cove	8.50–20.00	5.74–13.51
Coca-Cola (inside attraction)	$1.20	.81
Roll of Kodak film, 36 exposures, at Walgreens	6.99	4.73
Adult admission to Caribbean Gardens	15.00	10.14
Child admission to Caribbean Gardens	10.00	6.76
Adult admission to Teddy Bear Museum	6.00	4.05
Child admission to Klassix Auto Attraction	2.00	1.35

Keeping a Lid on Hidden Expenses

Be on the lookout for these not-so-nice surprises:

✔ **Sales tax:** Florida adds a 6 percent sales tax to most items, except groceries and medical services. Additionally, some communities have a local-option sales tax and a bed tax on hotel rooms that can push the tax total to 12 percent or higher.

✔ **Rental-car charges:** Sales tax, surcharges, and various other required add-ons could add 20 to 25 percent to the rates that rental-car companies will quote you. To avoid a last-minute shock, ask about these add-ons when you book.

✔ **Phoning home:** If ever there was a travel commandment that should not be broken, this is it: Thou shalt not make a telephone call from thy hotel room without first asking how much it will cost. Although some hotels don't charge for local calls, most do. And the charge for a long-distance call can be marked up by as much as 200 percent. Some hotels charge you even if you use your calling card. Save yourself a coronary and ask before you dial, or better yet, use pay phones — almost all hotels have them in their lobbies.

✔ **Minibar charges:** We are convinced that the hotel minibar is actually a small replica of Fort Knox. Although, in all fairness, gold may actually be cheaper than some of the items in these money-grabbers. Even looking isn't free; many of the minibars at better hotels have a built-in sensor system that charges you the minute you *touch* an item. Sure those peanuts are convenient, but are they worth the price of your kids' college tuition?

✔ **Tipping:** The number of people who forget to factor gratuities into their budget often surprises us. Gratuities generally run 15 percent for restaurant service and cab rides. (In the case of restaurants, double-check the bill before you tip. Many restaurants automatically add a gratuity to the check.) Housekeepers at your hotel may be worth $1 to $2 a day for cleaning your mess, making your beds, and keeping you in towels. Baggage handlers usually get $1 per bag (but zip if they lose the handles).

✔ **Park food:** As we mentioned earlier, those of you who spend time at the major theme parks and some smaller attractions, such as the Kennedy Space Center or Parrot Jungle, may be stuck paying more than your fair share for meals that aren't contenders for platinum-spoon awards.

Cutting Costs

Considering the number of warnings we've already dished out, by now you must be wondering whether you can afford this place. Of course you can. It's simply a matter of choosing a vacation that fits your budget. Florida isn't as pricey as some folks think. Sure, there are five-star crash pads that will steal your breath and a healthy chunk of your kids' inheritance, but the millions of tourists that arrive every year have created considerable competition, and that can result in bargains.

After you've settled on your accommodations and airfare, you can keep the other expenses in check by regulating what attractions you see, where you eat, and how much time you spend doing the free stuff or things that are included in your room rate. (A day at the motel pool is a tad cheaper than taking a family of four deep-sea fishing or visiting the Miami MetroZoo and Miami Seaquarium in one day.) There are plenty of ways — some little, some big — to cut costs.

✔ **Go in the off-season.** During nonpeak times — October and November, April and May, and the two weeks before Christmas — you'll find that the airlines and hotels slash their prices by as much as 50 percent. These are the best times of year to travel, if you're trying to save money (and avoid crowds).

✔ **Buy a package tour.** For many destinations, one call to a travel agent or packager can net you airfare, hotel reservations, a car, and some sightseeing or attractions tickets, all for much less than if you tried to put the trip together yourself. Even if you don't want to go with a complete package — say, if you want to buy your airfare with frequent-flyer miles or you just don't like what a full package offers — you can book room/car deals or other special packages directly through some hotels. (See Chapter 5 for more information in package tours.)

✔ **Always ask about discounts.** Membership in AAA, frequent-flyer plans, trade unions, AARP, the military, your company, or other groups may qualify you for discounted rates on plane tickets, hotel rooms, car rentals, and even meals. Many attractions also offer discounts to members of certain organizations. Ask about everything — you could end up pleasantly surprised.

✔ **Reserve a room with a kitchen.** Use these features to cook some of your meals. It may not feel as much like a vacation as snapping your fingers for service in a fine restaurant, but you'll save a heck of a lot of money this way. Even if you only make breakfast and an occasional bag lunch in the kitchen, you'll still save in the long run. This is also a good way to make sure that a hefty room-service bill won't shock you. Room service is among the costlier ways to eat, and the food quality often rivals cardboard.

✔ **Skip the room with a view.** Rooms with great views are the most expensive rooms in any hotel. Since you probably won't be hanging out in your room all day anyway, why pay the price? (See Chapter 7 for more about room rates and views.)

✔ **Ask if your kids can stay in your room with you.** A room with two double beds usually doesn't cost any more than one with a queen-size bed, and many hotels won't charge the additional-person rate, if the additional person is pint-size and related to you. Even if you have to pay $10 or $15 for a rollaway bed, you'll save a ton by not taking two rooms.

✔ **Pick up those free, coupon-packed visitor magazines.** Detailed maps, feature stories, dining and shopping directories, and discount coupons give these pocketsize giveaways a good wallop. One of the more common visitor magazines is the *Discount Guide to Florida,* which can be found for free at 12,000 locations around the state (give or take a few, of course). The guide offers discounted hotel and resort rates. Advance planners can get a copy by mail, for a $3 shipping fee, by calling ☎ **800-332-3948** from 8 a.m. to 8 p.m., weekdays.

✔ **Skip souvenirs.** Make your photographs and memories the best mementos of your trip. If you're worried about money, do without the T-shirts, seashells, key chains, salt-and-pepper shakers, mouse ears, and other trinkets. Set a spending limit and stick to it!

Chapter 4

Planning for Travelers with Special Needs

● ●

In This Chapter

▶ Traveling with a family

▶ Visiting Florida, senior-style

▶ Realizing a world without barriers

▶ Gaining another barrier-free view

● ●

*I*t's time to dispense a little advice for travelers with special needs. The last thing you want or need is a vacation that's too old, young, or restrictive for you or your lifestyle. There are so many things to see and do in Florida that anybody should be able to find something suitable. Many cities also provide specialized services for those with special needs, so if you need help, just ask.

Making Family Travel Fun

Florida is a kid-friendly destination. Most of the state's major attractions were designed with kids in mind; nearly all restaurants have special menus for young diners; and many hotels let youngsters stay in their parents' room at no extra charge. Many of Florida's beach resorts offer activities for kids, and in some cases, full daily programs to occupy their time. A number of hotels also offer baby-sitting services so moms and dads can have a night on their own. And Disney and Orlando cater to youngsters in triplicate, day or night.

If you have a chance, take a look at *Family Travel Times*, an excellent bimonthly newsletter that covers all aspects of family travel. Subscriptions cost $39 a year. Call ☎ **888-822-4388** or 212-477-5524 to subscribe. You can also peruse back issues on the newsletter's Web site at www.familytraveltimes.com.

Here are some general rules and reminders for your family to consider when planning a trip to Florida:

✔ **Discount coupons:** After you arrive, keep an eye out for coupons that discount meals and attractions. Some are two-for-one specials, while others offer a percentage taken off the regular price. You can find these coupons in giveaway newspapers and magazines in the lobbies of hotels and restaurants. Also, check the Friday entertainment sections in local newspapers.

✔ **Accommodations and children:** Kids under 12, and in many cases under 18, stay free in their parents' room in most hotels. If you're not sure of the policy at individual locations, ask when making a reservation. Look for places that have pools and other recreational facilities and then spend a no-extra-expense day or two away from costly tourist attractions.

✔ **Ground rules:** It's tough to be firm when the object is fun, but consider setting up rules on such things as bedtimes and souvenirs. It can soften the disappointment after you're here.

✔ **Lost and found:** Getting lost inside the larger tourist attractions and areas is as easy as remembering your middle name. In their guide maps, many attractions outline what to do if you or your child gets lost. If your kids are 7 or under, attach a nametag to the inside of their shirt or jacket. (If children are crying and scared, they may have trouble giving park staffers their name.) It's also a good idea for older kids and adults to choose a place to reunite if they get separated.

✔ **Staying safe:** Your home may be toddler-proof, but hotel rooms aren't. Bring blank plugs to cover outlets and whatever else is necessary to prevent an accident from happening in your room. Also, pack *sunscreen* and hats for the entire family, including infants and toddlers. If you forget to bring sunscreen, buy some at a convenience store or drugstore. Get one that has an SPF (sun protection factor) rating of 25 or higher. Young children should be slathered with sunscreen, even if they're in a stroller. Adults and children should also drink plenty of water to avoid dehydration during Florida's hot months, especially May through September.

✔ **Snack times:** If you're going to be spending much time on the road, on the beach, or in tourist attractions, bring some lightweight snacks in an easy-to-carry backpack. These snacks may save you headaches and money (concessions at attractions sometimes charge double what the free world charges).

✔ **Nap time:** Don't try to overextend yourselves in the touring department, because the only things you have to gain are hot, tired, and cranky kids. Take frequent breaks when touring the major attractions and, if possible, go back to your hotel room and spend a little downtime before hitting the sights again.

> ✔ **Playtime for parents:** It's your vacation too! If your hotel offers a babysitting service, book a sitter for the night and go out for a romantic dinner or another adult-oriented activity.

Planning Tips for the Senior Set

With the exception of kid-crazy Orlando, Florida is as popular among seniors (especially during the fall and winter months) as it is with the families that flock here during holidays and summers. Many Florida hotels, restaurants, and attractions roll out the red carpet for older travelers.

Keep in mind that although some of us may look the part, others don't. If you look younger than your years, consider yourself blessed and always carry some form of photo ID so you can take advantage of discounts. Minimum ages for discounts vary from 50 on up, so it never hurts to ask when making a reservation or buying an admission ticket.

If you're not a member of the **American Association of Retired Persons (AARP),** 601 E St. NW, Washington, DC 20049 (☎ **202-434-2277;** Internet: www.aarp.org/travel), do yourself a favor and sign up. Membership — open to anyone 50 or over — costs $8 per person or couple and entitles you to many discounts. Call AARP to obtain a free list of hotels, motels, and car-rental firms that offer discounts to AARP members.

Mature Outlook, P.O. Box 9390, Des Moines, IA 50306-9519 (☎ **800-336-6330**), is a program by Sears that offers discounts on car rentals, motels, and more. The $40 annual fee also includes department-store savings.

The Mature Traveler, a monthly 12-page newsletter on senior citizen travel, is available by subscription ($30 a year) from GEM Publishing Group, P.O. Box 50400, Reno, NV 89513-0400. GEM also publishes *The Book of Deals,* a collection of more than 1,000 senior discounts on airlines, lodging, tours, and attractions around the United States; it's available for $10 by calling ☎ **800-460-6676.** Another helpful publication is *101 Tips for the Mature Traveler,* available from **Grand Circle Travel,** 347 Congress St., Suite 3A, Boston, MA 02210 (☎ **800-221-2610** or 617-350-7500, fax 617-350-6206).

The **National Council of Senior Citizens**, 8403 Colesville Rd., Suite 1200, Silver Spring, MD 20910-3314 (☎ **301-578-8800**), is a nonprofit organization that publishes a newsletter six times a year (partly devoted to travel tips) and offers discounts on hotel and auto rentals; annual dues are $13 per person or couple.

Here are some additional ways to save:

✔ The **Hilton Senior Honors Program,** available to people 60 and older, provides discounts of up to 50 percent off hotel rooms. The annual membership is $50 per person, but because spouses stay for free, only one of you needs to join if you travel together. Call ☎ **800-432-3600** between 7 a.m. and 7 p.m. CST, Monday through Friday.

✔ The **Choice Hotels** group (**Comfort, Clarion, Sleep, Rodeway, Econo Lodge,** and **Friendship**) gives travelers 50 and older 30 percent off regular rates if they reserve in advance (10 percent off for walk-ins). The hotels set aside only a few rooms for these Senior Saver Discounts, so book early. Call ☎ **800-424-4777** for Econo Lodge, Rodeway, and Friendship Inns, and ☎ **800-221-2222** for the others.

✔ Most U.S. airlines sell senior airfare coupons for travelers 62 and older. Each coupon is good for one flight anywhere in the United States. You can buy a packet of four coupons for $542 to $596. Each coupon is valid for one-way travel.

✔ **Amtrak** offers a 15 percent discount on the lowest available coach fare (with certain travel restrictions) to people 62 and over. Contact Amtrak at ☎ **800-872-7245.**

Traveling Without Barriers

A disability shouldn't keep anyone from visiting most of Florida's popular tourist areas, and the major destinations do a lot to lift barriers.

You can get a free copy of the *Planning Guide for Travelers with Disability* from Visit Florida, P.O. Box 1100, Tallahassee, FL 32302-1100 (☎ **888-735-2872;** Internet: www.flausa.com). The major theme parks in Orlando all offer guidebooks that are specially geared to disabled guests. Ask for these publications at the parks' guest services desks when you arrive.

A World of Options, a 658-page book of resources for physically challenged travelers, covers everything from biking trips to scuba outfitters. The book costs $35 and is available from Mobility International USA, P.O. Box 10767, Eugene, OR 97440 (☎ **541-343-1284,** voice and TTY; Internet: www.miusa.org). Another place to check out is Access-Able Travel Source (Internet: www.access-able.com), a comprehensive database of travel agents who specialize in disabled travel. The database also serves as a clearinghouse for information about accessible destinations around the world. Also check out iCan online (www.ican.com), a network run by people with disabilities for people with disabilities, which will help you find accessible vacation spots and share stories with other disabled vacationers.

The **Moss Rehab Hospital** (☎ 215-456-9600) has been providing friendly and helpful phone advice and referrals to disabled travelers for years through its **Travel Information Service** (☎ 215-456-9603; Internet: www.mossresourcenet.org).

If you require special considerations, you may also want to consider joining a tour group that caters specifically to the physically challenged. One of the best operators is **Flying Wheels Travel**, P.O. Box 382, Owatonna, MN 55060 (☎ 800-535-6790; fax 507-451-1685). It offers escorted tours and cruises, as well as private tours in minivans with lifts. Another good company is **FEDCAP Rehabilitation Services**, 211 W. 14th St., New York, NY 10011. Call ☎ 212-727-4200 or fax 212-727-4373 for information about membership and summer tours. **The Guided Tour, Inc.** (☎ 215-782-1370) runs trips to Florida every 6 weeks and utilizes wheelchair-lift vans for some of the tours. Finally, **Wilderness Inquiry** (☎ 800-728-0719 or 612-379-3858) organizes Everglades excursions for the physically challenged.

If you're vision-impaired, contact the **American Foundation for the Blind**, 11 Penn Plaza, Suite 300, New York, NY 10001. Call ☎ 800-232-5463 for information on traveling with guide dogs.

You can also obtain a copy of *Air Transportation of Handicapped Persons* by requesting Free Advisory Circular No. AC12032, from the Distribution Unit, U.S. Department of Transportation, Publications Division, M-4332, Washington, DC 20590.

Many of the major car rental companies now offer hand-controlled cars for disabled drivers. Avis can provide such a vehicle at any of its locations in the United States with 48-hour advance notice; Hertz requires advance reservations of 24 to 72 hours at most of its locations. Likewise, Wheelchair Getaways (☎ 800-536-5518 or 606-873-4973; Internet: www.wheelchairgetaways.com) rents specialized vans with wheelchair lifts and other features for the physically challenged.

A handicap permit is required for parking in parking places designated for the disabled. Handicap permits from other states are honored, but a disabled license plate alone won't do the job.

Amtrak (☎ 800-872-7245) provides redcap service, wheelchair assistance, and special seats if you give 72-hours notice. Travelers with disabilities are also entitled to a 15 percent discount off the lowest available adult coach fare. Documentation from a doctor or an ID card proving your disability is required, however. Amtrak also provides wheelchair-accessible sleeping accommodations on long-distance trains. Amtrak permits service dogs aboard, and they travel free. For a free booklet called *Amtrak's America,* which includes a chapter detailing services for passengers with disabilities, call ☎ 800-872-7245, or go online to www.amtrak.com. TDD/TTY service is also available at 800-523-6590; or you can write to P.O. Box 7717, Itasca, IL 60143.

Internet users can surf over to www.disabilities.com/travel.htm, for a list of other sources dealing with travel or travel products for the disabled.

Planning Advice for Gay and Lesbian Travelers

Although Florida has a few pockets of intolerance, most of the state has active gay and lesbian contingents. Many of the large cities and several of the smaller coastal areas are especially receptive to gay and lesbian guests. Miami's South Beach and Key West are extraordinarily popular with gay and lesbian travelers, and Orlando's Gay Weekend in June attracts thousands.

You can get information about events for Gay Weekend, as well as events that occur throughout the year, from Gay, Lesbian & Bisexual Community Services of Central Florida, 934 N. Mills Ave., Orlando, FL 32803. Call ☎ **407-425-4527** or 407-843-4297, or check out the Internet: www.glbcc.org for more information. Welcome packets usually include the latest issue of *Triangle,* a quarterly newsletter (☎ **407-849-0099**) dedicated to gay and lesbian issues, and a calendar of events pertaining to Florida's gay and lesbian community. Though not a tourist-specific packet, the welcome packet includes information and ads for the area's clubs. *Watermark* is another gay-friendly publication that you can find in many Central Florida bookstores; it can also be ordered online at (www.amazon.com).

For state-specific information on the Net, try **The Gay Guide to Florida** at http://gay-guide.com; this site has a wealth of information, especially nightlife listings.

There are two good, biannual, English-language gay guidebooks, both focused on gay men but including information for lesbians as well. You can get the *Spartacus International Gay Guide* or *Odysseus* from most gay and lesbian bookstores and, often, from the large chain stores as well, or you can order them from **Giovanni's Room** (☎ **215-923-2960**) or **A Different Light Bookstore** (☎ **800-343-4002** or 212-989-4850; Internet: www.adlbooks.com). Both lesbians and gays may want to pick up a copy of *Gay Travel A to Z.* The **Ferrari Guides** (Internet: www.q-net.com) are yet another very good series of gay and lesbian guidebooks.

Out and About, 8 W. 19th St. #401, New York, NY 10011 (☎ **800-929-2268** or 212-645-6922; Internet: www.outandabout.com), offers guidebooks and a monthly newsletter packed with good information on the global gay and lesbian scene. Its Web site is especially comprehensive. A year's subscription to the newsletter costs $49.

Travel agencies include **Family Abroad,** servicing gay and lesbian travelers, (☎ **800-999-5500** **212-459-1800,** 212-459-1800) and **Above and Beyond Tours,** geared toward gay men, (☎ **800-397-2681;** Internet: www.abovebeyondtours.com).

Travelers can also contact the **International Gay & Lesbian Travel Association** (☎ **800-448-8550** or 954-776-2626; Internet: www.iglta.org). This organization connects travelers with service organizations and tour specialists, as well as hotels, airlines, and cruise specialists.

Part II
Ironing Out the Details

The 5th Wave By Rich Tennant

"Oh, quit looking so uncomfortable. This is Miami! No one wears a cape and formal wear in Miami."

In this part . . .

Okay. It's time to slide a little deeper into the lock-and-load mode. This part of the book opens by chatting about travel agents, package tours, and sources for bargain airfares. Then we talk about getting around Florida, zeroing in on a room that's right for you, and money matters, such as whether to use traveler's checks or credit cards. Finally, we discuss travel and medical insurance, making advance reservations for the fun things, and how to pack with the best of them.

So, if you're ready, sing a little traveling music with us!

Chapter 5

Getting to Florida

• •

In This Chapter

▶ Consulting a travel agent

▶ Choosing a package tour

▶ Buying an airline ticket

▶ Using alternate travel methods

• •

*G*etting there *isn't* half the fun for most travelers, especially those of us enduring airport lines, stewing over flight delays, or getting bumped involuntarily by airlines that overbook their flights (which seems to be virtually all of them). But the trip doesn't have to be an expensive hassle. It doesn't require a master's degree in planning, either. In this chapter, we cut through the baloney and make sure you have an easier time than those who didn't map out their campaign in advance.

Most of you are going to fly to Florida. But before you make those arrangements, you need to decide whether you want to do it yourself or use a hired gun.

Friend or Foe? Hiring a Travel Agent

The first task to complete after you decide where you want to go on vacation is deciding whether you want to book your vacation yourself or use a hired gun. Many Internet-savvy travelers choose to research and book airfares and hotel accommodations online, but if you prefer discussing your options with an expert, working with a travel agent is your best bet.

A good travel agent is like a good mechanic or plumber — hard to find, but invaluable once you latch on to the right one. The best way to find a five-star model is the same way you find a contractor or a doctor — word of mouth. Ask a friend who travels often if he or she has a favorite.

All travel agents can find you bargain rental-car rates, accommodations, or airfares. Good travel agents stop you from choosing the wrong deal, even if it is cheap. The best travel agents can help you with all aspects of your vacation: arranging decent rental rates, budgeting your time, booking better hotels with comparable prices, finding cheap flights that don't require five layovers, and recommending restaurants.

Travel agents work on commission, which is good news and bad news. The good news: You don't have to pay the commission — the airlines, resorts, and tour operators take care of payment. The bad news: Unscrupulous agents will try to persuade you to book vacations that earn them the most commission, while taking the least amount of their time to arrange. Unfortunately, these commissions lead to ugly news too.

The ugly news: Over the past few years, many airlines and some resorts have started eliminating or limiting travel-agent commissions. Therefore, some travel agents don't bother to book these services unless you specifically request them. In fact, some travel analysts predict that if more players in the travel industry follow suit, agents may start charging customers for their services. When and if that day arrives — and even now — you should consider using reservation agents associated with the airlines themselves. However, make sure that you receive a good deal. To do so, call the airlines two or three times (most have toll-free numbers), get a 24-hour confirmation number (the airlines will hold a reservation for 24 hours before making you book a ticket) for any rate that differs from previous quotes, go with the best rate, and cancel the others.

Travel agents also get a commission for booking you into mega-resorts, such as **Walt Disney World.** However, they're usually a better source of information than resort receptionists, who will answer questions but won't volunteer any money-saving tips. Shop around among airlines, too. (See the Appendix in the back of this book for the toll-free numbers and URLs of the major airlines.) Delta is a big player in the Florida packages arena, especially those with Disney as a destination (see "Packaging Your Travel" in this chapter).

If you want to grade a travel agent, do a little homework. Flip through our sections on accommodations in this book (see Chapter 7) and choose a few that appeal to you. If you have access to the Internet, check prices on the Web (see "Finding affordable airfare," later in this chapter). You can then take your notes and ask a travel agent to make the arrangements for you. Because they have access to better resources than the most complete travel Web site, travel agents should be able to offer you a better price than the one you can get yourself. Likewise, travel agents can issue your tickets or vouchers on the spot, and if they can't get your preferred hotel, they can recommend an alternative.

After you've digested the information on package tours in the next segment, you can ask your travel agent to book the package of your choice (at no added cost to you), plus add-ons, such as airport transfers and side trips. Using a travel agent can make life much easier — and cheaper — for you.

Packaging Your Travel

Package tours aren't the same as escorted tours. *Package tours* give you the opportunity to buy airfare, accommodations, and add-ons (optional items such as meal plans, rental cars or airport transfers, attractions passes, and so on) at the same time. Escorted tours place the details of the trip in someone else's hands while you sit back and enjoy the ride. We discuss the ins and outs of both deals in the following sections.

Buying package tours

For popular destinations, such as Florida, packages are the smart way to go because they often offer discounts that you could never get if you booked all the elements of your vacation separately. Package prices are low because they are sold in bulk to tour operators, who resell them to the public. It's kind of like buying your vacation at one of those mega-store membership discount clubs. Except here, the tour operator buys the 1,000-count box of garbage bags and resells them ten at a time, at a cost that undercuts what you'd pay at your neighborhood supermarket.

Four things can help you differentiate the real deals from the duds:

✔ **Research, research, research.** Do a little homework on Florida by reading this guide. Decide what cities in Florida you want to visit and pick some accommodations that you think you'll like. Compare the rack rates (standard hotel rates) that we list to the discount rates offered by the packagers to see what kinds of deals they offer, or whether they're just gussying up rack rates to make their full-fare offer *sound* like a deal. And remember: Don't just compare packagers to each other; compare the *deals* packagers offer on similar properties. What you save depends on the property you choose; most packagers offer bigger savings on specific properties.

✔ **Read the fine print.** When you compare packages, you don't want to compare apples and oranges. Make sure you know *exactly* what's included in the price you're quoted and what's not. Don't assume anything: Some packagers include everything but the kitchen sink, including plenty of extra discounts on restaurants and activities, while others don't include airfare. (Believe it or not, some airline packages don't include airfare because airlines know how fares can fluctuate better than anyone, and they don't want to get locked into a yearlong promise.)

✔ **Recognize your options.** Know what you're getting into and whether you can get yourself out of it. Before you commit to a package, make sure you know how much flexibility the package offers. Some packagers require ironclad commitments, while others will go with the flow, perhaps charging minimal fees for changes or cancellations. Make mental notes of the possibilities that might affect your situation, and ask all the right questions: What's the cancellation policy if my kid gets sick at the last minute and we can't go? What if the office calls me home three days into my vacation? What if we want to adjust our schedule and go west when the itinerary goes east?

✔ **Use your best judgment.** Stay away from fly-by-nights and shady packagers. If a package appears to be too good to be true, it probably is. Go with a reputable firm with a proven track record. Your travel agent can come in handy in this situation; he or she should be knowledgeable about different packagers, the deals they offer, and the general rate of satisfaction among their customers. If the agent doesn't seem savvy, take your business elsewhere.

Packages vary as much as garbage bags. Some packages offer a better class of hotels than others; some offer lower prices; some offer flights on scheduled airlines; and others book charters. In some packages, your choice of accommodations and travel days may be limited.

Taking an escorted tour

Some packages let you choose between escorted and independent vacations; others let you add escorted trips (also at prices lower than if you book them yourself). You may enjoy escorted tours, if you like to let bus drivers do the work while you sit back and catch the sights, or if you prefer having your day pre-planned. Escorted tours are the way to go if you want someone else to handle the details, while also controlling your destinations. Tours can get you maximum exposure to Florida, but they don't necessarily take you to all the places you want to see — and freedom is at an absolute minimum. However, with escorted tours, you know all your costs up front, and you won't experience many surprises.

Ask yourself these simple questions before buying an escorted tour:

✔ **What's the cancellation policy?** Can the company cancel your reservation, and can you cancel with a full refund either way? What are the conditions of cancellation? If you can receive a refund, how soon can you expect to receive it?

✔ **How packed is the schedule?** Is the tour trying to fit 25 hours of sights into a 24-hour day, or do you have time to relax, shop, and do other individual things? If you don't like getting out of bed at 7 a.m. and being on the road for 12 hours or more, an escorted tour may not be right for you.

✔ **How big is the group?** Smaller groups are more flexible, which means you won't have to spend time waiting on your traveling companions. Always ask about group size. Some tours have a minimum group size and may cancel if there aren't enough people. And if there are enough people, you may find the group too large for your preferences.

✔ **What does your tour include?** Don't assume anything. Always ask. You may have to get yourself to and from the airport, or you may have to pay for drinks to accompany the included box lunch. Can you opt out of activities that don't appeal to you, or does the bus take everyone to every stop? Are meals planned in advance? Can you choose an entrée or are you stuck with the tube steak du jour?

If you choose an escorted tour, think strongly about purchasing travel insurance (see Chapter 9), especially if the tour operator asks you to pay up front. But don't buy insurance from the tour operator! If they don't fulfill their obligation to provide you with the vacation you've paid for, you have no reason to think they'll fulfill their insurance obligations either. Obtain travel insurance through an independent agency.

Finding packagers

If you decide that you want to give package tours a try, your next course of action is to find the package that best fits your needs. To find travel packages, check the ads in the back of national magazines such as *Travel & Leisure* and *Condé Nast Traveler,* or those magazines that include travel arm sections, such as *Elegant Bride.* You can also check the travel section of your Sunday newspaper, but your best bets are the choices we outline in this section.

Some of the most popular Florida packages revolve around Orlando and its theme parks. The major parks themselves offer numerous packages:

✔ **Walt Disney World** (see Chapters 18 to 20) offers a dizzying array of packages, some of which include airfare, a room on or off Disney property, theme-park passes, a rental car, meals, a Disney cruise, and/or a stay at Disney's beach resort in Vero Beach. You can get more information about Disney packages by calling ☎ **800-828-0228** or 407-828-8101, heading online to `http://disney.go.com/DisneyWorld/intro.html`, or writing to Walt Disney World, Box 10000, Lake Buena Vista, FL 32830-1000. Ask for a *Walt Disney World Vacations* brochure or video.

✔ **Universal Studios** packages, although not on the same scale as Disney, have improved greatly, with the addition of the **Islands of Adventure** park (see Chapter 19), the **CityWalk** food-and-club district (Chapter 20), and the Portofino Bay Resort (Chapter 18). The menu includes rooms, VIP access to the parks, and discounts to other non-Disney attractions. Universal Studios also offers packages in conjunction with Carnival Cruise Line, some including travel and transportation. Contact **Universal Studios Vacations** at ☎ **888-322-5537** or 407-224-7000, or go online to `www.usevacations.com`.

✔ **SeaWorld** offers three-night packages that include rooms at a handful of Orlando hotels, car rental, tickets to SeaWorld (see Chapter 19), and in some cases, other parks. You can get information by calling ☎ **800-423-8368,** or online at `www.seaworld.com`.

The competition is not only stiff in Orlando but in other major Florida tourist destinations, including Miami, Fort Lauderdale, Daytona Beach, and Tampa/St. Petersburg. Check the packagers we list in this section to see what options they offer in your chosen destination.

Airline packages

Many airlines package their flights with lodging and other accommodations. When you pick an airline, you can choose one that offers frequent service to your hometown and allows you to accumulate frequent-flyer miles.

Delta Dream Vacations, the big fish in the pond, offers selections that can include round-trip airfare, lodging (including tax and baggage tips), a rental car with unlimited mileage or round-trip transfers from the airport, admission to some theme parks, accommodations, and so on.

Prices for Delta Dream Vacations usually vary depending on the package, property, departure city, and season. Call ☎ **800-872-7786,** or visit Delta online at www.deltavacations.com/disney.html.

Continental Airlines Vacations offers several packages that include airfare, car rental, and hotel stays at numerous Florida hotels and resorts. You can apply miles earned from the airline's frequent-flyer program to some packages, and you can make reservations with or without air service. Call ☎ **800-525-0280** for general information, or check out www.coolvacations.com online.

For other airline-package possibilities, see the phone numbers and Web sites for the various airlines listed in the Appendix in the back of this book.

Other package resources

Besides airline and theme park offerings, you can also find vacation packages elsewhere. **American Express Vacations** (☎ **800-941-2639;** Internet: http://travel.americanexpress.com/travel/personal) is one option. **Liberty Travel** (☎ **888-271-1584;** Internet: www.libertytravel.com) is one of the biggest vacation packagers in the Northeast and usually offers a number of good Florida deals.

Take a look at what some of the other package specialists can provide:

   ✔ If you're a linkster, you have several packagers from which to choose. **Golf Getaways** (☎ **800-423-3657;** Internet: www.golfgetaways.com), **Golf Travel Online** (☎ **888-486-4653;** Internet: www.gto.com), **Golfpac Vacations** (☎ **800-327-0878;** Internet: www.golfpacinc.com), and **golf.com** (Internet: www.golf.com) offer a slate of play-and-stay packages — from the most basic to the extraordinarily comprehensive.

✔ **Globus** repeatedly garners awards to lead the pack of tour operators. It balances scheduled sightseeing with leisure time and offers both escorted and independent tours. The company offers a 10-day escorted tour of Florida and the Bahamas.

To induce adults to bring their kiddies along, Globus grants a 10 percent discount on the land-only price to tour members under 18 that are accompanied by an adult. This company doesn't accept children under 8 for escorted tours, but kids of all ages are welcome on independent tours. For more information on Globus tours, contact your travel agent or check the Globus Web site at www.globustours.com.

✔ Many travelers swear by **Tauck Tours.** This tour company's attention to detail is legendary, and it offers two escorted tours of Florida, covering most of the major hot spots and tourist attractions. Individuals with special needs must travel with an able-bodied companion. For more information, call your travel agent or contact Tauck Tours (☎ **800-468-2825;** Internet: www.tauck.com).

✔ **SunStyle** (☎ **888-786-7895;** Internet: www.sunstyle.com), a wholesale operator, packages tickets, airfare, and car rentals.

✔ **Touraine Travel** (☎ **800-967-5583;** Internet: www.tourainetravel.com) offers a wide variety of Florida packages for mainstream travelers.

Information junkies should check out www.vacationpackager.com on the Internet. The site offers a search engine that can link you to many tour operators that offer Florida vacation packages.

Making Your Own Arrangements

Packages simply don't work for some people. Maybe you have your heart set on a city or resort that's not included in available package options, or maybe you want to use frequent-flyer miles for your tickets. Well, don't fret. This doesn't mean you'll get stuck paying rack rates for everything. The fact is that sometimes going a la carte saves a bundle — especially for destinations in South Florida, where packages frequently include many items that travelers won't use or don't need. Use the information that follows to get a decent price when booking your airfare.

Flying there

All of the major U.S. domestic carriers, many of the international ones, and some charter services offer regular flights into Florida's top four destinations. (In order, they are Miami, Orlando, Tampa, and Fort Lauderdale-Hollywood International Airports). Combined, this four-pack handles 92 million passengers per year. (See the Appendix in the back of the book for a list of the toll-free numbers and URLs for the major airlines.) And if the mainstream airports don't serve your preferred drop zone, the state has 13 more international and regional airports with limited jet traffic, meaning you may have to deal with an extra connection, but you shouldn't have trouble landing near most any Florida destination.

Finding affordable airfare

The airfare game is capitalism at its finest. Rarely do you pay the same fare for your ticket as the person sitting next to you on the plane. Airline ticket prices are based on the market — that means you — which translates into a roll of the dice, unless you know how to shop.

Business travelers and others who require flexibility usually pay the full fare price. However, if you can book your flight well in advance, don't mind staying at your destination over a Saturday night, or are willing to travel on a Tuesday, Wednesday, or Thursday, you can usually pay a fraction of the full fare price. Likewise, if you can take advantage of the discounts that flying with only a few days' notice offers, you can enjoy the benefits of cheaper airfare. On most flights, even the shortest hops, full-price fare is close to $1,000 or more, but an advance-purchase ticket, sometimes purchased as few as 7 or 14 days before the trip, can cut your ticket cost to $200 to $300. Obviously, planning ahead pays.

Periodically, airlines lower prices on their most popular routes. Although these sale-price fares have date-of-travel restrictions and advance-purchase requirements, you can't beat buying a ticket for (usually) no more than $400 for a cross-country flight. To take advantage of these airline sales, watch for ads in your local newspaper and on TV, and call the airlines or check out their Web sites (see the Appendix for Web addresses and phone numbers). Keep in mind, however, that airline sales often take place during low travel-volume seasons. In fact, finding an airline sale around the holidays or the peak summer vacation months of July and August is rare. On the other hand, November, December, and January (excluding holidays) often bring discounted and promotional fares, with savings of 50 percent or more.

Here are some tips for discovering the best values on airfare to Florida:

✔ Ask the airlines for their lowest fares and inquire about discounts for booking in advance or at the last minute. Decide when you want to go before you call, because many of the best deals are nonrefundable. Also, call more than once. Yes, being on hold that long is frustrating, but you'll probably get different rates each time, and one of the rates may be a bonanza.

✔ The more flexible you are about your travel schedule and length of stay, the more money you're likely to save. Flying during off times (at night, for instance) saves you money.

✔ Visit a large travel agency to find out about all of your available
options. Sometimes a good agent knows about fares that you
won't find on your own. Also, Internet providers offer travel sections that may include pricing comparisons.

✔ Several so-called no-frills airlines — low fares but no meals or
other amenities — fly to Florida. The biggest is Southwest Airlines
(☎ **800-435-9792;** Internet: www.iflyswa.com), which has flights
from many U.S. cities, including Jacksonville, West Palm Beach,
Fort Lauderdale, Orlando, and Tampa Bay.

✔ Consider joining a travel club, such as **Moment's Notice** (☎ **718-
234-6295**) or **Sears Discount Travel Club** (☎ **800-433-9383** for
information, or 800-255-1487 to join), that supplies unsold tickets
to its members at discounted prices. (You pay an annual fee to
receive the club's hot line number.) Of course, your choices are
limited to what's available, so you have to be flexible. Keep in
mind, however, that you may not have to join these clubs to get
such deals, because some airlines now unload unsold seats
directly through their Web sites.

Consolidators, also known as bucket shops, can also be a good place to
find low fares. *Consolidators* buy seats in bulk and sell them to the public
at prices below the airlines' discounted rates. Their small, boxed ads usually run in the Sunday travel sections of major newspapers, at the bottom
of the page. Before you pay, however, ask for a confirmation number from
the consolidator and then call the airline to confirm your seat. Be prepared to book your ticket with a different consolidator — there are many
to choose from — if the airline can't confirm your reservation.

Also, be aware that bucket-shop tickets are usually nonrefundable or
rigged with stiff cancellation penalties, often as high as 50 to 75 percent
of the ticket price. Among consolidators, **Council Travel** (☎ **800-
226-8624;** Internet: www.counciltravel.com) and **STA Travel** (☎ **800-
781-4040;** Internet: www.statravel.com) cater especially to young
travelers, but people of all ages can take advantage of their bargain-
basement prices. **Travel Bargains** (☎ **800-247-3273;** Internet: www.
1800airfare.com), formerly owned by TWA, offers deep discounts on
many other airlines, with a 4-day advance purchase. Other reliable consolidators include **1-800-FLY-CHEAP** (☎ **800-359-2432;** Internet: www.
1800flycheap.com) and **TFI Tours International** (☎ **800-745-8000** or
212-736-1140), which serves as a clearinghouse for unused seats.
Rebators, such as **Travel Avenue** (☎ **800-333-3335** or 312-876-1116)
and the **Smart Traveler** (☎ **800-448-3338** or 305-448-3338), rebate part
of their commission to you.

Booking great deals online

You can also find great deals on airfare on the Internet, along with hotel
and car-rental discounts. Among the leading online travel sites are

> ✔ **Arthur Frommer's Budget Travel Online** (www.frommers.com)
>
> ✔ **Lowestfare** (www.lowestfare.com)
>
> ✔ **Microsoft Expedia** (www.expedia.com)
>
> ✔ **Priceline** (www.priceline.com)
>
> ✔ **Travelocity** (www.travelocity.com)
>
> ✔ **The Trip** (www.thetrip.com)
>
> ✔ **Smarter Living** (www.smarterliving.com)

Each Web site has its own little quirks, but all provide variations of the same service. Simply enter the dates that you want to fly and the cities that you want to visit, and the computer searches for the lowest fares. Several other features are standard on these sites as well, including the ability to check flights at different times or dates in the hope of finding a cheaper fare, e-mail alerts when fares drop on a route that you've specified, and a database of last-minute deals that advertises super-cheap vacation packages or airfares for those who can get away at a moment's notice.

Another fantastic Web site is **Qixo** (www.qixo.com). This search engine allows you to compare the fares offered by ten major online booking sites — Expedia, Travelocity, and others — for a desired route. It also allows you to compare the hotel prices for many properties in major U.S. cities.

The comfort zone

Flying is fun for some folks, but if you're like us, you consider flying a necessary evil for getting to the real party. Some airlines have been adding an inch or so of legroom, but tourist class remains cramped, the cabin temperature is often too hot or too cold, and the air is dry enough to suck the spit out of a Saint Bernard. However, here are a few things you can do — some while you book your flight — to make your trip more tolerable.

✔ **Bulkhead seats** (the front row of each cabin compartment) have a little more legroom than normal plane seats. However, bulkhead seats also have some drawbacks. For example, bulkhead seats don't provide you with a place to put your carry-on luggage, except in the overhead bin, because there's not a seat in front of you. Likewise, you may find that these seats aren't the best places to see an in-flight movie.

✔ **Emergency-exit-row seats** also offer extra room. Airlines usually assign these seats at the airport on a first-come, first-served basis, so ask when you check in whether you can sit in one of these rows. Remember, though, that in the unlikely event of an emergency, you're expected to open the emergency exit door and help direct traffic. Remember, this job description doesn't include in-air emergencies. You'll be jeered or even wrestled to the ground by fellow passengers if you try to open the emergency door in mid flight.

✔ **Wear comfortable clothes.** Be sure to dress in layers, because climate-controlled aircraft cabins vary greatly in temperature and comfort levels. You won't regret taking a sweater or jacket that you can put on or take off, as your onboard temperature dictates. You can also grab one of the airlines' cozy blankets on the way back to your seat.

✔ **Bring some toiletries aboard on long flights.** Cabins are notoriously dry places. If you don't want to land in Orlando with the complexion of King Tut, take a travel-size bottle of moisturizer or lotion to refresh your face and hands at the end of your flight. If you're taking an overnight flight (the *red-eye*), don't forget to pack a toothbrush to combat your breath upon arrival.

Although some toiletries are helpful on airplane trips, some are dangerous. *Never* bring an unsealed container of nail polish remover into an airline cabin, because the cabin pressure causes the remover to evaporate and damage your luggage; the resulting smell won't help you gain any friends on your flight either. Likewise, if you wear contact lenses, wear your glasses for the flight, or at least bring some eye drops. You don't want to spend your hard-earned cash having your *soft* lenses surgically removed at a Florida hospital.

✔ **Jet lag** usually isn't a problem for flights within the United States, but some people coming from the West Coast are affected by the three-hour time change. For those individuals traveling across more than three time zones, jet lag is a distinct possibility. The best way to combat this time warp is to acclimate yourself to local time as quickly as possible. Stay up as long as you can for the first day, and then try to wake up at a normal time on the second day. Also, drink plenty of water during your first few days in town, as well as on the plane, to avoid dehydration.

✔ **If you're flying with kids,** don't forget chewing gum for ear-pressure problems (adults with sinus problems should chew as well), some toys to keep your angels entertained, extra bottles or pacifiers, and diapers. Even if you're kids aren't coming with you, keep in mind that many people on Florida flights *are* bringing their little darlings. Inbound, kids are often swinging from overhead compartments, excited about their journey to the Sunshine State. Outbound, they can fill all the luggage racks with souvenirs and stuffed toys before you can stow your briefcase.

Getting There Wingless

Can't stand to fly? Can't afford the extra expense? You're not alone. Each year, many people drive a car or hop a train to get to Florida. In this section, we explore the details of taking to the open road or riding the rails.

By car

Driving to Florida is a less expensive and potentially more scenic option than flying, but the distance may be so great that it eats up too much of your vacation.

Here's how far several cities are from Orlando. (If you're going to Miami, add about 200 miles to each figure; if you're only going to the Panhandle, subtract about 200.)

- ✔ Atlanta, 436 miles
- ✔ Boston, 1,312 miles
- ✔ Chicago, 1,120 miles
- ✔ Cleveland, 1,009 miles
- ✔ Dallas, 1,170 miles
- ✔ Detroit, 1,114 miles
- ✔ New York, 1,088 miles
- ✔ Toronto, 1,282 miles

Need directions? No problem. Use the following routes and once you're in Florida, pick up the highway that leads to your destination:

- ✔ From Atlanta, take I-75 South.
- ✔ From Boston and New York, take I-95 South.
- ✔ From Chicago, take I-65 South to Nashville and then I-24 South to I-75 South.
- ✔ From Cleveland, take I-77 South to Columbia, South Carolina, and then I-26 East to I-95 South.
- ✔ From Dallas, take I-20 East to I-49 South, to I-10 East, to I-75 South.
- ✔ From Detroit, take I-75 South.
- ✔ From Toronto, take Canadian Route 401 South to Queen Elizabeth Way South, to I-90 (New York State Thruway) East, to I-87 (New York State Thruway) South, to I-95 over the George Washington Bridge, and continue south on I-95.

AAA (☎ 800-222-4357) and some other automobile clubs offer free maps and optimum driving directions to their members.

By train

Amtrak trains (☎ 800-872-7245; Internet: www.amtrak.com) pull into several stations across Florida.

Amtrak's **Auto Train** allows you to bring your car to Florida without having to drive it all the way. The service begins in Lorton, Virginia — about a 4-hour drive from New York; 2 hours from Philadelphia — and ends at Sanford, Florida, about 23 miles northeast of Orlando. The Auto

Train departs Lorton and Sanford daily at 4:30 p.m., arriving at the other end of the line the next morning at 9 a.m. Rates for hauling your car range from $142 to $330; passenger rates are $93 to $182.

As with airline fares, you can sometimes receive discounts if you book train rides far in advance. However, you may find some restrictions on travel dates for discounted train fares, mostly around the very busy holiday periods. Amtrak offers money-saving packages, which include accommodations, car rentals, tours, and so on. For package information, call ☎ **800-321-8684.**

Chapter 6

Getting Around

. . . .

In This Chapter

▶ Traveling around Florida by car

▶ Pining away for a plane

▶ Chugging along on the choo-choo

▶ Riding the magic bus

. . . .

*F*lorida feeds on tourists — conservatively, about 50 million a year.
So, the tourism czars make sure that you and your fellow 49,999,999
million travelers can go from Point A to Point B as quickly as possible.
(After all, the faster you travel, the more time you have to spend your
hard-earned dollars.)

Some of you will fly to Florida and rarely venture more than 25 miles
from the airport. But others will do a little in-state traveling. In this
chapter, we provide some information on the four most popular ways
to get from Point A to Point B in Florida, for those of you who wish to
hit the road while you're here.

Driving Around Florida

You won't need a car if you stick to single-destination vacations, including Disney and Orlando, Miami, Fort Lauderdale, Key West, Daytona
Beach, and St. Petersburg. However, bringing or renting your own set of
wheels is the best and easiest way to see Florida's sights, especially if
you plan on visiting more than one city. Having a car is also a good way
to make sure you're not a prisoner of one resort or tour company.

The fact that traveling around Florida is easy and convenient, however,
doesn't mean that you won't spend much time on the road. The large
distances between the major cities can make for a long drive — 500
miles from Key West to Jacksonville, for example, is quite a haul — and
the traffic on the state's major highways will only make the trip longer.
See "Florida Driving Times and Distances" in this chapter to get a
better idea of the time you'll spend on the road to get to your chosen
destinations.

Florida Driving Times and Distances

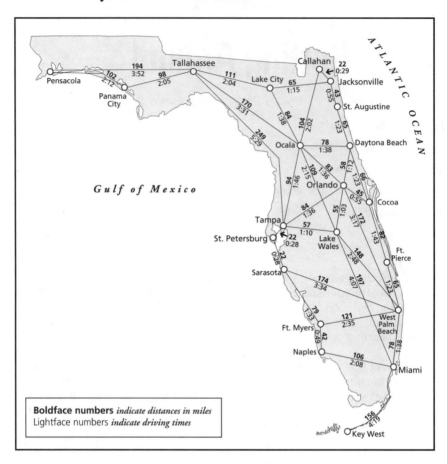

Boldface numbers *indicate distances in miles*
Lightface numbers *indicate driving times*

Minding the road rules

Here are a few tidbits about driving in Florida, some of which may be different than where you live:

✔ **Rush hour:** In Florida, rush hour generally runs from 7 to 9 a.m. and 4 to 6 p.m. on weekdays. Traffic during these times can be brutal in cities such as Miami, Orlando, and Tampa, more so if you use the interstates and other major highways. Most toll roads, on the other hand, tend to be less congested, so it does pay to pay up.

✔ **The more the merrier:** Several counties (most notably Miami-Dade) operate special High Occupancy Vehicle (HOV) lanes on their major roads and highways. In order to use these lanes (usually, but not always faster than the regular traffic lanes), you need to have a minimum number of passengers in the car (usually three). Do yourself (and other road-rage-prone drivers) a favor and don't get in an HOV lane if your car isn't carrying the requisite number of passengers. If you enter these lanes without the minimum number of passengers and you're lucky, and few people are that lucky, you'll only face some nasty hand gestures; otherwise, a not-so-friendly police officer will fine you several hundred dollars.

✔ **Red means go:** Florida law allows drivers to make a right turn on red, after coming to a full stop and making sure the coast is clear (unless signs say otherwise). If you're sitting at a red light, with your blinker on, and not turning right, you'll probably hear horns blaring. Chances are that the horns are in your honor, so *move it!*

✔ **Speed demons beware:** Posted speed limits are enforced pretty vigorously. The speed limits on Florida's interstates and major state and federal highways usually are 65 to 70 mph in rural areas. The limit is 55 mph on many other roads, but it dips as low as 30 mph in some neighborhoods and 10 to 20 mph in school zones. Fines for speeding begin at more than $150. Pay particular attention to construction and school zones, where limits are reduced and signs warn about fines being doubled. They're not kidding!

✔ **Buckle up:** It's illegal to drive without using a seat belt, and the local police actively ticket violators.

✔ **Safety issues:** Ask someone at your hotel's front desk, your rental-car agency, the local chamber of commerce, or the local police department about which routes in the area are safe for travel and which should be avoided. Be particularly wary of high-crime areas and ultra-rural roads. Also, be extra careful at night, especially regarding where you park. Try to stay in well-lit, public areas.

✔ **Permits:** A handicap permit is required for parking in places designated for the disabled. Handicap permits from other states are honored, but a disabled license plate alone won't do the job.

✔ **Emergencies:** In an emergency, you can reach the Florida Highway Patrol on a cell phone by dialing *FHP. From a regular phone, dial 911.

Renting some wheels

If you've ever rented a car, you probably already know that car-rental rates vary even more than those for airfares. The price depends on the size of the car, the length of time you keep it, where and when you pick it up and drop it off, where you take it, rental specials that may be available, and a host of other factors (including the phase of the moon and your astrological sign). Asking the following questions can help save you hundreds of dollars when renting a car:

✔ **Is the weekend rate lower than the weekday rate?** Ask if the rate for Friday-morning pickup is the same as the rate on Thursday night. If you're keeping the car five or more days, a weekly rate may be cheaper than the daily rate.

✔ **Will I be charged a drop-off fee if I return the car to a location that's different from where I rented it?** Some companies may assess a drop-off charge, while others, notably National, do not. Ask if the rate is cheaper if you pick up the car at the airport or a location in town.

✔ **May I have the price I saw advertised in the local newspaper?** Be sure to ask for that specific rate; otherwise, you may be charged the standard (higher) rate. Don't forget to mention membership in AAA, AARP, frequent flyer programs, and trade unions. These memberships usually entitle you to discounts ranging from 5 to 30 percent. Ask your travel agent to check any and all of these rates. Remember, too, that most car rentals are worth at least 500 miles on your frequent-flyer account.

If you want information about the major rental-car companies serving Florida, see the Appendix in the back of this guide.

Ringing up the cost of renting a car

On top of the standard rental prices, other optional charges apply to most car rentals. The *Collision Damage Waiver (CDW),* which covers what you would be required to pay for damage to the car in a collision, is charged on rentals in most states. However, many credit-card companies cover this expense. Check with your credit card company before you go, so that you can avoid paying this hefty fee (as much as $15 a day).

Car rental companies also offer additional liability insurance (if you harm others in an accident), personal accident insurance (if you harm yourself or your passengers), and personal effects insurance (if your luggage is stolen from your car). If you have insurance on your car at home, you're probably covered for most of these unexpected events. If your own insurance doesn't cover you for rentals, or if you don't have auto insurance, consider buying additional coverage (car rental companies are liable for certain base amounts, depending on the state). But, weigh the likelihood of getting into an accident or losing your luggage against the cost of extra coverage (as much as $20 a day, combined), which can significantly add to the price of your rental.

Some companies also offer refueling packages — you pay for an entire tank of gas up front. The price is usually fairly competitive with local gas prices, but you don't get credit for any gas remaining in the tank when you return the car. If you reject this option, you pay only for the gas you use, but you have to return the rental with a full tank or face charges of $3 to $4 a gallon for any shortfall. If a stop at a gas station on the way to the airport will make you miss your plane, by all means take advantage of the fuel purchase option. Otherwise, skip it.

You will also need to tack on some pretty hefty taxes — as much as 20 percent — to your base rental rate. Florida assesses a use tax of $2.05 per day, and additional local taxes add at least 6 percent to that total. If you rent your car in an airport, you might be charged an additional fee on top of the taxes. To estimate the true rental price, always ask for a rundown of all the applicable taxes and fees assessed on your car.

 Finally, youth does have its disadvantages when renting a car. Most rental companies have a minimum age requirement for renters, which usually range from 19 to 25, and some have a maximum age limit. When they do rent to the under-25 crowd, rental companies charge an extra $10 to $20 *per day* in young-renter fees. Most companies will also refuse to rent you a car if you have a poor driving record or you don't have a credit card.

Booking a rental on the Internet

Using the Internet can make comparison shopping and reserving a rental car much easier. All the major booking Web sites — **Travelocity** (www.travelocity.com), **Expedia** (www.expedia.com), **Yahoo! Travel** (www.travel.yahoo.com), and **Cheap Tickets** (www.cheaptickets.com), for example — offer search engines that can dig up discounted car-rental rates. Enter the size of the car you want, the pickup and return dates, and the city where you want to rent the car, and the server returns a price. You can then make your reservation through these sites.

Winging It

The commuter branches of several major airlines provide extensive service to many Florida cities. Fares for short hops are usually reasonable. The three most popular airlines for intrastate travel are

- ✔ **Continental:** ☎ 800-525-0820; Internet: www.cooltravelassistant.com
- ✔ **Delta:** ☎ 800-221-1212; Internet: www.delta.com
- ✔ **US Airways:** ☎ 800-352-0714; Internet: www.usair.com

Cape Air, a small commuter airline, flies between Key West, Fort Myers, and Naples, which means you can avoid backtracking to Miami from Key West if you are touring all of the state. Contact Cape Air at ☎ 800-352-0714 or visit the company Web site at www.flycapeair.com.

All major carriers offer service to Florida's busiest airports: Miami International (☎ 305-876-7000) and Orlando International (☎ 407-825-2001). Tampa International (☎ 813-870-8700) and Fort Lauderdale-Hollywood International (☎ 954-359-6100) are nearly as popular.

Most of the big-name domestic airlines serve the following international and regional airports. The airlines usually offer direct flights for intrastate travel, but if you use these airports as an arrival point from outside Florida, you may have to make an extra connection. This group includes

- Palm Beach International (☎ 561-471-7412)
- Southwest Florida International, in Fort Myers (☎ **941-768-4700**)
- Jacksonville International (☎ **904-741-2000**)
- Sarasota Bradenton International (☎ **941-359-2770**)

Many large domestic carriers, their express services, and commuter airlines serve this next tier in the airport food chain:

- Pensacola Regional (☎ **850-435-1746**)
- Orlando Sanford (☎ **407-322-7771**)
- St. Petersburg-Clearwater International (☎ **727-535-7600**)
- Daytona Beach International (☎ **904-248-8069**)
- Melbourne International (☎ **321-723-6227**)
- Key West International Airport (☎ **305-296-7223**)
- Panama City-Bay County International (☎ **850-763-6751**)

In most cases, your choice of airport will be based on an airport's proximity to your vacation base. For example, if your destination is the Pinellas County Gulf beaches (see Chapter 16 for details), you can save yourself a 1-hour drive from major airport in the area, Tampa International, if you get a flight into St. Petersburg-Clearwater International. This sort of thing is not always easy to do, however, since far fewer carriers serve the latter airport. Ditto for Key West versus Miami airports. If Key West is your goal, you'll save at least three hours in driving time by landing in Key West instead of Miami International. Don't worry, though. You'll still get to visit Miami's airport, in most cases, to catch an express or commuter flight to Key West.

See the Appendix in the back of this book for the toll-free telephone numbers and Web sites of the most popular airlines that serve Florida.

Riding the Tracks

Train travel from one Florida destination to another isn't terribly feasible, mainly due to sporadic scheduling and frequent stops and starts, as trains move from one station to the next. Getting from Daytona Beach to Fort Lauderdale, for example, takes 8½ hours by train, but by car the same trip takes less than 4 hours. However, if trains are in your travel plans, **Amtrak** (☎ **800-872-7245;** Internet: www.amtrak.com) runs trains to 50 cities in Florida, including Daytona, Fort Lauderdale, Key West, Miami, Orlando, Tampa, and St. Petersburg.

Bussing It

 Public transportation is available in cities and large towns, but the services are usually tailored to commuters rather than tourists. We give you the specifics for each region's public transportation services and availability in the destination chapters (see Chapters 10 through 23). **Greyhound** (☎ **800-231-2222;** Internet: www.greyhound.com) is an option for inter-city travel, but it has the same problems — slow and sporadic service — as train travel. It also doesn't give you the flexibility that a rental car does.

Chapter 7

Booking Your Accommodations

- -

In This Chapter

▶ Avoiding rack rates

▶ Getting the best for less

▶ Rating your accommodations options

▶ Shopping for a room online

▶ Finding a room without a reservation

- -

Some folks call a hotel, ask for a rate, and pay it — no questions asked. This practice is like going to a car lot and paying the sticker price. If this description hits a little too close to home, just read on. In this chapter, we show you how to find the best hotel rates and get the best room that your money can buy.

Avoiding Rack Rates (And Why You Don't Have to Pay Them)

Rack rates are the standard rates that hotels charge for their rooms. If you call a hotel for a rate or walk into a hotel to get a room for the night, you pay the room's rack rate. Hotels also post their rack rates on the backs of room doors (unless the spring breakers swipe them as a souvenir).

You don't have to pay rack rates. In fact, hardly anyone does. Perhaps, the best way to avoid paying the rack rate is surprisingly simple: Ask for a cheaper or discounted rate. The hotel's answer may pleasantly surprise you.

Room rates usually depend on many factors, not the least of which is how you make your reservation. For example, a travel agent may be able to secure a better price with certain hotels than you can, because hotels sometimes give agents special discounts as a reward for bringing in an abundance of return business.

Seasons also affect room rates, especially as occupancy rates rise and fall. Most Florida destinations are in peak season during summer and holidays (when kids are out of school and their families travel) and during winter (mainly between January and March when snowbirds come south). If a hotel is nearly full, it's less likely to offer you a discount. Likewise, if the hotel is nearly empty, an employee may negotiate a room rate with you, especially if the hotel is locally owned. Some resorts offer midweek specials, and downtown hotels often offer cheaper weekend rates.

Orlando, for the most part, doesn't have a normal pattern of high and low travel seasons. Blame two things for this phenomenon: Disney's year-round tourist appeal, and a convention schedule that never takes a breather. Many Orlando hotels do, however, offer lower rates from early January through March, from just after Labor Day to just before Thanksgiving, and for the first two weeks of December. If you plan to hit a destination during its busy season, your best shot at getting a discount is to reserve early — months in advance, if possible.

Please note that room prices are subject to change without notice, so even the rates quoted in this book may be different from the actual rate you receive when you make your reservation.

Getting the Best Room at the Best Rate

Finding the best hotel rate requires a bit of detective work. For example, reserving a room through the hotel's toll-free number, rather than calling the hotel directly, may result in a lower rate. However, the central reservations number may not know about discounts at specific locations. Case in point: Some franchises may offer a special group rate for a wedding or family reunion, but they may neglect to tell the central booking line. Your best bet is to call the local number *and* the toll-free number to see which one gives you a better deal.

Ask about discounts if you're a student, senior, military or government employee, or member of AAA or AARP. Also, if you own stock in a hotel company or in Disney, you may be eligible for some kind of a price break or other perk. When you settle on your destination, make sure to contact the local visitor information center (see the Appendix in the back of the book) by phone or via the Web to see if it has any discounts available.

When budgeting for your room, don't forget to allow for the combined sales and bed taxes that are charged in the state's various counties. In some parts of Florida, they add as much as 12 or 13 percent to your bill.

Lining Up the Lodgings

Although Florida sports a wide variety of accommodations, for the most part, this guide will concentrate on Florida's four main lodging types. We use a handy little code for the amount of dough you'll have to hand over when you decide to stay in these places. The explanation for the code is in the "Pricing our picks" section later in this chapter.

- ✔ **Resorts** usually offer just about everything you can get with a room. Features vary from property to property, but amenities are often in the $$$$ category. The resorts are usually right on the beach, in the best neighborhoods, or in the heat of the action. If you're so inclined, resorts can be one-stop destinations that offer package deals and good rates during the off-season. But keep in mind that you won't feel like part of the family, and they usually cost top dollar.

- ✔ **Hotels** sometimes have accommodations similar to resorts, but they're generally smaller and offer fewer activities and facilities. Hotels usually offer daily housekeeping service, one or more swimming pools, one or more lounges and restaurants, room service, and an activities desk. Hotels can be more intimate than a resort and often slightly cheaper, but they have fewer amenities and services. The locations may not be as good, and hotels can have thin walls.

 - ✔ **Motels,** whether chains or mom-and-pop operations, generally have basic rooms and amenities, the kind found in the $ and, in a few cases, the $$ categories. The rooms tend to be smaller, a good restaurant (or any restaurant) likely won't be on the premises, and their locations are often farther from the action. But the price is right, and most of us don't go on vacation to spend much time in the room.

- ✔ **Bed-and-Breakfasts** are plentiful in Florida and a good way to experience a home-style visit. The locations, usually situated outside of the tourist mainstream, will be a perk for some of you, particularly the kind of traveler who likes the feeling of staying in someone's home. Bed-and-breakfasts vary widely in size and services. On one end of the scale, some have tight quarters and shared baths, while others have private sitting areas, lavish amenities, and private whirlpool tubs. At either end, don't expect a great deal of service beyond breakfast, bed and towel service, and, sometimes, evening dessert or a glass of wine. Bed-and-breakfasts are hardly ever on the beach, so if your heart's set on that ocean view, you ought to consider another style of accommodation.

Inn Route, P.O. Box 6187, Palm Harbor, FL 34684 (☎ **800-524-1880;** Internet: www.florida-inns.com), publishes a nifty guide, *Inns of Florida,* which offers descriptions of a number of inns and bed-and-breakfasts in the state. Inn Route inspects all the listed properties.

In addition to the four main lodging categories, we also touch on a few **condominiums** and **vacation rentals.** These accommodations are good if you have a large family, like the spaciousness of a house or an apartment, or plan to stay in an area for a few weeks or longer. But, they tend to be pricey, and there usually isn't onsite management, so service is slow or nonexistent.

Pricing our picks

The hotels, motels, and resorts listed in the destination areas of this book (see Chapters 10 to 23) are grouped by price, from budget motels to very expensive rooms and apartments. The rates we quote in those chapters are per night, based on double occupancy. To give you a better idea on what you can expect to get for your money, here's a tally of the amenities that each price category offers:

- ✔ **$ ($50 to $100):** Accommodations at this level generally have pretty basic trimmings and limited space. They also tend to lean toward the no-frills side (although almost all come with swimming pools and air conditioning). Accommodations at the higher end of this category may have hair dryers and coffeemakers, TV with cable, kids' play areas, and sometimes offer free continental breakfasts. If they're multistory, they usually have an elevator.

- ✔ **$$ ($100 to $200):** Within this category, you will probably have a choice of king-size or double beds, a full range of amenities (coffeemakers, hair dryers, two TVs in two-room models, multiline phones, maybe modem lines, VCRs, free daily newspapers, and so on), designer shampoos, and room service. Rooms are slightly larger, and the pools may be joined by a whirlpool and fitness center. The continental breakfast probably has fresh fruit, granola, and muffins, rather than day-old doughnuts and those pint-size boxes of dry cereal. The hotel may even have a palatable onsite restaurant.

- ✔ **$$$ ($200 to $250):** Hotels at this level tack on guest-services desks where you can arrange sightseeing trips, attractions tickets, and restaurant reservations. They probably have large, resort-style pools with multiple whirlpool tubs (some of the higher-end rooms have their own), fitness centers, and, occasionally, small spas. Rooms have multiple phones, beds, and TVs. They also often have minibars and separate tubs and showers.

✔ **$$$$ ($250 and up):** With these accommodations, nothing is out-side the realm of possibility, including a world-class fitness center. In addition to the nicer amenities in the earlier price categories, many of the hotels here have concierge levels, loaded rooms, 24-hour room service, gorgeous pool bars, and live entertainment in their lounges. Some have full-service spas, gourmet restaurants, and tight security.

The view: To do or not to do

Views are one of the most heavily advertised amenities offered by hotels located in Florida's coastal cities. Sure it would be nice to see the sun disappear over the ocean from your hotel room, but is a room with a view worth the money? You might pay an extra $50, $100, or more per night for a beautiful view of sea oats, sand dunes, and frothy waves. If money's no object or if that restful view is the top priority of your vacation, then damn the torpedoes. Full speed ahead. But if you won't be hanging out in your room very much, you can find better ways to spend your money.

Want to know exactly what you get when the hotel offers you a view? Here's the scorecard:

✔ **Oceanfront:** This usually means your room is smack-dab on the beach, which is synonymous with being 8 feet under water, during a hurricane tide. It also means you're going to pay for that location. But it doesn't necessarily mean you actually get a view of the ocean, so ask. Some of Florida's less-than-reputable innkeepers advertise themselves as oceanfront because a room in a building faces the tides, even if your room doesn't. You also may not be able to walk straight out your door to the beach — many of these places are high-rises where it's highly recommended that you go down before you go out. Don't forget to ask about elevator service. Going down-stairs is a piece of cake; going up is a gravity-defying experience. Be sure to ask exactly what you're getting.

✔ **Ocean-view:** These rooms are usually guaranteed to be at the top of the price chart. Your shoulders will be squared to the beach, but you may not be oceanfront. You may actually be several hun-dred feet back, overlooking some shorter buildings. Again, remem-ber to ask. Remember, too, when staying in a high-rise, that if surf sounds are what's important, make sure you're on one of the first few floors. You won't be able to hear the waves above the fourth or fifth floors. Their sounds usually yield to the roar of airline engines or the complaints of high-flying gulls.

✔ **Partial ocean-view:** This is where semantics come into play. If you look east, at sunset on an odd-numbered Thursday . . . well, you get the idea. You may be able to see the surf from half of the windows in your L-shaped condo, or maybe you can see it if you press your nose into the glass and stare cross-eyed to the left. It may be a great deal or a great rip-off. Our best advice: Take it if it's offered, but don't pay a penny extra. **Note:** Panhandle destinations (see Chapter 23) offer a double whammy — sunrises to the left (east) and sunsets to the right (west), so a partial view may be more than enough.

✔ **Other views:** Depending on where you land in Florida, you may encounter a room with views of a marsh, garden, wildlife habitat, or any of Florida's other natural treasures, including waste-treatment plants. But don't buy in if the brochure promises a mountain view — there are none.

Finding the right room

If you're looking for general guidelines for getting a great room, here are some of our strategies:

✔ **Always ask for a corner room:** They're usually larger, quieter, closer to the elevator. Corner rooms have more windows and light than standard rooms, and they don't always cost more.

✔ **Steer clear of construction zones:** Be sure to ask if the hotel is renovating; if it is, request a room away from the renovation work. The noise and activity may be a bit more than you want to deal with on your vacation.

✔ **Request your smoking preference:** Be sure to ask for either a smoking or non-smoking room, if you have a preference. Otherwise, you're likely to get stuck with a room that doesn't meet your needs.

✔ **Inquire about the location of the restaurants, bars, and discos:** These areas of the hotel could all be a source of irritating noise. On the other hand, if you want to be close to the action, or if you have a disability that prohibits you from venturing too far very often, you may choose to be close to these amenities. (See Chapter 4 for more information about getting around if you have a disability.)

If you book your room through a travel agent, ask the agent to note your room preferences on your reservation. When you check in at your hotel, your preferences will pop up when the reception desk pulls your reservation. Special requests cannot be guaranteed, but it can't hurt to make them in advance. If you aren't happy with your room when you arrive, talk to the front desk. If they have another room, they should be happy to accommodate you, within reason.

Surfing the Web for Hotel Deals

You may be better off dealing directly with the hotels, but if you don't like haggling, online reservation services can act like airline consolidators (see Chapter 5 for more information). They buy hotel rooms in bulk and sell them to consumers for less than the rack rates. The

Internet also offers numerous sites that provide information on hotels or resorts in Florida. The biggest advantage that you get from using the Internet is that you can see the hotel or resort before you book your trip. Plus, you can book online and save yourself the aggravation of listening to a slew of annoying automated voice systems.

While the major travel booking sites (see Chapter 5 for details) offer hotel booking, your best bet is to use a site devoted primarily to lodging, because you may find properties that aren't listed on more general online travel agencies. Also, some lodging sites specialize in a particular type of accommodations, such as bed-and-breakfasts, which you won't find on the more mainstream booking services. Other sites, such as **TravelWeb** (see the Internet lodging list in this section), offer weekend deals on major chain properties, which cater to business travelers and have more empty rooms on weekends.

Here are a few of the better lodging sites:

- ✔ **Florida Travel Online** (www.floridatravelonline.com) is a wholesaler for hotel rooms, suites, and homes. Click the "Places To Stay" link to find a large database of hotels, which lists prices and other information for approximately 30 hotels and resorts. Clicking the individual hotel links gives you detailed information on each property.

- ✔ **Florida Hotel Network** (www.floridahotels.com) offers a centralized reservations service for accommodations in a variety of price ranges for major cities in Florida. If you want to book rooms for large groups, you can do it here.

- ✔ **All Hotels on the Web** (www.all-hotels.com) includes tens of thousands of listings throughout the world, although its name is something of a misnomer. Bear in mind, however, that each hotel has paid a small fee (of $25 and up) to be listed, so the site is not an objective list. It's more like a book of online brochures.

- ✔ **hoteldiscount!com** (www.180096hotel.com) lists bargain room rates at hotels in more than 50 U.S. and international cities, including Miami and Orlando. The cool thing is that hoteldiscount!com pre-books blocks of rooms in advance, so sometimes it offers rooms — at discount rates — at hotels that are sold out. This site is noted for delivering deep discounts in cities where hotel rooms are expensive. The toll-free number is printed all over this site (☎ 800-96-HOTEL); call it if you want more options than the ones listed online.

- ✔ **Places to Stay** (www.placestostay.com) lists one-of-a-kind places in the United States and abroad that you may not find in other directories, with a focus on resort accommodations. Again, the listing is selective — this isn't a comprehensive directory, but it can give you a sense of what's available.

✔ **TravelWeb** (www.travelweb.com) lists more than 26,000 hotels in 170 countries, focusing on chains such as Hyatt and Hilton, and you can book almost 90 percent of the listed hotels online. The "Click-It Weekends" feature, updated each Monday, offers weekend deals at many leading hotel chains.

Most of the visitor information centers are listed in the Appendix, in the back of this book, have links to some of the hotels in their areas. Also, many of the accommodations listings in Chapters 10 through 23 include Web addresses. And you can link to specific hotels at **Visit Florida** online (www.flausa.com) and **Absolutely Florida** online (www.funandsun.com), although getting to your desired choice on these sites will probably require some patience.

Arriving without a Reservation

There are a few places where arriving without a reservation can be a problem, although not necessarily an insurmountable one, during certain times of the year. These spots include Orlando in summer and school holiday periods, and most of Florida's Atlantic coast during winter (snowbirds) and spring break (higher-ed birds). The good news is that most Florida destinations never toss a shutout, so if you didn't follow our advice about reserving a room early, the odds are that you won't have to camp out in your car. Some of the best spots for last-minute shopping are the chain motels, many of which are listed in the Appendix in the back of the book. And don't overlook the visitor information centers listed in the Appendix. Many of them will try to get you into a hotel if you ask nicely.

Web wanderers can also find last-minute rooms at the **Accommodation Search Engine Network** online (www.ASE.net), which offers discounts of up to 30 percent off room rates. Fill out a form that records your choices in several categories — rates, types of hotels, facilities, recreation amenities, and so on. After the form is filled out, click the Search button on the page, and you receive a list of hotels or resorts that fit your selections.

Chapter 8

Managing Your Money

· ·

In This Chapter

▶ Sorting out your money options

▶ Preventing and recovering from theft

· ·

*T*ake a moment to ponder the meaning of the most important word in Florida's economic lexicon.

Tourism (tooo' riz-um): n. 1. Travel, particularly the kind that brings two sides together; one side providing food, shelter, and entertainment, in exchange for payment from the other; 2. A game of chance in which a bunch of business bigwigs attempt to relieve the unsuspecting of their assets; 3. A puzzling phenomenon in which visitors pay to do the things that natives leave town to avoid.

Regarding relieving others of their assets, Miami, Orlando, and the rest of Florida's Tourism A-Team make it sinfully easy to spend, spend, *and spend*. You can't turn a corner without finding a way to blow your budget. With that fact in mind, read this chapter for advice on accessing and guarding your money, so that you can keep the good times rolling in the Sunshine State. You will also read about what to do in case the bad times roll in and swipe your stash.

Paper, Plastic, or Pocket Change

You can choose from a number of payment options for your vacation expenses, including meals, souvenirs, and so on. In this section, we explore the available options to help you determine the one that's right for you.

 Some people like to wear a fat wallet, but carrying cash is your worst option for payment of vacation-related expenses. Lose it, and it's gone. Besides, these days, most of Florida's hotels, restaurants, and tourist attractions accept plastic, so there's little reason to stash a wad of cash in your pocket. Carry only enough for incidentals, such as transit fare, a cold beverage, a newspaper, and so on. We recommend carting around no more than $50 at a time. If you need more cash, you can get an advance on your credit card or use an ATM. (See the credit card and ATM sections in this chapter for more information.)

Carrying the cards: Charge!

Traveling with credit cards is a safe alternative to carrying cash. Credit cards also provide you with a record of your vacation expenses, after you return home.

Most major credit cards are accepted throughout Florida, though some places, such as the Walt Disney World parks and resorts, only accept American Express, MasterCard, and Visa. You can get cash advances from your credit cards at any bank (although you start paying hefty interest on the advance from the moment you receive the cash, and you don't receive frequent-flyer miles on an airline credit card). At most banks, you don't even need to go to a teller; you can get a cash advance at the ATM if you know your personal identification number (PIN). If you've forgotten your PIN or didn't even know you had one, call the phone number on the back of your credit card and ask the bank to send it to you. It usually takes between five and seven business days, though some banks will give the number over the phone, if you tell them your mother's maiden name or pass some other security clearance.

Finding an ATM ASAP

Florida, like most states, has an ample supply of 24-hour ATMs (automated teller machines) linked to national networks that almost always include your bank. You can find the machines at most malls, banks, and convenience stores, such as 7-Eleven and Circle K. Frequently, one or more ATMs are located inside theme parks and larger tourist attractions, as well as in shopping or downtown districts.

ATMs are a convenient way to bank 24 hours a day. Check the back of your ATM card to see which network your bank belongs to and look for ATMs that display your network's sign. You are probably connected to one of the two most popular networks: **Cirrus** (☎ 800-424-7787; Internet: www.mastercard.com/atm/) and **Plus** (☎ 800-843-7587; Internet: www.visa.com/atms). You may opt to call their toll-free numbers or visit their Web sites to obtain convenient locations in Florida.

If you need to make a face-to-face transaction, most Florida banks are open from 9 a.m. to 3 or 4 p.m., Monday through Friday, and many drive-ins are open between 9 a.m. and noon on Saturdays.

One downside to using an ATM is that, frequently, you are charged extra for using another bank's ATM. In Florida, you're assessed an average charge of $2.60, if you use an ATM that isn't affiliated with your bank. Your own bank may also assess a fee for using an ATM that's not at one of its branch locations. Some machines warn you of the extra charges before your transaction is complete. Also, remember some cards have a *daily* withdrawal limit, no matter what your balance is, so don't let your cash reserves get too low.

In addition, although an ATM card may be an amazing convenience when traveling in another country (put your card in the machine and out comes foreign currency, at an extremely advantageous exchange rate), banks are also likely to slap you with a foreign currency transaction fee, just for making them do the pounds-to-dollars conversion math. Given these sneaky tactics, reverting to traveler's checks may just be cheaper (though certainly less convenient).

Toting traveler's checks

Traveler's checks are a throwback to the days before ATM machines gave you easy access to your money. Because you can replace traveler's checks if they're lost or stolen, they are a sound alternative to stuffing your wallet with cash. However, you may have trouble cashing them in some places.

You can get traveler's checks at almost any bank. **American Express** offers checks in denominations of $20, $50, $100, $500, and $1,000. You pay a service charge that ranges from 1 to 4 percent of the total value of the checks that you receive. Call American Express (☎ **800-221-7282**) to purchase traveler's checks over the phone.

Visa (☎ **800-227-6811**) also offers traveler's checks, available at Citibank locations and several other banks across the country. Call the toll-free number for a complete list of bank locations. Visa traveler's checks come in denominations of $50, $100, $500, and $1,000, with service charges ranging from 1.5 to 2 percent. **MasterCard** also offers traveler's checks; call ☎ **800-223-9920** for a location near you.

AAA members can obtain traveler's checks without a fee at most AAA offices. Members should call their local office for details.

Keeping Your Money Safe (And What to Do If It's Stolen)

Florida's once-wholesome image has been tarnished in recent years by some well-publicized crimes against tourists, but some folks still let down their guards with disastrous results. Tourists are easy prey for thieves. Here are some tips to help you avoid this agonizing situation (or, at least, ease the pain if it happens):

✔ **Keep your purse slung diagonally across your chest, preferably under a jacket.** This goes whether you're inside attractions or strolling city streets. The best kind of purse to take is one that folds over, rather than one that just has a zipper on top. Do not sling your purse or camera over your chair when in a restaurant. When carrying a backpack, put both straps over your shoulder;

don't just sling one strap over one arm. Ideally you should use a money belt or a fanny pack to store cash, credit cards, and traveler's checks in.

✔ **If your hotel has an in-room safe, use it.** Stash excess cash, traveler's checks, and any other valuables that you don't need for immediate use. If your hotel room doesn't have a safe, put your valuables and cash inside the hotel's safety deposit box. In general, we recommend using an ATM machine and only withdrawing about $50 at a time.

✔ **Be extremely careful when using ATMs.** This is especially true at night and in poorly lit areas that are heavily traveled. Shield your access numbers from prying eyes, and never put anything in the trash that has your account number or other personal information on it.

✔ **If carrying traveler's checks, record the serial numbers of the checks.** Keep that list, to be used in case of an emergency, in a separate location from the checks. It's also a good idea to leave the serial numbers with a relative back home. Should your checks be stolen, call the issuer, give the serial numbers, and ask for instructions on getting your checks replaced.

Almost every credit-card company has a toll-free emergency number that you can call if your cards are lost or stolen. If a theft occurs, call as soon as possible to report your situation and stop any unauthorized transactions on your account. The credit-card company may be able to immediately wire you a cash advance on your credit card, and often, you can get you an emergency credit card within a day or two.

The issuing bank's toll-free number is usually printed on the back of the credit card. Make note of this number before you leave on your trip and stash it somewhere other than your wallet. If you forget to write down the number, you can call ☎ 800-555-1212 — directory assistance for toll-free numbers — to get the number. And because thieves may not swipe this guidebook — though it's worth its weight in gold — here are a few additional numbers for credit-card companies. The emergency number, in the United States, for **Citicorp Visa** is ☎ **800-336-8472.** **American Express** cardholders and traveler's checks users need to call ☎ **800-221-7282** for all money emergencies. **MasterCard** holders must call ☎ **800-307-7309.**

Odds are that if your wallet is gone, you've seen the last of it, and the police aren't likely to recover it for you. However, after you realize that it's gone, and you cancel your credit cards, you should still call the police. You may need their report number, later, for credit card or insurance purposes.

Chapter 9

Tying Up Last-Minute Loose Ends

● ●

In This Chapter

▶ Playing the insurance game

▶ Making long-distance reservations

▶ Stuffing your bags

▶ Traveling with pets

● ●

*T*he launch pad is just ahead. All you need to do is take care of a few last-minute details: Call NASA, stuff your bags with everything that's clean, water the geraniums, pay the rent, and finish 50 other eleventh-hour chores. Then you're on your way to Ponce de Leon's land of dreams!

Feel free to skip this chapter if you're not worried about insurance matters, advance reservations for restaurants and events, or packing pointers. Otherwise, join the rest of us.

Buying Travel Insurance: Good Idea or Bad?

There are three primary kinds of travel insurance: trip cancellation, lost luggage, and medical. Trip cancellation insurance is a good idea for some, but lost luggage and additional medical insurance don't make sense for most travelers. Be sure to explore your options and consider the following tips before you leave home:

✔ **Trip cancellation insurance:** Cancellation insurance is a good idea if

- You paid a large portion of your vacation expenses up front.

- You bought a package trip.

- A member of your party becomes ill.

- There's a death in the family, and you aren't able to go on vacation.

But remember, trip cancellation insurance costs approximately 6 to 8 percent of your vacation's total value.

✔ **Lost luggage insurance:** Your homeowner's insurance should cover stolen luggage, if your policy encompasses off-premises theft, so check your existing policies before you buy any additional coverage. Airlines are responsible for $2,500 worth of lost baggage on domestic flights, but that may not be enough to cover your sharkskin suit. Our best advice: Wear the sharkskin suit, or your favorite dress, on the plane, and if you're carrying anything else of substantial value, stow it in your carry-on bag.

✔ **Medical insurance:** Your existing health insurance should cover you, if you get sick while on vacation. (However, if you belong to an HMO, check to see whether you're fully covered when away from home.)

✔ **Credit cards:** Some credit cards (American Express and certain gold and platinum Visas and MasterCards, for example) offer automatic flight insurance in the case of death or dismemberment in an airplane crash.

If you still think you need additional insurance, make sure that you don't pay for more insurance than you need. For example, if you only need trip cancellation insurance, don't purchase coverage for lost or stolen property. Here's a list of some of the reputable issuers of travel insurance:

✔ **Access America,** 6600 W. Broad St., Richmond, VA 23230 (☎ **800-284-8300;** Fax 800-346-9265; Internet: www.accessamerica.com).

✔ **Travelex Insurance Services,** 11717 Burt St., Suite 202, Omaha, NE 68154 (☎ **800-228-9792;** Internet: www.travelex-insurance.com).

✔ **Travel Guard International,** 1145 Clark St., Stevens Point, WI 54481 (☎ **800-826-1300;** Internet: www.travel-guard.com).

✔ **Travel Insured International, Inc.,** P.O. Box 280568, 52-S Oakland Ave., East Hartford, CT 06128-0568 (☎ **800-243-3174;** Internet: www.travelinsured.com).

Combating Illness Away from Home

Fortunately, it's been two centuries since Florida has had a case of the plague, and there isn't an illness specific to the state. Mosquitoes and sand gnats are pains, but they don't carry malaria. Raw oysters can make you ill in some cases, especially if you have diabetes, a liver ailment, or stomach problems. And the sun can ruin a vacation if you stay out in it too long. Other than those problems, the illnesses you'll encounter here are the same ones you'll find most anywhere on Planet Earth.

Still, mishaps happen, and finding a doctor you trust when you're out of town is hard. Getting a prescription refilled is no piece of cake, either. So, here are some travel tips to help you avoid a medical dilemma while you're on vacation:

- ✔ **If you have health insurance, carry your identification card in your wallet.** If you don't think your existing policy is sufficient, purchase medical insurance for more comprehensive coverage.

- ✔ **Take all of your medications with you on the trip.** Remember to take a prescription for more if you think you'll run out.

- ✔ **Take an extra pair of contact lenses or glasses in case you lose them.**

- ✔ **Take over-the-counter medicines for common travelers' ailments like diarrhea or stomach acid.**

- ✔ **If you suffer from a chronic illness, talk to your doctor before taking your trip.** For conditions such as epilepsy, diabetes, or a heart condition, wear a **Medic Alert** identification tag to immediately inform any doctor about your condition and give him or her access to your medical records through Medic Alert's 24-hour hot line. Participation in the Medic Alert program costs $35 per year, with a $15 renewal fee. Contact the Medic Alert Foundation, 2323 Colorado Ave., Turlock, CA 95382 (☎ **800-432-5378**; Internet: www. medicalert.org). See Chapter 4 for more information about traveling with a disability.

If you do get sick, ask the concierge at your hotel to recommend a local doctor — including his or her own family doctor. This plan will probably produce a better recommendation than what you'll get from a referral number for physicians. If you can't get a doctor to help you right away, try the emergency room at the local hospital.

If your ailment isn't a life-threatening emergency, use a walk-in clinic. You may not get immediate attention, but you'll probably pay around $60, rather than the $300 minimum for just signing in at an emergency-room counter.

Be wary of doc-in-a-box facilities. In the last few years, travelers have experienced problems with disreputable companies, operating in tourist areas. You can get a reputable referral from **Ask-A-Nurse**, a free service open to everyone. (Ask-A-Nurse does ask whether you have insurance, but that's for information purposes only, so Ask-A-Nurse staff can track who uses the system.) Check the Yellow Pages for your destination — it's often listed under "Physicians and Surgeons Information."

You can fill your prescriptions at pharmacies such as Eckerd or Walgreens. Likewise, many discount stores, such as Kmart or Target, also have pharmacies, some with 24-hour service. You can find pharmacies and stores such as these in the White or Yellow Pages of the phone book.

To find a dentist, call **Dental Referral Service** (☎ **800-917-6453**). Staff can tell you the location of the nearest dentist who meets your needs. Phones are manned daily from 5:30 a.m. to 6 p.m.

Beating the Crowd: Reservations and Tickets

You'll want to spend your time in Florida on the beach or at attractions because your time is at a premium; the last thing you want to do is wile away precious hours waiting for a restaurant table or a theater ticket. Although, in most cases, an advance reservation (for dining and other activities) is not mandatory, having one will certainly make your day run more smoothly.

Reserving a table

Try to get a last-minute table in New York, San Francisco, and other world-class dining destinations, and you'll likely get turned back toward the sidewalk. However, getting a reservation in Florida is comparatively easy. In most cases, you can make same-day reservations or even walk into the restaurant when you feel your first hunger pangs. There are, of course, plenty of exceptions, such as **Yuca** on Miami's South Beach (see Chapter 10) and **Emeril's** in CityWalk in Orlando (see Chapter 18). Even at places that are less in demand, we recommend that you make reservations as far in advance as you can (including before you leave home) for any restaurant accepting them. You can find all the information you need to make a reservation in the dining listings in Chapters 10 to 23. After you arrive, your hotel's concierge or front desk can help with reservations, too.

Reserving a ticket and getting event information

Ticketmaster is the key player for reservations to most of Florida's major events, including concerts, shows, and pro sports events. If you know of an event that happens while you're in town, check first with your hometown Ticketmaster outlets to see if they sell tickets for the event. (If you live as close as Atlanta or New Orleans, they probably do.) Otherwise, go to the Ticketmaster Web site at www.ticketmaster.

com, or call the outlet in the city you'll be visiting. The Ticketmaster numbers for a few of Florida's larger cities are

✔ Fort Lauderdale: ☎ **954-523-3309**

✔ North Florida: ☎ **904-353-3309**

✔ Miami: ☎ **305-358-5885**

✔ Orlando: ☎ **407-839-3900**

✔ St. Petersburg: ☎ **727-898-2100**

✔ Tampa: ☎ **813-287-8844**

Most of the ticket outlets are open from 9 a.m. to 9 p.m., Monday to Friday, and 9 a.m. to 7 p.m., Saturday and Sunday.

You can pick up information on what's playing in your part of Florida from a few solid sources. Most of Florida's mid-size and larger daily newspapers publish an entertainment section on Friday that includes events, restaurants, and much more. Many of them have free online publications.

The **International Association of Convention & Visitor Bureaus** has a Web site at www.officialtravelinfo.com — another good place to find out what's happening during your stay. Use the site's links page to find your destination, and then choose the services or activities you want to see. The same goes for **Visit Florida** (☎ **888-735-2872;** Internet: www.flausa.com) and **Absolutely Florida** (☎ **305-865-9420;** Internet: www.funandsun.com), which include information on sightseeing, cultural events, accommodations, and more.

The visitor centers listed in Chapters 10 to 23 are also good sources of event, restaurant, and sightseeing information.

Reserving a green

Golfers can get information on many of Florida's courses and make reservations through **Golfpac** (☎ **800-327-0878** or 407-260-2288; Internet: www.golfpacinc.com). Or you can contact **Tee Times USA** by calling ☎ **800-374-8633** or visiting the Web at www.teetimesusa.com.

Gearing Up: Practical Packing Advice

To start packing for your trip, take everything you think you'll need and lay it out on the bed. Now get rid of half of it. It's not that the airlines won't let you take it all — they will, with some limits — but why do you want to get a hernia from lugging half of your house around with you? And remember, suitcase straps are particularly painful to sunburned shoulders. Use the tips in this section to avoid renting a moving truck to haul your luggage around Florida.

Packing criteria

When choosing your suitcase, think about how you'll be traveling. If you're going to haul your own luggage, a bag with wheels makes sense. Wheels become even more important if you have a substantial hike to your room, or it's on an upper floor of an inn that hasn't discovered elevators. Also, remember that hard-sided bags protect breakable items better than soft-sided ones, but they weigh more.

Florida is a laid-back place. Therefore, you can leave your formal wear — even your tie — at home, unless you're planning a special night out. Instead, bring casual clothes, including some comfortable walking shoes (a must) and airy shirts, blouses, shorts, skirts, or pants. If you come during the Sunshine State's microscopic winter (mainly January and February), you may need to layer your clothing. In fact, bring a light jacket or sweater and a thin rain poncho, anyway, but you probably won't need the jacket or sweater if you head south to Miami or the Keys. And don't forget all the necessary toiletries, medications (pack these in your carry-on bag so you have them if the airline loses your luggage), and a camera.

Packing pointers

When packing, start with the biggest, hardest items (usually shoes or sports equipment) first and then fit smaller items in and around them. Pack breakable items in between several layers of clothes or keep them in your carry-on bag. Put things that can leak, like shampoos or suntan lotions, in leak-proof plastic bags. Lock your suitcase with a small padlock (available at most luggage stores, if your bag doesn't already have one) and put an identification tag on the outside. Also, tying a colorful scarf around your suitcase handle makes it easier to spot your bag on the airport baggage carousel.

Some airlines allow two pieces of carry-on luggage per person, both of which must fit in the overhead compartment or under the seat in front of you, but others restrict passengers to one. (Ask when making your reservation.) Use carry-ons for valuables, medications, and vital documents first. You can then add a book, breakable items that you don't want to put in your suitcase, and a snack, if you have room. Also, carry the sweater or light jacket with you — cabins can feel like the Arctic, one minute, and a sauna, the next.

Discovering your carry-on limits

Because lost-luggage rates have reached an all-time high, consumers bring their possessions onboard to try to avert disaster. But planes are more crowded than ever, and overhead compartment space is at a premium. Some domestic airlines have started cracking down, limiting you to a single carry-on for crowded flights and imposing size restrictions to the bags that you bring onboard. The dimensions vary, but the strictest airlines say carry-ons must measure no more than 22 x 14 x 9 inches, including wheels and handles, and weigh no more than 40 pounds. Many airports already have x-ray machines that literally block any carry-on bigger than the posted size restriction. These measures may sound drastic, but keep in mind that many of these regulations are enforced only at the discretion of the gate attendants. If you plan to bring more than one bag aboard a crowded flight, make sure that your medications, documents, and valuables are consolidated in one bag, in case you're forced to check the second bag.

Here are some other essential packing tips:

✔ You can leave the snowshoes, ski masks, and thermal underwear at home, although some winter mornings in central Florida do get brisk. Winter weather usually follows a 3-day cycle: wet, windy and cold; colder and sometimes frosty; bright and beginning to warm. Therefore, *layered clothing* (a sweater, light jacket, and a sweatshirt) is a good idea if you visit Florida during our abbreviated winter season.

✔ The most common sign welcoming diners to Florida's restaurants states "Shirt and Shoes Required." It summarizes the Floridian way of life: casual, but not gross. Please, no short-shorts, tank tops, outer-underwear, or see-throughs in the dining room. (You may not care, but the rest of us are trying to eat.) Beyond these prohibitions, you won't encounter many rules for attire. Classier joints may insist on a coat, fewer yet a tie, but sports coats or — heaven forbid! — suits are pretty much a waste of time and luggage space. Slacks and a nice shirt or blouse are sufficient for almost any occasion, and nice shorts show up everywhere, even at night. Most hosts know you're taking a holiday, and they are more concerned about getting your business than enforcing the dress code, but within reason. See the preceding mention of outer-underwear.

✔ Want to look like a local? No problem. Avoid shirts that say "Yonkers and Proud of It." Ditto for wearing Bermuda shorts and sandals with *socks!!* Stay away from tank tops. Plaid is out, always. Sunglasses are cool in most cases, but not if you wear those freaky things that come with fishtails. And no real Floridian wears a thong or bikini in public, if he or she packs more than 20 extra pounds. Don't tie a sweater around your neck. Don't wear cowboy boots until you're 20 miles from either coast or polyester this side of the '70s. Also, don't try to look like a lobster. (See the next entry.)

✔ Protection from the sun is essential. You can get a blistering burn on the coolest and cloudiest of days in Florida. Bring a hat (preferably one with a brim) and sunglasses. Also, don't forget to bring sunscreen with an SPF (sun protection factor) rating of 25 or higher, preferably, the waterproof variety so you don't lose its benefits by sweating or swimming. Kids especially need protection from the sun.

✔ Don't forget an umbrella or poncho, regardless of the season. Florida is as wet as it is warm, and the umbrella and poncho prices in theme parks can cause a panic attack.

✔ Bring at least two pairs of shoes and plenty of socks so you can start each day with fresh, dry footwear. Your standby shoes are invaluable after a visit to one of the theme parks or water rides. Even if you stay off the flumes, waiting in line on hot days is tougher on the tootsies than marine boot camp. Many Florida veterans carry extra shoes and socks with them, changing footwear midway through their day.

✔ If you visit Florida from early spring to late fall, bring plenty of lightweight shirts (T-shirts work very well) and shorts to stay cool during the days. If there's a "dollar store" in your town, look for one of those trigger-controlled water misters that look like a short, squat bottle of glass cleaner. You may find one for $5 at home, while the going rate in tourist zones is $12 to $15. And for the sake of your fellow patrons, don't forget an extra swipe of deodorant.

✔ Don't forget bug repellent to feed the mosquitoes, sand gnats, and everything else that zeroes in our carbon dioxide emissions. Also, don't forget an anti-itch cream to take the sting out when the repellent fails.

Dragging along Fido and Fluffy

As sure as Lassie came home, some of you will get blind-sided into taking the furriest member of the family along on your vacation. Without warning, those warm, woeful eyes are going to get to you at the last minute. Isn't that how Morris or Old Blue avoids spending the vacation, year after year, in the kennel?

Well, taking along the family pet is really not a good idea, unless you plan well in advance. First of all, make sure your pets will be welcome at the places you're going to stay. Then, ask if your favorite attractions have kennels. In Florida, it's illegal to leave an animal inside a parked car because your pet could be left sweltering in the family, pardon the expression, hearse.

If you insist on dragging along your cat or dog, here are two sources of information on pet travel:

- ✔ **Travel Dog,** P.O. Box 19724, Sacramento, CA 95819 (Internet: www. traveldog.com) has state and city listings that include pet-welcoming motels, kennels, and more.

- ✔ The **American Veterinary Medical Association,** 1931 N. Meacham Road, Suite 100, Schaumburg, IL 60170 (☎ **847-925-8070;** Internet: www.avma.org), provides some general travel tips. If you visit the Web site, click on "Care for Animals" at the top of the page, scroll down to the "Animal Safety" section, and click on "Traveling with Your Pet."

We cannot recommend taking your pet on an airplane, but if you insist on flying with Fido, make sure to ask the airline or your travel agent about the airline's policy and fees regarding pets before you book your trip. Some airlines will not transport animals in their cargo holds, and others may charge a hefty fee to fly Fluffy to Florida. Also, keep in mind that almost all airlines will not carry pets as cargo during the hottest summer months.

Part III
South Florida

The 5th Wave   By Rich Tennant

"Maybe we shouldn't have gotten a time share so close to the Everglades."

In this part . . .

Some of you are already zeroing in on South Florida as your top-draft pick. Arguably, it has as much diversity as any other landing zone in Florida. Party lovers find it hard to resist the *salsa-fied* energy of Miami's South Beach (see Chapters 10 and 11) or the eclectic and electric lifestyle of Key West (see Chapter 12). And those of you who prefer to relax when vacationing aren't left out, thanks to such natural treasures as John Pennekamp Coral Reef State Park in Key Largo (Chapter 12), Bahia Honda State Park on Big Pine Key (Chapter 12), and the Everglades (Chapter 13).

The following five chapters offer all you need to know about the best places to eat, sleep, and be merry in the frequently frenetic, though sometimes soothing, south.

Ready to burn some rubber?

Chapter 10

Settling into Miami

. . . .

In This Chapter

▶ Getting there painlessly

▶ Moving around Miami

▶ Finding rooms that fit your budget

▶ Looking at what's cooking

. . . .

Miami is one heck of a multifaceted city. Biscayne Bay ripples in the sunset as the last speedboats come home for the night. Little Havana tickles the air with the intoxicating fragrance of paella. And South Beach sways with nighttime rhythms. This is as chic as *La Florida* gets. With the exception of theme parks and Mouse-ka-things, you can find just about everything worth finding in Florida in Miami.

The items that surprise first-timers most are the city's cultural and natural resources. Sapphire-blue water, gleaming quartz beaches, and tropical gardens are complemented by such showstoppers as **Villa Vizcaya, Biscayne National Park,** and **Bill Baggs Cape Florida State Recreation Area.** And yes, if you need an attraction fix, some of Florida's most enduring — among them, the **Miami Seaquarium** and **Metrozoo** — are here to delight you.

We'll chauffeur you to those as well as other attractions in Chapter 11, but for now let's get you here, through the check-in line, and parked at a dinner table.

Getting There

Most folks come by air because flying is convenient and in most cases reasonably economical. Trains can be tedious, and even rail buffs find them time consuming if they only have a week off. Ditto for drivers — they're staring at about 450 miles between the state line and Miami.

By plane

Touch down at **Miami International Airport,** which handles 34 million passengers annually. The tenth busiest airport in the world, it's served by more than 100 domestic and foreign airlines, offering direct links to 200 cities on five continents. The airport's 121 gates may seem overwhelming, but it isn't quite as complicated as it appears. For further information, call ☎ **305-876-7000;** or visit the airport's Web site, www. miami-airport.com.

If you are headed to the northern section of Miami you may be better off flying in and out of **Fort Lauderdale Hollywood International Airport.** Located in the middle of Broward County, it is actually closer to North Miami Beach and Aventura than Miami's own airport. See Chapter 14 for more on this airport. (☎ **954-359-6100;** Internet: www. co.broward.fl.us/fll.htm).

After picking up your luggage — the route to baggage claim is clearly marked — you can take advantage of a number of services:

- ✔ **Car rental desks** for Avis, Budget, Dollar, Hertz, National, Value, and Royal are on the first level near the baggage-claim exit. (See the Appendix for rental-car agency information.)

- ✔ **Customs** has two inspection areas. Passengers arriving at Concourses D, E, and F exit at Concourse E, Level 1. Those arriving at Concourses B and A exit at Concourse B, Level 3.

- ✔ **Foreign currency exchange booths** are at six locations on the second level and in the third level at B Greeters Lobby of the terminal. A booth at Concourse E operates 24 hours a day. If you're coming from another country, convert to U.S. dollars at a bank back home. The exchange rate may not be better, but you'll save on fees.

- ✔ The **24-hour information center** is on Level 2, at Concourse E across from the hotel. There are four other centers, including two at baggage claim on Level 1, Concourse D and G (11 a.m. to 7 p.m.). You can also get information by calling ☎ **305-876-7000.**

- ✔ A **full-service bank** is located on Level 4 of Concourse B. **ATMs** are also located at the Passenger Service Centers between Concourses B and C and between Concourses G and H on Level 2 of the Terminal. The bank is open 9 a.m. to 6 p.m. on weekdays, 10 a.m. to 4 p.m. on Saturdays.

Interstate 95, toll roads, and interior highways link Miami International Airport, 6 miles from downtown Miami and about ten miles from the beaches, to the tourist areas. As we mentioned earlier, all the major car-rental agencies are located at the airport, or they run shuttles to their nearby offices. If you're arriving at night and planning to rent a car, it's a smart idea to grab a cab to your hotel and have the agency deliver the car to you the next day. If you reserved your rental before you left home, head for your rental agency's desk after you've collected your baggage.

Cabs cost $1.50 to $3 to start the meter and $2 for each mile. So a one-way fare for up to five people from the airport to the beaches would range from $21.50 to $23. Taxis line up outside the airport's arrival terminals.

Super Shuttle is one of the city's busiest van services. Its rates from the airport to South Beach are $11.50 per person one way. That's not a bargain for larger families. For more information, call ☎ **305-871-2000;** or visit the shuttle's Web site, `www.supershuttle.com`.

We don't recommend using public buses. They're unreliable, and it can take an hour or more to travel the ten miles to South Beach.

By car

If you're coming by car, there are only two routes worth considering:

- ✔ Connect with Interstate 75 in north Florida and the Florida Turnpike (a toll road) at Wildwood.
- ✔ Ride Interstate 95 down the East Coast.

I-95 is the major north-south artery here. From it, you can reach the beaches, downtown, and points south. But it's the highway system's answer to bronchitis — it's highly congested and poorly marked, so it's easy to get lost. (See Chapter 5 for northerly routes into the city.)

By train

Amtrak has two trains departing daily from New York. That's the good news. The bad news: They take as long as 30 hours to reach Miami, and prices often aren't much better than that for airfare (and they're worse if you want a sleeper). See Chapter 5 for additional information on train travel in Florida, including Amtrak's Auto Train. You may also wish to phone ☎ **800-872-7245** or visit Amtrak's Web site, `www.amtrak.com`.

Orienting Yourself

Most of western Miami-Dade County is undeveloped, but areas east of I-75 — especially the coastal zone — are so saturated that the county has had to go to ten-digit dialing for local calls. (That means you need to dial the 305 or 786 area code followed by the seven-digit local number.)

Miami's modest herd of high-rises lies in the heart of the city, and you can see them from a wide radius, making them a good reference point. The airport is west; the beaches are east; Coconut Grove and the Keys are south.

The mainland — some parts of Miami lie on islands, which are connected to the mainland by causeways — is cut into quadrants: Northeast, Northwest, Southeast, and Southwest. The quadrants converge at the intersection of Flagler Street and Miami Avenue. Street numbering, in most cases, is reasonably simple. Leaving that intersection, you progress through First Street, Second Street, Third Street, and so on. A *NE, NW, SE,* or *SW* designation following the street number tells you which quadrant you're in. The same holds true for avenues, boulevards, terraces, places, and lanes. Also note that most streets run east-west, while avenues run north-south.

Miami Beach's layout is simpler. First Street is on its southern tip, and the streets progress north. Collins Avenue, alias *A1A,* makes the entire journey and, as on the mainland, is one of several streets that has more than one name or number. (If cases like this come up in hotel or attractions listings, we'll give you both names and/or numbers.)

One other point: Numbers on the mainland and island do not parallel each other. For instance, the 79th Street Causeway coming from the mainland reaches across Biscayne Bay to 71st Street on the beach.

Making Miami by Neighborhood

Miami-Dade County is a huge area that includes Miami, Miami Beach, Coconut Grove, Coral Gables, Aventura, Hialeah and a number of other cities. (Skip ahead to the "Miami at a Glance" map.) The sprawling metropolis is confusing at best for those who've never set foot in Miami and almost as baffling for those who have been here before. The street signs include both names and numbers to help you find your way, but they don't always lead you in a straight line because Miami is full of canals, causeways, parks, and other obstacles. Getting lost here is easier than acquiring a suntan on the beach.

We've broken the county into eight geographical regions that should help you navigate, or at least identify where you are when your trip to the beach somehow lands you in a swamp:

Coconut Grove

South Florida's best surfing zone, the Grove used to be a favorite haven for intellectuals and artists, but most have escaped to quieter digs.

Nevertheless, the neighborhood's major streets — Grand Avenue, Main Highway, and McFarlane Road — boast neat shops, unique restaurants, and an upscale crowd that makes for some neat people-watching at night. During the day you'll definitely get an eyeful at the always-interesting Haulover Beach. It's clothing-optional with an emphasis on *optional*. The architecture here has a decidedly Bahamian flavor. You'll find Bahamian-style frame homes built by early settlers from the Islands along Charles Street, and the Coconut Grove Goombay Festival, a street party, celebrates that island heritage. Don't stray far from the major tourist strips in this neighborhood at night.

Coral Gables

Mediterranean-style homes, palms, and plazas grace this grand dame of Miami-Dade County. At 70 years old, Coral Gables has just about the longest history in South Florida (albeit a short one by almost any other standard). Coral Gables, a stunning example of Florida's boom-style architecture — Spanish-tile roofs, coral-rock walls, carved plazas, and gurgling fountains — is a favorite of Latin Americans and a top-notch eating and shopping zone for everyone. You'll also find the **Miami Museum of Science** here.

Downtown Miami

Downtown offers good shopping and food, including merchants selling fresh pineapples and mangoes as well as some nice restaurants and a mall. Many tall buildings, brimming with corporate stiffs, lead the way to Brickell Avenue and Biscayne Bay. After you get a look at the **Miami Center** you'll be tempted to ask if something died on the top. Much to the chagrin of owners and tenants, a flock of big black turkey vultures love to roost on the center. Nobody knows why the birds have taken a liking to the building — maybe it's all the lawyers working inside.

This neighborhood is not the kind of place safety-conscious people hang around after dark.

Greater Miami

This zone encompasses everything from North Miami Beach to a large hunk of **Everglades National Park, Biscayne National Park,** and the **Florida Keys National Marine Sanctuary.** While many of these are pristine areas, towns such as Hialeah, Miami Springs, and Homestead tend to be congested with condos and shopping malls. None are particularly visitor-oriented, though we can make a few stops here later on in this chapter and the next.

Miami at a Glance

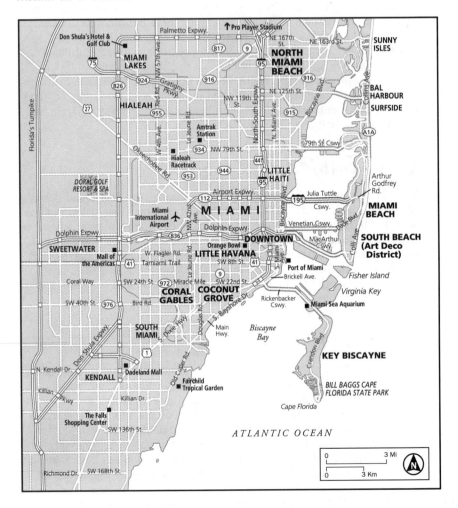

Little Havana

The Cuban community's epicenter is also Miami's most important cultural enclave. Southwest Eighth Street, locally called **Calle Ocho,** is the main thoroughfare. It's lined with everything from auto-repair shops to relatively inexpensive, ethnic eateries. If you stop, don't miss a *café cubano* or *café con leche* with buttered Cuban bread for breakfast or a deviled crab with hot sauce any time of day. While you enjoy, watch the community's elder statesmen, dressed in *guayaberas* (specially crafted white linen shirts), playing dominoes.

As much as we love it, this is another area you'd best leave when the sun does.

Miami Beach

Back in the '50s, this *was* Miami, also known as Havana North — or at least that's what the tourists thought. Back then, huge luxurious resorts offered shows featuring top stars, but many of those fabulous palaces have been converted into private condos. The hotels that endured are again thriving thanks to the renewed tourist trade. Right now, the biggest building on the block is the **Miami Beach Convention Center,** with more than 1 million square feet of exhibition space. The area's main thoroughfare, Collins Avenue, also known as A1A, links the north beach towns of Surfside, Bal Harbour (famous for shops including a huge alfresco mall and some elegant homes and hotels), Sunny Isles, and others to South Beach (see the section on "South Beach" in this chapter).

North Miami Beach

A residential area, North Miami Beach has shopping and dining, but it's not much of a tourist stop. The only noteworthy place to unpack your bags is the **Turnberry Resort.** Unlike its southern cousin, North Miami Beach is on the mainland.

South Beach

Miami isn't the hot destination it was in the middle of the twentieth century, but its rebirth as a tourist magnet has been led by this art-deco district, which international visitors (some Americans may be a bit skeptical about traveling here) find especially fascinating. The district, which stretches fewer than two miles on the south end of Miami Beach, had quite a remarkable transformation beginning in the early 1980s. Structures that had fallen into disrepair were renovated into pastel pink and vibrant yellow calling cards for the area. Today, South Beach, a magnet for photographers, models, and writers, has a large gay community, the best nightlife in South Florida, and some of the best places to eat anywhere in the Miami-Dade area.

Showing Street Smarts: Where to Get Information After Arrival

We urge you to plan in advance. Contact the visitor information folks listed in Chapter 11 and in the Appendix. If you call the **Greater Miami Convention and Visitors Bureau** before you arrive, ask for a copy of the free vacation planner, *TropiCool Miami.*

The **Miami Design Preservation League** (1234 Washington Ave., Suite 207, Miami Beach, ☎ **305-672-2014**) has an informative guide on South Beach's art-deco district. It's open 10 a.m. to 7 p.m., Monday through

Saturday. The **Greater Miami and the Beaches Hotel Association** (407 Lincoln Road, Miami Beach, ☎ **800-531-3553** or 305-531-3553) has information about accommodations and tours.

Getting Around Miami

A car is your best option for getting around the city as long as you have a reliable map (see the "Fast Facts" in Chapter 11). Taxis are a distant second — economical only if you're in a group of four or five. Public transportation is plodding and, except for South Beach, Miami isn't much of a walker's paradise.

By car

Most streets on the mainland and beaches are numbered, so it's easy to find your way around if you have a reliable map. (You can get one from one of the information sources listed under "Fast Facts" in Chapter 11, from AAA if you're a member, or from your car-rental agency.) Miami's attractions, beaches, restaurants, and hotels are spread out, making a car almost essential if you want to explore in a timely, cost-effective manner. If, on the other hand, you plan to camp at a resort or on South Beach and do your sightseeing by guided tour, you won't need a car. (Don't forget to allow delay time in your schedule for traffic congestion and, if you're going to or from the beaches, draw-bridge openings.)

Generally, there are plenty of parking spaces throughout Miami-Dade County (a major exception is South Beach), but parking can be expensive. Keep your pocket or wallet filled with quarters to feed the hungry meters or be prepared for fines of $20 or more. You can find parking garages and valet service in some areas. The going rate for valet is $3 to $20 depending on how much they think you need them. (If you're in South Beach and don't mind losing a little shoe leather, there are parking garages at 17th St. and Washington Ave., 7th St. between Washington and Collins Ave., and 13th St. between Collins and Ocean Dr. The cost is $1 an hour or $8 a day.)

See the Appendix for contact information about rental car agencies.

By taxi

Unless you can fill the cab (five passengers), this isn't a cheap way to travel, especially when you add a tip. However, a taxi is usually quick and direct, with fixed rates between certain points. Usually it's $1.50 to start the meter and $2 for each mile. The county's main cab companies are **Central,** ☎ **305-532-5555; Metro,** ☎ **305-888-8888**; and **Yellow,** ☎ **305-444-4444.**

By bus

Miami's public transit system offers little to recommend it. Bus routes almost universally are designed for commuters, not visitors. Even if buses go your way, they're slow, making too many stops and often requiring transfers and more time. For the record, the **Metro-Dade Transit System** (☎ 305-770-3131) operates the county's bus line. Fares are $1.25 plus 25 cents for each transfer.

By rail

The **Metro-Dade Transit System** (☎ 305-770-3131) also operates two trains in the county. **Metrorail** is a high-speed commuter train that runs between downtown Miami and the southern suburbs on a 21-mile elevated track. If you're staying in Coconut Grove or Coral Gables, you can park at the station and hitch a ride downtown, but it, too, isn't very tourist friendly. The fare is $1.25, and the line runs 6 a.m. to midnight daily. **Metromover,** a 4.4-mile elevated line, circles the downtown area, stopping at several downtown attractions and shopping areas. The fare is 25 cents, and it runs 6 a.m. to midnight.

Staying in Style

The following listings reflect the city's best choices in various price categories. In general, you can expect to pay the highest prices for the more upscale digs, as well as those in or near the beaches. Note that although rates in this chapter are per-night double, this is a kid-friendly state. Many accommodations let kids under 12 and in some cases under 18 stay free with parents or grandparents as long as you don't exceed the maximum occupancy of the room. Just to be safe, ask when booking your room.

The height of tourist season — the priciest period — is winter. Rates will be highest from November through March. The off-season is generally considered to run from mid-May through August, and rates are discounted by as much as 30 to 50 percent. If you're a beach buff, you can also save by staying at a hotel a few blocks off the water.

If you don't like dealing directly with hotels or haggling over rates, you can contact several reservations services in the area, including **Central Reservation Service** (☎ 800-555-7555; Internet: www.reservation-service.com); **Florida Hotel Network** (☎ 800-538-3616; Internet: www.floridahotels.com); and the **Greater Miami & the Beaches Hotel Association** (☎ 800-733-6426; Internet: www.gmbha.org).

Don't forget to allow for taxes. The combined sales, local-option and hotel bed taxes can add as much as 12.5 percent to your bill.

One last note: This is Florida. That means every hotel listed here has air conditioning and either has a pool or is on the ocean. These hotels also have television (most have cable and many have in-room movies) and telephones. Many also have hair dryers, coffee makers, and in-room safes.

Miami's Best Hotels

The Abbey Hotel

$$ South Beach

In summer, this boutique hotel can be one of the better deals on the beach. It's chic and typically deco-ish with 50 rooms set in a three-story building. The rooftop sundeck is a plus. Like many structures in this area, the Abbey Hotel has a long history and was recently revitalized. (Skip ahead to the "South Beach Accommodations" map.)

300 21st St., west of Collins Ave./A1A, east of Park Ave. ☎ *888-612-2239 or 305-531-0031. Fax: 305-672-1663. Internet:* www.abbeyhotel.com. *To get there: From the mainland take the Venetian Causeway across Biscayne Bay to Collins Ave., turn right to 21st St., turn right; hotel is on the left. Parking: $15 nightly. Rack rates: $139–$219 Dec–May and Oct–Nov, $89–$219 June–Sept. AE, CB, DC, DISC, MC, V.*

AmeriSuites Airport West

$$ West Miami

Although it lies a bit west of most of the action, AmeriSuites Airport West is close to malls and the Metrozoo. It has a fitness center and 126 suites that come with kitchenettes and free continental breakfast. Its rates during most of the year actually put this hotel in the $ category.

3655 NW 82nd Ave., west of the airport off 36th St. ☎ *800-833-1516 or 305-718-8292. Fax: 305-718-8295. Internet:* www.amerisuites.com. *To get there: From the airport, take Hwy. 836/Dolphin Expressway west to Palmetto Expressway, go north to NW 36th St., then west; turn left on 82nd Ave., hotel is on left. Parking: Free. Rack rates: $129–$169 Jan–Mar, $67–$109 Mar–Jan. AE, CB, DISC, MC, V.*

The Biltmore Hotel

$$$$ Coral Gables

On the National Register of Historic Places, the Biltmore has been a Coral Gables landmark for seven decades. Gangsters stayed here in its heyday, and during WWII it served as a VA hospital. Its copper-topped tower is visible most days from across the city. The Westin-owned hotel's 278 rooms are large and elegantly decorated; all of them overlook the Coral Gables Golf Course. The resort also has a fitness center, spa, ten tennis courts, and a spectacular 21,000-square-foot swimming pool. Other features include grand ballrooms and terraces, a choice of five restaurants, and an elaborate Sunday brunch. (See the "Accommodations Elsewhere in Miami" map, later in this chapter.)

1200 Anastasia Ave., 1 mile west of LeJeune Rd./42nd Ave. ☎ 800-727-1926 or 305-445-8066. Fax: 305-913-3159. Internet: www.biltmorehotel.com. *To get there: From I-95, take U.S. 1/South Dixie Hwy. southwest to LeJeune, go right to Anastasia, left to hotel. Parking: Valet $10. Rack rates: $239–$299 Apr–Sept, from $319 Oct–Apr. AE, CB, DISC, JC, MC, V.*

Casa Grande Suite Hotel

$$$$ South Beach

Located on Deco Drive, its 34 suites have a grande price too. Resembling well-appointed apartments, the rooms attract celebrities and quite a number of affluent Europeans. Each suite comes with full kitchen, mahogany and teak furnishings, a full range of luxurious amenities, twice daily maid service, and turn-down service. There's no pool, but the beach is a hop, skip and a jump away. Rooms facing the ocean can be loud, particularly when the real crowds arrive on weekends.

834 Ocean Dr., across from Lummus Park. ☎ 800-688-7678 or 305-672-7003. Fax: 305-672-3669. Internet: www.islandoutpost.com/CasaGrande. *To get there: From mainland take MacArthur Causeway across Biscayne Bay and continue on 5th St. to Ocean Dr., turn left; hotel is on left. Parking: $18 nightly. Rack rates: $295–$1,500 Oct–Mar, $195–$750 Apr–Sept. AE, DC, DISC, MC, V.*

Cavalier

$$$ South Beach

This trendy hotel has a great oceanfront location, close to many shops and restaurants. The Cavalier also offers some of the quietest rooms on hip (and often noisy) Ocean Drive. The eager-to-please staff is in tune with South Beach happenings. The hotel's 45 guest rooms feature a nice array of amenities and are decorated in decidedly bold prints and colors.

1320 Ocean Dr., opposite north end of Lummus Park. ☎ 800-688-7678 or 305-531-8800. Fax: 305-531-5543. Internet: www.islandoutpost.com/Cavalier. *To get there: From mainland take MacArthur Causeway across Biscayne Bay and continue on 5th St. to Ocean Drive, turn left; hotel is on left. Parking: valet, $16. Rack rates: $170–$375 Oct–Mar, $130–$275 Apr–Sept. AE, DC, DISC, MC, V.*

South Beach Accommodations

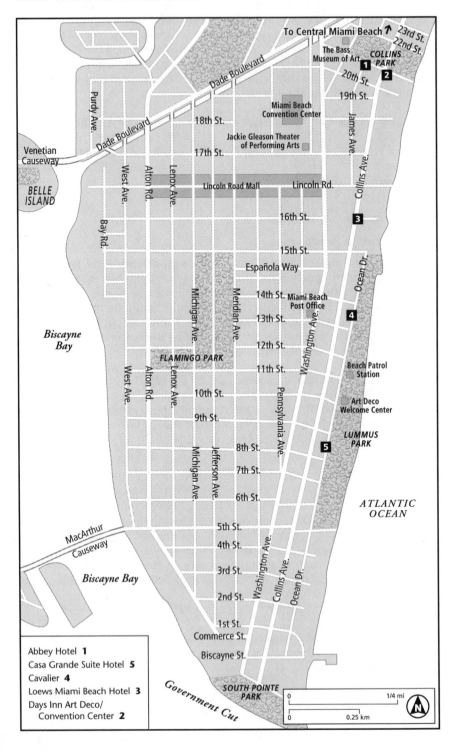

To Central Miami Beach ↑ 23rd St.
22nd St.

The Bass
Museum of Art
**COLLINS
PARK**
1
2

20th St.

19th St.

Miami Beach
Convention Center

James Ave.

Dade Boulevard

Purdy Ave.

18th St.

Jackie Gleason Theater
of Performing Arts

17th St.

Venetian
Causeway

West Ave.

Alton Rd.

Lenox Ave.

Lincoln Road Mall   Lincoln Rd.

Collins Ave.

**BELLE
ISLAND**

16th St.

3

Bay Rd.

15th St.

Ocean Dr.

Española Way

14th St. Miami Beach
Post Office

Meridian Ave.

13th St.

4

Michigan Ave.

**Biscayne
Bay**

12th St.

Washington Ave.

11th St.

Beach Patrol
Station

FLAMINGO PARK

Art Deco
Welcome Center

West Ave.

Alton Rd.

Lenox Ave.

10th St.

9th St.

Pennsylvania Ave.

**LUMMUS
PARK**

8th St.

5

Jefferson Ave.

7th St.

Michigan Ave.

6th St.

**ATLANTIC
OCEAN**

5th St.

4th St.

MacArthur
Causeway

3rd St.

Washington Ave.

Collins Ave.

Ocean Dr.

Biscayne Bay

2nd St.

1st St.

Commerce St.

Abbey Hotel **1**
Casa Grande Suite Hotel **5**
Cavalier **4**
Loews Miami Beach Hotel **3**
Days Inn Art Deco/
Convention Center **2**

Biscayne St.

Government Cut

**SOUTH POINTE
PARK**

0   1/4 mi

0   0.25 km

Courtyard by Marriott Miami Airport West

$$ West Miami

This reasonably priced hotel's 145 rooms (12 are suites) are set on four floors and have hair dryers, coffee makers, and in-room safes. Complimentary coffee is served in the lobby. The hotel's restaurant serves breakfast and dinner, and you can work off the calories in the exercise room or the whirlpool. Although it caters to business travelers, this hotel has a good location near several golf courses and malls, Key Biscayne, and Pro Player Stadium.

3929 NW 79th Ave., ☎ 800-321-2211 or 305-477-8118. Fax: 305-599-9363. Internet: www.courtyard.com/MIACA. To get there: From Miami airport, take LeJeune Road/42nd Ave. to 36th St., go through light and around a Miami Subs, which puts you on 36th; go to 79th Ave., turn right; hotel is on right. Parking: Free. Rack rates: $114–$159 Oct–Mar, $69–$119 Apr–Sept. AE, CB, DISC, MC, V.

Doral Golf Resort and Spa

$$$ West Miami

Home of the "Blue Monster" course, rated one of the top 25 in the country by *Golf* magazine, this well-known luxury resort, close to the airport, sports a number of world-class golf courses. The Doral's rooms are large, with big windows that provide a great view of the gardens — or sand traps. Standard accommodations come with private balconies or terraces. The resort has five restaurants, ranging from an outdoor grill to an elegant sit-down eatery. Other amenities include a full-service spa, an Arthur Ashe Tennis Center, and Camp Coral (a kids' day camp open 9 a.m. to 4 p.m. daily).

In addition to the usual taxes, all guests are charged an extra $13 nightly for the luxury of having door, bell, and room staff at their beck and call.

4400 NW 87th Ave. ☎ 800-713-6725 or 305-592-2000. Fax: 305-591-6630. Internet: www.doralgolf.com. To get there: From the airport, take LeJeune Road/42nd Ave. south to Hwy. 836/Dolphin Expressway, exit at 12th St., go right on 87th Ave.; hotel is on left after 36th St. Parking: $13 nightly. Rack rates: $245–$970 Oct–Mar, $155–$760 Apr–Sept. AE, DC, DISC, MC, V.

Doubletree Grand Hotel Biscayne Bay

$$ Downtown Miami

Here's a modern base with 152 large rooms and a nice view of Biscayne Bay, the Miami skyline, and the Dodge Island cruise ship port. You're also just a couple of minutes from South Beach and local attractions via land or water taxi. Rooms offer a nice array of amenities and private balconies overlooking the bay. The hotel has a full-service marina, a health club, sauna, steam room, a few restaurants, and a deli.

1717 N. Bayshore Dr., east of U.S. 1. ☎ **800-222-8733** *or 305-372-0313. Fax: 305-372-9455. Internet:* www.hilton.com/doubletree/hotels/MIABSDT/index.html. *To get there: Take I-395, exit left on Biscayne Blvd., then right on 15th St. to North Bayshore, to left and look for white building with a blue awning. Parking: $15 nightly. Rack rates: $139–$169 Oct–Mar, $129–$159 Apr–Sept. AE, DISC, MC, V.*

Fountainebleau Hilton Resort & Towers

$$$$ Miami Beach

A beach landmark, the Fountainebleau is as much of an attraction as a resort. You really ought to gawk even if, like us, you can't afford to stay. The guest register includes presidents, pageant contestants, and movie stars (Lucille Ball, Frank Sinatra, and Elvis Presley among others). The more than 1,200 rooms are elegant, and the 20-acre resort has a half-acre rock grotto pool with waterfalls, seven lighted tennis courts, a full-service spa, seven restaurants, and five lounges. There's also a 2-mile seaside boardwalk that leads to South Beach. (Skip ahead to the "Miami Beach Accommodations" map.)

The hotel's size tends to cause problems. The staff is overworked, and lines in the lobby area are frequently long.

4441 Collins Ave./A1A, just south of 46th St. Park. ☎ **800-445-8667** *or 305-538-2000. Fax: 305-531-9274. Internet:* www.fountainbleau.hilton.com. *To get there: From mainland, take Julia Tuttle Causeway to the island and Arthur Godfrey Rd. to Collins, turn left; hotel is ocean-side. Parking: $14 nightly. Rack rates: $249–$369, $199–$299 June–Aug. AE, CB, DC, DISC, MC. V.*

Hampton Inn

$$ Coconut Grove/Coral Gables

It's not the Ritz, but this branch of the Hampton Inn chain offers clean, basic hotel rooms at modest rates in a section of Miami overrun by $$$ and $$$$ hotels. There are 135 rooms, a Jacuzzi, a workout room, and free continental breakfast.

2800 SW 28th Terr., just east of U.S. 1. ☎ **800-426-7866** *or 305-448-2800. Fax: 305-442-8655. Internet:* www.hamptoninn.com. *To get there: From airport, take LeJeune Road/NW 42nd Ave. south to U.S. 1, left to 27th Ave., right and make the first right to hotel. Parking: Free. Rack rates: $104–$139 Oct–Mar, $99–$109 Apr–Sept. AE, CB, DC, DISC, MC, V.*

Hotel Sofitel Miami

$$$ Miami

Located only five minutes from the airport, this hotel's 281 rooms offer a decidedly French ambiance, and some them overlook a lagoon. The 15-story structure includes three two-bedroom apartments. It has a fitness room, restaurant, and two lighted tennis courts.

5800 Blue Lagoon Dr., just SW of the intersection of Hwy. 836/Dolphin Expressway and Red Rd. ☎ *305-264-4888. Fax: 305-262-9049. Internet:* www.accorhotel.com. *To get there: From airport, take LeJeune Road/42nd Ave. to Hwy. 836/Dolphin Expressway West, exit on 57th Ave.; hotel is at Red Road. Parking: Free. Rack rates: $159–$259 year-round. AE, DISC, MC, V.*

Hyatt Regency

$$$ Coral Gables

The Hyatt is an elegant, Mediterranean-style hotel within walking distance of the shops along Coral Gables' famous Miracle Mile. Some of the Spanish-themed rooms have balconies and whirlpools. The buildings that house them have arched entrances, grand courtyards, and tile rooms. The lobby has overstuffed chairs and marble floors. Amenities include a health club, fitness center, and two saunas.

50 Alhambra Plaza, downtown at Alhambra Plaza and Douglas Rd. ☎ *800-633-7313 or 305-441-1234. Fax: 305-441-0520. Internet:* www.hyatt.com. *To get there: From the airport, take LeJeune Rd./SW 42nd Ave. south to Coral Gables, turn left on Alhambra; hotel is 2 blocks on right. Parking: Valet $12, self $9 nightly. Rack rates: $179–$299 Oct–May, $159–$249 June–Sept. AE, CB, DISC, MC, V.*

Loews Miami Beach Hotel

$$$ South Beach

The first new hotel to open on South Beach in 30 years, this art-deco hotel is popular with business travelers headed for the nearby convention center. It has 857 luxurious rooms, 62 of which are suites. All offer data ports and a full array of luxury amenities; some have butler service. The hotel has a fitness center, a kids' camp, and three restaurants.

1601 Collins Ave./A1A, just north of Lummus Park. ☎ *800-235-6397 or 305-604-1601. Fax: 305-531-8677. Internet:* www.loewshotels.com. *To get there: From mainland, take MacArthur Causeway across Biscayne Bay and continue on 5th St. to Ocean Dr., turn left; hotel is on left. Parking: Valet $18, self $16 nightly. Rack rates: $199–$499 Oct–Mar, $159–$365 Apr–Sept. AE, DC, DISC, MC. V.*

Ocean Surf Hotel

$ Miami Beach

Though it's well north of the art-deco district, the Ocean Surf looks like it belongs on South Beach. The small art-deco hotel was built in 1940 and restored in 1997. The 49 rooms aren't fancy, but they're clean, cozy, and have all the standard amenities. The lobby area has a Keystone fireplace and a '40s and '50s Florida standard — terrazzo floors. You can watch the world go by from a funky front porch. Folks on a budget will appreciate the free continental breakfast.

Miami Beach Accommodations

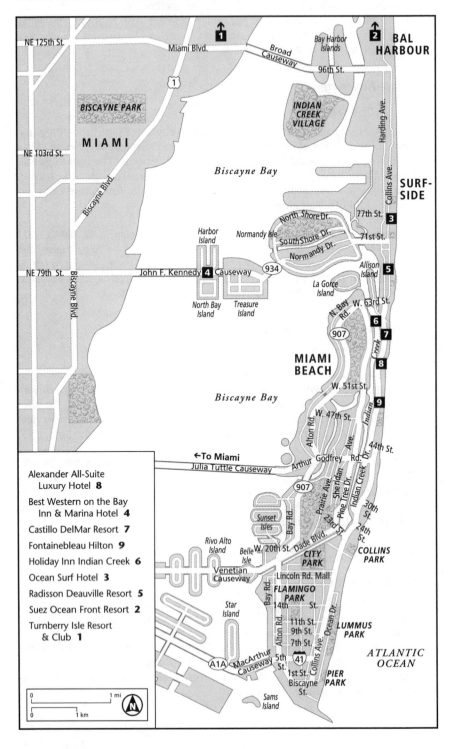

Alexander All-Suite
   Luxury Hotel **8**

Best Western on the Bay
   Inn & Marina Hotel **4**

Castillo DelMar Resort **7**

Fontainebleau Hilton **9**

Holiday Inn Indian Creek **6**

Ocean Surf Hotel **3**

Radisson Deauville Resort **5**

Suez Ocean Front Resort **2**

Turnberry Isle Resort
   & Club **1**

7436 Ocean Terr., just east of Collins Ave. and 75th St. ☎ *800-555-0411 or 305-866-1648. Fax: 305-866-1649. Internet:* www.oceansurf.com. *To get there: From the mainland, take the John F. Kennedy Causeway (Hwy. 934/NE 79th St.) to Collins, turn right to 75th, then left to the hotel. Parking: Free. Rack rates: $69–$139 Dec–Apr, $74–$124 Apr–Nov. AE, DISC, MC, V.*

Omni Colonnade Hotel

$$$ Coral Gables

Portions of this hotel are in an historic building erected by one of Coral Gables' founders, George Merrick. Guests enter the lobby from an escalator onto a wonderful pink-and-black marble floor under a domed ceiling and columns. The Colonnade's 157 rooms are quite large and contain old photographs, marble counters, and gold finished fixtures. Those with deep pockets will find suites with spiral staircases, mahogany tables and armoires, and crystal chandeliers. Amenities include a restaurant, sauna, Jacuzzi, health club, and rooftop sun deck with pool.

180 Aragon Ave., downtown at Aragon and Ponce de Leon Blvd. ☎ *800-843-6664 or 305-441-2600. Fax: 305-445-3929. Internet:* www.omnihotels.com. *To get there: From the airport, take LeJeune Rd./42nd Ave. south to Aragon Ave., go left, hotel is 3 blocks. Parking: Valet $11, self $10. Rack rates: $215–$459 Oct–Mar, $145–$360 Apr–Sept. AE, CB, DC, DISC, MC, V.*

Radisson Deauville Resort

$$ Miami Beach

Like most hotels on the beach, the Deauville had to renovate once stars such as Frank, Sammy, and Dino moved (and passed) on. Its 500+ rooms are tucked into a high-rise that sticks its chin out over the ocean. All come with a nice array of in-room amenities, and a chance to enjoy the resort's spa, exercise room, tennis courts, restaurant, bar, and 700 feet of private beach.

6701 Collins Ave./A1A, 67th St. at Collins. ☎ *800-333-3333 or 305-865-8511. Fax: 305-865-8154. Internet:* www.radisson.com. *To get there: From the mainland, take the John F. Kennedy Causeway (Hwy. 934/NE 79th St.) to Collins, turn right to 67th St.; hotel is on right. Parking: $16 nightly. Rack rates: $159–$219 Oct–Mar, $109–$139 Apr–Sept. AE, CB, DISC, MC, V.*

Turnberry Isle Resort and Club

$$$$ Aventura

Golfers, fitness fanatics, and those seeking luxurious pampering will find Turnberry an especially attractive choice. Set on 300 acres, its rooms have tiled bathrooms with whirlpool tubs that come in handy after a workout on one of the resort's 20 tennis courts or a round on one of two golf courses. The decor is Mediterranean, but the atmosphere will make you feel like you're in an exclusive, country-club neighborhood.

Turnberry has a renowned full-service spa, a marina, six restaurants, several bars, and a disco.

19999 W. Country Club Dr., ½ mile west of A1A off Hwy. 856. ☎ *800-327-7028 or 305-932-6200. Fax: 305-933-6560. Internet:* www.turnberryisle.com. *To get there: Go north on U.S. 1 to 199th St./Aventura Blvd., turn right and follow signs. Parking: Valet $8. Rack rates: $265–$555 Sept–May, $175–$355 June–Sept. AE, CB, DISC, MC, V.*

Runner-up Accommodations

If your favorites are full or you can't find one in the previous listings to satisfy your tastes and budget, here are a few more places to consider:

Alexander All-Suite Luxury Hotel

$$$$ Each of this stunning hotel's 150 suites, feature two baths, a full kitchen, and a balcony. The amenities and services are top-notch. *5225 Collins Ave./A1A, Miami Beach.* ☎ *800-327-6121 or 305-865-6500; Fax: 305-864-8525; Internet:* www.alexanderhotel.com.

Best Western on the Bay Inn & Marina

$ This modest hotel delivers small-but-clean rooms overlooking Biscayne Bay. *1819 79th St. Causeway.* ☎ *800-624-3961 or 305-865-7100; Fax: 305-868-3483; Internet:* www.bestwestern.com.

Castillo del Mar Resort

$$ This 17-story member of Miami Beach's Millionaire's Row offers newly renovated rooms with kitchenettes, and also has a beachside pool. *5445 Collins Ave./A1A.* ☎ *888-352-3224 or 305-865-1500; Fax: 305-861-7864; Internet:* www.castillodelmar.com.

Clarion Hotel-Miami Airport

$$ This hotel is near enough to the action on the beaches that its price and reputation make it a worthy alternate. *5301 NW 36th St.* ☎ *800-252-7466 or 305-871-1000; Fax: 305-871-4971; Internet:* www.hotelchoice.com.

Comfort Inn Airport

$$ It won't win any location or luxury points, but its 110 rooms are an economical base for exploring Miami. *5125 NW 36th St.* ☎ *800-228-5150 or 305-887-2153; Fax: 305-887-3559; Internet:* www.clarcom.com/comforteast.html.

Days Inn Art Deco/Convention Center

$ This budget-chain motel's location is its greatest feature — it's on South Beach, right at Collins Ave./A1A, but doesn't sport the hype or the price of many of its neighbors. *100 21st St., Miami Beach* ☎ *800-544-8313; 305-538-6631; Fax: 305-674-0954; Internet:* www.daysinn.com.

Fairfield Inn Miami Airport

$ You'll find 281 standard motel rooms at this budget choice, which also serves up a free continental breakfast and two tennis courts. *1201 NW LeJeune Rd./42nd Ave.* ☎ *800-228-2800 or 305-643-0055; Fax: 305-649-3997; Internet:* www.fairfieldinn.com.

Holiday Inn Indian Creek

$ This is a basic inn, but the price is right and you get a view of the ocean or the city. *6060 Indian Creek Dr., Miami Beach.* ☎ *800-519-3555 or 305-865-2565; Fax: 305-865-2506; Internet:* www.basshotels.com/holiday-inn.

Hyatt Regency Miami

$$$ A room here comes with a nice view of the Miami River, and the hotel is just a few steps from The Riverwalk and the shops at Bayside Marketplace. *400 SE 2nd Ave.* ☎ *800-633-7313 or 305-358-1234; Fax: 305-356-0529; Internet:* www.hyatt.com.

Riande Continental Bayside

$$ This downtown hotel offers friendly service and 247 rooms, many of them overlooking Biscayne Bay and the Port of Miami. *146 Biscayne Blvd.* ☎ *800-742-6331 or 305-358-4555; Fax: 305-531-5602; Internet:* www.hotelesriande.com.

Riviera Court Motel

$ The Riviera is a basic but clean mom-and-pop motel that's near the Miracle Mile. *5100 Riviera Drive, Coral Gables.* ☎ *800-368-8602 or 305-665-3528; Fax: 305-667-8993.*

Sheraton Biscayne Bay Hotel

$$ A short drive away from the best Miami has to offer, the hotel has 598 comfortable rooms overlooking the pool or the downtown skyline. *495 Brickell Ave.* ☎ *800-321-2323 or 305-373-6000; Fax: 305-374-2279; Internet:* www.sheraton.com.

Silver Sands Beach Resort

$$ The most affordable place on Key Biscayne, its 56 roomy rooms date to the 1950s, but were remodeled after Hurricane Andrew in 1992. *301 Ocean Dr., Key Biscayne* ☎ *305-361-5441; Fax: 305-361/5477; Internet:* www.silversandsmiami.com.

Accommodations Elsewhere in Miami

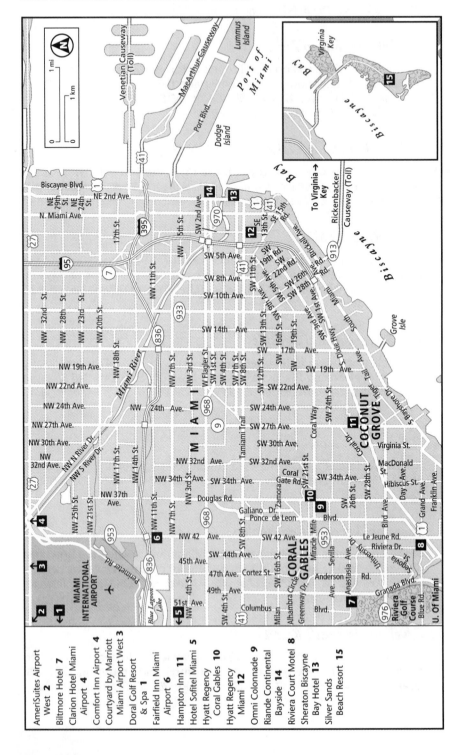

AmeriSuites Airport West **2**
Biltmore Hotel **7**
Clarion Hotel Miami Airport **4**
Comfort Inn Airport **4**
Courtyard by Marriott Miami Airport West **3**
Doral Golf Resort & Spa **1**
Fairfield Inn Miami Airport **6**
Hampton Inn **11**
Hotel Sofitel Miami **5**
Hyatt Regency Coral Gables **10**
Hyatt Regency Miami **12**
Omni Colonnade **9**
Riande Continental Bayside **14**
Riviera Court Motel **8**
Sheraton Biscayne Bay Hotel **13**
Silver Sands Beach Resort **15**

Suez Ocean Front Resort

$ It's kind of kitschy, but here's a basic landing zone if you want to be on a Miami-Dade beach, but as far north of the action as possible. *18215 Collins Ave.* ☎ *800-327-5278 or 305-932-0661; Fax: 305-937-0058; Internet:* www.suezresort.com.

Dining in Miami

There are so many restaurant choices — literally hundreds and hundreds of places in a city that's arguably one of the Southeast's best bets when it comes to culinary diversity. If you have a hankering for it (Cuban, kosher, Thai, Vietnamese, nouveau, Old World, you name it), you can find it here. Note, however, that competition is so stiff some places don't last three months. So don't be surprised if your No. 1 choice on these pages has disappeared by the time you land. Some great kitchens can't stand the heat. On the upside, look for less-than-conventional treats on the menu — fish battered in mushrooms or ribs injected with guava sauce. Miami is especially known for its fresh seafood and its Fusion cuisine, which combines the best of ethnic and continental cooking to create a fabulous dining experience.

Keep in mind that you won't be the only one looking to eat at the hottest restaurants in town. Dining out is a popular activity in Miami. To save yourself from headaches and an empty stomach, make reservations at the restaurants you want to sample or you may end up waiting several hours — and in the best of the best, several days.

Miami's Best Restaurants

Botticelli Trattoria

$ Coral Gables   ITALIAN

If you're traveling with kids and want a good meal for a great price, this is a good choice. The chicken and veal dishes in this nonsmoking restaurant are simple but tasty; the fresh pasta and seafood specialties — pasta primavera and the spicy seafood medley, for example — are better choices. Cap the meal with Italian cheesecake or fruit tarts drenched in caramel sauce.

1915 Ponce de Leon, just north of Alhambra Plaza. ☎ *305-444-3357; Internet:* www.coralgables.net/botticelli.htm. *Reservations strongly suggested. To get there: From airport, take LeJeune Rd./42nd Ave. south to 8th St., go left to Ponce de Leon, then right. Main courses: $10–$20 (most $16 and under). AE, DISC, MC, V. Open: 11:30am–2:30 p.m. and 5:30–11 p.m. Mon–Fri; 5:30–11 p.m. Sat.*

Caffe Abbracci

$$ Coral Gables   ITALIAN

Abbracci's staff serves delightfully prepared food in a fun — if somewhat loud — setting. The menu changes periodically, but might include snapper grilled with shiitake mushrooms or *frutti di mare* — an assortment of seafood in tomato sauce sprinkled over linguine. Try the salmon or tuna carpaccio for starters. This place gets really packed on weekends.

318 Aragon Ave., Aragon at Salzedo. ☎ *305-441-0700. Reservations required. To get there: Take LeJeune Rd./42nd Ave. south from airport, then east on Aragon. Main courses: $16–$28. AE, CB, DISC, MC, V. Open: 11:30 a.m.–3 p.m. and 6–11:30 p.m. Mon–Fri; 6–11:30 p.m. Sat–Sun.*

Casa Juancho

$$ Little Havana/Downtown   SPANISH/CUBAN

This is unquestionably one of Miami's best Latin restaurants. The ambitious menu offers mahi-mahi, clams, and shrimp in a garlic and white wine sauce; seafood and chicken paella; roast suckling pig; and sherry-cured rabbit in a brown sauce. You can make an entire meal out of one or two tapas ($5 to $14). On top of all these selections, this *casa* also has a dandy wine list, featuring many Spanish reserves.

2436 SW 8th St., just east of 8th and SW 25th Ave. ☎ *305-642-2452. Internet:* www . casajuancho.com. *Reservations suggested. To get there: From the airport, take LeJeune/42nd Ave. south to Tamiami Trail/SW 8th/Calle Ocho and go east. Main courses: $14–$40. AE, DISC, MC, V. Open: noon–midnight Sun–Thurs; noon–1 a.m. Fri–Sat.*

Chef Allen's

$$$ North Miami Beach   AMERICAN CONTEMPORARY

Foodies flock here for some of the best new-world cuisine in South Florida. Watch the chefs inside a glass-enclosed kitchen prepare goodies such as goat cheese-crusted lamb chops with lentils and roasted peppers, and mesquite-grilled soft shell crabs with pineapple salsa. Owner-chef Allen Susser's 16-year-old eatery stands out in a place where restaurants get flattened like wildlife on an interstate.

19088 NE 29th Ave., just east of U.S. 1/Biscayne Blvd. at 191st St. ☎ *305-935-2900. Internet:* www.chefallen.com. *Reservations suggested. To get there: Take U.S. 1 north to 191st St., turn right. Main courses: $24–$35, also $52 fixed–price menu. AE, DISC, MC, V. Open: 6–10:30 p.m. Sun–Thurs; 6–11 p.m. Fri–Sat.*

Chrysanthemum

$$ South Beach   CHINESE

"Mums" offers tasty Szechuan cuisine in an unpretentious (rare in South Beach) setting. The service is prompt and expert. The menu is dotted with items such as crispy duck in five-flavor spice and filet mignon in mandarin sauce. Seafood Delight (shrimp, scallops, and fish with vegetables) and lamb sautéed in a hot, spicy sauce are two local favorites. Vegetarians will find numerous specialties to choose from. (See the "South Beach Dining" map, later in this chapter.)

1248 Washington Ave., near City Hall. ☎ *305-531-5656. Reservations suggested. To get there: From mainland, take MacArthur Causeway/U.S. 41/A1A across Biscayne Bay to Washington, turn left. Main courses: $12–$20. AE, DC, MC, V. Open: 6–11 p.m., Tues–Sun.*

Fleming: A Taste of Denmark

$$ Kendall/Southwest Miami   DANISH

A smoke-free atmosphere, a cozy dining room, and a patio complement this restaurant's innovative menu. Specialties here include gravlax and *frikaeller* (Danish meatballs). If you want something a bit more continental, the staff also serves a veal chop in port wine with mushrooms, pan-seared salmon, and weinerschnitzel. (See this restaurant on the "Attractions in South Miami-Dade County" map in Chapter 11.)

8511 SW 136th St., just east of U.S. 1 on 136th. ☎ *305-232-6444. Reservations accepted. To get there: U.S. 1 south to 136th St., then east. Main courses: $11–$27. AE, MC, V. Open: 5:30–10:30 p.m. Tues–Sun.*

The Forge

$$$ Miami Beach   AMERICAN

The English oak paneling and Tiffany glass will give you an idea of the prices at this restaurant, even before you get a look at the menu. The caviar- (Beluga naturally) and escargot-eating money crowd stops in here regularly, although the atmosphere is more elegant than stuffy. When it comes to entrees, red meat rules at The Forge — from prime rib and the award-winning Super Steak to veal, rack of lamb, buffalo, and venison. There's an extensive wine list. (See the "Miami Beach Dining" map, later in this chapter.)

432 Arthur Godfrey Rd., ½ mile west Collins Ave./A1A. ☎ *305-538-8533. Reservations suggested. To get there: From mainland, take the Julia Tuttle Causeway into its merger with Arthur Godfrey Rd. Main courses: $24–$40. AE, DISC, MC, V. Open: 6 p.m.–midnight Sun–Thu; 6 p.m.–1 a.m. Sat–Sun.*

Grillfish

$ Coral Gables   SEAFOOD

Opened in 1999, this is the second Miami-Dade storefront for a small chain that also operates restaurants in Boston, Bethesda, and Washington, D.C. It's a good choice if you like marine cuisine grilled medium rare and you don't want to empty your wallet for it. Expect salmon, swordfish, wahoo, halibut, mahi-mahi, and shark. There are also a few pasta dishes. Most items are under $15. **Note:** Miami's other branch of Grillfish is on 1444 Collins Ave. (☎ 305-538-9908) in South Beach. (See the "Dining Elsewhere in Miami" map, later in this chapter.)

2325 Galiano Ave., corner of Argon and Galiano. ☎ *305-445-6411. Reservations recommended. To get there: From the airport, take LeJeune Rd./42nd Ave. south to Aragon, left 3 blocks. Main courses: $10–$20. (lunch $9–$11.50). AE, DC, DISC, MC, V. Open: noon–2:30 p.m. and 5:30 p.m.–till Mon–Fri; 5:30 p.m.–till Sat–Sun.*

Monty's Stone Crab & Seafood House

$$$ South Beach   SEAFOOD

The nicest thing about Monty's: It's a more affordable and arguably better option than the more famous Joe's Stone Crab (see listing under "Runner-up Restaurants"). Don't miss the she-crab soup for starters before diving into the restaurant's headliner — stone crabs, which are in season October through May. During the season, you might find all-you-can-eat specials for $50 to $70 (medium vs. large). Skip the crabs during the off-season, when frozen claws are sold (unfrozen on your plate, of course) for the same amount. Meat and pasta are on the menu, in case someone in your party doesn't like seafood. **Note:** Monty's also has a branch in Coconut Grove, on 2550 S. Bayshore Dr.; ☎ 305-858-1431.

300 Alton Rd., located at the south end of the beach. ☎ *305-673-3444. Internet:* www.montysstonecrab.com. *Reservations suggested. To get there: From mainland, take MacArthur Causeway/A1A to Alton, go right. Main courses: $15–$39, AE, DC, MC, V. Open: 5:30–11 p.m. Sun–Thurs; 5:30 p.m.–midnight Fri–Sat.*

Norman's

$$$ Coral Gables   NEW WORLD

Owner Norman Van Aken is a perennial award winner, with trophies or at least kudos from *Bon Appetit, Conde Nast, Food & Wine, Gourmet, GQ,* the James Beard Foundation, *Wine Spectator,* and Zagat. His restaurant features an open kitchen, a professional staff, and a tasteful atmosphere. Chef Norman will delight you with his Asian and Caribbean-inspired dishes, which include a pork tenderloin served with browned Haitian grits, and venison *au poivre.* And don't skimp on the front end here, the appetizers — a gazpacho-and-crab cocktail with Grey Goose vodka, for example — are excellent.

21 Almeria Ave., 3 blocks south of Miracle Mile, just west of Douglas Rd. ☎ *305-446-6767. Internet:* www.normans.com. *Reservations recommended. To get there: From the airport, take LeJuene Rd./42nd Ave. south to Coral Way/Miracle Mile, go left to 37th Ave./Douglas, turn right, go 3 blocks to Almeria, turn right. Main courses: $26–$46. AE, CB, DISC, MC, V. Open: 6–10:30 p.m. Mon–Thurs; 6–11 p.m. Fri–Sat.*

South Beach Dining

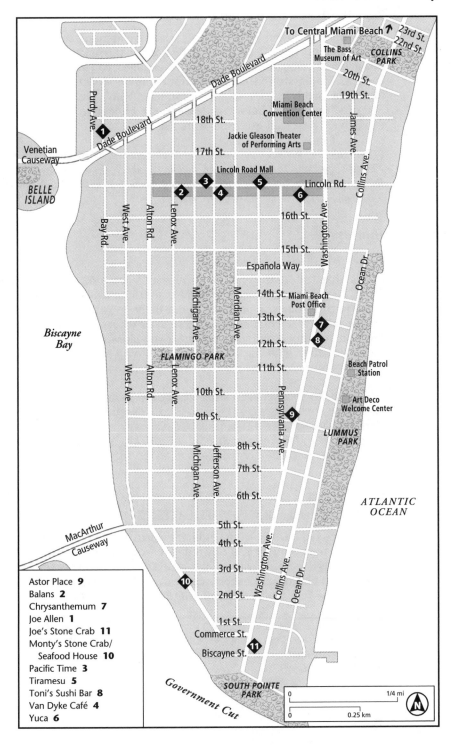

To Central Miami Beach ↑ 23rd St.
22nd St.

The Bass
Museum of Art
COLLINS
PARK

Dade Boulevard

20th St.

Purdy Ave.

19th St.

Miami Beach
Convention Center

18th St.

Dade Boulevard

James Ave.

Collins Ave.

Jackie Gleason Theater
of Performing Arts

17th St.

Venetian
Causeway

Lincoln Road Mall

BELLE
ISLAND

3

5

Lincoln Rd.

2

4

6

16th St.

West Ave.

Alton Rd.

Lenox Ave.

Bay Rd.

Washington Ave.

Ocean Dr.

15th St.

Española Way

14th St.

Miami Beach
Post Office

Michigan Ave.

Meridian Ave.

13th St.

*Biscayne
Bay*

7

12th St.

8

Beach Patrol
Station

FLAMINGO PARK

11th St.

Art Deco
Welcome Center

West Ave.

Alton Rd.

Lenox Ave.

10th St.

9th St.

9

LUMMUS
PARK

8th St.

Michigan Ave.

Jefferson Ave.

Pennsylvania Ave.

7th St.

6th St.

*ATLANTIC
OCEAN*

MacArthur
Causeway

5th St.

4th St.

Washington Ave.

Collins Ave.

Ocean Dr.

3rd St.

10

2nd St.

Astor Place **9**
Balans **2**
Chrysanthemum **7**
Joe Allen **1**
Joe's Stone Crab **11**
Monty's Stone Crab/
   Seafood House **10**
Pacific Time **3**
Tiramesu **5**
Toni's Sushi Bar **8**
Van Dyke Café **4**
Yuca **6**

1st St.

Commerce St.

11

Biscayne St.

Government Cut

SOUTH POINTE
PARK

0   1/4 mi

0   0.25 km

Pacific Time

$$$ South Beach   PACIFIC RIM

Chef-owner Jonathan Eisman works wizardry in a bustling atmosphere that frequently hosts a celebrity or two. While the Asian-Fusion menu at this award-winning establishment often changes, you may find delicacies such as ginger-stuffed catfish tempura, honey-roasted Peking duck, Mongolian lamb salad, and grouper infused with sake and served on a bed of shredded shallots. For dessert, the chocolate bomb is sinfully explosive. There's an extensive wine list.

915 Lincoln Rd., between Jefferson and Michigan Ave. ☎ *305-534-5979. Reservations suggested. To get there: From mainland, take Venetian Causeway to Alton Rd. and go right, then left on Lincoln. Main courses: $17–$35. AE, DISC, MC, V. Open: 6–11 p.m. Sun–Thurs; 6 p.m.–midnight Fri–Sat.*

Tiramesu

$$ Miami Beach   ITALIAN

Here's an eatery that gained in popularity when it moved off of Ocean Drive. The restaurant specializes in Northern Italian cuisine, and pastas come in three sizes (small, large, and belly up to the trough, bucko). Vegetarians get several selections, such as wheat rigatoni with beans, broccoli, tomatoes, and mushrooms. If you like seafood, don't overlook the grilled tuna with basil sauce or fusilli with salmon and tomatoes. There's a very good wine list.

721 Lincoln Road, midway between the Atlantic and Biscayne Bay. ☎ *305-532-4538. Internet:* www.tiramesurestaurant.com. *Reservations suggested. To get there: From mainland, take Venetian Way Causeway east to Alton, turn right, then left on Lincoln. Main courses: $11–$22. AE, DC, MC, V. Open: noon–4 p.m. and 5:30 p.m.–midnight Sun–Thurs; noon–4 p.m. and 5:30 p.m.–1 a.m. Sat–Sun.*

Wolfie's

$ Miami Beach   JEWISH/DELICATESSEN

Open since 1954, Wolfie's is a landmark worth a visit for people-watching alone. It's something of a sit-down deli married to an old-style cafeteria. The menu is decorated with soups, salads, burgers, and desserts, as well as favorites like lox and bagels, and the portions are huge. If you want a taste of New York while in Miami, this 24-hour joint is the place to go.

21st St. and Collins Ave., across from Collins Park. ☎ *305-538-6626. Reservations not accepted. To get there: From mainland, take Venetian Causeway into Dade Blvd. and go to Washington, turn right, then left on 21st. Main courses: $4–$16. MC, V. Open: 24 hours daily.*

Miami Beach Dining

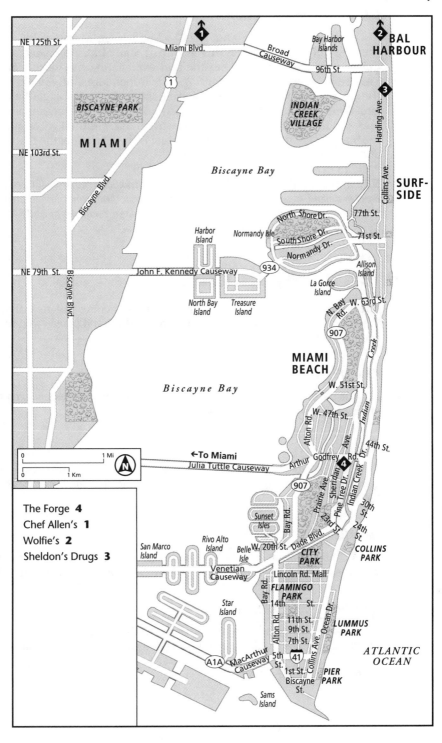

NE 125th St.
Miami Blvd.
Broad Causeway
Bay Harbor Islands
BAL HARBOUR

96th St.

1

BISCAYNE PARK

INDIAN CREEK VILLAGE

Harding Ave.

M I A M I

NE 103rd St.

Biscayne Blvd.

Biscayne Bay

Collins Ave.

SURF-SIDE

North Shore Dr.
77th St.

Harbor Island
Normandy Isle
South Shore Dr.
71st St.

NE 79th St.
John F. Kennedy Causeway
934
Normandy Dr.

Allison Island

La Gorce Island

North Bay Island
Treasure Island

N. Bay Rd.
W. 63rd St.

907

MIAMI BEACH

W. 51st St.

Biscayne Bay

W. 47th St.

Indian Creek

Alton Rd.

44th St.

0   1 Mi
0   1 Km

←To Miami
Julia Tuttle Causeway

Arthur Godfrey Rd.

Sheridan Ave.

Pine Tree Dr.

Indian Creek Dr.

4

907

The Forge **4**
Chef Allen's **1**
Wolfie's **2**
Sheldon's Drugs **3**

Sunset Isles

Prairie Ave.

30th St.

24th St.

COLLINS PARK

San Marco Island

Rivo Alto Island

Belle Isle

W. 20th St. Dade Blvd.

23rd St.

CITY PARK

Bay Rd.

Venetian Causeway

Lincoln Rd. Mall

Alton Rd.

FLAMINGO PARK

Star Island

14th St.

11th St.
9th St.
7th St.

Collins Ave.
Ocean Dr.

LUMMUS PARK

MacArthur Causeway

A1A

5th St.

41

1st St.
Biscayne St.

PIER PARK

ATLANTIC OCEAN

Sams Island

YUCA

$$$ South Beach   CUBAN

It's pronounced "*You*-ka" not "*Yuck*-a" and is an acronym for Young Upscale Cuban Americans. (It's also the name of a staple vegetable in Cuban American kitchens, but the first explanation has more pizzazz.) The menu is peppered with cutting-edge Cuban fare, but you may have trouble reading it. If you don't speak Spanish, the staff will gladly translate. When available, the guava-injected ribs are a crowd pleaser as is the pork tenderloin, which you can cut with a fork. On the lighter side try the plantain-coated dolphin. Ask for a seat near the front of the restaurant and away from the noisy kitchen area.

501 Lincoln Rd., at Drexel. ☎ 305-532-9822. Reservations required. To get there: From mainland, take Venetian Way Causeway east to Alton, turn right, then left on Lincoln. Main courses: $20–$36. AE, DISC, MC, V. Open: noon–4 p.m. and 6–11 p.m. Sun–Thurs; noon–4 p.m. and 6 p.m.–midnight Fri–Sat.

Runner-up Restaurants

The good thing about a town where restaurants come and go is that there is always fresh blood. Here are some additional places that might satisfy your cravings.

Astor Place Bar & Grill

$$$ It packs a solid reputation for seafood dishes. *956 Washington Ave., inside the Hotel Astor, South Beach. ☎ 305-672-7217.*

Balans

$ A British import that delivers bangers and mash and some Thai favorites. Best of all, it's affordable. *1022 Lincoln Rd., South Beach. ☎ 305-534-9191.*

Joe Allen

$$ It has the appeal of its Manhattan parent, and salads, pizza, and, your old favorite, meat loaf. *1787 Purdy Ave., Miami Beach. ☎ 305-531-7007.*

Joe's Stone Crab Restaurant

$$$ Arguably Miami's best-known eatery, it's snobby and too pricey for the value received, but some folks feel compelled to visit. It's only open during stone-crab season, mid-October to mid-May. *11 Washington Ave., South Beach. ☎ 305-673-0365.*

Dining Elsewhere in Miami

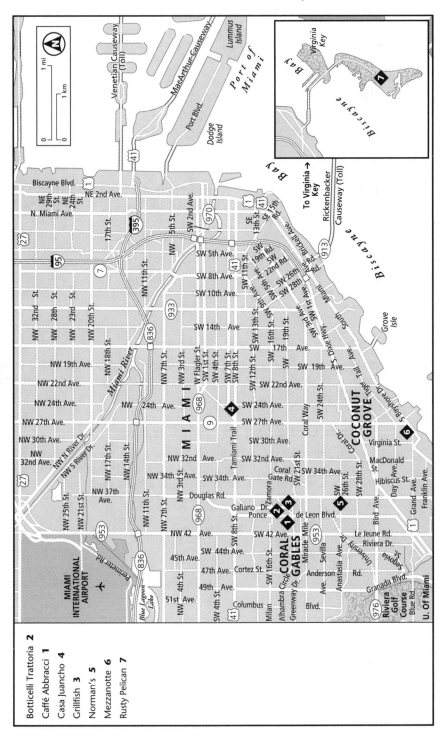

Botticelli Trattoria **2**
Caffé Abbracci **1**
Casa Juancho **4**
Grillfish **3**
Norman's **5**
Mezzanotte **6**
Rusty Pelican **7**

Mezzanotte

$$ A popular, upscale, noisy bistro where you can dig into a hearty Italian meal. It's not unusual for your neighbors to come over and dance on your table. *3390 Mary St., adjacent to the Mayfair Shops at Mary and Florida Streets, Coconut Grove.* ☎ *305-448-7677.*

The Rusty Pelican

$$ This spot features a great view and a menu filled with steaks and seafood. *3201 Rickenbacker Causeway, Key Biscayne.* ☎ *305-361-3818.*

Sheldon's Drugs

$ An old-fashioned drugstore counter that offers basic food — including a great piece of pie — at an exceptionally good price. *9501 Harding Ave., Miami Beach.* ☎ *305-866-6251.*

Shula's Steak House

$$$ This restaurant — bursting with Miami Dolphins' memorabilia — lives up to a reputation for serving monster steaks and great seafood. *7601 Miami Lakes Dr., Miami Lakes.* ☎ *305-820-8102.*

Toni's Sushi Bar/Japanese Restaurant

$$ Slip off your shoes, belly up to one of the tables, and enjoy some of the freshest sushi on the beach. *1208 Washington Ave., South Beach.* ☎ *305-673-9368.*

Van Dyke Café & Upstairs at the Van Dyke

$$ A magnet for the see-and-be-seen set, the service and food (sandwiches, pizza, seafood, and chicken) are pretty good by South Beach standards. *846 Lincoln Rd., South Beach.* ☎ *305-534-3600.*

Chapter 11

Exploring Miami

● ●

In This Chapter

▶ Visiting must-see attractions and sights

▶ Touring the city with sample itineraries

▶ Shopping your way through Miami

▶ Having some after-dark fun

● ●

*N*ow that you had a chance to catch your breath and suck down
some calories, it's time to start turning turnstiles. We'll visit the
day shift first, exploring some of Miami's top attractions, museums,
and parks. We'll also give you some shopping pointers. Then, as the
sun sinks into the Everglades, we'll start painting the town whatever
color suits you.

So, with your permission . . .

Seeing the Top Sights

Miami is full of interesting places to visit, and no matter what your
preference — a day spent touring museums or one strolling through
gardens of exceptional beauty, for example — you will find something
here that will hold your attention. (Skip ahead to the "Central Miami
Attractions" map.)

American Police Hall of Fame and Museum

Ever wanted to sit in an electric chair (without someone throwing the
switch, of course)? You can climb into a hot seat here, as well as see 11,000
other exhibits in a building that also has a memorial to 6,000 officers who
have died in the line of duty. Other displays include a guillotine and, on a
sobering note, a clock keeping track of today's U.S. murder rate. Allow
between 2 and 2½ hours, but more if you're a crime-and-punishment type.

3801 Biscayne Blvd./US 1, two blocks north of the US 1/I-95 junction. ☎ *305-
573-0070. Internet:* www.aphf.org. *To get there: Take I-95 to US 1 and go north 2
blocks. Admission: $7.50 adults, $6.50 seniors, $4 kids 6–11. Open: 9 a.m.–5 p.m. daily.*

Central Miami Attractions

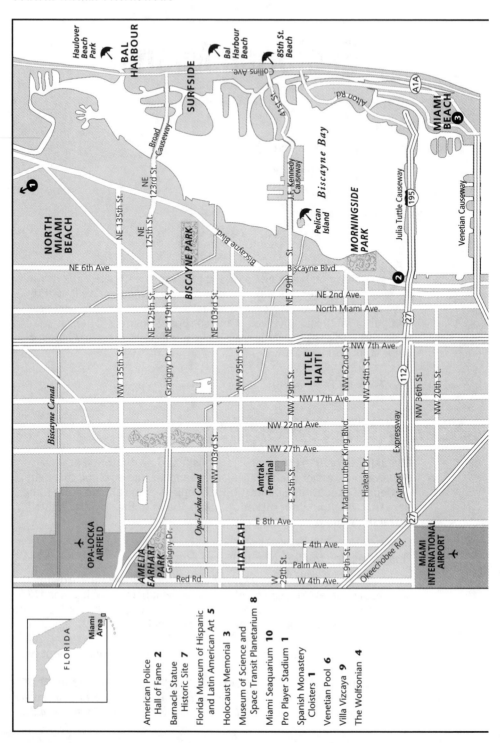

FLORIDA

Miami Area

American Police Hall of Fame **2**
Barnacle Statue Historic Site **7**
Florida Museum of Hispanic and Latin American Art **5**
Holocaust Memorial **3**
Museum of Science and Space Transit Planetarium **8**
Miami Seaquarium **10**
Pro Player Stadium **1**
Spanish Monastery Cloisters **1**
Venetian Pool **6**
Villa Vizcaya **9**
The Wolfsonian **4**

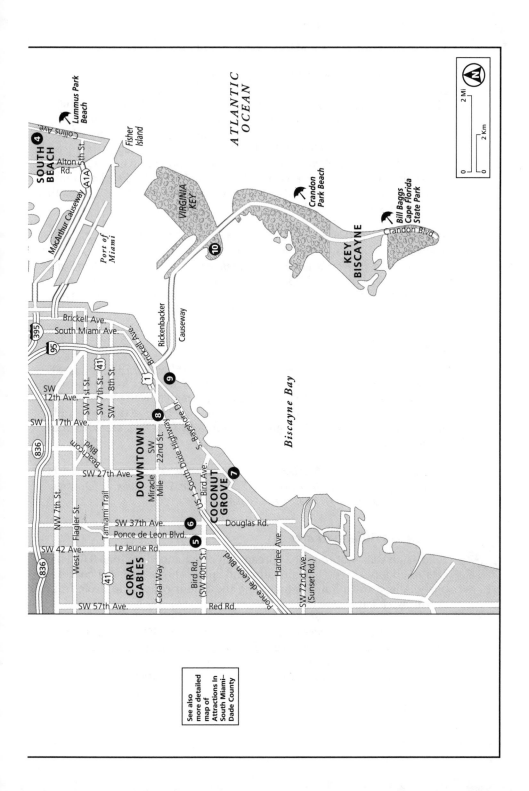

ATLANTIC
OCEAN

Lummus Park
Beach

SOUTH
BEACH ➍

Collins Ave.
5th St.
Alton
Rd.
A1A

Fisher
Island

MacArthur Causeway

Port of
Miami

VIRGINIA
KEY

Crandon
Park Beach

Bill Baggs
Cape Florida
State Park

Crandon Blvd.

KEY
BISCAYNE

➓

Rickenbacker
Causeway

Brickell Ave.
South Miami Ave.

Brickell Ave.

395

95

41

SW
12th Ave.

SW 1st St.
SW 7th St.
SW 8th St.

➒

➑

SW
17th Ave.

836

SW
22nd St.

DOWNTOWN

Beacom
Blvd.

SW 27th Ave.

Biscayne Bay

➐

S. Bayshore Dr.

US-1 South Dixie Highway

Bird Ave.

COCONUT
GROVE

Miracle
Mile

NW 7th St.

Tamiami Trail

Flagler St.

SW 37th Ave.
Ponce de Leon Blvd.

Le Jeune Rd.

➏

➎

Douglas Rd.

Hardee Ave.

SW 42 Ave.

836

41

CORAL
GABLES

West

Coral Way

Bird Rd.
(SW 40th St.)

Ponce de Leon Blvd.

SW 72nd Ave.
(Sunset Rd.)

SW 57th Ave.

Red Rd.

2 Mi

2 Km

0

0

See also
more detailed
map of
Attractions in
South Miami–
Dade County

Biscayne National Park

Mangroves, coral reefs, and tiny keys form this 181,000-acre refuge, most of which is occupied by water. Hiking hounds can take advantage of 1½- and 7-mile trails through Elliott Key's hardwood hammocks and mangroves, but you have to hitch a boat ride from the park's concessionaire, **Biscayne National Underwater Park** ($21 per person, ☎ **305-230-1100**). Other possibilities include renting a canoe ($8 an hour, $22 a half day) or a kayak ($11 an hour), taking a glass-bottom boat tour ($19.95 adults, $17.95 seniors, $12.95 kids under 12; 10 a.m. and 1 p.m. daily), going on a snorkeling trip ($29.95 including gear, 1:30 and 5:30 p.m), and going scuba diving ($44.95 for a two-tank dive including tanks, 8:30 a.m.). Reservations are recommended for boat tours. With the time it takes to reach the park, allow all day to see it.

9700 SW 328th St., Convoy Point Visitor Center. ☎ 305-230-7275 or 305-230-1100. Internet: www.nps.gov/bisc *and* www.biscayne.national-park.com. *To get there: Take the Florida Turnpike and its Homestead extension south to Exit 6 (Speedway Blvd.), go left to SW 328th/N. Canal Dr., go left again and continue about 5 miles to entrance on the left. Admission: It's free, but there are concession fees (see preceding information). Open: 8 a.m.–5:30 p.m. daily.*

Coral Castle

Lovesick Latvian Edward Leedskalnin moved to Miami in 1923 and spent 25 years chipping away at huge boulders to make a palace for his 15-year-old, would-be bride. This 100-pound, 5-foot-tall man moved pieces of rock that weighed as much as 35 tons, but he couldn't move the love of his life. She was a no show. A 25-minute audio tour tells Ed's story. Plan to spend 1½ to 2 hours.

28655 S. Dixie Hwy./US 1. ☎ 305-248-6344. Internet: www.coralcastle.com. *To get there: Take U.S. 1 south to SW 286th St. Admission: $7.75 adults, $6.50 seniors 62 and older, $5 kids 7–11. Open: 9 a.m.–6 p.m. daily.*

Everglades Alligator Farm

Take a noisy airboat tour of a spread that's home to more than 3,000 big sets of choppers. See live alligator and snake shows that run continuously. Allow 4½ to 5 hours including the 2-hour-round-trip drive from downtown Miami.

40351 SW 192nd Ave., 2 miles west of Florida Turnpike. ☎ 305-247-2628. Internet: http://everglades.com. *To get there: Follow US 1 south to Palm Drive/SW 344th St., go west/left to SW to 192nd Ave., left to entrance. Admission: $14.50 adults, $8 kids 4–10 ($5 less if you don't want to ride the airboat). Open: 9 a.m.– 6 p.m. daily.*

Miami Metrozoo

Still classy, this city zoo has been hammered by slumping attendance since Hurricane Andrew destroyed a number of exhibits, and money problems forced the zoo to keep them closed. Now, with the Zoological Society of Florida in its driver's seat, the zoo intends to reopen an aviary in 2002 and has already launched exhibits featuring 700 critters, including apes, white tigers, black rhinos, and clouded leopards. The animals live in natural outdoor settings sprinkled across some of the park's 290 acres. There's also a nice petting zoo and kids playground. At a comfortable pace, you can see the zoo in about 4 hours.

12400 SW 152nd St., 152nd St. at 124th Ave. ☎ *305-251-0400. Internet:* www. metro-dade.com/parks.metrozoo.htm. *To get there: Take US 1 south to 152nd Street/Coral Reef Dr., go right/west past the Florida Turnpike to 124th. Admission: $8 adults, $4 kids 3–12. Open: 9:30 a.m.–5:30 p.m. daily.*

Miami Museum of Science & Space Transit Planetarium

Techno types of all ages love this combination museum, planetarium, and wildlife center, which offers 140 exhibits available for inspection, some of which let you explore the universe. You can surf the Internet at the speed of light, play virtual basketball, scale a climbing wall, and test the speed of your fastball. The planetarium has laser shows, and the wildlife center has reptiles and birds of prey on display. Allow 3 to 4 hours inside, depending on how long you want to play. (See the "Attractions in South Miami-Dade County" map, later in this chapter.)

3280 S. Miami Ave./Bayshore Dr., south of Rickenbacker Causeway. ☎ *305-646-4200 or 305-646-4420 (planetarium show times). Internet:* www.miamisci. org. *To get there: It's on South Miami/Bayshore, just south of the Rickenbacker Causeway. Admission: $9 adults, $7 seniors and students, $5.50 kids 3–12, half price after 4:30 p.m. Open: 10 a.m.–6 p.m. daily.*

Miami Seaquarium

Lolita the killer whale stars in a show that's been a mainstay since 1971. But some of her fans, unhappy over the size of her quarters and her years of service, have launched a Free Willy-style drive (for the record, Internet: www.freelolita.net). Other shows, which feature bottlenose dolphins and Salty the sea lion, are less controversial. The Miami Seaquarium's other critters include sharks, manatees, eels, sea turtles, alligators, and an aviary that's home to lorikeets and doves. Some shows feature audience participation. The 750,000-gallon Tropical Reef Aquarium is a throwback exhibit where a diver feeds loggerhead turtles, moray eels, and an assortment of fish. You can spend all day here if you take a relaxed pace.

4400 Rickenbacker Causeway, in Biscayne Bay. ☎ *305-361-5705. Internet:* www. miamiseaquarium.com. *To get there: Take the causeway from U.S. 1 near Little Havana and go east halfway across Biscayne Bay. Admission: $21.95 adults, $15.95 kids 3–9. An annual pass is just $5 more per person. Open: 9:30 a.m.–6 p.m. daily.*

Monkey Jungle

It's no lie when they say this is a place where humans are caged and primates run wild. Screened trails run through the 30-acre preserve, inadvertently created when a man released six monkeys here in 1933. The crew now includes orangutans, golden lion tamarinds, and macaques that keep up a lively chatter.

After 60 years of monkey business, it has a real smell of the jungle, so it isn't for the faint of nose. Allow about 2½ hours to see the park.

14805 SW 216th St., between South Miami and Homestead. ☎ *305-235-1611. Internet.* www.monkeyjungle.com. *To get there: Take U.S. 1 south to Cutler Ridge and head west 2 miles on 216th St. Admission: $13.50 adults, $8 kids, 4–12. Open: 9:30 a.m.–5 p.m. daily.*

Parrot Jungle and Gardens

Back in the early '30s, nature lover Franz Scherr cut a trail through some coral rock, paid someone to ship him a dozen macaws, and on opening day entertained 100 guests who paid 25 cents each. Fast-forwarding three-quarters of a century, Parrot Jungle and Gardens is a tad larger. Cockatoos have joined the macaws — so have flamingoes, lories, tortoises, alligators, crocodiles, and hundreds of exotic plants. The three-times-a-day shows include a parrot show, reptile encounter, creatures of the night, and apes and monkeys. The park also has a petting zoo. You can see it all in 3 to 4 hours.

Parrot Jungle will move to Watson Island at some point in 2002, and its already hefty admissions fees will increase at that time. Call the park before you go if you plan to visit it after 2001.

If you have Internet access, surf over to the attraction's Web site, where you can download a coupon that offers a discount on admission.

11000 SW 57th Ave./Red Rd., 5½ miles south of Coral Gables. ☎ *305-666-7834. Internet:* www.parrotjungle.com. *To get there: Follow U.S. 1 to 57th/Red Rd. and go south 2½ miles. Admission: $14.95 adults, $9.95 kids 3–10. Open: 9:30 a.m.–6 p.m. daily.*

Villa Vizcaya Museum & Gardens

An Italian-style villa and formal gardens make this museum one of the premiere attractions in Miami. Built in 1916, this was the winter residence of James Deering. His cozy "little" bungalow and its 34 public rooms show some of the opulence reserved for the wealthy in the early twentieth century. Adorned with 400- and 500-year-old furnishings and art, the villa is one of two National Historic Landmarks in the county. Guided tours are often available. Allow 2–2½ hours, more if you're really into art and architecture.

3251 S. Miami Ave./Bayshore Dr. ☎ *305-250-9133. To get there: It's on South Miami/Bayshore, south of the Rickenbacker Causeway. Admission: $10 adults, $5 kids 6–12. Open: 9:30 a.m.–5 p.m. daily.*

More Cool Things to See and Enjoy

Behind the front line, there's an army of things to do in Miami that are less expensive and more leisurely. Some of these appeal to folks who have special interests — whether that means being an art buff, a golfer, an avid fisherman, or a pro-sports fan.

Visiting museums, gardens, parks, and more

Some of Miami's best museums and parks not only provide you with a wonderful day's entertainment and education, they do it for much less than many of the city's more popular attractions. Here's a sampling of some of the city's coolest offerings:

✔ **Barnacle State Historic Site,** 3485 Main Hwy., Coconut Grove (☎ 305-448-9445), was built in 1891 as the home of naval architect Ralph Munroe. Now a museum in the state park system, rangers lead tours of the spot four times a day. It's open Friday through Monday from 9 a.m. to 4 p.m.; admission is $1.

✔ **Bill Baggs Cape Florida State Recreation Area,** 1200 S. Crandon Blvd., Key Biscayne (☎ 305-361-5811), is a barrier island that's home to one of our favorite beaches (see Chapter 24 for more on Miami's beaches). Sand, surf, the Cape Florida lighthouse, and a Miami rarity — seclusion — are the ingredients of this winner. Ranger-led tours, a food stand, and rentals (bikes, chairs, umbrellas, roller blades, aqua bikes, kayaks, and more) are pluses. It's open daily from 8 a.m. to sunset. Admission is $5 per carload, including a $1 toll.

✔ **Florida Museum of Hispanic and Latin American Art,** 4006 Aurora St., Coral Gables (☎ 305-444-7060; Internet: www. latinoweb.com/museo), has permanent and changing exhibits featuring Latin American artists, and its historic downtown location is close to other galleries. Open Tuesday through Friday from 11 a.m. to 5 p.m. and Saturday from 11 a.m. to 4 p.m. Admission is free.

✔ **Gold Coast Railroad Museum,** 12450 SW 152nd St., Miami (☎ 888-608-7246 or 305-253-9963; Internet: www.goldcoast-railroad. org), features models as well as more than 30 pieces of historic equipment, including Zephyr cars and Florida East Coast Railroad steam engines. The site, where damage caused by Hurricane Andrew is still being repaired, is adjacent to the Metrozoo. Open

Monday through Friday from 11 a.m. to 3 p.m., and Saturday through Sunday from 11 a.m. to 4 p.m. Admission is $5 for adults, $3 for kids 3 to 12.

✔ **Holocaust Memorial,** 1933 Meridian Ave., Miami Beach (☎ 305-538-1663), features a photo mural and a Memorial Wall built in tribute to the 6 million Jews who died before and during WWII. The centerpiece is a statue that depicts thousands of victims crawling into the open hand of freedom. Open daily from 9 a.m. to 9 p.m. Admission is free.

✔ **Miccosukee Indian Village & Airboat Tours,** U.S. 41, 30 miles west of Miami (☎ 305-223-8380), offers airboat rides, guided tours, alligator wrestling demonstrations, and Native American arts and crafts exhibits. And because the village lies on a reservation, you'll also find cheap cigarettes and legal gambling. Open daily from 9 a.m. to 5 p.m. Admission costs $5 to $12 for adults, and $3.50 to $8.50 for kids 5 to 12.

✔ The **Spanish Monastery Cloisters,** 16711 W. Dixie Hwy., N. Miami Beach (☎ 305-945-1461), is one of the oldest monasteries in the Western Hemisphere. Dating back to 114, the cloisters were built in Spain and later moved here in pieces. Open Monday through Saturday 10 a.m. to 4 p.m. and Sunday from 1 p.m. to 5 p.m. Admission is $4.50 for adults, $2.50 for seniors 55 and older, and $1 for kids 11 and under.

✔ **Venetian Pool,** 2701 DeSoto Blvd., Coral Gables (☎ 305-460-5356), lets you follow in the strokes of Esther Williams and Johnny Weissmuller by taking a dip in this pool, which is fed by underground artesian wells. Hours vary seasonally so call ahead before you go, but be warned that they're sometimes *very* slow to answer the telephone. Admission is $5 to $12 for adults, and $2 to $4 for kids 3 to 12.

✔ **The Wolfsonian,** 1001 Washington Ave., Miami Beach (☎ 305-531-1001), is located in the heart of the art-deco district. It has some 70,000 American and European sculptures, photographs, ceramics, and other treasures dating from 1885 to 1945. Open Tuesday and Friday through Saturday from 11 a.m. to 6 p.m., Thursday from 11 a.m. to 9 p.m., and Sunday from noon to 5 p.m. Admission is $5 adults, $3.50 students and seniors.

Golfing

Golf is everywhere in Miami, and there are a number of excellent courses to satisfy your tee-time cravings. For golfing information online, haul your clubs over to www.golf.com and www.floridagolfing.com. If you like surfing the old-fashioned way, request course information from the **Florida Sports Foundation** (☎ 850-488-8347), or from **Florida Golfing** (☎ 877-222-4653). Here are just a few of the courses you can play while in Miami:

Attractions in South Miami-Dade County

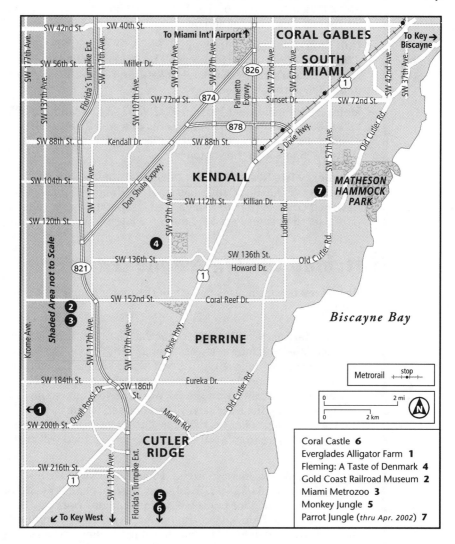

Coral Castle **6**
Everglades Alligator Farm **1**
Fleming: A Taste of Denmark **4**
Gold Coast Railroad Museum **2**
Miami Metrozoo **3**
Monkey Jungle **5**
Parrot Jungle (*thru Apr. 2002*) **7**

✔ **Don Shula's Golf Club,** 7601 Miami Lakes Dr., Miami Lakes
(☎ **305-820-8106),** has a flat course with plenty of water and tight,
tree-lined fairways. It's a par 72. Greens fees are $86 to $110 in
winter, $41 to $65 in summer.

✔ **Doral Resort Silver Course,** 5001 NW 104th Ave., Miami (☎ **305-
477-1906),** is a par 71 that tests all facets of your game with bunkers, lakes, and trees. The "Island Hole" is the course's signature.
Greens fees are $111 and up in winter, $41to $65 during the
summer.

✔ **Doral Resort Gold Course,** 4400 NW 87th Ave., Miami (☎ **305-592-2030**), is the home of the challenging "Blue Monster." It's a par 70. Greens fees are $111 and up in winter, $66 to $85 in the summer.

✔ **Golf Club of Miami,** 6801 Miami Gardens Dr., Miami (☎ **305-829-8449**), offers a course designed by Robert Trent Jones that may be Miami's best value. Greens fees are $66 to $85 in winter, under $25 in the summer.

✔ **Melreese International Links,** 1802 NW 37 Ave., Miami (☎ **305-633-4583**), has 97 bunkers and 6 acres of water. Fairways have rolling hills and lots of sand. Greens fees are $66 to $85 during winter, $25 to $40 in the summer.

✔ **Turnberry Isle Resort & Club,** 19999 W. Country Club Dr., Aventura (☎ **305-932-6200**), has a pair of Robert Trent Jones–designed courses (par 70 and 72) and a reputation as a golfer's paradise. Greens fees are $111 and up winter, $25 to $65 summer.

Watching the big-league teams

The Miami area has franchises in each of the major sports. The line-up is as follows:

✔ **Florida Marlins:** Pro Player Stadium, 2269 NW 199th St., Miami (☎ **305-623-6100;** Internet: `www.flamarlins.com`). The Sunshine State's lovable worst-to-first-to-worst Major League Baseball team was assembled, and then dismantled by founding owner Wayne Huizenga. The Marlins won the '97 World Series, only to find Big Wayne shedding the huge payroll he amassed to win it, which left the team sucking cellar lint. The Marlins play their regular season home games here from April to September. To attend will cost you $2 to $45.

✔ **Florida Panthers:** Broward Arena, 1 Panthers Pkwy., Fort Lauderdale (☎ **954-835-8275;** Internet: `www.flpanthers.com`). What do Miami and ice hockey have in common? Nothing. The team is north of here, and doesn't even play in the city proper. But that's close enough for Miamians to think it's theirs. The National Hockey League season runs November to April. It will set you back $14 to $65 to cheer from the stands.

✔ **Miami Dolphins:** Pro Player Stadium, 2269 NW 199th St., Miami. (☎ **305-623-6100;** Internet: `www.miamidolphins.com`). It's been a long time since 1972's perfect season, but fan support remains high — high enough that it's hard to get tickets to the eight regular season home games (September to January) or the preseason, either. And it isn't cheap either, a ticket costs $27 and up — way up!

✔ **Miami Heat:** Miami Arena, 1 SE 3rd Ave., Miami (☎ **305-577-4328;** Internet: www.nba.com/heat). The Heat hoopsters entered the National Basketball Association in 1988–89 and spent the first two years digging out of the cellar. By their tenth season they had 50 wins in an 82-game schedule and their second Atlantic Division title. The season runs November through May. Tickets run from $14 to $70.

Fishing

Several saltwater species are common to all South Florida, including redfish, trout, snook, Spanish and king mackerel, sailfish, grouper, and snapper.

Charters for small groups (up to four people) begin at about $225 per half day and $400 for 8 hours of inshore fishing and about double that for deep-sea excursions. Rates on large party boats usually start at $25 ($40 for all day). Here are a couple of places where you can get a guide for your fishing expedition:

✔ The **Miami Beach Rod & Reel Club,** 208 S. Hibiscus Island, Miami Beach (☎ **305-531-1233;** Internet: www.rnfl.com/rodreel), is an excellent source of guides. It has 17 affiliated guides in Miami, Fort Lauderdale, and the Keys.

✔ Internet users can get plenty of information at **Florida Charter Captains** online (www.fishfla.com), which breaks the state into several regions and profiles guides in each area.

✔ **Florida Charter Fishing Guide** online (www.flafish.com/flafish1.htm), is another good Internet source that groups Florida guides geographically.

Laying down some bets

You can wager your hard-earned money on the athletic ability of humans or animals at several places. There is live and simulcast action at:

✔ **Calder Race Course** (☎, **305-625-1311**), 2269 NW 199th St., Miami. Horse racing.

✔ **Flagler Greyhound Track** (☎ **305-649-3000**), 401 NW 38th Court, Miami. Dog racing.

✔ **Hialeah Park** (☎ **305-885-8000**), 2200 E. 4th Ave., Hialeah Horse racing.

✔ **Miami Jai Alai Fronton** (☎ **305-633-6400**), 3500 NW 37th Ave. Jai Alai — Duh!

Seeing Miami by Guided Tour

Sometimes it's fun to leave all of the decision-making to someone else. Miami has several organized tour options. If you need help deciding which tour would be appropriate for you, ask your hotel's concierge for a recommendation.

A bus tour

The oldest and arguably one of the most reliable operators is **Miami Nice Excursions,** 18430 Collins Ave., Miami Beach (☎ **305-949-9180**). The company offers knowledgeable guides and will pick you up from your hotel. Mini-bus tours range from city sightseeing ($32 for adults, $17 for kids 4 to 12) to longer and more expensive ones that travel to Key West, the Everglades, and the Kennedy Space Center.

Walking tours

The **Biltmore Hotel Tour,** 1200 Anastasia Ave., Coral Gables, is a free guided tour (Sundays only at 1:30, 2:30, and 3:30 p.m.) of this wonderful old hotel. You must make a reservation by calling ☎ **305-445-1926.**

The **Miami Design Preservation League,** 1001 Ocean Dr., South Beach (☎ **305-672-2014**), conducts 90-minute guided tours of the art-deco district on Thursdays at 6:30 p.m. and Saturdays at 10:30 a.m. ($10). If a self-guided tour is more your speed, the league offers an audiotape tour seven days a week for a cost of $5.

A bike tour

Art-Deco Cycling Tour, 601 5th St., South Beach (☎ **305-674-0150**), gives you a chance to see the district on wheels. The two-hour tour is conducted the third Sunday of the month, beginning at 10:30 a.m. The cost of $20 includes a vehicle from the Miami Beach Bicycle Center.

Sightseeing Itineraries

We're going to give you 3- and 4-day attack plans that will keep you as much as possible within one geographical area each day. If one or more of the sights or activities here don't appeal to you, simply replace it with one of the ones we've mentioned elsewhere in this chapter. Most of these itineraries presume you have your own set of wheels. If you don't, you can see many of the following sights on the guided tours. The shopping and nightlife options referenced in this section are explained fully later in this chapter.

Miami in 3 Days

On **Day 1,** rise, shine and beat it to the **Metrozoo,** where you can spend most of the day being charmed by the tigers, rhinos, leopards, and koalas. Time and mood permitting, leave after lunch and head north, spending the rest of the afternoon at **Monkey Jungle** or **Parrot Jungle and Gardens** before stopping for dinner at **Grillfish** in Coral Gables.

On **Day 2,** plan to spend most of your day at the **Miami Seaquarium,** enjoying the shows and antics of the killer whale, dolphins, sea lions, and other critters. Head back to the mainland at 2 or 3 p.m., so you have time to visit **Vizcaya.** Then enjoy dinner at **Norman's** in Coral Gables before capping the evening at **Murphy's Law Irish Pub.**

Plan to spend **Day 3** on South Beach. Visit the **Holocaust Memorial** and **The Wolfsonian,** saving some time to shop along the Lincoln Road Mall and ogle architecture on Collins Avenue. Have lunch at **YUCA;** then enjoy a dinner feast of claws at **Monty's Stone Crab & Seafood House.** End the day partying at **The Clevelander.**

Miami in 4 Days

Enjoy the 3-day itinerary, then add a **Wild Card Day** where and when it fits your mood and schedule. Actually, we're giving you two options to consider:

- ✔ If you want to do a little shopping, aim north and start at the **Aventura Mall** or the shops on Biscayne Boulevard/U.S. 1, but make sure to save time to browse through the **Bal Harbour Shops.** Then have a late dinner at **Chef Allen's.**

- ✔ If you'd rather spend the day on more sights and shows, go south to Florida City for the toothy show at the **Everglades Alligator Farm,** and then work your way north, grabbing a fast lunch on the road before buying your tickets for the **Miami Museum of Science & Space Transit Planetarium** in Coconut Grove. You're already in the neighborhood, so have dinner at **Caffe Abbracci.**

Shopping

With a dozen malls and a crush of other retail centers, Miami is a major shopping mecca for Florida, the Southeast, and the Caribbean. Best of all, the area offers much more than tourist trinkets. The 10 million people who visit every year lug everything home from hand-rolled cigars to electronics to imports from the Caribbean.

Before we outline Miami's neighborhoods and the shops you can find in them, here are a few basic ground rules:

✔ Most stores are open 10 a.m. to 6 p.m. Monday through Saturday and noon to 5 p.m. Sunday. Those in malls and major shopping centers keep their doors open as late as 9 or 10 p.m., except on Sunday.

✔ The state and local sales taxes add 6.5 percent to all purchases except food and medicine.

✔ If you don't want to haul it home with you, most stores will ship your purchase for you, though we recommend using some discretion. If you don't know the store, it's safer to make your own arrangements through a carrier such as United Parcel Service (☎ 800-742-5877), or the post office (skip ahead to "Fast Facts" for more on mailing packages).

Burning some bucks

When you feel the urge to splurge on a shopping spree, here are the best places to empty your wallet:

✔ **Aventura:** A 2-mile string of shops on Biscayne Blvd./U.S. 1 stretches north from Miami Gardens Drive. Storefronts include Best Buy, Circuit City, Loehmann's, Marshall's, and Sports Authority. You'll also find the mammoth Aventura Mall (see "Crawling through the malls" later in this chapter).

✔ **Calle Ocho:** Little Havana's main shopping district is "8th Street" between SW 27th and SW 12th Avenues. In addition to tantalizing smells, you can find everything from hand-rolled cigars to baked goods to Latin CDs and tapes.

✔ **Coconut Grove:** The Grove's roomy sidewalks, particularly along Main Highway and Grand Avenue, are very shopper-friendly. You can find them lined with cafes as well as boutiques, clothiers, and import stores for shopping or browsing. The Grove is also the home of CocoWalk (see the following section on malls).

✔ **Coral Gables/Miracle Mile:** Actually, it's the Miracle Half-Mile, and it's peppered with men's and women's clothing stores, bridal shops, and some of the trendier chains, such as Old Navy. Miracle Mile is also the home of several good restaurants.

✔ **Downtown Miami:** If you like to bargain, Flagler Street west of Biscayne Boulevard is a good place to try your luck finding watches and jewelry, luggage, shoes and other leather goods. But it's also a place where you can get hustled if you're not careful.

✔ **South Beach:** Some hip clothing stores (Armani, Benneton, and others) line Collins and Washington Avenues between 6th and 9th Streets, which also are good places to see art deco architecture. The seven-block Lincoln Road Mall offers a dizzying array of cafes, shops, and galleries.

Crawling through the malls

Because most of Miami's shopping gets done in malls that could qualify as neighborhoods in and of themselves, here are a few of the best in town:

✔ **Aventura Mall:** This mega mall — 250 stores fill up 2.3 million square feet — is home to retail giants such as Macy's and Lord and Taylor, as well as smaller local outfits. Stock up some energy at the mall's plethora of restaurants, or let your kids run down their batteries inside the mall's playground. The mall also has a 24-screen movie theater. At Biscayne Blvd. and 196th St., Aventura (☎ 305-935-1110; Internet: www.shopaventuramall.com).

✔ **Bal Harbour Shops:** Considered by many to be one of the most prestigious shopping places in the world, Bal Harbour's headliners include Neiman Marcus, Saks Fifth Avenue, Cartier, Channel, Armani, Christian Dior, Gianni Versace, Gucci, and Tiffany. It's worth a look even if you can't afford the lofty prices. 9700 Collins Ave., Bal Harbour (☎ 305-866-0311; Internet: www.balharbourshops.com).

✔ **Bayside Marketplace:** This waterside shopping area features all the mall regulars, including Benneton, Brookstone, The Disney Store, Guess?, Key West Cargo, Sammy Goody, Speedo Fitness, and Sharper Image. 401 Biscayne Blvd., Miami (☎ 305-577-3344; Internet: www.baysidemarketplace.com).

✔ **CocoWalk:** In addition to such name tenants as Banana Republic and Victoria's Secret, this mini mall has specialty stores selling cigars, books, cutlery, clothing, fragrances, and more. It also has a movie theater and several outdoor cafes. 3015 Grand Ave., Coconut Grove (☎ 305-444-0777; Internet: www.cocowalk.com).

✔ **The Falls:** Macy's, Bloomingdales, Coach, and The Disney Store are flanked by 100 other shops (Ann Taylor, Crabtree & Evelyn, and Papyrus), a few restaurants, and a movie theater. 8888 SW 136th St., Miami (☎ 305-255-4570; Internet: www.thefallsshoppingcenter.com).

You can find scores of other places to test your credit line or liquidate your traveler's checks at **Miami International Mall,** ☎ 305-593-1775, State Road 836 at NW 107th Ave.; and **Dadeland Mall,** ☎ 305-655-6226, Kendall Drive at U.S. 1.

Lighting Up the Night

After the sun goes down, Miami really raises the decibel level. You can rock 'n' roll, rumba and samba, or just swill and chill. For an up-to-the-minute scorecard, see the **Miami Herald's** "Weekend" section on

Fridays. Tickets for specific events, concerts, plays, and other perform-ances can be booked through **Ticketmaster** (☎ **305-358-5885;** Internet: www.ticketmaster.com).

You also can get recorded information from the **Planet Radio Stuff to Do Hotline** (☎ **305-770-2513**), and the **Zeta Concert Hotline** (☎ **305-770-2515**).

Toasting the town

If a mixed drink is more your style than mixing it up on the dance floor, you can find a host of bars waiting to help you blast off on an alcoholic adventure.

- ✔ The **Clevelander Hotel,** 1021 Ocean Drive, South Beach (☎ **305-531-3485**), has a funky little bar with plastic cups, a beachy feel, and (best of all) no cover charge. Drinks are half price from 5 to 7 p.m., Monday through Friday.

- ✔ **The Forge,** 432 41st St., Miami Beach (☎ **305-538-8533**), is a trendy restaurant/bar known for its fabulous people watching, especially on Wednesday, which is "models" night. Call well in advance if you want a table so you can gawk while you eat. There's no cover.

- ✔ **Molly Malone's,** 166 Sunny Isles Blvd., North Miami (☎ **305-948-3512**), is a mellow bar that caters to the folks who appreciate good lagers and ales mixed with darts and a little eight-ball. There's no cover charge.

- ✔ **Murphy's Law Irish Pub,** 2977 McFarlane Dr., Coconut Grove (☎ **305-446-9956**), is a friendly neighborhood bar known as a hangout for those who want to escape the *in* bar scene. There's a big-screen TV for sports events and usually live music on the weekends.

- ✔ **Rose Bar at the Delano,** 1685 Collins Ave., South Beach (☎ **305-672-2000**), is one of the hottest of the many beach bars. The in-crowd and its wannabes hang at the Rose or on its deck. The drinks are rather pricey, but there's no cover.

Clubbing

South Beach is home to some of the hottest — and often snootiest — dance clubs in America, so you can find plenty of opportunities to shake your booty. To get past the velvet rope, dress hip (such as wear-ing black) and arrive before midnight.

✔ **Bash,** 655 Washington Ave., South Beach (☎ **305-538-2274**), gets into themed nights that feature disco, funk, and even fashion shows. It's open 10 p.m. to 5 a.m. Thursday through Saturday. There's a $15 to $20 cover charge, and the doormen like to play God deciding who gets in.

✔ **Bermuda Bar,** 3509 NE 163rd St., North Miami (☎ **305-945-0196**), has DJs and theme nights several times a week (Thursday means salsa, and there are Saturday dance parties). The cover is $10 to $30 after 9:30 p.m., depending on the night and event.

✔ **Living Room at the Strand,** 671 Washington Ave., South Beach (☎ **305-532-2340**), is another place that Miami's models and their pursuers mingle. The cover charge is $8 to $20 cover charge, and hours are 11:30 p.m. to 5 a.m., Wednesday to Sunday.

✔ **Mango's,** 900 Ocean Dr., South Beach (☎ **305-673-4422**), has a funky Brazilian beat, and the patio bar area literally pulsates. The cover is $5 to $15.

Splashes of culture

It may be more acclaimed for its clubs and bars, but Miami does have a respectable number of cultural institutions. If Beethoven and Bach have more appeal than hard rock, you won't have a problem finding a place to hear a little night music.

The **Concert Association of Florida,** 555 17th St., South Beach (☎ **305-532-3491**) is always up to speed on upcoming performances. Season after season, world-renowned dance companies and seasoned virtuosi (Itzhak Perlman, Andre Watts, and Kathleen Battle to name a few) punctuate its schedules.

If you're a fan of orchestral music, you're in luck. Miami is home to three excellent symphonic orchestras.

✔ The **Florida Philharmonic Orchestra,** 1243 University Dr., Miami. (☎ **800-226-1812**), is the best of its kind in South Florida.

✔ The **Miami Chamber Symphony,** 5690 N. Kendall Dr., Kendall (☎ **305-672-0552**), which regularly features international soloists.

✔ The **New World Symphony,** 541 Lincoln Rd., South Beach (☎ **305-673-3331;** Internet: www.nws.org), which offers innovative performances, and often gives free concerts.

The **Florida Grand Opera,** 1200 Coral Way, Miami (☎ **800-741-1010** or 305-854-1643), will open a new headquarters in late 2001. The respected company regularly features singers from top houses in both America and Europe.

The highly acclaimed **Miami City Ballet,** Ophelia and Juan Jr. Roca Center (on Collins and 22nd Street Ave.), Miami Beach (☎ **305-929-7000**), runs through a repertoire of more than 60 ballets in a given season.

Fast Facts

Area Code

Miami's two area codes are **305** and **786.** All *local* calls made inside Miami-Dade County require *10-digit dialing:* The area code + the seven-digit local number. Calls from Miami to the Keys (see chapter 12), which are in the 305 area code, require a 1 + 305 or 0 + 305 preceding the seven-digit number. Those will be billed as long distance. The 786 area code is starting to be used for new numbers in southern Miami-Dade County.

American Express

There are three offices in the area. The ones in downtown **Miami** (330 Biscayne Blvd., ☎ **305-358-7350**) and in **Bal Harbour** (9700 Collins Ave., ☎ **305-865-5959**) are open 10 a.m.–6 p.m., Monday through Saturday. The **Coral Gables** office (32 Miracle Mile, ☎ **305-446-3381**) is open 10 a.m.–6 p.m., Monday through Friday.

Doctors

In an emergency, dial ☎ **911**. For a physician referral, call the Dade County Medical Association at ☎ **305-324-8717,** 9 a.m.–5 p.m., Monday through Friday, or see the hospital listings following.

Emergencies

Dial ☎ **911** for police, fire, and ambulance service.

Hospitals

Cedars Medical Center, Miami ☎ **305-325-5511**

Jackson Memorial Hospital, Miami ☎ **305-585-1111**

Parkway Regional Medical Center, North Miami ☎ **305-651-1100**

Hialeah Hospital, Hialeah ☎ **305-693-6100**

HealthSouth Doctors' Hospital, Coral Gables ☎ **305-666-2111**

Mount Sinai Medical Center, Miami Beach ☎ **305-674-2121**

Internet Access

You can find several listings for internet cafes in Miami's Yellow Pages including **Café and Internet of America**, 12536 N. Kendall Dr., Miami (☎ **305-412-0100;** Internet: www.cafeina.net).

Mail

There are U.S. post offices at 2200 NW 72nd Ave., Miami (west of the airport); 1300 Washington Ave., South Beach; and 3191 Grand Ave., Coconut Grove. To locate other postal offices, call ☎ **800-275-8777.**

Maps

The information sources listed in the following sections are great ones to hit up for maps before or after you land. (Trust us: Good maps are necessities, because it's easy to get lost in Miami, and this city's bad neighborhoods are no place to get lost.) Rental-car agencies are another good source (including those at the airport) and so are convenience stores that sell maps for $3–$5.

Newspapers

The **Miami Herald** (Internet: www.herald.com) is the major daily, and visitors shouldn't miss the paper's "Weekend" entertainment guide, which comes out on Friday. There's also a Spanish-language paper, **El Nuevo Herald** (Internet: www.elherald.com).

Pharmacies

The Yellow Pages are filled with national and local pharmacies, including the 24-hour **Walgreens** pharmacies at 1845 Alton Road in South Beach (☎ **305-531-8868**), and at 5731 Bird Road at SW 40th Street (☎ **305-666-0757**).

Police

Dial ☎ **911.**

Safety

Miami is a large city and has all the crime that one would normally associate with a major metropolis. We don't recommend walking alone after dark and be wary about driving anywhere in downtown Miami. Stick to well-lit and known tourist areas and even then be aware of your surroundings. Keep your eyes peeled for bright orange sunbursts on highway exit signs; they will direct you tourist-friendly zones. Use a map (see preceding information on maps) to familiarize yourself with the city and make sure you know where you're going and your route before driving anywhere. Never stop on a highway and get out of your car if you can avoid it and always keep your doors locked. Some car rental agencies will rent you a cell phone for the duration of your trip, this way you can get immediate assistance should you require it.

Smoking

Unlike tobacco states and most areas of Europe, Florida is continually restricting smokers. Most restaurants and hotels still have smoking areas or rooms, and even more bars still allow you to light up. But most public buildings prohibit smoking, and some tourist attractions won't let you light up in many areas, including some that are outside.

Taxes

The sales and local-option taxes throughout Miami-Dade County add 6.5 percent to most purchases except medicines and groceries. The hotel and restaurant taxes push the total to between 9.5 and 12.5 percent.

Taxis

It's $1.50–$3 to start the meter and $2 for each mile. See Chapter 10 for more information.

Transit Info

For **Metrorail** and **Metromover** schedule information call ☎ **305-770-3131**. See Chapter 10 for more transit information.

Weather Updates

For a recording of current conditions and forecast reports, call the local office of the **National Weather Service** at ☎ **305-229-4522**, or check out the national office's Web site at www.nws.noaa.gov. You can also get information by watching the **Weather Channel** (Internet: www.weatherchannel.com).

Gathering More Information

The **Greater Miami Convention and Visitors Bureau,** 701 Brickell Ave., Miami, FL 33131 (☎ **800-933-8448** or 305-539-3063; Internet: www.tropicoolmiami.com) is the best source of specialized information about Miami. Even if you don't have a specific question, call ahead to request its free magazine, *Destination Miami,* which includes several good, easy-to-use maps and other useful contact numbers. The office is open weekdays from 9 a.m. to 5 p.m.

Especially good sources of information are the local chambers of commerce. The **Greater Miami Chamber of Commerce,** 420 Lincoln Rd, no. 20. Miami Beach, FL 33139 (☎ **305-350-7700;** Internet: www. greatermiami.com) can supply you with a local neighborhood map and tourist information, as can the **Coral Gables Chamber of Commerce,** 50 Aragon Ave., Coral Gables, FL 33134 (☎ **305-446-1657,** Internet: www.gableschamber.org), and the **Coconut Grove Chamber of Commerce,** 2820 McFarlane Rd., Miami, FL 33133 (☎ **305-444-7270**).

If you are hooked into the Internet, surf over to www.goflorida.com. It provides a vast array of information on accommodations, dining, and entertainment options throughout Miami and South Florida. You can also check out Miami-Dade County's official Web site at www.co. miami-dade.fl.us, which offers up-to-date information on county parks, sports, and attractions, such as the Miami Metrozoo, and cultural events.

Chapter 12

Unlocking the Keys

· ·

In This Chapter

▶ Fishing for snapper, grouper, and marlin

▶ Snorkeling and diving for sunken treasure

▶ Swimming with dolphins

▶ Visiting Hemmingway's retreat

· ·

South Florida has two kinds of conchs: those that land in chowder and those that land where they please. The latter — Florida Keys natives — are born with a birthright to go against the grain and indulge in a little wacky behavior — traits that are carried out to the nth degree in the Keys' southernmost city, Key West.

The most famous of Florida's islands, Key West has threatened to secede from the Union and establish a *Conch Republic* three times (and counting). The top pastimes in Key West are fishing and getting fried (in a Bacardi sense), and not necessarily in that order. It's a city whose melting-pot character has long made Key West a home for pirates, preachers, gun runners, and gays, all of whom live more or less peacefully on a 3½-mile sandbar some locals call "paradise."

Of course, paradise isn't for everyone, including those Conchs (pronounced *konks*) who settled to the north in towns and on islands with far less razzle-dazzle, but an equal amount of charm.

In this chapter we show you the many faces of the Keys, including those where the only action is diving after a 300-year-old shipwreck, landing a tarpon, or swimming with dolphins.

Getting a Clue about the Keys

Four hundred islands are spread across this 150-mile chain, but only a few dozen are inhabited, and fewer yet are developed into something a mainstream tourist would want to see. We subdivided them into five mini-regions: Key Largo, Islamorada, Marathon, the Lower Keys, and Key West. You'll find them in the same sequence if you drive from the mainland, leaving Florida City on U.S. 1 and crossing Barnes and Blackwater Sounds. Skip ahead to the map of the Florida Keys for an overview of the area.

John Pennekamp Coral Reef State Park on Key Largo will be your first stop; then you greet the **Florida Keys Wild Bird Rehabilitation Center** on Tavernier before landing on Islamorada, where you can meet the pet tarpons at **Robbie's Pier** and the unique plants of Lignumvitae Key. In the third area, Marathon, we take you inside the **Dolphin Research Center** for an unusual swimming lesson. Then we can head over **Seven-Mile Bridge** as we zero in on the Lower Keys, home of the **Bahia Honda State Recreation Area,** which has one of our favorite beaches, and the **National Key Deer Refuge.** Saving the most raucous for last, we arrive in Key West, home to sunset parties, Hemingway's ghost, and a cemetery where you'll die laughing.

Choosing Your Transportation

Most folks fly into the Keys because flying is convenient and, in most cases, relatively economical. If you are visiting the Upper or Middle Keys, your best bet is to book a flight to **Miami International Airport** (☎ 305-876-7000; Internet: www.miami-airport.com) and then rent a car to drive to Key Largo, Islamorada, or Marathon. The airport is served by more than 100 airlines, including 42 foreign carriers, and virtually every rental agency in the U.S. is at or near it (see the Appendix for rental agency telephone numbers and Web sites; see Chapter 10 for more airport information).

Unless you're a glutton for punishment, there's only one good way to get to the Lower Keys and Key West. Lock onto a commuter or other low-level option from Miami International Airport; it beats the long — 3 to 4 hours, depending on your destination — drive from Miami. Commuters will plant you at **Key West International,** ☎ 305-296-7223, which is about 25 minutes south of the Lower Keys. This airport is served by about a half dozen major carriers or their partners, and Avis, Hertz, Budget, and Dollar. (See the Appendix for rental agency telephone numbers and Web sites.)

Taking a train to the Keys can be tedious, and even rail fans find that train travel is time consuming if a vacation is of limited duration. **Amtrak** (☎ 800-872-7245; Internet: www.amtrak.com) has two trains leaving daily from New York — that's the good news. The bad news: They take 30 hours to reach Miami (the furthest south they go), and the prices aren't much better than airfare (and they're worse if you want a sleeper). Amtrak's Miami station is 5 miles from the airport and arguably the best in terms of rental-car options.

The Florida Keys

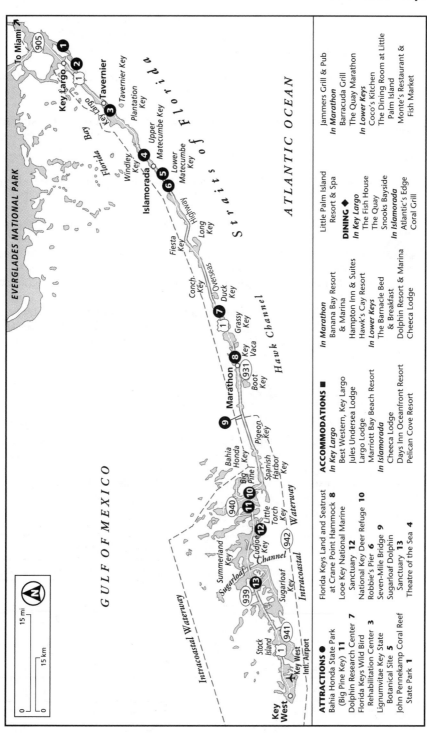

ATTRACTIONS ●
Bahia Honda State Park
(Big Pine Key) **11**
Dolphin Research Center **7**
Florida Keys Wild Bird
Rehabilitation Center **3**
Lignumvitae Key State
Botanical Site **5**
John Pennekamp Coral Reef
State Park **1**
Florida Keys Land and Seatrust
at Crane Point Hammock **8**
Looe Key National Marine
Sanctuary **12**
National Key Deer Refuge **10**
Robbie's Pier **6**
Seven-Mile Bridge **9**
Sugarloaf Dolphin
Sanctuary **13**
Theatre of the Sea **4**

ACCOMMODATIONS ■
In Key Largo
Best Western, Key Largo
Jules Undersea Lodge
Largo Lodge
Marriott Bay Beach Resort
In Islamorada
Cheeca Lodge
Days Inn Oceanfront Resort
Pelican Cove Resort
In Marathon
Banana Bay Resort
& Marina
Hampton Inn & Suites
Hawk's Cay Resort
In Lower Keys
The Barnacle Bed
& Breakfast
Dolphin Resort & Marina
Cheeca Lodge
Little Palm Island
Resort & Spa

DINING ◆
In Key Largo
The Fish House
The Quay
Snooks Bayside
In Islamorada
Atlantic's Edge
Coral Grill
Jammers Grill & Pub
In Marathon
Barracuda Grill
The Quay Marathon
In Lower Keys
Coco's Kitchen
The Dining Room at Little
Palm Island
Monte's Restaurant &
Fish Market

Traveling to the Keys by car can also be a drag; from the Florida/Georgia border to Key Largo is 500 miles. From the north, take the Florida Turnpike south along the East Coast. Just after Fort Lauderdale, take Exit 4 — the Turnpike Extension, which is marked for Homestead/Key West. This goes to U.S. 1 in Florida City, the only road into the Keys.

From the West Coast, come across I-75 (Alligator Alley) to the Miami exit and go south to the Turnpike Extension.

Alligator Alley is not the best of roads, so make sure to check your tires and fill up your tank before you get on it. Also, if at all possible, drive it during daylight hours only.

From Miami International Airport, take LeJeune Road south to Hwy. 836 West and the Turnpike Extension; then go south to U.S. 1 and the Keys.

Given one highway and the liberal use of mile markers for addresses and reference points (skip ahead to "Marking every mile," the next section in this chapter for more information), it's next to impossible to get lost driving here. Unless — due to the Mob, the IRS, or your ex-spouse — you want to get lost. The speed limit throughout the Keys is no higher than 55 mph, and there are occasional passing lanes. Reaching the Upper Keys is a piece of cake, but if you're going further south, driving gets tedious, sometimes aggravating. If you have the time and budget and you want to drive down U.S. 1, consider taking two days to travel from one end to the other.

Marking every mile

U.S. 1/the Overseas Highway is the Keys' version of Main Street. The best way to find something is to know the mile marker (MM) that's nearest that destination. Used in place of addresses in many cases, the little green mile-marker signs adorn the roadside every mile, starting south of Florida City with MM 127 and running south to MM 1 in Key West. For a general guide to the Mile Marker system, see Table 12-1.

Table 12-1	The Keys' Mile-Marker Guide		
City	*Mile Marker*	*Miles from Miami*	*Driving Time from Miami*
Key Largo	110–87	58	1.5 hours
Islamorada	86–66	76	2 hours
Marathon	65–40	111	2.5 hours
Lower Keys	39–9	128	3 hours
Key West	8–0	159	4 hours

Seeing the Keys in 5 Days

If you want to comfortably take in all of the Keys' highlights, plan on spending 5 days. This itinerary is designed for folks who fly into Key West. If you make Miami your landing zone, you can ad lib by reversing our directions and traveling north to south. This itinerary is also designed for travelers who have a car. If you don't have a car, following this itinerary is nearly impossible unless you have a chauffeur.

Day 1 begins with you on the **Conch Train** or **Old Town Trolley,** acquainting yourself with Key West. The **Audubon House & Tropical Gardens** give you a closer look at the area. The **Banana Cafe** is the spot for lunch. Adjourn to the **Ernest Hemingway Home and Museum** and the **Key West Cemetery. Mangia, Mangia** staff prepares your evening meal. Afterward celebrate your first night at **Capt. Tony's.**

On **Day 2,** head to **Islamorada.** Have an early lunch at **Jammers Grill & Pub,** and spend most of the afternoon at **Theatre of the Sea.** Feed the tarpon at **Robbie's Pier** before grabbing dinner at the **Coral Grill.** To end your day, have a nightcap at your hotel bar.

Rise early on **Day 3** and scoot to **John Pennekamp Coral Reef State Park,** where you can spend the day on watersports. Have dinner at **The Quay** or **Snook's Bayside.**

Day 4 sends you south to **Marathon** for some quality marine-mammal time at the **Dolphin Research Center.** Have a late lunch at **Barracuda Grill** and then aim your sedan back to **Key West** for a late dinner at **Cafe Marquesa.**

Begin **Day 5** at the **Key West Aquarium; Turtle Kraals** provides lunch. The **Mel Fisher Maritime Heritage Museum** should be your before-dinner attraction; then head to the **Banana Cafe,** followed by the **Sunset Celebration at Mallory Square** and a nightcap at **Sloppy Joe's.**

Laying Back in Key Largo

The Upper Keys are a refuge for many South Floridians who love the region's laid-back lifestyle and lack of congestion. Key Largo attracts saltwater fishermen and scuba divers, but other than natural marine resources, outfitters, motels, and restaurants, there's not much here. It's either hit the water or hit the road out of town.

Getting to Key Largo is a no-brainer. After you exit the mainland, U.S. 1 (the Overseas Highway) is the only route through the Keys. Buses and other kinds of public transportation don't exist here. So the way to get around is by car or on one of those you-have-to-go-where-we-want-to-go tours. See Chapter 5 for more on group tours.

Key Largo's Best Hotels

The first and largest Florida key, Key Largo offers a wide variety of accommodations, from chain hotels to full-scale resorts. Most hotels are right off U.S. 1 or on the waterfront. Most accommodations combine a laid-back atmosphere with extensive facilities, so you can do as much or as little as you want. Unless otherwise noted, all listings include air conditioning, televisions, and a pool. As with much of coastal Florida, winter (December through April) is peak season. And don't forget to add an additional 11.5 percent room tax to your hotel rate.

Best Western Key Largo

$$ Key Largo

Rooms here are one-bedroom, split-level mini-suites with kitchens, and the hotel has a cozy location near John Pennekamp Coral Reef State Park. Furnishings are motel-style but comfy. Rates include a free continental breakfast.

201 Ocean Dr., MM 99.8. ☎ *800-462-6079 or 305-451-5081. Fax: 305-451-4173. Internet:* www.keysdirectory.com/bestwestern/index.html. *To get there: From the north, take U.S. 1/Overseas Hwy. to Ocean Dr., turn right/east. Parking: free. Rack rates: $150–$175 Dec–Apr; $100–$125 May–Nov. AE, CB, DISC, MC, V.*

Jules' Undersea Lodge

$$$$ Key Largo

These novel accommodations make for an interesting stay if you can afford the high price tag and if you're a diver — or want to be. You eat, sleep, and swim with the fishes — five fathoms below the surface. The conventional plan includes gourmet dinner and breakfast. The European plan is cheaper but its meals are lighter. Dive gear and out-the-hatch dives are included. Jules' Undersea Lodge is popular with the honeymoon crowd.

51 Shoreland Dr., MM 103.2. ☎ *305-451-2353. Fax: 305-451-4789. Internet:* www.jul.com. *To get there: At MM 103.2, go right/east on Shoreland. Parking: free. Rack rates: $325 per person American ($275 groups of 4–6); $225 per person European ($175 for 4–6). AE, DISC, MC, V.*

Largo Lodge

$-$$ Key Largo

The cottages at this lodge are "Old Keys-style," meaning that they're designed more for divers and fishermen than for folks after fancy digs. However, they're bright and reasonably comfy, with kitchenettes and screened porches. There's no pool, and guests must be 16 or older.

101740 U.S. 1/Overseas Hwy., MM 101.7, ☎ *800-468-4378 or 305-451-0424. No fax. Internet:* www.largolodge.com. *To get there: MM 101.7, bay-side. Parking: free. Rack rates: $115 Dec–Apr, $85 May–Nov. AE, MC, V.*

Marriott Bay Beach Resort

$$$ Key Largo

This mammoth resort's 153 rooms overlook the island or Florida Bay and are decorated in a tropical style. Most rooms have balconies or patios. Suites have kitchens. Amenities include a health spa, three small beaches, tennis courts, and a kids' club that is open Wednesday to Sunday ($20 for a half day; $40 for a full day, including lunch).

103800 U.S. 1/Overseas Hwy., MM 103.8. ☎ *800-932-9332 or 305-453-0000. Fax: 305-453-0093. Internet:* www.marriottkeylargo.com. *To get there: At MM 103.8, bay-side. Parking: free. Rack rates: $265–$295, suites $635 Dec–Apr; $169–$219, suites $419 May–Nov. AE, DC, DISC, MC, V.*

Key Largo's Best Restaurants

Unquestionably, this is a seafood lover's destination. During the season, Florida lobster will be offered on many menus. The local favorites also include grouper, trout, swordfish, tuna, mahi-mahi, and crab. If you're not a seafood lover, all restaurants do offer meat and poultry entrees. And don't forget to try a slice of Key lime pie — it's almost a mandatory dessert in the Keys.

The Fish House

$$ Key Largo   SEAFOOD

This fun spot serves up great local seafood. Conch (in a salad, floating in chowder, or fried) is one headliner. So are oysters, shrimp, and yellowtail snapper. The service is fast and the atmosphere relaxed. If you want to bring the catch of the day back home with you, there's a fish market on premises.

102401 U.S. 1/Overseas Hwy., MM 102.4. ☎ *888-451-4665 or 305-451-4665. No fax. Internet:* www.fishhouse.com. *Reservations aren't accepted. To get there: MM 102.4 ocean-side. Main courses: $5–$14 lunch, $9–$27 dinner; kids' menu $5–$10. AE, DISC, MC, V. Open: 11:30 a.m.–10 p.m., daily.*

The Quay

$$ Key Largo SEAFOOD/STEAKS

This waterfront restaurant offers dining with a spectacular view of the Keys' famous sunsets. You can chow down on seafood (broiled lobster tails, blackened swordfish) or meat dishes (prime rib) in the air-conditioned indoor dining room. The outdoor Dockside Bistro offers conch, prawns, ribs, and steaks.

102050 U.S. 1/Overseas Hwy., MM 102. ☎ *305-451-0943. Internet:* www.quayrest. com. *Reservations accepted. To get there: MM 102 bay-side, just past Holiday Inn. Main courses: $12–$31 ($11–$15 dockside). AE, DISC, MC, V. Open: 4–10 p.m. daily.*

Snooks Bayside

$$ Key Largo AMERICAN

Seafood, steaks, chicken, and veal are featured on the daily menu and brunch on Sunday. Snooks has a nice wine list, and the dining room has a view of Florida Bay. An outdoor terrace accommodates fresh-air fans.

99470 U.S. 1/Overseas Hwy., MM 99.9. ☎ *305-453-3799. Reservations suggested. To get there: Look for it at Key Largo's only traffic light, by Marina Del Mar Bayside. Main courses: $15–$28. AE, DISC, MC, V. Open: 11:30 a.m.–10:30 p.m. Mon–Sat, 10 a.m.–10:30 p.m. Sun.*

Frolicking with fauna

Much of the doings here are related to water — Florida Bay to the west and the Atlantic Ocean to the east.

Dolphins Plus

Key Largo

One of a few swim-with-the-dolphins programs around the Keys, Dolphins Plus gives you a briefing before you get into the water. This is a dolphin-contact sport. You need to be a good swimmer (despite the free flotation vest) and comfortable in water that's taller than you are. If you just want to watch, you can do it from high and dry. Allow 2 hours.

31 Corinne Place. ☎ *305-451-1993. Internet:* www.dolphinsplus.com. *To get there: Turn east/left at the stop light at MM 99.9, go 1 block, take the first right, go another block, then left on Ocean Shores Dr. and go several blocks to a bridge, turning right just before it. Admission: $125 for a dolphin swim (minimum age, 10; $10 to observe ($5 for kids 7 years old and older). Open: 9 a.m.–5 p.m. daily.*

Florida Keys Wild Bird Rehabilitation Center

Tavernier

Want a close look at hawks, great blue herons, roseate spoonbills, brown and white pelicans, white ibises, and snowy egrets? Look no further. You can see the staff feeding pelicans at 3:30 p.m. Allow 30 to 60 minutes; more if there's a photographer in your group.

93600 U.S. 1/Overseas Hwy., MM 94. ☎ *305-852-4486. To get there: Heading south, the bird sculptures on your right will point the way. Admission: donation. Open: 8 a.m.–6 p.m. daily.*

John Pennekamp Coral Reef State Park

This 188-square-miler is mostly underwater but shallow enough that snorkelers can easily see its 40-something varieties of coral, 650 species of fish, and a very tall statue. The visitors' center, which has a large aquarium and other tanks inside, should be your first stop. Not getting wet is a shame, but if you insist on staying dry, take the glass-bottom boat tour. For most, this is an all-day outing.

U.S. 1/Overseas Hwy., MM 102.5. ☎ *305-451-1202 or 305-451-1621. Internet:* www.pennekamp.com. *To get there: It's on the ocean side, just a tad south of where U.S. 1 comes from the mainland. Admission: $5 for a vehicle plus 50 cents per passenger; $1.50 for foot soldiers or bicyclists. Open: 8 a.m.–5 p.m. daily.*

Touring the waters

Boaters should head for **John Pennekamp Coral Reef State Park,** named for a late newspaper editor/environmentalist, which offers hourly ($27–$50), half day ($90–$185), and full day ($160–$325) rentals of 19- to 28-foot motorboats. Diving- and dive lesson-packages are available, too. Call ☎ **305-451-1202** or 305-451-6325 for details.

Arguably, the Keys offer some of the finest underwater fun anywhere in the United States. Even if you're not a certified scuba diver or lack the time to get certified here, you can still enjoy it. All it takes is a mask, snorkel, and fins.

John Pennekamp Coral Reef State Park and **The Key Largo National Marine Sanctuary** (☎ 305-451-1621) are Key Largo's signature underwater sights. In addition to coral reefs and fish, the park features *Christ of the Deep,* a 9-foot, 4,000-pound bronze sculpture that stands in 25 feet of water. If you're a diver, you'll love Molasses Reef's abundant sea life and the Elbow, which has several shipwrecks.

Other area outfitters include **Conch Republic Divers,** MM 90.3 (☎ **800-274-3483** or 305-852-1655; Internet: www.conchrepublicdivers.com); and **Keys Diver Snorkel Tours,** MM 100, (☎ **888-289-2402** or 305-451-1177; Internet: www.keysdiver.com).

Prices vary, but snorkel tours start at $30, dive tours at $50.

Fishing may be the Keys' favorite pastime. Sport fish, such as bonefish, tarpon, and marlin, are plentiful in the Keys, as are tasty treats, such as grouper, yellowtail snapper, and red snapper. Inshore rates generally are $225 for a half-day and $400 for eight hours. Double that price for deep-sea expeditions. Charter operators include **Back Country Adventures** (☎ **305-451-1247**) and **Sailor's Choice** (☎ **305-451-1802**).

Shopping

Key Lime Products, 95231 U.S. 1/Overseas Hwy., MM 95 ocean-side (☎ **305-853-0378;** Internet: www.keylimeproducts.com), sells some funky items made from the namesake fruit. The shelves are lined with the usual (pies, jellies, and candy), as well as more unusual gifts (hair- and skin-care products, pasta, cheesecakes, salsa, and soap).

For a real Keys-style shopping experience, head for the weekend flea market held Saturday and Sunday at MM 103.5 (☎ **305-664-4615**). Dozens of vendors sell a wide variety of merchandise — antiques, T-shirts, shoes, books, among others — from 9 a.m. to 5 p.m.

Lacking karaoke

Folks tend to party here at any hour, acting under the premise that it's 5 p.m. somewhere on the planet. Most of the action is at motel bars. Other options include **Snapper's Waterfront Saloon & Raw Bar,** 139 Seaside Ave., MM 94.5 ocean-side (☎ **305-852-5956**), which is open nightly and usually has a band on weekends. **Snook's Bayside** (see the listing under "Key Largo's Best Restaurants" earlier in this chapter) has a guitar player on Thursday night and duets Friday and Saturday.

Enjoying Islamorada Is Easier than Pronouncing It

The next major key south of Key Largo is not going to dethrone Walt Disney World as the top tourist draw, but Islamorada ("the purple island") has a lot of daytime fun and even a few places to keep you entertained at night. The unofficial capital of the Upper Keys, it has the most area's best atmosphere, food, and lodging. If you fish, you can find more fishing boats per square mile here than in any other vacation destination. First, though, here are some basics.

Think car. Trains, public transit, and taxis that travel the entire length of the islands are nonexistent in the Keys, and it's next-best-to impossible to get lost: The Overseas Highway (U.S. 1), which takes 3 hours to travel from end to end, is the only thoroughfare through the Keys. Even if you plant yourself at one resort, with the possible exception of Key West, you're going to need a car to get to the islands from Miami.

Islamorada's Best Hotels

Sport fishing rules in Islamorada, and the hotels and resorts cater to the anglers who come to participate in annual fishing events or to just kick back and enjoy the emerald waters. Depending on your budget, you can choose from several accommodations options in Islamorada, including camping, guest houses, bed-and-breakfast inns, and resorts.

Unless otherwise noted, all listings include air conditioning, televisions, and a pool. As with much of coastal Florida, winter (December through April) is peak season. Also, remember to add an additional 11.5 percent room tax to your hotel rate.

Cheeca Lodge

$$$$ Islamorada

A dignitary broke a bottle of bubbly across the Cheeca's bow in 1949. Legend has forgotten the dignitary, but the lodge remains one of the better places to turn out the lights in the Keys. It has a casual air but features the amenities of a classy resort: 27 acres of beachfront, 9 holes of par-3 golf, lighted tennis courts, and a good restaurant. It also has three pools, hot tubs, and kids' programs. The Cheeca's 203 rooms have balconies/patios, and some of them have kitchenettes or microwaves.

U.S. 1/Overseas Hwy. at MM 82. ☎ *800-327-2888 or 305-664-4651. Fax: 305-664-2893. Internet:* www.cheeca.com. *To get there: Just look for it at MM 82. Parking: free. Rack rates: $175–$425 May–Nov, $250–$1,500 Nov–May. AE, CB, DC, DISC, MC, V.*

Days Inn Oceanfront Resort

$$ Islamorada

By Days Inn standards, this is a small motel — just 36 units — but it offers a choice of standard rooms, efficiencies, and suites. The suites have washer-dryer combos, and some accommodations have balconies. The oceanfront location offers a great view; there's a small dock. Local restaurants will deliver.

82749 U.S. 1/Overseas Hwy., MM 82.7. ☎ *800-325-2525 or 305-664-3681. Fax: 305-664-9020. Internet:* www.floridakeys.net/daysinn. *To get there: Look for it ocean-side at MM 82.7. Parking: free. Rack rates: $7–$169; suites $9–$245. AE, CB, DC, DISC, MC, V.*

Pelican Cove Resort

$$$ Islamorada

Balconies or patios are notable features of this secluded oceanfront resort's 63 rooms and suites. Some accommodations have views of the ocean or marina; some have kitchens. All come with mini refrigerators and free continental breakfast. The resort has a freshwater pool, a whirlpool, tennis court, and an outdoor Jacuzzi.

84457 U.S. 1/Overseas Hwy., MM 84.5. ☎ *800-445-4690 or 305-664-4435. Fax: 305-664-5134. Internet:* www.pcove.com. *To get there: It's at MM 84.5, behind Theater of the Sea. Parking: free. Rack rates: $18–$325 Dec–Apr, $125–$255 May–Nov. AE, CB, DC, DISC, MC, V.*

Islamorada's Best Restaurants

Seafood isn't the only show in town, but passing up the chance to have it so fresh is a shame. Also, if you want to increase your dining choices, shop for restaurants in Key Largo, which is discussed earlier in this chapter, and Marathon, coming up a bit later.

Atlantic's Edge

$$$ Islamorada   SEAFOOD

This may be the fanciest restaurant in the Keys, but that's relative — a sports jacket for men may even be a bit too much. Steaks, chicken, pasta, and rack of lamb keep landlubbers happy, but seafood rules this ocean-front restaurant's menu. Specialties include dolphin and Thai-spiced snapper. Everything is fresh, and the service is professional. The chef will cook the fish you caught that afternoon for $15 per person.

81801 U.S. 1/Overseas Hwy., ocean-side in the Cheeca Lodge (see under "Islamorada's Best Hotels"). ☎ *305-664-4651. Reservations suggested. To get there: It's near MM 82. Main courses: $25–$36. AE, CB, DC, DISC, MC, V. Open: 5:30–10 p.m. nightly.*

Coral Grill

$$ Islamorada   SEAFOOD

This old war horse has regular menu service or, if you're hungry, a seafood buffet full of fried, broiled, and baked fish and shellfish. Brunch is offered on Sundays.

83532 U.S. 1/Overseas Hwy. ☎ *305-664-4803. Reservations aren't necessary. To get there: It's at MM 83.5. Main courses: $10–$25. AE, DISC, MC, V. Open: 4:30–9:30 p.m. Tues–Fri, 4:30–10 p.m. Sat, noon–9 p.m. Sun.*

Jammers Grill & Pub

$ **Islamorada** **AMERICAN**

A game room, big-screen TVs, and Friday- and Saturday-night DJs crank up the volume. The dolphin sandwich (grilled, blackened, or broiled) and shrimp combo platters are popular selections. Prime rib, chicken, T-bones, or barbecued ribs round out the menu.

86701 U.S. 1/Overseas Hwy., MM 86.7. ☎ *305-852-8786. Reservations aren't necessary. To get there: MM 86.5. Main courses: $6–$18. MC, V. Open: 11 a.m.–11 p.m. daily.*

Exploring Islamorada

Fully exploring the wonder of Islamorada requires a bit of imagination and patience, but it can be done.

Lignumvitae Key State Botanical Site

Lignumvitae Key

This 280-acre island is one of the backcountry islands, so you need to catch a boat. But if you want to see the Keys as they used to be, this one (it means "wood of life" in Latin) is worth a trip. In addition to its namesakes, Lignumvitae is home to mahogany, strangler fig, and gumbo-limbo trees. The lush hammocks also shelter several bird species, but bring mosquito repellent. Because of a limit on visitors, calling ahead is advisable. Due to the ferry schedule, it's a half-day event.

Leave from Robbie's Pier, MM 77.5 (see the next entry). ☎ *305-664-9814. To get there: Look for the Hungry Tarpon sign on the right, just past the Indian Key channel. Admission: Robbie's runs a ferry twice a day (9:30 a.m. and 1:30 p.m.) for $15 per person. Reservations are a good idea. Open: The park is open dawn till dusk.*

Robbie's Pier

Islamorada

This is the closest most folks get to a tarpon. Tarpons put up a whale of a fight when hooked, but at dockside, they're peaceful. The ones cruising for handouts at Robbie's (you can buy tarpon chow for $2) are about 50 pounds, but you may get lucky enough to see one four times that size. Allow an hour if you come early or late.

U.S. 1 at MM 77.5. ☎ *305-664-9814. Internet:* www.robbies.com. *To get there: Under Hungry Tarpon sign just past Indian Key channel. Admission: $1 (free if you take the Lignumvitae ferry). Open: 8 a.m.–5 p.m. daily.*

Theatre of the Sea

Islamorada

This aging park, opened in 1946, offers dolphin and sea lion shows, a chance to swim with dolphins, and a guided boat tour that gives you a decent glimpse of captive stingrays, sharks, turtles, and sea lions. The swims are 9:30 a.m., noon, and 2 p.m. daily and last an hour, including instruction. Expect to spend 2 hours (3 if you do the swim).

U.S. 1/Overseas Hwy., MM 84.5. ☎ 305-664-2431. Admission: $16.75 adults, $10.75 kids 3–12; dolphin swim $110. Open: 9:30 a.m.–4 p.m. daily.

Pursuing outdoor delights

If you're a skipper, you can rent a boat and chart your course from **Robbie's Pier,** located on U.S. 1/Overseas Hwy. at MM 77.5. (☎ **305-664-9814;** Internet: www.robbies.com), where 14- to 27-footers rent for $75–$225 half day, $95–$325 full day. **Bud n' Mary's Marina** (☎ **800-742-7945** or 305-664-2461; Internet: www.budnmarys.com/index.html) has outdoor and pontoon boat rentals for $90–$160 per half day and $140–$240 for a full day.

The diving magnet for this region is a sunken Spanish galleon, **The Eagle,** dating to 1733. Little is left, but the galleon is still a favorite of divers. Curators have added many authentic touches, including seven concrete cannon replicas and a ship's anchor from the eighteenth century. The ship, nearly a football field long in 110 feet of water, is a magnet for grouper, tarpon, and jack.

Sea Raven Dive Boat at Lookout Lodge, 87770 U.S. 1/Overseas Hwy., MM 88 (☎ **800-870-1772** or 305-852-9915; Internet: www.searavendiver.com), is a respected local charter ($29 snorkelers; $47–$56 divers). The same goes for **Lady Cyana Divers,** MM 85.9 (☎ **800-221-8717** or 305-664-8717). The outfit charges $25 for snorkelers, $40 and up for divers.

The rod-and-reel crowd will find catching bonefish, tarpon, and marlin a thrill. Grouper, yellowtail snapper, and mahi-mahi make great meals. Inshore rates are generally $225 a half day, $400 for eight hours; double that for deep-sea excursions.

Robbie's, 84500 U.S. 1/Overseas Hwy. (☎ **877-664-8498** or 305-664-9814; Internet: www.robbies.com) and **Reef Runner,** 176 Coral Rd. (☎ **305-852-3660**), are two reliable outfitters and offer a number of expeditions.

Lighting up the night

You haven't lived until you've experienced Big Dick and the Extenders at **Woody's Saloon and Restaurant** (☎ **305-664-4335**), MM 81.5. Big is a large, often profane Native American whose shtick is particularly stinging if you climb into a front table. His band takes the stage about 10 p.m. and holds court until 4 a.m., Wednesday through Saturday. Dick appears in time for an adult comedy show at 11 p.m. On a tamer front, the **Green Turtle Inn,** MM 81.5 (☎ **305-664-9031**) has piano music from Tuesday through Sunday; it's open from noon to 10:30 p.m. The **Lorelei Restaurant,** MM 82 (☎ **305-664-4338**) features nightly guitar and other music at its Cabana Bar. The restaurant is open from 6 a.m. to 10 p.m. daily; the bar stays open until 2 a.m.

Meandering Through Marathon

Marathon is another sleepy hollow where motels are a bit thin, and restaurants are thinner. But there's a bright side: Marathon has one of the better dolphin-swim programs. See "Exploring Marathon" later in this chapter for further details.

Marathon has no public transportation, so a car is essential. U.S. 1, also known as the Overseas Highway, boasts most of the action in the Keys, except for Key West. Almost every place you'll visit uses a mile marker as a reference point. Getting lost is hard to do.

Marathon's Best Hotels

Marathon, in the heart of the Keys, offers the modern conveniences of a bustling commercial community and has a number of resort hotels. Even though Marathon is growing, it still retains its nineteenth-century-fishing-village charm, so you'll also find a sprinkling of guesthouses and bed-and-breakfasts.

Unless otherwise noted, all listings include air conditioning, televisions, and a pool. As with much of coastal Florida, winter (December through April) is peak season. And don't forget to add an additional 11.5 percent room tax to your hotel rate.

Banana Bay Resort & Marina

$$ Marathon

Though **Banana Bay Resort & Marina** may not make the next issue of *Better Resorts & Marinas,* this early-1950s, fish camp-turned-inn offers a warm welcome. The grounds are lush, overflowing with banyans and palms. The moderately sized rooms are comfortable, and some have private balconies. A free continental breakfast is served, and a restaurant, Tiki Bar, whirlpool, and two tennis courts are available on the premises.

U.S. 1/Overseas Hwy. at MM 49.5. ☎ *800-226-2621 or 305-743-3500. Fax: 305-743-2670. Internet:* www.bananabay.com. *To get there: Look for sign at MM 49.5. Parking: free. Rack rates: $135–$210 Jan–Mar, $105–$195 Apr–May, $85–$160 June–Dec; $15 per child over 5. AE, DC, DISC, MC, V.*

Hampton Inn & Suites

$$ Marathon

Rooms here are clean and a couple of notches above typical motel fare. All have patios or balconies. The suites have kitchenettes and sleeper sofas. There's free continental breakfast, an exercise room, and an onsite laundry.

U.S. 1/Overseas Hwy. at MM 48. ☎ *800-426-7866 or 305-743-9009. Internet:* www. hampton-inn.com. *To get there: Look for sign at MM 48. Parking: free. Rack rates: $199–$319 Feb–Apr and Dec, $119–$209 May–Nov and Jan. AE, CB, DC, DISC, MV, V.*

Hawk's Cay Resort

$$$ Duck Key/Marathon

This 60-acre island resort has 176 rooms, suites, and villas. The atmosphere is casual, and the accommodations are reasonably large (views account for most of the price differences) and are equipped with balconies and small refrigerators. Suites have sitting areas, sofa sleepers, and wrap-around terraces. **Hawk's Cay** has two pools, a beach, a small fitness area, eight tennis courts, a Jacuzzi, a kids' club (open to kids 3 to 12; cost is $25 to $35 per day Monday through Friday, and $25 on weekend nights), and a lagoon with five dolphins.

U.S. 1/Overseas Hwy at MM 61. ☎ *888-443-6393 or 305-743-7000. Internet:* www. hawkscay.com. *Fax: 305-743-5215. To get there: At MM 61 north of Marathon. Parking: free. Rack rates: $230–$285 Jan–Apr (suites $435–$875), $190–$260 May–Dec (suites $335–$775); plus $5–$10 daily resort fee. AE, DC, DISC, MC, V.*

Marathon's Best Restaurants

The cuisine in Marathon, such as that in the rest of the Keys, revolves around seafood. Fish, crabs, lobsters, and scallops are your best bets. If you prefer your dinner off the hoof, however, you'll also find basic burgers, poultry, and the like. If you want to increase your dining options, you can also look for places to eat in nearby Islamorada and the Lower Keys, which are also discussed in this chapter.

Barracuda Grill

$$ Marathon BISTRO/SEAFOOD

A husband-and-wife-team runs this casual spot, where the grilled tuna and pan-seared snapper are very tasty. If you want a break, the rack of lamb or pork tenderloin roasted in red onions and figs are good respites. The American wine list is good.

MM 49.5, bay-side. ☎ *305-743-3314. Reservations aren't necessary. To get there: Look for the sign between MM 49 and 50. Main courses: $16–$30. AE, DISC, MC, V. Open: 6–10 p.m. Wed–Sat.*

The Quay Marathon

$$ Marathon   STEAK/SEAFOOD

This **Quay Marathon** isn't related to the restaurant of the same name in Key Largo, but it has a nice selection of dolphin, grouper, yellowtail snapper, shrimp, and lobster as well as steaks, veal, and chicken. Seating is indoor and outdoor.

U.S. 1/Overseas Hwy. at MM 54. ☎ *305-289-1810. Reservations suggested. Main courses: $13–$33. AE, CB, DC, DISC, MC, V. Open: 11:30 a.m.–10 p.m. Sun–Thurs; till 11 p.m. Fri–Sat.*

Exploring Marathon

The options here are lean in terms of numbers, but Marathon has one of our favorite critter encounters at its famous Dolphin Research Center. If you want to take a tour of the area, **Latigo Yacht Charters,** in the Marathon Marina, 1021 11th St. (☎ **305-289-1066;** Internet: www.latigo.net) offers several options aboard a 56-foot motor yacht. A bed-and-breakfast cruise ($420 per couple) is one option that includes dinner, beer, wine, champagne, breakfast, and snorkeling.

Dolphin Research Center

Marathon

This is our blue-light special: No other dolphin experience is as organized and informative. The center's primary goal is caring for the animals, and several experiences are interactive. *Dolphin Encounter,* the hands-down favorite, allows you to swim with bottlenose beauties. The cost is $110 for ages 5 and older; reservations and English comprehension are required. *Dolphin Splash* lets you get in the door without a dolphin swim. The price is $60, kids under 3 get in free. *Tips on Training* puts you behind the scenes to see training techniques and touch a dolphin. The cost is $35 for adults, $30 for kids 4 to 12. Guided tours can also give you the basics about the mammals. Allow 2 to 3 hours.

U.S. 1 at MM 59. ☎ *305-289-1121 or 305-289-0002 (reservations). Internet:* www.dolphins.org. *To get there: Look for the 30-foot dolphin statue. Reservations: must be made six weeks in advance. Admission: Guided tours $12.50 adults, $7.50 kids 4–12. For special programs, see the preceding paragraph. Open: 9:30 a.m.–4 p.m. daily.*

Florida Keys Land & Sea Trust at Crane Point Hammock

Marathon

The lagoon in the trust's Children's Museum has bonnethead sharks and more, Casa Iguana has 3- to 6-foot namesakes, and Los Ninos de los Cayos is an interactive pirate vessel with a cannon, skeletons, and treasure. Outside, a 2-mile trail winds through several habitats, and reserved guided tours show off an archaeological site. Allow 3 to 4 hours.

5550 U.S. 1/Overseas Hwy. ☎ 305-743-9100. To get there: It's at MM 50.5. Admission: $7.50 adults, $6 seniors 65 and older, $4 kids 6 and older. Open: 9 a.m.– 5 p.m. Mon–Sat (May–Nov), 10 a.m.–5 p.m. Sun.

Seven-Mile Bridge

Marathon

The bridge is not your typical tourist attraction, but you can't avoid a peek. It takes nine minutes to cross, and there's nothing else to do but gawk and marvel. Opened in 1982, the architectural wonder cost $45 million. Its crowning achievement is the fact that the **Seven-Mile Bridge** apex is the highest point in the Keys. Locals and tourists use a 4-mile stretch of the old bridge for hiking, fishing, and sunsets.

Between MMs 40 and 47. To get there: It's south of Marathon. Admission: The best things in life are free. Open: Always, unless you or one of the other gawkers hits another gawker— or a wall.

Outdoor pursuits

Boaters should try **Biggs Watersports,** 4650 U.S. 1/Overseas Hwy. (☎ 305-743-8090; Internet: www.biggswatersports.com), which rents outboards ($70 to $110 for a half day), WaveRunners ($60 per hour), and kayaks ($45 to $50 for a half day).

Popular diving sites include the **Adelaide Baker,** a wrecked steamer whose twin stacks lie in 25 feet of water; **Thunderbolt,** a 188-foot wreck at a depth of 115 feet, and **Coffin's Patch,** a series of six reefs brimming with coral and fish.

Prices vary by outfitter, but snorkel tours usually begin at $25 and dive tours at $60. Marathon's charter fleet includes **Marathon Divers,** 12221 U.S. 1/Overseas Hwy. (☎ 800-724-5798 or 305-289-1141), and **Capt. Hook's Marina & Dive Centers,** 11833 U.S. 1/Overseas Hwy. (☎ 800-278-4665).

As in the rest of the Keys, the fish are always biting in Marathon. In addition to having many of the more common inshore species, this area has more than its share of blue and white marlin, mako shark, and blackfin tuna thanks to offshore depths that reach up to 1,100 feet.

Local charters include small-party boats, such as **Florida Keys Fly Fishing,** 253 29th St., (☎ **305-743-6010**), which charges $300 per half day, $400 for a full day. **Black Ghost Outfitting,** MM 50, P.O. Box 501324, Marathon, Florida Keys, 33050 (☎ **305-743-9666**), where excursions run $275 per half day, $400 for a full day.

Escaping to the Lower Keys

If you want to be near but not in the middle of zany Key West, the Lower Keys is the place. Despite being close to ground zero, Big Pine, Summerland, and Sugarloaf Keys are as quiet and natural as the major keys get.

 The car is king in the Keys. Except for Key West, you won't find a trace of public transportation in the Lower Keys. Rental agencies are few and far between, which means you'll need to drive here in your own car, one rented on the mainland, or one rented in Key West. The Overseas Highway (U.S. 1), as always, is your major reference point, and mile markers should help prevent you from getting lost.

The Lower Keys' Best Hotels

If you're looking for national chains, you won't find them in the more than 50 islands that make up the Lower Keys. Most accommodations here are vacation rental homes, with most rentals offering two- to three-bedroom units, some with oceanfront views. Except for a few small properties and one or two resorts, this section of the Keys is undeveloped.

We can only tell you in the following listings about air conditioning, pools, and televisions if a property doesn't have them. And, as always, don't forget to tack on the 11.5 percent room tax to your hotel rate.

If a back-to-nature experience appeals to you, the area does offer some great camping. **Bahia Honda State Recreation Area** (see the listing for the park, later in this chapter), which features 80 camping sites, is loaded with facilities and outdoor activities. A site costs $26 for a maximum of four people and includes electricity. Cabins — under construction at press time — hold up to eight people. Equipped with linens, kitchenettes, and utensils, the cabins run from $100 to $150 depending on the season. For more information, or to reserve a site, call ☎ **305-872-2353.**

The Barnacle Bed & Breakfast

$$ Big Pine Key

This older, Caribbean-style inn was forced into refurbishment after Hurricane Andrew and now has a range of well-sized rooms and cottages.

A full breakfast is included in the rates, and all rooms have small refrigerators. Guests have access to a hot tub, paddleboats, and kayaks, and can take advantage of diving and fishing programs. Kids under 16 aren't welcome.

1557 Long Beach Dr. ☎ *800-465-9100 or 305-872-3298. Fax: 305-872-3863. Internet:* www.thebarnacle.net. *To get there: Cross Spanish Harbor Bridge (MM 33) and take first left onto Long Beach, then 1 mile and look for sign on left. Parking: free. Rack rates: $95–$140 Dec–May, $85–$140 June–Nov. DISC, MC, V.*

Dolphin Resort & Marina

$$ Little Torch Key

Located 30 minutes from Key West, **Dolphin Resort & Marina** is close to the action but outside of the clutter. The resort features a wide variety of suites and rooms. Many rooms have full kitchens and porches; larger suites can hold six people. There isn't a pool, but if you are looking to fish, the resort has close ties to local fishing guides and will help you arrange a charter.

U.S. 1 at MM 28.5. ☎ *800-553-0308. Internet:* www.dolphinresort.com. *To get there: Bay-side at MM 28.5. Parking: free. Rack rates: $99–$189 Dec–Apr, $79–$169 May–Nov. AE, DISC, MC, V.*

Little Palm Island Resort & Spa

$$$$ Little Torch Key

Presidents and kings have been known to drop in at the exclusive **Little Palm Island Resort & Spa.** The resort's 28 suites are housed in thatched-roof villas on an island 3 miles into the Atlantic. Most suites are duplexes with king-size beds, living areas, and whirlpools. Rooms don't have telephones, televisions, or alarm clocks. The five-acre island has a lagoonlike pool and waterfall. Rates include use of a fitness center, kayaks, canoes, rods and reels, and snorkeling gear. Kids under 16 aren't welcome, and all the suites are smoke-free. Plan on paying a 10 percent service charge.

28500 U.S. 1/Overseas Hwy. ☎ *800-343-8567 or 305-872-2524. Fax: 305-872-4843. Internet:* www.littlepalmisland.com. *To get there: Look for the Little Palm Island Ferry Service sign at MM 28.5 ocean-side. Parking: free. Rack rates: $850–$1,600 Jan–Apr, $750–$1,500 May–June and Oct–Dec, $550–$1,200 July–Sept. AE, CB, DC, DISC, MC, V.*

The Lower Keys' Best Restaurants

Unfortunately, the Lower Keys don't have many dining options. Aside from the following eateries, your best restaurant bet is to try the one with the most cars parked in front of it. We can tell you from experience that if a storm rears up during hurricane season, every establishment shuts up tight. You may want to keep a few snacks in your room.

Coco's Kitchen

$ Big Pine Key   CUBAN/NICARAGUAN

This tiny storefront offers a Cuban-accented menu that includes black beans and rice, shredded beef, roast pork, grouper, and flan. The menu also offers a sprinkling of Caribbean and Italian cooking, but go Latin when you dine here.

283 Key Deer Blvd., in the Winn-Dixie shopping center. ☎ *305-872-4495. Reservations aren't necessary. To get there: Turn at the traffic light at MM 30.5 and stay in the left lane. Main courses: $5–$16. Credit cards aren't accepted. Open: 7 a.m–7:30 p.m. Mon–Sat.*

The Dining Room at Little Palm Island

$$$ Little Palm Island   FRENCH/FLORIBBEAN

If you aren't keeping track of your dining budget, go dressy casual, grab the island ferryboat, and head to this resort restaurant. Choose from a menu that leans toward French and Floribbean (that's Florida and Caribbean flavors colliding). The menu changes, but it may include pan-seared snapper with lobster dumplings, crab cakes with vegetables, or roast chicken in a tarragon-Riesling sauce. The wine list is extensive.

28500 U.S. 1/Overseas Hwy. ☎ *800-343-8567 or 305-872-2524. Fax: 305-872-4843. Internet:* www.littlepalmisland.com. *To get there: Look for the Little Palm Island Ferry Service sign at MM 28.5 ocean-side. Main courses: $30–$43. AE, CB, DC, DISC, MC, V. Open: 7:30–10 a.m., 11:30 a.m.–2:30 p.m., 6:30–10 p.m. daily.*

Monte's Restaurant & Fish Market

$ Summerland Key   SEAFOOD

Dress cool because Monte's is old-style — no air conditioning. This is a no-frills place, but the restaurant's staff make up for it with a gut-busting seafood basket and raw bar. Lobster tail, at $17, is the only thing that goes above the $ threshold. Beer and wine are the only relaxants sold here.

Just off U.S. 1 at MM 25, Summerland Key 33042. ☎ *305-745-3731. Reservations aren't necessary. Main courses: $9–$17. Don't bring the credit cards. Open: 9 a.m.– 10 p.m. Mon–Sat; 11 a.m.–9 p.m. Sun.*

Exploring the Lower Keys

This is outdoorsville. If you want to commune with nature in a tranquil and relatively unspoiled setting, this is the place to be. Unlike their neighbors to the north and Key West in the south, the Lower Keys are devoid of spring-break crowds and have little nightlife. Unless you go south to Key West, you won't even be able to find a tourist trap.

Bahia Honda State Recreation Area

Big Pine Key

This is the only state park in the Lower Keys and the only natural beach in the entire chain. Its 524 acres are made of dunes, coastal mangroves, and hammocks. The white-sand beach has deep water close to shore, making this venue good for diving and snorkeling. (You may find starfish floating only 3 feet below the surface of the water.) Snorkel trips to **Looe Key Reef** depart two to three times daily, and the cost is $24.95 for adults, $19.95 for kids under 18, and $5 for equipment rental. (See Looe Key National Marine Sanctuary later in this chapter under "Taking it to the water.") While you're here, climb aboard what's left of Henry Flagler's rail line and treat yourself to a panorama of the nearby keys.

36850 U.S. 1/Overseas Hwy. ☎ 305-872-2353. For diving/snorkeling trips, call ☎ 305-872-3210. Internet: www.bahiahondapark.com. Reservations recommended for snorkeling. To get there: at MM 37, 12 miles south of Marathon. Admission: $5 per couple and 50 cents for each additional person. Open: 8 a.m.–5 p.m.

National Key Deer Refuge

Big Pine Key

Key deer — no larger than medium-sized dogs — are making a last stand on this isle. Thanks to pollution, vanishing habitats, and speeding cars, only 300 deer are left. The deer sanctuary has a marked trail (Watson Hammock) where you might get a glimpse of a deer if you come early or late in the day. If you do see one, please don't feed the deer. The animals' tiny bodies aren't built for people food.

☎ 305-872-2239. To get there: Weekdays, go to the ranger station at MM 30.5 in the Winn-Dixie plaza. Otherwise, go to Big Pine Key's lone traffic light and take Key Deer Boulevard back, then the left fork. Admission: Just waltz in; it's free. Open: The ranger station is open 8 a.m.–5 p.m. Mon–Fri. The refuge is open daily, during daylight hours.

Taking it to the water

Divers will find that the **Looe Key National Marine Sanctuary** boasts exceptionally dramatic reefs due to a ban on spear fishing as well as coral and shell collecting. You can see barracuda, tarpon, and moray eels at a depth of less than 35 feet, and some of the marine life swims right up to your mask. Prices begin at $30 for snorkelers and $60 for divers. **Looe Key Reef Resort and Dive Center,** U.S. 1/Overseas Hwy., at MM 27.5, Ramrod Key (☎ 305-872-2215), is one of the area's better diving operators.

Fishermen love a fight. The Keys' favorite fighters are bonefish (3 to 15 pounds), tarpon (usually 40 or 50 pounds but as big as 200), and permit, which reach 25 pounds. **Back Country Guide Service,** 472 Sands Rd., Big Pine Key (☎ **800-663-5780** or 305-872-9528) charges $275 per half day and $375 for a full day aboard an 18-footer with little sun relief. **Grouch Charters,** MM 24.5, Summerland Key (☎ **305-745-1172**), takes $350 for four people per half day, and $475 for a full day on an offshore boat.

If you want to take a specialized tour of the area, **Gale Force Charters,** at Sugarloaf Marina on Sugarloaf Key, MM 17 (☎ **305-745-2868;** Internet: www.galeforcecharters.com) offers ecotours and snorkeling trips. Tour price is $150 for 2 people.

Going Key West, Young Man

Paradise? That may be stretching things when you describe Key West. There's traffic, prices are high, it's hot, the decibel level can split an oak, and franchises have usurped Hemingway's hideaway. Did we mention that cruise ships dock here?

But Key West does combine some of the natural treasures of the Keys (fishing and other water sports) with some of the rum-and-then-some fun of a destination that also has bars, restaurants, weird shows, and weirder people. (See an overview of "Key West" coming up.) And the gay lifestyle of many residents and tourists is openly accepted, which makes Key West one of the more progressive cities east of the Mississippi.

The island is small, and there are enough transportation options that you won't need a car, unless you're planning on touring some of the other Keys. Taxis from the airport to town run $3.50 to $7 per person for two or more, depending on your destination. **Five Sixes Taxi** (☎ **305-296-6666**) and **Friendly Cab Co.** (☎ **305-295-5555**) are two of the regulars. Rates are $1.75 for the first .2 mile and 45 cents for each additional .2 mile.

Key West's downtown parking and traffic are annoying, however, so your best bet for getting around may lie on two wheels. If you're staying on the key, consider renting a bike (from $8 a day and $30 a week) or moped ($30 and $100, respectively) from **Moped Hospital,** 601 Truman Ave., (☎ **305-296-3344**). **Tropical Bicycles & Scooters,** 1300 Duval St., (☎ **305-294-8136**) rents bikes for $8.50 a day and $35 a week; scooters are $29 and $129, respectively.

Key West's Best Hotels

Here's a city with a melting-pot character that permits a large, liberal base to mingle with crusty natives, called Conchs (pronounced *konks*), and with Miami wheeler-dealers. The wealth of places to stay in Key West ranges from bed-and-breakfasts to hotel chains and upscale resorts. If you plan on coming to town during one of the island's special events or during the holidays, reserve well in advance because rooms become scarce and many places require minimum stays.

You should also keep in mind that prices skyrocket during high season and special events, so finding a prime room for a reasonable price can be difficult. **Vacation Key West** (☎ **800-595-5397** or 305-295-9500; Internet: www.vacationkw.com) is a hotel reservation service in Key West that may be able to get you a last-minute deal in some of the larger hotels and motels. Vacation Key West also represents a few guesthouses. The service can often get you discounts of 20 to 30 percent at some of the major chains on the island and also offers car rental discounts.

Unless otherwise noted, all listings include air conditioning, televisions, and a pool. As with much of Florida, winter (December through April) is peak season. Key West assesses and additional hotel tax of 11.5 percent, so don't forget to budget for this when selecting your accommodations.

Island City House Hotel

$$$ Key West/Old Town

This small resort's 24 rooms have kitchens and share a junglelike courtyard that is home to a Jacuzzi. Rooms facing this courtyard are the best of the bunch. The wraparound verandas on the main building are great for casual strolls or kicking back. Most rooms (from studios to two-bedroom suites, some dating to 1880) have king-size beds and antique furnishings. A complimentary continental breakfast is served in the garden.

411 Williams St., at Eaton St. ☎ *800-634-8230 or 305-294-5702. Fax: 305-294-1289. Internet:* www.islandcityhouse.com. *To get there: It's 3 blocks north of Duval on Eaton. Parking: free if you can find it on the street. Rack rates: Studios $145–$175 Dec–May, $115 June–Nov; 1-bdr suites $175–$240 Dec–May, $135–$175 June–Nov; 2-bdr suites $230–$315 Dec–May, $185–$210 June–Nov. AE, CB, DC, DISC, MC, V.*

La Pensione

$$ Key West/Old Town

This Classic-Revival mansion's nine rooms are pretty intimate. The bed-and-breakfast was built in 1891, and the comfortable rooms all have king-size beds and private baths. Some rooms have French doors that open onto verandas, where you can enjoy a made-to-order breakfast (included). Room Nine is the largest in the house. Telephones and televisions are lacking, but the service is friendly and first-rate. Kids aren't welcome.

809 Truman Ave. ☎ *800-893-1193 or 305-292-9923. Fax: 305-296-6509. Internet:* http://lapensione.com. *To get there: It's between Windsor and Margaret Streets. Parking: free. Rack rates: from $98 May–Dec, $158–$168 Dec–May. AE, DC, DISC, MC, V.*

Key West

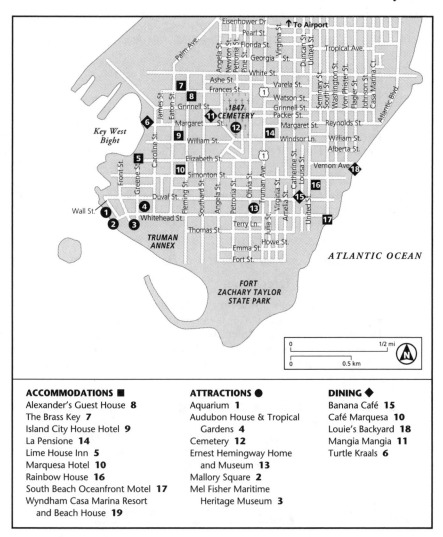

ACCOMMODATIONS ■
Alexander's Guest House **8**
The Brass Key **7**
Island City House Hotel **9**
La Pensione **14**
Lime House Inn **5**
Marquesa Hotel **10**
Rainbow House **16**
South Beach Oceanfront Motel **17**
Wyndham Casa Marina Resort
  and Beach House **19**

ATTRACTIONS ●
Aquarium **1**
Audubon House & Tropical
  Gardens **4**
Cemetery **12**
Ernest Hemingway Home
  and Museum **13**
Mallory Square **2**
Mel Fisher Maritime
  Heritage Museum **3**

DINING ◆
Banana Café **15**
Café Marquesa **10**
Louie's Backyard **18**
Mangia Mangia **11**
Turtle Kraals **6**

Marquesa Hotel

$$$ Key West/Old Town

Oversize furnishings, four-poster beds, and marble baths complement this 40-room inn, a perennial award-winner. Rooms and suites are scattered throughout four buildings; some have living areas and private porches. Two pools and two waterfalls help you forget the rush-hour traffic back home, and Cafe Marquesa (skip ahead to "Key West's Best Restaurants") serves dinner nightly. The hotel provides a free daily newspaper, wine on your arrival, and a Saturday night cocktail party.

600 Fleming St., Key West 33040. ☎ *800-669-4631 or 305-292-1919. Fax: 305-294-2121. Internet:* www.keywest.com/marquesa.html. *To get there: It's at the corner of Fleming and Simonton. Parking: free. Rack rates: $245–$380 Dec–Apr, $220–$320 May–June and Sept–Nov, $155–$265 June–Aug. AE, DC, MC, V.*

South Beach Oceanfront Motel

$$ Key West/South Beach

View the ocean or walk to Duval Street from this motel but don't expect many frills. (Only two rooms have a view of the ocean; the rest overlook the pool.) Three of the 47 rooms are efficiencies, which offer shaded balconies. An onsite dive shop offers scuba and snorkeling lessons.

508 South St. ☎ *800-354-4455 or 305-296-5611. Fax: 305-294-8272. Internet:* www.oldtownresorts.com/southbeach.htm. *To get there: On the ocean at Duval. Parking: free. Rack rates: $169–$230 Jan–Apr, $99–$179 May–Dec. AE, MC, V.*

Wyndham Casa Marina Resort & Beach House

$$$ Key West/Oceanfront

This luxurious resort, built in 1921 by the heirs of Florida magnate Henry Flagler, has 311 comfortable rooms. Decorated in tropical colors, many of the rooms come with balconies, and all the rooms have a full array of amenities. The property's facilities include three tennis courts, a whirlpool, an exercise room, a massage room, a sauna, and Flagler's Steakhouse.

1500 Reynolds St. ☎ *800-626-0777 or 305-296-3535. Fax: 305-296-4633. Internet:* www.casamarinakeywest.com. *To get there: From airport, go west on Roosevelt Blvd., 1 mile to Atlantic Blvd., turn left, one mile to Reynolds St., right; hotel is on left. Parking: free self, $10 valet. Rack rates: $245–$395 Jan–Apr, $179–$319 May–June and Oct–Nov, $149–289 July–Sept. AE, CB, DC, DISC, MV, V.*

Key West's Best Restaurants

You can find a tempting array of food choices on Key West, with many different cuisines represented. If your tastes run more toward food of the fast variety, many national chains have franchises along Roosevelt Boulevard. Fresh fish and seafood, as in the rest of Florida, are usually your best bets on a menu, and don't visit here without trying a slice of authentic Key lime pie. Quality Key lime pie will be pale yellow, not green.

Restaurants, for the most part, offer a relaxed and casual atmosphere. Many offer outdoor dining so patrons can get a good look at the spectacular Key West sunsets. Note, however, that many don't offer onsite parking.

Banana Cafe

$$ Key West/Old Town FRENCH

Like many of Key West's restaurants, this eatery is situated in a century-old house that was built near the end of the island's maritime heyday. The provincial entrees include sliced duck breast in green peppercorn sauce; rack of lamb in sautéed apples and Madeira wine sauce; and shrimp, mussels, scallops, and fish in Provençal tomato sauce served over saffron egg fettuccine. A jazz band plays here on Thursday nights.

1211 Duval St. ☎ 305-294-7227. Internet: www.banana-cafe.com. *Reservations suggested. To get there: On Duval, two blocks south of Truman. Main courses: $15–$20. AE, DC, DISC, MC, V. Open: 8 a.m.–3 p.m. and 7–11 p.m. daily.*

Cafe Marquesa

$$$ Key West/Old Town AMERICAN

Fine wine, formal service, and sinfully delicious seafood are the headliners at this hotel restaurant. The theater-style kitchen here produces such hits as pan-seared yellowfin tuna dusted in peppercorns, and Florida lobster tail and scallops in Thai basil sauce and Asian vegetables. This is a smoke-free restaurant.

600 Fleming St. ☎ 800-869-4631 or 305-292-1919. Internet: www.marquesa.com/cafe.html. *Reservations suggested. To get there: It's in the Marquesa Hotel at Simonton and Fleming. Main courses: $21–$31. AE, DISC, MC, V. Open: 7–11 p.m. daily.*

Louie's Backyard

$$$ Key West/South Beach CARIBBEAN/AMERICAN

This smoke-free old house has a deck surrounded by sea grapes that's perfect for watching a glorious Key West sunset. The menus include Sunday brunch (grilled rabbit sausage with potato pancakes), a range of marine cuisine (grilled yellowfin tuna with papaya and wasabi), and red meats (spice-rubbed venison loin). Service is usually good but can turn chilly in peak periods.

700 Waddell Ave. ☎ 305-294-1061. Internet: www.louiesbackyard.com. *Reservations suggested. To get there: Head south of Truman on Simonton to South Street, east to Vernon, south to Waddell. Main courses: $25–$45. AE, DC, MC, V. Open: 11:30 a.m.–3 p.m., 6:30–10 p.m. daily.*

Mangia Mangia

$ Key West/near Old Town ITALIAN

This much-venerated Italian trattoria serves inexpensive yet good food in a low-key atmosphere. Specialties include a variety of homemade pastas in marinara or pesto sauce, and scallops sautéed in garlic and butter, then tossed in spinach fettuccine. The family-run spot is a favorite with locals. You can eat in the small indoor dining room or on the small outdoor patio.

900 Southard St. ☎ *305-294-2469. Internet:* www.mangia-mangia.com. *Reservations not necessary. To get there: Corner of Margaret and Southard Streets. Main courses: $9.50–$15.50. AE, MC, V. Open: 5:30–10 p.m. daily.*

Turtle Kraals

$ Key West/North End   SOUTHWESTERN/SEAFOOD

Built on the site of an old turtle cannery, Turtle Kraals attracts lots of locals to a converted waterfront warehouse that serves up Southwestern dishes and excellent seafood. Specials include Bahamian seafood stew (shrimp, scallops, and fish in a garlic-and-tomato sauce), grilled chicken enchiladas, and mango crab cakes. Blues bands play here on most nights.

213 Margaret St. ☎ *305-294-2640. Internet:* www.turtlekraals.com. *Reservations not necessary. To get there: Corner of Margaret and Caroline Streets. Main courses: $7–$16. DISC, MC, V. Open: 11 a.m.–10:30 p.m. Mon–Sat, noon–10:30 p.m.*

Exploring Key West's Major Attractions

In addition to the attractions mentioned here, Key West throws two grand parties (and nightly mini ones) during the year. The first is **Hemingway Days** (☎ **305-294-4440**; Internet: www.hemingwaydays.com), which is held each July and includes a ton of fun. Festivities include everything from Papa look-alike contests and a fishing tournament to literary events and a street fair. **Fantasy Fest** (☎ **305-296-1817**; Internet: www.fantasyfest.net) covers the 10 days leading up to Halloween. Activities include balls, parades, a celebrity look-alike contest, and beach and toga parties.

Now, on with the rest of the show.

Audubon House & Tropical Gardens

Key West/Old Town

Painter and bird fancier John James Audubon didn't own the place, but he spent a few nights here in 1822. Rare Audubon prints and antiques are joined by a self-guided audio tour that takes about 30 minutes. You can also wander the grounds, which contain orchid and herb gardens.

205 Whitebread St. ☎ *877-281-2473 or 305-294-2116. Internet:* www.audubonhouse.com. *To get there: It's between Greene and Caroline Streets. Admission: $7.50 adults, $3.50 kids 6–12. Open: 9:30 a.m.–5 p.m. daily.*

Ernest Hemingway Home and Museum

Key West/Old Town

In this case, the namesake did live here and probably would roll over in his grave if he saw what happened to one of his favorite cities, as well as his image. Papa is the biggest celebrity to hit Key West, and his mug is plastered on everything from T-shirts to beer mugs. This Spanish-colonial house dates to 1851, 80 years before the author landed. Descendants of his six-toed cats rule the grounds. A self-guided tour of the house and grounds takes about an hour.

907 Whitebread St. ☎ *305-294-1136. Internet:* www.hemingwayhome.com. *To get there: It's between Truman Avenue and Olivia Street. Admission: $8 adults, $5 kids 6–12. Open: 9 a.m.–5 p.m daily.*

Key West Aquarium

Key West/Port Area

Born in 1934, **Key West Aquarium** is the oldest continuous attraction on the island. A touch tank contains sea cucumbers and anemones. Watch the daily shark and turtle feedings (not to each other, of course). A large aquarium sports eels, barracudas, tarpons, and more. Allow 3 hours.

1 Whitebread St. ☎ *800-868-7482 or 305-296-2051. Internet:* www.keywestaquarium.com. *To get there: North end of Whitebread St. Admission: $8 adults, $4 kids 4–12. Open: 10 a.m.–5:30 p.m. daily.*

Key West Cemetery

Key West/Old Town

Key West Cemetery is as strange and crowded as the city it serves, which underscores the notion that Key Westers keep their senses of humor even in death. Epitaphs include such parting thoughts as: "His beautiful little spirit was a challenge to love," for a Yorkshire terrier buried beside his mistress; "Now I know where he's sleeping at night," for a wayward husband deserving a proper send-off from his wife; "I told you I was sick," for a woman who apparently had trouble getting her friends and physician to listen; and "The buck stops here," for a native whose spirit pretty much epitomizes the local lifestyle. Allow 1 to 3 hours depending on your interest in the dead.

At Margaret and Angela Streets. ☎ *305-294-8380 for tours. Admission: Free; 90-minute tours are $20. Open: dawn to dusk daily.*

Mel Fisher Maritime Heritage Museum

Key West/Old Town

The namesake treasure hunter has gone to that great salvage yard in the sky, but his life's work remains on display. During his heyday, Fisher was usually at odds with state and federal regulators over the multimillion-dollar booty he found at the bottom of the sea. Exhibits include some of the gold he claimed from the wreck of treasure ships, such as the *Nuestra Senora de Atocha*. This is a good stop if you're into pirates and treasure hunting. Most folks stick around from 1 to 2 hours.

200 Greene St. ☎ *305-294-2633. Internet:* www.melfisher.org/home.htm. *To get there: At Greene and Whitebread Streets. Admission: $6.50 adults, $4 students, $2 kids under 6. Open: 9:30 a.m.–5 p.m. daily.*

Seeing Key West by guided tour

You can see Key West in an organized fashion in several ways. **Sharon Wells' Biking & Walking Guide to Key West** (☎ **305-294-8380;** Internet: www.seekeywest.com) offers plenty of touring choices in the $20 to $25 range. Themes include architecture, the Key West Cemetery, and an island overview.

The **Conch Train** (☎ **800-868-7482** or 305-296-6688) is one of two island tours operated by Historic Tours of America. It's tacky and touristy (a Jeep disguised to look like a locomotive pulls you around), but enduring this 90-minute special is almost required by the Tourists' Honor Code. You may want to hear a running, usually tongue-in-cheek narrative and explore an overview of Key West sights. Catch it at Mallory Square or the Welcome Center near U.S. 1/Overseas Hwy. and North Roosevelt; the tours depart every half-hour from 9 a.m. to 4:30 p.m. daily. The cost is $18 for adults, $9 for kids between 4 and 12. The **Old Town Trolley** (☎ **800-868-7482** or 305-296-6688) offers the same sort of humorous tours at the same prices, but you can get off and reboard at any of the trolley's 14 stops. Choose the trolley if you're staying at one of the hotels along the trolley route, or in the case of bad weather — the Conch Train doesn't have a roof.

Ghost Walk (☎ **305-294-9255;** Internet: www.hauntedtours.com), is a 90-minute, 1-mile hike through the city's historic district offered by the Key West Tour Association. The spooky but fun experience costs $18 for adults (you can find $3-off coupons everywhere; if you can't, the staff discounts the cost anyway) and $10 (no discount) for kids 3 to 12. The tour leaves nightly at 8 p.m. from the Holiday Inn La Concha at 430 Duval St., Old Town. Getting there 15 minutes early is smart; so are day-before reservations.

Several local vessels offer short sightseeing excursions, and some go to **Fort Jefferson** in nearby **Dry Tortugas National Park.** The fort, known as the "Gibraltar of the Gulf," was built on Garden Key in the mid-nineteenth century. In a cluster of seven coral islands, the Dry Tortugas, Fort Jefferson gave the United States control of navigation in the Gulf of Mexico. The walls are 8 feet thick and 50 feet high. Its main claim to fame, though, was as a Civil War prison for the Union Army. The fort's most famous inmate was Dr. Samuel Mudd, the Maryland surgeon who unwittingly set the broken leg of John Wilkes Booth, President Lincoln's assassin. Today, it's a favorite of bird watchers. (Tens of thousands of orioles, swallows, and terns pass through each spring.) Divers and snorkelers may see leatherback, green, and Atlantic Ridley sea turtles. For more information, call the **National Park Service, ☎ 305-242-7700.**

The catamaran **Sunny Days (☎ 305-296-5556;** Internet: www. sunnydayskeywest.com) makes runs to the Dry Tortugas from its dock at the end of Elizabeth and Greene Streets (arrive by 7:30 a.m.). The 8½-hour excursion includes continental breakfast, lunch, soft drinks, snorkeling gear and a guided tour. The ride costs $85 for adults, $75 for seniors and students, $50 for kids under 6. **Yankee Freedom (☎ 800-926-5332** or 305-294-7009; Internet: www.yankee-fleet.com) makes the same run from Key West Seaport, 240 Margaret St. The fare for this 100-foot catamaran is $95 for adults, $85 for seniors and college students, and $60 for kids. The price includes continental breakfast, lunch, snorkeling gear, and a tour.

The 130-foot, 1939 schooner **Western Union (☎ 305-292-1766;** Internet: www.schoonerwesternunion.com) is the last tall ship built in Key West. Berthed at Schooner Wharf, 202 William St., the schooner is used for 2-hour afternoon cruises ($30 per person, including beer, wine, and champagne) and sunset sails ($50 per person, including beer, wine, champagne, conch chowder, and live entertainment). The 74-foot schooner **Wolf (☎ 305-296-9694;** Internet: www.schoonerwolf.com) sails from 201 Williams St. Its 2-hour day trips ($25 per person) include soda. Sunset cruises ($30) include champagne, beer, soda, and music.

Seaplanes of Key West (☎ 800-950-2359 or 305-294-0709; Internet: www.seaplanesofkeywest.com) offers 4- and 8-hour snorkeling/ sightseeing excursions to the Dry Tortugas National Park. Rates are $159 per half day and $275 for a full day, including snorkel equipment, sodas, and water. If you want lunch, bring your own. It's based out of Key West Airport.

Outdoor adventures

Key West continues the Florida Keys' strong water sports theme. Key West also delivers the chain's only legitimate golf course.

The southernmost city has several good sites for diving and snorkeling. Resting 65 feet below the surface, **Joe's Tug** is a good place to see moray eels, barracudas, and jacks. **Nine-Foot Stake** is a reef where you can encounter soft coral and juvenile marine life at 10 to 25 feet.

At The Water's Edge offers a reservations service (☎ 305-766-2240; Internet: http://hometown.aol.com/doitallman/keywest.html). Local outfitters include **No Wake Charters,** 201 William St., Key West (☎ 305-294-3912; Internet: www.nowakecharters.com), which uses a 31-foot sailboat for private half-day ($175 for 2) and full-day ($325 for 2) charters. The trip includes round-trip transportation from your hotel. **Southpoint Divers,** 714 Duval St. (☎ **800-891-3483** or 305-292-9778; Internet: www.southpointdivers.com), offers two-tank scuba trips for $40 if you have gear and $70 if you need to rent all your equipment.

Bonefish, tarpon, and permit are some of the inshore fishing prizes. Grouper and snapper are common on reefs or around wrecks. Marlin, sailfish, blackfin tuna, wahoo, and dolphin are just a few of the creatures lurking in the depths. Party boat rates average about $35 for a full day; charters that take four to six anglers are about $550.

At The Water's Edge is a reservations service (☎ **305-766-2240;** Internet: http://hometown.aol.com/doitallman/keywest.html). You can also go straight to guides, such as **Key West Flats Fishing,** 903 Eisenhower, at the Harborside Motel (☎ **305-294-7670;** Internet: keywestflatsfishing.com), or **Lethal Weapon Charters,** 245 Front St., at the Key West Hilton Resort & Marina (☎ **305-296-6999;** Internet: www.lethalweaponcharters.com).

There is a drought of good golfing in the Keys, but the **Key West Golf Club,** 6450 E. College Rd., MM 4.5, and then turn on College Road (☎ **305-294-5232;** Internet: www.keywestgolf.com) can come to the rescue of desperate duffers. This 6,526-yard 18-holer was designed by Rees Jones and is open to the public. Mangroves and water spell many hazards. Greens fees are $40 to $70 from June to October, $65 to $110 from November to May.

Seeing Key West in 3 Days

Even if you don't have a car, much of the following itinerary can be accomplished using the bicycle, scooters, or taxi options listed earlier under "Going Key West, Young Man." For a more extensive itinerary that covers the entire Keys area, see "Seeing the Keys in 5 Days," earlier in this chapter.

On **Day 1,** climb aboard the **Conch Train** or **Old Town Trolley** to get acquainted; then get a closer look at the **Audubon House & Tropical Gardens;** have lunch at the **Banana Cafe;** then adjourn to the **Ernest Hemingway Home and Museum** and the **Key West Cemetery.** Have dinner at **Mangia, Mangia,** and then celebrate your first night at **Capt. Tony's.**

Start **Day 2** at the **Key West Aquarium;** grab lunch at **Turtle Kraals;** then do the **Mel Fisher Maritime Heritage Museum** before an early dinner at the **Banana Cafe,** followed by the **Sunset Celebration at Mallory Square** and a nightcap at **Sloppy Joe's.**

Day 3 is dedicated to a boat or seaplane trip to **Dry Tortugas National Park,** where you can snorkel, tour **Fort Jefferson,** and eat a picnic lunch. (The alternate is a fishing or diving trip.) Dine at **Louie's**

Backyard, then toast the day at the **Hog's Breath Saloon.**

Keeping a bit of the Keys for yourself

If you fall in love with local seafood and worry about post-pig-out depression, you can find the cure at **Key West Seafood,** 517 Duval St. (☎ 800-292-9853 or 305-292-4774; Internet: www.keywestseafood.com). It ships fresh stone crab claws (only from October through May), lobster tails, shrimp, fish, and Key lime pie overnight. **Nellie & Joe's** (☎ 800-546-3743; Internet: www.keylimejuice.com) is Key West's oldest and best known bottler. Thirty years ago, the happy couple started pouring Key-lime juice into long-neck beer bottles and corking them. Today, the selection includes lemon juice and marinades. Although this wholesaler doesn't have its own storefront, you can find its products in local stores, or you can order by phone or online. **Peppers of Key West,** 291 Front St. and 602 Greene St. (☎ 800-597-2823; Internet: www.peppersofkeywest.com), has an exhaustive selection of hot sauces. The **Saltwater Angler,** in the Hilton Resort & Marina at 243 Front St. (☎ 800-223-1629 or 305-296-0700; Internet: www.saltwaterangler.com), features high-end fishing tackle as well as tropical clothes and gear. In addition to the aforementioned stores, most bars in town sell T-shirts and other trinkets bearing their logos.

If you like the nightlife . . . if you like to boogie . . .

Capt. Tony's, 428 Greene St., is the center of a local debate. Is this the original Sloppy Joe's that Hemingway wrote about? Many insist that it is. Even if it isn't, Capt. Tony's is a delightful dive named for former owner/mayor Tony Tarracino. Folks get so caught up in the action here that many leave undergarments hanging from the ceiling. Call ☎ 305-294-1838 to warn them you're coming.

The **Hog's Breath Saloon,** 400 Front St. (☎ 800-826-6969 or 305-292-2032; Internet: http://hogsbreath.com), comes with the motto: "Hog's Breath Is Better Than No Breath." It's exceptionally lively, and like most of the town, the saloon is raucous and sometimes raunchy. But as long as you're a consenting adult (why else would you be in Key West?), drink up and expect such events as a homemade bikini contest where the combatants wear coconuts or water-filled plastic bags. The reigning **Sloppy Joe's,** 201 Duval St. (☎ 305-294-5717; Internet: www.sloppyjoes.com), has live music evenings and is often packed with tourists. The atmosphere is mellower at **Jimmy Buffett's Margaritaville,** 500 Duval St. (☎ 305-292-1435; Internet: www.margaritaville.com), where parrot heads down tasty margaritas, but Jimmy doesn't. He left the place to the tourists years ago.

The **Sunset Celebration at Mallory Square,** behind the Clinton Street Market at the west end of Duval (near the cruise-ship docks), happens most days, even if it's a bit overcast. One of the island's most unusual theaters, Sunset Celebration is a show where dwarfs juggle fruit, aging hippies sing Janis Joplin's songs (sometimes a little off-key), and someone always swallows a flaming sword or walks a high wire. The performance is free, though handouts are widely solicited. For more information call ☎ 305-292-7700 or surf over to http://sunsetcelebration.org.

Coming out to enjoy the gay scene

Key West has a very active gay and lesbian social scene. Some of the best nightlife in town can be found in predominantly gay clubs that welcome anybody with an open mind. The **Epoch** (☎ 305-296-8521) at 623 Duval St. picks up where the Copa left off. A 1995 fire destroyed the latter, a legendary hot spot. This new dance club was built in its place, specializing in a wide range of loud, Loud, LOUD soundzzz. **One Saloon,** 524 Duval (☎ **305-296-8118**), is another high-flying late-nighter among male partygoers. The same goes for the **801 Bourbon Bar** at 801 Duval (☎ **305-294-4737**).

Considering the island's popularity with gay and lesbian travelers, it's no wonder that Key West boasts a number of hotels that cater specifically to gays and lesbians. Here are a few of the best in town:

✔ One of the city's best known and respected inns, **Alexander's Guest House,** 1118 Fleming St. (☎ **800-654-9919** or 305-294-9919; Internet: www.alexghouse.com), has won an Editor's Choice Award from *Out & About* magazine four years running. Its 17 rooms have private baths, cable TV, and refrigerators. Some have full kitchens, verandas, and king-size beds. Rates ($145–$300 Dec–Apr, $80–$160 Apr–Dec) include continental breakfast (served poolside if the weather permits) and evening cocktails.

✔ The **Lime House Inn,** 219 Elizabeth St. (☎ **800-374-4242** or 305-296-2978, toll-free from the UK, 0800-89-8961; Internet: www.gaykeywestfl.com/limehs.html), is another favorite. This three-story Victorian, built in 1850, is on the National Register of Historic Places. Its rooms come with refrigerators, coffee makers, and voice mail. Most have private baths and kitchenettes. The grounds have gardens and a clothing-optional pool with spa. Rates are $75–$120 Apr–Dec, $120–$185 Dec–Apr.

✔ **Rainbow House,** 525 United St. (☎ **800-749-6696** or 305-292-1450; Internet: www.rainbowhousekeywest.com), is among Key West's better establishments catering solely to women. It offers rooms and suites, all with queen-size beds, TVs, telephones, and private baths. Rainbow House has two clothing-optional pools, a sun deck, and two hot tubs. Rates ($69–$149 May–Dec, $109–$229 Dec–Apr) include continental breakfasts.

✔ The **Brass Key,** 412 Francis St. (☎ **800-932-9119** or 305-296-4719; Internet: www.brasskey.com), offers rooms and suites with private baths, voice mail, TV/VCRs, and refrigerators. The grounds are filled with palms, jasmines, bougainvilleas, and hibiscuses. Amenities include verandas, sun decks, a pool, and spa. Rates ($85–$210 Apr–Dec; $140–$305 Dec–Apr) include a buffet breakfast.

See Chapter 4 for more information on gay and lesbian travel.

Fast Facts

Area Code

It's **305** throughout the Keys.

Currency Exchanges

Convert your cash at the airport. You'll be hard pressed to find a bank in the Keys that can or will convert your money to U.S. dollars.

Hospitals

Mariners Hospital, Tavernier ☎ **305-852-4418**

Lower Keys Health System, Key West ☎ **305-294-5531**

Information

For a free vacation kit, call the **Florida Keys and Key West Visitors Bureau** (☎ **800-352-5397** in U.S. and Canada, or 305-296-1552; Internet: www.fla-keys.com). You can write to the bureau at P.O. Box 1146, Key West, FL 33041, or when you're in town, stop in at 3406 N. Roosevelt Blvd., Suite 201.

Mail

Find the nearest post office location by dialing ☎ **800-275-8777.**

Newspapers

The *Key West Citizen* (☎ **305-294-6641**) is the Keys' only daily. Its "Paradise" section, published Thursdays, has things to do and see, mainly in the city but also in some of the other keys. The *Miami Herald* also circulates here, as does *USA Today.*

Taxes

The hotel tax is 11.5 percent, and there's a sales tax of 7.5 percent on most other items.

Weather Updates

For a recording of current conditions and forecast reports, call the local office of the **National Weather Service** at ☎ **305-229-4522,** or check out the national Web site at www.nws.noaa.gov. You can also get information by watching the **Weather Channel** (Internet: www.weatherchannel.com).

Chapter 13

The Everglades

In This Chapter

▶ Hiking through cypress and swamp

▶ Biking to the bush and beyond

▶ Dining out in the Glades

▶ Viewing panthers, manatees, and crocodiles

▶ Experiencing outdoor adventures

"*L*eave only your footprints behind for the next generation," maintains Chief James Billie, the current leader of the Seminole Tribe of Florida. The truth is, leaving any kind of tracks in the Glades is next best to impossible. Mostly swamps, the Glades are curiously appealing to developers. Just add a little fill or fertilizer and . . . voilà! Instant riches!

The Everglades are also a magnet to naturalists, animal lovers, and those seeking peace and quiet just an hour's drive from the madness of Miami.

Introducing the Everglades

Highways, agricultural runoff, and other fingerprints of civilization have partially destroyed Florida's largest wetland. Plants and animals have disappeared; the water has been poisoned; and habitats have been turned into subdivisions.

But parts of the Everglades remain untouched, leaving this spot, at least for now, primordial and unique. Actually, **Everglades National Park** is one of the most beautiful wildernesses in the continental United States. The park is basically a 40-mile-wide river, full of dense vegetation, which runs in super slo-mo; a gallon of water takes nearly a month to move from one end to the other. (Skip ahead to the map for an overview of "The Everglades.")

Everglades National Park lies in the southernmost part of mainland Florida, reaching from Everglades City on the west coast down to Cape Sable and a state of mind called Flamingo. Then, the park goes along the bottom of Florida to where the mainland gives way to the Keys. The

The Everglades

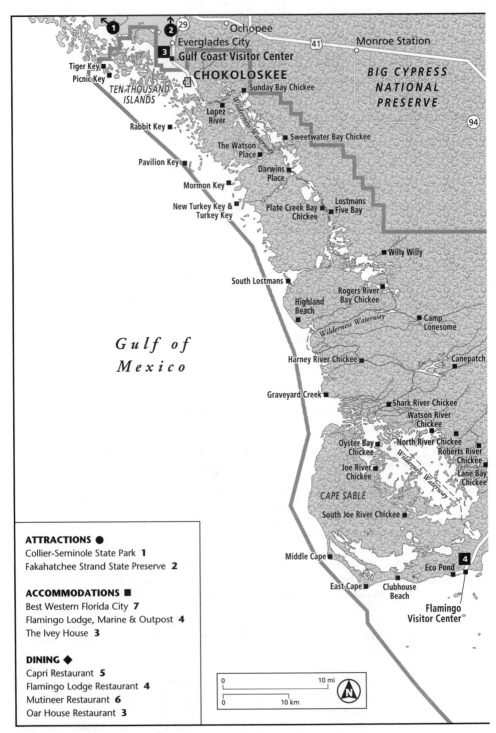

Ochopee
Everglades City
Gulf Coast Visitor Center
Monroe Station
41

CHOKOLOSKEE

Tiger Key
Picnic Key
TEN THOUSAND ISLANDS

BIG CYPRESS NATIONAL PRESERVE

94

Sunday Bay Chickee

Lopez River

Rabbit Key

Wilderness Waterway

Sweetwater Bay Chickee

The Watson Place

Pavilion Key

Darwins Place

Mormon Key

New Turkey Key & Turkey Key

Plate Creek Bay Chickee

Lostmans Five Bay

Willy Willy

South Lostmans

Rogers River Bay Chickee

Highland Beach

Camp Lonesome

Wilderness Waterway

Gulf of Mexico

Harney River Chickee

Canepatch

Graveyard Creek

Shark River Chickee

Watson River Chickee

Oyster Bay Chickee

North River Chickee

Roberts River Chickee

Joe River Chickee

Lane Bay Chickee

CAPE SABLE

South Joe River Chickee

Wilderness Waterway

ATTRACTIONS ●
Collier-Seminole State Park **1**
Fakahatchee Strand State Preserve **2**

ACCOMMODATIONS ■
Best Western Florida City **7**
Flamingo Lodge, Marine & Outpost **4**
The Ivey House **3**

DINING ◆
Capri Restaurant **5**
Flamingo Lodge Restaurant **4**
Mutineer Restaurant **6**
Oar House Restaurant **3**

Middle Cape

Eco Pond
4

East Cape
Clubhouse Beach

Flamingo Visitor Center

0 — 10 mi
0 — 10 km
N

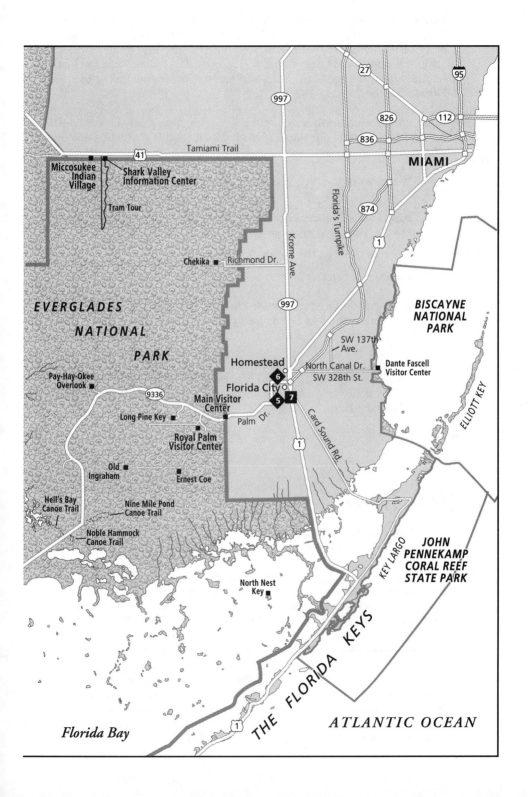

park's supporting cast includes **Big Cypress Swamp** to the north and its namesake national preserve, **Fakahatchee Strand State Preserve,** and **Collier-Seminole State Park.** Combined, these four include the ancestral homes of the Seminole and Miccosukee Indians and the last habitats for scores of plant, tree, and animal species, including the Florida panther.

Although the area brims with natural wonders, it certainly is not a destination for everyone. But the Glades may be a good fit if you like places where

 ✔ TV, a rare commodity, gets fuzzy reception.

 ✔ If you can find a newspaper, the front-page headline may be "Mayor Crowns Miss Speckled Perch" (and the film critic may not differentiate *The Perfect Storm* from *The Tempest*).

 ✔ Bugs rule the day, the night, and the in between.

 ✔ Domino's doesn't deliver.

If these factors aren't enough to discourage you, consider also that: It's hot in the winter; the sun in this part of Florida can cause a nasty burn; and bull frogs' pickup lines are one of the few forms of nightlife.

Did we mention kids? Most children may marvel when they see eagles, manatees, and river otters for the first time in the wild, but the magic wears off for many kids when they discover video games and thrill rides don't exist here.

But if you consider all this and you're still psyched, then welcome to the Everglades!

Getting There

The Glades are just about as remote as Florida gets. Unless you come on a see-Florida-by-bus tour, the modes are inconvenient.

If you don't want to fly Everglades-Or-Bust Airlines, you're going to need a rental car for the last leg of your trip. The best option is to fly into Miami (see Chapter 10 for airport information), rent a car, and then head for the Glades. To get there from the airport, take I-95 south to the Dolphin Expressway/Hwy. 836; go west to the West Dade Expressway/ Hwy. 821; then south to U.S. 41/Tamiami Trail, and then head west.

You can attack from the west, but **Southwest Florida International Airport** in Fort Myers is the only realistic landing zone (see Chapter 17 for more on the airport), and it's 70 miles from the western fringe of the Glades. If you opt for this route, after you're on the ground, take I-75 south to Naples and then head west to the Glades.

Getting Around

Without an airboat, a car is the only way around the Glades. That said, this is a wilderness region. Some of these roads, even the major highways, can be pretty remote, and signs of civilization are few and far between. A breakdown is the last thing you want to suffer on the more remote roads, especially if you're traveling at night. So have a solid plan if you're coming or getting around by car. Don't take chances with your gas level and skip the adventure routes or anything that could leave you stranded. Our advice: Carry a cell phone in case of an emergency. You can often get a cell phone as an add-on to your rental car, so ask at the rental agency (see Chapter 6 for more on car rentals). Also, check — then double-check — directions to activities, accommodations, and restaurants. Travel in daylight only. If a road looks suspicious, find another route or activity.

Looking at a regional road map (see the "Maps" entry in "Fast Facts" at the end of this chapter), you can see that straight paths from any given point A to point B are often nonexistent. So, make sure you allow enough time in your schedule. The major east-west roads are I-75/Alligator Alley (north end) and U.S. 41/Tamiami Trail central. The north-south roads are Hwy. 29 (west) and Hwy. 997 (east). Additionally, from Florida City south of Miami, take Hwy. 9336 and follow the signs to Everglades National Park and **Ernest F. Coe Visitor Center.** The highway continues southwest to the **Flamingo ranger station** on the park's south end. The other entrances include Everglades City (west) at U.S. 41/Tamiami Trail and **Shark Valley** (east) at U.S. 41/Tamiami Trail.

The Everglades' Best Hotels

The Everglades is clearly a sparsely developed area with only a meager smattering of places to stay. In addition to the following listings, check out the hotels in Miami (see Chapter 10) and those in Fort Myers and Naples (see Chapter 17) if you want more options. Also see the campgrounds listed under "Exploring the Everglades" later in this chapter.

Best Western Florida City

$ **Florida City**

This two-story, standard-style inn caters to a business clientele and has all the modern comforts. Suites have microwaves, coffee makers, and small refrigerators. There's a Jacuzzi and a small pool. Local phone calls, a daily newspaper, and continental breakfast are included in the room rate. **Note:** A 3-day stay is often required during high season; ask when you reserve.

411 S. Krome Ave. ☎ *888-981-5100 or 305-246-5100. Fax: 305-242-0056. Internet: www.bestwestern.com. To get there: Just off U.S. 1, south of the Florida*

Turnpike. Parking: Free. Rack rates: $89–$104 (suites $144) Dec–Apr, $69–$94 (suites $125) May–Nov. AE, DC, DISC, MC, V.

Flamingo Lodge, Marina & Outpost Resort

$$ Flamingo/Everglades National Park

If you want to stay inside the park, this resort is your only choice. Its 103 motel units and 24 cottages overlook Florida Bay. The cottages are larger and have kitchenettes, but don't offer televisions. Choose from a host of outdoor activities. In many ways, the resort feels like a backwoods camp, and the scenery is great.

1 Flamingo Lodge Hwy. ☎ **800-600-3813** *or 941-695-3101. Fax: 941-695-3921. Internet:* www.flamingolodge.com. *To get there: From Miami, head south on U.S. 1, turn right on Palm Drive/Hwy. 9336/SW 344th St. and follow the signs. Parking: Free. Rack rates: $95–$135. AE, DC, DISC, MC, V.*

The Ivey House

$ Everglades City

This former boarding house has ten rooms with shared baths, plus a cottage with a private bath. Two decks are available for those who want a smoke or drink, and a large living room for getting-to-know-yous. Breakfast is included. TVs and phones are in common areas and the cottage. The Ivey House is also a good base for outdoor recreation (see canoeing and biking sections later in this chapter). **Note:** It's closed June through October.

107 Camellia St. ☎ *941-695-3299. Fax: 941/695-4155. Internet:* www.iveyhouse. com. *To get there: Off Hwy. 29, 1 block behind Circle K Convenience store. Parking: Free. Rack rates: $70 Jan–May ($125 cottage), $50–$55 Nov–Dec ($90 cottage). MC, V.*

The Everglades' Best Restaurants

As with places to stay, the Glades offer relatively few dining choices. If you're after some diversity, consider some of the Miami (Chapter 10) or Fort Myers/Naples (Chapter 17) dining options, or test your survival skills.

Capri Restaurant

$ Florida City   ITALIAN/AMERICAN

The main attractions at this fortresslike restaurant — open since 1958 — are pasta, local seafood, beef, and salads. The reasonably large portions of Italian fare come at a moderate price.

935 N. Krome Ave. ☎ *305-247-1542. Reservations accepted. To get there: It's just west of U.S. 1 off Hwy. 997 Main courses: $7–$18. AE, MC, V. Open: 11 a.m.–10 p.m., Mon–Thurs; till 11 p.m., Fri–Sat.*

Flamingo Lodge Restaurant

$$ **Flamingo SEAFOOD**

Located in Everglades National Park, the Flamingo Lodge Restaurant's views of Florida Bay complement a menu featuring shrimp scampi, steaks, chicken, pastas, and fresh fish served grilled, blackened, or fried. Sandwiches, salads, and conch chowder are the lighter luncheon fare. The prices are pretty reasonable.

1 Flamingo Lodge Hwy. ☎ *941-695-3101. Internet:* www.flamingolodge.com. *Reservations suggested. To get there: From U.S. 1 south of Miami, turn right on Palm Drive/Hwy. 9336/SW 344th St. and follow the signs to the park. Main courses: $11–$22. AE, DC, DISC, MC, V. Open: 7–10 a.m., 11:30 a.m.–3 p.m., 5:30–9 p.m., daily.*

Mutineer Restaurant

$$ **Florida City SEAFOOD/STEAK**

If you're a seafood freak, this is a good place to chow down. Fresh marine cuisine, including stuffed grouper, blackened snapper, and frog legs sautéed in garlic fill the menu. You can also order steaks, chicken, and ribs. There's a lunch buffet ($7.50, 11 a.m.–3 p.m., Mon–Sat), a kids' menu, and a petting zoo.

11 SE 1st Ave./U.S. 1. ☎ *305-245-3377. Internet:* www.mutineer.com. *Reservations aren't necessary. To get there: It's at the light just south of the Florida Turnpike. Main courses: $12–$27. AE, DC, DISC, MC, V. Open: 11 a.m.–10 p.m., daily.*

Oar House Restaurant

$ **Everglades City SEAFOOD**

This dinerlike establishment offers seafood baskets and regional specialties, including gator tail, turtle, and frog legs. Reasonable prices, a selection of cardiac-friendly options, and waitresses who call everyone "hon" make this a good place to stop for a bite.

305 Collier Ave. ☎ *941-695-3535. Reservations are a good idea in winter. To get there: It's south of U.S. 41/Tamiami Trail off Hwy. 29. Main courses: $8–$18. MC, V. Open: 6 a.m.–9 p.m. Mon–Sat, 6 a.m.–2 p.m. Sun.*

Exploring the Everglades

If you missed our hints earlier, glitter and glitz aren't expected to land in the Glades' region until Y3K. Just about everything to do in the Glades is natural or relates to nature. Although there are more places here to visit than most people realize, the headliner is (drum roll, please): Everglades National Park.

Everglades National Park

The park was dedicated by President Harry Truman in 1947, the same year Marjory Stoneman Douglas immortalized this corner of the world in her book, *The Everglades: River of Grass.* Douglas died in 1998 at 107, after dedicating her life to saving the Glades.

The park remains one of the few natural places to see endangered species, such as American crocodiles, West Indian manatees, and, on an incredibly rare evening or early morning, Florida panthers. Unfortunately, many of the park's creatures are in severe decline else-where — fewer than 50 panthers are alive in the wild today — so a trip here may be your only opportunity to catch a glimpse of this kind of wildlife.

Just the facts

Here are all the facts (wouldn't Sergeant Friday be proud?) you'll need to know before heading into the park:

- ✔ **Admission:** It's $10 per vehicle or $5 per person if you're on a motorcycle. Your admission pass is good for seven days. (Sorry, there's no shorter option.) Florida residents should consider get-ting an annual Everglades Park Pass ($20), and U.S. citizens 62 and over can snag a Golden Age Pass ($10) that's good for life.

- ✔ **Getting There:** Some of the park's northern reaches are accessible off U.S. 41/Tamiami Trail and Hwy. 29. You can get to its eastern and southern areas off State Road 9336, but much of the park has no easy access.

- ✔ **Information:** Write to **Everglades National Park,** 40001 Hwy. 9336, Homestead, FL 33034-6733, call ☎ **305-242-7700**, or visit `www. everglades.national-park.com` on the Internet.

- ✔ **Peak Season:** It runs from November through April.

- ✔ **Ranger Programs:** More than 50 programs are conducted during peak season, and cost nothing more than the standard park admission. Regular walking tours include **Glades Glimpses,** a 50-minute outing discovering some of the area's flora and fauna, and **Anhinga Ambles,** a similar walking program that lasts 20 minutes. Check ahead for schedules unless you want to do the miles of hiking and biking trails on your own.

- ✔ **Visitor Centers:** The park's five naturalist- and ranger-staffed cen-ters are

    - **Ernest F. Coe Visitor Center** (☎ **305-242-7700**), located at the main entrance to the park on Hwy. 9336, west of Florida City. It's open 8 a.m. to 5 p.m. daily.

- The **Royal Palm Visitor Center** (☎ 305-242-7700) is situated 4 miles west of the main entrance. It has a small nature museum and is open daily from 8 a.m. to 4 p.m.

- **The Flamingo Visitor Center** (☎ 941-695-3311), located 38 miles southwest of the main entrance on Hwy. 9336, offers interactive nature displays and exhibits. It's open daily from 8 a.m. to 5 p.m.

- The **Gulf Coast Visitor Center** (☎ 941-695-3311), at the western entrance to the park, in Everglades City off Hwy. 29, has exhibits on the local wildlife and offers information on boat tours. It's open daily from 7:30 a.m. to 5 p.m.

- The **Shark Valley Visitor Center** (☎ 305-221-8776), on U.S. 41/Tamiami Trail, 15 miles west of Hwy. 997, is in the northern reaches of the park. The small center is open daily 8:30 a.m. to 5:30 p.m.

Enjoying the park

Preparation is the key to a good experience in Everglades National Park. (The Boy Scouts really do know what they are talking about!) Here are a few things to keep in mind before you arrive:

✔ **Bike Rentals:** You can rent bikes at the **Shark Valley Tram Tours** (☎ 305-221-8455), adjacent to the Shark Valley Visitor Center (see "Just the facts" preceding this section), for $4.25 per hour.

✔ **Climate, Clothing and Mosquitoes:** The Everglades is mild and pleasant from December through April, though *rare* cold fronts may bring you face to face with chilly, 58-degree conditions. Summers are wire-to-wire hot and humid — 90 degrees and 90 percent humidity or *worse!* Afternoon thunderstorms are common, and the mosquitoes are ferocious, so bring repellent. Wear comfortable sportswear in winter; loose-fitting pants, long-sleeved shirts, and slap on the sunscreen in summer.

✔ **Supplies:** Bring your own water and snacks (they're not available in most areas), but keep in mind that snacks aren't allowed on the interpretive trails, which are marked for self-guided hikers.

Camping out

If you really want to get back to nature, try camping overnight in the Everglades. Three campgrounds have tent and RV sites, restrooms, and water but no electrical hookups. We hope you like your showers cold. All three sites are open year-round. To make reservations, call ☎ 800-365-2267 (U.S. only), 301-722-1257, or 888-530-9796 with a TDD for the hearing-impaired. Reservations should be made at least 30 days in advance. Sites are $14 nightly for a maximum of 8 people.

✔ **Long Pine Key Campground:** Seven miles from the main entrance, just off the main road, the campground has 108 drive-up sites for tents and RVs. There are restrooms, water, phones, a sewer dump station, and fresh-water fills but no showers. A nearby picnic area has fire grates. The camp also has a fishing pond, an amphitheater for winter programs, and several hiking trails.

✔ **Flamingo Campground:** Located at the end of the main park road in Flamingo, the campground has 234 drive-in sites, including 55 with a view of the water. There are cold-water showers, two dump stations, picnic tables, grills, and a public telephone. Flamingo has an observation tower, hiking and canoe trails, and a store with limited groceries and camping supplies.

✔ **Chekika:** Located 6 miles west of Krome Avenue/Hwy. 997 on SW 168th Street, southwest of Miami, Chekika has 20 sites for RVs and tents, with water basins for filling jugs, a dump station with a freshwater fill, hot showers, and a fishing pond.

Big Cypress National Preserve

Not as well known as its national-park neighbor, this preserve is a part of the larger, 2,400-square-mile Big Cypress Swamp, and home to an incredible array of wildlife, including alligators, bald eagles, black bears, wood storks, and rare Florida panthers. While a portion of the preserve is swampland, it also has dry prairies, marshes, sloughs, hardwood uplands, mangroves, and cypress forests. The preserve's name refers to the vast amount of cypresses that once blanketed the entire area. Loggers killed most of the virgin trees in the 1930s and 1940s. Those that remain are mainly dwarf pond cypresses, but you can still find the occasional 700-year-old bald cypress within the 728,000-acre sanctuary.

Big Cypress was established as a northwest buffer to Everglades National Park and includes the ancestral home of the Seminole and Miccosukee Indians. It's accessible from either coast via I-75/Alligator Alley (north) and U.S. 41/Tamiami Trail (south).

You will find Big Cypress rather lean on visitor amenities; this is true wilderness. So unless you're into roughing it, an afternoon of exploration will suffice.

Here are a few items that will help make your visit more enjoyable:

✔ **Admission:** It doesn't get much cheaper than free.

✔ **Information:** Call ☎ 941-695-4111, write to **Big Cypress National Preserve Headquarters,** HCR 61, Box 110, Ochopee, FL 34141, or surf over to www.nps.gov/bicy. Request a map and specialized information on the preserve.

- **Lodging and Camping Facilities:** Eight primitive campgrounds are available to the public, seven of which are free: Bear Island, Midway, Burns Lake, Monument, Loop Road, Pinecrest, and Mitchell's Landing. None have water or restrooms. Dona Drive Campground ($4 per night) has an RV dump station. Call the preserve's headquarters for more information on camping here.

- **Oasis Visitor Center:** It's located 20 miles east of Ochopee (55 miles east of Naples) on U.S. 41/Tamiami Trail. There's a 15-minute film about the preserve as well as exhibits on its flora and fauna. Pick up a free trail map here before heading into Big Cypress. It's open daily from 8:30 a.m. to 4:30 p.m.

- **Programs and Activities:** Ranger-led hikes, canoe trips, bike rides, and campfire programs at the campgrounds are offered during the winter season. If you go during the rainy season, prepare to hike through ankle-deep water on some of the trails.

- **Supplies:** As far away from civilization as you can get, the preserve has no stores, gas stations, or restaurants. Make sure to pack plenty of snacks and water, and fill up your tank before you set off.

Fakahatchee Strand State Park

Located in the area's southwest corner, this second preserve in the Big Cypress Swamp is something of a secret, but discovery may be just over the horizon. The Fakahatchee was Hollywood's choice for the upcoming screen version of *The Orchid Thief,* a nonfiction book based on the story of a man obsessed with poaching a rare flower. Some fear the book and movie will do for Fakahatchee what *Midnight in the Garden of Good and Evil* did for Savannah. That remains to be seen.

For now, the park is a long way from the big time. While Everglades National Park gets more than 1 million visitors a year, some 130,000 motorists drive through the Fakahatchee, but only a few stop to enjoy it. Part of the blame rests with the swamp's inhospitable nature. It's pretty wild and not easily accessible. To get here, the best route involves taking I-75/Alligator Alley from Naples or Fort Lauderdale, exiting on Hwy. 29 and going 14 miles south to the ranger station on Jane's Scenic Drive.

Searching for skunk apes

The Everglades' answer to Bigfoot and Yeti, Skunk Apes are supposed to be big, hairy, and very aromatic (imagine rotten eggs and fresh dung with a trace of road-kill skunk). Legend has it that these man-apes live in abandoned alligator dens, which would account for the smell and their muddy-brown appearance. The 7-foot, 300-pound (or more) creatures supposedly love lima beans. If all this sounds fascinating to you, just ask one of the many willing storytellers, but so far there's little proof of them or their lima-bean fixation.

Those who come will find bald cypresses, the largest stand of royal palms in North America, and ghost orchids along the 11-mile Jane's Scenic Drive, an improved dirt road. Visits near dawn and dusk may give you a glimpse of a black bear, bobcat, or Everglades mink, but don't count on it. Fox squirrels, wood storks, roseate spoonbills, snowy white egrets, and great blue herons are commonly observed. Stay on the main road and don't be tempted by those dirt spur roads that go to the swamp's wilder areas.

Considering the remoteness of the location, you won't find many visitor-oriented amenities here, but keep in mind the following:

- ✔ **Admission:** This is another freebie.

- ✔ **Information:** Call ☎ **941-695-4593,** write to P.O. Box 548, Copeland, FL 33926, or go to www.abfla.com/parks/ FakahatcheeStrand/fakahatchee.html.

- ✔ **Programs and Activities:** While this preserve is self-guided, there's a 2,000-foot boardwalk meandering through virgin cypress trees at Big Cypress Bend, which is about 3 miles west of Hwy. 29 on U.S. 41. From November through February, rangers lead swamp walks at 10 a.m., the third Saturday of the month. They're limited to 15 people, and reservations are required; call ☎ **941-695-4593** for more information or to make a reservation.

- ✔ **Supplies:** This is the boonies — bring plenty of food and water, and top off your gas tank before you arrive.

Collier-Seminole State Park

In the early 1940s, Barron Collier, a wealthy advertising executive and developer, laid the framework for a park that went into the state ledger in 1947. It's named for him and the tribe that has long made the area its home.

The park's 6,430 acres have a wealth of vegetation and wildlife common to the region. The rare royal palms, salt marshes, mangrove and cypress swamps, and pine flatwoods give it diversity. Its critters include brown pelicans, wood storks, bald eagles, red-cockaded woodpeckers, American crocodiles, black bears, and fox squirrels. Panthers, the state animal, and manatees, the state marine mammal, may also be seen (very occasionally).

The park also has fishing, boating, picnicking, canoeing, and several hiking trails. To get here, head for the entrance, 17 miles east of Naples on U.S. 41/Tamiami Trail.

Unlike the nature preserves, the park offers a bit more for visitors to see and do. If you decide to visit, keep the following in mind:

- **Admission:** $5 per vehicle.

- **Information:** Call ☎ **941-394-3397** or write to Collier-Seminole State Park, 20200 U.S. 41 S., Naples, FL 33961. Information is available online at www.dep.state.fl.us/parks/District_4/ CollierSeminole. Also, a Seminole-style log fort at the park's entrance houses a small information center.

- **Programs and Activities:** A 6.5-mile hiking trail winds through pine flatwoods and cypresses; a self-guided trail features a boardwalk system and observation platform overlooking the salt marsh. Rangers lead tours through the park from December to April. You can see plant and wildlife exhibits in the park's interpretive center. Boat tours down river ($8.50 for adults, $5.50 for kids 6 to 12 years) are available from a concessionaire.

Outdoors in the Everglades

This isn't theme-park central, but there are plenty of outdoor activities in the Everglades to keep you occupied.

Cycling enthusiasts should head for **Shark Valley Tram Tours** (☎ **305-221-8455**) in Everglades National Park (see the information on the Shark Valley Visitor Center in "Just the facts," earlier); it rents bikes for $4.25 per hour. The area has one of the top cycling venues in South Florida, a 17-mile loop that has no traffic except other peddlers. **Everglades City** has a 4-mile paved trail across the scenic causeway to Chokoloskee Island. You can rent wheels at **The Ivey House**, 107 Camellia St. (☎ **941-695-3299**), for $3 an hour and $15 a day from November to May.

If you want to go canoeing, Everglades National Park has four marked trails, 4 to 22 miles long, with starting points from the Flamingo area. You can also take on all or parts of the 99-mile Wilderness Waterway from Flamingo to Everglades City. Visitors' centers (see "Everglades National Park" earlier in this chapter) distribute maps. You can rent canoes at the **Flamingo Lodge, Marina & Outpost Resort** in Everglades National Park, at the southwest end of Hwy. 9336 (☎ **941-695-3101**; Internet: www. flamingolodge.com), for $8 an hour and $22 for a half day ($12 and $30, respectively, for a family-size model). **North American Canoe Tours,** 107 Camellia St., at the Ivey House in Everglades City (☎ **941-695-4666**), rents canoes for $25 a day (November to May). This outfitter also leads canoe tours starting at $40 a half day and $50 a full day.

The Everglades is not renowned for fishing. There are few guide services; the coast is so remote or inhospitable it discourages most surf fishermen. The shallow character of the Glades makes freshwater fishing frustrating.

Flamingo Lodge, Marina & Outpost Resort is the exception (☎ 941-695-3101; Internet: www.flamingolodge.com) in Everglades National Park. Several guides go after redfish, snook, tarpon, and trout out of the marina. An excursion costs $210 per half day for 2; $300 for a full day.

If you want a few more selections to choose from while you are in the Everglades area, we list some more fishing options in Chapter 17.

Organized Tours

Billie Swamp Safari, HC-61, Box 46, Clewiston, Florida 33440 (☎ 800-949-6101 or 941-983-6101; Internet: www.seminoletribe.com/safari) offers a unique way to see the landscape. The Seminole Tribe of Florida has opened some 2,000 acres of its Big Cypress Reservation to **eco-tours.** The tours include a ride in a swamp-buggy (a big truck with monster tires) over hardwood hammocks, wetlands, and sloughs that are home to white-tailed deer, bison, wild hogs, hawks, bald eagles, and alligators ($20 for adults, $10 for kids 6 to 12). You also can take an airboat ride ($10 adults) or watch a snake-and-alligator show ($8 for adults, $4 for kids). To get there from Naples or Fort Lauderdale, take I-75 to Exit 14; then go north 19 miles to the Big Cypress Seminole Indian Reservation.

Flamingo Lodge, Marina, & Outpost, at the southwest end of Hwy. 9336 in Everglades National Park (☎ 941/695-3101; Internet: www.flamingolodge.com), offers 2-hour back-country cruises ($16 for adults, $8 for kids 6 to 12) and 90-minute Florida Bay cruises ($10 for adults, $5 for kids 6 to 12), among other tours.

Wooten's, in Ochopee, 35 miles southwest of Naples on U.S. 41/Tamiami Trail (☎ 800-282-2781; Internet: www.wootens.com), conducts 30-minute airboat and swamp-buggy tours through the Glades ($13.50 ages 7 and up, free 6 and under). A combination ticket ($35) is good for both tours, an alligator show, and a self-guided tour of the animal exhibits.

Fast Facts

Area Code

It's 305 to the east and 941 to the west.

Hospitals

The nearest are **Homestead Hospital,** 160 N.W. 13th St., Homestead, FL (☎ 305-242-3535), and **Naples Community Hospital,** 350 7th St. N., Naples, FL (☎ 941-436-5111).

Information

For information on the area, contact the Everglades Area Chamber of Commerce (☎ 941-695-3941; Internet: www.florida-everglades.com). Although not particularly well designed, the Web site offers some valuable advice, including maps, fishing tips, event listings, and a wildlife photo gallery.

Mail

There are U.S. post offices at 301 Collier Ave. in Everglades City and 333 W. Palm Dr. in Homestead. To find a post office location anywhere in the United States, call ☎ **800-275-8777.**

Maps

Ask the Chamber of Commerce (see "Information" earlier in this section) for a detailed map, or, if you're renting a car, ask the rental agency for a map. You can also buy maps at some convenience stores for $3–$5.

Newspapers

The Naples Daily News (☎ **941-262-3161**; Internet: www.naplesnews.com), and the **Miami Herald** (☎ **305-350-2111**; Internet: www.herald.com) are the two major papers.

Pharmacies

There are **Walgreens** pharmacies at 861 NE 8th St. in Homestead (☎ **305-245-0395**) and at 12784 U.S. 41/Tamiami Trail in Naples (☎ **941-530-1356**).

Taxes

Florida's sales tax is 6 percent. Hotels here add another 3 percent.

Weather Updates

For a recording of current conditions and forecast reports, call the local office of the National Weather Service at ☎ **305-229-4522,** or check out the Web site: www.nws.noaa.gov. You can also get information by watching the Weather Channel on the Internet: www.weatherchannel.com.

Chapter 14

The Gold Coast

In This Chapter

▶ Traveling in the appropriate mode

▶ Planting yourself in the right places

▶ Finding a menu that fits your wallet

▶ Filling your days with the choicest spots

Miami refugees have to go somewhere. Many crash-land in Broward and Palm Beach Counties, just north of Miami on the east coast, also known as the upper Gold Coast. Add transplanted snowbirds and the millions of tourists who come to bask on some of Florida's most glamorous beaches, and the resulting explosion has builders desperately trying to satisfy the demand for more hotels, restaurants, shops, and attractions.

On the downside, of course, this means that Florida has another east coast landing zone with too many sweaty bodies. But you can find some relief and cut-rate deals if you come during the off-season, which runs from May through October.

Finding the Gold Coast's Attractions

Most of the action is close to the water. Start your voyage in Broward County at Hollywood's **World Fishing Center** and then float over to Fort Lauderdale, home of the **International Swimming Hall of Fame** as well as shopping venues, such as **Sawgrass Mills.**

Crossing the line into Palm Beach County, you can take the grand tour of Boca Raton; be sure to include the **International Museum of Cartoon Art.** Then you can move on to Palm Beach and West Palm Beach, the home of **Lion Country Safari.**

Note that the cities and towns on the Gold Coast are close enough in proximity that you can mix and match many of the restaurants and attractions.

Heads up, now. The rocket is primed.

Fort Lauderdale, Hollywood, and Beyond

When it comes to coastal development in Florida, the upper Gold Coast is second only to Miami. The beach highways (A1A/Ocean Blvd./Atlantic Blvd.) and U.S. 1 are well developed, offering many places to stay and eat, numerous things to do, and 23 miles of coast. On the quieter side, Hollywood is quaint but growing, sort of like Miami's South Beach without the tourist glut, parking fees, and attitude.

Getting there

An aerial attack is the easiest, quickest, and most economical way to get here from most places. Florida highways and rail service make car and train travel good secondary options, but the highway route is time consuming, and taking a train is virtually as expensive as buying an airline ticket.

By plane

Fort Lauderdale Hollywood International Airport (☎ 954-359-6100; Internet: www.co.broward.fl.us/fll.htm) is Florida's fourth largest airport, transporting almost 14 million passengers per year. Thirty-three domestic, foreign, and commuter airlines land here. **Avis, Budget, Dollar, National,** and **Royal** have rental-car desks in the lower-level baggage claim areas; other car-rental agencies are located nearby (see the "Quick Concierge" in the back of this book for telephone numbers and Web sites). Taxis and shuttles (see "Getting Around," a little later in this chapter) are on the same level. The same goes for **Tri-County Airport Express** (☎ 800-244-8252 or 954-561-8888), which offers several ride options, and limousine services, such as **Broward Limousine** (☎ 954-791-3000) and **Elite Limousine** (☎ 954-563-2122).

Here are sample rates from the airport to Fort Lauderdale Beach:

- ✔ **Taxi:** $14 to $18 for up to five
- ✔ **Limousine:** $65 for up to eight
- ✔ **Shuttle:** $7 to $11 per person

If you want an additional option, **Miami International Airport** (☎ 305-876-7000; Internet: www.miami-airport.com) is only an hour's drive south of Fort Lauderdale and welcomes more than 100 airlines, including 42 foreign carriers. Also, some airlines may offer discounts if you fly into one airport instead of another. So, if you're on a tight budget, check to see if you can reduce your airfare by flying into Miami instead of Fort Lauderdale.

By car

If you're coming from Florida's west coast, I-75 and U.S. 41/Tamiami Trial are your best choices. I-95 and Florida's Turnpike are the best routes to drive on from the east coast;. both require a 350- to 400-mile journey after you cross the Florida/Georgia line. U.S. 1 (East Coast) and U.S. 27 (West Coast) are additional options if you don't mind passing through small towns.

By train

 Amtrak (☎ **800-872-7245;** Internet: `www.amtrak.com`) runs two trains a day out of New York, but they take 28 to 30 hours to reach Fort Lauderdale. Amtrak rides from other cities, however, can take much longer.

The price of train travel in the United States isn't much better than the cost of airfare. If you want a sleeper car, the price is usually worse. Unless your heart is set on a train trip, you can most likely do better traveling in the air than on the ground. See Chapter 5 for more Amtrak information.

Getting around

If you stick to the tourist-friendly coastal cities and the areas immediately adjacent to them, you can find a number of user-friendly transportation options at your disposal.

By bus

Broward County Public Transit (☎ **954-357-8400;** Internet: `www.broward.org/bct/welcome.htm`) has 250 buses covering 30 routes. The fare is $1 for adults, 50 cents for seniors and kids taller than 40 inches (bring exact change). Buses run from 5:30 a.m. to 10 p.m., Monday through Saturday.

 If you stay on the beach and limit your goings, you can get away with using public transportation. Like many other Florida transit systems, however, Broward County's is designed for commuters, not tourists. Unless you really don't want to rent a car, we can't recommend this public transit system as an efficient way to get around the area.

By car

Less expensive than taking cabs and more efficient than public transit, driving is the best way to get around Fort Lauderdale. The main north-south routes are U.S. 1/Federal Highway, A1A/Ocean Boulevard on the beach side (for scenic reasons), and I-95 (for longer hauls). The primary east-west thoroughfares are I-595, Hallandale Beach Boulevard/Hwy. 858, Hollywood Boulevard/Hwy. 820, Sheridan Street/Hwy. 822, SW 24th

Street/Hwy. 84, Griffin Road/Hwy. 818, Broward Boulevard/Las Olas/Hwy. 842, Sunrise Boulevard/Hwy. 838, Oakland Park Boulevard/Hwy. 816, and Commercial Boulevard/Hwy. 870.

If you plan on driving around, invest in a map (see "Maps" in "Fast Facts" at the end of this section on Fort Lauderdale). That said, the Fort Lauderdale grid is pretty simple to navigate; traffic, except during rush hour, isn't particularly nasty. Most streets have numbers, but names are given to the main thoroughfares, such as those that run from the west to the beaches and back. The exception is the 17th Street Causeway, which is the east-west road that leads to Port Everglades, a major shipping and cruise port, before turning north into A1A (the road that travels along the beach). All the major streets, except Broward, run across bridges over the Intracoastal Waterway.

Although numbered streets grow consecutively between named boulevards, you can find some exceptions. For the most part, however, Andrews Avenue divides the city between east and west, and Broward Boulevard divides north and south. Streets run east and west; avenues run north and south. Also, all addresses are assigned to one of four quadrant designations: NE, NW, SE, and SW. A street address that's NE is north of Broward Boulevard and east of Andrews Avenue.

By taxi

Taxi fares for up to five passengers are $2.45 for the first mile and $1.75 for each additional mile. The biggest cab company in the area is **Yellow Cab/Checker** (☎ **954-565-5400**).

Unless you happen to be at a major hotel, hailing a taxi can be next to impossible; so call ahead.

By train

Tri-Rail (☎ **800-874-7245** or 954-942-7245) is a 67-mile commuter line that connects Palm Beach, Broward, and Miami-Dade Counties. As is often the case, this public transit line isn't very tourist friendly. Six commuter stations are located in the Greater Fort Lauderdale area. Round-trip fares range from $3.50 to $9.25.

By trolley

Beach Trolley (☎ **954-946-7320**) offers a narrated sightseeing tour, as well as daylong shuttle service to 25 or so shops, restaurants, and attractions along A1A. Available from 9 a.m. to 5 p.m. on weekdays, the tour and the shuttle cost $10 each. Maps and pickup service are available at most major hotels.

By water taxi

The upper Gold Coast is one of the few places in the United States where you can call a taxi and have a boat pick you up. The marine highway is the Intracoastal Waterway. In addition to sightseeing, the boat stops include boutiques and eateries along Las Olas Boulevard.

Water Taxi of Fort Lauderdale (☎ 954-467-0008) sells one-way tickets for $7.50, round-trippers for $14, and a day pass for $16. Taking a water taxi is cheaper than renting a car, as long as you want to stay in its service area. Water taxis run from 10 a.m. until midnight on weekdays and until 2 a.m. on weekends.

Staying in the Fort Lauderdale Area

Fort Lauderdale's beach zone is teeming with hotels and motels in every style, size, and price range. (See the map for an overview of "Fort Lauderdale" later in this chapter.) If you are on a tight budget, look for a hotel in Hollywood, where rates are often cheaper. Many accommodations let kids under 12 years (and sometimes under 18) stay free if you don't exceed the maximum-room occupancy. To be safe, though, ask when booking a room.

Sales and hotel taxes add 11 percent to your bill. Also note that winter (December to April) is peak season, and rates can be 50 percent higher than during the rest of the year.

If you are traveling during high season and can't find a room that you're happy with, or you don't want to deal directly with the hotels, you can choose from two good booking services. The **Central Reservation Service** (☎ 800-555-7555; Internet: www.reservationservice. com), and **Florida Hotel Network** (☎ 800-538-3616; Internet: www. floridahotels.com) will make lodging arrangements after you tell them your needs.

The area's best hotels

Best Western Pelican Beach Resort

$$ Fort Lauderdale Beach

This beachfront hotel's 110 units include standard rooms, efficiencies, and one-bedroom suites with kitchens. The rooms are clean and comfortable; those with an ocean view cost more. A free continental breakfast buffet is part of the package.

2000 N. Atlantic Blvd./A1A. ☎ *800-525-6232 or 954-568-9431. Fax: 954-565-2622. Internet:* www.introweb.com/pelican. *To get there: It's on A1A, less than 1 mile south of Oakland Park Boulevard. Parking: Free. Rack rates: $100–$210 Dec–Apr, $75–$120 May–Nov. AE, CB, DC, DISC, MC, V.*

Fort Lauderdale

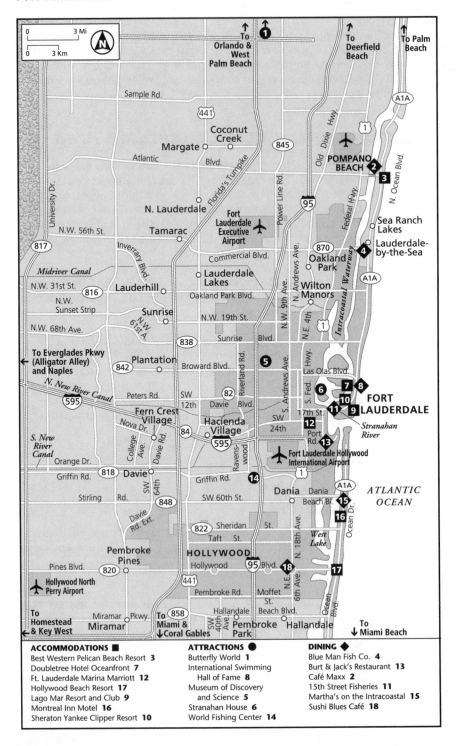

ACCOMMODATIONS ■
Best Western Pelican Beach Resort **3**
Doubletree Hotel Oceanfront **7**
Ft. Lauderdale Marina Marriott **12**
Hollywood Beach Resort **17**
Lago Mar Resort and Club **9**
Montreal Inn Motel **16**
Sheraton Yankee Clipper Resort **10**

ATTRACTIONS ●
Butterfly World **1**
International Swimming
  Hall of Fame **8**
Museum of Discovery
  and Science **5**
Stranahan House **6**
World Fishing Center **14**

DINING ◆
Blue Man Fish Co. **4**
Burt & Jack's Restaurant **13**
Café Maxx **2**
15th Street Fisheries **11**
Martha's on the Intracoastal **15**
Sushi Blues Café **18**

Doubletree Hotel Oceanfront

$$ Fort Lauderdale Beach

This hotel's great location off the Intracoastal Waterway affords guests easy access to the beach, shops, and nightlife along Las Olas Boulevard. All 230 rooms come with a good assortment of amenities and have a view of the ocean or the skyline and Stranahan River. A fitness center and restaurant are also onsite.

440 Seabreeze Blvd./A1A. ☎ *800-222-8733 or 954-524-8733. Fax: 954-467-7386. Internet:* www.doubletreeoceanfront.com. *To get there: It's just south of Las Olas on A1A. Parking: self $9 per day. Rack rates: $179–$239 Oct–Apr, $109–$179 May–Sept. AE, CB, DC, DISC, MC, V.*

Fort Lauderdale Marina Marriott

$$ Fort Lauderdale Riverfront

Located right off the Intracoastal Waterway, about a mile from the beaches, this resort's 580 rooms offer patios or balconies. In addition to a large selection of in-room amenities, the hotel has numerous recreational facilities, a 32-slip marina, two restaurants, a health club, sauna, and whirlpool.

1881 SE 17th St. ☎ *800-433-2254 or 954-463-4000. Fax: 954-527-6705. Internet:* www.marriotthotels.com/FLLFL. *To get there: It's riverfront on A1A, 1 mile east of U.S. 1. Parking: $5 self, $8 valet per day. Rack rates: $179–$259 Dec–Apr, $129–$189 May–Nov. AE, CB, DC, DISC, MC, V.*

Hollywood Beach Resort Hotel

$$ Hollywood Beach

This 1920s resort lacks warmth, and the facilities are pretty basic. The hotel's location and price, however, make it a good choice for many travelers. All accommodations, from small studios to one-bedroom suites, have fully equipped kitchens and views of the Atlantic Ocean or Intracoastal Waterway. Laundry facilities are available onsite.

101 N. Ocean Dr./A1A. ☎ *800-331-6103 or 954-921-0990. Fax: 954-920-9480. Internet:* www.florida.com/hollywoodbeach. *To get there: It's on Ocean Dr./A1A, just south of Hollywood Blvd. Parking: Valet only, $9/day. Rack rates: $114–$220 Dec–Apr, $78–$159 May–Nov. AE, DC, DISC, MC, V.*

Lago Mar Resort and Club

$$$ Fort Lauderdale Beach

Located in the Harbor Beach area, this family-oriented hotel has a mix of traditional rooms and suites, many with balconies and views, and some with kitchens. It has four pools (one is a palm-lined lagoon), mini golf, two tennis courts, a kids' playground, and four restaurants. During traditional school vacation times, the hotel offers many supervised activities for children.

1700 S. Ocean Dr./A1A. ☎ *877-524-6627 or 954-523-6511. Fax: 954-524-6627. Internet:* www.lagomar.com. *To get there: From 17th St. Bridge, go east to where A1A turns north along ocean. Parking: Free. Rack rates: $125–$210 ($185–$480 suites) Nov, $195–$245 ($305–$685 suites) Dec–Apr, $115–$150 ($150–$380 suites) May–Oct. AE, CB, DISC, MC, V.*

Montreal Inn Motel

$ **Hollywood**

Cut from very basic cloth, the Montreal offers clean, affordable rooms, efficiencies, and one-bedroom apartments. The Montreal Inn is not the Ritz, but this motel is a safe bet for those on a tight budget. The beach is 100 paces due east, and several restaurants are a few blocks away.

324 Balboa St. ☎ *954-925-4443. Fax: 954-926-7487. Internet:* www.montrealinn. com. *To get there: Between A1A and the ocean off Sheridan Avenue. Parking: Free, self. Rack rates: $66–$93 Dec–Mar, $43–$73 Dec–Apr. AE, DISC, MC, V.*

Sheraton Yankee Clipper Resort

$$ **Fort Lauderdale Beach**

This longtime resident is worth seeing if only to reminisce about its heyday in the '50s and '60s. Should you decide to stay, the resort's 501 rooms are decorated in a tropical fashion and equipped with all the modern comforts. The resort has three pools, has a fitness center, and offers several kids' programs.

1140 Seabreeze Blvd./A1A. ☎ *800-958-5551 or 954-524-5551. Fax: 954-523-5376. Internet:* www.sheratonclipper.com. *To get there: On A1A 2½ miles south of Sunrise. Parking: $5 self, $8 valet. Rack rates: $159–$239 Dec–Apr, $99–$149 May–Aug, $129–$199 Sept–Nov. AE, CB, DC, DISC, MC, V.*

Runner-up accommodations

If you can't find lodging in the previous listings to satisfy your tastes and budget, here are a few more places to consider:

The Bahama Hotel

$ **Fort Lauderdale Beach** This modest hotel has a yesterday's beach feel and offers decent rooms and efficiencies, a gym, and a good onsite restaurant. *401 N. Atlantic Blvd./A1A.* ☎ *800-622-9995 or 954-467-7315. Fax: 954-467-7319. Internet:* www.bahamahotel.com).

Beau Rivage Beach Resort

$ Fort Lauderdale Beach   This small property offers rooms, efficiencies, and 1- and 2-bedroom apartments in a nicely landscaped setting. *2025 N. Ocean Blvd./A1A. ☎ 800-901-0111 or 954-563-4577. Fax: 954-563-4588. Internet:* www.ssl-online.com/beaurivage.

Hyatt Regency Pier Sixty-Six

$$$ Fort Lauderdale   This luxury resort offers 388 rooms with balconies, a full range of recreational activities and facilities, a spa, and a 142-slip marina on the Stranahan River. *2301 SE 17th St./A1A. ☎ 800-633-7313 or 954-525-6666. Fax: 954-728-3551. Internet:* www.hyatt.com.

Dining out in the Fort Lauderdale Area

Much like Miami, Broward County has virtually any kind of cuisine you can imagine. The largest collection of restaurants in town is along Las Olas Boulevard. Seafood is, not surprisingly, a good bet in this area.

Don't forget to add 6 percent local sales tax to your budget.

If you have a car, try some of the Palm Beach-area restaurants described later in this chapter or the Miami restaurants in Chapter 10.

The area's best restaurants

Blue Moon Fish Co.

$$ Lauderdale-by-the-Sea   CONTINENTAL/SEAFOOD

Weather permitting, dine al fresco and watch the yachts glide by on the Intracoastal Waterway or eat in the art-deco dining room of this casually elegant restaurant. The open kitchen dishes out excellent seafood, such as sea bass in a macadamia-nut crust and oak-roasted swordfish. A raw bar and a nice wine list are available, too.

4405 W. Tradewinds Ave., Lauderdale-by-the-Sea. ☎ 954-267-9888. Internet: www.bluemoonfishco.com. *Reservations suggested. To get there: On the Intracoastal, north of Commercial Blvd. Main courses: $19–$29. AE, MC, V. Open: 11:30 a.m.–3 p.m. daily; 6–10 p.m. Sun–Thurs, 6–11 p.m. Fri–Sat.*

Burt & Jack's Restaurant

$$$ Port Everglades/Fort Lauderdale   STEAKS/SEAFOOD

This waterfront restaurant, housed in a Mediterranean-style villa, offers fine — and smoke-free — dining in a semiformal setting. (Guys must wear jackets.) Specialties include rack of lamb, steaks, veal and pork chops, scallops, broiled swordfish, sautéed mahi-mahi, and Maine lobsters — at three pounds and up — that bust the price chart.

Berth 23, Port Everglades. ☎ 954-522-5225. Internet: www.burtandjacks.com. *Reservations urged. To get there: take I-595 east to the end; then follow signs to Port Everglades. Main courses: $15–$35. AE, MC, V. Open: 5–10 p.m. nightly.*

Cafe Maxx

$$$ Pompano Beach   SEAFOOD/FLORIBBEAN

Chef Oliver Saucy's award-winning restaurant offers global cuisine in a contemporary setting. Home-grown vittles don't get much better than the sweet-onion crusted yellowtail snapper in Madeira sauce or the Indonesian-spiced wahoo and shrimp. Landlubbers can feast on duck in sweet-and-sour pineapple sauce. If you want to eat here on a weekend, reserve a cozy booth well in advance

2601 E. Atlantic Blvd. ☎ 954-782-0606. Internet: www.cafemaxx.com. *Reservations suggested. To get there: Just east of U.S. 1, across from a Publix Supermarket. Main courses: $22–$32. AE, MC, V. Open: 5:30–10:30 p.m. Mon–Sat, 5:30–10 p.m. Sun.*

15th Street Fisheries

$$$ Fort Lauderdale   SEAFOOD

Open for more than 20 years, this restaurant offers a winning combination of fresh Florida seafood, friendly service, and great views of the Stranahan River. Ignore the exotic dishes (kangaroo and ostrich) and stick to such local favorites as tuna mignon, sautéed snapper, dolphin Oscar, lemon scallops, stuffed flounder, alligator, or stone crabs (in season October to May).

1900 SE 15th St. ☎ 954-763-2777. Internet: www.15streetfisheries.com. *Reservations accepted. To get there: I-595 east to U.S. 1, left 1½ miles to 15th, right to end of street. Main courses: $15–$38. AE, MC, V. Open: 5–9 p.m. Sun–Thurs, 5–10:30 p.m. Fri–Sat.*

Martha's on the Intracoastal

$$$ Hollywood   CONTINENTAL

The dress code in the Tropical Grille upstairs is much more casual than in the dining room below, but the formal Supper Club, down the stairs, offers live musical entertainment. Both dining rooms offer a sexy menu of New World cuisine, including veal loin medallions, roast duckling, rack of lamb, horseradish-roasted salmon, and scrumptious seafood cioppino. The restaurant also offers a popular Sunday brunch and has a great wine list.

6024 N. Ocean Dr. ☎ 954-923-5444. Internet: www.marthasrestaurant.com. *Reservations suggested. To get there: On A1A between Dania Boulevard Bridge*

and Sheridan. Main courses: $18–$32. AE, MC, V. Open: 11:30 a.m.–3 p.m. and 4 p.m.–midnight daily.

Sushi Blues Café

$$ Hollywood NEW JAPANESE

Any restaurant that survives more than 10 years in South Florida is doing things right. This small storefront eatery is the place to try something out of the ordinary, such as sake-steamed salmon, snapper in a wasabi-dijon-herb crust, or chicken stuffed with crab, asparagus, and cheese. The Sushi Blues Band performs here on Friday and Saturday (see Sushi Blues again later under "Living the Nightlife" later in this chapter).

1836 S. Young Circle. ☎ *954-929-9560. Internet:* www.sushiblues.com. *Reservations recommended. To get there: From Hollywood Boulevard, go south on Young Circle; it's on the right. Main courses: $14–$30. AE, MC, V. Open: 6 p.m.–midnight Sun–Thurs, 6 p.m.–2 a.m. Fri–Sat.*

Runner-up restaurants

If you're after more options, try one or more of these spots.

Chez Porky's

$ Pompano Beach This inexpensive choice serves mainly Cajun fare, including spicy sautéed shrimp and bourbon-soaked steaks. *105 SW 6th St.* ☎ *954-946-5590.*

The Left Bank

$$$ Fort Lauderdale This attractive restaurant tempts diners with Provençal-style cuisine and an award-winning wine list. *214 SE 6th Ave.* ☎ *954-462-5376. Internet:* www.theleftbank.com.

Samba Room

$$ Fort Lauderdale This Cuban bar and cafe offers up Latin-Fusion cuisine and such traditional treats as arroz con pollo and paella. *350 E. Las Olas Blvd.* ☎ *954-468-2000. Internet:* www.ftlauderdalenow.com/Samba.html.

Exploring Fort Lauderdale, Hollywood, and Beyond

Despite the upper Gold Coast's size and tenure as a tourist destination, relatively few attractions are here. The beaches, however, more than make up for the lack of sights.

Seeing the top attractions

Butterfly World

Coconut Creek

Here's your chance to walk among a bazillion or so butterflies and hummingbirds. (Can you feel a Hitchcock moment coming?) Butterfly World also boasts a botanical garden, breeding lab, and museum — a final resting place for those not quick enough to beat the nets. Allow 1 to 2 hours if you're into color and garden critters.

3600 W. Sample Road. ☎ *954-977-4400. Internet:* www.introweb.com/butterfly. *To get there: 4 miles west of I-95. Mon–Sat, 1–5 p.m. Sun. Admission: $10 adults, $5 kids 4–12. Open: 9 a.m.–5 p.m.*

International Swimming Hall of Fame

Fort Lauderdale

This is a neat tribute to aquatic heroes, including the definitive Tarzan, Olympian, and charter-member Johnny Weissmuller; seven-time (1972) Olympic champ Mark Spitz; and former lifeguard and collegiate swimming team captain, President Ronald Reagan. There's an interactive area, two swimming pools, a theater, photos galore, and artifacts dating to the 1500s. Allow 1½ to 2 hours.

1 Hall of Fame Drive. ☎ *954-462-6536. Internet:* www.ishof.org. *To get there: 1 block west of A1A, 1 block south of Las Olas. Admission: $5 families or $3 adults, $1 kids and seniors. Open: 9 a.m.–7 p.m. daily.*

Museum of Discovery and Science

Fort Lauderdale

Children and adults alike enjoy this *infotaining* experience. Allow 3 to 4 hours to see the museum's scientific playground, space-flight simulator, ecology area with living turtles and sharks, virtual volleyball game, Internet area, and five-story IMAX theater.

401 SW 2nd St. ☎ *954-467-6637. Internet:* www.mods.org. *To get there: Take Broward Boulevard east to 5th, right to the garage. Admission: $8.50 adults, $7.50 kids and seniors including IMAX, $6 and $5 without. Open: 10 a.m.–5 p.m. Mon–Sat, noon–5 p.m. Sun.*

Stranahan House

Fort Lauderdale

Built in 1901 as a trading post, Stranahan House is the city's oldest standing structure and an example of Florida-frontier architecture. This is a pleasant way to spend an hour or so if you're a museum or architecture buff; otherwise skip it.

335 SE 6th Ave. ☎ *954-524-4736. Internet:* www.stranahanhouse.com. *To get there: It's on 6th at Las Olas. Admission: $5 adults, $2 kids under 12. Open: 10 a.m.–4 p.m. Wed–Sat, 1–4 p.m. Sun.*

World Fishing Center

Dania Beach

It may smell a little fishy, but if you're one of America's 60 million rod-and-reelers, you'll think that you're in angler's heaven. The 32-million-dollar complex includes a Fishing Hall of Fame, an honor roll of folks who caught the really big ones, and a collection of vintage lures. Fishing fans will spend at least 2 hours here.

If the World Fishing Center baits your hook, drop in next door at **Bass Pro Shops Outdoor World** (☎ **954-929-7710;** Internet: www.outdoor-world.com), where a 160,000-square-foot showroom sells fishing, hunting, boating, and golfing goodies.

300 Gulf Stream Way. ☎ *954-927-2628. Internet:* www.igfa.org. *To get there: Go west of I-95 on Griffin Road to Anglers Ave. and south. Admission: $9 adults, $7 seniors, $5 kids 6–12. Open: 10 a.m.–6 p.m. daily.*

Visiting more cool sights

Beyond the first tier, Fort Lauderdale offers many other sights, including some items that will appeal to folks with special interests.

Baseball and spring training

The **Baltimore Orioles** (☎ **954-776-1921**) train at Fort Lauderdale Stadium, 5901 NW 12th Ave. Tickets cost $6 to $12. Workouts begin in mid-February, and games are played during March.

Beaches

Broward County's coastline has 23 miles of beaches, the best of which is **Hollywood Beach,** extending from Sheridan to Georgia Streets. Hollywood Beach appeals to sassy teens, growing families, and brazen tourists (as well as locals) willing to hide things in a string bikini or less. This area also has a 3-mile boardwalk lined with T-shirt and souvenir shacks, mini-golf places, snack bars, and panhandlers. **Fort Lauderdale Beach** has similar expanses as well as the recently renovated **Promenade,** a dining, nightlife, and retail complex on A1A between Las Olas and Sunrise Boulevards.

Fishing

The saltwater pickings are the same farther south: redfish, trout, snook, mackerel, sailfish, grouper, and snapper. Charters for small groups (up to four people) inshore begin at about $275 for a half day, $425 for a full day; deep-sea excursions are about double that. Rates on large party boats start at $35 per half day, $50 for a full day. **Action Sportfishing** (☎ 954-423-8700; Internet: www.actionsportfishing. com) and **Hillsboro Inlet Marina** (☎ 954-943-8222) are a couple of the area's more notable outfitters.

Golfing

More than 50 golf courses offer tee times to the public in the Fort Lauderdale area. For information on golfing in the region, surf over to www.golf.com and www.floridagolfing.com. If you're getting information the old-fashioned way, request course information from the **Florida Sports Foundation** (☎ 850-488-8347) or **Florida Golfing** (☎ 877-222-4653).

Here is a small sampling of the courses available in the area:

- ✔ The **Carolina Club,** 3011 Rock Island Rd., Margate (☎ 954-753-4000), has a par-72 course with tough water hazards and a lot of doglegs. Greens fees are $66 to $85 in the winter and $25 to $40 in the summer.

- ✔ The **Crystal Lake Country Club,** 3800 Crystal Lake Dr., Pompano Beach (☎ 954-943-2902) offers a fun-but-forgiving course with narrow fairways. Greens fees are $41 to $65 during the winter and $25 to $40 in summer.

- ✔ **Hillcrest Golf Club,** 4600 Hillcrest Dr., Hollywood (☎ 954-983-3142) is one of the area's prettiest courses and has an island green on the ninth hole. Greens fees are $41 to $65 during winter and $25 to $40 in summer.

Touring

Beach Trolley, ☎ 954-946-7320, operates a 90-minute, narrated sightseeing tour as well as a daylong shuttle service to 25 or more restaurants, shops, and attractions along A1A. Both tours cost $10 each and run from 9 a.m. to 5 p.m. weekdays. Pickup service is available at most major hotels.

Several companies offer waterfront cruises. **Jungle Queen,** 801 Seabreeze Blvd./A1A in Bahia Mar Marina, Fort Lauderdale (☎ 954-462-5596; Internet: www.junglequeen.com), runs 3-hour sightseeing ($11.50) and 4-hour dinner cruises ($25.95 adults, $13.75 kids 4 to 12) aboard a riverboat. **Riverfront Cruises,** 301 SW 1st Ave., Fort Lauderdale (☎ 954-267-3699; Internet: www.riverfrontcruises. com), uses motor yachts for 90-minute tours on New River and the Intracoastal Waterway ($14).

Water Taxi of Fort Lauderdale (☎ 954-467-0008) travels the Intracoastal Waterway. In addition to sightseeing, the water taxi stops at boutiques and eateries along Las Olas Boulevard. One-way tickets are $7.50, round-trippers are $14, and an all-day pass is $16. You can call for pickup or hail one from 10 a.m. until midnight on weekdays, until 2 a.m. on weekends.

Shopping

Fort Lauderdale has the same kind of shops and malls that you can find in most major cities. Most stores are open from 10 a.m. to 6 p.m. from Monday through Saturday, and from noon to 5 p.m. on Sunday. Those shops located in malls and major shopping centers keep their doors open as late as 9 or 10 p.m., except on Sunday.

Hitting the best shopping areas

- ✔ **Antique Row:** Hundreds of shops line Dania's *old stuff* district on Federal Highway/U.S. 1, just south of the airport. Most upscale shops are overpriced, but some smaller ones offer bargains.

- ✔ **Hallandale Beach Boulevard:** You can find deep discounts on off-brand shoes, bags, and jewelry in a string of stores east of Dixie Highway and the railroad tracks.

- ✔ **Las Olas Boulevard:** Bargains are hard to find here, but this is arguably Fort Lauderdale's trendiest shopping area. Hundreds of boutiques, galleries, and restaurants can keep you browsing and buying at least for a full day along Las Olas.

Shopping at the next best spots

Mall shopping may very well be the favorite local sport, and a number of excellent places can bust your bank account. **Broward Mall,** 8000 W. Broward Blvd., Plantation (☎ **954-473-8100**) has 120 stores with such anchors as Burdines, Sears, and JCPenney. **The Galleria,** 2414 E. Sunrise Blvd., Fort Lauderdale (☎ **954-564-1036**) offers Neiman Marcus, Lord & Taylor, Saks, Dillard's, and 150 other shops. Bargain hunters should head for **Sawgrass Mills,** Flamingo Road at W. Sunrise Blvd. in Sunrise (☎ **800-356-4557** or 954-846-2300). The largest outlet mall in the world, Sawgrass Mills sports 270 outlet stores, including Neiman Marcus, Ann Taylor, Saks, and DKNY.

Living the Nightlife

If you're still hankering for some action after a day at the beach, you can find plenty after the sun goes down. Fort Lauderdale is home to hundreds of bars and clubs that cater to a wide range of tastes. In addition to the hot spots listed in the following sections, check out Friday's entertainment section in the local newspaper, the *Sun-Sentinel.* Tickets for specific events, concerts, plays, and other performances can be booked through **Ticketmaster,** (☎ **954-523-3309;** Internet: www.ticketmaster. com).

Bars

Most of the large, modern hotels have lounges that liven up after dark. A particularly good one is the **Pier Top Lounge** (☎ **954-525-6666**) in the Hyatt Regency Pier Sixty-Six at 2301 SE 17th St. (A1A and 17th Street

Causeway). Live jazz can be heard from Tuesday through Saturday at 9 p.m. Other popular watering holes include **Crabby Jack's,** 1015 S. Federal Hwy./U.S. 1, Deerfield Beach (☎ **954-429-3770**); **Durty Harry's,** 3214 E. Atlantic Blvd./A1A, Pompano Beach (☎ **954-783-7060**); and **River Rock Cafe,** 2528 N. Federal Hwy./U.S. 1, Fort Lauderdale (☎ **954-537-3527**).

Clubs

The **Iguana Cantina,** 300 SW 1st Ave., Fort Lauderdale (☎ **954-527-6601;** Internet: www.iguanacantina.com) has dancing parties, ladies' nights, and more. The cover ranges from $2 to $10, depending on the event. **O'Hara's Pub and Jazz Cafes,** 722 E. Las Olas Blvd., Fort Lauderdale (☎ **954-524-1764**), and 1903 Hollywood Blvd., Hollywood (☎ **954-925-2555;** Internet: www.heatbeat.com/oharasjazzcafe.html), are moody clubs with live music. You pay anywhere from $3 to $12 as a cover. **Sushi Blues,** 1836 S. Young Circle, Hollywood (☎ **954-929-9560;** Internet: www.sushiblues.com.), has live jazz and blues on Friday and Saturday nights. The cover is usually $10.

Music venues

The **Broward Center for Performing Arts,** 201 SW 5th Ave., Fort Lauderdale (☎ **800-564-9539** or 954-462-0222) has large and small theaters that feature everything from comedy and drama to jazz and opera.

Fort Lauderdale and Hollywood in 2 Days

If you don't have a car, you can still see the sights by using one of the companies listed under the "Touring" section earlier in this chapter. On **Day 1,** get acquainted with the area by taking the **Beach Trolley** or **Riverfront Cruises** sightseeing tour, do lunch at **Mark's Las Olas,** and then visit the **International Swimming Hall of Fame.** If you have kids or a young heart, finish the day at the **Museum of Discovery and Science.** Try **Burt & Jack's** for dinner; then unwind a little at **O'Hara's Pub and Jazz Cafe.** Spend most of **Day 2** using the **Water Taxi of Fort Lauderdale** as your vehicle to discover the boutiques, galleries, and restaurants on **Las Olas Boulevard,** where you can ad lib lunch. Go Cuban for dinner at the **Samba Room.** If you have a car, take a midafternoon detour to **Hollywood Beach** and its boardwalk, bringing a change of clothes so you can feast at **Sushi Blues.** (If it's Friday or Saturday, stick around for the jazz and blues.)

If you're looking to lengthen your itinerary and broaden your range, see "Palm Beach County in 3 Days," later in this chapter, or check out the touring-Miami options in Chapter 11.

Fast Facts

Area Code

The local area code is **954**.

American Express

There's an office at 3312 NE 32nd St., Fort Lauderdale (☎ **954-565-9481**).

Doctors

You can get referrals from the Broward County Medical Association at ☎ **954-714-9477**.

Hospitals

Florida Medical Center, 5000 W. Oakland Park Blvd., Fort Lauderdale (☎ **954-735-6000**); **Broward General Medical Center**, 1600 S. Andrews Ave., Fort Lauderdale (☎ **954-776-6000**); **Memorial Regional Hospital**, 3501 Johnson St., Hollywood (☎ **954-987-2000**); **University Hospital and Medical Center**, 7201 N. University Dr., Tamarac (☎ **954-721-2200**).

Information

Contact the **Greater Fort Lauderdale Convention & Visitors Bureau**, 1850 Eller Dr., Fort Lauderdale (☎ **800-227-8669**, 800-356-1662, or 954-765-4466; Internet: www. sunny.org.)

Internet Access

You'll find several listings in the Yellow Pages including **Cybernation**, 2635 E. Oakland Park Blvd., Fort Lauderdale (☎ **954-630-0223**), and **Hard Drive Cafe**, 1942 Hollywood Blvd., Hollywood (☎ **954-929-3324**).

Mail

There are U.S. post offices are located at 6240 W. Oakland Park Blvd., Fort Lauderdale, and 1801 Polk St., Hollywood. To find a location near your hotel, call ☎ **800-275-8777**.

Maps

The information source in this section is a great ones to hit up for maps before or after you land. Rental-car agencies are another good source (including those at the airport), and so are convenience stores, which sell maps for $3–$5.

Newspapers

The **Sun-Sentinel** (☎ **954-356-4000**) publishes its entertainment section on Friday.

Pharmacies

Local 24-hour pharmacies include **Walgreens**, 2355 NE 26th St., Fort Lauderdale (☎ **954-561-3880**), and **Eckerd**, 1701 E. Commercial Blvd., Fort Lauderdale (☎ **954-771-0660**).

Taxes

State sales tax is 6 percent. Hotels add 5 percent for a total of 11 percent.

Taxis

Generally, it's $2.45 for first mile, $1.75 per additional mile. The major company is Yellow Cab/Checker (☎ **954-565-5400**).

Transit Info

Broward County Public Transit (☎ **954-357-8400**), charges $1 for adults, 50 cents for seniors and kids over 40 inches (bring exact change).

Weather Updates

For a recording of current conditions and forecast reports, call the local office of the **National Weather Service** at ☎ **305-229-4522**, or check out its Web site at www. nws.noaa.gov. You also can get information by watching the **Weather Channel** (Internet: www.weatherchannel.com).

Palm Beach, West Palm Beach, and Boca Raton

The ritzy reputations of Palm Beach and Boca, the playgrounds of the Pulitzers, Rockefellers, and Kennedys, may be enough to scare away budget-conscious travelers. But these areas have changed a great deal in the last quarter of a century. While the wealthy still winter here, they no longer own the franchise, and affordable places have grown up around them. As we show you in the next several pages, Palm Beach and Boca offer plenty of cool, and relatively cheap, things to do.

Getting there

Unless you don't mind a long car or train ride, flying here is your best bet. Modern interstate highways and rail lines do, however, make car and train travel secondary options.

By plane

Palm Beach International Airport (☎ **561-471-7412;** Internet: www.pbia.org) welcomes 16 domestic carriers and Air Canada and serves about 6 million passengers a year. **Alamo, Avis, Budget, Dollar, Enterprise, Hertz,** and **National** rental-car agencies are stationed on level one. Hotel shuttles and taxis also depart from level one.

Fort Lauderdale-Hollywood International Airport (☎ **954-359-6100;** Internet: www.co.broward.fl.us/fll.htm) is a second option and has about double the airlines that Palm Beach does.

See the "Quick Concierge" in the back of the book for more information on airlines and rental-car companies.

By car

I-75 and U.S. 41 invade from the west. I-95 and Florida's Turnpike are the best routes to use when driving in from the north. If you're on a tight budget, use I-95 because the turnpike's tolls are high. (You'll pay $9 driving here from Orlando.) U.S. 1 and U.S. 27 are options if you don't mind passing through small towns and traffic lights. It's 300 to 350 miles from the state line to here.

By train

Amtrak (☎ **800-872-7245;** Internet: www.amtrak.com) has a station in West Palm Beach at 201 S. Tamarind Ave. (☎ **561-832-6169**).

Getting around

Like its neighbors to the south — Broward and Miami-Dade Counties —
Palm Beach County is relatively easy to navigate because most of the
development is along the coast. Traffic, although not quite as bad as in
the Miami area, can be bad enough; you may want to leave the driving
to someone else.

By bus

Palm Tran (☎ 561-841-4200), runs routes throughout the county. The
fare is $1 for adults and 50 cents for kids 3 to 18. It runs from 6 a.m. to
7 p.m. Monday through Friday, from 8 a.m. to 6 p.m. Saturday, and from
10 a.m. to 4 p.m. on Sunday. Free route maps are available by calling
☎ 561-233-4-BUS.

Free shuttles operate in downtown West Palm Beach on weekdays from
9 a.m. to 4 p.m. Look for the bright pink buses when you're downtown.
For more information, call ☎ **561-833-8873.**

By car

The same roads that get you here are the primary north-south thor-
oughfares (I-95, A1A, and U.S. 1). Common east-west routes include
Palmetto Park Road (Boca Raton), Atlantic Avenue/Hwy. 806 (Delray
Beach), and Okeechobee Road/Hwy. 704 (West Palm and Palm Beach).

By taxi

Sunshine Cab (☎ 561-832-8500) in West Palm Beach and **Metro Taxi**
(☎ **561-391-2230**) in Boca Raton are two of several taxi companies in the
area. It will cost you $1 to start the meter and $1.80 a mile thereafter.

By train

Tri-Rail (☎ **800-874-7245** or 954-942-7245) is a commuter service running from Palm Beach County to Broward and Miami-Dade Counties.
Round-trip fares range from $3.50 to $9.25.

Staying in Palm Beach County

Palm Beach County tends to be pricey, with most accommodations
falling into either the luxury or chain-hotel categories. (Skip ahead to
the map for an overview of "Palm Beach and Boca Raton.") If you don't
find anything that fits your budget in the listings that follow, check out
the chain-hotel numbers and Web sites in the "Quick Concierge" at the
back of this book.

Palm Beach and Boca Raton

ACCOMMODATIONS ■
Best Western Sea Spray **2**
The Breakers **5**
Delroy Beach Marriott **13**
Palm Beach Hawaian Inn **10**
PGA National Resort & Spa **1**

DINING ◆
Café L'Europe **7**
My Martini Grille **6**
Snappers Seafood
 and Pasta **11**
Testa's **4**
32 East **12**

ATTRACTIONS ●
Henry Morrison
 Flagler Museum **3**
International Museum
 of Cartoon Art **14**
Lion Country Safari **16**
Palm Beach Zoo at
 Dreher Park **8**
Morikami Museum
 and Japanese Gardens **15**
South Florida Science
 Museum **9**

Florida Hotel Network (☎ 800-538-3616; Internet: www.floridahotels.com) can take care of your hotel arrangements after you tell the folks there your specific needs. You can also try **Palm Beach Accommodations** at ☎ 800-543-SWIM. This booking service specializes in long-term rentals, but it does represent other kinds of accommodations.

Many accommodations let kids under 12 (and sometimes under 18) stay free if you don't exceed the maximum occupancy. But, to be safe, ask when booking. Also, pools and air conditioning are part of the deal unless otherwise noted here.

Don't forget the 10 percent sales and hotel taxes.

The area's best hotels

Best Western Sea Spray

$$ Palm Beach Shores/Singer Island

The Best Western Sea Spray may be basic motelville, but the rooms are clean, and the location is good — right off the beach, it offers a great view of the Atlantic Ocean. Some efficiencies are available. A restaurant and a lounge with entertainment nightly are onsite.

*123 Ocean Ave./A1A. ☎ **800-330-0233** or 561-844-0233. Fax: 561-844-9885. Internet: www.bestwestern.com. To get there: PGA Boulevard/Hwy. 786 east to Ocean Avenue/A1A, then south. Parking: Free. Rack rates: $90–$150 Dec–Apr, $60–$95 May–Nov. AE, CB, DC, DISC, ME, V.*

The Breakers

$$$$ Palm Beach

Speaking of Palm Beach without mentioning this grand dame is impossible, but this resort's royal-sized rates make it better for sightseeing than staying. The 1920s, Great Gatsby-style resort epitomizes Palm Beach luxury. Guest rooms range from 250-square-foot standards (ask for a corner room, which offers a bit more room for the same price) to ocean-front suites that are double that. All rooms have a full array of luxurious and modern amenities, including robes and PlayStations. The resort has two golf courses, 14 tennis courts, seven restaurants, and four bars.

*1 S. County Rd. ☎ **888-273-2537** or 561-655-6611. Fax: 561-659-8403. Internet: www.thebreakers.com. To get there: Okeechobee Boulevard east to South County Road, turn left. Parking: Free, self, $16 valet. Rack rates: $380–$2,700 Jan–Apr, $280–$1,780 May, $250–$1,750 June–Dec. AE, CB, DC, DISC, MC, V.*

Delray Beach Marriott

$$$ Delray Beach

Located halfway between Boca Raton and Palm Beach, this hotel — popular with business travelers — has 342 rooms and suites equipped with the usual array of modern amenities. The hotel overlooks the ocean and is within walking distance of boutiques, galleries, cafes, restaurants, and nightlife. You can skip a rental car if you aren't interested in seeing some of the area's outermost attractions; A car is a must, however, if you want to venture into the downtown or West Palm Beach area.

10 N. Ocean Blvd./A1A. ☎ ***800-228-9290*** *or 561-274-3200. Fax: 561-274-3202. Internet:* www.marriotthotels.com/PBIDR. *To get there: Just north of Atlantic Avenue on A1A. Parking: $6 self, $8 valet. Rack rates: $270–$390 Jan–Apr, $110–$260 May–Sept, $140–$390 Oct–Dec. AE, DISC, MC, V.*

Palm Beach Hawaiian Ocean Inn

$$ Palm Beach

Rooms at this oceanfront property range from standard-motel issue and efficiencies to suites. This is a plain-Jane place to stay, but it's on the ocean and in a fairly good location (just a bit south of Palm Beach posh). There's a restaurant and bar on the premises.

3550 S. Ocean Blvd./A1A. ☎ ***800-457-5631*** *or 561-582-5631. Internet:* www. palmbeachhawaiian.com. *To get there: Lantana Road/Hwy. 812 east to Dixie Hwy./U.S. 1, south to Ocean Ave., east to Ocean Blvd. Parking: Free. Rack rates: $150–$240 Dec–Apr, $90–$160 May–Nov. AE, MC, V.*

PGA National Resort & Spa

$$$ Palm Beach Gardens

This golfers' paradise (five championship courses) also has 19 tennis courts, an excellent spa, a fitness center, a croquet complex, and nine pools to help you burn off some of the calories you may pick up in its nine restaurants. Standard rooms have marble foyers and large bathrooms. Suites come with patios or balconies. Cottages include two bedrooms, two baths, a living room, and kitchen.

400 Avenue of the Champions. ☎ ***800-633-9150*** *or 561-627-2000. Fax: 561-622-0261. Internet:* www.pga-resorts.com. *To get there: 2 miles west of I-95 exit 57. Parking: Free, self, $10 valet. Rack rates: $360–$1,400 Dec–Apr, $230–$800 May–Sept, $290–$1,200 Oct–Nov. AE, DC, DISC, MC, V.*

Runner-up hotels

The Colony Palm Beach

$$–$$$ Palm Beach   This British-flavored boutique hotel offers cheery rooms, luxurious suites, and a prime location only 100 yards from the beach. *155 Hammon Ave.* ☎ ***800-521-5525*** *or 561-655-5430. Fax: 561-659-8104 Internet:* www.thecolonypalmbeach.com.

Embassy Suites

$$ **Boca Raton** Just east of I-95, this branch of the well-known chain offers 2- and 3-room suites, free cooked-to-order breakfasts, and a full range of facilities. *661 NW 53rd St.*☎ *800-362-2779 or 561-994-8200. Fax: 561-995-9821. Internet:* www.embassysuites.com.

Dining out in Palm Beach County

Palm Beach has some of the finest restaurants in Florida, and you'll pay royally to dine with the upscale types who winter here. The dress code is a tad more formal as well; most men wear blazers, and ladies sport classy dresses when dining out. Boca has its fair share of pricey seafood and steak joints, but the atmosphere is a bit more casual.

If you have a car, you can easily get to the Fort Lauderdale and Hollywood restaurants mentioned earlier in this chapter.

Don't forget to allow for the 6 percent sales tax.

The area's best restaurants

Café L'Europe

$$$ **Palm Beach** **CONTINENTAL**

This award-winning restaurant offers romantic dining and superb service. Seafood and steaks are your best bets. For deep-pocketed starters, there's a grand caviar bar ($16.50 to $87). The main events include sea bass steamed in papilotte with spinach, zucchini, and garlic; a grilled veal chop with potato cake; and a luscious cut of pan-seared sesame tuna in ginger vinaigrette.

331 S. County Rd. ☎ *561-655-4020. Internet:* www.cafeleurope.com. *Reservations required. To get there: Okeechobee Blvd. over the Intracoastal to South County Road, right to Brazilian Avenue. Main courses: $22–$36. AE, DISC, MC, V. Open: noon–3 p.m. Tues–Sat, 6–10 p.m. daily.*

My Martini Grille

$$ **West Palm Beach** **AMERICAN**

This hot spot on Clematis Street offers diners good food and great service in a somewhat noisy atmosphere. The menu includes beef, veal, and pork kebobs; crispy duck in mango glaze; shrimp, scallops, and calamari swimming in angel-hair pasta; and a range of steaks. The three-dozen or so martinis on the menu are pricey — one selection, made with Louis XIII vodka, costs a cool $120 — so if you're on a tight budget, sip something before coming.

225 Clematis. ☎ *561-832-8333. Internet:* www.pbol.com/clematis/martini_info.html. *Reservations recommended. To get there: From Okeechobee*

Boulevard go north on Olive to Clematis. Main courses: $16–$28. (Martinis average $8–$10.) AE, DC, DISC, MC, V. Open: 5 p.m.–2 a.m. Mon–Sat.

Snappers Seafood & Pasta

$ Boynton Beach   SEAFOOD

Located near the Boynton Beach Mall, Snappers offers a respectable wine list to go with shellfish (broiled lobster tails, steamed crab, fried oysters), seafood platters (shrimp and scallops), fresh fish (grilled or blackened mahi-mahi), and pasta (shrimp, snapper, crawfish, and andouille sausage with fettucine). Most dinner entrees are priced under $18, and a good lunch can be had for less than $10.

398 N. Congress Ave. ☎ *561-375-8600. Internet:* www.snappers.com. *Reservations suggested. To get there: Take Congress south from West Palm past Old Boynton Beach Boulevard; it's in the Oakwood Square shopping center. Main courses: $8–$28. AE, MC, V. Open: 11:30 a.m.–10 p.m. Sun–Thurs, 11:30 a.m.–11 p.m. Fri–Sat.*

Testa's

$$ Palm Beach   SEAFOOD

Family owned and operated for 75 years (there's a Maine location, too), Testa's has indoor and al fresco dining and a menu loaded with south Florida staples (stone crabs and seared tuna) and a few novelties (almond-crusted prawns and a seafood marinara with lobster, mussels, shrimp, scallops, and fish). If you're here in season, the restaurant's massive omelette buffet, served 11 a.m. to 2 p.m. on Sundays, is a fantastic bargain at only $12.95.

221 Royal Poinciana Way. ☎ *561-832-0992. Internet:* www.pbol.com/testas. *Reservations required in winter. To get there: 4 blocks east of Flagler Memorial Bridge on A1A. Main courses: $14–$23. AE, CB, DC, DISC, MC, V. Open: 7 a.m.– midnight daily (till 11 p.m. in summer).*

32 East

$$ Delray Beach   AMERICAN

Eat indoors or out at this casual restaurant. Fish is front and center, but there's plenty for landlubbers as well. Menu standards include oak-roasted snapper with avocado salsa, roasted chicken breast in mustard-butter sauce, and grilled yellowfin tuna served with rice and a spring roll. The wine list is pretty extensive.

32 E. Atlantic Ave. ☎ *561-276-7868. Internet:* www.32east.com. *Reservations suggested. To get there: On mainland between Swinton Boulevard and SE 1st Avenue. Main courses: $14–$28. AE, DISC, MC, V. Open: 5:30–10 p.m. daily.*

Runner-up restaurants

If you're looking for something a little different, try one of these:

Fandango Grill Restaurant

$$ **West Palm Beach** Southern cuisine rules the kitchen, which dishes out such rib-stickers as red-chile pasta, blue-cornmeal catfish, and chicken-fried steak. *901 Village Blvd.* ☎ *561-616-0900. Internet:* http://members.aol.com/fandangoFL.

No Anchovies Pastaria

$$ **Palm Beach Gardens** This casual family restaurant delivers a nice selection of Italian dishes, including pastas, pizzas, and salads. *2650 PGA Blvd.* ☎ *561-622-7855 and 1901 Palm Beach Lakes Blvd., West Palm Beach.* ☎ *561-684-0040. Internet:* www.noanchovies.com.

Exploring Palm Beach, West Palm Beach, and Boca Raton

Cartoons, critters, and museums provide much of the action in Palm Beach County, which also has some beautiful beaches, several parks, and the sport of kings — polo.

The top attractions

Henry Morrison Flagler Museum

Palm Beach

This estate, billed as the *Taj Mahal of North America,* was a gift from railroad and oil magnate Henry Flagler to his third wife. Built in 1902 to the tune of $4 million, the museum has a marble entry and 55 antique-filled rooms, including a Louis XIV music room. Guided tours are available. Outside, you can look at *The Rambler* — Flagler's private rail car. Allow 2 hours.

1 Whitehall Way. ☎ *561-655-2833. Internet:* www.flagler.org. *To get there: Go north on A1A, left on Worth Avenue, west to Coconut Row, right .8 mile to the museum. Admission: $7 adults, $3 kids 6–12. Open: 10 a.m.–5 p.m. Tues–Sat, noon–5 p.m. Sun.*

International Museum of Cartoon Art

Boca Raton

The works of artists from 50 countries are housed in a collection of 160,000 drawings that includes comics, gags, editorial cartoons, and more. A single artist's work — such as that of the late Charles Schulz, who created

Peanuts — is usually featured for months at a time. There's also a toon-town hall of fame. The museum will keep you busy for 2 to 4 hours.

201 Plaza Real. ☎ *561-391-2200. Internet: www.cartoon.org. To get there: On U.S. 1, 2 blocks north of Palmetto Park Road in Mizner Park. Admission: $8 adults, $6 seniors, $4 kids 6–12. Open: 10 a.m.–6 p.m. Tues–Sat, noon–6 p.m. Sun.*

Lion Country Safari

Loxahatchee

The featured attractions are well fed. But just in case, convertibles and pets are not allowed. You have to keep your car windows up as you drive through. You can rent cars for $6 per 1½ hours, and pets can stay in a kennel for a $5 refundable deposit. Park residents also include gibbons, wildebeests, rhinos, and elephants. There's also a walking tour, a cruise, and a kids' petting zoo (no meat-eaters here, of course). Allow at least 2 and as much as 4 hours to see everything.

2000 Lion Country Safari Road. ☎ *561-793-1084. Internet: www. lioncountrysafari.com. To get there: It's 15 miles west of West Palm Beach on Southern Boulevard. Admission: $15.50 adults, $10.50 seniors and kids 3–9. Open: 9:30 a.m.–5:30 p.m. daily.*

Palm Beach Zoo at Dreher Park

West Palm Beach

A compact 22 acres, this zoo has 500 animals, including tigers, giant tortoises, kangaroos, and wallabies. There's an elevated boardwalk that allows you to see deer, shore birds, and plants. The kids' zoo gives little ones a chance to dirty their hands and clothing. Figure on spending about 1½ to 2½ hours here, more if you walk like a sloth.

1301 Summit Blvd. ☎ *561-533-0887. Internet: www.palmbeachzoo.org. To get there: From I-95, take Summit Boulevard to Parker, right, then left on Summit. Admission: $6 adults, $5 seniors, $4 kids 3–12. Open: 9 a.m.–5 p.m. daily.*

Seeing and doing more cool things

If you're into museums, there are two excellent ones in the area.

Museums

The **Morikami Museum and Japanese Gardens,** 4000 Morikami Park Road, Delray Beach (☎ 561-495-0233; Internet: www.morikami.org), was once home to a short-lived agricultural community. Today, it's the only U.S. museum dedicated to living Japanese culture and features gardens, trails, art, artifacts, and bonsai. It costs $5.25 for adults, $4.75 for seniors, and $3 for kids 6 to 18. The museum is open Tuesday through Sunday from 10 a.m. to 5 p.m.

The **South Florida Science Museum,** 4801 Dreher Trail N., West Palm Beach (☎ 561-832-1988; Internet: www.sfsm.org/index.htm), beckons with hands-on exhibits, laser shows, and a planetarium. Admission to the museum costs only $6 for adults, $4 for kids 3 to 17; if you add on a visit to the planetarium and a laser show, admission costs $10 for adults, $8 for kids 3 to 17.The museum is open Monday through Thursday from 10 a.m. to 5 p.m., Friday from 10 a.m. to 6 p.m., and Sunday from noon to 6 p.m.

Baseball and spring training

The **St. Louis Cardinals** and **Montreal Expos** (☎ 561-966-3309) share Roger Dean Stadium at 4751 Main St. in Jupiter. Tickets run from $5 to $17 and go fast, so it's smart to call for them in advance. Workouts begin in mid-February; games are played through March.

Beaches

John D. MacArthur Beach State Park, 2 miles south of PGA Boulevard and U.S. 1 on A1A, North Palm Beach (☎ 561-624-6950), has a 1,600-foot boardwalk running through 760 acres of submerged land, hammocks, and mangroves. Expect to see ibises, herons, and skittish fiddler crabs. Its nature center features displays and a video on the barrier island, and there's a footbridge to the dune area and Atlantic Ocean. Take Blue Heron Boulevard across the Intracoastal and turn north on Ocean Boulevard. Admission is $5 per vehicle.

Other good beaches include

- ✔ **Juno Beach:** On A1A, 1 mile north of the town. This is an undeveloped beach with lifeguards.

- ✔ **Carlin Park:** On A1A, south of Indiantown Road, Jupiter. Here you'll find 3,000 feet of rocky beach with lifeguards and trails.

- ✔ **Lantana Park:** State Road 12 and A1A, 1 mile east of Lantana. Lantana Park is an undeveloped beach with lifeguards.

- ✔ **Spanish River Park:** 3000 N. A1A, Boca Raton. This 46-acre park offers more than half a mile of beachfront manned by lifeguards.

Diving

Local favorites include **Breakers Reef,** a 45- to 60-foot dive that's usually packed with fish; the **Esso Bonaire,** a tanker lying at 150 feet; and **Northwest Doubles,** an 80- to 90-footer where you'll find many tropicals and maybe some reef sharks. Tours begin at $40 per person for divers and snorkelers.

Charter operators include **Coral Island Charters** (☎ 888-889-3483 or 561-745-9286; Internet: www.coralislandcharters.com) in North Palm Beach; **SS Minnow** (☎ 561-848-6860; Internet: www.ssminnow.charters.com) in Palm Beach Gardens; and **Splashdown Divers** (☎ 561-736-0712) in Boynton Beach.

Fishing

The **Palm Beach County Fishing Club** (☎ 561-832-6780) is a good place to start. For $10, the club sends you a bunch of information on camps, charters, and tournaments. Call, or write to P.O. Box 468, West Palm Beach, FL 33402, but allow four weeks for delivery. If you want to be a bit more spontaneous, **Capt. Bob** (☎ 561-842-8823), in the Riviera Beach Marina at the foot of 13th Street, is a 65-foot party boat that offers 4-hour trips twice a day except Wednesday. The cost is $25 for adults, $20 for kids 11 and under.

Golfing

On the Internet, go to www.golf.com and www.floridagolfing.com for a full list of local courses. You also can call **Florida Golfing** (☎ 877-222-4653). Three good places to play are

- **Delray Beach Golf Club,** 2200 Highland Ave., Delray Beach (☎ 561-243-7380) has a course that is a bit long in the tooth (1923) but is still a challenge at 6,900 yards. Greens fees run under $25 in summer, $41 to $65 in winter.

- The **PGA National Resort & Spa,** 400 Avenue of the Champions, Palm Beach Gardens (☎ 561-627-2000) has five courses and is home to the headquarters of the PGA. Greens fees run $86 to $110 in summer, $120 to $145 in winter.

- **The Village Golf Club,** 122 Country Club Drive, Royal Palm Beach (☎ 561-793-1400), offers a course that is rated one of the 20 toughest in south Florida. Greens fees run under $25 in summer, $41 to $65 in winter.

Playing polo

The **Palm Beach Polo & Country Club,** 11809 Polo Club Road, Wellington, 10 miles west of I-95 off Forest Hills (☎ 561-798-7110), puts on a pro season that peaks with the $100,000 World Cup in March. Matches take place at 3 p.m. on Sundays from January through April. Tickets cost $7 to $40.

Organized Touring

Loxahatchee Everglades Airboat Tours, 15490 Loxahatchee Road, Boca Raton (☎ 800-683-5873 or 561-482-6107), offers swamp tours on 6- to 20-passenger models. The cost is $30 for adults, $10 for kids 6 to 10, and children 5 and under get in free.

Shopping

Palm Beach has some fabulous — and fabulously expensive — shopping, but pickings in this part of the Gold Coast are generally a little leaner than in Fort Lauderdale. Most shops, however, have the same kind of hours as that city: 10 a.m. to 6 p.m. Monday through Saturday and noon to 5 p.m. on Sunday. Stores inside malls and major shopping centers are open as late as 9 or 10 p.m., except on Sunday.

Seeking out the area's best shopping

Even if you don't like shopping, visiting **Worth Avenue** is a Palm Beach tradition (☎ **561-659-6906**). Often referred to as "the Rodeo Drive of the South," it stretches four blocks from South Ocean Boulevard to Coconut Row and offers more than 200 upscale shops and boutiques. Although you won't find many bargains, the people-watching is worth every minute.

Hitting the malls

Boynton Beach Mall, 801 N. Congress Ave. (☎ **561-736-7900**), houses 150 shops, including Macy's and Burdines. The **Gardens of the Palm Beaches Mall,** 3101 PGA Blvd., Palm Beach Gardens, (☎ **561-775-7750**), has 180 tenants, including Saks, Bloomingdale's, and Macy's. **Town Center Mall** (☎ **561-368-6000**) in Boca Raton sports Bloomingdale's, Lord & Taylor, and Saks. It's west of I-95 on Glades Road between St. Andrews and Butts Road. And, one of the few places you can get a real bargain in Palm Beach County, the **Palm Beach Outlet Center,** 5700 Okeechobee Blvd., West Palm Beach, features upscale clothing, luggage, and other items at discounted prices.

Living the Nightlife

From culture to classic rock, Palm Beach rivals Fort Lauderdale when it comes to after-dark offerings.

Cultural corner

Staffers at the **Palm Beach County Cultural Council,** 1555 Palm Beach Lakes Blvd., West Palm Beach (☎ **800-882-2787** or 561-471-2901), can give you information on everything from museums to theater.

The **Palm Beach Opera,** 415 S. Olive Ave., West Palm Beach (☎ **888-886-7372;** Internet: www.pbopera.org) has a season running from October to April. The **Raymond F. Kravis Center for the Performing Arts,** 701 Okeechobee Blvd., West Palm Beach (☎ **800-572-8471** or 561-832-7469; Internet: www.kravis.org), takes center stage in the local cultural scene. Its 2,500 indoor seats and amphitheater host more than 300 performances each year, from the **Doobie Brothers** to the 70-piece **Boca Pops.**

Bars

Café L'Europe, 331 S. County Rd. (☎ **561-655-4020**), has a piano bar in its bistro, which is open six nights a week; a jazz combo plays here on Friday and Saturday evenings. **Clematis Street** in the heart of downtown West Palm Beach (☎ **561-833-8873;** Internet: www.downtownclematis. com) has a rocking street fest every Thursday night. Many of the street's storefronts offer live and canned music including **Respectable Street Café,** 518 Clematis (☎ 561-832-9999); **Spanky's Sports Bar,** 500 Clematis (☎ 561-659-5669); and **Rooney's Irish Pub,** 213 Clematis (☎ 561-833-7802;** Internet: www.rooneyspub.com).

Clubs

Hugh Jorgan's, 96 NE 2nd Ave., Delray Beach (☎ 561-272-7887; Internet: www.hughjorgans.com), is a rollicking dueling-piano bar that has shows at 8 p.m. Wednesday through Saturday. (A $5 to $10 cover is charged on Friday and Saturday.) Look for it inside Love's Drugs. Meanwhile, disco rules at **Polly Ester's** — a small chain with clubs in New York, Chicago, DC, Philly, San Francisco, and other cities. This branch, at SE 1st Street and 1st Avenue in Boca Raton (☎ 561-447-8955; Internet: www.pollyesters.com), is a local favorite, particularly among the college crowd on Fridays and Saturdays beginning at 9 p.m. The cover is usually under $10.

Palm Beach County in 3 Days

On **Day 1,** spend the morning seeing the Real Florida on **Loxahatchee Everglades Airboat Tours** out of Boca Raton. Grab lunch on the fly and make it an afternoon at the **International Museum of Cartoon Art** in Boca; then have dinner at **32 East** in Delray Beach or at **Snapper's Seafood & Pasta** in Boynton Beach. If you still have energy and it's Wednesday through Saturday, burn the midnight oil at **Hugh Jorgan's** in Delray Beach.

Start **Day 2** at **Lion Country Safari** in Loxahatchee, have lunch at **Testa's** in Palm Beach, and then spend the afternoon at the **South Florida Science Museum** or the **Palm Beach Zoo at Dreher Park.** Try **My Martini Grille** for dinner or, if you're hankering for some nightlife again, head to **Clematis Street** in West Palm Beach to eat and party.

Day 3 is for beach-goers. Spend the day at **John D. MacArthur Beach State Park** in North Palm Beach before grabbing dinner at **Café L'Europe** in Palm Beach. If you're looking to broaden your experience, try the Fort Lauderdale and Hollywood itinerary earlier in this chapter.

Fast Facts

Area Code

The local area code is **561.**

American Express

Adventure Travels, 30 SE 7th St., Boca Raton (☎ 561-395-5722); **Palm Beach International Travel Service,** 226-A Royal Palm Way, Palm Beach (☎ 561-833-2626). Both offices are open 9 a.m.–5 p.m. weekdays.

Hospitals

JFK Medical Center, 5301 S. Congress Ave., Atlantis (☎ 561-965-7300); **St. Mary's Hospital,** 901 45th St., West Palm Beach (☎ 561-650-6126).

Information

For information, brochures, and maps, contact the **Palm Beach County Convention and Visitors Bureau,** 1555 Palm Beach Lakes Boulevard, Suite 204, West Palm Beach, FL 33401 (☎ **561-471-3995;** Internet: www. palmbeachfl.com).

Mail

There are U.S. post offices at 401 S. County Rd., Palm Beach, and 8185 Via Ancho Rd., Boca Raton. To find a location near your hotel, call ☎ **800-275-8777.**

Maps

The information source in this section is a great one to hit up for maps before or after you land. (Trust us: Good maps are necessities because getting lost is easy in this part of the state.) Rental-car agencies are another good source (including those at the airport) and so are convenience stores, which sell maps for $3–$5.

Newspapers

The **Palm Beach Post (☎ 561-820-4100;** Internet: www.gopbi.com/partners/ pbpost/epaper/editions/today), publishes a weekly entertainment section on Friday.

Pharmacies

There are **24-hour Walgreens** at 2501 Broadway, Riviera Beach (☎ **561-848-6464**), and 7561 N. Federal Hwy./U.S. 1, (☎ **561-241-9802**). For more information on stores in this chain, you can also check out Internet: www.walgreens.com.

Taxes

The sales tax is 6 percent; the hotel tax is an additional 4 percent.

Transit Info

Palm Tran (☎ 561-841-4200), operates routes throughout the county. The fare is $1 for adults and 50 cents for kids 3–18. It runs 6 a.m.–7 p.m. Mon–Fri, 8 a.m.–6 p.m. Sat, and 10 a.m.–4 p.m. Sun.

Weather Updates

For a recording of current conditions and forecast reports, call the local office of the **National Weather Service** at ☎ **305-229-4522** or check out the service's Web site at Internet: www.nws.noaa.gov. You also can get information by watching the **Weather Channel** (Internet: www. weatherchannel.com).

Part IV
The Gulf Coast

The 5th Wave   By Rich Tennant

SHELLING ON FLORIDA'S WEST COAST

©RICHTENNANT

"Oooo! Back up, Robert. There must be a half dozen Lightening Whelks here."

In this part . . .

Tampa traditionally attracts more business travelers than tourists, but the Busch Gardens theme park and other attractions are trying to change that. St. Petersburg and Clearwater add a few more fun spots and arguably the Gulf Coast's best beaches. The area also chips in big-league baseball, football, and hockey.

South of Tampa Bay, Sarasota's cultural offerings are hard to overlook; the natural beauty of Sanibel, Captiva, and a ton of other islands beckons; the rich history of Fort Myers invites exploration, and the wealth of Naples and Marco Island, which lie just on the fringe of the Everglades, attracts millions of visitors each year.

Chapter 15

Tampa

● ●

In This Chapter

▶ Bringing your car with you

▶ Mapping out your itinerary beforehand

▶ Roller coasting through Tampa's top theme park

▶ Dining out and dancing to the tunes of flamenco

● ●

The commercial center of Florida's west coast, Tampa is better known as a haven for high-tech industry than as a magnet for visitors. Nevertheless, Tampa attracts tourists in droves with its signature theme park, **Busch Gardens,** and exceptional sports venues. The city of Tampa is also a major port for cruise ships bound for Mexico and the Caribbean. For an overview of Tampa's attractions, see the "Tampa Attractions" map later in this chapter.

Real baseball (not just spring training) is the newest attraction in the tourist-friendly Tampa area, but baseball is played just across the bay (see Chapter 16 for information on the Devil Rays and more St. Petersburg fun). In this chapter, we take you to **Busch Gardens,** which rivals Orlando's best theme parks. We also highlight the city's smaller attractions, including the **Florida Aquarium, Lowry Park Zoo,** and **Museum of Science and Industry.** And for those of you who truly come alive when the sun goes down, we also take a look at the Ybor-City club scene. Although this isn't the place to spend a week, the city's premiere attractions definitely merit a look.

Getting to Tampa

As is the case with most Florida cities, taking an aerial highway in the sky is the quickest and, in many cases, the most convenient way to get here. Train travel from the Northeast takes 25 to 28 hours, but those coming by car face a 4½- to 5-hour drive after crossing the Florida-Georgia line.

By plane

Florida's third largest airport, **Tampa International Airport** (☎ 813-870-8700; Internet: www.tampaairport.com) handles about 15.1 million passengers, half the amount of second-ranked Orlando. More than 30 domestic and foreign lines land at TIA.

Hook up with ground transportation on level one, the baggage claim area, which has public buses and taxis — **Tampa Yellow** (☎ 813-253-0121), and **United Cab** (☎ 813-253-2424). The average fare from the airport to downtown Tampa is $14. Level one is also home to **Avis, Budget, Dollar, Hertz,** and **National** rental desks (see the "Quick Concierge" in the back of the book for telephone numbers); eight other agencies have shuttle service to offsite locations. Level three has ATMs, information booths, first-aid stations, currency exchanges, and mail drops.

Much smaller than Tampa International, **St. Petersburg-Clearwater International Airport** (☎ 727-535-7600; Internet: www.stpeteclwairport.com) handles mostly charter flights operated by six smaller American and Canadian carriers. **Alamo, Avis, Budget, Dollar, Enter-pise, Hertz,** and **National** operate rental desks here, and there are plenty of taxis. The average cab fare from the airport to St. Petersburg and the beaches is $30.

By car

Cruise along I-75, the primary north-south route, with I-275 being the spur that cuts through downtown Tampa and St. Petersburg. I-4 is an option if you're arriving from I-95 and the east coast. U.S. 301, 41 and 19 are options only if you want to take a marginally scenic route, and you have a strong tolerance for bumper-to-bumper traffic.

By train

Amtrak (☎ 800-872-7245; Internet: www.amtrak.com) has a station in Tampa at 601 Nebraska Ave. If you bring your car with you on your vacation, drive to Lorton, Virginia (4 hours driving time from New York, 2 hours from Philadelphia); then put yourself and your car on Amtrak's Auto Train out of Lorton. The train stops in Sanford, about 90 minutes east of Tampa. Passenger rates on the Auto Train run from $93 to $182, and the cost of transporting the car ranges from $142 to $330.

Orienting Yourself to Tampa

Most streets in Tampa have names, making the need for a map (see "Fast Facts" at the end of this chapter) reasonably important. Some of the most common streets found in this guide include Dale Mabry (west side), Fowler Avenue and Busch Boulevard (north side), 7th Avenue and Broadway (Ybor City), and Kennedy Boulevard, Tampa and Ashley Streets (downtown). For the most part, the downtown and its museums are dead center, with Busch Gardens due north on I-275, Ybor City's clubs and memories east on I-4, the airport and business areas west on I-275, and St. Petersburg, Clearwater, and their Gulf beaches 60 minutes farther west, traffic willing.

Tampa by neighborhood

Despite its business-destination image, Tampa has plenty of places to stay, eat, party, and play, including Busch Gardens, Florida Aquarium, Lowry Park Zoo, and Ybor City. Downtown also has a modern perform- ing arts center and a pedestrian mall. As you move to the peripheries, you can come across other towns, including Temple Terrace (north), Brandon and Plant City (east), and Riverview and Ruskin (South).

Street smarts: Getting information after arriving

The **Tampa/Hillsborough Convention & Visitors Association,** 400 N. Tampa St., (☎ **800-448-2672** or 813-223-2752; Internet: www.gotampa. com) is your best bet for advance information. The association also operates an information center downtown at Madison and Ashley. The downtown center is open from 9 a.m. to 5 p.m. daily. See the "Quick Concierge" at the back of the book for general Florida information sources.

The **Tampa Bay Visitor Information Center (☎ 813–985-3601)** is located near Busch Gardens at 3601 E. Busch Blvd. The privately owned center sells discounted attractions tickets and has many brochures regarding things to do in the area. The helpful staff will also book hotels and car rentals for you. It's open Monday through Saturday from 9 a.m. to 5:30 p.m., Sunday from 9 a.m. to 2 p.m.

Getting Around Tampa

The best way to get around the Tampa area is to drive, because the city's public transportation system isn't ideal for traveling to the major tourist spots.

 Rush hour — the worst of which occurs from 7 to 9 a.m. and 4 to 6 p.m. — causes severe traffic backups on Dale Mabry, Kennedy Boulevard, I-4, I-275, and I-275's Howard Franklin Bridge (locals refer to it as the "Howard Frankenstein"), which leads to St. Petersburg. Because Dale Mabry and I-275 are frequently used when exiting the airport, allow plenty of time to get to your hotel, — or back to the airport if your flight is wrapped around either peak period.

By car

Tampa is in the cross hairs of I-4 and I-75/275. The latter two split north of town. I-75 goes around the city to the east toward Brandon, and then south toward Sarasota (see Chapter 17). I-275 cuts through the heart of downtown and continues across Tampa Bay to St. Petersburg. Tampa is laid out in a grid, but like many of Florida's cities, it relies on named streets. So if you're coming by car, or going to be using a rental while you're here, get a map (see "Fast Facts" at the end of this chapter). If you belong to AAA or another motor club, ask for a map. Major roads here include Florida Avenue, which separates the east and west portions of the city, and Kennedy Boulevard/State Road 60/Adamo Drive, which divides Tampa's north and south.

By taxi

You won't find taxis cruising the streets, but they usually line up at hotels, performance venues, and train stations. **United Cab** (☎ 813-253-2424), and **Yellow Cab** (☎ 813-253-0121) are the major taxi companies in Tampa. The meter starts at $1.25, and it's another $1.75 per mile. Fares are for up to five people.

By bus

HARTline, Tampa's public transportation system, serves the city and the suburbs. Fares are $1.15 (exact change is required). For information, call ☎ **813-623-5835** or 813-254-4278, or check out its Web site, www.hartline.org. As is often the case, city buses aren't the best choice to get to and from tourist areas.

Staying in Tampa

High season in Tampa runs from January to April, but peak season rates in this neck of the woods aren't as high as the rates for properties near the beaches. Downtown and the area near the airport are mostly commercial, so hotels in these areas — although close to many of Tampa's attractions — are usually filled with businessmen, bankers, and convention attendees during the week. (Just ahead, see the map of "Tampa Accommodations and Dining.") You may also find a number of national chain hotels in these zones. See the "Quick Concierge" in the back of the book for a listing of chain hotel numbers and Web sites.

Because Tampa actively caters to business travelers, visitors can often get excellent rates on weekends, especially in the downtown area. And, if you plan on visiting Busch Gardens, ask whether a hotel offers special discount packages. Also, many accommodations let kids under 12 and sometimes under 18 stay free if you don't exceed the maximum room occupancy. To be safe, though, ask when booking a room.

Sales and hotel taxes add 11.75 percent to your bill.

If you don't want to haggle, the **Florida Hotel Network** (☎ **800-538-3616;** Internet: www.floridahotels.com) can take care of making accommodations arrangements for you.

Tampa's best hotels

AmeriSuites Tampa Airport

$$ **West Side**

This property is conveniently situated just a few miles from the airport and right off I-275. Some of its 126 rooms and suites have kitchenettes. Work off the free breakfast buffet in the hotel's health club, or its heated outdoor pool.

4811 W. Main St. ☎ ***800-833-1516*** *or 813-282-1037. Fax: 813-282-1148.* www. amerisuites.com. *To get there: From the airport, take Spruce to Westshore, then right to Main. Parking: Free. Rack rates: $139–$159 Dec–Apr, $89–$119 May–Nov; suites $109–$179. AE, DC, DISC, MC, V.*

Best Western All Suites

$$ **North Side**

Located right behind Busch Gardens, Best Western's 150 suites have recliners, two TVs, balconies, refrigerators, microwaves, data ports, and sleeper sofas. Other features include a free country-style breakfast buffet, a hot tub, an onsite restaurant, and a free daily newspaper. The upstairs suites are the best of the bunch.

3001 University Center Dr. ☎ ***800-786-7446*** *or 813-971-8930. Fax: 813-971-8935. Internet:* www.bestwestern.com. *To get there: At I-275 and Busch. Parking: Free. Rack rates: $99–$129 Dec–Apr, $99–109 May–Nov. AE, CB, DC, DISC, MC. V.*

Doubletree Guest Suites/Busch Gardens

$$ **North Side**

This property's 129 suites offer kitchenettes with refrigerators, sofa beds, two-line telephones, and data ports. A continental breakfast and daily

Tampa Accommodations & Dining

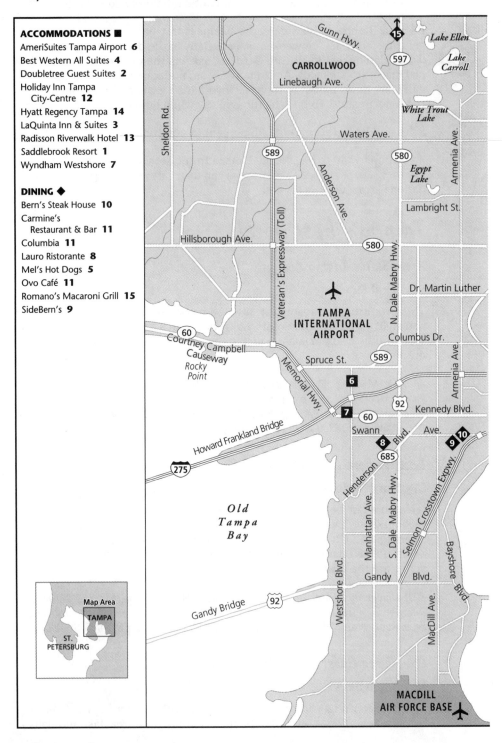

ACCOMMODATIONS ■
AmeriSuites Tampa Airport **6**
Best Western All Suites **4**
Doubletree Guest Suites **2**
Holiday Inn Tampa
 City-Centre **12**
Hyatt Regency Tampa **14**
LaQuinta Inn & Suites **3**
Radisson Riverwalk Hotel **13**
Saddlebrook Resort **1**
Wyndham Westshore **7**

DINING ◆
Bern's Steak House **10**
Carmine's
 Restaurant & Bar **11**
Columbia **11**
Lauro Ristorante **8**
Mel's Hot Dogs **5**
Ovo Café **11**
Romano's Macaroni Grill **15**
SideBern's **9**

Gunn Hwy.
Lake Ellen
597
Lake Carroll
CARROLLWOOD
Linebaugh Ave.
White Trout Lake
Waters Ave.
580
Egypt Lake
Armenia Ave.
Sheldon Rd.
589
Anderson Ave.
Lambright St.
Veteran's Expressway (Toll)
Hillsborough Ave.
580
N. Dale Mabry Hwy.
Dr. Martin Luther
60
Courtney Campbell Causeway
Rocky Point
TAMPA INTERNATIONAL AIRPORT
Spruce St.
589
Columbus Dr.
Armenia Ave.
Memorial Hwy.
6
7
92
Kennedy Blvd.
60
Swann
8
Blvd.
Ave.
9 **10**
Howard Frankland Bridge
275
685
Henderson
Old Tampa Bay
Manhattan Ave.
S. Dale Mabry Hwy.
Selmon Crosstown Expwy.
Bayshore Blvd.
Westshore Blvd.
Gandy
Blvd.
MacDill Ave.
Map Area
TAMPA
ST. PETERSBURG
Gandy Bridge
92
MACDILL AIR FORCE BASE

newspaper are also included in your rate. Less than 1 mile from Busch Gardens, the hotel runs a free shuttle on mornings and afternoons to the theme park.

11310 N. 30th St. ☎ *800-222-8733 or 813-971-7690. Fax: 813-972-2252. Internet:* www. doubletree.com. *To get there: South of Fowler Avenue on 30th. Parking: Free. Rack rates: $99–$139 Dec–Apr, $79–$119 May–Nov. AE, DISC, MC, V.*

Holiday Inn Tampa City-Centre

$$ Downtown

Located close to the Tampa Bay Performing Arts Center, its 312 rooms have data ports and tea makers; some have microwaves and refrigerators. Upper floors overlook the Hillsborough River (but don't expect foliage — after all, this is the city). A cocktail lounge, two restaurants, laundry facilities, and a complimentary airport shuttle are also available.

111 W. Fortune St. ☎ *800-513-8940 or 813-223-1351. Fax: 813-221-2000. Internet:* www.basshotels.com/holiday-inn. *To get there: Just south of I-275's Ashley Street exit. Parking: Free. Rack rates: $123–$153 Jan–Apr, $79–$101 May–Dec. AE, CB, DC, DISC, MC, V.*

Hyatt Regency

$$$ Downtown

Situated in the business district, near the Performing Arts and Convention Centers, this recently renovated hotel caters to the corporate crowd. All 521 rooms have data ports, and mini-refrigerators are available on request. The Hyatt also touts a small fitness center with NordicTrack equipment, a heated outdoor pool with rooftop sundeck, a lounge, and an onsite restaurant.

2 Tampa City Center, ☎ *800-233-1234 or 813-225-1234. Fax: 813-204-3095. Internet:* www.tampa.regency.hyatt.com. *To get there: South from I-275 on Ashley to Jackson, east on Tampa Street. Parking: valet $10/day. Rack rates: $204–$244 Dec–Apr, $165–$224 May–Nov. AE, DC, DISC, MC, V.*

La Quinta Inn & Suites

$$ North Side

This property is a shade on the upscale side, but La Quinta's 105 rooms are still standard motel fare. The rooms have all the standard amenities, including data ports, and a free continental breakfast is included in your rate. The property also has a good location: only 1½ miles from Busch Gardens.

3701 E. Fowler Ave. ☎ *800-687-6667 or 813-910-7500. Fax: 813-910-7600. Internet:* www.flhotels.com/tampa/laquinta_977.html *To get there: Take the*

Fowler Avenue exit off I-275 east to the motel. Parking: Free. Rack rates: $105–$129 Dec–Apr, $89–$119 May–Nov. AE, CB, DC, DISC, V.

Radisson Riverwalk Hotel

$$$ Downtown

The hotel sits on the banks of the not-so-scenic metro leg of the Hillsborough River, but the Radisson Riverwalk is a good option if you're after a central location. The hotel's 286 large rooms, last remodeled in 1998, come with data ports, and a free daily newspaper. Two restaurants, a bar, fitness center, and sauna are also onsite.

200 N. Ashley St. ☎ **800-333-3333** *or 813-223-2222. Fax: 813-221-5292. Internet:* www. radisson.com. *To get there: Take Ashley Street exit off I-275. Parking: valet $7. Rack rates: $209–$259 Dec–Apr, $159–$229 May–Nov. AE, CB, DC, DISC, MC, V.*

Saddlebrook Resort

$$$ Far North

This resort, 25 minutes north of Tampa, is a dandy landing zone for golfers (36 holes plus an Arnold Palmer school), tennis players (45 courts and a Harry Hopman school), and self-indulgent types (the spa features out-of-this-world treatments). All accommodations have data ports and fully stocked bars; suites come with kitchens and balconies or patios. Although the resort is heralded as a corporate retreat, many mainstream tourists stay here, too. After you park yourself here, everything's within walking distance, and the year-round *Cool Stuff* program is a winner for kids, ages 4 to 12. Golf, tennis, and spa packages are also available.

5700 Saddlebrook Way, Wesley Chapel, ☎ **800-729-8383** *or 813-973-1111. Fax: 813-973-4504. Internet:* www.saddlebrookresort.com. *To get there: Off I-75 east on Hwy. 54.* **Note:** *the following rates are per person, double occupancy, and include breakfast and dinner daily. Rack rates: $185 rooms, $197–$267 suites Jan–May; $160 rooms, $182–$242 suites Oct–Jan; $120 rooms, $132–$165 suites May–Sept. AE, DC, DISC, MC, V.*

Wyndham Westshore

$$$ West Side

Corporate suits usually patronize the Wyndham Westshore, which is attached to a business center located near the airport. The hotel's 324 comfortable rooms come with free coffee, data ports, and a free week-day newspaper. A fitness center, an 11-story atrium, heated pool, and a restaurant are onsite.

4860 W. Kennedy Blvd. ☎ **877-999-3223** *or 813-286-4400. Fax: 813-286-4053. Internet:* www.wyndham.com. *To get there: It's on Kennedy, south of I-275 and west of Westshore. Parking: Free. Rack rates: $204–$224 Dec–Mar, $184–$204 Apr–Nov. AE, DC, DISC, MC, V.*

Runner-up accommodations

Sometimes the upper echelons just don't make the earth move for you. If that's the case, here are some more options. Other than accommodations near Busch Gardens, these hotels usually cater to business travelers, meaning they may be a shade more expensive, but are most likely upscale and have a good assortment of amenities.

Baymont Inn & Suites

$ **Off Busch Blvd.** A good place for the cost-conscious to rest their heads, this motel features spacious rooms, a free continental breakfast, and a great location near Busch Gardens. *9202 N. 30th Blvd.* ☎ *800-428-3438 or 813-930-6900. Fax 813-930-0563. Internet:* www.baymontinns.com.

Sheraton Suites Tampa Airport

$$ **Only ten minutes from Raymond James Stadium** This newly renovated hotel's two-room suites offer numerous amenities, including refrigerators. *4400 W. Cypress St.* ☎ *888-713-3330 or 813-873-8675. Fax: 813-879-7196. Internet:* www.sheraton.com.

Dining Out in Tampa

Not exactly a culinary hotbed, Tampa touts a respectable number of good restaurants offering numerous types of cuisine in a wide range of prices. You'll also find plenty of fast-food joints, especially near Busch Gardens.

Don't forget to add 6.75 percent local sales tax to your budget. And if you have a car, try some of the St. Petersburg-Clearwater restaurants in Chapter 16.

Tampa's best restaurants

Bern's Steak House

$$$ **Midtown** **STEAKS**

This local institution offers an atmosphere akin to that of an exclusive club. Long regarded as Tampa's premiere steak house, the restaurant's lost a star and a little luster over the years, but it's still a favorite among many travelers and locals. Although you can order other things on the menu, such as seafood, coming to Bern's to eat anything but the aged beef — sold in 62 cuts — is a sin. Bern's is also home to the world's largest wine list — more than 85,000 bottles are stored on the premises.

1208 S. Howard Ave. ☎ *813-251-2421. Reservations required. To get there: I-275 south on Armenia to Azeele, left a block to Howard, then left. Main courses: $15–$35. AE, DC, DISC, MC, V. Open: 5–11 p.m. daily.*

Carmine's Restaurant & Bar

$ Ybor City CUBAN

The place is noisy, and tables don't match the chairs. But the large number of locals dining here attests to Carmine's quality as a good ethnic experience. No need to get fancy here — settle for a Cuban sandwich, a bowl of garbanzo bean soup, and a fashionable local beer, such as Ybor Gold.

1802 E. 7th Ave. ☎ *813-248-3834. Reservations not required. To get there: I-4 to 21st Street, go south to 7th/Broadway, then right. Main courses: $5–$16. Credit cards not accepted. Open: 11 a.m.–11 p.m. Mon–Tues, 11–1 a.m. Wed–Thurs, 11–3 a.m. Fri–Sat, 11 a.m.–6 p.m. Sun.*

Columbia

$$ Ybor City CUBAN/SPANISH

Among Tampa's finest restaurants, from the frenetic Flamenco dancers in the main dining room to the ceramic-tile exterior, the Columbia is truly a Latin experience (ask to sit in the patio room for a bright time, although it's tough to pass on those dancers). Built in 1905, this restaurant is the dean of Tampa's restaurants. The *paella* is a traditional dish of shrimp, scallops, squid, clams, fish, and mussels in a mound of yellow rice. Served with black beans and rice, the *boliche* is a melt-in-your-mouth-tender eye of round, stuffed with chorizo. Several newer Columbia restaurants are located in a handful of other Florida cities, but none can touch the Ybor-City Columbia, which has to appease the city's fickle Latin diners.

Rumor has it that eating the Columbia's boliche while listening to the soulful strains of flamenco can be a powerful aphrodisiac.

2117 E. 7th Ave. ☎ *813-248-4961. Internet:* www.columbiarestaurant.com. *Reservations recommended. To get there: from I-4 go south on 21st Street, then left on 7th. Main courses: $14–$33. AE, DC, DISC, MC, V. Open: 11 a.m.–10 p.m. Mon–Thurs, 11 a.m.–11 p.m. Fri–Sat, noon–9 p.m. Sun.*

Lauro Ristorante

$$ West Side ITALIAN

Chef and owner Lauro Medaglia dishes out excellent Northern Italian cuisine that attracts locals and tourists alike. His classically decorated trattoria offers a romantic atmosphere and excellent service. Think about sampling the Dover sole, crab, veal, duck, and (for organ lovers) sweetbreads, which are all done in middle-Italy style. The pastas and sauces are standouts.

3915 Henderson Blvd. ☎ *813-281-2100. Internet:* www.lauroristorante.com. *Reservations suggested. To get there: On Henderson, a shade south of Kennedy Boulevard. Main courses: $11.50–$22.50. AE, MC, V. Open: 11:30 a.m.–2 p.m. Mon–Fri, 5:30–10 p.m. daily.*

Mel's Hot Dogs

$ North Side/Busch Gardens   AMERICAN

Few guidebooks are bold enough to offer a hot-dog stand as one of its top dogs, but few stands can match Mel's. Roll up your sleeves up and join some of Tampa's movers, shakers, and hot-dog makers at this compact red-and-white cottage. Most of the hot-dog selections are served with French fries and a choice of coleslaw or baked beans. Mel also sells burgers, bratwurst, and more.

4136 E. Busch Blvd. ☎ *813-985-8000. Internet:* www.mels-hotdogs.com. *Reservations? Ha! To get there: From I-275 go east 2 miles and look away from Busch Gardens. Main courses: $4–$9. Credit cards? Ha, again! Open: 11 a.m.–9 p.m. daily.*

Ovo Café

$ Ybor City   INTERNATIONAL

This small cafe offers twists on standard international fare, attracting a sophisticated clientele on weekdays, and clubbers on weekends. Ovo serves several creative salads (try the chicken feta), smoked-tuna sandwiches, shrimp bisque, and desserts that literally will rock your taste buds. Woo-hoo!

1901 E. 7th Ave. ☎ *813-248-6979. Reservations not required. To get there: From I-4 go south on 21st Street and right on 7th/Broadway. Main courses: $8–$15 (sandwiches $6–$8; pizzas $8–$10). AE, MC, V. Open: 11 a.m.–4 p.m. Mon–Tues, 11–2 a.m. Wed–Sat, 11 a.m.–10 p.m. Sun.*

Romano's Macaroni Grill

$ West Side   ITALIAN

Sure, Romano's is a small chain, but there's a nice family atmosphere (you can definitely hear the buzz of conversation), and most of Tampa's better restaurants are oriented toward the business crowd. The staff will put jug wine on your table and trust you after the first glass. The entrees (veal picatta, chicken marsala, shrimp scampi, and a meaty lasagna) are reasonably priced and pretty tasty.

14904 N. Dale Mabry. ☎ *813-264-6676. Internet:* www.macaronigrill.com. *Reservations not necessary. To get there: From I-275 take Dale Mabry north 14 miles and look for it on the left. Main courses: $7–$17. AE, MC, V. Open: 11:30 a.m.– 9:30 p.m. daily.*

SideBerns

$$ Midtown   ASIAN/FLORIBBEAN

This child of Bern's Steak House (discussed earlier in this chapter) is trying to come of age as an alternative to its daddy. After trying out and discarding several menus, the restaurant settled on something the management calls "One World Cuisine," which is actually a mix of Pacific Rim, African, Asian, and Florribean. Try such delicacies as Szechuan-glazed grouper, lemon confit organic chicken, or chorizo-scaled sea bass. The casually elegant restaurant offers indoor seating in a light and airy dining room, as well as covered outdoor seating.

2208 W. Morrison St. (at Howard St.) ☎ *813-258-2233. Internet:* www.zip2. com/tampa/bernssteakhouse. *Reservations suggested. To get there: I-275 south on Armenia to Azeele, left a block to Howard, then left and around the corner. Main courses: $14–$23. AE, DC, DISC, MC, V. Open: 6–10 p.m. daily.*

Runner-up restaurants

Tampa has several other proven favorites featuring French and Cuban recipes as well as seafood served Florida-style. Try some of these on for size:

Ceviche Tapas Bar

$$ South Side   This restaurant serves about 45 old-style, Spanish tapas made with mussels, sea bass, roast pork, quail, and more. *2109 Bayshore Blvd.* ☎ *813-250-0203.*

Four Green Fields

$ Downtown   A friendly thatched-roof pub, it delivers Irish stew, shepherd's pie, and plenty of feel-good Irish music. *205 Platt St.* ☎ *813-254-4444. Internet:* www.fourgreenfields.com.

Le Bordeaux

$$ Midtown   This French bistro offers excellent classical French cuisine on its oft-changing menu. *1502 S. Howard Ave.* ☎ *813-254-4387.*

Exploring Tampa

Although the city lacks five-star beaches, Tampa exceeds St. Petersburg-Clearwater in the number of attractions available.

Tampa Attractions

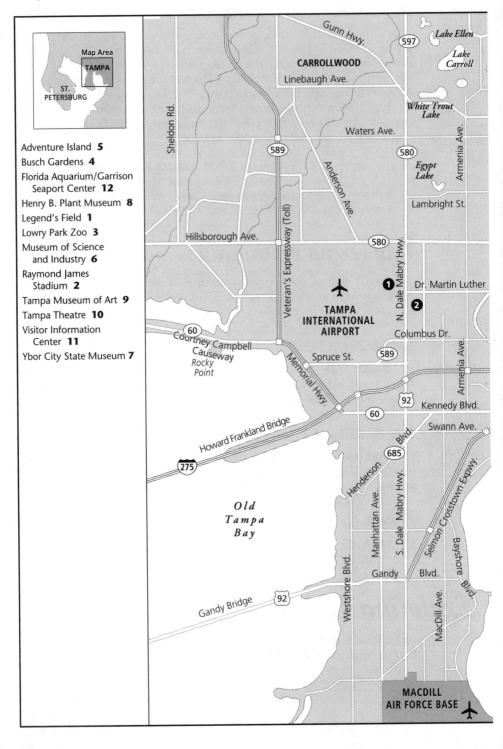

Adventure Island **5**
Busch Gardens **4**
Florida Aquarium/Garrison
    Seaport Center **12**
Henry B. Plant Museum **8**
Legend's Field **1**
Lowry Park Zoo **3**
Museum of Science
    and Industry **6**
Raymond James
    Stadium **2**
Tampa Museum of Art **9**
Tampa Theatre **10**
Visitor Information
    Center **11**
Ybor City State Museum **7**

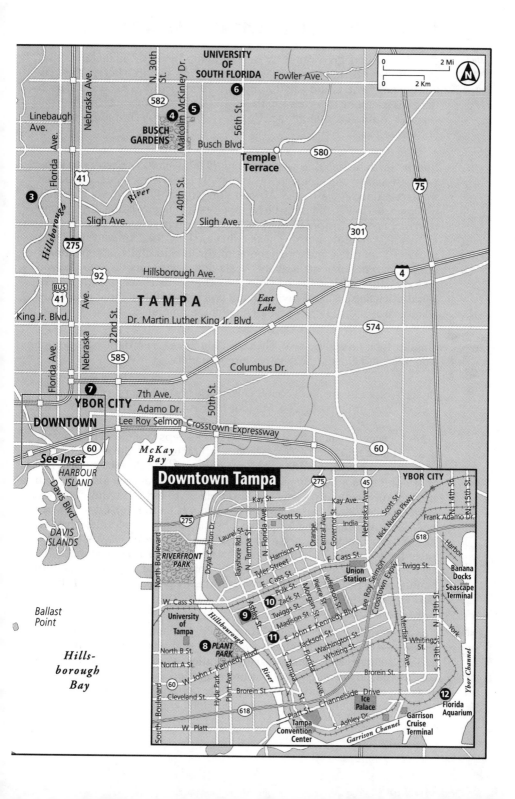

Going into the bush: Busch Gardens

This Tampa park grew out of a brewery. In the 1960s, the main (and only) attractions at **Busch Gardens** were a bird show and free beer. (You may be thinking, who could ask for anything more?) Today, however, Busch Gardens is among Florida's top theme parks. Two things set it aside from **Disney's Animal Kingdom** (see Chapter 19) in nearby Orlando: its coasters and critters.

Busch Gardens has five — count 'em, *FIVE*!! — roller coasters to keep your adrenaline and stomach levels high. The newest is *Gwazi*, a wooden wonder named for a fabled African lion with a tiger's head. This $10-million ride slowly climbs to 90 feet, before turning, twisting, diving, and *va-rrroommming* to speeds of 50 mph — enough to give you air time (also known as weightlessness). These twin coasters, the Lion and the Tiger, provide 2 minutes and 20 seconds of thrills and chills, steep-banked curves, and bobsled maneuvers. At six different points on the ride, you feel certain you're going to slam the other coaster as you hit 3.5 Gs. (That's science's way of saying that if you weigh 100 pounds, your body will feel like 350.) There's a 54-inch height minimum.

Smaller than an airline seat, Gwazi's 15-inch seat is a tight squeeze for thin folks and close to misery for larger models.

Busch's other four roller coasters are made of steel. *Kumba* covers 4,000 feet of tract at 60 mph. The 143-foot-high roller coaster jerks you with sudden turns (54-inch height minimum). *Montu* musses your hair at speeds exceeding 60 mph while the G-force keeps you plastered to your seat (54-inch minimum). *The Python*, a tad tamer, runs through a double spiraling corkscrew and a 70-foot plunge (48-inch minimum). *The Scorpion* offers a high-speed 60-foot drop and 360-degree loop (42-inch minimum). Busch's critters have fewer places to hide and, therefore, are easier to see than those at **Animal Kingdom** (Chapter 19). *Edge of Africa* and the *Serengeti Plain* allow views of lions, hippos, crocodiles, hyenas, and other animals that seem to roam free. (The *Serengeti,* by the way, recently got a facelift. This roller coaster's 29 acres now have hills, 700 trees, 32 kinds of edible grass, and 300 animals that are encouraged to wander closer to the tourist-carrying trains by placing food, cool shade, and water misters nearby.)

For an extra $15 over the admission price, you and 19 others can join a guide on a 30-minute *Serengeti Safari Tour* that gives you an ultra-close look at animals, and a chance to feed giraffes, gazelles, and more. (Tours are limited; advance reservations are suggested, and children must be at least 5 years old.) And up to 200 people per day can take a 30-minute truck tour that lets you pet a giraffe and feed antelopes.

In spring 2001, Busch is adding *Rhino Rally*. The attraction starts off as an off-road safari ride in 16-passenger Land Rovers that take guests within 15 feet of elephants, white rhinos, antelopes, cape buffalo, and other animals. After a few adventures, the Rovers drive over a shaky pontoon bridge that's washed out by a mock flash flood. The vehicles and passengers spiral downriver in what amounts to a raft ride. (Don't worry, the vehicles remain attached to a track under water.) The ride lasts 8 minutes.

Nairobi's Myombe Reserve, home to gorillas, has a baby animal nursery, petting zoo, turtle and reptile displays, and an elephant exhibit. *The Congo* features rare white Bengal tigers. For a good view, try the monorail, sky ride, and *Trans-Veldt Railway*.

The park's three water rides provide welcome relief from the summer heat. *Tanganyika Tidal Wave* and the *Stanley Falls* flume ride are splashy fun. The *Congo River Rapids* ride is very similar to Kali River Rapids in Animal Kingdom.

In addition to the animals, your kids will love the treehouse, rides (56-inch height maximum), and Dumphrey the Dragon in *Land of the Dragons*, as well as the sandy dig site at *King Tut's Tomb* and the friendly lorikeets of *Lory Landing*.

Buy your tickets in advance at the **Tampa Bay Visitor Information Center** (see "Street smarts: Getting information after arriving" earlier in this chapter), across Busch Boulevard from the park's entrance, to avoid long lines and save a couple of dollars.

Busch Gardens usually offers a special that lets you buy a second-day ticket for $12 per person.

Did we mention free beer if you're 21 or older? You can sample Anheuser-Busch products at the **Hospitality House.**

Busch Gardens is located at 3000 E. Busch Blvd. at McKinley Drive/N. 40th Street. From Orlando, take I-4 west to the U.S. 41 exit, go right (north) on Fla. 583. The route to the park is well marked, and it's 90 minutes from Orlando. Park hours are 9:30 a.m.—6 p.m. daily; however, the park sometimes opens as early as 9 a.m. and closes as late as 8:30 p.m. Admission costs $47.95 for adults, $38.95 kids 3–9, excluding tax. FlexTicket pricing is $197 for adults, $158 for kids for a 10-day pass that also includes unlimited admission to **Universal Studios Florida, Islands of Adventure, SeaWorld,** *and* **Wet 'n Wild.** *Parking is $6. Call ☎ 800-423-8367 or 813-987-5283 or visit its Web site at* www.buschgardens.com *for more information.*

Seeing other top sights

Busch Gardens may be Tampa's top attraction, but several other city sights are worthy of your attention, and most of them won't empty your wallets as fast as the theme park will.

Adventure Island

North Side/Next to Busch Gardens

This Busch-owned water park offers 36 acres of wet fun. The A-list attractions here include the **Key West Rapids,** a 700-foot tube run; **Tampa Typhoon,** a seven-story, adrenaline-pumping water slide; and **Gulf Scream,** another body slide that gets you lickity-splitting at 25 mph. This all-day affair also has picnic areas and a volleyball complex.

10001 McKinley Dr. ☎ 813-987-5600. Internet: www.adventureisland.com. *To get there: It's on the east side of Busch Gardens. Admission: $25 adults, $23 kids 3–9. Parking: $4. Open: 10 a.m.–5 p.m., sometimes later, daily, mid Feb–Nov.*

Florida Aquarium

Downtown

Its 4,300 animals and plants include 550 of Florida's native species. The galleries explore wetlands, bays, beaches, coral reefs, and the creatures that live in them. Numerous interactive exhibits, including a 600-gallon touch pool, make this a great place to take younger children, who can also watch divers regularly feed sharks and other marine life. You can rent audio tours in English and Spanish that take you on an interactive journey through Florida's water world. Allow 2 to 4 hours to see everything.

701 Channelside Dr. ☎ 813-273-4000. Internet: www.flaquarium.org. *To get there: Take Kennedy Boulevard to 13th Street, turn right and follow the signs. Admission: $12 adults, $11 seniors, $7 kids 3–12. Parking: $4. Open: 9:30 a.m.–5 p.m. daily.*

Lowry Park Zoo

North Side

Dating back to the early 1930s, the Lowry faced extinction 20 years ago, but park lovers got Tampa's oldest zoo on track. Today's version is rated among the top small zoos in the nation. The zoo's 1,500 tenants include manatees, Komodo dragons, and red pandas. The park has a free-flight aviary, a birds-of-prey show, a kids' petting zoo, a hands-on discovery center. By the way, Lowry Zoo has one of Florida's three manatee hospital and rehabilitation centers. It's also a sanctuary for panthers and red wolves. It takes 4 to 6 hours to enjoy the zoo.

7530 N. Boulevard. ☎ 813-935-8552. Internet: www.lowryparkzoo.com. *To get there: Exit I-275 on Sligh Avenue and follow the signs 1 mile west. Admission: $8.50 adults, $7.50 seniors, $5 kids 3–11. Parking: Free. Open: 9:30 a.m.–5 p.m. daily.*

Museum of Science and Industry

North Side

Kids can touch stuff and discover by doing. (Okay, adults can play, too.) The **Amazing You** lets you explore the body, **Diplodocus Dinosaurs** offers a close look at our earliest giants, and **Our Place on the Planet: An Exhibition of Florida** focuses on environmental issues. The museum has 450 hands-on, minds-on exhibits, including space and hurricane simulators, a planetarium, an IMAX theater, and several traveling exhibits. Plan to stick around for 3 to 4 hours.

4801 Fowler Ave. ☎ *813-987-6300. Internet:* www.mosi.org. *To get there: 2 miles east of I-275 on Fowler. Admission: $13 adults, $11 seniors, $9 kids 2–13. Parking: Free. Open: 9 a.m.–5 p.m. daily.*

Ybor City

East of downtown

The liveliest section in Tampa and the epicenter of the city's Latin culture, Ybor City was born in 1885 when Cuban exile Don Vicente Martinez Ybor (pronounced *"EEEEE-bore"*) moved his cigar business from Key West to a palmetto patch east of Tampa. Hailed as the *cigar capital of the world* until the industry high-tailed it to South and Latin America 60 years ago, Ybor is still a good spot to pick up a hand-rolled cigar. The **Ybor State Museum,** 1818 9th Ave. (☎ **813-247-6323;** $2 admission), heralds Cuban exiles and spans half a block, including a restored worker's home and the historic **Ferlita Bakery.**

It may not be on par with some other cities' hippest spots, but the district is loaded with excellent restaurants, shopping, and nightlife. Just west of 21st Street, there's a wall-to-wall run of clubs, cafes, and galleries. If you come after dark, however, stick to well-lit and well-traveled areas. Allow 2 to 4 hours to hit the major spots.

The National Historic District stretches for 110 red-brick blocks, but most of the action happens along an eight-block stretch of 7th Avenue/East Broadway (I-4 east to 21st Street, south to Broadway). The best way to see this charming slice of yesterday is on foot. Parking spaces are available on Broadway.

Seeing and doing more cool things

An army of less-expensive-and-more-leisurely things to do is waiting for you behind the front line. Some of these attractions and activities appeal to those of you with special interests — whether you're an art buff, a golfer, or a pro-sports fan.

Taking in some culture: Museums and more

Here are three options for visitors who are culturally inclined:

✔ **Henry B. Plant Museum:** Now on the University of Tampa campus, the museum is in the south wing of what used to be the Tampa Bay Hotel. The 1891 structure has turn-of-the-century art, furnishings, and fashions. Its Russian spires are a prominent part of the skyline. It's at 401 W. Kennedy Blvd. (☎ **813-254-1891;**

Internet: www.plantmuseum.com). Admission costs $5 for adults, $2 for kids under 12.

✔ **Tampa Museum of Art:** The museum's collection includes permanent and changing exhibits housed in eight galleries, with more than 7,000 pieces displayed. Classical and Mediterranean antiquities and twentieth-century American art are its specialties. The museum is located at 600 N. Ashley Dr. (☎ 813-274-8130; Internet: www.tampamuseum.com). Admission is $5 for adults, and $3 for kids over 6.

✔ **Tampa Theatre:** Architecture is the calling card these days at this 1926 classic, but films and concerts are presented here during the year. It has balconies, replicas of Roman sculptures, and one of those ghostly Wurlitzers. Speaking of ghosts, this old house is said to be haunted by Foster Finely, a projectionist who worked here for 35 years. Tours are only available on an irregular basis. Call in advance for prices. The theater is at 711 Franklin St. (☎ 813-274-8981; Internet: www.tampatheatre.org).

Playing around: Sports and more

The newest attraction to hit Tampa Bay took quite a while to get here, but baseball has arrived. The regular-season big leagues — courtesy of the Tampa Bay Devil Rays — actually play across the bay in St. Petersburg (see Chapter 16). But you can see the New York Yankees's spring training at **Legends Field** on North Dale Mabry Highway (☎ 813-287-8844), where tickets will set you back $5 to $13.

If you decide to see a game while you're in Tampa and you're from a big-league-baseball town, you won't suffer price shock when arriving at the ballpark. When the national pastime finally landed in the Tampa Bay area, however, some locals thought its theme song should have said: "Buy me some peanuts and Cracker Jack — on the installment plan."

Prices at concession stands and restaurants under the dome at St. Petersburg's **Tropicana Field** are anything but civilized.

Expect to pay:

✔ Up to $7 for a burger

✔ $10 to park in the same time zone

✔ $5 if you want this Bud to be for you

✔ $5 for those Cracker Jacks

Heck, it's only $5 for sushi — yes, you heard right, *sushi* at a ball park.

The average price for a family of four is about $125. In fairness, though, that ranks about in the middle of the major leagues. And you can find bargains. If you're not affected by altitude sickness you can snag $3 seats in the outfield. You can use the water fountain instead of the beer or soda carts. And there's free parking — 1 mile away if you don't mind riding the shuttle or hiking.

If you prefer other sports to the national pastime, you will find an abundance of options open to you, including

- ✔ **Fishing:** Our best advice for anglers is to head across the bay to St. Petersburg-Clearwater (Chapter 16), but several guides can get you there, including Dave Markett (☎ **813-962-1435**).

- ✔ **Football:** The **Tampa Bay Buccaneers** have risen from the ashes of two decades of frustration to show, well, a little promise. They play preseason games in August and eight regular-season games in the fall and early winter at Raymond James Stadium at 4201 N. Dale Mabry Highway (☎ **813-879-2827**; Internet: www.buccaneers.com).

- ✔ **Golf:** You can find a ton of tee-time fun on the Internet at www. golf.com and www.floridagolfing.com. If you prefer to do your research the old-fashioned way, request course information from the **Florida Sports Foundation** (☎ **850-488-8347**), or **Florida Golfing**, (☎ **877-222-4653**). Some of the more popular courses here are

  - **Saddlebrook,** north of Tampa (☎ **813-973-1111**). Greens Fees: $70-$130.

  - **Summerfield,** in Riverview, (☎ **813-671-3311**). Greens Fees: under $25.

  - **Tournament Players Club,** in Tampa, (☎ **813-949-0091**). Greens Fees: $41 to $110.

Seeing Tampa by guided tour

If you're a foot soldier, there are several good walking tours around town. You can join a twice-monthly, 1-hour guided tour of the **Tampa Theatre.** The tour costs $5. Call ☎ **813-274-8981** for dates and times. The Ybor City State Museum offers a weekly Walking Tour of Historic Ybor City on Saturdays at 10:30 a.m. The price is $4, and you can call ☎ **813-247-6323,** for more information. For a spooky time, try **Ybor City's Ghost Walks** (☎ **813-242-9255**). A tour costs $12.50 for adults, $7 for kids 12 and under; tours start at 7 p.m. from Thursday through Saturday and at 4 p.m. on Sundays.

Shopping

At the risk of redundancy, Florida isn't generally known as a paradise for shoppers, but Tampa does offer a couple of funky areas that are worth browsing. Malls are generally open from 10 a.m. to 9 p.m. (noon to 6 p.m. on Sunday); individual shops are usually open from 10 a.m. to 6 p.m. Monday through Saturday.

Tampa's best shopping areas

✔ **Ybor City:** You may encounter an aged craftsman or woman hand-rolling cigars in the string of clubs, restaurants, and shops that run through this core area (an eight-block stretch of 7th Avenue/ East Broadway, which is south of I-4 east off the 21st Street exit). You can find Caribbean trinkets at the open air market. **Centro Ybor,** a seven-acre shopping, entertainment, and restaurant area opened in late 2000 on Eighth Avenue, hosting a museum, an Improv-style comedy club, retail shops, an art gallery, and a 20-screen theater.

✔ **Channelside:** This spot at 615 Channelside Dr., near the Florida Aquarium (see "Seeing other top sights," earlier in this chapter), has a half dozen eateries, a nine-screen theater, and a few retailers, including a Ron Jon's Surf Shop.

✔ **Old Hyde Park Village:** Located south of downtown (748 S. Village Circle, ☎ 813-251-3500), this landing zone has a collection of 60-some shops, eateries, and more in an Old World, outdoor setting. Standouts here include Ann Taylor and Austin-Hyde leather goods.

Hitting the malls

Tampa and the surrounding areas certainly have their share of malls. **Brandon TownCenter,** 459 Brandon TownCenter (☎ 813-661-6255; Internet: www.shopbtc.com) has 120 stores including Burdines, Abercrombie & Fitch, Dillard's, and Banana Republic. **Citrus Park Town Center,** 8021 Citrus Park Town Center (☎ 813-926-4644; Internet: www.citrusparktowncenter.com) has an equal number of shops led by Burdines, Dillard's, Brooks Brothers, and Eddie Bauer. **Westshore Plaza,** 250 Westshore Plaza (☎ 813-286-0790; Internet: www.westshoreplaza.com) has 100 stores, including FAO Schwartz and Saks Fifth Avenue.

Living the Nightlife

You can find bars and clubs scattered throughout the Tampa Bay area, but none are as concentrated as those in Ybor City. Stroll along 7th Avenue between 15th and 20th Streets, where you can find a host of stylish clubs catering to the 20s-and-under set. If you prefer your evenings to have a more cultural tone, you will have a number of options to choose from.

To find out what's playing where, don't forget to peruse a copy of the "Friday Extra" section in *The Tampa Tribune.* You can get the latest arts information, 24 hours a day, from **Artsline** at ☎ 813-229-2787.

Bars

Four Green Fields, at 205 Platt St./Downtown (☎ **813-254-4444;** Internet: www.fourgreenfields.com) is a friendly thatched-roof pub with friendlier Irish music. **Frankie's Patio,** 1920 E. 7th Ave., Ybor City (☎ **813-248-3337**) is a warehouse-style club featuring DJs and an exceptional variety of live musical acts. The **Green Iguana Bar & Grill,** 4029 S. Westshore Blvd. (☎ **813-837-1234**), and 1708 E, 7th Ave., Ybor City (☎ **813-248-9555;** Internet: www.greeniguana.com) attracts the young professional crowd with live music nightly.

Clubs

The **Columbia Restaurant's** Flamenco dancers perform nightly, Monday through Saturday. The show is $6 plus the cost of dinner. The restaurant is located at 2117 E. 7th Ave., Ybor City (☎ **813-248-4961;** Internet: www.columbiarestaurant.com). **Side Splitters Comedy Club** showcases stand-up pros on most nights of the week. It's at 12938 N. Dale Mabry Highway, (☎ **813-960-1197**). Shows are usually scheduled on Tuesday, Wednesday, and Sunday at 8:30 p.m., and on Saturdays at 8 and 10 p.m. There's a cover of $6 to $8.

Cultural centers

The **Tampa Bay Performing Arts Center,** 1010 MacInnes Place (☎ **800-955-1045** or 813-229-7827) is a four-theater complex that stages Broadway plays, concerts, operas, and other special events. The **Off-Center Theater,** inside the Performing Arts Center, features local artists in music, dance, comedy, and other productions. For information, call ☎ **813-221-1001.**

Sightseeing Itineraries

We're going to give you 2- and 3-day plans that will keep your dance cards full but not wear you out. If one or more of the sights or activities following sounds unappealing, replace it with one of those elsewhere in this chapter or from across the bay (see Chapter 16). These presume you have a car.

Tampa in 2 Days

On **Day 1,** hot-foot it to **Busch Gardens,** where you can spend the day riding any or all of the five roller coasters, getting close to the not-so-wildlife, and enjoying the park's other rides and shows. But don't get caught paying theme park prices for lunch. Get your hand stamped for return entry and leave the park in favor of **Mel's Hot Dogs,** just up the boulevard. Later, go to the **Columbia Restaurant** for the dinner show, then finish the evening at the **Green Iguana Bar & Grill.**

Spend the first half of **Day 2** at **Lowry Park Zoo.** Grab lunch on the fly, then visit the **Museum of Science and Industry** in the afternoon. If either of those options doesn't appeal to you, replace it with the **Florida Aquarium.** Have dinner at the **Ovo Café** and then visit the **Blues Ship** or one of the other clubs around Ybor City.

Tampa in 3 Days

Follow the **Day 1** itinerary under "Tampa in 2 Days," the section preceding, first going to **Busch Gardens,** grabbing lunch at **Mel's Hot Dogs,** and then dinner and the show at the **Columbia,** and finishing at the **Green Iguana.**

When you buy your Busch Gardens tickets, take the second-day discount option and return on **Day 2,** which lets you see the park at a more relaxed pace. Or spend Day Two at **Adventure Island,** Busch's adjacent water park. (Of course, this plan won't work in winter; so if you're coming when the island is closed, go to plan C, visiting the **Florida Aquarium, Henry B. Plant Museum,** and **Tampa Museum of Art,** all of which are downtown.) Enjoy a leisurely dinner at **Bern's Steakhouse,** and then lift a pint or two and sing along with the gang at **Four Green Fields.**

On **Day 3,** spend your morning and early afternoon at **Lowry Park Zoo,** grab lunch on the fly, and then finish the day at the **Museum of Science and Industry.** Have dinner at the **Ovo Café,** and then party a little in some of the clubs around Ybor City.

Fast Facts

Area Code

The local area code is **813.**

American Express

There's a travel service center at One Tampa City Center, (☎ **813-273-0310**). It's open 9 a.m.–5 p.m. weekdays.

Doctors

If you need a physician referral, ask the **Hillsborough County Medical Association** (☎ **813-253-0471**). You can turn to **Ask-A-Nurse** (☎ **813-870-4444**) with health questions.

Hospitals

Hospitals servicing the area are: St. Joseph's Hospital, 3001 Martin Luther King Blvd. (☎ **813-870-4000**); Tampa General Hospital, 2 Columbia Dr. (☎ **813-251-7000**); and University Community Hospital, 3100 Fletcher Ave. (☎ **813-971-6000**).

Information

The **Tampa/Hillsborough Convention & Visitors Association,** 400 N. Tampa St., (☎ **800-448-2672** or 813-223-2752; Internet: www.gotampa.com) is your best bet for tourist information.

The **Ybor City Chamber of Commerce** (☎ **877-934-3782** or 813-248-3712; Fax: 813-247-1764; Internet: www.yborg.com) has a visitors center that dispenses information at 1800 E. 9th Ave. (at 18th St.) from 9 a.m. to 5 p.m. Monday–Friday.

Mail

U.S. post offices are located at 9748 N. 56th St., Temple Terrace, and 5201 W. Spruce St., Tampa Airport. Call ☎ **800-275-8777**.

Maps

The information sources preceding are great organizations to hit up for maps before or after you land. (Trust us: Good maps are necessities because getting lost in Tampa is easy.) Rental-car agencies are another good source (including those at the airport), and so are convenience stores, which sell maps for $3–$5.

Newspapers

The Tampa Tribune (☎ **813-259-7711**) publishes an extremely useful weekly entertainment section called "Friday Extra."

Pharmacies

A 24-hour Walgreens is located at 15602 N. Dale Mabry Highway (☎ **813-264-7722**; Internet: www.walgreens.com), and a 24-hour Eckerd at 3714 Henderson Blvd. (☎ **813-876-2485**; Internet: www.eckerd.com).

Safety

Tampa has all the crime that's associated with a large city. We don't recommend walking alone after dark, and you should be wary about driving in the downtown area. Stick to well-lit and known tourist zones and even then be aware of your surroundings. Never stop on a highway and get out of your car if you can avoid it. Always keep your doors locked.

Taxes

The sales and local-option taxes equal 6.75 percent in Hillsborough County. Hotels add another 5 percent for a total of 11.75 percent.

Taxis

Generally, it costs $1.25 to get into a taxi and $1.75 per mile. The major companies in Tampa are **United Cab** (☎ **813-253-2424**), and **Yellow Cab** (☎ **813-253-0121**).

Transit Info

Hillsborough Area Regional Transit or **HARTline,** (☎ **813-623-5835** or 813-254-4278), runs buses throughout the county, although the routes are not especially tourist friendly. Bus fare is $1.15.

Weather Updates

For a recording of current conditions and forecast reports, call the local office of the **National Weather Service** at ☎ **813-645-2506,** or check out the Web site, www.nws.noaa.gov. You also can get information by watching the **Weather Channel** (Internet: www.weatherchannel.com).

Chapter 16

St. Petersburg, Clearwater, and Beaches

● ●

In This Chapter

▶ Dancing around the Suncoast's ocean critters

▶ Fishing for grouper, amberjack, and sea bass

▶ Going insane on the primary north-south highway

▶ Stretching along the touristy St. Petersburg shore

● ●

*U*nlike Tampa across the bay, St. Petersburg can never be described as a business center. The city was built with visitors in mind, and it shows. And if you're looking for sun and sand, this 28-mile long stretch of shoreline and barrier islands along Florida's Gulf Coast is *beachville*.

And because a trip to the beach is pretty much a must on any St. Pete visitor's dance card, we offer the following five tips for staying healthy while having fun in the sun:

✔ **The Jellyfish Jitterbug:** If you see one, it may be too late. These translucent wave riders are common on the Gulf beaches. While their sting is far from deadly, it's painful enough, and their washed-up carcasses can still ruin the moment. If they sting you, meat tenderizer helps relieve the pain; the creature's venom is pure protein, and tenderizer breaks it down.

✔ **The Stingray Shuffle:** Rays are another unpleasant item you may encounter when going to the beach. They love to snooze on the bottom of the ocean. Most folks who get hit by the poisonous spines on their backs and tail step directly down on them. If you shuffle your feet as you walk through the water, stingrays usually skedaddle.

✔ **The Crispy Critter:** Sunburn or its evil twin, sun poisoning, can nail anyone, but fair-skinned tourists on their first few days at the beach are the most vulnerable. So take the slow approach. Get a little sun at a time and keep applying a sunscreen that's rated 25 or higher. Getting a tan is okay, but who wants to look like raw meat (or spend a few nights in a hospital)?

✔ **The Red Tide Hide:** All you can do is hide when the marine blight, known as the red tide comes to the beach. This phenomenon occurs when a microscopic marine algae — appearing as red patches in the water — begins to multiply at a higher rate than normal. The tide poisons fish. The stink from the dead fish washing up on the beach is monstrous. If red tide lands, you have to hunker down in your room or eat your losses and move to another coast. The Florida Marine Research Institute maintains a Web site for red tide watch at `www.fmri.usf.edu`.

✔ **The Sand Wedgie:** Sitting in the surf and letting the waves lap at your lower extremities is fun while you build a sandcastle on a scorching hot day. But unless your swimsuit is airtight, pesky grains of sand that have the same effect on your skin as tenderizer has on protein can get into areas best left untouched. As soon as you're done building, take a dip or shower to wash away the invaders.

Okay, now that you've been warned, let's get to the introductions.

Searching the Suncoast: What's Where?

Pinellas County is a narrow peninsula. The sun-drenched beaches in the St. Petersburg/Tampa section of the county — a zone appropriately nicknamed the Suncoast — are an especially popular tourist draw. With a handful of exceptions, much of this region's action takes place along or near the Gulf Coast.

Most of those exceptions are in St. Petersburg's downtown, where the **Salvador Dalí Museum, the Pier, the Bayfront Center, Tropicana Field** (home of the Tampa Bay Devil Rays), and **Florida International Museum** are the cornerstone attractions. **Fort DeSoto Park** is at the southern end of the beaches, which continue north to the Clearwater area and some of its showpieces, such as the **Clearwater Marine Aquarium** and **Ruth Eckerd Hall.** Before hitting the county line, you may also have a chance to visit **Caladesi Island State Park,** one of our favorite beaches, and the Greek community of Tarpon Springs, with its famous **Sponge Docks.**

St. Petersburg and Beaches

The southern half of Pinellas County is the west coast's biggest tourist zone, mainly due to the beaches and the Gulf of Mexico. As you travel around, you may run into a few interior areas, such as Kenneth City and Pinellas Park (north), Seminole (northwest), and South Pasadena and Gulfport (south). But we concentrate on the most popular zones downtown or along the coast: **St. Pete Beach, Treasure Island, Madeira Beach, Redington Beach,** and **Indian Rocks Beach.**

Getting there

Your only convenient option to get directly to St. Petersburg or its beaches is by plane, although driving is a possibility. (See the "Downtown St. Petersburg" map later in this chapter.)

By plane

St. Petersburg-Clearwater International Airport (☎ 727-535-7600; Internet: www.stpete-clwairport.com) courts six smaller American and Canadian carriers, including American Trans Air and Canada 3000. **Avis, Hertz, National,** and **Enterprise** have car-rental desks at the airport. You can also get a ride into town from **Yellow Cab** (☎ 727-799-2222), and **St. Pete Taxi of Clearwater** (☎ 727-799-8294). Standard rates are $1.50 to start the meter and $1.60 per mile.

If you want a greater variety of arrival and departure options, consider flying into **Tampa International,** ☎ 813-870-8700; Internet: www.tampaairport.com. (See "Getting to Tampa" in Chapter 15 for more information.)

By car

Those of you who are highway heroes have three choices by car:

- ✔ **U.S. 19:** This highway, also known as Instant Insanity, is a constantly clogged artery down most of Florida's lower Gulf Coast.

- ✔ **I-75/275:** This road brings you across the Florida/Georgia border and down the state's midsection. North of Tampa, take the I-275 option (it bears right, through Tampa, across Tampa Bay, and then into St. Petersburg).

- ✔ **I-95/I-4/I-275:** I-95 gets you into the state along the east coast, where you can pick up I-4 in Daytona Beach and ride it onto I-275, and from there into Tampa and St. Petersburg.

Getting around

When you consider that St. Petersburg was designed with tourists in mind, it should come as no surprise that this is one of the easiest cities in Florida to navigate. Thank city planners who wanted to keep things simple.

By car

St. Petersburg is easy to navigate because, with only a few exceptions, street numbers are used rather than names. Think of Central Avenue as Ground Zero. Avenues run north and south. They grow (1st, 2nd, and so on) in either direction from Central. Streets climb higher as they move west from downtown. You'll find a few exceptions, most notably the northeast and southeast addresses that are on the city's east side, which

Downtown St. Petersburg

ACCOMMODATIONS ■
Hilton St. Petersburg **5**
Renaissance Vinoy Resort **1**

DINING ◆
The Moon Under Water **2**

ATTRACTIONS ●
Florida International Museum **4**
Great Explorations Hands-on
 Museum **3**
Salvador Dalí Museum **6**
The Pier **3**

are numbered in reverse of the procedure preceding. In some cases, the Beaches use St. Petersburg's street-numbering system, in others they use names. The main beach road is Gulf Boulevard/Hwy. 699.

By bus

The **Pinellas Suncoast Transit Authority** (☎ 727-530-9911) serves the entire county. The fare is $1.25 per ride. Unless you don't mind a slow, often nontourist pace, skip it.

You can also try **Looper: the Downtown trolley** (☎ 727-571-3440), which runs past all the downtown attractions every 30 minutes from 11 a.m. to 5 p.m. daily except Thanksgiving and Christmas. Rides cost 50 cents per person.

By taxi

In general, it costs $1.50 to get into a cab and $1.60 a mile thereafter. **Yellow Cab** (☎ 727-799-2222), and **St. Pete Taxi of Clearwater** (☎ 727-799-8294) are among the taxi companies that operate in St. Petersburg.

Staying on the Suncoast

St. Petersburg has a wide range of accommodations, from hotels and motels to condominiums. Numerous chain motels lie along U.S. 19. The high season runs from January to April, and many hotels offer significant off-season discounts.

The **St. Petersburg/Clearwater Area Convention & Visitors Bureau,** 14450 46th St. N., Clearwater (☎ 727-464-7200; Internet: www. floridasbeach.com) publishes a brochure listing members of its Superior Small Lodgings program; all of which have been inspected and certified for cleanliness and value. Visitors can also call the bureau's free reservations service at ☎ 800-345-6710.

You can also book a hotel room through the **Florida Hotel Network** (☎ 800-538-3616; Internet: www.floridahotels.com), but be advised that on the Web site you need to click on Tampa to find lodgings in St. Petersburg and St. Pete Beach.

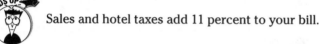

Sales and hotel taxes add 11 percent to your bill.

The Suncoast's best hotels

Alden Beach Resort

$$ St. Pete Beach

Located on the south end of the beaches, its 140 suites have fully equipped kitchenettes and a separate living area with a sofa bed. Some suites have private balconies overlooking the Gulf. The resort has numerous recreational facilities, including two tennis courts, a playground, whirlpools, and a game room.

5900 Gulf Blvd. ☎ **800-237-2530** *or 727-360-7081. Fax: 727-360-5957. Internet:* www. aldenbeachresort.com. *To get there: 2 miles north of Pinellas Bayway/Hwy. 682. Parking: Free, self. Rack rates: $110–$195 Feb–Apr; $85–$140 Jan, May–Aug; $75–$130 Sept–Dec. AE, CB, DC, DISC, MC, V.*

Beach Haven

$ St. Pete Beach

Here's an old-style (1950s), beachfront property that offers family warmth and a modernized interior. There are five motel rooms (with shower-only bathrooms), as well as tropically decorated one- and two-bedroom efficiencies. The property has a large beach deck, barbecue grills, a coin-operated laundry, and is near several restaurants.

4980 Gulf Blvd. ☎ **727-367-8642**. *Fax: 727-360-8202. Internet:* www. beachhavenvillas.com. *To get there: 1.2 miles north of Pinellas Bayway. Parking: Free, self. Rack rates: $88–$144 Feb–Apr, $77–$120 Dec–Jan, $65–$107 May–Aug, $55–$92 Sept–Nov. MC, V.*

Don CeSar Beach Resort and Spa

$$$ St. Pete Beach

Opulent is the best word to describe the Don, the beach's most famous landmark, since its first guest signed the register in 1928. The *Pink Palace,* so dubbed for its color and architecture, offers 345 rooms, suites, and guest houses overlooking the Gulf of Mexico or Boca Ciega Bay. A full-scale spa, fitness center, and restaurant are available onsite. Even if it's beyond your budget, the Don's worth a stop as a tourist attraction.

Most rooms are in the $$$ range, but some cost more; rates do not include a $15 per couple per night resort fee.

3400 Gulf Blvd. ☎ **800-637-7200** *or 727-360-1881. Fax: 727-367-3609. Internet:* www. doncesar.com. *To get there: At 34th Ave. and the Pinellas Bayway. Parking: Free, self. Rack rates: $294–$824 Feb–Apr; $229–$699 Jan, May, Oct–Dec; $169–$564 June–Sept. AE, DISC, MC, V.*

Hilton St. Petersburg

$$ Downtown

The hotel's 333 rooms are spread among 15 floors and have views of Tampa Bay, the Bayfront Center, and/or other downtown landmarks. Standard rooms are basic but modern and clean. A small fitness center, an onsite restaurant, and a lobby bar are available.

333 1st St. S. ☎ **800-774-1500** *or 727-894-5000. Fax: 727-823-4797. Internet:* www. hilton.com. *To get there: I-275 to I-175, exit 5th Ave. South, go east to 1st St.,* and then north. Parking: $8 valet. Rack rates: $135–$185 Nov–Apr, $95–$125 May–Oct. AE, CB, DC, DISC, MC, V.

Renaissance Vinoy Resort

$$$ St. Petersburg/Downtown

This old beauty rests on Tampa Bay and is even more of a showpiece than the Don. Built in 1925 and restored in 1992, the Vinoy has 360 luxuriously appointed rooms, many offering bay views. The resort features graceful arches, marble floors, a marina, an 18-hole golf course, a 14-court tennis complex, two croquet courts, five restaurants, and a health club and spa.

501 5th Ave. NE. ☎ **800-468-3571** *or 727-894-1000. Fax: 727-894-1970. Internet:* www. renaissancehotels.com. *To get there: 2 miles east of I-375 (off I-275) on 4th Av., north to Beach Dr., go left, then right on 5th. Parking: $8 a day self, $12 valet. Rack rates: $269-$329 Jan–Apr; $229–$299 Dec, May, Oct–Nov; $129–$179 June–Sept. AE, DC, DISC, MC, V.*

Tradewinds Sandpiper Hotel and Suites

$$ St. Pete Beach

The Sandpiper is one of three connecting Tradewinds properties. (The others are Tradewinds Island Grand and Sirata Beach Resort.) The hotel's 56 standard rooms have refrigerators, wet bars, toasters, and dishware; the 103 suites offer separate bedroom and living areas, as well as full kitchens. There's a fitness center and kids' program to keep the little ones from ruining your tan. An additional nightly resort fee of $10 is charged to cover some of the amenities.

6000 Gulf Blvd. ☎ **800-237-0707** *or 727-367-6461. Fax: 727-360-3848. Internet:* www. tradewindsresort.com. *To get there: 2 miles north of the Pinellas Bayway. Parking: $8 a day. Rack rates: $159–$318 Feb–Apr, $125–$239 May–Dec, $125–$229 Jan. AE, CB, DC, DISC, MC, V.*

Runner-up hotels

Here are a few other places to park yourself. You can also check out the major hotel chains listed in the "Quick Concierge" in the back of this book.

Island's End Resort

$$ St. Pete Beach   This small hideaway, situated right off the beach, offers five one-bedroom cottages with kitchens and excellent value. *1 Pass-A-Grille Way.* ☎ **727-360-5023**; *Fax: 727-367-7890. Internet:* www. islandsend.com.

Buccaneer Beach Resort

$ Treasure Island   A 40-something-year-old property with 70 rooms (some with kitchens and multiple bedrooms) and pocket-friendly rates.

10800 Gulf Blvd. ☎ *800-826-2120 or 727-367-1908. Fax: 727-367-4890. Internet:* www.bucbeachresort.com.

Schooner Motel

$ Madeira Beach The Schooner is far from fancy, but the motel's rooms have refrigerators, microwaves, and coffee makers. *14500 Gulf Blvd.* ☎ *800-573-5187 or 727-392-5167. Internet:* www.schoonermotel.com/index.html.

Thunderbird Beach Resort

$ Treasure Island This '50s-style motel has a lush pool area, a location right on the Gulf, and well-equipped rooms and efficiencies. *10700 Gulf Blvd.* ☎ *800-367-2473 or 727-360-2800. Fax: 727-360-4330. Internet:* www.gotampabay.com/thunderbird.

Dining out on the Suncoast

The Suncoast is another destination made for seafood lovers, and you can find fresh fish dishes on almost every menu. Carnivores won't go hungry; plenty of menus brim with meat and poultry items, too. Families and those on a tight budget can find many national chain restaurants and fast-food joints along the major thoroughfares.

If you have a car, try some of the ones listed later in this chapter under "Clearwater." And don't forget to add 7 percent sales tax to your meal budget.

The Suncoast's best restaurants

Hurricane Seafood Restaurant

$ Pass-a-Grille/St. Pete Beach SEAFOOD

A favorite haunt of locals and tourists, the Hurricane, situated just across from Pass-a-Grille Beach, offers a large selection of fish (served blackened, jerk-style, and more), shellfish, and a belly-busting Class 5 Hurricane Combo (flounder, shrimp, crab cake, clam strips, and scallops). The rooftop bar offers magnificent views at sunset.

807 Gulf Way. ☎ *727-360-9558. Internet:* www.thehurricane.com. *Reservations not accepted. To get there: From the Bayway, go south on Gulf Blvd. to 22nd Ave., turn right, then left on Gulf Way and go 12 blocks. Main courses: $10–$17. AE, MC, V. Open: 8–1 a.m. daily.*

La Vigna Ristorante

$$ Redington Shores SOUTHERN ITALIAN

Intimate booths in an elegant setting, and a buzzing kitchen complement a menu bursting with such Italian treats as farfalle with chicken, wild mushrooms, and sun-dried tomatoes; and linguine in tomato broth with clams, mussels, calamari, and shrimp. The service is excellent, and the wine list is extensive.

17807 Gulf Blvd. ☎ *727-392-8001. Reservations recommended. To get there: Just south of Hwy. 694 on Gulf Blvd. Main courses: $11–$20. AE, MC, V. Open: 4:30–10 p.m. Tues–Sun.*

The Moon Under Water

$ St. Petersburg/Downtown   MIDDLE EASTERN/FAR EASTERN

This restaurant, a pleasant change of pace from seared steaks and Florida-style seafood, takes its cue from the cuisine of former British outposts. Eat on the outdoor verandah or inside the British-colonial dining room. Entrees range from pot pies to minced spiced beef, and fiery Indian curries. Wash your meal down with an Irish, English or Australian beer.

332 Beach Dr. ☎ *727-896-6160. Reservations for six or more. To get there: Between 3rd and 4th aves. Main courses: $10–$17. AE, DC, DISC, MC, V. Open: 11:30 a.m.–11 p.m. daily.*

Ted Peters' Famous Smoked Fish

$ South Pasadena   SEAFOOD

This open-air eatery is an institution in these parts. We've been eating Ted's best since the early '60s, but he's been around at least a decade longer. Some folks bring the fish they caught for the staff to smoke (at $1 a pound), others figure fishing is a waste of time and come right to Ted's table for mullet, mackerel, salmon, and other fish that have been slowly cooked over red oak. Enjoy the smell and sip a cold one while you wait for your order.

1350 Pasadena Ave. ☎ *727-381-7931. Reservations — sorry, not here! To get there: 1 mile south of Central Ave. Main courses: $10–$18. Leave the credit cards at home. Open: 11 a.m.–7:30 p.m. Wed–Mon.*

The Wine Cellar

$$ North Redington Beach   CONTINENTAL

The Wine Cellar, an elegant family-run restaurant, is a good destination for a special evening out. It has an intimate atmosphere, professional service, and — surprise! — a great wine list. Entrees include pecan-crusted grouper in red-pepper salsa, beef Wellington, veal marsala, and Dover sole filleted at your table. Most entrees are under $28, and the five-course special is $35.

17307 Gulf Blvd. ☎ *727-393-3491. Internet:* www.thewinecellar.com. *Reservations recommended. To get there: 2½ miles north of Madeira Beach Causeway at 173rd Ave. Main courses: $15–$39. AE, DC, MC, V. Open: 4:30–11 p.m. Tues–Sun.*

Runner-up restaurants

Here are a few more options worthy of consideration:

Basta's

$ **St. Petersburg** This restaurant serves up a nice selection of Italian favorites in a refined setting. *1625 4th St. S.* ☎ *727-894-7880. Internet:* www. bastas.net.

Harbourside Grill

$ **Madeira Beach** Head here for a wide and reasonably priced selection of local and not-so-local fish, including grouper, swordfish, mahi-mahi, and snapper. *13115 Gulf Blvd.* ☎ *727-393-3448. Internet:* www.gotampabay. com/restaurants/harbourside.

Keystone Steak and Chop House

$$ **St. Petersburg** This New York–style chophouse dishes out Angus filets, NY strips, and more. *320 4th St. N.* ☎ *727-822-6600.*

Crab Shack

$ **St. Petersburg** The Crab Shack specializes in steamed, blue crabs and smoked mullet, but you can also order soft-shelled crabs, shrimp, catfish, and grouper. *11400 Gandy Blvd.* ☎ *727-576-7813. Internet:* www. crabshack.com.

Exploring St. Petersburg

You won't find theme parks or roller coasters, but there are some dandy beaches and many other things to see and do in St. Petersburg, especially if you have a car and can visit Tampa (see Chapter 15) and Clearwater.

Touring the top sights

Florida International Museum

St. Petersburg

First opened in 1995, the museum's permanent exhibits now include the Kennedy Collection, which has full-size recreations of the Oval Office and Rose Garden. View changing exhibits on loan from the Smithsonian Institution, the National Portrait Gallery, and others. An audio guide is given to visitors as part of the admission price. Allow 2 to 3 hours to take in the major exhibits.

100 2nd St. N. ☎ *800-777-9882 or 727-822-3693. Internet:* www.floridamuseum. org. *To get there: 1 block north of Central Ave. on 2nd. Admission: $14 adults, $13 seniors, $6 kids 6 and over. Open: 9 a.m.–6 p.m. Mon–Sat, noon–6 p.m. Sun.*

Great Explorations Hands-On Museum

St. Petersburg/Downtown

While the Hands-On Museum is not on the same level as Tampa's Museum of Science and Industry, it's user-friendly and geared to kids. Children can don lab coats and become vets, get familiar with spiders and snakes, or dabble in a ton of other hands-on experiments. Allow 2 to 3 hours to see the museum.

800 2nd Ave. NE. ☎ *727-821-8992. Internet:* www.greatexplorations.org. *To get there: It's on the 3rd floor of The Pier. Admission: $4 ages 3–55, $2 for 56 and older. Open: 10 a.m.–5 p.m. Mon–Sat, noon–5 p.m. Sun.*

Salvador Dalí Museum

St. Petersburg/Downtown

Wow, did this guy have a *different* perspective of Spaceship Earth! St. Petersburg, of all places, has the world's largest collection of what George Carlin would call Dalí's "stuff" — including a melting clock. The museum offers tours and has a little shop of oddities for souvenirs. Unless you're a Dalí-maniac, spending 2 hours here is plenty.

1000 3rd St. S. ☎ *727-823-3767. Internet:* www.daliweb.com. *To get there: On 3rd, 10 blocks south of Central. Admission: $9 adults, $7 senior, $5 students over 10. Open: 9:30 a.m.–5:30 p.m. Mon–Sat, noon–5:30 p.m. Sun.*

Seeing and doing more cool things

Visitors will find many things, beyond the city's first-tier attractions, to occupy their time. Some of the ones listed following appeal to those with special interests, some are free for the taking.

✔ **Baseball:** The **Tampa Bay Devil Rays** play their 81-game, regular season, home schedule (April to October) at Tropicana Field, 16th Street at 4th Avenue South (☎ **800-326-7297** or 727-898-7297; Internet: www.devilray.com). Tickets run $8 to $160; parking is $4 to $10. The Rays also play spring training games in March at nearby Al Lang Stadium, 2nd Avenue at 1st Street South (☎ **727-825-3137**). Tickets cost $3 to $12.

✔ **Beaches:** Pinellas County is lined with public beaches from one end of Gulf Boulevard/Hwy. 699 to the other. **Pass-a-Grille** and **St. Pete Beach** are in the south, near the Pinellas Bayway. **Treasure Island** is in the middle, a west extension of Central Avenue and the Treasure Island Causeway. **Madeira Beach** lies on the northern end. The best things in life are free, though all these beaches do have metered parking, so bring a reasonable amount of change.

✔ **Fishing: Hubbard's Marina** at John's Pass Village and Boardwalk, between Treasure Island and Madeira Beach (☎ **800-755-0677** or 727-393-1947; Internet: www.hubbardsmarina.com), offers half-day

($30) and full-day ($52.50) charters aboard a party boat. Grouper, amberjack, sea bass, and red snapper are among the catches.

✔ **Parks: Fort DeSoto Park,** 3500 Pinellas Bayway (☎ 727-582-2267), on Mullet Key, is a 900-acre county park with a neat old Spanish-American War-era fort (its cannons were never fired in anger). Fort DeSoto is a good place for the kids to explore, but bring plenty of insect repellent. The park also has playgrounds, picnic shelters, and 7 miles of beach. There's an 85-cent toll to drive into the park. A concessionaire, known as the Camp Store, rents canoes for $16 an hour or $32 for a full day (☎ 727-864-1991).

Seeing the shore by guided tour

Hubbard's Marina at John's Pass Village and Boardwalk, halfway between Treasure Island and Madeira Beach (☎ 800-755-0677 or 727-393-1947; Internet: www.hubbardsmarina.com) offers a 2-hour dolphin watch and sightseeing cruise. It costs $12 for adults, $6 for kids 11 and under. There's also a 6-hour snorkeling tour with a barbecue lunch that costs $37 for adults, $25 for kids.

Shopping

Haslam's Book Store, 2025 Central Ave., St. Petersburg (☎ 727-822-8616; Internet: www.haslams.com) is one of our favorite places to browse. Dating back to 1933, its collection has grown to more than 350,000 volumes, making Haslam's Florida's largest bookstore.

John's Pass Village and Boardwalk, 12901 Gulf Blvd., Madeira Beach (☎ 727-391-7373) is a new, made-to-look-old shopping area that features restaurants, galleries, saloons, and boutiques — most of which are over-priced. It's a nice place for a stroll and a little browsing though. A ton of other souvenir shacks lining Gulf Boulevard peddle T-shirts, shells, and other trinkets.

On the mall front, among the area's most notable malls is **Tyrone Square Mall,** 6901 22nd Ave. N., St. Petersburg (☎ 727-345-0126), which has 170 stores anchored by Burdines and Dillard's.

Living the nightlife

In addition to the following listings, you can get up-to-the-minute enter-tainment information each Thursday in the "Weekend" section of the *St. Petersburg Times.*

Bars

Cadillac Jack's, 145 107th Ave., Treasure Island (☎ 727-360-2099; Internet: www.cadillacjacks.net) has a cigar and martini bar, as well as live music nightly (blues, jazz, and Big Band). The cover is

usually around $5. **Gator's Café,** 12754 Kingfish Dr., Treasure Island
(☎ 727-367-8951; Internet: www.gatorscafe.com) is a sports bar
that also offers entertainment ranging from DJs to local and regional
musicians (oldies, disco, and more). A $3 cover is charged after 9 p.m.
Ringside Cafe, 2742 4th St. N., St. Petersburg (☎ 727-894-8465; Internet:
www.ringsidecafe.com) specializes in the blues on Friday and Saturday nights. The cover depends on the act playing; usually it's $2 and up.

Performing arts

The **Bayfront Center** and the **Mahaffey Theater,** 400 1st St. S., St.
Petersburg (☎ 727-892-5767 or 727-892-5700) present a variety of
Broadway plays, ice shows, big bands, and circuses.

North Pinellas and Beaches

The North Pinellas area isn't Grand Tourist Central, but its beaches do
a jam-up business in summer (families) and winter (snowbirds). Inland,
the major cities include Clearwater, Dunedin, Largo, and Palm Harbor.
On the coast, you come across **Bellair Beach, Clearwater Beach,** and
Sand Key. (See the "St. Pete and Clearwater Beaches" map, later in
this chapter.) The Greek community of **Tarpon Springs** anchors the
north end.

Getting there

Like St. Petersburg, reaching Clearwater by the sky is best. For details
on getting here via airplane, see "Getting there" in the "St. Petersburg"
section of this chapter.

Those of you coming by car will have a choice of three routes:

- **U.S. 19,** where the traffic is beyond frustrating.

- **I-75/275,** which cuts through the center of the state from the
  Florida/Georgia border, and then runs into Tampa and Pinellas
  County.

- **I-95/I-4/I-275:** I-95 gets you into the state along the East coast,
  where you can pick up I-4 in Daytona Beach and ride it onto I-275,
  which takes you through Tampa into Clearwater.

Getting around

The beaches sector primarily uses a named street system, so navigating
isn't as easy as in St. Petersburg. This is, however a smaller area, so its
harder to get really lost. If you do take a wrong turn, keep in mind that
the water is in the west. If you're driving, pick up a map (see "Fast Facts"
at the end of this chapter), and you shouldn't have a problem.

St. Pete & Clearwater Beaches

ACCOMMODATIONS ■

Alden Beach Resort **8**

Beach Haven **9**

Don Cesar Beach
   Resort and Spa **10**

Tradewinds Sandpiper Hotel
   and Suites **7**

The Beach House **14**

Safety Harbor Resort & Spa **2**

Sheraton Sand Key Resort **16**

Westin Innisbrook Resort **1**

DINING ◆

Britt's Beachside Café **13**

Hurricane Seafood
   Restaurant **11**

Johnny Leverock's Seafood
   House **15**

La Vigna Ristorante **4**

Salt Rock Grill **3**

Seafood & Sunsets
   at Julie's **12**

Ted Peters' Famous
   Smoked Fish **6**

The Wine Cellar **5**

By bus

The **Pinellas Suncoast Transit Authority** (☎ 727-530-9911), serves the entire county. The fare is $1.25 per ride. The Jolley Trolley (☎ 727-445-1200) provides service in the Clearwater beach area, from downtown to the beaches as far south as Sand Key. It costs 50 cents per person, 25 cents for seniors.

By car

U.S. 19 (known to the locals frequently ensnared in its traffic tie-ups as U.S. #@%$#!!) is the main north-south highway. Hwy. 611 runs the same route to the far east, Alt. U.S. 19 does it to the west, and Gulf Boulevard does it on the beach. The primary east-west roads are East Bay Drive/Hwy. 686 (Largo), Gulf to Bay Boulevard/Hwy. 60 (Clearwater), and Curlew Road/Hwy. 586 (Dunedin).

By taxi

Yellow Cab (☎ 727-799-2222), **St. Pete Taxi of Clearwater** (☎ 727-799-8294), and **BATS Taxi** (☎ 727-367-3702) are a few of the local taxi companies. It's $1.50 to get in a cab and $1.60 a mile thereafter.

Staying in North Pinellas County

Because the beaches tend to fill up year-round, it's wise to make hotel reservations early. It is possible to get discount packages during the summer, so ask when you reserve your room.

This area is loaded with condominium rentals, many of them in a building just off the beach. If you plan on staying here a week or more, it may pay to look into this option. Two local agents that offer a number of rental choices are **Excell Vacation Condos** (☎ 800-733-4004 or 727-391-5512; Internet: www.islandtime.com/vacation) and **JC Resort Management** (☎ 800-535-7776 or 727-397-0441; Internet: www.jcresort.com).

The **Florida Hotel Network** (☎ 800-538-3616; Internet: www.floridahotels.com) will make accommodations arrangements for you, if you don't want the hassle of haggling or dealing with motel clerks.

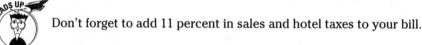

Don't forget to add 11 percent in sales and hotel taxes to your bill.

The area's best hotels

The Beachouse

$$ Clearwater Beach

These well-kept suites have small kitchens, king-size beds, and a non-smoking, adults-only atmosphere. Because there only are five units, reserving early is best.

421 Hamden Dr. ☎ *727-461-4862. Internet:* www.thebeachouse.com. *To get there: From I-275 take Hwy. 60 west to the Gulf, take the roundabout left on Gulf Blvd. to Hamden, then right 1 block to the inn. Parking: Free, self. Rack rates: $65–$185 Nov–Mar, $50–$165 Apr–Oct. MC, V.*

Safety Harbor Resort & Spa

$$ Safety Harbor

This Mediterranean-style, 22-acre resort floats above natural mineral springs west of Tampa Bay. All 193 rooms offer data ports and complimentary mineral water, and most have views of the grounds or Tampa Bay; the deluxe rooms have balconies and dressing areas. The resort has numerous recreational facilities and a full-service spa offering numerous treatments and fitness programs.

105 N. Bayshore Dr. ☎ *800-458-5409 or 727-726-1161. Fax: 727-726-4268. Internet:* www.safetyharborspa.com. *To get there: Hwy. 60 east to Bayshore, left 3 miles. Parking: Free, self. Rack rates: $149–$229 Jan–Mar, $119–$179 June–Sept, $99–$139 Dec–May. AE, DC, DISC, MC, V.*

Sheraton Sand Key Resort

$$ Sand Key/Clearwater Beach

One of this resort's best virtues is its location, away from the tourist glitz. Located next to Sand Key Park, the 10-acre resort has a large, white-sand beach and is popular with water-sports enthusiasts. All rooms have coffee makers, balconies with a view of the Gulf or bay, and Nintendo. Its summertime **Kids Camp** program (open 9 a.m. to 2 p.m. weekdays) costs $18 per day. Other facilities include a restaurant, fitness and tennis centers, and an onsite store.

1160 Gulf Blvd. ☎ *800-325-3535 or 727-595-1611. Fax: 727-596-8488. Internet:* www.beachsand.com. *To get there: Gulf to Bay/Hwy. 60 west to the roundabout, go right to southwest corner, follow the beach road across the Sand Key Bridge. Parking: Free, self. Rack rates: $165–$250 Feb–Apr, $135–$220 Jan, May–Dec. AE, DC, DISC, MC, V.*

Westin Innisbrook Resort

$$$ Palm Harbor

This 1,000-acre mini city has 700 luxurious rooms and suites, 72 holes of golf, a golf school, a tennis and fitness center, six restaurants, and six pools, including the $3.4-million **Loch Ness Monster Pool & Spa.** A **Kids Club** (open 9 a.m. to 5 p.m. daily, for ages 5 to 12, at $20 to $35 a day), allows parents time to work on their swings. Of course, you pay for what you get.

36750 U.S. 19 N. ☎ *800-456-2000 or 727-942-2000. Fax: 727-942-5578. Internet:* www.westin-innisbrook.com. *To get there: It's about 3 miles north of Hwy. 584 on U.S. 19. Parking: Free. Rack rates: $275–$500 Dec–Apr, $225–$465 May–Nov, $130–$350 May–Aug. AE, DC, DISC, MC, V.*

Runner-up accommodations

Here are a few other options. You also can consider listings for St. Petersburg (earlier in this chapter) and Tampa (Chapter 15):

The Belleview Biltmore Resort and Spa

$$$ **Clearwater** A 292-room Victorian palace with creaking wood floors has a championship golf course and a full-service spa laid out in a nineteenth-century setting. *25 Belleview Blvd.* ☎ *800-237-8947 or 727-442-6171. Fax: 727-441-4173. Internet:* www.belleviewbiltmore.com.

Hilton Clearwater Beach

$$ **Clearwater Beach** This 10-acre beachfront resort has 425 rooms decorated in Hilton's modern though impersonal style. *400 Mandalay Ave.* ☎ *800-774-1500 or 727-461-3222. Fax: 727-446-2371. Internet:* www.hilton.com/hotels/PIECBHF.

Radisson Suite Resort on Sand Key

$$$ **Clearwater Beach** An all-suite resort that offers two-room waterfront suites with balconies, microwaves, and coffee makers; a kids' program; and a 35-foot waterfall cascading into the pool. *1201 Gulf Blvd.* ☎ *800-333-3333 or 727-596-1100. Fax: 727-595-4292. Internet:* www.RadissonSandKey.com.

Dining out in North Pinellas County

Seafood is the name of the game when dining in the Clearwater area, but you can find plenty of other choices if marine cuisine doesn't make your mouth water. Budget-minded travelers can find a host of fast-food joints and chain restaurants off the main highways that lead to the beaches, and in the tourist zones.

Don't forget to add 7 percent sales tax to your meal budget.

The area's best restaurants

Britt's Beachside Café

$ **Clearwater Beach** **SEAFOOD**

Britt's is a casual place offering indoor and outdoor seating with a great view of the Gulf. The tasty cuisine features wraps (blackened-chicken Caesar), seafood (ginger shark and grouper Creole), and a good jambalaya. Live entertainment is provided a few evenings each week.

201 S. Gulfview Blvd. ☎ *727-461-5185. Internet:* www.brittscafe.com. *Reservations accepted. To get there: Take Gulf to Bay/Hwy. 60 across the causeway, go* *left as you enter the beach, then right at the next light and veer around the curve (in the Beach Towers Hotel). Main courses: $5–$17. MC, V. Open: 11–2 a.m. Mon–Fri, 8:30–2 a.m. Sat–Sun.*

Johnny Leverock's Seafood House

$ Clearwater Beach   SEAFOOD

This is one of 12 Florida restaurants that still carry the name of the guy who built the first one in 1948. The restaurant is right off the water, and you can dine indoors or out; the atmosphere is decidedly casual. The vittles are tasty, but they're chain-style seafood — crab-cakes imperial, garlic-shrimp scampi, and a few platters. Most entrees are under $16.

551 Gulf Blvd. ☎ 727-446-5884. Internet: www.leverocks.com. *Reservations accepted. To get there: It's just north of the Sand Key bridge. Main courses: $8–$22. AE, DISC, MC, V. Open: 11:30 a.m.–10 p.m. daily.*

Salt Rock Grill

$$ Indian Shores   STEAKS/SEAFOOD

This waterfront restaurant offers diners a great view of the Gulf. Inside, you'll find a laid-back beach attitude to go with wood-fired steaks, chicken, and seafood. Try the Havana-style pork tenderloin or the rock-shrimp penne for a real treat. Chomp on a cigar or sample a martini in the restaurant's bar.

19325 Gulf Blvd. ☎ 727-593-7625. Internet: www.saltrockgrill.com. *Reservations accepted. To get there: It's ¼ mile north of the Hwy.694/Park Blvd. bridge. Main courses: $9–$30. AE, DC, DISC, MC, V. Open: 4–10 p.m. Sun–Thurs, till 11 p.m. Fri–Sat.*

Seafood & Sunsets at Julie's

$ Clearwater Beach   SEAFOOD/SANDWICHES

This sidewalk cafe has a wonderful sunset view on the beach, a perfect accompaniment to its menu, which is headlined by a great fried-grouper sandwich. Other Key West-inspired favorites include charbroiled mahi-mahi in herb sauce, barbecued shrimp on a skewer, and a conch sandwich. Most entrees cost under $17.

351 S. Gulfview Blvd. ☎ 727-441-2548. Reservations not accepted. To get there: It's 3 blocks south of Pier 60. Main courses: $8–$22. AE, MC, V. Open: 10 a.m.–10 p.m. daily.

Runner-up restaurants

In addition to this brief second-tier list, don't overlook the restaurants in Chapter 15 (Tampa) and earlier in this chapter (St. Petersburg), which are all within driving distance of the beaches.

Big Ben Pub

$ Clearwater Beach   Big Ben's offers traditional pub grub (steak-and-kidney pie, bangers and mash, shepherd's pie, and Cornish pasty) and a big-screen telly that airs soccer, rugby, and cricket. *731 Bayway Blvd.* ☎ **727-446-8809.** *Internet:* www.bigbenpub.com.

Frenchy's Café

$ Clearwater Beach   Frenchy's has hung around for two decades thanks to a dandy grouper sandwich, gumbo, and its peanut butter pie. *41 Baymont St.* ☎ *727-446-3607. Internet:* www.clearwaterbeach.com/FRENCHY/original.html.

Sweetwater's

$$ Clearwater   The menu lacks imagination, but it has some pleasant offerings, including blackened mahi-mahi and filet mignon, as well as a decent children's menu. *2400 Gulf to Bay Blvd.* ☎ *727-799-0818. Internet:* www.sweetwatersrest.com-clearwater/open.htm.

Exploring Clearwater

The beaches are the main draw in this area. If you tire of the surf and sand, however, a handful of other attractions can help fill your time. Keep in mind that this area's major showstoppers are of the natural variety. So if you prefer hanging out in museums, head into St. Petersburg.

Touring the top sights

Caladesi Island State Park

Dunedin

Caladesi is among our favorites. Cars and trucks aren't allowed, so noise and carbon dioxide are minimal. The 3-mile island's résumé includes sea grasses, small dunes, and a variety of birds, including blue herons. If you're lucky, you may see some resident dolphins performing off the beach, and in summer you can probably see the crawl marks left by nesting loggerhead turtles. The park is only accessible by boat, and there's a 4-hour maximum stay.

3 Causeway Blvd. ☎ *727-469-5918. To get there: Use the ferry ($7 adults, $3.50 kids 3–12,* ☎ *727-734-5263) from Honeymoon Island State Recreation Area (see following). Admission: No charge beyond the $4 for Honeymoon Island. Open: Ferry runs hourly from 10 a.m.–5 p.m.*

Clearwater Marine Aquarium

Clearwater Beach

This aquarium is dedicated to rehabilitating or providing a permanent home for injured marine mammals (dolphins and otters), as well as sea turtles. On Sundays and Mondays, a 5½-hour, trainer-for-a-day program is offered. The program is limited to one person per day and costs $125. Otherwise, allow 2 to 4 hours to see all the exhibits.

249 Windward Passage. ☎ *888-239-9414 or 727-441-1790. Internet:* www.cmaquarium.org. *To get there: Hwy. 60 west to Island Way, right to Windward. Admission: $6.75 adults, $4.25 kids 3–12. Open: 9 a.m.–5 p.m. Mon–Fri, 9 a.m.–4 p.m. Sat, 11 a.m.–4 p.m. Sun.*

Honeymoon Island State Recreation Area

Dunedin

While it's not as appealing as neighboring Caledesi Island (see earlier in this section), this public park features ospreys, mangroves, and dunes, as well as swimming, fishing, and picnic areas. There are also bathhouses where you can change. If you throw in a side trip to Caledesi, this can be an all-day affair.

3 Causeway Blvd. ☎ *727-469-5918. To get there: From Clearwater go north on U.S. 19, then west on Curlew Rd., which ends at the park. Admission: $4 per vehicle. Open: 8 a.m.–dusk daily.*

Tarpon Springs

To a touristy degree, this old riverfront neighborhood re-creates the sights, sounds, and tastes of a Greek village. It also remembers this town's sponge-diving heyday. The **Cultural Center,** 101 S. Pinellas Ave. (☎ 727-942-5605) showcases historical exhibits. **Spongeorama,** 510 Dodecanese Blvd. (☎ 727-943-9509) offers a museum and a movie about the town's past. Also on Dodacanese Boulevard are the neighborhood's historic **Sponge Docks,** where sponges are still sold today. **St. Nicholas Greek Orthodox Cathedral,** 18 Hibiscus Ave. (☎ 727-937-3540) is a replica of St. Sophia's in Constantinople and has beautiful icons, stained glass, and sculptured marble. All these attractions are free. You can see most of the town in about 4 hours.

Tarpon Springs lies along the Anclote River and is bordered to the west by the Gulf of Mexico. To get there: From U.S. 19, follow Tarpon Ave. (the extension of Hwy. 582) west to Pinellas Ave., go right to Dodecanese, then left.

Doing more cool things

Most folks come to this region to sample an old Florida attraction — the shore. But if you can't go on vacation without hitting the greens at least once, or if you yearn to watch the Boys of Summer get into shape, here are a few of your options.

> ✔ **Beaches:** North Pinellas beaches are every bit as attractive as those in the southern part of the county, but they are fewer in number. The star is Clearwater Beach, which lies at the west end

of Hwy. 60. Information on all the Gulf beaches can be found on the Web at www.gulfbeaches-tampabay.com.

✔ **Golf:** If you want to get out your clubs while on vacation, information on courses in the area is available on the Internet at www.golf.com and www.floridagolfing.com. If you prefer to do your research the old-fashioned way, request course information from the **Florida Sports Foundation** (☎ 850-488-8347), or **Florida Golfing,** (☎ 877-222-4653). Some of the more popular courses here are:

- **Bardmoor Golf Club:** 7979 Bayou Club Blvd., Largo (☎ 727-392-1234). Greens fees: $40 to $65 summer, $66 to $85 winter.

- **Belleview Biltmore Golf Club:** 1501 Indian Rocks Rd., Clearwater (☎ 727-581-5498). Greens fees: $25 to $40 year-round.

- **Lansbrook Golf Club:** 4605 Village Center Dr., Palm Harbor (☎ 727-784-7333). Greens fees: under $25 summer, $40 to $65 winter.

✔ **Spring Training:** The **Philadelphia Phillies** (☎ 727-442-8496; Internet: www.phillies.com) play at Jack Russell Stadium, 800 Phillies Dr., Clearwater. Tickets costs $6 to $12. The **Toronto Blue Jays** (☎ 727-733-0429; Internet: www.bluejays.com), make camp at Grant Field, 373 Douglas Ave., Dunedin. Tickets run $9 to $13. Workouts begin in mid-February, and games are played through March.

Seeing the area by guided tour

Starlite Cruises, 25 Causeway Blvd., Clearwater Beach (☎ 800-444-4814 or 727-462-2628; Internet: www.starlitecruises.com), runs 2- to 3½-hour sightseeing, lunch, dinner, and dancing cruises out of the Clearwater City Marina. Cruise prices run from $10.50 to $35.

Captain Nemo's Pirate Cruise also runs out of the Clearwater Marina (☎ 727-446-2587; www.captainmemo.com) and uses a replica of a pirate ship for sightseeing and champagne cruises that are often escorted by dolphins. The cruises cost $28 to $30 adults, $22 teens, $18 kids.

Shopping

This is not a major shopping zone, so if you came to exercise your credit card, go elsewhere. If you're desperate enough, consider browsing through **Boatyard Village,** 16100 Fairchild Dr., Clearwater (☎ 727-535-4678), which has a number of rather unremarkable shops, galleries, and restaurants on Tampa Bay. Mall-aholics can gather at **Countryside Mall,** U.S. 19 and Hwy. 580, Clearwater (☎ 727-796-1079), which houses some 180 stores.

Living the nightlife

Many of the beach's restaurants usually offer some form of entertainment when the sun goes down, and you can find many bars in the same area. Club-wise, there are three popular ones. **Club Liquid Blue,** 22 N. Fort Harrison, Clearwater (☎ **727-446-4000;** Internet: www.clubliquidblue. com) is a dance, martini, and cigar venue that features DJs and, on some nights, live radio. On most nights there is no cover. **The Living Room,** 13707 57th St. N., Clearwater (☎ **727-531-0332;** Internet: www. livingroomclearwater.com) features local bands from Tuesday through Sunday. On most nights there is no cover, but on Saturdays there's a cover of $7 after 8 p.m. **New York, New York** 18573 U.S. 19 N., Clearwater (☎ **727-539-7441**), is something of a sports bar, but offers live music on most nights (oldies to Top 40). There is no cover.

On the performing arts front, Clearwater's **Ruth Eckerd Hall,** 1111 McMullen Booth Rd. (☎ **727-791-7400**) ranks as one of the state's finest centers, featuring musicals, dance, and a variety of other performances during the year.

For more information on cultural offerings, the *St. Petersburg Times* (☎ **727-893-8111;** Internet: www.sptimes.com) puts out an entertainment and dining guide called "Weekend," each Thursday.

Suggested Itineraries

Because St. Petersburg and the Clearwater areas are so close to each other, zigzagging through both sections of the Suncoast while on your trip is not a major hassle. To help you make the best use of your time, we give you the following 3- and 4-day itineraries, expanding our turf just a little in the latter.

The Suncoast in 3 Days

Day 1 is for museum lovers. Sleep in a bit and then arrive at the **Salvador Dalí Museum** in downtown St. Petersburg by 10 a.m. Grab lunch at **The Moon Under Water** and then divide your afternoon between the **Florida International Museum** and the **Great Explorations Hands-On Museum.** Wind up your day with a meal at the **Hurricane Seafood Restaurant.**

On **Day 2,** it's time to go *au natural.* Start your day in South Pinellas County, sunning and swimming at **Pass-a-Grille Beach,** grab a quickie lunch on the road, and then fill your afternoon at **Fort DeSoto Park** before having your dinner outdoors-style at **Ted Peters' Famous Smoked Fish.** If you're in a party mood, end the evening at **Cadillac Jack's. Day Two Option B:** If you're more inclined to avoid the crowds at the beaches, go north and spend the day at **Honeymoon Island**

State Recreation Area and **Caladesi Island State Park,** and then eat dinner at **Frenchy's Cafe.**

Head north on **Day 3,** spending the morning kicking around **Tarpon Springs,** where you can grab lunch before heading to the **Clearwater Marine Aquarium.** End your day at **Seafood & Sunsets at Julie's.**

The Suncoast and Tampa in 4 Days

Follow the 3-day itinerary preceding, and on **Day 4,** head over to **Busch Gardens in Tampa** (see Chapter 15), an all-day affair. Cap off your trip with a dinner at the **Columbia Restaurant,** where the flamenco dancing shows are sure to end your vacation on a high note.

Day-Tripping to Weeki Wachee, Homosassa Springs, and Crystal River

We're traveling north on this run:

Weeki Wachee Springs (☎ 877-469-3354; Internet: www.weekiwachee. com) opened in 1946 and still features its meat-and-potatoes mermaid shtick. The mermaids spend most of their stage time cavorting under-water in a crystal-clear spring, sucking on air hoses and trying to make it look like they really can see the snowbirds 75-feet-and-a-thick-glass-window away. The attraction also has a water park, **Buccaneer Bay,** which is open from late spring to early fall; a wilderness cruise; and canoe rentals (they cost $31 a day). The springs are open to scuba divers (☎ 352-597-4300; Internet: www.Neptune-Divers.com). The springs are at U.S. 19 and Hwy. 50, 45 miles north of Clearwater, and are open from 10 a.m. to 3 p.m. in winter (6 p.m. in summer) daily. Admission costs $16 adults, $12 for kids 3 to 10.

Just 15 miles north of Weeki Wachee is **Homosassa Springs State Wildlife Park, 4150 U.S. 19** (☎ 352-628-5343; Internet: www.citruscounty-fl. com/statepark.html), which lets you see manatees without getting wet. This southwest Citrus County tourist attraction is a permanent home for injured manatees, as well as a rehabilitation center. However, the manatees are only part of the show. The park has an underwater observatory where you get another angle on the manatees as well as thousands of fish. Nature trails wind through the habitats of several other permanent residents, including eagles, owls, red-tail hawks, otters, and an ornery black bear. The park is open from 9 a.m. to 5 p.m. daily. Admission costs $8 for adults, $5 for kids 3 to 12, and includes a 30-minute narrated boat ride.

If you want to take a swim with some manatees, you can do so in Crystal River, located about 7 miles north of Homosassa Springs. The region's warm springs and federal sanctuaries attract these slow-moving, endangered marine mammals every winter, from November to March. They also reside in some of the local rivers during the warmer months. There are a number of dive shops in Crystal River on U.S. 19 that offer sightseeing and snorkeling tours beginning at $25 to $30. They also rent fins, masks, and wet suits. Operators include the **Crystal Lodge Dive Center** (☎ 352-795-6798), and **American Pro Diving Center** (☎ 352-563-0041; Internet: www.americanprodive.com).

If you choose to do only one of the preceding activities, you can do it in a long day trip of about 5 to 7 hours. You can get information by calling ☎ 800-587-6667 or checking out the Internet: www.visitcitrus.com. You can also contact the **Citrus County Chamber of Commerce,** 28 NW Hwy. 19, Crystal River (☎ 352-795-3149).

Fast Facts

Area Code

The local area code is **727.**

American Express

You can get some travel services at Bowen Keppie Travel, 825 Court St., Clearwater, (☎ 727-442-2131). It's open 8:30 a.m.–5 p.m. weekdays.

Hospitals

Area hospitals include **Bayfront Medical Center,** 701 6th St. S., St. Petersburg (☎ 727-823-1234) and **Morton Plant Hospital,** 300 Pinellas St., Clearwater (☎ 727-462-7000).

Information

For advance information on both St. Petersburg and Clearwater, contact the **St. Petersburg/Clearwater Area Convention & Visitors Bureau,** 14450 46th St. N., Clearwater (☎ 800-345-6710 or 727-464-7200; Internet: www.stpete-clearwater.com).

Another good source of tourist information is the **St. Petersburg Area Chamber of Commerce,** 14450 46th St., N., Clearwater

(☎ 727-895-6326; Internet: www.stpete.com).

Internet Access

You'll find listings for several internet cafes in the local Yellow Pages, including the **Internet Outpost Café,** 7400 Gulf Blvd., St. Pete Beach (☎ 727-360-7806, Internet: www.iocafe.net), and the **Surf-N-Sip Internet Café,** 19455 Gulf Blvd., Indian Shores (☎ 727-517-2543; Internet: www.surfnsip.com).

Mail

There are U.S. post offices at 1299 66th St. N., St. Petersburg; 250 Corey Ave., St. Pete Beach; and 1281 S. Lincoln Ave., Clearwater. To locate a post office near your hotel, call ☎ 800-275-8777.

Maps

The information sources preceding are great organizations to hit up for maps before or after you land. Rental-car agencies are another good source (including those at the airport), and so are convenience stores, which sell maps for $3–$5.

Newspapers

The *St. Petersburg Times* (☎ 727-893-8111) is the local paper and puts out an entertainment and dining guide called "Weekend" each Thursday.

Pharmacies

There are 24-hour **Walgreens** (Internet: www.walgreens.com) at 900 49th St. N., St. Petersburg (☎ 727-327-8801) and at 1801 Gulf to Bay/Hwy. 60, Clearwater (☎ 727-441-8694).

Taxes

A sales tax of 7 percent is assessed on everything except groceries and medicine. The hotel tax raises the tax total to 11 percent on rooms.

Taxis

Taxis cost $1.50 to get in and $1.60 per mile. **Yellow Cab** (☎ 727-799-2222), and **St. Pete Taxi of Clearwater** (☎ 727-799-8294) are two of the major cab companies in the area.

Transit Info

The Pinellas Suncoast Transit Authority (☎ 727-530-9911) operates the region's public bus system. The fare is $1.25 per ride.

Weather Updates

For a recording of current conditions and forecast reports, call the local office of the **National Weather Service** at ☎ 813-645-2506, or check out Internet: www.nws.noaa.gov. You also can get information by watching the **Weather Channel** (Internet: www.weatherchannel.com).

Chapter 17

Sarasota, Fort Myers, and Naples

● ●

In This Chapter

▶ Encountering an albino python in Naples

▶ Following footpaths through grapes, palms, and mangroves

▶ Showstopping museums: From Ringling to Imaginarium

▶ Retreating to the beaches in the Land of 10,000 Islands

● ●

*B*efore we get into the nitty-gritty details about this area of Florida, here's a little multiple-choice pop quiz.

A *green flash* is

1. What happens when you eat Tuesday's oysters on Friday.

2. A religious experience usually encountered after too many frozen margaritas.

3. A brief, brilliant, rarely seen flare that occurs as the last tip of the sun disappears beneath the horizon.

We're sure that you know that the correct — and, yes, it is correct — answer *is* number three.

Unfortunately, most people never see one, but you may when you visit the southwestern coast of Florida. Those who do get something far better than seashells to take home. Meteorologists say that a green flash requires the right atmospheric brew (heavy on the greens, light on the reds) for the setting sun to ignite this explosion of color. It also takes a flat horizon and cloudless sky. If everything adds up, a green flash probably will steal your breath.

But even if you don't see a flash, you can still find plenty to write home about. The Sarasota-Fort Myers-Naples region of Florida is called the *Land of 10,000 Islands.* That may be a stretch, but there are a ton of them, and most have never met a bulldozer. If you like civilization, well, don't fret that, either. There's plenty to fill your date book here.

Southwest Florida: What's Where?

Down south, Florida's Collier County, which includes Naples and Marco Island, woos more millionaires per capita than any other county east of the Mississippi. While you're in town, you can cruise **Millionaire's Row** in Olde Naples, as well as some of the boutiques and galleries that keep the rich from getting too idle.

Thirty miles north, Fort Myers and Fort Myers Beach are as quiet and quaint as they were when **Thomas Edison** and **Henry Ford** built their winter homes here.

Just offshore, **Sanibel** and **Captiva** are two of the region's island gems.

Sarasota, which is the home of the **Asolo Theatre** and **Ringling Museum,** is this region's largest city. It's flanked by Anna Maria Island, St. Armands Key, Longboat Key, and Casey Key, a line of barrier islands that separate the Gulf of Mexico and Sarasota Bay.

 On the downside, the Sarasota-Fort Myers-Naples region is spread far and wide. There are few day-filling activities, and you will occasionally have to drive for a spell before reaching your next stop.

Sarasota and Bradenton

Sarasota has grown into something of an upscale retirement community, similar to Marco Island and, to a lesser degree, Naples to the south. (Skip ahead to the map for an overview of "Sarasota and Bradenton.") That's good news, because the city caters to its residents with a wide variety of cultural attractions and events. Bradenton, Sarasota's often-overlooked neighbor, remains more of a casual fishing village and blue-collar town.

Getting there

The cities' location on the south side of Tampa Bay means that coming here is best by air, but we do give those of you who prefer to leave your feet on the ground another option.

By plane

Sarasota-Bradenton International Airport (☎ 941-359-2770; Internet: www.srq-airport.com) north of downtown off University Parkway between U.S. 41 and U.S. 301, is served by a half dozen major airlines or their partners, including **Continental, Delta, Northwest, TWA,** and

US Airways. **Alamo, Avis, Budget, Dollar, Hertz,** and **National** have rental counters in the terminal. The taxi fleet here includes **Yellow Cab** (☎ 941-955-3341), **Green Cab** (☎ 941-922-6666), and **Diplomat Taxi** (☎ 941-359-8294). The standard fare is $2.10 to start the meter, plus $1.50 per mile.

Another option is to fly into **Tampa International** (☎ 813-870-8700; Internet: www.tampaairport.com), which offers more arrival and departure choices (see Chapter 15 for more information). You will likely get a better airfare — and if you're renting a car, a better rental price — by flying into Tampa, which is about 1½ to 2 hours north of Sarasota.

By car

I-75 is the primary route into Sarasota from the north, and it's about 5 to 6 hours from the Florida-Georgia line to Sarasota. If you prefer I-95, take it to Daytona Beach; and then follow I-4 to I-75 before heading south.

Getting around

If you're a do-it-yourself type, start by getting a map. You can get a map in advance from the information sources listed in "Fast Facts" at the end of this chapter. You can also get a map, after you land, from your rental-car company or at a local convenience store.

By car

U.S. 301 and U.S. 41/Tamiami Trail are the major north-south arteries on the mainland; the Gulf to Mexico Drive (Hwy. 789) is the main island road. The largest east-west thoroughfares in Sarasota are Hwy. 72 (Stickney Point Road), Hwy. 780, University Parkway, and (to the islands) Ringling Causeway, which deposits you on Lido Beach. Hwy. 70 (53rd Avenue), Hwy. 684 (Cortez Road), and Hwy. 64 (Manatee Avenue) are the main roads in Bradenton.

By public transit

Sarasota County Area Transit, or SCAT (☎ 941-316-1234), runs regularly scheduled bus service. A 50-cent fare will take you to stops in the city and St. Armands, Longboat, and Lido Keys. It runs from 6 a.m. to 7 p.m. Monday through Saturday.

By taxi

Taxi companies include **Yellow Cab** (☎ 941-955-3341), **Green Cab** (☎ 941-922-6666), and **Diplomat Taxi** (☎ 941-359-8294). The standard fare is $2.10 plus $1.50 per mile.

Sarasota and Bradenton

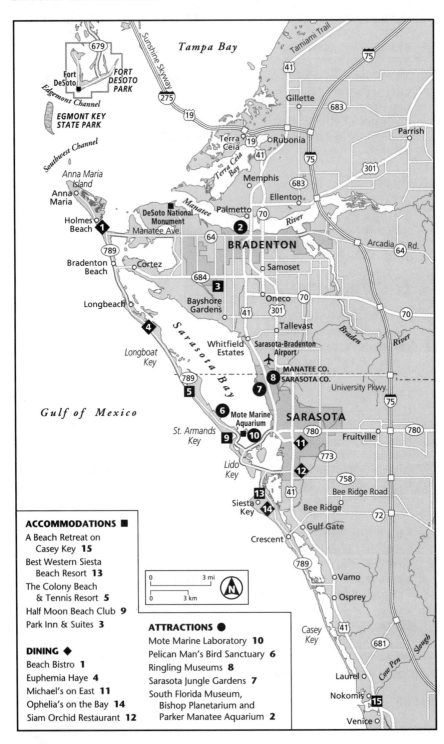

ACCOMMODATIONS ■

A Beach Retreat on
  Casey Key **15**
Best Western Siesta
  Beach Resort **13**
The Colony Beach
  & Tennis Resort **5**
Half Moon Beach Club **9**
Park Inn & Suites **3**

DINING ◆

Beach Bistro **1**
Euphemia Haye **4**
Michael's on East **11**
Ophelia's on the Bay **14**
Siam Orchid Restaurant **12**

ATTRACTIONS ●

Mote Marine Laboratory **10**
Pelican Man's Bird Sanctuary **6**
Ringling Museums **8**
Sarasota Jungle Gardens **7**
South Florida Museum,
  Bishop Planetarium and
  Parker Manatee Aquarium **2**

Staying the night

The beaches in this area are loaded with condominiums, but you will find a number of other lodging options. In downtown Sarasota and on U.S. 41, just south of the airport, you can find a number of modern-chain hotels. See the "Quick Concierge" at the back of the book for hotel reservation numbers and Web sites.

You can leave the reserving to someone else by contacting the **Florida Hotel Network** (☎ 800-538-3616; Internet: www.floridahotels.com). You can also call the free reservation service operated by the **Bradenton Area Convention and Visitors Bureau** at ☎ 800-4-MANATEE.

High season here runs from January to April, but rates along the beaches remain high year-round, so if you're looking for a bargain, stick to the downtown area.

Don't forget Sarasota's 10 percent hotel tax and Bradenton's 9 percent.

The area's best hotels

A Beach Retreat on Casey Key

$ Nokomis

It may be a bit spartan, but this cantaloupe-colored inn is clean, comfortable, and delightfully inexpensive. And the Gulf and beach are only a few steps away. The inn offers newly remodeled studios, small efficiencies with full kitchens, and multiple-bedroom models.

105 Casey Key Road. ☎ *941-485-8771. Fax: 941-966-3758. Internet:* www.venice-fla.com/beachretreat.htm. *To get there: U.S. 41 south to Albee Rd., right 2 miles to Nokomis; motel is on right. Parking: Free. Rack rates: $98–$135 Dec–Apr, $75–$120 May–Sept, $68–$105 Oct–Nov. MC, V.*

Best Western Siesta Beach Resort

$$ Siesta Key

This Mediterranean-style, two-story structure sports standard hotel rooms, efficiencies with microwaves, and one- and two-bedroom suites, some of which are equipped with two-person Jacuzzis. It's older but well maintained. Beach access is right across the street.

5311 Ocean Blvd. ☎ *800-223-5786 or 941-349-3211. Fax: 941-349-7915. Internet:* www.siestakeyflorida.com. *To get there: West on Clark Rd./Hwy. 72, right on Midnight Pass, left on Beach Rd.; go ¾ mile. Parking: Free. Rack rates: $139–$249 Feb–Apr, $129–$199 Dec–Jan, $89–$149 May–Nov. AE, DC, DISC, MC, V.*

The Colony Beach & Tennis Resort

$$$$ Longboat Key

If you can stand the sticker shock, this beachside resort offers modern and luxurious one- and two-bedroom suites, lanais, and beach houses. All accommodations have kitchens with microwaves, refrigerators, and dishwashers; baths have whirlpools. The resort has 21 hard- and soft-surface tennis courts (court time is included in your rate), a fitness center and spa, and programs for kids 3 to 13 (also included in the price of your room).

1620 Gulf of Mexico Dri. ☎ *800-282-1138 or 941-383-6464. Fax: 941-383-7549. Internet:* www.colonybeachresort.com. *To get there: 1 mile north of the Ringling Causeway. Parking: Free. Rack rates: $395–$1,195 Feb–Apr, $270–$975 Jan and May, $195–$895 June–Sept.*

Half Moon Beach Club

$$ St. Armands Key/Lido Beach

All rooms, efficiencies, and suites in this beachfront motel come with a patio or balcony, refrigerator, and coffee maker. Some of the spacious rooms have kitchenettes with a microwave, and a few rooms sport Gulf views. The art-deco property also has an onsite restaurant and a guest laundry.

2050 Ben Franklin Dr. ☎ *800-358-3245 or 941-388-3694. Fax: 941-388-1938. Internet:* www.halfmoon-lidokey.com. *To get there: Ringling Causeway to Lido Beach, south to Ben Franklin. Parking: Free. Rack rates: $139–$269 Feb–Apr, $119–$189 May–Jan. AE, DC, DISC, MC, V.*

Park Inn & Suites

$$ Bradenton

All rooms are housed in a three-story building that wraps around the courtyard/pool area. All the spacious rooms have data ports and hair dryers; some have Jacuzzis. A free continental breakfast is served. There's an onsite pub, and numerous restaurants are within walking distance. The inn is 6 miles from Bradenton Beach.

4450 47th St. West. ☎ *800-437-7275 or 941-795-4633. Fax: 941-795-0808. Internet:* www.parkinnclubbradenton.com. *To get there: Manatee Ave./Hwy. 64 west to 43rd, left to Cortez Rd., right to 47th, left to inn. Parking: Free. Rack rates: $109–$139 Jan–Apr, $94–$124 May–Dec. AE, CB, DISC, MC, V.*

Runner-up accommodations

In addition to the first tier accommodations preceding, here are a few more equally good options for your snoozing pleasure.

The Beach Inn

$$ **Holmes Beach** This small inn features six clean and comfortable units that were remodeled in 1998. *101 66th St.* ☎ *800-823-2247 or 941-778-9597. Fax: 941-778-8303. Internet: www.thebeachinn.com.*

Harrington House Bed & Breakfast

$$ **Holmes Beach** This cozy inn still exudes the ambiance of its birth year, 1925. *5626 Gulf Drive.* ☎ *888-828-5566 or 941-778-5444. Fax: 941-778-0527. Internet: www.harringtonhouse.com.*

The Resort at Longboat Key Club

$$$ **Longboat Key** This upscale resort offers 232 luxurious rooms and suites, 45 holes of golf, 38 tennis courts, and 500 feet of private beach. *301 Gulf of Mexico Drive.* ☎ *800-237-8821 or 941-383-8821. Fax: 941-383-0359. Internet: www.longboatkeyclub.com.*

Dining out in the Sarasota region

A veritable bounty of upscale restaurants caters to the tastes of Sarasota locals, but there are also plenty of places to dine that won't put a king-size dent in your budget. As in most Florida cities, your best bet is to stick to local seafood, which is almost always fresh and well prepared.

Don't forget to allow for the 7 percent sales tax.

The area's best restaurants

Beach Bistro

$$$ **Holmes Beach** **INTERNATIONAL**

The Bistro gets high marks from *Wine Spectator, Zagat, Florida Trend* magazine, and others thanks to an impressive wine list, excellent cuisine, a romantic dining room that offers views of the Gulf, and great service. Some of the restaurant's better entrees include pan-seared grouper in a coconut-and-cashew crust, roast duck in pepper sauce, and herb-rubbed rack of lamb.

6600 Gulf Drive. ☎ *941-778-6444. Internet:* www.beachbistro.com. *Reservations recommended. To get there: At Gulf and 66th. Main courses: $28–$45 ($23–$30 for smaller portions). AE, DC, DISC, MC, V. Open: 5:30–10 p.m. daily.*

Euphemia Haye

$$–$$$ **Longboat Key** **CONTINENTAL**

Another highly decorated establishment, this 20-year-old restaurant combines a great menu (peppered and pan-fried steak, snapper baked in a pistachio crust), an extensive wine list, and a darling second-floor loft that offers salads, lighter bites, and desserts. Its unique cuisine and romantic and friendly atmosphere have won this restaurant *Florida Trend's* Golden Spoon award seven years running.

5540 Gulf of Mexico Drive. ☎ 941-383-3633. Internet: www.euphemiahaye.com. *Reservations suggested. To get there: Take Hwy. 789 7.8 miles north of New Pass Bridge. Main courses: $15–35. CB, DISC, MC, V. Open: 5–10 p.m. Sun–Thurs, 5–10:30 p.m. Fri–Sat.*

Michael's on East

$$ Sarasota CONTINENTAL

A consistent award-winner, Michael's serves contemporary cuisine to a primarily business-oriented clientele in a plush dining room. This is the place in Sarasota for a power lunch, and its wine list packs some punch as well. Try the wonderful Chilean sea bass with vegetable couscous and artichoke hearts or the grilled fillet of beef with wild mushroom ragout and asparagus.

1212 East Ave. S. ☎ 941-366-0007. Internet: www.bestfood.com/moe. *Reservations recommended. To get there: On U.S. 41/Tamiami Trail in Midtown Plaza at junction of Bahia Vista Dr. Main courses: $16.50–$32. AE, DISC, MC, V. Open: 11:30 a.m.–2 p.m. Mon–Fri and 5:30–10 p.m. nightly.*

Ophelia's on the Bay

$$ Siesta Key AMERICAN

The casually elegant Ophelia's continues our string of award winners. The glass-walled dining rooms offer a romantic atmosphere and wonderful views of the bay, or you can dine on an outside patio. The staff is thoroughly professional, and there's a good wine list. The menu offers modern American options, such as a mixed grill of ragout of curried lamb, mango-and-rum glazed breast of duck, and pistachio-crusted prawns.

9105 Midnight Pass Rd. ☎ 941-349-2212. Internet: www.opheliasonthebay. com. *Reservations suggested. To get there: 3 miles south of Stickney Point Rd. Main courses: $15–$32. AE, DC, DISC, MC, V. Open: 5–10 p.m. daily.*

Siam Orchid Restaurant

$ Sarasota THAI

This 13-year-old Thai restaurant offers an exotic atmosphere, friendly service, and a good wine list. House specials include *goong tod* (well-seasoned fried shrimp) and a platter of shrimp, mussels, and lobster tail on stir-fried noodles. Many entrees cost under $15 including the *pad talay* (mixed seafood with vegetables).

4141 Tamiami Trail/U.S. 41. ☎ *941-923-7447. Internet:* www.siamorchidrestaurant.com. *Reservations suggested. To get there: Go south on U.S. 41 to Robinhood St., then make a right and head into the 4141 Plaza. Main courses: $9–$24. In the 4141 Plaza at Robinhood St. AE, DISC, MC, V. Open: 11 a.m.–2 p.m. Mon–Fri, 5–9:30 p.m. daily.*

Runner-up restaurants

Here's another group of eateries to keep you flush with dining choices.

Anna Maria Oyster Bar

$ **Bradenton** A casual, generally inexpensive place to wade into shrimp, crab, lobster, and grouper fixed many ways, including in a walnut crust. *6906 14th St. W.* ☎ *941-758-7880. Internet:* www.oyster-bar.com.

Café on the Bay

$$ **Longboat Key** It serves up treats such as shrimp stuffed with blue crab, along with a view of the Intracoastal Waterway. *2630 Harbourside Dr.* ☎ *941-383-0440. Internet:* www.cafeonthebay.com.

Café L'Europe

$$ **St. Armands Key** The chef here has spent 25 years perfecting a menu that's brimming with such continental temptations as potato-crusted grouper, cioppino, paella, bouillabaisse, and osso buco. *431 St. Armands Circle.* ☎ *941-388-4415. Internet:* www.neweuropeancuisine.com.

Exploring Sarasota and Bradenton

Visitors won't find any theme parks here, but there is a nice mix of things to do for plant, animal, and art lovers.

Touring the top sights

Mote Marine Laboratory

Longboat Key

Stare into a shark's eye or count a barracuda's teeth. Meet manatees Hugh and Buffett, enjoy a 30-foot touch tank, and find out a lot about nature in the river and estuary displays. Don't forget to stick your head around the corner to see the marine mammal hospital or the brand new sea turtle and aquaculture exhibits. Allow 2 to 4 hours to see everything.

1600 Ken Thompson Pkwy. ☎ *941-388-4441. Internet:* www.mote.org. *To get there: From St. Armands Circle, go north toward Longboat Key and follow the signs. Admission: $10 adults, $7 kids 4–17. Open: 10 a.m.–5 p.m. daily.*

Pelican Man's Bird Sanctuary

Sarasota

Dale Shields started this MASH unit for feathered patients in 1989, and today the 2-acre sanctuary in Ken Thompson Park has 200 walking-wounded birds. There's a viewing area, hospital, recovery and rehabilitation areas, and a gift shop. You can adopt a pelican for $25. When you go, the pelican stays (but you get a picture). Allow an hour.

1708 Ken Thompson Pkwy. ☎ *941-388-4444. Internet:* www.pelicanman.org. *To get there: From St. Armands Circle, go north and follow the signs. Admission: Free, but donations are welcome. Open: 10 a.m.–5 p.m. daily.*

Ringling Museums

Sarasota

This 60-acre showstopper, once the home of showman John Ringling, is Sarasota's Big Top. Combined, the **Baroque Art Gallery, Museum of the Circus,** and the Ringling residence, **Ca'd'Zan,** house a ton of European and American art, some of it dating back 500 years. The Circus Museum preserves the gusto of one of America's most spectacular eras; and when you tour Ca'd'Zan (House of John), you'll see a grand terra-cotta palace of stained glass, whimsical carvings, and personal mementos of John and Mable Ringling. Plan on spending about 4 hours if you want to see everything.

5401 Bayshore Rd. ☎ *941-359-5723 or 941-351-1660 (recording). Internet:* www.ringling.org. *To get there: U.S. 41 north to University Pkwy. and follow the signs. Admission: $9 adults, $8 seniors 55 and over, kids 12 and under free. Open: 10 a.m.–5:30 p.m. daily.*

Sarasota Jungle Gardens

Sarasota

Jungle trails meander through 240 species of trees, plants, flowers, and leopards. Rounding out the menu are bird and reptile shows, a kids' jungle (a petting area and energy-burning playground), and free-roaming flamingos that will eat from your hand. Plan to spend 3 to 4 hours here.

3701 Bayshore Rd. ☎ *877-861-6547 or 941-355-1112. Internet:* www.sarasotajunglegardens.com. *To get there: Take U.S. 41 north to Myrtle and turn left. Admission: $10 adults, $8 seniors 62 and over, $6 kids 3–12. Open: 9 a.m.–5 p.m. daily.*

South Florida Museum, Bishop Planetarium, and Parker Manatee Aquarium

Bradenton

Snooty, the oldest captive-born manatee in our galaxy, headlines this attraction. Born in 1948, the Snootster and his sidekick "Mo" live in the 60,000-gallon aquarium. The trifecta adds astronomy, natural history, and cultural exhibits; a hands-on room; and laser-light shows in the planetarium. Allow 4 hours to explore the total experience.

201 10th St. W. ☎ *941-746-4131. Internet:* www.sfmbp.com. *To get there: Take Manatee Ave./Hwy. 64 west to 10th St. and turn right. Open: 10 a.m.–5 p.m. Tues–Sat, noon–5 p.m. Sun. Admission: $7.50 adults, $6 seniors, $4 kids 5–12.*

Seeing and doing more cool stuff

Visitors with special interests, or those who just want to work on their tans, will find a number of other things to occupy their time. Some of the better options include

- **Baseball:** The **Pittsburgh Pirates** (☎ 941-747-3031), use McKechnie Field, 17th Avenue and 9th Street West, for training camp. Tickets cost $6 to $9. The **Cincinnati Reds** (☎ 941-954-4464 or 941-334-3309) pitch their tents at Sarasota's Ed Smith Stadium, 2700 12th St. Tickets run $5 to $12. Workouts begin in mid-February, and games are played through March.

- **Beaches:** Swim in several places located along the barrier islands, from Holmes Beach to Casey Key. Sarasota's Siesta Beach is just ¼-mile long, but Siesta is also 500-feet wide. The sand granules are soft and squeaky under your toes and the Gulf's waters soothe. Go west on Hwy. 72 over U.S. 41 and the Intracoastal Waterway to the end at Midnight Pass, and then turn right. The beach is free.

- **Fishing:** The **Flying Fish Fleet** (☎ 941-366-3373), at Marina Jack's, U.S. 41 at Island Circle, Sarasota, offers half-day rates of $30 for adults and $18 for kids under 15 on big boats, and $395 for private charters (up to six people).

- **Gardens: Selby Botanical Gardens,** 811 South Palm Ave., Sarasota (☎ 941-366-5731) has been called a "supernova in the constellation of botanical gardens." The star attraction, a collection of more than 6,000 orchids, commands the most attention. The 11-acre complex also has an open-air museum of some 20,000 colorful plants. Admission costs $8 for adults and $4 for kids 6 to 11. The gardens are open 10 a.m. to 5 p.m. daily.

- **Golf:** The **Bobby Jones Golf Complex,** 1000 Circus Blvd., Sarasota (☎ 941-365-4653) is a 45-hole municipal course where greens fees run under $25 year-round. The **Legacy Golf Club,** 8255 Legacy Blvd., Bradenton (☎ 941-907-7067) has sand and water hazards on all 18 of its holes. Greens fees run $25 to $40 in summer, and $66 to $85 in winter. **Tatum Ridge Golf Links,** 421 Tatum Road, Sarasota (☎ 941-378-4211) has 18 holes set among wetlands. Greens fees here run under $25 in summer, and $25 to $40 during the winter.

Shopping

Sarasota and Bradenton offer little in terms of unique merchandise, but the former does have a unique shopping district. **St. Armands Circle** on St. Armands Key is a fun place to window shop or splurge a little (more like a lot — you pay more here than in other areas). The circle is an outdoor zone of 150 trendy specialty shops, art galleries, and cafes. It's on par with Palm Beach's Worth Avenue and Park Avenue in Winter Park. To get there, follow Hwy/780 across the Ringling Causeway until you see the circle. For more information, call ☎ 941-388-1554.

On the conventional side, JCPenney, Burdines, Parisian, and Sears anchor the **Sarasota Square Mall,** U.S. 41 and Geneva Road (☎ 941-922-9609). **Desoto Square Mall,** U.S. 301/U.S. 41/1st Avenue at Cortez Road, Bradenton (☎ 941-747-5868), has Burdines, Dillard's, Sears, and JCPenney.

Living the nightlife

In addition to these listings, the *Sarasota Herald-Tribune* (☎ 941-953-7755; Internet: www.newscoast.com/xwelcome.cfm) publishes a Friday entertainment edition called "Ticket." The *Bradenton Herald* (☎ 941-748-0411; Internet: bradenton.com) publishes "The Weekender" on Friday.

Bars and clubs

All the following clubs have no cover charge.

Cha Cha Coconuts, 417 St. Armands Circle, Sarasota (☎ 941-388-3300) is a restaurant and canned-music bar in the Margaritaville tradition. The **Gator Club,** 1490 Main St., Sarasota (☎ 941-366-5969; Internet: www.thegatorclub.com), has live Top 40 and rhythm and blues every night. **The HayeLoft** atop the Euphemia Haye restaurant, 5540 Gulf of Mexico Drive, Longboat Key (☎ 941-383-3633; Internet: www.euphemiahaye.com), offers live jazz Friday through Tuesday and blues on Wednesday and Thursday.

Performing arts

The **FSU Center for the Performing Arts,** 5555 N. Tamiami Trail/U.S. 41, Sarasota (☎ 800-361-8388 or 941-351-8000; Internet: www.asolo.org), is the home of the **Asolo Theatre,** Florida's official state theater. The center's large and small stages present various performances throughout the year. There's also an actors-in-training program. Tickets to performances run from $13 to $39.

The **Van Wezel Performing Arts Center,** 777 N. Tamiami Trail/U.S. 41, Sarasota (☎ **941-953-3366;** Internet: www.vanwezel.org), commands the bayfront skyline with a seashell-shaped hall. The acoustics here are great, and year-round programs range from ballet to jazz and musical comedy. The **Sarasota Ballet** (☎ **941-351-8000;** Internet: www.sarasotaballet.org) performs at the center from October to April, and it also stages performances at the FSU Center. Tickets cost $11 to $45.

Seeing Sarasota and Bradenton in 3 Days

The following game plan pretty much requires that you have a set of wheels. It's also only a suggestion. Feel free to add or subtract items in order to suit your tastes. Or tell us to take a hike and do things your own way.

Spend the morning of **Day 1** at the **Mote Marine Lab** and grab lunch on the run. Then fill in your afternoon at the **South Florida Museum, Bishop Planetarium,** and **Parker Manatee Aquarium.** Have a leisurely dinner at **Euphemia Haye;** then close out your evening upstairs at **The HayeLoft.**

On **Day 2,** head to **Sarasota Jungle Gardens** in the morning, do lunch at **Siam Orchid** (if it's a weekday), and then tour the **Ringling Museums** in the afternoon. **Ophelia's on the Bay** is a great place for dinner, and if the mood and the event calendar strike you, think about an evening performance at the **Asolo Theatre.** If the Asolo isn't open, head out to **Stan's Idle Hour Seafood Restaurant** (see "Living the nightlife" later in this chapter) in Goodland, which offers its own brand of theatrical entertainment.

Day 3 is ultra casual. Take a quickie tour of **Pelican Man's Bird Sanctuary,** and then spend the rest of the day wearing sun block on **Siesta Key** or one of the other barrier-island beaches before having dinner at **Café on the Bay.**

Fort Myers, Sanibel, Naples, and Marco Island

Marco Island and, to a lesser degree, Naples can stake a legitimate claim to being west Florida's wealthiest areas per capita. Fort Myers Beach and its island neighbors — Sanibel and Captiva — are among the area's most popular tourist magnets. Tough zoning laws and campaigns to protect the local ecology should help keep the area's natural wonders, if not untouched, then certainly unspoiled. Travels in this half of the chapter stay close to the coast. (See the "Fort Myers, Sanibel & Naples" map on the following page.)

If you're interested in heading farther south to see the **Everglades,** check out Chapter 13.

Getting there

Most out-of-state visitors opt for the shortest travel time between home and holiday — that means coming by air. **Southwest Florida International Airport** in Fort Myers (☎ **941-768-4700;** Internet: www.swfia.com) is served by about two dozen American, Canadian, and European airlines or their partners, including **Continental, Delta, Northwest/ KLM, TWA, US Airways, Air Canada,** and **LTU International** (see the Appendix for telephone number and Web site information). **Alamo, Avis, Budget, Dollar, Hertz,** and **National** have desks at the airport. **Superior Airport Shuttle** (☎ **888-397-9571** or 941-267-4777; Internet: www.superiorairportshuttle.com) will get you to most southwest Florida destinations from the airport. Here are a few one-way rates for up to three passengers: Fort Myers, $16 to $35; Sanibel and Captiva, $37 to $56; Naples, $38 to $56; and Marco Island, $56 to $70.

If you do decide to come by car (and we can't recommend it), expect a 7- to 8-hour drive from the Florida-Georgia state line. I-75 is the primary route from the north. If you prefer to drive in from the East Coast, take I-95 to Daytona Beach; then take I-4 to I-75 and head south. (See the "Fort Myers, Sanibel & Naples" map, on the following page.)

Getting around

Top to bottom, this area is about 60 miles long, though the tourist zones pretty much hug the coastline and barrier islands. Unless you're going to be relatively stationary, you'll need to have a car.

By car

U.S. 41/Cleveland Avenue/Tamiami Trail is the primary north-south road on the mainland. Hwy. 865/Estero Boulevard runs between Fort Myers Beach and Bonita Beach. Hwy. 78/Pine Island Road connects that island with North Fort Myers, while Hwy. 867/McGregor Boulevard leads the way from Fort Myers to Sanibel and Captiva.

You will definitely need a map to navigate the area without accidentally ending up in the Gulf — or Louisiana for that matter. You can obtain good maps from the information sources listed in "Fast Facts" at the end of this chapter.

Fort Myers, Sanibel & Naples

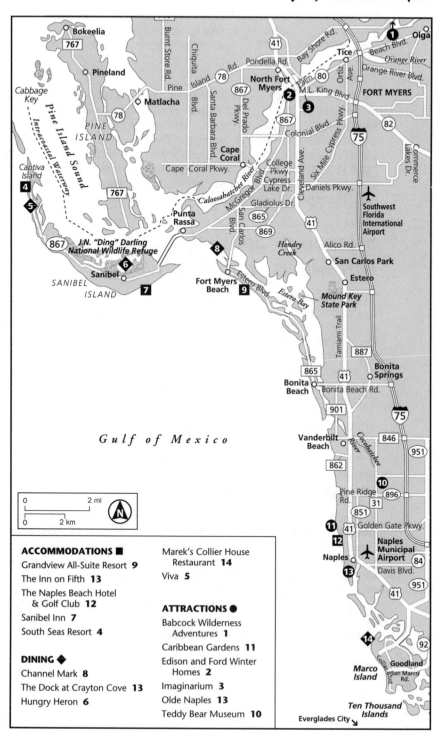

Bokeelia
767
Olga
1
Pineland
Tice
Bay Shore Rd.
Beach Blvd.
41
Pondella Rd.
Orange River
Cabbage Key
Matlacha
78
North Fort Myers
Palm
80
Orange River Blvd.
Rd.
867
FORT MYERS
M.L. King Blvd.
Ortiz Ave.
2
3
82
PINE ISLAND
Burnt Store Rd.
Pine Island Blvd.
Chiquita Blvd.
Santa Barbara Blvd.
Del Prado Pkwy.
867
Colonial Blvd.
75
78
Cape Coral
College Pkwy
Six Mile Cypress Pkwy.
Cleveland Ave.
Commerce Lakes Dr.
Captiva Island
4
Cape Coral Pkwy.
Cypress Lake Dr.
Daniels Pkwy.
5
767
Caloosahatchee River
McGregor Blvd.
Gladiolus Dr.
Southwest Florida International Airport
Pine Island Sound
Intracoastal Waterway
J.N. "Ding" Darling National Wildlife Refuge
Punta Rassa
865
869
41
867
San Carlos Blvd.
Hendry Creek
Alico Rd.
San Carlos Park
8
Estero
Sanibel
6
Fort Myers Beach
9
Estero Blvd.
Estero Bay
Mound Key State Park
SANIBEL ISLAND
7
Tamiami Trail
887
Gulf of Mexico
865
Bonita Springs
Bonita Beach
41
Bonita Beach Rd.
75
901
Vanderbilt Beach
Corkscrew River
846
951
862
Pine Ridge Rd.
10
896
851
31
11
41
Golden Gate Pkwy.
12
Naples Municipal Airport
Naples
84
Davis Blvd.
13
951
41
14
92
Marco Island
Goodland
San Marco Rd.
Ten Thousand Islands
Everglades City

0   2 mi
0   2 km

ACCOMMODATIONS ■
Grandview All-Suite Resort **9**
The Inn on Fifth **13**
The Naples Beach Hotel & Golf Club **12**
Sanibel Inn **7**
South Seas Resort **4**

DINING ◆
Channel Mark **8**
The Dock at Crayton Cove **13**
Hungry Heron **6**

Marek's Collier House Restaurant **14**
Viva **5**

ATTRACTIONS ●
Babcock Wilderness Adventures **1**
Caribbean Gardens **11**
Edison and Ford Winter Homes **2**
Imaginarium **3**
Olde Naples **13**
Teddy Bear Museum **10**

By taxi

Yellow Cab (☎ **941-332-1055** in Fort Myers and ☎ **941-262-1312** in Naples) is the major taxi company in the area. Fares cost $2.75 to $3.75 for the first mile and $1.50 per mile thereafter (up to five passengers).

By bus

Public transportation should be used only as a last resort, because in most cases it caters to commuters, not tourists. **Lee Tran** (☎ **941-275-8726**), operates buses in the Fort Myers and beach areas from 6 a.m. to 9:45 p.m. Monday through Saturday. The fare is $1 for adults, 50 cents for seniors, and kids under 42 inches get on free. The **Naples Trolley** (☎ **941-262-7300**) makes 25 stops in the downtown and the beach area and allows riders to get on and off the trolley throughout the entire day. Fares run $14 for adults and $6 for kids 3 to 12.

Staying in Sanibel, Naples, Fort Myers, and Captiva

As with the rest of South Florida, room rates are highest in the winter, and even motels far removed from the beaches charge premium rates from mid-December through April (although January sees somewhat lower rates in Sanibel and Captiva). Rates drop by as much as 50 percent during the off-season, so if you're on a tight budget, the timing of your vacation will be crucial. Also, keep in mind that hotels can pack in the crowds during high season, so make sure to reserve a room well in advance.

Accommodations in Southwest Florida range from small motels to condominiums to major resorts. Fort Myers is home to a branch of seemingly every chain hotel on the planet, Sanibel offers a host of old-fashioned cottages and condominiums, and Naples has some of the most expensive resorts in the region.

Several reservation services can help get you decent rates or find you a hotel room during a particularly busy time of year. The **Lee Island Coast Visitor and Convention Bureau** operates a free reservation service (☎ **800-733-7935**) that covers lodging in the Fort Myers and Sanibel areas. **Sanibel and Captiva Central Reservations, Inc.** (☎ **800-325-1352**; Internet: www.sanibel-captivarents.com) will book you into condos and cottages on the islands. **Florida Hotel Network** (☎ **800-538-3616**; Internet: www.floridahotels.com) will make arrangements for you in many locations in Southwest Florida.

Sales and hotel taxes add 9 percent to your bill.

The area's best hotels

Grandview All-Suite Resort

$$ Fort Myers Beach

All 75 of this 14-story resort's comfortable suites have sleeper sofas, full kitchens, and balconies with views of the gardens, island, or Gulf. The resort offers recreational programs, boat rentals, and a stretch of private beach.

8701 Estero Blvd. ☎ *941-765-4422. Fax: 941-765-4499. Internet:* www. grandviewfl.com. *To get there: San Carlos/Hwy. 865 across the causeway to Estero Blvd. and ½ mile to the resort. Parking: Free. Rack rates: $145–$225 Jan–Apr, $80–$129 May–Dec. AE, DISC, MC, V.*

The Inn on Fifth

$$ Old Naples

Located in reborn Olde Naples, this Mediterranean-style boutique hotel is only 6 blocks away from the beach. Its 87 large-and-comfortable rooms have French doors that lead to balconies or terraces. All rooms come with terry robes, data ports, coffee and coffee makers, and a free continental breakfast. An onsite restaurant, bar, and fitness center and spa are also available.

699 5th Ave. S. ☎ *888-403-8778 or 941-403-8777. Fax 941-403-8778. Internet:* www. naplesinn.com. *To get there: Pine Ridge Rd. to U.S. 41, south 5 miles to 5th, go right 2½ blocks. Parking: Free self and valet. Rack rates: $209–$369 Jan–Apr; $149–$279 Oct–Dec, Apr–May; $109–$249 June–Sept. AE, CB, DC, DISC, MC, V.*

The Naples Beach Hotel & Golf Club

$$ Naples

This hospitable, upscale resort is unique in that it has been family owned since 1946. Its 318 tropically decorated rooms are large and comfortable, sporting data ports, minibars, and balconies. Set on 125 acres, the resort has a dandy spa, a kids' club that offers free activities to children ages 5 to 12, and a front-row view of the Gulf of Mexico.

851 Gulf Shore Blvd. N. ☎ *800-237-7600 or 941-261-2222. Fax: 941-261-7380. Internet:* www.naplesbeachhotel.com. *To get there: From Pine Ridge Rd., go south on U.S. 41/Tamiami Trail 4 miles and, at the resort's golf club, turn right on South Golf Dr. Parking: Free. Rack rates: $205–$340 Dec–Apr, $115–$250 May and Oct–Nov, $95–$200 June–Sept. AE, CB, DISC, MC, V.*

Sanibel Inn

$$$ Sanibel

Look for hummingbirds and butterflies in the gardens on this 8-acre resort set on a nature preserve. Accommodations here include standard rooms, efficiencies, and one- and two-bedroom apartments. Rattan furnishings keep with the island's motif, and all rooms have a microwave, refrigerator, and a screened balcony or patio. An onsite restaurant, recreational programs, and two tennis courts are also available.

937 E. Gulf Drive. ☎ *800-965-7772 or 941-472-3181. Fax: 941-481-4947. Internet:* www.sanibelinn.com. *To get there: McGregor Blvd./Hwy. 867 Causeway to East Gulf Dr. and the inn. Parking: Free. Rack rates: $285–$465 Jan–Apr, $215–$279 May, $159–$239 June–Dec. AE, DISC, MC, V.*

South Seas Resort

$$$ Captiva

This 330-acre resort is set on 2½ miles of beach that provide some of Florida's finest shelling. South Seas has 18 tennis courts, a nine-hole golf course, a fitness center, five restaurants, and a sailing school where you might see manatees and loggerhead turtles. The comfortable accommodations here range from standard hotel rooms to luxurious three-bedroom villas, and all come with balconies or porches. Rates don't include $8 per person daily service charge.

5400 South Seas Plantation Rd. ☎ *800-965-7772 or 941-481-3636. Fax: 941-481-4947. Internet:* www.ssrc.com or www.south-seas-resort.com. *To get there: Follow Hwy. 869 across the Sanibel Causeway and continue 16 miles to the resort. Parking: Free. Rack rates: $190–$1,000 Holidays–May, $145–$550 Oct–Dec, $115–$495 June–Sept. AE, DISC, MC, V.*

Runner-up accommodations

In addition to the following, check out the chains listed in the Appendix in the back of this guide for more lodging possibilities.

Edgewater Beach Hotel

$$$ Naples This all-suite resort on Millionaire's Row is a bit more elegant, though a little stuffier, than the Naples Beach Hotel & Golf Club. *1901 Gulf Shore Blvd. N.* ☎ *800-821-0196 or 941-403-2000. Fax: 941-403-2100. Internet:* www.edgewaternaples.com.

Olde Naples Inn & Suites

$$ Naples Located near the beach and shopping, the Olde Naples has courtyards that many of its rooms, efficiencies, and suites open onto. *801 3rd St. S.* ☎ *800-637-6036 or 941-262-5194. Fax: 941-262-4876. Internet:* www.oldenaplesinn.com.

Sandpiper Gulf Resort

$$ Fort Myers Beach A clean, family feel is evident in this resort's Gulf-side rooms, which have kitchens and convertible sofas. *5550 Estero Blvd.* ☎ *800-584-1449* or *941-463-5721. Fax: 941-463-5721. Internet:* www.sandpipergulfresort.com.

Dining out in Sanibel, Naples, Fort Myers, and Marco Island

The good news is that restaurants in the affluent areas of Southwest Florida — especially the islands — couldn't afford to stay in business if they didn't churn out good food. So if fine dining tickles your fancy, your luck runneth over. And you need not be a millionaire to feast like a king, although a bulging wallet will certainly help. Those travelers on very tight budgets, or in search of that must-have Big Mac, will find chain restaurants and fast-food joints strung along U.S. 41 from Fort Myers all the way to Naples.

Don't forget to allow for the 7 percent sales tax.

The area's best restaurants

Channel Mark

$$ Fort Myers Beach SEAFOOD

Try this tropical restaurant for a relaxing waterside lunch or a romantic evening out. Every seat in the house has a view of Hurricane Bay and its passing boats. The menu offers creative twists on seafood dishes, and house specialties include a scrumptious grouper topped with shrimp and poached in parchment paper, and honey-and-bacon grilled shrimp.

19001 San Carlos Blvd. ☎ *941-463-0117. Internet:* www.channelmark.com. *Reservations not accepted. To get there: On San Carlos, just before the bridge to Estero Island. Main courses: $11–$32. AE, DC, DISC, MC, V. Open: 11 a.m.–10 p.m. Sun–Thurs, till 11 p.m. Fri–Sat.*

The Dock at Crayton Cove

$ Olde Naples SEAFOOD/FLORIBBEAN

This lively old standard on the city dock has been offering great water-front dining since 1976. Visitors and locals frequent the restaurant, which dishes out Floribbean-inspired seafood. Options include a crispy rum-and-molasses barbecued duck, and an assortment of sandwiches, includ-ing a crab-salad BLT. The bar features daily happy hours and makes a great margarita.

1200 5th Ave. S. ☎ *941-263-2734. Internet:* http://dockcraytoncove.com. *Reservations not accepted. To get there: It's on 12th Ave. at Naples Bay (at the City Dock). Main courses: $8.50–$20. AE, DISC, MC, V. Open: 11 a.m.–midnight daily.*

Hungry Heron

$ Sanibel   AMERICAN/SEAFOOD

This family restaurant — Sanibel's most popular — has a tropical decor and a menu bursting with nearly 300 items, including 35 for kids. Disney movies and cartoons play on multiple screens while families chow down on big sandwiches, pasta, and shellfish. All-you-can-eat specials (prime rib, gulf shrimp, and so on) are featured throughout the week.

2330 Palm Ridge Rd. ☎ *941-395-2300. Internet:* www.hungry-heron.com. *Reservations not accepted. To get there: It's at Palm Ridge and Periwinkle Way (in Palm Ridge Plaza). Main courses: $7–$16. AE, DISC, MC, V. Open: 11 a.m.–9:30 p.m. daily.*

Marek's Collier House Restaurant

$$ Marco Island   CONTINENTAL

Both the indoor and verandah dining rooms of this restaurant — Marco Island's finest — offer a relaxed-but-refined dining experience. Chef/owner Peter Marek, a triple gold-medal winner at the World Culinary Olympics, has cooked for Queen Elizabeth, and you're sure to dine royally at his home base. House specials include shrimp stuffed with spicy crabmeat and wrapped in filo, and rack of lamb with garlic and rosemary. There's an extensive wine list.

1231 Bald Eagle Drive. ☎ *941-642-9948. Internet:* www.mareksrestaurant.com. *Reservations suggested. To get there: It's 1 mile north of Collier Blvd./Hwy. 951. Main courses: $18–$32.50. AE, MC, V. Open: 5:30–9:30 p.m., closed Sept. 15–Nov. 30.*

Viva

$$$ Captiva   INTERNATIONAL

This restaurant, housed in an avant-garde building, beckons with sharp angles, natural light, and fine art. Sharing space with an art gallery, the dining room also sports an open kitchen. The seafood side of the ledger includes dover sole and blackened yellowfin tuna. The menu also features coq au vin, grilled veal chops, and duck à l'orange. There's an excellent wine list. Viva is smoke-free.

15050 Captiva Drive. ☎ *941-395-9494. Internet:* www.viva-captiva.com. *Reservations suggested. To get there: Hwy. 869 across the Sanibel Causeway and continue 15 miles. Main courses: $22–$34. AE, DISC, MC, V. Open: 5:30–10 p.m. Mon–Sat (2:30–5 p.m. tea time), noon–3 p.m. Sun.*

Runner-up restaurants

In case you haven't gotten hungry yet, here are three more places where you can pack on some extra vacation pounds.

Morgan's Forest

$$ Sanibel   This restaurant features a tasty selection of seafood and pasta, although one could get lost in the faux (Okay, hokey!) rain-forest motif. *1231 Middle Gulf Dr.* ☎ *941-472-4100. Internet:* www.morgansforest.com.

The Beach Pierside Grill

$ Fort Myers Beach   This small eatery specializes in fried and broiled seafood (grouper, shrimp, and oysters). *1000 Estero Blvd.* ☎ *941-765-7800. Internet:* www.piersidegrill.com.

Stan's Idle Hour Seafood Restaurant

$ Goodland   This spot is notable as much for its sideshows (Stan singing, the Goodland Mullet Festival, and the Buzzard Lope Queens) as for its seafood. Note: In the summer, Stan keeps occasional hours, so call in advance. *Hwy. 892* ☎ *941-394-3041. Internet:* www.stansidlehour.com.

Exploring Fort Myers, Sanibel, Naples, and Marco Island

There aren't many major attractions in this area of Florida, but if you like old things, animals, and the great outdoors, you'll find plenty to do.

Touring the top sights

Babcock Wilderness Adventures

Punta Gorda

You take a 90-minute, swamp-buggy tour of a ranch and Telegraph Cypress Swamp. (Reservations are required; no handicapped access.) In addition to the naturalist-narrated tour (you may see an alligator or eagle), there's a small museum and some ranch critters. Allow 2-plus hours in addition to driving time. (It's 45 minutes north of Fort Myers.)

8000 Hwy. 31. ☎ *800-500-5583. Internet:* www.babcockwilderness.com. *To get there: On Hwy. 31 off Hwy. 80, east of I-75. Admission: $18 adults, $10 kids 3–12. Open: 9 a.m.–3 p.m. daily Nov–May, morning only May–Oct (call for times).*

Caribbean Gardens

Naples

Larry Tetzlaff and friends run an attraction where big cats (tigers, cara-cals, and clouded leopards) and primates are the focal point of a con-servation theme. The agenda here includes cat shows, boat rides, and closer encounters with kangaroos, gators, and an albino python. You can easily fill 3 to 4 hours if you like wild things.

1590 Goodlette-Frank Rd. ☎ *941-262-5409. Internet:* www.caribbeangardens. com. *To get there: South on U.S. 41 to entrance sign just before Golden Gate Pkwy. Admission: $15 adults, $10 kids 4–15. Open: 9:30 a.m.–5:30 p.m. daily.*

Edison and Ford Winter Homes

Fort Myers

Thomas Edison and Henry Ford were neighbors and friends. Edison's 14-acre riverfront estate includes his lab, garden, vintage cars, and 200 phonographs. He spent his winters in what he dubbed "Seminole lodge," from 1886 to 1931. Ford arrived at his 3-acre estate in 1916. His home, known as "Mangoes," has a 1914 Model T and a 1917 Model T Truck. Guided and self-guided tours are available. Figure on spending about 2 to 3 hours here.

2350 McGregor Blvd. ☎ *941-334-7419. Internet:* www.edison-ford-estate.com. *To get there: West on Colonial to McGregor; turn right and continue to the houses. Admission: $11 adults, $5.50 kids 6–12 including guided tour. Open: 9 a.m.–5:30 p.m. Mon–Sat, noon–5:30 p.m. Sun.*

Imaginarium

Fort Myers

This neat, hands-on aquarium and museum lets you stand in a Florida thunderstorm without getting wet, watch Elvis the eel slither through coral, get blown away in the Hurricane Experience, and lost in the Amazing Maze. Allow 2 hours to see all the exhibits.

2000 Cranford Ave. ☎ *941-337-3332. To get there: Just east of downtown. Admission: $6 adults, $3 kids 3–12. Open: 10 a.m.–5 p.m. Tues–Sat.*

Olde Naples

This city grew up around a beach and boat pier. Some of the homes built by well-to-do Northerners in the early part of the twentieth century remain today. **Millionaire's Row,** a long, palm-studded block of these fab-ulous homes runs from Gulf Shore Boulevard to the beach. In addition to that rich architecture, the district is a tree-lined package of clubs, shops, restaurants and sidewalk cafes, boutique hotels, a 1,000-foot fishing pier, and a sugar-sand beach. Some of the area's highlights include **Palm Cottage,** 137 12th Ave. S. (☎ **941-261-8164**), built in 1895 and now the home of the Collier County Historical Society; and **Tin City,** 1200 5th Ave. S., an old oyster-processing plant that's now the home of 40 or so shops and restaurants. Plan to spend 4 to 6 hours here depending on your tolerance for browsing.

Olde Naples reaches north from 12th Ave. South to Central and west from 9th St. to the Gulf of Mexico.

Teddy Bear Museum

Naples

If 4,000 stuffed bears from around the globe sound like fun, this museum is for you. There's a gift shop if you feel the urge to bring something huggable home. Unless you're a teddy fanatic, you can see everything in about 90 minutes.

2511 Pine Ridge Rd. ☎ 941-598-2711. Internet: www.teddymuseum.com. *To get there: On Pine Ridge/Hwy. 896 east of Airport Rd. Admission: $6 adults, $4 seniors 60 and older, $2 kids 4–12. Open: 10 a.m.–5 p.m. Wed–Sat, 1–5 p.m. Sun.*

Seeing and doing more cool stuff

Here are some more ways, especially for sports and outdoors enthusiasts, to fill your days.

- ✔ **Baseball:** The **Texas Rangers** play at Charlotte County Stadium in Port Charlotte, 2300 El Jobean Rd. (☎ **941-625-9500**). Tickets cost $7 to $9. The **Boston Red Sox** take the field at City of Palms Park, 2201 Edison Ave., Fort Myers (☎ **941-334-4700**), and it will set you back $10 to $11 to see a game. The **Minnesota Twins** play at Hammond Stadium in the Lee County Sports Complex, 14100 Six Mile Cypress Pkwy., Fort Myers (☎ **800-338-9467**), and tickets run $9 to $12. Workouts begin in mid-February, with games played through March.

- ✔ **Beaches, Parks, and Preserves:** The **Corkscrew Swamp Sanctuary,** 375 Sanctuary Rd., Naples (☎ **941-348-9151**) is an 11,000-acre preserve with a 2¼-mile boardwalk running through the prairie and hammock homes of wild orchids, wood storks, and virgin bald cypresses, some of which are 500 years old. Admission costs $8 adults, $3.50 kids 6 to 18. **Delnor-Wiggins Pass State Recreation Area,** 11100 Gulf Shore Dr., Naples (☎ **941-597-6196**), has things that other parts of Florida have lost: sea oats, sea grapes, cabbage palms, wading birds, manatees, and loggerhead nests. Its boardwalks lead to nature areas, and the swimming is good, but stay out of the pass to avoid undertows. Admission is $4 per car. **J.N. "Ding" Darling National Wildlife Refuge,** 1 Wildlife Dr., Sanibel (☎ **941-472-1100**), is Sanibel Island's finest hour, a 6,000-acre preserve that offers footpaths through sea grapes, sabal palms, and mangroves that provide homes to such critters as spoonbills, mangrove cuckoos, alligators, and a few American crocodiles. A visitors center and a 5-mile Wildlife Drive are available. Admission is $5 for vehicles.

✔ **Fishing:** The main event happens in mid-July, when hundreds of anglers arrive in Boca Grande for the **World's Richest Tarpon Tournament** (☎ 941-964-2283) and a shot at the $100,000 grand prize. Small party charter rates start at about $250 per half day and $450 for a full day (for up to six people). You can find guides through the **Boca Grande Fishing Guides Association** (☎ 941-964-1711), **Jensen's Marina** on Captiva Island (☎ 941-472-5800), **Naples City Boat Dock** in Olde Naples (☎ 941-434-4693), and **Cedar Bay Marina** on Marco Island (☎ 800-906-2628 or 941-394-9333).

✔ **Golf:** You can find local golf information on the Web at www.golf. com and www.floridagolfing.com. If you like surfing the old-fashioned way, request course information from the **Florida Sports Foundation** (☎ 850-488-8347), or **Florida Golfing** (☎ 877-222-4653). Some of the more popular local options are

- **Cypress Woods,** 3525 North Brook Drive, Naples (☎ 941-592-7860), whose course has hills and tree-lined fairways. Greens fees: $25 to $40 in the summer, and $41 to $65 during winter.

- **Eagle Ridge,** 14589 Eagle Ridge Drive, Fort Myers (☎ 941-768-1888), which has big greens and water on 17 of its holes. Greens fees: under $25 in the summer, and $41 to $65 in the winter.

- **Marriott's Golf Club,** 400 S. Collier Blvd., Marco Island (☎ 941-793-6060), which has water hazards on 16 holes and well-bunkered greens. Greens fees: $25 to $40 summer, and $86 to $110 during the winter.

Seeing the area by guided tour

Several tour companies offer visitors a chance to explore Naples and its surroundings through a variety of means. Some of the sightseeing options in this corner of Florida also give you a chance to experience the Everglades, but for a deeper look at this wonderful wilderness, see Chapter 13.

By air

Casablanca Air in Naples (☎ 941-431-1133; Internet: www. casablancaair.com) offers biplane tours out of **Naples Municipal Airport,** 160 Aviation Blvd., including one where you get to take the controls. Tours cost $70 to $205. There are also tours, which run $300 to $650, for up to six people in a modern plane. All these tours last 15 to 30 minutes; destinations include the Gulf of Mexico and parts of the Everglades.

By airboat and van

Fossil Expeditions of Fort Myers (☎ **800-304-9432** or 941-368-3252; Internet: www.fossilexpeditions.com) offers 6-hour, hands-on, fossil-collecting tours in the Everglades that include an airboat ride. Tours run $60 for adults, $50 for kids 12 and under. The company also offers a 4½-hour Everglades Eco-Tour by van that includes a pickup at most Sanibel or Fort Myers Beach motels, which runs $60 for adults, and $55 for kids 12 and under.

By trolley

Naples Trolley Tours (☎ **941-262-7300;** Internet: www.naples-trolley. com) are an often humorous, narrated introduction to the city, including Olde Naples and some of its century-old estates. The trolleys make 22 stops at area shops, restaurants, and hotels. You can get on and off at stops at your leisure. It costs $14 for adults, and $6 for kids 3 to 12 for all-day passes.

Shopping

Shoppers will find the same theme in this region that exists in most of Florida: We have few unique products other than seashells, T-shirts, and other cheap trinkets.

Olde Naples, which was ground zero for the city's original settlement, is the only true shopping district in this sector. In addition to yesterday's architecture, this downtown district has clubs, shops, restaurants, and sidewalk cafes. Olde Naples reaches north from 12th Avenue South to Central and west from 9th Street to the Gulf of Mexico. **Tin City,** 1200 5th Ave. S., an oyster-processing plant in a past life, now houses 40 or so shops, plus restaurants, boat charters, and tours.

Finding the second-best shopping spots

In the north, **Sanibel Factory Stores** (☎ **941-454-1616**) has such outlets as Big Dog Sportswear, Etienne Aigner, and Reebok. To get here from I-75, go west on Daniels Parkway to Cypress Lake; then make a left on Summerline. Remember our standard outlet warning: Know what the retail price is so you can tell if you're really getting a bargain. **Edison Mall,** Cleveland Avenue/U.S. 41 at Winkler in Fort Myers (☎ **941-939-5464**), is anchored by Burdines, Dillard's, Sears, and JCPenney.

In the south, **Coastland Center Mall,** U.S. 41 between Golden Gate Parkway and Fleischmann (☎ **941-262-2323**) is anchored by Sears, JCPenney, Burdines, and Dillard's. The **Village at Venetian Bay,** 4200 Gulf Shore Blvd. N., Naples (☎ **941-261-6100**) features 50 canalside shops, including clothiers and art galleries.

Buying special souvenirs

Okay, some of you are dying to put a shell next to your ear and pretend to hear the ocean. Here's your shot. **The Shell Factory,** 2787 N. Tamiami Trail/U.S. 41, North Fort Myers (☎ **800-474-3557** or 941-995-2141), is tacky, touristy, free, and it's crammed with 5 million shells, sponges, pieces of coral, and fossils.

Living the nightlife

In addition to the listings in this section, get up-to-the-minute entertainment information from the local newspapers: The *News Press* in Fort Myers (☎ **941-335-0200;** Internet: http://news-press.com) and the *Naples Daily News* (☎ **941-262-3161;** Internet: www.naplesnews.com). Also, keep in mind that most hotels on the beaches and coast offer live or canned music at night; so do clubs sprinkled around **Olde Naples.** (See "Touring the top sights" following "Exploring Fort Myers, Sanibel, Naples, and Marco Island" earlier in this chapter.)

Bars

Remember the pop quiz we gave you at the beginning of the chapter? Well, there's another kind of green flash here. The **Green Flash Restaurant,** Sanibel-Captiva Road, Captiva Island (☎ **941-472-3337)** has a ten-seat bar, but because the restaurant faces east, the only way to see the flash that is sometimes caused by the setting sun is to sip your beer out back. **The Beached Whale,** 1249 Estero Blvd., Fort Myers Beach (☎ **941-463-5505**), has bands four or five nights a week. **Stan's Idle Hour Seafood Restaurant,** Hwy. 892, Goodland (☎ **941-394-3041;** Internet: www.stansidlehour.com), is famous — well, within local circles — for its sideshows. There's a little song (Stan and others are not quite ready for prime time), a little dance (the **Buzzard Lope Queens,** a mondo bizarro feathery fiasco), and a little seltzer in your pants (the **Goodland Mullet Festival,** always held the weekend before the Super Bowl in conjunction with crowning a Buzzard Lope Queen). Other treats include November's Polish Oktoberfest (yes, Oktoberfest in November) and the men's legs contest in March. Stan's is open daily from 11 a.m. to 10 p.m. or later, November through April, and from 11 a.m. to 10 p.m., Friday through Sunday, the rest of the year.

Performing arts

The **Barbara B. Mann Performing Arts Hall,** 8099 College Pkwy. SW, Fort Myers (☎ **800-440-7469** or 941-481-4849; Internet: www.bbmannpah. com), stages concerts and Broadway-style shows. The **Philharmonic Center for the Arts,** 5833 Pelican Bay Blvd., Naples (☎ **800-597-1900** or 941-597-1900; Internet: www.naplesphilcenter.org), offers Broadway, country, dance, jazz, and pop performances.

Suggested itineraries

In this section we give you two options, one covering the northern reaches of Southwest Florida, the other covering the south. If you want to stretch the organized portion of your itinerary, feel free to combine the two. As always, most of these excursions require a car.

Seeing Fort Myers and Sanibel in 2 Days

Day 1 is dedicated to the real Florida. Grab a bag lunch and climb into a **Fossil Expeditions** van to hunt everything from shark's teeth to dinosaur bones. (Featured alternate: Do the company's Everglades Eco-Tour.) If time permits, spend a late-afternoon hour or two at **The Shell Factory.** Then have dinner at the **Hungry Heron** and a nightcap at **The Beached Whale.**

On **Day 2,** begin at **Babcock Wilderness Adventures;** then head south and do lunch at **The Beach Pierside Grill.** After lunch, tour the **Edison and Ford Winter Homes.** Then, depending on your mood, see **Imaginarium** or take the self-guided wildlife drive at **J.N. "Ding" Darling National Wildlife Refuge.** End your day with dinner at the **Channel Mark.**

Seeing Naples and Marco Island in 2 Days

Spend a long morning on **Day 1** at **Caribbean Gardens,** and then grab lunch on the fly before crashing on the beach at **Delnor-Wiggins Pass State Recreation Area.** Head for **Stan's Idle Hour Seafood Restaurant** for a casual dinner, and stick around for some of the later shenanigans.

Day 2 sends you to the **Teddy Bear Museum** for a quick visit, and then you're off to **Olde Naples** to shop and ogle the architecture. Plan on having lunch at **The Dock at Crayton Cove,** and put on your evening feed bag at **Marek's Collier House Restaurant.**

Fast Facts

Area Code

The local area code is **941.**

American Express

Travel service offices include **Palmer Ranch Travel,** 8443 S. Tamiami Trail/U.S. 41, Sarasota (☎ **941-924-0144**); **A to Z Travel,** 13401 Summer line Rd., Fort Myers (☎ **941-489-2122**); and **A to Z Travel Center,** 5034 Airport Rd., Suite 304, Naples (☎ **941-262-3300**).

Hospitals

The major area hospitals are **Sarasota Memorial Hospital,** 1700 S. Tamiami Trail/U.S. 41 (☎ **941-917-9000**); **Columbia Blake Medical Center,** 2020 59th St. W., Bradenton (☎ **941-792-6611**); **Lee Memorial Hospital,** 2776 Cleveland Ave., Fort Myers (☎ **941-437-5211**); and **Naples Community Hospital,** 350 7th St. N., Naples (☎ **941-436-5000**).

Information

The best information sources for the Sarasota-Bradenton area are the **Sarasota Convention & Visitors Bureau**, 655 N. Tamiami Trail/U.S. 41, (☎ **800-522-9799** or 941-957-1877; Internet: www.sarasotafl.org), and the **Bradenton Area Convention & Visitors Bureau** (☎ **800-462-6283** or 941-729-9177; Internet: www.floridaislandbeaches.org). Both bureaus offer maps, brochures, and tourist information.

Your best sources of information for Naples and the surrounding territory are the **Lee Island Coast Visitor & Convention Bureau**, 2180 W. 1st St., Suite 100, Fort Myers (☎ **800-237-6444** or 941-338-3500; Internet: www.LeeIslandCoast.com), and **The Naples Area Chamber of Commerce**, 895 5th Ave. S., Naples (☎ **941-262-6141**; Internet: www.naples-online.com).

Other good sources of information are the **Greater Fort Myers Chamber of Commerce** (☎ **800-366-3622** or 941-332-3624; Internet: www.fortmyers.org), the **Sanibel-Captiva Islands Chamber of Commerce** (☎ **941-472-1080**; Internet: www.sanibel-captiva.org), and **Visit Naples** (☎ **800-605-7878**; Internet: www.visit-naples.com).

Internet Access

Java Java, 860 5th Ave. S., Naples, (☎ **941-435-1180**; Internet: www.javajavanaples.com), is an Internet cafe that offers access to e-mail and the World Wide Web.

Mail

There are U.S. post offices at 1661 Ringling Blvd., Sarasota; 815 4th Ave. W., Bradenton; 1200 Goodlette Rd. N., Naples; and at 1350 Monroe St., Fort Myers. For branches near your hotel, call ☎ **800-275-8777**.

Maps

The information sources listed that precede this section are great places to ask for a map. Rental-car agencies are another good source (including those at the airport), as are local convenience stores, which sell good maps for $3–$5.

Newspapers

The *Sarasota Herald-Tribune* (☎ **941-953-7755**; Internet: www.newscoast.com/xwelcome.cfm), the *Bradenton Herald* (☎ **941-748-0411**; Internet: bradenton.com), the *News Press* in Fort Myers (☎ **941-335-0200**, Internet: http://news-press.com), and the *Naples Daily News* (☎ **941-262-3161**; Internet: www.naplesnews.com) are the four major papers.

Pharmacies

There are 24-hour **Walgreens** at 3901 S. Tamiami/U.S. 41, Sarasota (☎ **941-926-2522**); 4220 Manatee Ave. W., Bradenton (☎ **941-749-1561**; Internet: www.walgreens.com); and Cleveland Avenue/U.S. 41 and Woodland Boulevard, Fort Myers (☎ **941-939-2142**; Internet: www.walgreens.com). There's a 24-hour **Eckerd** at 5296 Tamiami Trail/U.S. 41 N., Naples (☎ **941-261-1395**; Internet: www.eckerd.com).

Taxes

The sales tax in Sarasota and Bradenton is 7 percent on almost everything except groceries and medicine. Sarasota adds on another 3 percent for a total of 10 percent on hotel rooms. That total is 9 percent in Bradenton.

Fort Myers and Naples assess a standard 6 percent state sales tax on most goods except groceries and medicine. Both add 3 percent for a total of 9 percent tax on hotel rooms.

Taxis

Generally, in Sarasota and Bradenton it's $2.10 to get in the cab, plus $1.50 per mile thereafter. The fleet includes **Yellow Cab** (☎ 941-955-3341), **Green Cab** (☎ 941-922-6666), and **Diplomat Taxi** (☎ 941-359-8294).

Cab fare in the rest of the region costs $2.75–$3.75 for the first mile and $1.50 per mile thereafter (up to five passengers). **Yellow Cab,** (☎ 941-332-1055 in Fort Myers and ☎ 941-262-1312 in Naples), is the major taxi company in the area.

Transit Info

Sarasota County Area Transit or SCAT (☎, 941-316-1234), runs buses in the city and St. Armands, Longboat, and Lido keys. The fare is 50 cents. Buses run from 6 a.m. to 7 p.m. Monday through Saturday.

Lee Tran (☎ 941-275-8726), operates buses in the Fort Myers and beach areas. The fare is $1 adults, 50 cents seniors, kids under 42 inches free. **Naples Trolley** (☎ 941-262-7300), makes 25 stops in the downtown and beach area. An all-day pass costs $14 adults, $6 kids 3–12.

Weather Updates

For a recording of current conditions and forecast reports for Sarasota, call the local office of the **National Weather Service** at ☎ 813-645-2323. For conditions in and around Naples, call the Miami office of the **National Weather Service** at ☎ 305-229-4522, or check out the Web site, www.nws.noaa.gov. You can also get information by watching the **Weather Channel** (Internet: www.weatherchannel.com).

Part V
Visiting Central Florida: Mickey Mania

The 5th Wave   By Rich Tennant

Of all the theme hotels in Orlando, you had to pick one whose theme was The Great Depression!

In this part . . .

*I*f you know only one thing about Florida's geography, it's probably that Orlando and Walt Disney World are smack-dab in the middle of the bull's-eye.

These locations are worlds unto themselves, especially Mickeyville, which owns 47 square miles of things to keep you busy. When you add Universal Orlando, SeaWorld, and several wannabes to the mix, there are enough options to drive you screaming from Cinderella's Castle.

Fear not: This part divides and conquers. The first chapter gets you here, helps you find a bed, and suggests a few dining options. The second chapter devotes itself to Orlando's major shrines — the theme parks. Finally, the third chapter takes a look at the city's smaller attractions, shopping, and nightlife.

Chapter 18

Settling into Walt Disney World and Orlando

In This Chapter

▶ Landing and getting your bearings

▶ Pillow talk — accommodations

▶ Refueling in Orlando's restaurants

▶ Character dining and dinner shows

*W*elcome to Orlando, a land dominated by a king-size rodent, and a modern utopia to many of the young and young-at-heart. For those of us who have been around a while, Walt Disney World is a mystery: Some day, it will run out of gas. (Won't it?) But to the millions who make the pilgrimage here — a group that includes Super Bowl champs, a prince or two, and regular folks — it's a national shrine. A crowded shrine at that.

Walt Disney's Florida legacy is still growing, 35 years after his death. At current count, Orlando has eight major theme parks (see Chapter 19), 80 or so smaller attractions nearby (see Chapter 20), some 110,000 hotel rooms, and an avalanche of restaurants.

In this chapter we get you into town, tell you how to get around, outline the best places for you to lay your head at the end of the day, and give you options for refueling your system. Making choices in this town doesn't require a doctorate in dodging dilemmas, but deciding a few things before the landing gear lowers will allow you to spend more time cozying up to the Mouse.

Getting There

A significant majority of travelers have limited vacation time — that's why most people fly to Orlando. Some of you may have a little more leisure time, however, so we give you information on the three most common means of arrival.

By plane

If you're coming by airplane, you will most likely fly into **Orlando International Airport** (☎ 407-825-2001; Internet: http://fcn.state.fl.us/goaa). Orlando has direct or nonstop service from 70 American and 25 international cities. Forty scheduled airlines, and as many charters, feed 28 million people into these terminals annually. The most frequently used carriers include **Delta, American, American West, British Airways, Canadian Airlines, Continental, Midway, Northwest, Southwest, TWA,** and **US Airways.** (See the "Quick Concierge" in the back of the book for the telephone numbers and Web sites of the major air carriers.)

The way to baggage claim is clearly marked. (You land at level three, take a shuttle to the terminal, and then go to level two.)

If you need cash, ATMs are located in the arrival and departure terminals near the three pods of gates (1 to 29, 30 to 59, and 60 to 99). There are also ATMs located where the shuttles deposit you in the main terminal. If you need to convert your pounds, francs, and so on to U.S. dollars, you can find currency exchanges (open 9:30 a.m. to 9 p.m.) opposite of the ATMs at gate pods 1 to 29 and 60 to 99 in the air terminal. In the main terminal, they're located where shuttles arrive from gates 1 to 29.

All major car-rental companies are located at the airport (on level one) or nearby. Check out the Appendix in the back of this book for the toll-free numbers of the major rental companies. You can find other vehicle-rental company services online at http://fcn.state.fl.us/goaa.

At the Orlando International Airport, arriving passengers can find information at The Magic of Disney and Disney's Flight of Fantastic, two shops located in the A and B terminals, respectively. They sell Disney multi-day park tickets, make dinner show and hotel reservations, and provide brochures. Facilities are open daily from 6 a.m. to 9 p.m. The **Universal Studios** and **SeaWorld** stores in the airport offer similar services and hours.

The airport is a 25-minute hop, skip, and long jump from **Disney World,** and 20 minutes from downtown. **Mears Transportation Group** (☎ 407-423-5566) is the major shuttle player. It runs vans between the airport (you board outside baggage claim) and all Disney resorts and official hotels, as well as most other area properties, every 15 to 25 minutes. Round-trip fare to downtown Orlando or International Drive is $21 for adults ($14 for kids 4 to 11); it's $25 for adults ($17 for kids) to Walt Disney World/Lake Buena Vista or Kissimmee/U.S. 192.

QuickTransportation/Orlando (☎ 888-784-2522 or 407-354-2456; Internet: www.quicktransportation.com) offers shuttle service that is a bit more personal. Employees greet you at the airport's baggage claim department (with a sign bearing your name). This company is 10 to 15 percent more expensive than Mears, but QuickTransportation comes for you, not a full load of tourists, and this company only goes to your resort. This is a good option for a group of four or more.

Taxis are another option if your party has enough people. The standard rates for **Ace Metro** (☎ 407-855-0564) and **Yellow Cab** (☎ 407-699-9999) are $2.50, for the first mile, and $1.50 a mile, thereafter. The one-way charge from the airport to Disney for up to five people in a cab, or seven people in a van, is about $42. A trip to International Drive is $26; to downtown it's $17. Vans and taxis load on level two of the airport.

Some hotels offer free shuttle service to and from the airport, so make sure to ask when booking your room.

By car

Driving to Orlando is a less expensive and potentially more scenic option, unless the distance is so great that making the road trip eats up too much of your vacation.

Here's how far several cities are from Orlando: Atlanta, 436 miles; Boston, 1,312 miles; Chicago, 1,120 miles; Cleveland, 1,009 miles; Dallas, 1,170 miles; Detroit, 1,114 miles; New York, 1,088 miles; and Toronto, 1,282 miles.

Folks coming from the West and Midwest usually connect with I-10 in north Florida and then follow I-75 to the Florida Turnpike. From inland eastern cities, take I-75 into Florida. Those coming down the coastal route can take I-95 to Daytona Beach and then I-4 to Orlando.

By train

Amtrak trains (☎ 800-872-7245) pull into two central stations: 1400 Sligh Blvd., between Columbia and Miller Streets in downtown Orlando, and 111 Dakin Ave., at Thurman Street in Kissimmee. Amtrak's Auto Train allows you to bring along the family sedan without having to drive it all the way. The service begins in Lorton, Virginia — about a 4-hour drive from New York; 2 hours from Philadelphia — and ends at Sanford, Florida, about 23 miles northeast of Orlando. The Auto Train departs Lorton and Sanford daily at 4:30 p.m., arriving at the other end of the line the next morning at 9 a.m. Rates for hauling your car range from $142 to $330; passenger rates are $93 to $182.

Amtrak offers money-saving packages to Orlando, including accommodations (some at Walt Disney World resorts), car rentals, tours, and so on. For package information, call ☎ **800-321-8684.**

Orienting Yourself in Orlando

Orlando's major artery is Interstate 4. Locals call it I-4 or that #@$*%^#!! road, because it runs at a snail's pace, especially during the weekday rush hour (7 to 9 a.m. and 4 to 6 p.m.). I-4 runs diagonally across the state from Tampa to Daytona Beach. Exits from I-4 — they're mostly well-marked — lead to all **Walt Disney World** properties, **Universal, SeaWorld,** International Drive, U.S. 192, Kissimmee, Lake Buena Vista, Church Street Station, downtown Orlando, and Winter Park. (Skip ahead to the "Orlando Neighborhoods" map.)

The Florida Turnpike crosses I-4 and links with I-75 to the north. U.S. 192, a major east-west artery, reaches from Kissimmee to U.S. 27, cross-ing I-4 near the Walt Disney World entrance road. Farther north, the BeeLine Expressway toll road (or Florida 528) goes east from I-4, past Orlando International Airport to Cape Canaveral and the Kennedy Space Center. The East-West Expressway (also known as Florida 408) is another toll road that bypasses the tourist Meccas.

Ordering Orlando by Neighborhood

We've broken Orlando into seven geographical areas:

- ✔ **Walt Disney World:** The area is big, and little tourist parks, resorts, restaurants, shops, and trimmings are scattered across 30,500 acres. Oh, and Disney isn't actually in Orlando — it's south-west of the city, off I-4 on west U.S. 192. Stay here and discover that convenience has its price — rooms can cost double what they cost in nearby Kissimmee.

   A major section of **Walt Disney World, Downtown Disney,** is the general name that Disney gives to its two night-time entertainment areas, **Pleasure Island** and **Disney's West Side,** plus its shopping complex, **Downtown Disney Marketplace.** The area is filled with restaurants, shops, and dance clubs of all types and prices. Downtown Disney is actually in Lake Buena Vista although it's a part of **Walt Disney World.**

- ✔ **Lake Buena Vista:** This Disney next-door neighbor is where you'll find "official" (Disney-approved but not Disney-owned) hotels. It's close to Downtown Disney and Pleasure Island. This charming area has manicured lawns, tree-lined thoroughfares, and free transportation throughout the realm. The major north-west/ northeast road is Highway 535, or Apopka-Vineland Road. **Note:** North of the Palm Parkway, however, Apopka-Vineland Road changes becomes Highway 435.

- ✔ **Celebration:** Imagine living in a Disney world. Celebration is an attempt to re-create a squeaky-clean, Mickey-magic town. It will eventually have thousands of residents living in Disney homes, which start at about $200,000. Celebration's downtown area is, however, designed for tourists. It has some first-rate, if pricey, shops and restaurants. Celebration is located off U.S. 192.

✔ **Kissimmee:** This area has a tacky side: It's loaded with T-shirt shops and every burger barn known to Western civilization. But, Kissimmee is just a short drive (10 to 15 miles) from the Wizard of Disney, and, with plenty of modest motels, it's a good choice for those on a budget. The town centers on U.S. 192/Irlo Bronson Memorial Highway.

✔ **International Drive (Hwy. 536):** Can you say tourist Mecca? Known as **I-Drive,** this area extends 7 to 10 miles north of the Disney kingdom, between Highway 535 and the Florida Turnpike. From bungee jumping and ice skating to dozens of themed restaurants, this stretch of road is *the* tourist strip in Central Florida. I-Drive also offers numerous hotels and shopping areas. It is the home to the Orange County Convention Center and offers easy access to **SeaWorld** and **Universal Studios.** The road runs north-south.

✔ **Downtown Orlando:** Right off I-4 East, Downtown Orlando's headliner is the **Church Street Station** entertainment and shopping complex. There are loads of clubs, shops, and restaurants in the heart of the city. Dozens of antiques shops line **Antique Row** on Orange Avenue near Lake Ivanhoe.

✔ **Winter Park:** Just north of downtown Orlando, Winter Park offers **Park Avenue,** a collection of upscale shops and restaurants, along a cobblestone street. Winter Park has little if any kid-appeal, and it's too far north to use as a home base, if you plan on spending much time at the Disney parks.

Showing Street Smarts: Getting Information on Arrival

After you've landed, one of the best places for up-to-date information is the concierge or the front desk at your hotel (and they're even better if you're staying on a Disney property).

If you're in the International Drive area, stop at the official **Orlando Visitors Center,** 8723 International Drive (four blocks south of Sand Lake Road), for information. Or, give the center a call at ☎ 407-363-5872.Friday's "Calendar" section in the *Orlando Sentinel* also includes a lot of tourist-friendly information on dining and entertainment. See "Fast Facts" at the end of Chapter 20 for additional information sources.

Getting Around Orlando

Tens of millions of people visit Orlando's theme parks yearly, and the city's tourism czars want to make going from Point A to Point B as easy as 1-2-3. The faster you can get around town, the more time you can spend in the parks and attractions (and the more money you spend).

Still, unless you spend your entire vacation inside Walt Disney World or Universal, you're going to have to deal with slow-downs, such as rush hour (weekdays, 7 to 9 a.m. and 4 to 6 p.m.) and peak period crowds (weekends and summers are the worst).

One way you shouldn't travel around Orlando is on foot. This city isn't conducive to strolling. Within the safe confines of the theme parks, you'll have no problems hoofing around (in fact, you're on your feet quite a bit), but walking anywhere outside of the theme parks is a thrills-and-chills experience that most people want to avoid. Wide roads that are designed to move traffic quickly and a shortage of sidewalks, streetlights, and crosswalks are to blame.

Here are some of the more conventional ways of getting around.

Disney transportation system

If you're going to stay at a **Walt Disney World** resort or official hotel (see "Staying the Night in Orlando" later in this chapter) and spend the majority of your time in Disney parks, then you can skip a rental car. There's a free transportation network that runs throughout Disney World. Buses, ferries, water taxis, and monorails operate from 2 hours prior to the Disney parks' opening until two hours after closing. There's also service to various Disney shopping areas, nightclubs, and smaller attractions.

In addition to being free, the system saves you the cost of a rental car, gas, and the $7 parking charge at the attractions. But you're at the mercy of Disney's schedule. Sometimes you have to take a ferry to catch a bus to get on the monorail to reach your hotel. It can take an hour or more to get somewhere that's right across the lagoon from you.

By car

If you're on an extended stay — more than a week — you'll probably want to rent a car for at least a day or two to venture beyond the tourist areas. (Yes, there *is* life beyond the theme parks.) See the "Quick Concierge" at the back of this book for toll-free numbers of various car-rental agencies. Also, you can check out "Orienting Yourself in Orlando" and "Ordering Orlando by neighborhood," earlier in this chapter, for navigational tips.

Orlando Neighborhoods

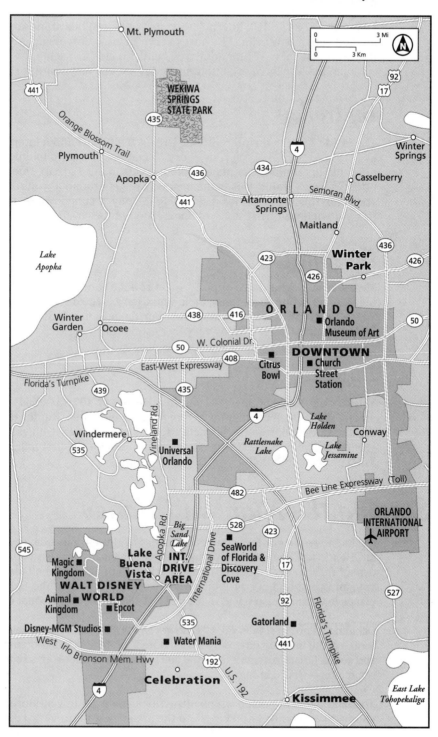

By bus

Lynx (☎ 407-841-8240; Internet: www.golynx.com) bus stops are marked with a paw print. The buses serve **Disney, Universal,** and **International Drive** ($1 for adults, 25 cents for kids and seniors; $10 for an unlimited weekly pass), but their routes are not very visitor-oriented.

By trolley

The **I-Ride Trolley** on International Drive (☎ 407-354-5656; Internet: www.iridetrolley.com) runs every 15 minutes, 7 a.m. to midnight (75 cents for adults, 25 cents for seniors, kids under 12 free). Due to I-Drive's heavy traffic, this is the best way to get around, if you're staying in this area or at least spending the day. It cuts down on the hurry-up-and-wait frustration of bumper-to-bumper traffic.

By shuttle

Mears Transportation Group (☎ 407-423-5566) operates shuttle buses to all major attractions, including **Cypress Gardens, Kennedy Space Center, Universal Studios, SeaWorld,** and **Church Street Station,** among others. Rates vary by destination.

By taxi

Yellow Cab (☎ 407-699-9999) and **Ace Metro** (☎ 407-855-0564) are among the taxicab companies serving the Orlando area. But for day-to-day travel to and from the attractions, cabs are expensive, unless your group has five or more people. Rates cost $2.50, for the first mile, and $1.50 per mile, thereafter.

Staying the Night in Orlando

Unlike the seedier or less competitive areas of Florida, almost every hotel in Orlando has been built or renovated in the past 20 years, so you can expect reasonably modern trimmings. (Hotel appliances won't shock you, and you don't need rabbit ears to see what's on the tube.) Most places in Orlando also try to make kids feel like Mickey's personal guests.

Deciding where to stay in the city, however, isn't all that easy, because rooms come in many different flavors: hotels, motels, bed-and-breakfasts, and so on. Orlando's more than 100,000 rooms make choosing a room seem a bit overwhelming.

The best bet is to decide which attractions you want to visit during your stay and book a hotel close to the area you want to visit. For example, if you're visiting **Walt Disney World,** stay in a Disney resort, if you don't mind paying a little extra; on Hwy. 535/Apopka-Vineland Road, if you want to save a few bucks; or the Kissimmee end of U.S. 192, if you want to save even more. Although not Disney-owned, "official" Disney hotels in Lake Buena Vista offer many of the privileges Disney resort guests enjoy, often for less money than the better Disney resorts. If you're planning your trip around **Universal** Orlando, consider one of its hotels or, as is the case with SeaWorld fans, one of those along International Drive.

 Many accommodations let kids under 12 (and in some cases under 18) stay free, as long as you don't exceed the maximum occupancy of the room. But to be safe, ask when booking your room.

 Don't forget to allow for taxes. The combined sales taxes, local-option taxes, and hotel add-ons increase your bill by 11 to 12 percent, depending on where you choose to stay.

If you're considering booking a room at a Disney resort, be sure to ask, when calling **Central Reservations** (☎ 407-934-7639) or the **Walt Disney World Travel Company** (☎ 800-327-2996), about any discounts available to members of AAA or other auto clubs, AARP, frequent-flyer programs, or other groups. Also, ask about meal plans that could save you money or packages that include your room, tickets, and airfare.

If you don't like dealing with hotels or haggling over rates, there are several reservations services in the area. These include **Central Reservation Service** (☎ 800-555-7555; Internet: www.reservation-service.com) and **Florida Hotel Network** (☎ 800-538-3616; Internet: www.floridahotels.com).

All listings in this chapter have one of the Florida *musts* — air-conditioning. We only tell you if one doesn't have the other — a swimming pool. Ditto for television and telephones.

Accommodations in Orlando and Walt Disney World

The area's best hotels

 ### Best Western Lake Buena Vista

$$ Lake Buena Vista/Official WDW Hotel

This 18-story high-rise is a great place to view the Disney fireworks without braving the crowds in the parks. The 325-unit lakefront hotel is located on prime property along Hotel Plaza Boulevard and is within walking distance of **Downtown Disney Marketplace.** The rooms are large, and some come with balconies and views of the lake. Amenities include Nintendo, coffee makers, free local calls, an onsite restaurant, several pools, a playground, baby-sitting service, and free shuttles to Disney parks. (See the "Accommodations & Dining in Walt Disney World & Lake Buena Vista" map, later in this chapter.)

2000 Hotel Plaza Blvd. ☎ *800-348-3765 or 407-828-2424. Fax: 407-828-8933. Internet:* www.orlandolodging.com. *To get there: Located between Buena Vista Dr. and Apopka-Vineland Rd./Fla. 535, across from the Doubletree Hotel. Parking: Free. Rack rates: $109–$199. Ask about AAA discounts and packages. AE, CB, DC, DISC, JCB, MC.*

Celebration Hotel

$$$ Kissimmee

Located in the Disney-run town of Celebration, this hotel has a three-story, wood-frame design straight out of 1920s Florida. All rooms have TVs with Nintendo, speaker phones with voice mail and data ports, high-speed Internet access, ceiling fans, safes, hair dryers, and makeup mirrors. Suites and studios have refrigerators and wet bars. Other amenities include a pool, Jacuzzi, and fitness center. You can walk to shops and restaurants. An 18-hole golf course is nearby. (See the map for "Other Orlando Area Accommodations & Dining," later in this chapter.)

700 Bloom St. ☎ *888-499-3800 or 407-566-6000. Fax: 407-566-1844. Internet:* www.celebrationhotel.com. *To get there: Take I-4 to Exit 25A/U.S. 192, go east to second light, then right on Celebration Ave. Parking: Free. Rack rates: $165–$255, $205–$470 for studios and suites. 115 units. AE, DC, DISC, MC, V.*

Courtyard by Marriott

$$ Lake Buena Vista/Official WDW Hotel

The Courtyard is a moderately priced hotel located close to **Downtown Disney Marketplace's** shops and restaurants. The Marriott chain has broken the mold with the Courtyard, which attracts more families than business travelers. Rooms are standard size (not microscopic, but you won't forget you're in a hotel), and most come with balconies. There's a small reception area located in a 14-story atrium, a full-service restaurant, a cocktail lounge, and a deli that specializes in pizza. Ask about a schedule for the hotel's free transportation to the Walt Disney World parks at the guest services desk.

1805 Hotel Plaza Blvd. ☎ *800-223-9930 or 407-828-8888. Fax: 407-827-4623. Internet:* http://courtyard.com/MCOLB/. *To get there: Located between Lake Buena Vista Dr. and Apopka-Vineland Rd./Fla. 535, close to the Hilton Royal Plaza Hotel. Parking: Free. Rack rates: $99–$169. Discounts for AAA members, check for package rates. 323 units. AE, CB, DC, DISC, JCB, MC, V.*

Disney All-Star Movie Resort

$ **Walt Disney World**

Kids aren't the only ones amazed by the, uh, aesthetics of this resort. When did you last see architecture as inspiring as Goliath-size Dalmatians leaping from balconies? And the low (by Mickey standards) rates will thrill some parents. The All-Star resort in the "Runner-up accommodations" listings, later in this chapter, is pretty much the same — expect small rooms and postage-stamp bathrooms. But you're still "on property," and you're enjoying the lowest prices your Mouse bucks can buy. There's a full-size pool with a *Fantasia* theme and a food court that serves pizza, pasta, sandwiches, and family-dinner platters.

1991 W. Buena Vista Dr. ☎ *407-934-7639 or 407-939-7000. Fax: 407-939-7111. Internet:* http://asp.disney.go.com/disneyworld/db/seetheworld/ resorts/facilities/index.asp?id=813. *To get there: Disney All-Star Resorts are located close to Animal Kingdom, Blizzard Beach, and Winter Summerland. Parking: Free. Rack rates: $74–$104. 1,900 units. AE, MC, V.*

Disney's Beach Club Resort

$$$$ **Walt Disney World**

The Beach Club is within walking distance of **Epcot,** a plus for those who want to spend more than a day at that park. The resort has a Cape Cod theme and a posh atmosphere. Kids and adults love the resort's three-acre, free-form swimming pool, Stormalong Bay. Guest rooms are about 400 square feet and come with one king-size or two queen-size beds. All units come with double vanities, a tub/shower combination, ceiling fans, and balconies. It's a nice upscale resort destination, especially if you want to stay only a short distance from the Disney parks.

1800 Epcot Resorts Blvd. ☎ *407-934-7639 or 407-934-8000. Fax: 407-934-3850. Internet:* http://asp.disney.go.com/disneyworld/db/seetheworld/ resorts/facilities/resorts.asp?id=280. *To get there: Take Buena Vista Dr. and turn west on Epcot Resorts Blvd. Parking: Free self and valet. Rack rates: $269–$545. 597 units. AE, MC, V.*

Disney's BoardWalk

$$$$ **Walt Disney World**

More than any other Disney property, the BoardWalk appeals to couples and singles looking for a sliver of yesterday. The 1920s-era "seaside" resort overlooks a village green and lake. The bed-and-breakfast-style accommodations are larger than those in the moderate Disney resorts, with rich cherry-wood furnishings, two queen beds, a child-size daybed, a midsize bathroom, balconies, and ceiling fans. The atmosphere is

Accommodations & Dining in Walt Disney World & Lake Buena Vista

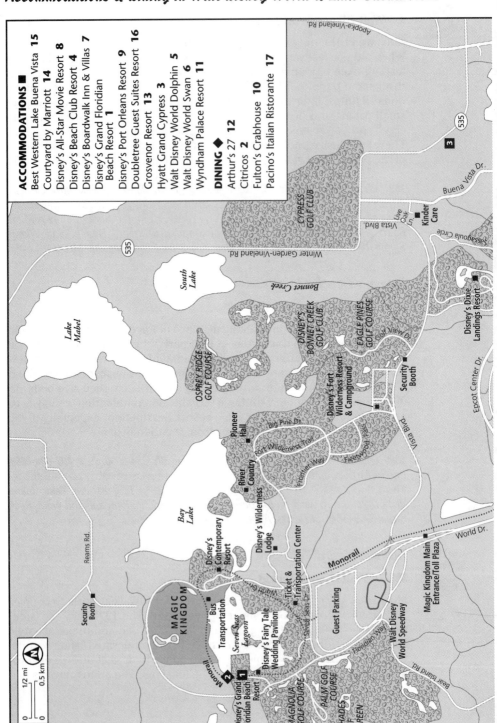

ACCOMMODATIONS ■
Best Western Lake Buena Vista **15**
Courtyard by Marriott **14**
Disney's All-Star Movie Resort **8**
Disney's Beach Club Resort **4**
Disney's Boardwalk Inn & Villas **7**
Disney's Grand Floridian
   Beach Resort **1**
Disney's Port Orleans Resort **9**
Doubletree Guest Suites Resort **16**
Grosvenor Resort **13**
Hyatt Grand Cypress **3**
Walt Disney World Dolphin **5**
Walt Disney World Swan **6**
Wyndham Palace Resort **11**

DINING ◆
Arthur's 27 **12**
Citricos **2**
Fulton's Crabhouse **10**
Pacino's Italian Ristorante **17**

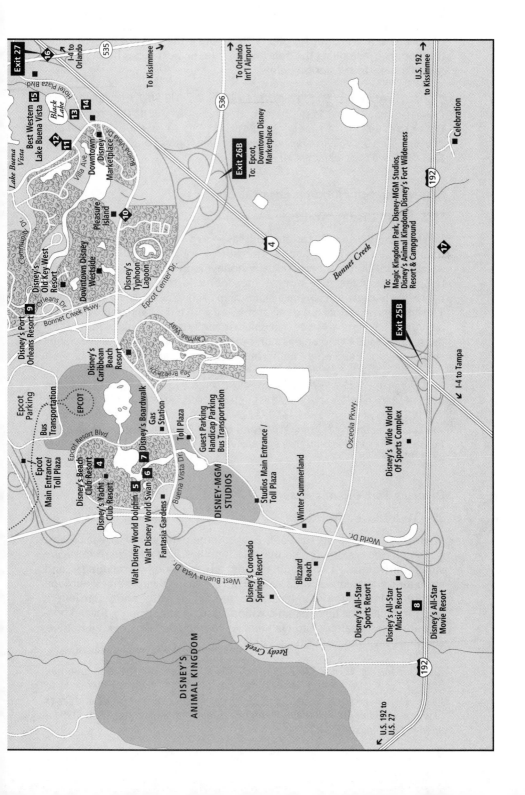

homey, but the creature comforts are first class. The property connects to a quarter-mile boardwalk, lined with shops, restaurants, and street performers, leaving guests plenty to do once the sun goes down. Note that rooms overlooking the boardwalk have the best views but tend to be noisy, thanks to the action below.

2101 N. Epcot Resorts Blvd. ☎ *407-934-7639 or 407-939-5100. Fax: 407-934-5150. Internet:* http://asp.disney.go.com/disneyworld/db/seetheworld/ resorts/facilities/resorts.asp?id=281. *To get there: Located north of Buena Vista Dr., on Epcot Resorts Blvd. Parking: Free self and valet. Rack rates: $269–$730. 378 units, 532 villas. AE, MC, V.*

Disney's Grand Floridian Resort & Spa

$$$$ Walt Disney World

You won't find a more luxurious address — in a Victorian sense anyway — than this 40-acre Great Gatsby-era resort. It's a great choice for couples seeking a bit of romance, especially honeymooners who aren't on a tight budget. The opulent, five-story, domed lobby hosts afternoon teas accompanied by piano music. In the evenings, an orchestra plays big-band tunes. The large guest rooms are richly furnished with chintz and mahogany and include either sunny private balconies or verandas overlooking formal gardens. The Grand Floridian has a first-rate health club and spa, a marvelous swimming pool, and offers numerous recreational activities.

4401 Floridian Way ☎ *407-934-7639 or 407-824-3000. Fax: 407-824-3186. Internet:* http://asp.disney.go.com/disneyworld/db/seetheworld/resorts/ facilities/resorts.asp?id=282. *To get there: Located in the far northwest corner of the Walt Disney World property, on Floridian Way, just north of the Polynesian Resort. Parking: Free self and valet. Rack rates: $304–$480. 933 units. AE, MC, V.*

Disney's Port Orleans Resort

$$ Walt Disney World

This resort, resembling turn-of-the-twentieth-century New Orleans (okay, a cleaned-up version), is a good bet for families. The midsize rooms have small bathrooms, two double beds, cherry-wood furnishings, and wrought-iron balconies. Kids love the larger-than-Olympic-size Doubloon Lagoon swimming pool and its serpent-shaped water slide. Gardeners will appreciate the landscaping, which features stately oaks, formal boxwood hedges, azaleas, and jasmine. A food court, cafe, cocktail lounge, and pool bar round out the facilities.

2201 Orleans Dr. ☎ *407-934-7639 or 407-934-5000. Fax: 407-934-5353. Internet:* http://asp.disney.go.com/disneyworld/db/seetheworld/resorts/ facilities/resorts.asp?id=279. *To get there: Located off of Bonnet Creek Pkwy., next to the Dixie Landings Resort. Parking: Free. Rack rates: $124–$189 for up to 4. 1,008 units. AE, MC, V.*

Doubletree Guest Suites

$$$ Lake Buena Vista/WDW Official Hotel

This seven-story, all-suite hotel is a good choice for large families. Young patrons get their own check-in desk, where they receive a chocolate-chip cookie. There's also a children's theater, game room, and video arcade. The one-bedroom suites can sleep up to six and are delightfully decorated. You'll also find a TV in the bathroom, a wet bar, refrigerator, microwave oven, and full living rooms and dining areas. Guests have access to several recreational facilities, including two pools, a whirlpool, a fitness room, and tennis courts. It's within walking distance of Downtown Disney Marketplace and has free transportation to all of the parks.

2305 Hotel Plaza Blvd. ☎ *800-222-8733 or 407-934-1000. Fax: 407-934-1011. Internet:* www.doubletreeguestsuites.com. *To get there: Just west of Apopka-Vineland Rd./Fla. 535, turn into the entrance to Downtown Disney Marketplace. Parking: Free self and valet. Rack rates: $169–$399. 229 units. AE, CB, DC, DISC, JCB, MC, V.*

Grosvenor Resort

$$ Lake Buena Vista/Official WDW Hotel

For traditional styling, plenty of stay-at-home entertainment, and a moderate price tag for a central location, head for the Grosvenor. This moderately priced resort has a 19-story epicenter that features inviting rooms decorated in shades of mauve and green. There are also five-story wings with tower and garden rooms that are larger and provide better views. The Grosvenor also hosts a Saturday-night mystery dinner theater and Disney character breakfasts. Other amenities include a 24-hour food court, a pool bar, and a lounge where sporting events are aired on a large-screen TV.

1850 Hotel Plaza Blvd. ☎ *800-624-4109 or 407-828-4444. Fax: 407-828-8192. Internet:* www.grosvenorresort.com. *To get there: Turn west off Fla. 535 onto Hotel Plaza Blvd., close to Downtown Disney Marketplace. Parking: Free self and valet. Rack rates: $145–$175. 626 units. AE, CB, DC, DISC, JCB, MC, V.*

Hyatt Regency Grand Cypress

$$$$ Lake Buena Vista

Here's a palatial resort that makes you wonder if you've fallen asleep and awakened in Bangkok. The opulent public areas are decorated with gold-tinted dragon gods and huge model junks made of jade. The main lobby has palms and parrots, such as LuLu, who waves to passersby. The atrium is 18-stories high and has inner and outer elevators. (Ride the outer ones for a real adrenaline rush.) Spacious rooms are a welcome respite from the crowded parks. You can get lost in the half-acre swimming pool, which flows through rock grottoes. The pool is spanned by a rope bridge and contains 12 waterfalls and two steep water slides. Relax on a sand beach, play tennis on 12 courts, or try your luck on the Jack Nicklaus–designed golf course.

One Grand Cypress Blvd. ☎ ***800-233-1234*** *or 407-239-1234. Fax: 407-239-3800. Internet:* www.grandcypress.com. *To get there: From I-4, take exit 27/Fla. 535 North to the second light. Parking: Free self, $8 valet. Rack rates: $335–$465. 750 units. AE, CB, DC, DISC, JCB, MC, V.*

The Peabody Orlando

$$$$ International Drive

Welcome to the home of the famous Marching Mallards, five ducks that waddle into the lobby fountain at 11 a.m. and then exit to a posh rooftop pool at 5 p.m. Their home is in the thick of all the action I-Drive has to offer, including attractions, restaurants, and shopping. Guest rooms, even the standard ones, are lavishly furnished and decorated. The suites are fabulous and five times larger than the oversize standard rooms. The hotel's ambiance, which extends to its top-rated restaurants, isn't duplicated anywhere in Orlando. (See the map for " Accommodations & Dining on International Drive" later in this chapter.)

Seniors thinking about staying here should take advantage of the hotel's over-50 price perks.

9801 International Dr. ☎ ***800-732-3639*** *or 407-352-4000. Fax: 407-351-0073. Internet:* www.peabody-orlando.com. *To get there: Located between the BeeLine Expwy. and Sand Lake Rd., across the street from the Orange County Convention Center. Parking: Free self and valet. Rack rates: $330–$1,000 and up. Ask about packages, holiday/summer discounts, and senior rates for those over 50. 891 units. AE, CB, DC, DISC, JCB, MC, V.*

Portofino Bay Resort

$$$$ International Drive/Universal Orlando

If you're spending the bulk of your time at Universal and have deep pockets, this is a great choice. The hotel is designed to look like the Mediterranean seaside village of Portofino, Italy. Furnishings are top notch. All rooms have fluffy king-size beds and cloud-soft pillows that will have you begging to know where to buy them (alas, it's Italy). The bathrooms have marble tubs. The rooms are state-of-the-art "smart rooms" that provide security and adjust room temperature. Family suites have kid-theme rooms, and butlers are available in 26 of the villas. The Portofino has eight restaurants, a spa and fitness center, playground, and two bocci courts.

5601 Universal Blvd. ☎ ***888-322-5541*** *or 407-503-1000. Fax: 407-224-7118. Internet:* www.uescape.com/resorts/. *To get there: Located off I-4, take exit 30/ Kirkman Rd./Hwy. 435 and follow the signs to Universal Orlando, where the resort is located). Parking: $10 per day. Rack rates: $235–$770 and up. 750 rooms. AE, CB, DC, MC, V.*

Other Orlando Area Accommodations & Dining

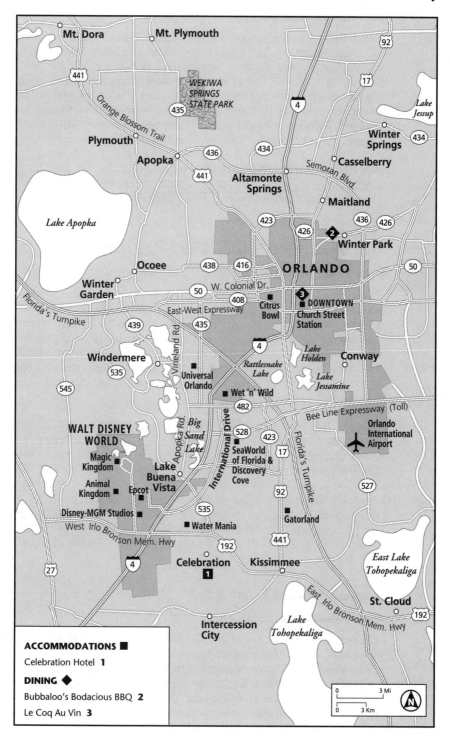

Mt. Dora
Mt. Plymouth
92
441
17
WEKIWA SPRINGS STATE PARK
435
4
Orange Blossom Trail
Lake Jessup
Plymouth
Winter Springs
434
Apopka
436
434
Casselberry
441
Semoran Blvd
Altamonte Springs
Maitland
Lake Apopka
423
436
426
426
2
Winter Park
Ocoee
438
416
ORLANDO
50
Winter Garden
50
W. Colonial Dr.
3
Florida's Turnpike
408
DOWNTOWN
East-West Expressway
435
Citrus Bowl
Church Street Station
439
4
Lake Holden
Conway
Windermere
Rattlesnake Lake
Lake Jessamine
535
Universal Orlando
545
Wet 'n' Wild
Bee Line Expressway (Toll)
482
Orlando International Airport
WALT DISNEY WORLD
Big Sand Lake
528
423
Apopka Rd.
International Drive
SeaWorld of Florida & Discovery Cove
17
Florida's Turnpike
Magic Kingdom
Lake Buena Vista
Animal Kingdom
Epcot
92
527
Disney-MGM Studios
535
West Irlo Bronson Mem. Hwy
Water Mania
Gatorland
441
192
East Lake Tohopekaliga
27
4
Celebration
Kissimmee
1
St. Cloud
East Irlo Bronson Mem. Hwy
192
Intercession City
Lake Tohopekaliga

ACCOMMODATIONS ■
Celebration Hotel **1**
DINING ◆
Bubbaloo's Bodacious BBQ **2**
Le Coq Au Vin **3**

0   3 Mi
0   3 Km

Summerfield Suites

$$$ International Drive

These two-bedroom suites can sleep up to eight people (if you're really into togetherness). Balconies overlook a courtyard filled with rustling palms. Sun-seekers will feel immediately at home in a suite that's more than just a bedroom. Units have homey features, such as an iron and ironing board, full kitchen, TV in the living room and bedrooms, and multiple telephones. A daily continental breakfast is free; you can purchase extra courses. The hotel has a pool, kiddie pool, fitness center, and video arcade. A shuttle to Walt Disney World costs $7 per person.

8480 International Dr. ☎ *800-830-4964 or 407-352-2400. Fax: 407-238-0778. Internet:* www.summerfieldsuites.com. *To get there: Located between the Bee Line Expwy. and Sand Lake Rd. Parking: Free. Rack rates: $209–$319. AE, CB, DC, DISC, MC, V.*

Walt Disney World Dolphin/Walt Disney World Swan

$$$$ Walt Disney World

These two resorts, located on a single property and connected by a walkway, are close to Downtown Disney. They offer a chance to stay on Magic Mickey's property without being bombarded by rodent decor. Both Westin-owned hotels have larger-than-life statues (you can't miss them) of swans and dolphins on the roofs. The luxurious rooms are fairly large, with two queen-size beds and first-class amenities; some of the units come with balconies. (The Swan's rooms are a bit smaller.) Guests are encouraged to dine at both resorts.

Dolphin: 1500 Epcot Resorts Blvd. ☎ *800-227-1500 or 407-934-4000. Fax: 407-934-4884. Internet:* www.swandolphin.com. *To get there: Located off Buena Vista Dr., next to Walt Disney World Swan. Parking: Free self and valet. Rack rates: $295–$465 and up. Inquire about packages. 1,509 units. AE, CB, DC, DISC, JCB, MC, V.*

Swan: 1200 Epcot Resorts Blvd. ☎ *800-248-7926, 800-228-3000, or 407-934-3000. Fax 407-934-4499. Internet:* www.swandolphin.com. *To get there: Located off Buena Vista Dr., next door to the Walt Disney World Dolphin. Parking: Free self and valet. Rack rates: $295–$465 and up. Inquire about packages. 758 units. AE, CB, DC, DISC, JCB, MC, V.*

Wyndham Palace Resort & Spa

$$$ Lake Buena Vista/Official WDW Hotel

The hotel's spacious accommodations — most with lake-view balconies or patios — are within walking distance of Downtown Disney Marketplace. It's an ideal spot for honeymooners or those looking for a romantic weekend getaway. The appealing rooms are equipped with bedroom and bathroom phones, safes, and ceiling fans. There also are one- and two-bedroom suites that have living and dining rooms, 65 hypoallergenic rooms, and 20 rooms equipped for travelers with limited mobility.

1900 Buena Vista Dr. ☎ *800-327-2990 or 407-827-2727. Fax: 407-827-6034. Internet:* www.bvp-resort.com. *To get there: Off Fla. 535, turn in the entrance to Downtown Disney Marketplace; the hotel is on Hotel Plaza Blvd.) Parking: Free self and valet. Rack rates: $209–$500 and up. 1,014 units. AE, CB, DC, DISC, MC, V.*

Runner-up accommodations

Something in the preceding list of accommodations didn't catchy your fancy or finances? No problem. Here are some others that might.

Cypress Glen at Lake Buena Vista

$$$$ **Lake Buena Vista** This art-deco bed-and-breakfast — just a 15-minute drive from the Disney parks — has arguably the best suite in all of Orlando, and the service is first-rate. *10336 Centurion Ct., off Fla. 535.* ☎ *407-909-0338. Fax: 407-909-0345. Internet:* www.cypressglen.com.

Disney's All-Star Music Resort

$ **Walt Disney World** Like its sister, the All-Star Movie Resort (see the listing under "The area's best hotels," preceding this section), this location repeats the bare-bones room theme, with mutant-size drums and other instruments adorning the exterior. *1801 W. Buena Vista Dr.* ☎ *407-934-7639 or 407-939-6000. Fax: 407-939-7222. Internet:* http://disney.go.com/disneyworld/index2.html.

Disney's Coronado Springs Resort

$$ **Walt Disney World** Sporting a Southwest theme, this Disney option features a Mayan temple-inspired swimming pool and an excellent food court. *1000 Buena Vista Dr.* ☎ *407-934-7639 or 407-934-6632. Fax: 407-939-1001. Internet:* http://disney.go.com/disneyworld/index2.html.

Disney's Wilderness Lodge

$$$$ **Walt Disney World** Patterned on a national park lodge, this Disney hotel offers modest-sized rooms, a sand beach, and an immense serpentine swimming pool. *901 W. Timberline Dr.* ☎ *407-934-7639 or 407-824-3200. Fax: 407-824-3232. Internet:* http://asp.disney.go.com/disneyworld/db/seetheworld/resorts/facilities/resorts.asp?id=284).

Hampton Inn at Universal Studios

$ **International Drive** It isn't fancy, but it's close (3 blocks) to Universal Orlando, 1 mile from the heat of International Drive's tourist traps, and 4 miles from SeaWorld. *5621 Windhover Dr.* ☎ *800-231-8395 or 407-351-6716. Fax: 407-363-1711. Internet:* www.go2orlando.com/sponsor/hamptoninn.

Accommodations & Dining on International Drive

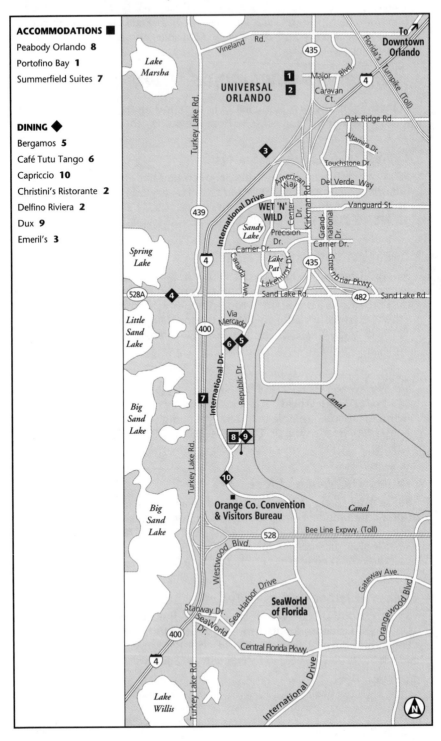

ACCOMMODATIONS ■
Peabody Orlando **8**
Portofino Bay **1**
Summerfield Suites **7**

DINING ◆
Bergamos **5**
Café Tutu Tango **6**
Capriccio **10**
Christini's Ristorante **2**
Delfino Riviera **2**
Dux **9**
Emeril's **3**

Holiday Inn Nikki Bird Resort

$$ **Kissimmee** Just minutes from Downtown Disney, this family favorite lets children eat free in the hotel's restaurant. *7300 Irlo Bronson Memorial Hwy./U.S. 192.* ☎ *800-206-2747 or 407-396-7300. Fax: 407-396-7555. Internet:* www.basshotels.com/holiday-inn.

Holiday Inn Sunspree Resort Lake Buena Vista

$$ **Lake Buena Vista** Kids get the royal treatment at this family-oriented resort, which offers a wide array of activities for children. *13351 Lake Buena Vista, off Fla. 535 near the Crossroads Shopping Center.* ☎ *800-366-6299 or 407-239-4500. Fax: 407-239-7713. Internet:* www.kidsuites.com.

Homewood Suites Maingate

$$ **Lake Buena Vista** This moderately-priced resort, only 2 miles from Walt Disney World, offers well-equipped suites and accepts pets. *8200 Palm Pkwy.* ☎ *800-225-5466 or 407-465-8200. Fax: 407-465-0200. Internet:* www.homewood-suites.com.

Dining Out in Orlando

Hungry yet? You can pick and choose from almost 4,000 restaurants in Orlando. We've gone through the contenders, picked those that are worth considering, and listed them as follows for you to review in alphabetical order. Because many of you will spend a lot of time in the Walt Disney World area, we give special attention to dining choices there. All the restaurants that we list have kids' menus, with entrees usually costing $5 and under.

All sit-down restaurants inside the Disney parks require park admission, with one exception: the Rainforest Café at Animal Kingdom. If you spend all day in the parks, you may find it more convenient to eat inside at one of their restaurants, but you'll probably pay an average of 25 percent more than you would in the outside world. Also, keep in mind that alcohol isn't served in the Magic Kingdom and that all Walt Disney World restaurants are *smoke-free*.

Don't forget to allow for the 7 percent sales tax when estimating your dining budget.

Orlando's Best Restaurants

Arthur's 27

$$$ **Lake Buena Vista** **INTERNATIONAL**

Come, first, for the 27th-floor sunsets and a spectacular view of the Wizard of Disney's fireworks. Romantic and mellow, this place has the feel of a 1930s supper club, minus the billowing clouds of cigarette smoke. You can choose from selections such as pan-seared breast of squab with chestnut risotto or steamed scallops and poached oysters with black capellini pasta. There's also an impressive wine list.

1900 Lake Buena Vista Dr., ☎ *407-827-2727. Internet:* `http://orlando.diningguide.net/data/d101542.htm.` *To get there: Just north of Hotel Plaza Blvd., in the Wyndham Palace Resort & Spa. Parking: Free self and validated valet. Reservations required. Main courses: $20–$30, fixed-price menu $49–$60. AE, DC, DISC, MC, V. Open: 6:30–10:30 p.m. daily.*

Bergamo's

$$ International Drive Area   NORTHERN ITALIAN

Bergamo's is almost always packed, and the singing waiters here are nearly as much fun as the food. For example, you may find Broadway show tunes and opera mixed with roasted veal and steamed mussels, among other treats. Even if you don't eat, this is a good spot to park your keister and enjoy the show over cocktails.

8445 International Dr. ☎ *407-352-3805. To get there: Take I-4 Exit 39/ Sand Lake Rd. east to International Dr. and head south; it's in the Mercado shopping center off Universal Blvd. Parking: Free. Reservations recommended. Main courses: $12–$37. AE, DC, MC, V. Open: 5–10 p.m. Sun–Thurs, 5–11 p.m. Fri–Sat.*

Bubbaloo's Bodacious BBQ

$ Near North   BARBECUE

Smoke billows from the chimney of this real-pit barbecue joint. The atmosphere is informal, but watch the sauces. Even the mild may be too hot for tender palates; the killer sauce comes with a three-alarm warning — it's meant only for those with asbestos taste buds and a ceramic-lined tummy. The pork platter with fixins is a deal and a half. It comes with beans and slaw. Monday through Friday you'll find daily specials that include chicken, meat loaf, turkey, and open-face roast-beef sandwiches with gravy and vegetables. And, it wouldn't be a barbecue without plenty of brew on hand.

1471 Lee Rd. ☎ *407-295-1212. To get there: From I-4, take Lee Rd. exit, the restaurant is on left, next to a dry cleaner. Parking: Free. Reservations not accepted. Main courses: $5–$8. AE, MC, V. Open: 10 a.m.–9:30 p.m. Sun–Thurs, 10 a.m.–10:30 p.m. Fri–Sat.*

Cafe Tu Tu Tango

$ International Drive   TAPAS

Located in the Doubletree Castle Hotel, this colorful eatery reminds many of a loft in Barcelona. The all-appetizer menu features treats from Latin

America, Asia, the Caribbean, the Middle East, and the United States. This is an ideal spot for sampling different types of cuisine. This tapas bar, where every order comes in a miniature size, is a great spot for grazing. Try the Cajun-style egg rolls, tuna sashimi with noodles and spinach in soy vinaigrette, and dozens of other chi-chi appetizers. For dessert, have guava cheesecake with strawberry sauce. **Note:** Ordering several tapas and drinks can turn this into a $$$ restaurant.

8625 International Dr. ☎ 407-248-2222. To get there: Located just west of the Mercado Shopping Center. Parking: Free. Reservations recommended. Tapas $3.75–$8.55 (even those with small appetites will want two or three). AE, DISC, MC, V. Open: 11:30 a.m.–11 p.m. Sun–Thurs, 11:30 a.m.–midnight Fri–Sat.

Capriccio

$$ International Drive TUSCAN/NORTHERN ITALIAN

The decor is chic and elegant, with a black-and-white tile floor, but the showcase is a kitchen with wood-fired pizza ovens. The pizzas and pastas are heavenly, and the pan-seared tuna is a nice off-speed pitch. When the crusty bread lands, dip it into a puddle of extra-virgin olive oil. (Ask for a dribble of Parmesan in the bottom.) The wine list is extensive.

9801 International Dr. ☎ 407-352-4000. Internet: www.peabodyorlando.com. To get there: Take I-4 to Exit 29/Sand Lake Rd., then head east to International Dr. Go South to Peabody Orlando hotel. Parking: Free self and validated valet. Reservations recommended. Main courses: $12–$22, Sunday buffet; $29 adults, $13 kids 5–12. AE, CB, DC, DISC, JCB, MC, V. Open: 6–11 p.m. Tues–Sun.

Christini's Ristorante

$$$ International Drive ITALIAN

Numerous awards and trophies, attesting to the high standard of service offered by restaurateur Chris Christini, line the walls of this restaurant. It can be hard to decide on a main course, but one of the house specialties is a veal chop, broiled and seasoned with fresh sage and served with applesauce. If you're in the mood for pasta, try the rigatoni served in a Parmesan fennel cream sauce with shredded sweet Italian sausages.

7600 Dr. Phillips Blvd. ☎ 407-345-8770. Internet: www.christinis.com. To get there: Take I-4 Exit 29/Sand Lake Rd. West to the Marketplace shopping plaza (on right). Parking: Free. Reservations recommended. Main courses: $20–$40. AE, CB, DC, MC, V. Open: 6 p.m.–midnight daily.

Citricos

$$$ Walt Disney World AMERICAN

The chef of this bright and airy restaurant makes a statement with citrus- and Mediterranean-infused flavors that also feature a Florida link. Crab and lobster in Parmesan are among the starters. Main courses include red-snapper carpaccio with bell pepper and melon salsa and Florida oyster and bay scallop risotto. For dessert, the citrus soufflé or the chocolate ravioli with licorice ice cream are hard to resist. Citricos has a well-stocked wine cellar; one of the best in the world.

4401 Floridian Way. ☎ *407-824-3000. Internet:* http://asp.disney.go.com. *To get there: Located in Disney's Grand Floridian Resort and Spa. Parking: Free. Reservations recommended. Main courses: $19–$36. AE, MC, V. Open: 5:30 p.m.– 10 p.m. daily.*

Delfino Riviera

$$$ **Universal Orlando**   **MEDITERRANEAN**

Located above a piazza overlooking the other Portofino Bay (not the one in Italy, alas), this restaurant's atmosphere is pretty romantic. This is the hotel's signature ristorante, complete with strolling musicians and crooners. The chef's table has six seats, and 20 more can dine on a balcony that offers a view of the commoners sitting below. There's also a terrace for outdoor dining. First-course options include champagne-baked oysters and citrus-cured sturgeon in grapefruit vinaigrette. Try the pasta treats, such as lobster and champagne risotto. For the main course, the chef works magic on sea bass roasted with mushrooms and potatoes in Chianti sauce.

1000 Universal Studios Blvd. ☎ *407-503-1415. Internet:* www.uescape.com. *To get there: Located in the Portofino Bay Hotel. Parking: $6. Reservations recommended. Main courses: $20–$32. AE, MC, V. Open: 6–10 p.m. Mon–Sat.*

Dux

$$$ **International Drive**   **HAUTE CUISINE**

Think posh with a capital P — that's what comes to mind when you slip inside these walls. The restaurant's name honors a family of ducks that splash all day in the marble fountains in the Peabody's grandly formal lobby. This location is a favorite of celebrities, who dine here after shooting (movies, not tourists, of course) at Universal Studios and Disney-MGM. The menu changes with the seasons. Possibilities include lamb chops basted with Hunan barbecue sauce and grouper grilled in Cajun spices. Choose a wine from its long, inspired list.

9801 International Dr. ☎ *407-345-4550. Internet:* http://www.peabodyorlando. com/. *To get there: Located in the Peabody Orlando. Parking: Free self and validated valet. Reservations recommended. Main courses: $19–$45. AE, CB, DC, DISC, JCB, MC, V. Open: 6–10:30 p.m. daily.*

Emeril's

$$$ Universal Orlando   NEW ORLEANS

Get a mouthful and eyeful in this ultra-modern showplace, the Florida home of culinary genius Emeril Lagasse, star of *Emeril Live* on cable TV's Food Network. Large abstract paintings cover the walls of a two-story restaurant that looks like an old warehouse. The second floor has a 12,000-bottle wine gallery and a cigar room. If you want a show, we highly recommend trying to get one of the eight counter seats where you can watch the chefs working their Creole magic, but to get one you'll need to make reservations excruciatingly (at least a month) early. The lunch menu features many dinner delights, including entrees such as pecan-crusted redfish. (It's easier to get a reservation for lunch.) You can also expect New Orleans barbecue shrimp and smoked chicken, and andouille sausage gumbo. Jackets are recommended for gents, even though that goes against the grain after a long day in the parks.

1000 Universal Studios Blvd. ☎ *407-224-2424. Internet:* www.uescape.com/citywalk/. *To get there: Located in CityWalk. Parking: $6. Reservations required, as far in advance as possible. Main courses: $17–$25 lunch, $18–$35 dinner. AE, DISC, MC, V. Open: 11:30 a.m.–2:30 p.m., 5:30–10 p.m. daily, until 11 p.m. Fri–Sat.*

Fulton's Crab House

$$$ Downtown Disney/Pleasure Island   SEAFOOD

Lose yourself in a world of brass, shining mahogany, and river charts, while you dine inside a Mississippi Delta-style paddle-wheeler. The catch of the day can be presented charcoal-grilled, broiled, fried with a dusting of cornmeal, blackened, or steamed. The cioppino is a feast of lobster, clams, mussels, red potatoes, and corn. Or, have the filet mignon with whipped potatoes. The wine list is comprehensive, and there's a full bar. For dessert, don't miss the milk-chocolate crème brûlée.

Aboard the riverboat at Pleasure Island ☎ *407-939-3463. Internet:* www.fultonscrabhouse.com. *To get there: Located in Pleasure Island, next to the Lego store. Parking: Free self, $5 valet. Reservations not accepted. Main courses: $16–$44. AE, MC, V. Open: 4 p.m.–midnight daily.*

Le Coq Au Vin

$$ South Orlando   FRENCH

Affordability and good food make this a solid choice, if you're on a budget. Owner-Chef Louis Perrotte loves country cooking and changes his menu seasonally, presenting such dishes as a grouper fillet encrusted with toasted pecans or a center-cut Black-Angus steak served with a dollop of peppercorn sauce. You might run into rack of lamb, braised rabbit, or grilled salmon, depending on when you touch down. (If you want to eliminate the mystery, call first.) This restaurant has a bistro atmosphere and regulars who attest to its staying power. Some insist this is Florida's best French restaurant, especially if you're after a bargain. Perrotte serves beer and wine.

4800 S. Orange Ave. ☎ 407-851-6980. Internet: www.orlandoweekly.com/dining/results.asp. *To get there: From I-4, take the Colonial Dr./ Hwy. 50 exit east to Orange Ave and head south. Parking: Free. Reservations required. Main courses: $12–$25. AE, DC, MC, V. Open: 11:30 a.m.–2 p.m. and 5:30–10 p.m. Mon–Fri, 5:30–10 p.m. Sat, 5:30–9 p.m. Sun.*

Pacino's Italian Ristorante

$$ Kissimmee   ITALIAN/MEDITERRANEAN

The hand-painted ceiling of this restaurant contains fiber optics that create an aura of dining under the stars, but there's also a patio if you want the real thing. Some servers can be a little aloof, making it really feel like Italy, but the food's price and taste make up for the service. House specialties include twin veal chops, ziti with sweet Italian sausage, a challenging 32-ounce porterhouse steak, *fruitti di mare* (a plate literally bursting with clams, calamari, shrimp, and scallops sautéed with white wine and herbs), and Australian lobster tail. The pizza is good, too.

5795 W. Hwy. 192/Irlo Bronson Memorial Pkwy. ☎ 407-396-8022. Internet: www.pacinos.com. *To get there: Located 2 miles east of I-4. Parking: Free. Reservations accepted. Main courses: $10–$27 (most are under $20). AE, MC, V. Open: 4–11 p.m. daily.*

Runner-up restaurants

The following Disney restaurants don't take typical reservations, but all Walt Disney World eateries have *priority seating,* which means that you get the next available table once you arrive. To make a priority seating reservation, call ☎ 407-939-3463.

Akershus

$$ World Showcase at Epcot's Norway pavilion   This lovely restaurant offers the traditional hot and cold dishes of a Scandinavian smorgasbord. ☎ *407-939-3463. Internet:* http://disney.go.com.

B-Line Diner

$$ Peabody Orlando hotel   This '50s-style diner serves such staples as chicken pot pies and huge omelets. *9801 International Dr.* ☎ *407-345-4460. Internet:* www.peabodyorlando.com.

Bahama Breeze

$$ International Drive   Dine in a Bahamian straw-market setting on Caribbean-inspired cuisine, including coconut curry chicken. *8849 International Dr.* ☎ *407-248-2499.*

Bob Marley — A Tribute to Freedom

$ **Universal Orlando's CityWalk** This combination of a club and eatery is modeled after the late singer's home in Kingston and serves traditional Jamaican dishes. ☎ *407-224-2262.* *Internet:* www.uescape.com/citywalk.

Coral Reef

$$$ **Epcot/Living Seas Pavilion** The name of the game is seafood at this restaurant, which offers a fabulous view of the Living Seas aquarium. ☎ *407-939-3463.* *Internet:* http://asp.disney.go.com.

Ming Court

$$ **International Drive** Locals flock to this restaurant, which satisfies the palate with innovative twists on traditional Chinese cuisine. *9188 International Dr.* ☎ *407-351-9988.* *Internet:* http://orlando.citysearch.com/E/V/ORLFL/0001/90/72/.

Race Rock

$ **International Drive** This NASCAR-themed restaurant serves up steaks, chicken, and burgers. *8986 International Dr.* ☎ *407-248-9876.* *Internet:* http://orlando.citysearch.com/E/V/ORLFL/0001/90/51/.

Rainforest Café

$$ **Downtown Disney** Marketplace and Animal Kingdom A jungle setting and animatronic critters bolster a decent menu of California-influenced dishes. ☎ *407-827-8500.* *Internet:* www.rainforestcafe.com.

Disney character dining

The 8-and-under crowd usually gets starry-eyed when characters show up to say howdy, sign autographs, pose for photos, and encourage them to eat their okra. Characters turn out at mealtimes at several Disney parks, attractions, and resorts. These get-togethers are incredibly popular. Translation: One-on-one interaction is somewhat brief.

You may not find a seat if you show up to a character appearance unannounced, so call to make reservations as far in advance as possible.

Prices for Disney character meals are pretty much the same, no matter where you dine. Breakfast prices average $14 for adults and $8 to $10 for children 3 to 9. Dinners, which are only available in some places (see the listings in this section and under "Dinner Shows" on p. 347), run $19 to $22 for adults and $9 to $13 for children 3 to 9. In general, the character presentations, at all the meals that we list in this chapter, rate a B — the food rates a B–. The character luau at **Walt Disney World's Polynesian Resort** is a bit better in both categories, so naturally it costs you a few more clams.

To make priority-seating reservations (these reservations don't lock down a table, but they do give you the next available table after you arrive) for any Disney character meal, call ☎ **407-939-3463**.

 Although we mention specific characters in the following list, be advised that Walt Disney World frequently changes their lineups, so don't promise the kids a specific character, or you may get burned. Also, keep in mind that you'll have to tack on the price of park admission to all character meals that are held inside the theme parks. Now here are our picks for the top players.

Chef Mickey's

The whimsical Chef Mickey's is the home of buffet breakfasts (eggs, breakfast meats, pancakes, fruit, and so on) where you can meet and be greeted by the Magic Mouse and various pals. Chef Mickey's character buffet dinners come with a salad bar, you-peel-em-you-eat-em shrimp, soups, hot entrees, breads, carved meats, vegetables, and an ice-cream bar with a great variety of toppings.

In Disney's Contemporary Resort, 4600 N. World Dr. Character breakfast: $14.95 adults, $7.95 children 3–9. Character dinner: $19.95 adults, $8.95 children 3–9. (Listed prices do not include park admission.) Open: 7–11:30 a.m., 5–9:30 p.m. daily.

Cinderella's Royal Table

This Gothic castle — the focal point of the Magic Kingdom — is the setting for daily character breakfasts. The menu has standard fare — eggs, bacon, Danish pastries, and fresh breads. Hosts vary, but Cinderella always makes an appearance. This is one of the most popular character meals in the park, so reserve far in advance. This meal is a great way to start your day in the Magic Kingdom.

In Cinderella's Castle, the Magic Kingdom. Character breakfast: $14.95 adults, $8.95 children 3–9. (Listed prices do not include park admission.) Open: 8–10 a.m. daily.

Liberty Tree Tavern

This colonial-style, eighteenth-century pub offers character dinners hosted by Mickey, Goofy, Pluto, Chip 'n' Dale, and Tigger (some or all of them, anyway). Meals are fixed-price and offer a salad of mixed greens, roast turkey with mashed potatoes, cornbread, and warm apple crisp with vanilla ice cream for dessert. Food-wise, it's the best character meal in the World.

In Liberty Square, the Magic Kingdom. Character dinner: $19.95 adults, $9.95 children 3–9. (Listed prices do not include park admission.) Open: 4 p.m.–park closing daily.

1900 Park Fare

Big Bertha — a 100-year-old French band organ that plays pipes, drums, bells, cymbals, castanets, and the xylophone — provides music. Mary Poppins, Winnie the Pooh, Goofy, Pluto, Chip 'n' Dale, and Minnie appear at the elaborate buffet breakfasts of traditional eggs, French toast, bacon, and pancakes. Beauty and the Beast and friends appear at nightly buffets, which feature prime rib, stuffed pork loin, fresh fish, and more.

In Disney's Grand Floridian Beach Resort, 4401 Floridian Way. Character breakfast: $15.95 adults, $9.95 children 3–9. Character dinner: $21.95 adults, $12.95 children 3–9. Open: 7:30–11:30 a.m., 5:30–9 p.m. daily

Dinner shows

Disney and Orlando have a reasonably busy dinner-show scene, but their offerings aren't like what you'll find in such high-flying cultural centers as Paris, New York, and London. Shows at Disney and in Orlando offer fun, not critically acclaimed drama. Most shows focus on entertaining the most important VIPs — kids. Therefore, in many instances, dinner theater in Orlando is a little like eating in front of the television set. The shows serve meals that are a cut above a TV dinner, but don't come expecting a primo dining experience. The admission prices listed under the following shows include dinner.

Arabian Nights

If you're a horse fan, this show is a winner. It stars virtually every breed of horse on the planet, from chiseled Arabians to muscular quarter horses to Royal Lipizzaner stallions. Many locals rate this performance number one among Orlando dinner shows. On most nights, the show opens with a ground trainer working one-on-one with a black stallion. The continuous action includes wild-west trick riders, a dual-dressage performance, a cowgirl thrill show, Native American riders, and treats, such as horse skiing, soccer, and chariot races. The meal, served during the 2-hour show, includes salad, prime rib, vegetables, rolls, dessert, sodas, and wine.

*6225 W. Irlo Bronson Memorial Hwy. ☎ **800-553-6116** or 407-239-9223. Internet: www.arabian-nights.com. To get there: Take U.S. 192,east to I-4 at Exit 25A). Parking: Free. Reservations recommended. Admission: $37 adults, $24 kids 3–11. Shows: Daily, times vary.*

Hoop-Dee-Doo Musical Revue

This is Disney's most popular show, so make your reservations *early.* Feast on a down-home, all-you-can-eat barbecue (country-fried chicken, smoked ribs, salad, corn on the cob, baked beans, baked bread, strawberry shortcake, and coffee, tea, beer, sangria, or soda). While you stuff yourself silly in Pioneer Hall, performers in 1890s garb lead you in a foot-stomping, hand-clapping high-energy show that includes a lot of jokes that you haven't heard since second grade. **Note:** Be prepared to join in the fun or the singers and the rest of the audience will humiliate you.

3520 N. Fort Wilderness Trail. ☎ *407-939-3563. Internet:* http://disney.go.com/DisneyWorld/intro.html. *To get there: Located at Walt Disney World's Fort Wilderness Resort and Campground. Parking: Free self. Reservations required. Admission: $44 adults, kids 3–11. Shows: 5, 7:15, 9:30 p.m. nightly.*

Polynesian Luau Dinner Show

This delightful 2-hour dinner show is a big favorite with kids, all of whom are invited on the stage. It features a colorfully costumed cast of hyper-active entertainers from New Zealand, Tahiti, Hawaii, and Samoa, performing hula, warrior, ceremonial, love, and fire dances on a flower-filled stage. Arrive early. There's a pre-show highlighting Polynesian crafts and culture (lei making, hula lessons, and more). The all-you-can-eat meal includes a big platter of fresh island fruits, barbecued chicken, roast pork, corn, vegetables, red and sweet potatoes, pull-apart cinnamon bread, beverages, and a tropical ice-cream sundae.

1600 Seven Seas Dr. ☎ *407-939-3463. Internet:* http://disney.go.com/DisneyWorld/intro.html. *To get there: Located at Disney's Polynesian Resort. Parking: Free self and valet. Reservations required. Admission: $44 adults, $22 kids 3–11. Shows: 5:15 and 8 p.m. Tues–Sat.*

Chapter 19

The Theme Parks

- -

In This Chapter

▶ Cruising the Congo, Amazon, and Nile Rivers

▶ Purchasing tickets and passes

▶ Riding colorful rockets into a brilliant galaxy

▶ Seeing all-star parades, fireworks, and shows

- -

*F*inally, we're off to the parks — Disney's Fab Four (**Magic Kingdom, Epcot, Disney-MGM Studios,** and **Animal Kingdom**), Universal's Dynamic Duo (**Universal Studios Florida** and **Islands of Adventure**), plus the marine scene at **SeaWorld** and **Discovery Cove.**

You know you won't be alone. But do you know how much company you're going to have? Combined, these eight theme parks attract more than *63 million* visitors a year — 40 million of which invade the four Disney parks. And, all these folks are bent on riding the same rides, eating at the same restaurants, and standing in the same lines as you. You can have much more fun at all the theme parks in Orlando, if you arrive knowing which parks and attractions suit your tastes and which you should avoid. So, we help you rank them in this chapter.

All these parks will take at least a full day.

Walt Disney World

Disney's four main theme parks line the western half of this 30,500-acre world. (Skip ahead to the "Walt Disney World" map.) The **Magic Kingdom** is the original attraction. With 15.2 million visitors a year, it's busier than any other U.S. theme park. **Epcot** is the third busiest theme park, welcoming 10.1 million visitors a year, followed by **Disney-MGM Studios,** at 8.7 million, and **Animal Kingdom,** with 8.6 million visitors a year.

All theme parks consider everyone 10 and older an adult, and the prices we give you don't include the 6 percent sales tax.

Walt Disney World

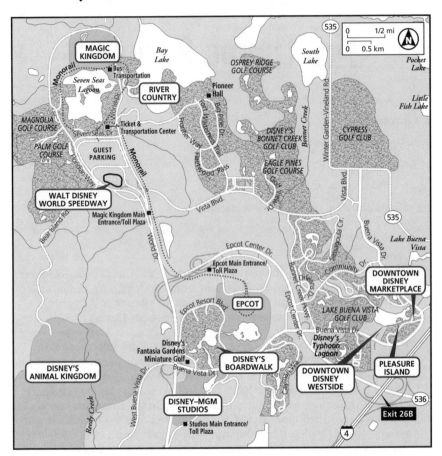

Pricing theme parks

Single-day admission costs $48 for adults and $38 kids 3 to 9. Walt Disney World Park Hopper Tickets allow unlimited access to multiple parks over several days. Options range from the 4-day pass ($192 adults, $152 kids 3 to 9) to the 7-day variety ($306 adults, $247 kids). Some passes include access to Walt Disney World's water parks (see Chapter 20 for information on **Typhoon Lagoon, Blizzard Beach,** and **River Country**) and **Pleasure Island.** Get more information on the parks and on prices for Disney's admissions passes by calling ☎ **407- 824-4321** or checking out http://disney.go.com/disneyworld/ index2.html.

If you're driving to the theme parks, parking costs $7 per day. In the Size XXXL Magic Kingdom lot, you'll probably want to ride the tram to the gate. At Epcot, Disney-MGM, and Animal Kingdom, it's faster to walk unless you have small children or sore feet.

Don't forget to make a note of your parking area and row. After a day spent standing in line, listening to screaming kids, and being tapped out by cash registers, you'll have a hard time remembering the location of your car.

Getting the most out of Walt Disney World

Most of the parks open at 9 a.m. throughout the year. They remain open at least until 6 p.m., and often as late as 11 p.m. or midnight during peak periods. The exception is Animal Kingdom, which opens at 8 a.m. and closes at 6 p.m. (slightly later during summer).

Lines at Disney and the other big parks can be incredibly long and irritating. A 20-minute wait is considered short, and 45 minutes to 1 hour is common at the primo rides. Consider getting a **FASTPASS** (skip ahead in this chapter for more on this) ticket to shorten your line time.

Here are a few other ways to beat the lines:

- ✔ Come during off periods: mid-October through November and mid-April to late May. The worst times to visit are during the holidays, spring break, and summer vacations.

- ✔ Arrive early and head straight for a primo ride, preferably one that is away from the entrance. Most folks stop at the first one they see.

- ✔ If you don't like the parades held each afternoon in the various parks, skip them and get on rides instead. Lines are shortest when most visitors are lining the parade route.

- ✔ Most rides and shows have signs telling you how long you'll have to wait.

- ✔ Ask or read the health and height restrictions at the rides before you get in line, in order to avoid wasting time on one that isn't for you.

- ✔ Disney hotel guests get into the parks 90 minutes before the swarm on select days. (Ask the front desk at your hotel for information.) The exception is Animal Kingdom, which doesn't offer this feature.

- ✔ Get a show schedule as soon you enter the park. You'll find the schedules at the turnstiles and in park shops. The rides are non-stop, but shows run at specific times.

- ✔ Want to avoid standing in line as long as other guests? Yet you're not flush enough to hire a stand in? Disney parks have installed a ride-reservation system called FASTPASS. You go to the ride, feed your ticket into a turnstile, and get an assigned time to return.

When you go back, you get into a shorter line and climb aboard. This express-lane feature is offered at more than a dozen (and counting) Walt Disney World rides. **Note:** This works for only *two rides at a time;* you must go on the two rides you've reserved before you make another FASTPASS reservation.

Finally, if you want to know all there is to know about Central Florida and its parks, purchase a copy of *Walt Disney World & Orlando For Dummies* by Jim and Cynthia Tunstall (Hungry Minds, Inc.).

The Magic Kingdom

Those attendance figures that we mention at the beginning of this chapter prove the Magic Kingdom's staying power. It remains number one, even though it has changed little since it opened in 1971. Even newer additions to the park, such as ExtraTERRORestrial Alien Encounter and Timekeeper, fall short of the 3-D dynamics that you'll find at other parks, but the kingdom is still the fairest of them all.

Main Street, U.S.A.

Though it's considered one of the kingdom's lands, Main Street is an entry zone. **Main Street Cinema** is one of the few attractions (we call it that in the loosest sense) in this area. You don't have to pay admission to watch the theater's cartoons, including vintage ones like 1928's *Steamboat Willie.* But you do have to stand — there are no seats. You also can catch the **Walt Disney World Railroad** here. This steam-powered train makes a 15-minute loop around the park, with stops in Frontierland and Mickey's Toontown Fair.

We recommend passing through Main Street quickly, when you arrive. You have to return this way at the end of the day, and if you're inclined to visit the shops, you can do it then.

Tomorrowland

Disney overhauled Tomorrowland in 1994 because it was becoming more like Yesterday-ville. It originally presented a twenty-first century without computers or answering machines. Thanks to *Star Wars* director George Lucas and others, today's version is high tech. Here's a sampling of what you'll find:

✔ **Astro Orbiter:** Astronaut wannabes, especially those who are 6 and under, love whirling high into the galaxy. Unfortunately, the orbiter has ridiculously long lines, so skip it if you're on a tight timetable.

✔ **Buzz Lightyear's Space Ranger Spin:** On this ride, you go to infinity and beyond in an interactive space adventure in which you help Buzz defend the Earth's supply of batteries from the evil Emperor Zurg. You fly an XP-37 space cruiser armed with twin lasers and a joystick that's capable of spinning the craft. (Space Rangers who get motion sickness should sit this attraction out. There's enough space debris flying around without your help.) While you cruise through space, you collect points by blasting anything that smells remotely like Zurg. Your hits trigger light, sound, and animation effects. Together, you and Buzz trash the Zurgmeister and his evil henchmen, saving the galaxy.

✔ **ExtraTERRORestrial Alien Encounter:** George Lucas helped design this extremely popular ride, which is another white-knuckle treat. After you're locked and loaded, something goes terribly wrong with your teletransporter's aim, and it sucks in a disgusting meat-eating creature from some part of deep space. The lights alternate on and off, but mainly off, and the alien busts loose. Then, with only a strobe light showing you the way, you're treated to down drafts from the alien's flapping wings, liquid spritzes (mucous if you prefer to think that way) on your face, and a little blast of hot breath on the back of your neck near the end.

✔ **Space Mountain:** Imagine a roller coaster. Then imagine it in the dark. This ride, *ExtraTERRORestrial Alien Encounter,* and *Big Thunder Mountain Railroad* (we talk about it later in this chapter) are the three **Magic Kingdom** attractions that teens and other thrill junkies bolt for first. So get here early or save it for the off hours, such as lunch or parade time. Space Mountain, a classic roller coaster, spins and plunges plenty (though it seems faster, it never tops 28 mph). Grab a front seat for the best ride.

✔ **Timekeeper:** IMAX and Circle-Vision combine with Disney AudioAnimatronics on this 360° movie. The Timekeeper is a robotic version of Robin Williams, who has a sidekick named *9-Eyes.* Williams's character takes you to the age of dinosaurs and then forward to medieval times, before he inadvertently kidnaps Jules Verne and yanks him on a reluctant trip into outer space.

✔ **Tomorrowland Speedway:** Kids, especially those ages 4 to 9, like slipping into these Indy-car knockoffs; but older children, teens, and adults find the lines and the steering less than stellar — especially those who are used to go-karts or the Malibu Grand Prix. The top speed is 7 mph, and a thick iron bar separates your tires; so you're pretty much kept on track. You have to be a minimum of 52 inches tall to drive alone.

✔ **Tomorrowland Transit Authority:** This elevated people-mover winds around *Tomorrowland* and into *Space Mountain* on a lazy ride that encourages you to nod off if it's late in the day and you've covered 4 or 5 miles on the old pedometer. There's usually no wait.

✔ **Walt Disney World Carousel of Progress:** A Disney oldie that was retooled in 1993, this 22-minute show takes up too much time and space for a presentation that lacks wow power. It uses AudioAnimatronics to trace the technological progress society has made since the Gas Light era.

Mickey's Toontown Fair

Head off cries of "Where's Mickey?" by taking young kids (2 to 8) to this two-acre site as soon as you arrive. *Toontown* gives kids a chance to meet Disney characters, including Mickey, Minnie, Donald Duck, Goofy, and Pluto. The **Magic Kingdom's** smallest land is set in a whimsical collection of candy-striped tents. *The Barnstormer at Goofy's Wiseacres Farm* is a mini roller coaster designed to look and feel like a crop duster that flies slightly off course and right through the Goofmeister's barn. *Donald's Boat* is an interactive fountain, with enough surprises to win squeals of joy (and relief on hot days). *Minnie's Country House* gives kids a chance to play in her kitchen, while *Mickey's Country House* features garden and garage playgrounds, plus a chance to meet the big cheese himself. And *Mickey's Toontown Hall of Fame* offers continuous meetings with Disney favorites.

Fantasyland

The rides and attractions here are based on classic Disney movies, as well as some of the more recent additions to the treasure chest of films. Young kids will want to spend lots of time here. Here's a list of *Fantasyland's* major attractions:

✔ **Cinderella's Castle:** This symbol of the **Magic Kingdom** sits at the end of *Main Street,* in the center of the park. It's a favorite for family photos, and if you land at the right time you can meet Cinderella, but there's really nothing to do here but gawk.

✔ **Cinderella's Golden Carousel:** In the late 1960s, Disney imagineers found this old beauty — it was built in 1917 — and brought it to the Magic Kingdom, where it was restored in time for the park's opening. It's a delight for kids, as well as carousel lovers of all ages. The organ plays — what else? — such Disney classics as "When You Wish Upon a Star" and "Twist and Shout."

✔ **Dumbo, the Flying Elephant:** This attraction doesn't do much for adrenaline-addicted older kids, but it's a favorite for ages 2 through 5. Dumbo's ears keep them airborne for a gentle, circular flight, with some little dips. If your little ones are dying to ride Dumbo, get here as soon as you enter the park — the wait times for this ride are brutal!

✔ **It's a Small World:** Young kids and most parents love this attraction; teens and other adults find it a real gagger. Nevertheless, pay your dues — every Disney visitor ought to be required to ride it at least once. You glide around the world in small boats, meeting Russian dancers, Chinese acrobats, and French cancan girls — and every one of them sings a tune that eats its way into your brain and refuses to stop playing for months.

✔ **Legend of the Lion King:** Simba and friends star in this jungle stage show. Kids under 4 may get fussy; those over 10 may find it childish. Showtimes are listed outside the theater and on the guide map that's available at the park entrance.

✔ **Mad Tea Party:** You make this tea party wild or mild, depending on how much you choose to spin the steering wheel in the teacup that acts as your chariot. The ride is based on *Alice in Wonderland* and is suitable for ages 4 and up.

✔ **The Many Adventures of Winnie the Pooh:** It features the cute-and-cuddly little fellow along with Eeyore, Piglet, and Tigger. You board a golden honey pot and ride through a storybook version of the Hundred Acre Woods, keeping an eye out for Heffulumps, Woozles, Blustery Days, and the Floody Place. This has become a favorite of kids 2 to 8 and their parents.

✔ **Peter Pan's Flight:** Another popular ride among visitors under 8, this ride begins with a flight over London — adults find the night-time tableau almost worth the line's long waits — in search of Captain Hook, Tiger Lily, and the Lost Boys.

✔ **Snow White's Scary Adventure:** Your journey takes you to the dwarfs' cottage and the wishing well, ending with the prince's kiss to break the evil spell. It's less scary now than it was years ago, when it was really dark, menacing, and surprisingly void of its namesake. She now appears in several friendly scenes, though kids younger than 5 still may get scared.

Liberty Square

This re-creation of Revolutionary-era America will infuse you with colonial spirit in no time at all. Historical touches (such as the 13 lanterns symbolizing the original colonies) may be lost on younger guests, but they'll delight in seeing a fife-and-drum corps and the opportunity to pose for a picture, while locked in the stocks. Here are some of the other hits in *Liberty Square:*

✔ **Boat Rides:** A steam-powered stern-wheeler called the *Liberty Belle* and one (sometimes two) keelboats depart *Liberty Square* for scenic cruises along the Rivers of America. The passing landscape sort of looks like the Wild West. Both vessels ply the same route and provide a restful interlude for foot-weary park-stompers.

✔ **Hall of Presidents:** American-history buffs age 10 and older most appreciate this show, which can be a real squirmer for young children. The hall is an inspiring production based on painstaking research. Pay special attention to the roll call of Presidents. The animatronic figures are incredibly lifelike — they fidget, whisper, and talk to the audience.

✔ **Haunted Mansion:** Although this park favorite has changed little over the years, it continues to offer great special effects and a grand atmosphere. You may chuckle at the corny tombstones lining the entrance, but the ride doesn't get much scarier than spooky music, eerie howling, and things that go bump in the night. The ride is best for those 6 and older.

Frontierland

Rustic log cabins, wooden sidewalks, swinging saloon doors, and other Old West trimmings help set the mood in this re-creation of an old frontier town. Attractions here include

✔ **Big Thunder Mountain Railroad:** The lines don't lie: This rocking railroad is a park favorite. The ride is something of a low-grade roller coaster with plenty of corkscrew action. It has enough of a reputation that even first-time visitors make a beeline for it. So, if you can't get to it as soon as the park opens, **FASTPASS** is your best bet. Or, give it a try late in the day (many coaster veterans maintain that the ride is even better after dark) or when a parade pulls most visitors away from the rides.

✔ **Country Bear Jamboree:** The stars of this 15-minute animatronic show are bears that croon country-and-western tunes. The audience gets caught up in the hand-clapping, knee-slapping, foot-stomping fun as Trixie, decked out in a satiny skirt, laments lost love as she sings "Tears Will Be the Chaser for Your Wine." Teddi Barra descends from the ceiling in a swing to perform "Heart We Did All That We Could," and Big Al moans "Blood in the Saddle."

✔ **Diamond Horseshoe Saloon Revue & Medicine Show:** Fancy ladies, honky-tonk pianos, and gamblers entertain you in a seven-times-a-day show that's fun for ages five and up. Marshall John Charles sings and banters with the audience, Jingles the Piano Man plays honky-tonk, and there's a magic act — all with lots of humor and audience participation.

✔ **Frontierland Shootin' Arcade:** Combining state-of-the-art electronics with a traditional shooting-gallery format, this arcade presents an array of 97 targets (slow-moving ore cars, buzzards, and gravediggers) in an 1850s boomtown. To keep things authentic, newfangled electronic firing mechanisms loaded with infrared bullets are concealed in genuine buffalo rifles. Fifty cents fetches 25 shots.

✔ **Splash Mountain:** Although it isn't as thrilling as the *Jurassic Park River Adventure* at **Islands of Adventure** or **SeaWorld's** *Journey to Atlantis, Splash Mountain* is a nifty flume ride with a substantial vertical drop and a good splash factor (around 200 megatons worth of wet). If you're lucky enough to have some real heavyweights in the front seat, look for a little extra explosion on the 40 mph, five-story downhill. In summer, this ride can offer sweet relief from the heat.

✔ **Tom Sawyer Island:** You can explore *Injun Joe's Cave* and tackle swinging bridges that threaten to throw you into a gaping chasm. It's a good place for kids to lose a little energy and for moms and dads to relax.

Adventureland

Kids can envision life in the jungle while walking through dense tropical foliage (complete with vines) or marauding through bamboo and thatch-roofed huts. This section's best attractions are

✔ **Enchanted Tiki Room:** Upgraded over the years, the show's newest cast member is Iago of *Lion King* fame. This attraction is set in a large, hexagonal, Polynesian-style dwelling with a thatched roof, bamboo beams, and tapa-bark murals. Other players include 250 tropical birds, chanting totem poles, and singing flowers that whistle, tweet, and warble. The nine-minute show runs continuously throughout the day.

✔ **Jungle Cruise:** This 10-minute, narrated voyage on the Congo, Amazon, and Nile Rivers offers glimpses of animatronic animals, foliage, a temple-of-doom-type camp, and lots of surprises. Some of the boat's captains can get their passengers pretty rowdy, but this old-style ride might seem pretty hokey to some visitors.

✔ **Pirates of the Caribbean:** In this oldie-but-goodie, after walking through a long grotto, you'll board a boat headed into a dark cave. Therein, elaborate scenery and hundreds of animatronic figures re-create a Caribbean town overrun by a boatload of buccaneers. With cheerful yo-ho-ho music playing in the background, passengers pass through the line of fire into a raging pirate raid and a panorama of almost fierce-looking pirates swigging rum, looting, and plundering.

✔ **Swiss Family Treehouse:** The story of the shipwrecked Swiss Family Robinson comes alive in this attraction made for swinging, exploring, and crawling fun. It's simple and void of all that high-tech stuff that's popular in today's parks. On busy days, be prepared to stand in a slow-moving line. The attraction is also hard for some physically challenged visitors to navigate. Kids 4 to 12 have a blast.

Parades and fireworks

Disney excels at producing fanfare, and the parades and firework displays in the following list are among the best of their kind in the world.

- **Disney's Magical Moments Parade:** With relatively few floats, all showcasing Disney movies, your interest in this parade depends on how much time you're willing to take away from the attractions. The parade includes lots of dancers and extras, but it presents a chance to dodge the mainstream and hit a primo ride, while the crowds are thin. If you decide to go, go early — seats on the curb disappear fast. *Magical Moments* is at 3 p.m. year-round. It runs from *Main Street* to *Liberty Square* and *Frontierland.*

- **Fantasy in the Sky Fireworks:** This is an explosive display that's held nightly during the summer and on holidays, as well as selected evenings the rest of the year (consult your schedule). The fireworks are preceded by Tinker Bell's magical flight from Cinderella's Castle. Suggested viewing areas are *Liberty Square, Frontierland,* and *Mickey's Toontown Fair.* Disney hotels close to the park (Grand Floridian, Polynesian, Contemporary, and Wilderness Lodge) also offer excellent views.

- **SpectroMagic:** This after-dark display replaces the **Main Street Electrical Parade,** a Disney classic that racked up 500 performances during its most recent — and final — Walt Disney World run. The SpectroMagic production combines fiberoptics, holographic images, clouds of liquid nitrogen, old-fashioned twinkling lights, and classic Disney tunes. Show times vary with seasons. The 20-minute parade is held every night during summer and other peak times, and Thursday through Saturday in the off-season.

Entering Epcot

Grab a big pot. Stir in equal measures of theme park and museum and then add movies, street performers, and interactive exhibits. What do you have? **Epcot.** Think of Epcot as a trip around the world — without the jet lag, though some say it's just as draining if you try to experience it in one day.

Walt Disney wanted this "Experimental Prototype Community Of Tomorrow" to be a high-tech city of 20,000 residents. But, when it was built 15 years after his death, it was more theme park than community. Epcot is divided into two sections. **World Showcase** lets you experience exotic, far-flung lands without a passport, or you can sit in a sidewalk cafe, munching some of the best pastries this side of Paris. In **Future World,** you can ride into the third millennium aboard thrill rides that use cutting-edge technology.

Of all the Disney parks, this one appeals least to younger children; it's better suited to the imaginations and fantasies of older children and adults.

Future World

Most visitors enter **Epcot** through _Future World,_ the northern section of the park (although it appears on the bottom of your guide map). _Spaceship Earth,_ that thing that looks like a giant, silver golf ball meant for a club the size of Gibraltar, is at the center of _Future World._ Exhibits here focus on discovery, scientific achievements, and technology, in areas spanning from energy to undersea exploration.

Innoventions

The crescent-shaped buildings to your right and left, just beyond _Spaceship Earth,_ showcase cutting-edge technology. Robot host Tom Morrow 2.0 welcomes you to nine exhibits, including three-dimensional body images, a huge, high-definition TV screen, and a place where you can create video e-mail to send to your friends. Kids love _Video Games of Tomorrow_ — 34 stations sponsored by Sega. There's also an offbeat game show, _The Broadband Connection,_ which explains communications in a way a 7-year-old can understand.

Journey Into Imagination

Even the fountains at this attraction are magical — shooting water snakes through the air. There are also a number of high-tech gadgets, but the main attraction is the 3-D _Honey I Shrunk the Audience_ show, based on the Disney film _Honey I Shrunk the Kids._ Inside, mice terrorize you, and, after you're shrunk, a large cat adds to the trauma. Then, a giant 5-year-old gives you a good shaking. Vibrating seats and creepy tactile effects enhance the dramatic 3-D action. Finally, everyone returns to proper size — everyone, that is, but the family dog, which creates a final surprise.

The Land

If agriculture doesn't interest you, skip _Living with the Land,_ a 13-minute boat ride through a simulated rain forest, an African desert, and the American plains. New farming methods and experiments ranging from hydroponics to plants growing in simulated Martian soil are showcased in real gardens.

Live footage and animation mix in _Circle of Life,_ a 15-minute, 70mm motion picture based on _The Lion King._ According to the story line, Timon and Pumbaa are building a monument to the good life called Hakuna Matata Lakeside Village, but their project, as Simba points out, is damaging the savanna for other animals.

The Living Seas

The Living Seas pavilion has a 5.7 million-gallon aquarium filled with more than 4,000 sharks, barracudas, rays, dolphins, and other reef fish. You start off with a film demonstrating the formation of the Earth and the seas as a means to support life. You then descend to *Seabase Alpha,* where a short ride offers you stunning views of the pavilion's marine residents. After the ride, you're free to explore an ocean research base of the future. *The Living Seas* also has two manatees living in terribly tight quarters.

Spaceship Earth

The show inside Epcot's icon includes a slow-track journey back to the roots of communications, beginning with an AudioAnimatronic Cro-Magnon shaman, and ending in outer space.

Compared to other Disney wizardry, this one is a real dud. If you *have* to see it, do it later in the day as you're leaving. The lines will be shorter.

Test Track

General Motors and Disney sank $60 million into this long-time-coming marvel of GM engineering and Disney imagineering. You can wait in line for more than an hour during peak periods, so consider using FAST-PASS. While in line, you'll snake through displays about corrosion, crash tests, and more. The five-minute ride follows a track that looks like an actual highway. It includes braking tests, a hill climb, and tight S-curves in a six-passenger "convertible." There's also a 12-second burst of speed that gets your heart pumping to the tune of 65 mph.

Universe of Energy

Ellen's Energy Adventure, a 32-minute ride, features comedian Ellen DeGeneres as an energy expert tutored by Bill Nye the Science Guy to be a *Jeopardy!* contestant. An animated movie depicts the Earth's molten beginnings, its cooling process, and the formation of fossil fuels. You then tour a 275-million-year-old, storm-wracked landscape where giant AudioAnimatronic dragonflies, pterodactyls, dinosaurs, earthquakes, and streams of molten lava surround you. The show ends on an upbeat note — a vision of an energy-abundant future and Ellen as a new *Jeopardy!* champion.

Wonders of Life

The *Making of Me,* starring Martin Short, is a captivating 15-minute motion picture combining live action with animation and spectacular in-utero photography to create the sweetest introduction imaginable to the facts of life.

The presentation may prompt some questions from young children; therefore, we recommend it for ages 10 and up.

Body Wars reduces you to the size of a cell for a medical rescue mission inside the human immune system. This motion-simulator takes you on a wild ride through gale-force winds in the lungs and pounding heart chambers.

Engineers designed this ride from the last row of the car, so that's the best place to sit to get the most bang for your buck.

In the funny *Cranium Command*, Buzzy, an AudioAnimatronic brain-pilot-in-training, is charged with the seemingly impossible task of controlling the brain of a typical 12-year-old boy during traumas that include meeting a girl and a run-in with the school principal.

World Showcase

The 11 miniature nations here open at 11 a.m. daily and surround a 40-acre lagoon. All the countries have authentic, indigenous architecture, landscaping, background music, restaurants, and shops. Art exhibits, dance performances, and films are among the area's strongest selling points. All the employees in each pavilion are natives of the country represented.

Most of these nations offer some kind of live entertainment throughout the day. Check your guide map/show schedule when you enter the park; you can also find schedules posted near the entrance to each country.

The American Adventure

This attraction's 29-minute *CliffsNotes* dramatization of U.S. history utilizes a 72-foot rear-projection screen, rousing music, and a large cast of lifelike animatronic figures, including narrators Mark Twain and Ben Franklin. You follow the voyage of the *Mayflower,* watch Jefferson writing the *Declaration of Independence,* and witness Matthew Brady photographing a family that the Civil War is about to divide. You can also witness Pearl Harbor and the *Eagle* heading toward the moon. Teddy Roosevelt discusses the need for national parks; Susan B. Anthony speaks out on women's rights; and Frederick Douglass discusses slavery. The *Voices of Liberty* singers perform folk songs in the Main Hall while you're waiting for the show.

Canada

The pavilion's highlight attraction is *O Canada!* — a dazzling, 18-minute, Circle-Vision 360° film that shows our northern neighbor's scenic wonders, from sophisticated Montréal to the thundering flight of thousands of snow geese departing the St. Lawrence River.

The architecture and landscape in *Canada* include a mansard-roofed replica of Ottawa's nineteenth-century, French-style Château Laurier and an Indian village, complete with a rough-hewn log trading post and 30-foot totem-pole replicas.

China

Epcot's version of this Asian land includes a half-size replica of Beijing's Temple of Heaven, a summer retreat for Chinese emperors. Gardens simulate Suzhou, a city in China, with miniature waterfalls, fragrant lotus ponds, and bamboo groves.

The highlight of this area is *Wonders of China,* a 20-minute, Circle-Vision 360° film that explores 6,000 years of dynastic and communist rule, as well as the breathtaking diversity of China's landscape.

France

This pavilion focuses on France's *belle epoque* (Beautiful Age) — 1870 to 1910 — when French art, literature, and architecture ruled. You enter via a replica of the beautiful cast-iron Pont des Arts footbridge over the "Seine," and the grounds include a ¹⁄₁₀-scale model of the Eiffel Tower, which was built from Gustave Eiffel's original blueprints.

Impressions de France, an 18-minute film shown in a palatial, sit-down theater à la Fontainebleau, offers a scenic journey through diverse French landscapes. It's projected on a vast, 200° wraparound screen and enhanced by the music of French composers.

Be sure to stop at the pavilion's *Boulangerie Patisserie* for tasty pastries.

Germany

Enclosed by castle walls, *Germany* offers bratwursts, oompah bands, and a rollicking atmosphere. The clock tower is embellished with whimsical glockenspiel figures that herald each hour with quaint melodies. The pavilion's outdoor biergarten was inspired by medieval Rothenberg and features a year-round Oktoberfest.

If you're a model-train fanatic or visiting with young kids, don't miss the exquisitely detailed version of a small Bavarian town, complete with working train station, located between *Germany* and *Italy.*

Italy

One of the prettiest *World Showcase* pavilions, *Italy* lures you over an arched stone footbridge to a replica of Venice's intricately ornamented pink-and-white Doge's Palace. Other architectural highlights include the 83-foot bell tower of St. Mark's Square, Venetian bridges, and a central piazza enclosing a version of Bernini's Neptune Fountain.

Japan

The central pagoda is modeled after Nara's Horyuji Temple, built in 700 A.D. The building to its right is a replica of Kyoto's Imperial Palace. If you have some leisure time, enjoy the pebbled footpaths and the other traditional touches. Exhibits ranging from eighteenth-century Bunraki puppets to samurai armor are displayed in the *White Heron Castle,* a replica of the Shirasagi-Jo, a seventeenth-century fortress.

Make sure that you include a performance of traditional Japanese music and dance in your schedule. It's one of the best shows in the *World Showcase.*

Mexico

The music of marimbas and mariachi bands hits you, as you approach this festive showcase, fronted by a towering Mayan pyramid modeled on the Aztec temple of Quetzalcoatl (god of life) and surrounded by dense Yucatán jungle landscaping. Inside the pavilion, you find a museum of pre-Colombian art and artifacts.

El Rio del Tiempo (River of Time) is an 8-minute cruise through Mexico's past and present. Passengers get a close-up look at the Mayan pyramid and the erupting Popocatepetl volcano.

Morocco

The *Medina* (old city), entered via a replica of an arched gateway, leads to a traditional Moroccan home and the narrow, winding streets of the *souk,* a bustling marketplace where all kinds of handcrafted merchandise are on display. The *Medina's* rectangular courtyard centers on a replica of the ornately tiled Najjarine Fountain in Fez, the setting for musical entertainment. There's also a replica of the Koutoubia Minaret, the prayer tower of a twelfth-century mosque in Marrakesh.

The *Royal Gallery of Arts and History* contains an ever-changing exhibit of Moroccan art, and the Center of Tourism has a continuous, three-screen slide show. A guided tour of the pavilion, *Treasures of Morocco,* runs from noon to 7 p.m. daily.

Norway

The Norway pavilion's stave church, styled after the thirteenth-century Gol Church of Hallingdal, features changing exhibits. There's also a replica of Oslo's fourteenth-century Akershus Castle, and other buildings that simulate the red-roofed cottages of Bergen and the timber-sided farm buildings of the Nordic woodlands.

Norway includes a two-part attraction. *Maelstrom,* a boat ride in a dragon-headed Viking vessel, travels through Norway's fjords and mythical forests to the music of Peer Gynt. Along the way, you see polar bears prowling the shore, and then you are turned into frogs by trolls that cast a spell on your boat. The watercraft crashes through a narrow gorge and spins into the North Sea, where a storm is in progress (don't worry — this is a relatively calm ride). The storm abates, a princess' kiss turns you into a human again, and you disembark to a tenth-century Viking village to view the 70mm film *Norway.*

United Kingdom

The U.K. pavilion evokes Merry Olde England through its *Britannia Square* — a formal London-style park complete with a copper-roofed gazebo bandstand, a stereotypical red phone booth (it really works!), and a statue of the Bard. Four centuries of architecture are represented along quaint cobblestone streets. Troubadours and minstrels entertain in front of a traditional British pub where you can grab a pint.

Don't miss the Old Globe Players, who present delightfully wacky performances of Shakespeare in the square. There is a lot of audience participation, and you may be tapped to try your hand at Hamlet — forsooth!

Fireworks and more

Epcot's millennium celebration ended Dec. 31, 2000, but the park is continuing its *Illuminations* display. It's a blend of fireworks, lasers, and fountains in a display that's signature Disney. The show is well worth dealing with the crowds that flock to the parking lot at its conclusion.

This display is very popular and draws a lot of people, but there are tons of good viewing points around the lagoon. However, it's best to stake your claim to a primo place a half hour or so before show time, which is listed in your entertainment schedule.

Disney-MGM Studios

Anyone who loves movies or the golden age of Hollywood will enjoy wandering the realistic streets, shops, sets, and back lots of this 110-acre combination theme park and working studio. Many films are shot here throughout the year, so you never know whether you're seeing slapstick or an actual taping. That's part of the fun. Wander the neighborhoods, which include Hollywood and Sunset Boulevards, where art deco movie sets recall the golden age of Hollywood. New York Street is lined with miniature renditions of the Empire State and Chrysler Buildings. It's also an impromptu stage where street actors perform a range of sidewalk fun.

Checking out the best of Disney-MGM

Unlike the **Magic Kingdom** and **Epcot,** you can pretty much see **Disney-MGM's** 110 acres of attractions in one day, if you arrive early. Here's a rundown of the best Disney-MGM has to offer:

✔ **Backlot Tour:** This 35-minute behind-the-scenes tour starts on foot and finishes in a tram. Two victims — um, volunteers — get soaked as special effects experts orchestrate fake deluges and submarine battles. After the demonstrations, you board a tram for a ride through Disney's costume department (the world's largest), sets from popular (and not-so-popular) TV shows and movies, and the domain of the special-effects wizards. The best comes when you reach *Catastrophe Canyon,* where an "earthquake" causes a tanker truck to explode, rocking the tram. Then a very large, *VERY WET* wave throws 70,000 gallons of water your way.

✔ **Backstage Pass:** A furry flurry of Dalmatians and the villainous Cruella De Vil are the stars of Disney's live-action remake of *101 Dalmatians* and this 25-minute walking tour. The stark, eerie movie sets are among the top attractions during the tour, and Wizzer, the most fluid of the canine actors, is featured in a film about the life of a four-pawed star.

✔ **Bear in the Big Blue House — Live on Stage!** Younger audiences like this 15-minute show, where Bear, Ojo, Tutter, Treelo, Pip, Pop, and Luna perform some of their favorite songs from the whimsical Disney Channel series.

✔ **Beauty and the Beast Live on Stage:** A 1,500-seat, covered amphitheater provides the stage for this 25-minute, live Broadway-style production of *Beauty and the Beast* adapted from the movie version. Musical highlights include the rousing "Be Our Guest" opening number and the poignant title song, featured in a romantic waltz-scene finale. Arrive early to get a good seat.

✔ **Disney's Doug Live!** The Nickelodeon star comes to life on stage, and through his words and actions, explains why being 12 is tough. This 30-minute show combines live performances and animation while Doug and his friends interact. The show requires volunteers: four adults (to play The Beets) and one child (as Quail Man).

✔ **The Great Movie Ride:** A slow journey down MGM's memory lane, it starts in the 1930s using incredibly lifelike animatronic versions of Jimmy Cagney, John Wayne, and Clint Eastwood to recreate some of their most memorable roles. Live bandits then show up and blow up the bank. One of the bad guys kidnaps you and your mates, but he goes the wrong way and runs into the space thing from *Alien.* Younger children could be frightened, and the older teens will be bored with this ride.

✔ **Honey, I Shrunk the Kids Movie Set:** An 11,000-square-foot playground where everything is larger than life, it has a 30-foot-tall thicket of grass, three-stories-high mushroom caps, and a friendly ant that makes a suitable seat. Play areas include a massive cream cookie, a 52-foot garden hose with leaks, cereal loops that are 9-feet wide and cushioned for jumping, and a waterfall that cascades from a leaf to a dell of fern sprouts. It's great for small children.

✔ **Hunchback of Notre Dame: A Musical Adventure:** Dozens of singers and dancers tell the story of Quasimodo in a 32-minute live performance geared to all ages. The human cast, aided by puppets, follows the Disney animated score and story line in which Quasimodo ultimately loses more than his beloved Esmeralda.

✔ **Indiana Jones Epic Stunt Spectacular:** *Spectacular* is a good word for this 30-minute, rock-'em, sock-'em extravaganza, *guaran-double-teed* to keep you entertained and on the edge of your seat. The show is held in a big, open-air pavilion and uses many adult volunteers. It begins with Indy rappelling down from the rafters, and the nifty special effects soon have him dodging spikes, falling into a pit of molten something-or-other, surviving two ax-wielding gargoyles, grabbing a priceless amulet, and then outrunning fire, steam, and a large boulder that nearly flattens him — all before the first commercial break. It may be a little intense for kids under 6.

✔ **Jim Henson's Muppet*Vision 3D:** This in-your-face, 25-minute spectacle allows the humor of the late Jim Henson to live on through Miss Piggy, Kermit, and the gang. A delight for all ages, this production is a chuckler that mixes some pretty good 3-D effects and sensory gags with puppets and a live-action character or two. You'll encounter flying Muppets, cream pies, cannonballs, high winds, fiber-optic fireworks, bubble showers, and even an actual spray of water. Kids in the first row can interact with the characters.

✔ **The Magic of Disney Animation:** Disney characters come alive at the stroke of a brush or pencil, as you tour glass-walled animation studios and watch artists at work. Walter Cronkite and Robin Williams explain what's going on via video monitors. They also star in a very funny eight-minute Peter Pan-themed film about the basics of animation. The 35-minute tour, recommended for ages eight and up, also includes a grand finale of magical moments from classic Disney films.

✔ **Rock 'n' Roller Coaster:** WOW! This inverted roller coaster — the fastest in Orlando — is one of the best thrill rides that Walt Disney World has to offer and is certainly not a ride for younger kids or folks with neck or back problems, faint hearts, or a tendency toward motion sickness. It's a fast-and-furious, indoor ride that puts you in a 24-passenger stretch limo, outfitted with 120 speakers that blare Aerosmith at 32,000 watts! A flashing light warns you to "prepare to merge as you've never merged before," and faster than you can scream, "Stop the music!" (around 2.8 seconds, actually), you shoot from 0 to 60 mph and into the first gut-tightening inversion at 5 Gs.

✔ **Sounds Dangerous Starring Drew Carey:** Drew Carey provides laughs while dual audio technology provides some incredible hair-raising effects during a 12-minute mixture of movie and live action at ABC Sound Studios. You feel like you're right in the middle of the action of a TV pilot featuring undercover police work and plenty of amusing mishaps.

✔ **Star Tours:** Your journey to a place far, far away begins with a winding walk (a line) through a bunch of *Star Wars* 'droids and a pre-ride warning about high turbulence, sharp drops, and sudden turns. *Star Tours* is a virtual ride where you go nowhere, but you feel like you do. The ride starts kind of slow, but it finishes fast, as you soar through space in a good-guy fighter, with R2-D2 and C-3PO helping you make passes through the canals of Lord Vader's mother ship.

✔ **The Twilight Zone Tower of Terror:** If you like leaving your stomach at several levels, you'll love this ride. Its legend says that during a violent storm on Halloween night 1939, lightning struck the Hollywood Tower Hotel, causing an entire wing and an elevator full of people to disappear. And you're about to meet them as you star in a special episode of *The Twilight Zone*. After various spooky adventures, the ride ends in a dramatic climax: a terrifying, 13-story free-fall into *The Twilight Zone!* At 199-feet, it's the tallest Walt Disney World attraction. You must be 40 inches tall to ride.

✔ **Voyage of the Little Mermaid:** Hazy lighting helps paint a picture of an underwater world in a 17-minute show that combines live performances, movie clips, puppetry, and special effects. Sebastian sings "Under the Sea," Ariel performs "Part of Your World," and the evil, tentacled Ursula, 12 feet tall and 10 feet wide, belts out "Poor Unfortunate Soul."

Parades and fireworks

It's hard not to be in awe of the choreography, laser lights, and fireworks that are the core of **Fantasmic!,** a 25-minute extravaganza. Shooting comets, great balls of fire, and animated fountains are among the special effects that really amaze the audience. The cast includes 50 performers, a giant dragon, a king cobra, and 1-million gallons of water — most of it orchestrated by a sorcerer mouse that looks very familiar. The ample amphitheater holds 9,000 souls. If you want to avoid a real traffic jam after the show, arrive up to 60 minutes early and sit on the right (the theater empties right to left).

Mulan — The Parade is a short one, celebrating Disney's 36th full-length animated feature. It's based on the story of a young, high-spirited girl who saves her father's life by disguising herself as a man and joining the Chinese army in his place. It's performed afternoons (weather permitting) along Hollywood Boulevard.

Animal Kingdom

The biggest knock against Disney's fourth theme park is that it's as animal friendly as it is people friendly. The critters here can escape the heat, and your view, if they choose. If your timing is right, you'll see African lions, giraffes, cheetahs, white rhinos, lowland gorillas, and hippos. You'll also bump into some that may be new to you, such as bongos (the antelopes, not the drums) and naked mole rats.

Your best bet for animal viewing is to arrive in time for the park's opening (usually 8 a.m., but sometimes an hour earlier) or to come here around closing. Most creatures are on the prowl at those times, not at midday. Like **Magic Kingdom,** this park has several areas or *lands.*

The Oasis

This is your introduction to **Animal Kingdom,** but many folks, ready to get to the action, launch their way through *The Oasis,* overlooking the fact that this is one of the better places to see animals early in the day. The lush vegetation, streams, grottoes, and waterfalls on either side of the walkway are good places to see wallabies, miniature deer, anteaters, sloths, iguanas, tree kangaroos, otters, and macaws.

Safari Village

After you pass through *The Oasis,* you head straight into *Safari Village,* which is the hub for the five lands scattered around **Animal Kingdom.** This is another animal-viewing area, where you may see wood ducks, flamingos, kangaroos, and small-clawed otters walking around the *Tree of Life.*

The attractions in this section of the park include:

- ✔ **It's Tough to Be a Bug!** Take the walkway through the Tree of Life's 50-foot base, grab a pair of 3-D glasses, and settle into a sometimes creepy-crawly seat. Based on the Disney-Pixar film, *A Bug's Life,* the special effects in this multimedia adventure are pretty impressive. While it may not be a good choice for kids under four (it's dark and loud) or bug haters, this attraction is a fun and sometimes-poignant look at life from a smaller perspective. After you put on your bug-eye glasses, all of your senses are awakened by the stars, including ants, beetles, spiders, and — oh, no! — a stinkbug.

- ✔ **Tree of Life:** The 14-story *Tree of Life* is Animal Kingdom's icon. The manmade tree and its carved animals are the work of Disney artists, teams of which worked for more than a year on its carved, free-form animal sculptures. It's not as tall or imposing as other icons, but it is impressive. It has 8,000 limbs, 103,000 leaves, and 325 mammals, reptiles, amphibians, bugs, birds, dinosaurs, and Mickeys carved into its trunk, limbs, and roots. When you view the tree, it seems as if a different animal appears from every angle.

Camp Minnie-Mickey

Youngsters love this place. It's a favorite hangout for several Disney characters from the forest and jungle, including Simba from *Lion King* and Baloo from *The Jungle Book*. Mickey, Minnie, Goofy, Pluto, Donald, Daisy, and a variety of other stars also make appearances from time to time around this woody retreat, which resembles an Adirondack summer camp. The big guns here are

- ✔ **Festival of the Lion King:** *Festival of the Lion King* at the Lion King Theater is a rousing 28-minute show that's the best in **Animal Kingdom** and one of the top three in all of **Walt Disney World.** The eight-times-per-day extravaganza celebrates nature's diversity with a talented, colorfully attired cast of singers, dancers, and life-size critters that lead the way to an inspiring sing-along. The action takes place both onstage and around the audience.

- ✔ **Pocahontas and Her Forest Friends:** The wait to see *Pocahontas and Her Forest Friends* can be nightmarish, and the 15-minute show isn't close to the caliber of *Festival of the Lion King* and *Tarzan Rocks!* In this show, Pocahontas, Grandmother Willow, and some forest creatures hammer home the importance of treating nature with respect.

Africa

Enter through the town of Harambe, which means "coming together," in Swahili. Costumed employees greet you as you enter the buildings. The whitewashed structures, built of coral stone and thatched with reed brought from Africa, surround a central marketplace, rich with local wares and colors. The best attractions here include:

- ✔ **Conservation Station:** This area of Africa offers a behind-the-scenes look at how Disney cares for animals inside the park. *Conservation Station* includes the Affection Section, where you can cuddle some friendly animals, explore their habitats, and find out how they're cared for and fed.

- ✔ **Kilimanjaro Safaris:** This attraction is one of the few rides and the best animal-viewing venue in the kingdom. But remember what we told you about the animals being scarce during the middle of the day, especially in the heat of summer. After you hit the end of the line, you board a large truck, and then you're off on a bouncy ride through what pretends to be Africa. The animals are real and include black rhinos, hippos, antelopes, Nile crocodiles, zebras, wildebeests, and a male lion that, if your timing is right, might offer a half-hearted roar toward some gazelles that are safely out of reach.

Arrive early! Lines can be 1 hour long or worse and definitely consider using FASTPASS, unless you can get there within 15 minutes
of the park's opening.

✔ **Pangani Falls Exploration Trail:** You can get a pretty good look at
birds and the ever-active mole rats along the trail, but the gorillas
are very hard to spot, and small viewing areas in various parts of
the other habitats make it hard to see other elusive animals. Lines
that grow to three or more people deep, when critters do material-
ize, can also make viewing difficult.

Asia

Disney's imagineers have outdone themselves in creating the mythical
kingdom of *Anadapour.* The intricately painted artwork at the front is
appealing, and it also helps make the lines seem to move a little faster.
Also, watch for (with little prior announcement) the appearance of
local youngsters performing Asian dances. The top attractions here are

✔ **Flights of Wonder:** Mixing live-animal action with a Disney character show, *Flights of Wonder* has undergone several transformations
since the park opened. It's a low-key break that has a few laughs,
but it's not much by bird-show standards.

✔ **Kali River Rapids:** White-water fanatics will scoff, but for a theme-
park raft ride, it's pretty good — slightly better, we think, than
Congo River Rapids at **Busch Gardens** (see Chapter 15), but not as
good as *Popeye & Bluto's Bilge-Rat Barges* in **Islands of Adventure**
(see later in this chapter). It has churning water that mimics real
rapids and optical illusions that make you wonder if you're about
to go over the falls. You *will* get wet. And lines are frequently long.

✔ **Maharajah Jungle Trek:** Disney keeps its promise to provide up-
close views of animals with this exhibit. If you don't show up in
the midday heat, you'll see Bengal tigers through the thick glass.
Nothing but air divides you from dozens of giant fruit bats hanging
in what appears to be a courtyard. Some of the bats have
wingspans of 6 feet. (If you have a phobia, you can bypass this
area, but the bats are harmless.) There are also chances to see
giant Komodo dragons, playful gibbons, and other monkeys.

Dinoland, U.S.A.

Here's Disney's attempt to capitalize on the dinosaur craze inspired by
Jurassic Park. To enter this area, you pass under Olden Gate Bridge, a
40-foot-tall Brachiosaurus reassembled from excavated fossils. The
best attractions here are

✔ **The Boneyard:** Kids love this play area, and it's a great place for parents to catch a second wind. Little ones can slide and climb over a simulated paleontological site, and they can squeeze through the fossils and skeletons of a triceratops and a brontosaurus.

✔ **Dinosaur:** This ride hurls you through darkness in a CTX Rover time machine past an array of snarling dinosaurs that are a little hokey. It's far from a smooth ride, and some kids may find the dinosaurs and darkness frightening. However, *Dinosaur* is as close as **Animal Kingdom** comes to a thrill ride — a herky-jerky, twisting-turning, bouncey-jouncey ride in which you and 20 other passengers try to save the last dinosaur worth saving.

✔ **Cretaceous Trail:** Wander leisurely back in time as you stroll down a path filled with living plants and animal species that have survived since the dinosaurs. A Chinese crocodile, Florida soft-shelled turtle, and red-legged seriema (a long-neck bird) are among the residents on this trail.

✔ **Tarzan Rocks!** This 28-minute, five-times-per-day show pulses with music and occasional aerial theatrics. Phil Collins's movie soundtrack supports a cast of 27, including tumblers, dancers, and in-line skating daredevils who really get the audience into the act. The costumes and music are pretty spectacular, second in Animal Kingdom only to *Festival of the Lion King* in *Camp Minnie-Mickey.*

Sometimes criticized for being too passive, Animal Kingdom is jumping into the coaster craze, though their entry is a tame one. *Primeval Whirl* won't have any inversions, when it opens in Dinoland U.S.A., at about the time this guide hits bookstores. It will, however, have a lot of spinning action. On a smaller scale, so will *Triceratop Spin,* a kids' ride designed along the same lines. Both attractions will be located in a new area called Dino-Rama, which also will have carnival-style games.

Universal Orlando

Team Universal's original park, **Universal Studios Florida,** is similar to **Disney-MGM Studios** in that it spends a ton of time and money to plug its movies and characters. Here, that means visitors get a healthy dose of *Earthquake, Terminator, Back to the Future,* Barney, Yogi Bear, *Jaws, E.T.,* and many more. Its second park, **Islands of Adventure,** rules Orlando in thrill rides, thanks to *Dueling Dragons, the Incredible Hulk Coaster, Jurassic Park River Adventure,* and *Dudley Do-Right's Ripsaw Falls.*

Single-day tickets cost $48 for adults, $38 for kids 3 to 9. That total doesn't include the 6 percent sales tax or, for those of you driving to the park, the $7 parking charge. For more information on tickets and on Universal's other admissions options (including multi-day passes) call ☎ **407-363-8000** or check out www.uescape.com on the Web.

Universal has also teamed with other parks to offer **FlexTickets.** A seven-day, four-park pass to **Universal Studios Florida, Islands of Adventure, Wet 'n Wild** (see Chapter 20), and **SeaWorld** costs $159.95 for adults and $127.95 for children 3 to 9. A ten-day, five-park pass that adds **Busch Gardens** in Tampa (see Chapter 15), is $198 for adults and $159 for children 3 to 9.

Universal Express is a line-beating program offered to guests buying certain multi-day passes. It offers early admission and faster access to the rides (maximum 15-minute wait) from 7 to 10 a.m. Universal also is experimenting with **Fast Track**, a system similar to Disney's **FASTPASS,** on certain rides.

Universal Studios Florida

Universal matches **Disney** stride for stride, and in some cases is a half step ahead, when it comes to cutting-edge rides. Real as well as virtual thrills, terrific special effects, mammoth screens, and 3-D action are part of its successful mix. The rides and shows at Universal are located in six different zones: *Hollywood, New York, Production Central, San Francisco, Woody Woodpecker's KidZone,* and *World Expo.*

Hollywood

This area is to the right of the Front Lot, where you enter. The main streets are Rodeo Drive, Hollywood Boulevard, and Sunset Boulevard. Here's a list of the best that Hollywood has to offer:

✔ **Terminator 2: 3-D Battle Across Time:** This attraction is billed as "the quintessential sight and sound experience for the twenty-first century!" and the park has little need to be modest about its claim. The director who made the movie, Jim Cameron, supervised this $60 million production. Live actors and six giant Cyborgs interact with Arnie, who appears onscreen (actually there are three huge screens). The crisp 3-D effects are among the best in Orlando. (When liquid mercury falls from the screen, cold water really hits your legs.) It's a must-see, but little kids may find it a bit intense.

✔ **Gory, Gruesome & Grotesque Horror Make-up Show:** This show is a fantastic Hollywood presentation that gives you a behind-the-scenes look at how monster makeup is done, including the transformation scenes from such movies as *The Fly,* and *The Exorcist.*

✔ **I Love Lucy, A Tribute:** This show is a remembrance of America's queen of comedy.

New York

New York is near the back of the park and includes rides and shows along 42nd and 57th streets, Park Avenue, and Delancy Street. The premiere attractions in this section are

- ✔ **Kongfrontation:** King Kong has returned to the Big Apple. As you stand in line in a replica of a grungy, graffiti-scarred New York subway station, CBS newsman Roland Smith reports on Kong's terrifying rampage. Everyone must evacuate to Roosevelt Island, so it's all aboard the tram. Cars collide and hydrants explode below, the tram malfunctions, and, of course, you encounter Mr. Banana Breath — all 40 feet and 12,000 pounds of him. He terrifies you and fellow passengers by dangling the tram over the East River.

- ✔ **Twister — Ride it Out:** The curtain rises in the movie town of Wakita, where Universal engineers have created a five-story funnel cloud by injecting 2-million cubic feet of air per minute (that's enough to fill four full-size blimps). Power lines spark and fall, an oak splits, and the storm rumbles at a rock-concert level as cars, trucks, and a cow fly about, while the audience watches from just 20-feet away. In the finale, the floor begins to buckle at your feet.

Production Central

Production Central is directly behind and to the left of the Front Lot. Its main thoroughfares are Nickelodeon Way and 7th and 8th Avenues. Here are some of the area's highlights:

- ✔ **The Funtastic World of Hanna-Barbera:** Yogi Bear is the pilot of this motion-simulator/spaceship that travels through the galaxy in an effort to rescue Elroy Jetson from the evil Dick Dastardly. The ride includes lots of rock 'n' roll — dips, dives, and blasts of air when things explode. You hurtle through Bedrock, Scoobie's Haunted Castle, and finally Jetsonville before — drat it! — Dick gets foiled again.

- ✔ **Nickelodeon Studios Tour:** Tour the soundstages where Nick shows, such as *Kenan & Kel* and the *Mystery Files of Shelby Woo* are produced, view concept pilots, visit the kitchen where Gak and green slime are made, play game shows, such as *Double Dare 2000,* and try new Sega video games. This 45-minute behind-the-scenes tour is a fun escape from the hustle of the midway, and there's a lot of audience participation. One child volunteer always gets slimed.

> ✔ **Other Production Central Shows:** *Stage 54* is an oft-changing area. *Alfred Hitchcock's Theater* is a tribute to the master of suspense, in which Tony Perkins narrates a reenactment of the famous shower scene from *Psycho*, and where *The Birds* — as if the original movie wasn't scary enough — becomes an in-your-face 3-D movie. There's also an audience-participation segment in which some volunteers relive frightening scenes.

San Francisco

This L-shaped zone faces the waterfront, and its attractions line The Embarcadero and Amity Avenue.

> ✔ **Beetlejuice's Rock 'n' Roll Graveyard Revue:** Horrible creatures, such as Dracula, Wolfman, the Phantom of the Opera, Frankenstein and his bride, and Beetlejuice, show up to scare you silly. Their funky rock musical has pyrotechnic special effects and MTV-style choreography. It's loud and lively enough to scare some small children and aggravate many older adults. Young teens seem to like it the most.
>
> ✔ **Earthquake — The Big One:** Sparks fly shortly after you board a BART train. The whopper — 8.3 on the Richter scale! — hits as you pull into the Embarcadero Station, and you're left trapped as vast slabs of concrete collapse around you, a propane truck bursts into flames, a runaway train comes hurtling at you, and the station floods (65,000 gallons of water cascade down the steps).
>
> ✔ **Jaws:** As your boat heads into a seven-acre, 5-million-gallon lagoon, an ominous dorsal fin appears on the horizon. What follows is a series of attacks from a three-ton, 32-foot-long, mechanical, great white shark that tries to sink its urethane teeth into your hide — or at least into your boat's hide. A 30-foot wall of flame, caused by burning fuel, surrounds the boat, and you'll truly feel the heat in this $45-million attraction.

> ✔ **The Wild, Wild, Wild West Stunt Show:** Stunt people demonstrate falls from three-story balconies, gun and whip fights, dynamite explosions, and other Wild West staples. This is a well-performed, lively show that's especially popular with foreign visitors who have celluloid visions of the American West.

Woody Woodpecker's KidZone

This section of the park contains rides and attractions sure to please the littlest members of your party. If you're traveling with a number of youngsters, plan on spending a lot of time here. Some of the highlights include:

✔ **A Day in the Park with Barney:** Set in a park-like theater-in-the-round, this 25-minute musical stars the Purple One, Baby Bop, and BJ. It uses song, dance, and interactive play to deliver an environmental message. This show can be the highlight of your youngster's day. The playground next door has chimes to ring, tree houses to explore, and lots of other things to intrigue little visitors.

✔ **E.T. Adventure:** For many families, this ride alone is worth the admission price. You soar with E.T., who is on a mission to save his ailing planet, through the forest and into space aboard a star-bound bicycle. You also meet some new characters Steven Spielberg created for the ride, including Botanicus, Tickli Moot Moot, Horn Flowers, and Tympani Tremblies.

✔ **Woody Woodpecker's Nuthouse Coaster:** This is the top attraction in the *KidZone*. Sure, it's a kiddie coaster, but the *Nuthouse Coaster* will thrill some moms and dads, too. Although it's only 30 feet at its peak, this ride offers quick, banked turns while you sit in a miniature steam train.

The ride only lasts 50 seconds, and waits can be 30 minutes, but few kids will let you miss it.

✔ **More to Do in Woody Woodpecker's KidZone:** *Fievel's Playland* is a wet, western-themed playground with a house to climb and a small water slide. *Curious George Goes to Town* has water- and ball-shooting cannons, plus a huge water tower that empties (after an alarm), drenching anyone who doesn't run for cover. Nearby, *Animal Actors Stage* offers a 20-minute show featuring Babe, Beethoven, Benji, and Lassie.

World Expo

The smallest zone in **Universal Studios Florida** offers a lot of punch in its two rides. *World Expo* is on Exposition Boulevard, between *San Francisco* and *KidZone*. The top attractions here are

✔ **Back to the Future — The Ride:** *Back to the Future* offers you a chance at time travel in a simulator made to look like a DeLorean. Six to eight of you are packed into a car, after a video briefing from Christopher Lloyd, also known as Dr. Emmett Brown. Biff the Bully has stolen another DeLorean, and you have to catch him. The fate of the universe is in your hands. The huge screen makes this ride very intense, but if you didn't heed the ride's warnings and begin to feel some of the symptoms, just stick your neck out of your car — literally. You can see the other cars, lending the very true perspective that you're really only in a theater.

✔ **Men in Black: Alien Attack:** Board a six-passenger cruiser, and you'll buzz the streets of New York, using laser tag-style guns to splatter 80 kinds of bug-eyed terrorists. This four-minute ride relies on 360° spins rather than speed for its thrill factor. At the ride's conclusion, a giant roach swallows you, and you must then blast your way out (getting doused with bug guts — warm water) for your efforts. Will Smith rates you as galaxy defender, atomically average, or bug bait.

Islands of Adventure

Universal's second park opened in 1999 with a vibrantly colored, cleverly themed collection of fast, fun rides wrapped in a 110-acre package. Roller coasters thunder above its pedestrian walkways, water rides careen through the center of the park, and theme restaurants are camouflaged to match their surroundings, adding to your overall immersion in the various "islands" in this adventure.This $1 billion park is divided into six areas: the *Port of Entry,* where you'll find a collection of shops and eateries, and the themed sections: *Seuss Landing, Toon Lagoon, Jurassic Park, Marvel Super Hero Island,* and *The Lost Continent.* **Islands of Adventure** has a large menu of thrill rides and coasters, plus a growing stable of play areas for younger guests.

Ten of the 12 major rides at Islands of Adventure have minimum heights (from 40 to 54 inches), so if you have very young children, you're better off at another park.

Port of Entry

Think of the Port as the park's starting line. The entire race is before you, but the creators of **Islands of Adventure** want to juice you slowly. The aesthetics in *Port of Entry* resemble a faraway marketplace that you'd find in Indiana Jones, where the park pushes stuff like junk food, souvenirs, and other completely unnecessary things while you're still suffering from ticket shock. From here, you can walk to the five other islands dotting the lagoon.

Seuss Landing

The main attractions in *Seuss Landing,* a ten-acre island, are aimed at the younger set, though anyone who loved the good Doctor as a child will enjoy some nostalgic fun on the colorful rides.

> ✔ **Caro-Seuss-El:** This not-so-ordinary carousel replaces the traditional wooden horses with seven whimsical Seussian characters (54 total mounts), including Cowfish, the elephant birds from *Horton Hatches an Egg,* and Mulligatawnies. They move up and down, as well as in and out. Pull the reins to make their eyes blink or heads bob, as you twirl through the riot of color surrounding the ride.

✔ **The Cat in the Hat:** All aboard the couch! In this case, they're six-passenger futons that steer 1,800 people an hour through 18 show scenes. Any Seuss fan will recognize the giant candy-striped hat looming over the entrance and probably many of the scenes from the chaotic journey. It's one of the signature experiences of **Islands of Adventure,** though you may find it tame.

✔ **If I Ran the Zoo:** *If I Ran the Zoo* is an interactive playland for kids who enjoy everything from flying water snakes to a chance to tickle the toes of a Seussian animal. The 19 play stations are a nice place to let your kids burn off some excited energy.

✔ **One Fish, Two Fish, Red Fish, Blue Fish:** On this attraction, your controls allow you to move your funky fish up or down 15 feet, as you spin around on an arm attached to a hub. Watch out for squirt posts, which spray unsuspecting riders who don't follow the ride's rhyme scheme (and sometimes the ones who do follow it). Riders must be 48 inches or taller to ride without an adult.

Marvel Super Hero Island

If you're a thrill junkie, you'll love the twisting, turning, stomach-churning rides on this island that's filled with building-tall murals of Marvel Super Heroes. Children can meet some of their favorite heroes in front of *The Amazing Adventures of Spider-Man.* Spidey's ride is just one of the many highlights on this island.

✔ The **Amazing Adventures of Spider-Man:** *The Amazing Adventures of Spider-Man* is a primo ride that combines moving vehicles, filmed 3-D action, and special effects themed around the original web master. The script: While you're on a yawn-able tour of the *Daily Bugle* newspaper — *yikes!* — the boys in black hats steal the Statue of Liberty. Your mission is to help Spidey get it back. Passengers wearing 3-D glasses squeal, and computer-generated objects alternately fly toward their 12-person cars, which twist, spin, plunge, and soar through this comic book universe. There's also a simulated 400-foot drop that feels an awful lot like the real thing.

✔ **Dr. Doom's Fearfall:** Look! Up in the sky! Uh-oh, it's you falling 200 feet, if you're courageous enough to climb aboard. This towering metal skeleton provides screams that you can hear far into the day and night. The plot line: You're touring a lab when something goes horribly wrong, as Doctor Doom tries to cure you of fear. You're fired to the top of the ride, with feet dangling, and dropped in intervals, leaving your stomach at several levels. The fall feels like the *Tower of Terror* at **Disney-MGM Studios,** but with the additional sensation of hanging free.

✔ **Incredible Hulk Coaster:** This ride is sure to knot your shorts and stomach, as it literally rockets from a dark tunnel into the sunlight, while accelerating from 0 to 40 mph in two seconds. Although it's only two-thirds the speed of Disney-MGM's *Rock 'n' Roller Coaster,* this ride is in broad daylight and you can *see* the asphalt! After launching, you spin upside down 128 feet from the ground, feel weightless, and careen through the center of the park over the heads of other visitors. Coaster lovers will be pleased to know that this ride, which lasts 2 minutes and 15 seconds, includes seven rollovers and two deep drops.

Toon Lagoon

More than 150 life-size, sculpted cartoon images let you know you've entered *Toon Lagoon,* which is dedicated to your favorites from the Sunday funnies.

✔ **Comic Strip Lane:** Beetle Bailey, Hagar the Horrible, and Dagwood and Blondie are just a few of the 80 characters in this comic-strip neighborhood. This attraction is fun for visuals and passive moments, but it's also a site to skip, if you're on a tight schedule.

✔ **Dudley Do-Right's Ripsaw Falls:** Although this island is pretty Popeye-happy, the heroic Dudley has a splashy flume ride that drops 75 feet at 50 mph. Your mission is to save the fair Nell from Snidely Whiplash. The boats take you around a 400,000-gallon lagoon and plunge you 15 feet below the water's surface, but this is mainly hype — the water is contained on either side of you. **Note:** You *will* get very wet, despite the contained water.

✔ **Me Ship, The Olive:** This three-story boat is a family-friendly playland with dozens of interactive activities from bow to stern. Kids can toot whistles, clang bells, or play the organ. *Sweet Pea's Playpen* is a favorite of younger guests. Kids six and up love *Cargo Crane,* where they can drench riders on Popeye & Bluto's Bilge-Rat Barges (see the next section).

✔ **Popeye & Bluto's Bilge-Rat Barges:** Here's another water special — a churning, turning, twisting, listing raft ride with the same kind of vehicle as *Kali River Rapids* at Disney's **Animal Kingdom,** but this one's faster and bouncier. You'll get wet from mechanical devices, as well as the water cannons fired by guests at *Me Ship, The Olive* (see earlier in the chapter). The 12-passenger rafts bump and dip their way along a course lined with villains, most notably Bluto and Sea Hag, and a twirling octopus boat wash.

Jurassic Park

All the basics from Steven Spielberg's wildly successful films and some of the high-tech wizardry are incorporated into this lushly landscaped tropical locale that includes a replica of the visitors center from the movie. Expect long lines at the *River Adventure* and pleasant surprises at the *Discovery Center,* both described in the following section.

✔ **Camp Jurassic:** This play area, designed along the same lines as *The Boneyard* in Disney's **Animal Kingdom,** has everything from lava pits with dinosaur bones to a rain forest. Watch out for the spitters (you'll get wet) that lurk in dark caves. The multilevel play area offers plenty of places for kids to crawl, explore, and lose a little steam. Keep a close eye on young children, because it's easy to get turned around inside the caverns.

✔ **Discovery Center:** Relax while you discover something new. The center has life-size dinosaur replicas and some interactive games, including a sequencer that lets you combine your DNA with a dinosaur's, as well as the *Beasaur* exhibit, where you can see and hear as the dinosaurs did. You can also play *You Bet Your Dinosaur* (a game show originally called *You Bet Jurassic*) and scan the walls for fossils. The highlight is watching a tiny velociraptor hatch in the lab.

✔ **Jurassic Park River Adventure:** The adventure of this attraction begins slowly, but it soon throws you into a world of stormy skies and five-story dinosaurs, including a T-Rex, the most unrelenting, fearsome bully to walk the planet. To escape, you take a heart-stopping 85-foot plunge in a flume that's steep and quick enough to leave your fingerprints embedded in the restraining bar's padded foam. Did we mention that you'll get soaked?

✔ **Pteranodon Flyers:** The 10-foot metal frames and simple seats of this high-flying ride look flimsy. The landing is bumpy and you'll swing side to side throughout. Unlike the traditional gondolas in sky rides, on *Pteranodon Flyers,* your feet hang free from the two-seat, skeletal flyer and there's little but a restraining belt between you and the ground. Now that we've scared you, this is a kiddie ride — single passengers must be between 36 and 56 inches; adults can climb aboard *only* when accompanying someone that size.

✔ **Triceratops Encounter:** Meet a "living" dinosaur and find out about the care and feeding of the 24-foot-long, 10-foot-high Triceratops from its trainers. The creature's responses to touch include realistic blinks, breathing, flinches, and leg movements. You can touch this heavyweight dino, as it turns its head and groans.

The Lost Continent

Although the millennia are mixed — ancient Greece with medieval forest — **Universal** has done a good job creating a foreboding mood in this section of the park, where the entrance is marked by menacing stone griffins.

- ✔ **Dueling Dragons:** The timer on this puppy is only set for 2½ minutes, but it comes with the usual health warnings and a scream factor of 11 on a 10-point scale. True coaster crazies love this intertwined set of leg-dangling racers that climb to 125 feet, invert five times, and on three occasions, come within 12 inches of each other as the two dragons battle, and you prove your bravery by tagging along. (Ride greeters ought to pass out diapers and a sedative.) The *Fire Dragon* can reach speeds of up to 60 mph, while the *Ice Dragon* only makes it to 55 mph.

- ✔ **The Eighth Voyage of Sindbad:** The mythical sailor is the star of a stunt demonstration that takes place in a 1,700-seat theater decorated with blue stalagmites and eerie, gloomy shipwrecks. The show includes six water explosions and 50 pyrotechnic effects including a 10-foot circle of flames. It doesn't, however, come close to the quality of the *Indiana Jones* stunt show at Disney-MGM Studios.

- ✔ **The Mystic Fountain:** This interactive "smart" fountain delights younger guests. It can see and hear, leading to a lot of kibitzing with those who stand before the stone fountain, suitably named "Rocky." If you get close enough, you may even get a surprise shower. It's a real treat for 3- to 8-year-olds.

- ✔ **Poseidon's Fury: Escape from the Lost City:** Clearly, *Poseidon's Fury* is the park's best show, although that may be a hollow compliment in a park that's decidedly weak in the show department. The Keeper, a ghostly-white character, leads you on a journey where you become trapped in a battle between the evil Poseidon, god of the sea, and Zeus, king of the gods. From a small room, you proceed through a 42-foot vortex — where 17,500 gallons of water swirl around you, barrel-style — and into the Temple of Poseidon. In the battle royale, the gods hurl 25-foot fireballs at each other. It's more interesting than frightening but still offers a thrill.

SeaWorld

Though it's a distant seventh (out of eight) in Orlando's theme-park wars, **SeaWorld** still manages to attract 4.7 million visitors a year by delivering a more relaxed pace with several animal encounters. This modern marine park focuses more on discovery than on thrill rides, though it offers its share of excitement with *Journey to Atlantis*, a steep flume-like ride, and *Kraken*, a floorless roller coaster. Park prices

Single-day admission is $48 for adults, $38 for kids 3 to 9, plus the 6 percent sales tax and $7 parking. **SeaWorld** also has teamed with **Universal** and other parks selling **FlexTickets**. A seven-day, four-park pass to **Universal Studios Florida, Islands of Adventure, Wet 'n Wild,** and SeaWorld is $159.95 for adults and $127.95 for children 3 to 9. A ten-day, five-park pass that adds **Busch Gardens** in Tampa, is $197.95 for adults and $158.95 for children 3 to 9. For more information, call ☎ 800-327-2424 or surf over to www.seaworld.com.

SeaWorld attractions

SeaWorld explores the mysteries of the deep in a format that combines wildlife-conservation awareness with laid-back fun. Close encounters with marine life are the major draw here, but you'll also find some excellent shows and thrill rides.

✔ **Clyde & Seamore Take Pirate Island:** A lovable sea lion-and-otter duet, with a supporting cast of walruses and harbor seals, stars in this fish-breathed comedy that comes with a swashbuckling conservation theme. The show is corny, but it's a refreshing break from all the high-tech rides and shows at the other theme parks.

✔ **Intensity Games Water Ski Show:** It's hard to top this show, a crowd-pleaser for more than 15 years. The hyper-competition stars some of the most skilled athletes on water. The 20-person team includes world-class skiers, wake-boarders, and stunt men and women from across the United States performing non-stop aquabatics.

✔ **Journey to Atlantis:** Taking a cue from Disney's imagineers, SeaWorld has come up with a flume ride that carries the customary surgeon-general's warning about heart problems, neck or back ailments, pregnancy, seizures, dizziness, and claustrophobia. The story line of this attraction involves a battle of good versus evil, but what really matters is the *drop* — a wild plunge from 60 feet with luge-like curves and a shorter drop thrown in for good measure.

✔ **Key West at SeaWorld:** It's not quite the way Hemingway saw it, but this five-acre sliver of paved paradise is a tree- and flower-lined Caribbean village that offers island food, street vendors, and entertainers. It has three animal habitats: *Stingray Lagoon,* where you get a hands-on encounter with harmless southern diamond and cownose rays; *Dolphin Cove,* a habitat for bottlenose dolphins set up for visitor interaction; and *Sea Turtle Point,* home to endangered and threatened species. Shortly after this area opened, the dolphins made a game of teasing visitors by swimming just out of arm's reach. But they soon discovered there are advantages to human interaction — namely smelt.

Speaking of smelt, you get a half dozen of them (to feed the dolphins) for $3, or two trays for $5, and it's real easy to be melted by the dolphins' begging.

✔ **Key West Dolphin Fest:** At the partially covered, open-air Whale and Dolphin Stadium, Atlantic bottlenose dolphins perform flips and high jumps, swim at high speeds, twirl, do the backstroke, and give rides to trainers. Some false killer whales, or Pseudocra crassidens, also make an appearance to the accompaniment of calypso music. The tricks are impressive, but if you've seen a traditional tourist-park dolphin show, you already know the plot.

✔ **Kraken:** SeaWorld's deepest venture into thrill rides, *Kraken* is named for a massive, mythological, underwater beast kept caged by Poseidon. This twenty-first-century version involves floorless, open-sided 32-passenger trains that plant you on a pedestal high above the track. When the monster breaks loose, you climb 151 feet, fall 144 feet, reach 65 mph, go underground three times (spraying bystanders with water — or worse if you're weak of stomach), and make seven loops over a 4,177-foot course. It may be the longest 3 minutes, 39 seconds of your life.

✔ **Manatees: The Last Generation?** This exhibit is as close as most people get to the endangered West Indian manatees. Underwater viewing stations, innovative cinema techniques, and interactive displays combine for a tribute to these gentle marine mammals.

✔ **Penguin Encounter:** The *Penguin Encounter* transports you, via a moving sidewalk, through Tuxedoville. The stars of the show are on the other side of a Plexiglas shield. You get a glimpse of them as they preen, socialize, and swim at bullet speeds in a 22-degree habitat. You can also see puffins and murres in a similar, but separate, area.

✔ **The Shamu Adventure:** Everyone comes to SeaWorld to see the big guy, and he and his friends don't disappoint. This featured event is a well-choreographed show, planned and carried out by very good trainers and very smart Orcas. The whales really dive into their work! The fun builds until the video monitor flashes an urgent "Weather Watch" and one of the trainers utters the warning: "Uh-oh!" Hurricane Shamu is about to make landfall. At this point, many folks remember the splash-area warnings, posted throughout the grandstand. Those who didn't pay attention when they arrived get one last chance to flee. The Orcas then race around the edge of the pool, creating huge waves of icy water that profoundly soak everything in range.

✔ **Shamu's Happy Harbor:** This three-acre play area has a four-story net tower with a 35-foot crow's-nest lookout, water cannons, remote-controlled vehicles, and a water maze. It's one of the most extensive play areas at any park and a great place for kids to unwind. Bring extra clothes for the tots (or for yourself) because the Harbor isn't designed to keep you dry.

✔ **Terrors of the Deep:** This attraction, formerly called *Shark Encounter,* was improved by the addition of some 220 species. Pools out front have small sharks and rays (feeding isn't allowed). The interior aquariums have big eels, beautiful lionfish, hauntingly still barracudas, and the fat, bug-eyed pufferfish.

This tour isn't for the claustrophobic: You walk through a Plexiglas tube beneath hundreds of millions of gallons of water. Also, small children may find the swimming sharks a little too much to handle.

✔ **Trainer for a Day:** Expect to invest a sizable chunk of your day and budget in this 7½-hour program (7 a.m. to 2:30 p.m.). You and one other person work side by side with a trainer, preparing meals and feeding the animals, finding out basic training techniques, and sharing lunch. It costs $349 and is limited to two people per day, so make reservations very early. You must be 13 or older, at least 52 inches tall, able to climb, and able to lift and carry 15 pounds of vittles. Call ☎ **407-370-1382** for more information.

✔ **Wild Arctic:** *Wild Arctic* combines a high-definition adventure film with flight-simulator technology to evoke breathtaking Arctic panoramas. After a hazardous flight over the frozen north, visitors emerge at a remote research base, home to four polar bears (including star residents and polar twins Klondike and Snow), seals, walruses, and white beluga whales. Kids may find the bumpy ride a little much, but there's a separate line for those who want to skip the thrill-ride section.

More SeaWorld fun

Other SeaWorld attractions include *Pacific Point Preserve,* a 2½-acre natural setting that duplicates the rocky northern Pacific Coast home of California sea lions and harbor seals (more smelt opportunities here), and *Tropical Rain Forest,* a bamboo and banyan-tree habitat that's home to cockatoos and other birds.

Hawaiian Rhythms is a dance troupe that entertains in an outdoor facility at Hawaiian Village (if you care to join, grass skirts and leis are available). The 5½-acre acre *Anheuser-Busch Hospitality Center* offers free samples of Anheuser-Busch beers. Next door, stroll through the stables and you may catch a glimpse of the famous Budweiser Clydesdale horses being groomed.

Discovery Cove

SeaWorld's second theme park is a $100-million number that cost one-tenth the sticker price of **Islands of Adventure,** but has an admission price that is four times higher. **Discovery Cove** has two admissions options: $199 per person, plus 6 percent sales tax, regardless of age, if you want to swim with the dolphins, or $99 if you can skip that luxury. Discovery Cove is an all-inclusive park that provides plenty of elbow-room — there's a limit of 1,000 guests per day. The all-inclusive nature of the park means that ticket prices include just about everything you'll need, from lunch to your towel and locker to swimming/snorkeling gear and your activities. Activities include

- ✔ Swimming near (but on the other side of Plexiglas from) black-tip sharks and barracudas.

- ✔ Snorkeling around a 1.3-million-gallon tank containing a coral reef with brightly colored tropical fish and another tank with gentle rays.

- ✔ Touching and feeding 300 exotic birds in the 100-foot-long aviary hidden under a waterfall.

- ✔ Cooling off under foaming waterfalls.

- ✔ Soaking up the sun on the beaches.

- ✔ Enjoying the soothing waters of the park's pools and rivers (freshwater and saltwater).

- ✔ Encountering dolphins for 30 minutes, under the supervision of a trainer, if you choose the dolphin experience. Guests must be 6 or older, though we recommend that children be at least 8, to avoid scares from things that go bump on and under the water.

- ✔ Visiting **SeaWorld** with seven days of unlimited admission.

To get to Discovery Cove, follow these directions to SeaWorld: If you're driving south from Orlando, take Exit 28 off I-4 and follow the signs. If you're heading northeast from Tampa, use exit 27A.

For up-to-the-minute information on this park, call ☎ **877-434-7268** or go to www.discoverycove.com on the Web. If visiting this extravagant park sounds like your cup of tea, we recommend making a reservation far in advance, just in case many other travelers choose to do the same.

Chapter 20

Exploring the Rest of Orlando

. . . .

In This Chapter

▶ Driving a racecar: An adults-only thrill

▶ White-water rafting: More than a spectator sport

▶ Shopping for everything from trinkets to rarities

▶ Living it up after the sun goes down in Orlando

▶ Getting out of town: Cypress Gardens

. . . .

*I*n addition to the five major theme parks, a ton of other attractions will help you get a break from the forced-march feeling that you can get from visiting the A-Team. These are places that you can visit in 2 to 6 hours without taking out a second mortgage to get inside. Considering Disney's corner on the Orlando market, it shouldn't come as a surprise that many of the most popular smaller attractions in town fall under the Disney umbrella. If, however, you prefer to leave Walt's wonderland for something a little more peaceful, intellectual, or cultural, numerous attractions that are far from Mickey-Mouse operations await you.

Seeing the Top Smaller Attractions

We start with the Disney also-rans and then get into some of the other things that you can do in less than a day (and for less than $50 a head) in and around O Town.

The never-ending world of Disney

Destination Disney never seems to run out of things to do. It's really a well-planned plot. (See an overview of "Other Disney Attractions" later in this chapter.) Eisner and company know that if they can entice you to stay on property and throw enough attractions at you, they get all your dough, instead of having to share it with others.

To the tune of "When You Wish Upon A Star," we offer the next level.

Other Disney Attractions

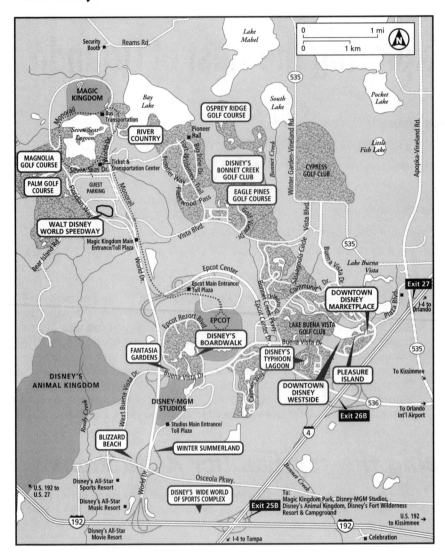

 ## *Blizzard Beach*

Near Disney-MGM Studios

The newest of Disney's water parks is a 66-acre "ski resort" situated in the midst of a tropical lagoon. Major attractions include *Cross Country Creek,* a 2,900-foot tube ride around the park; *Ski-Patrol Training Camp,* a preteen area with a rope swing and slides; *Meltaway Bay,* a 1-acre, relatively calm wave pool; and *Steamboat Springs,* Walt Disney World's longest white-water raft ride (1,200 feet of rushing waterfalls).

But the headliner here is *Summit Plummet.* Read every speed, motion, vertical-dip, wedgie, and hold-onto-your-breastplate warning and then test your bravado in a bullring, a space shuttle, or any other of your death-defying hobbies, as a warm-up. This puppy starts pretty slow, with a lift ride (even in Florida's 100-degree dog days) to the 120-foot summit, where you board the world's fastest body slide. You can easily spend the day in this park.

On World Dr. ☎ 407-560-3400. To get there: Located just north of the All-Star Sports and Music resorts. Admission: $30 adults, $24 kids 3–9. Open: 10 a.m–5 p.m. daily, extended to 9 a.m.–8 p.m. during peak times, such as summer.

DisneyQuest

Downtown Disney West Side

Meet the world's most interactive video arcade, with everything from old-fashioned pinball with a new-fangled twist to virtual rides. Here are some of the best virtual rides.

- *Aladdin's Magic Carpet Ride* puts you astride a motorcycle-like seat while you fly through the 3-D Cave of Wonders.

- *Hercules in the Underworld,* one of the best interactive games, is based on the Disney film *Hercules.* You and three others assume the roles of Herc, Mel, Pegasus, and Phil, the cute little round guy who seems to be from the same family as Pan. You race through a time-and-space continuum, gathering lightning bolts and dodging obstacles (including Hades) in the underworld. Fail and you crash and burn — for eternity.

- *Invasion: An Extraterrestrial Alien Encounter* has the same kind of theme and intensity as the Hercules game. Your mission is to save colonists from intergalactic bad guys. One player flies the module, while others fire an array of weapons. (We're contractually bound to tell you that the Starship Tunstall crashed and burned five times.)

- *Mighty Ducks Pinball Slam* is an interactive, life-size game in which the players ride platforms and use body language to score points.

- *The Create Zone* is for those with an inventive mind. Bill Nye the Science-Turned-Roller-Coaster Guy helps you create the ultimate loop-and-dipster, which you then can ride in a simulator. Bring your own motion-sickness medicine.

- *Animation Academy* provides some quiet time for those who need it, by way of a mini-course in Disney cartooning. There are also snack and food areas. A typical theme-park meal and drink at the food areas runs about $12 per person. There's no specific children's menu, but the servings are plentiful and can easily be enough for two. **Note:** Crowds are heaviest after dark.

Off of Buena Vista Dr. ☎ 407-828-4600. To get there: Located adjacent to Pleasure Island and Downtown Disney. Admission: $29 adults, $23 kids 3–9 for unlimited play. Open: 10:30 a.m.–midnight daily.

Disney's Wide World of Sports

South of Disney-MGM Studios

This 200-acre complex has several baseball and softball fields, six basketball courts, 12 lighted tennis courts, a golf driving range, and six sand volleyball courts. *NFL Experience* is one of the most popular attractions. Ten drills test your running, punting, passing, and receiving skills. You can dodge cardboard defenders and run a pass pattern, while a machine shoots you a pass. Depending on your stamina, interest, and the size of the crowds, the experience lasts 45 minutes to several hours.

South Victory Way, just north of U.S. 192. ☎ 407-939-1500. Internet: http:// disney.go.com/disneyworld/index2.html. *To get there: Take Exit 25/U.S. 192 West off of I-4 to World Drive. Make a right on to the Osceola Parkway, then another right at Victory Way. Admission: Prices vary by venue; NFL Experience $9 adults, $7 kids 3–9. Open: Daily, but hours vary by venue.*

Richard Petty Driving Experience

Walt Disney World Speedway

This is your chance to race as the pros race, in a 600-horsepower NASCAR Winston-Cup racecar. How real is it? You must sign a two-page waiver with words like "DANGEROUS," "CALCULATED RISK," and "UPDATE YOUR WILL!" before getting into a car. At one end of the spectrum, you can ride shotgun for a couple of laps at 145 mph. At the other end, you can spend 3 hours to 2 days finding out how to drive the car yourself and racing other daredevils for 8 to 30 laps of excitement (for a cool $350 to $1,200). You must be 18 years old to ride in the car.

Located on World Drive at Vista Boulevard just off U.S. 192. ☎ 800-237-3889. To get there: Take I-4 to exit 26-B/Epcot Center Drive and head west to World Drive. Make a right on to the Osceola Parkway and follow it 5 miles to the speedway. Admission: Adults only, $90–$1,200, varies by seasons and hours, so call ahead.

River Country

Near Magic Kingdom

One of the many recreational facilities at the Fort Wilderness Resort campground, this water park is fashioned after Tom Sawyer's swimming hole. Kids can scramble over boulders that double as diving platforms for a 330,000-gallon pool. This is a good half-day experience.

On Big Pond Dr. ☎ 407-824-4321. To get there: Located east of Magic Kingdom. Admission: $15.95 adults, $12.50 kids 3–9. Open: 10 a.m.–5 p.m. daily, and sometimes 10 a.m.–7 p.m.

Typhoon Lagoon

Near Downtown Disney

The fantasy setting for this water park is a storm-ravaged tropical island strewn with tin-roofed structures, surfboards, and other wreckage left by a "great typhoon." Headline attractions include *Castaway Creek,* a 2,100-foot raft and tube venue; *Ketchakiddie Creek,* an area just for the under 4-foot set; *Shark Reef,* where you can snorkel with the fish that live on a simulated coral reef; *Typhoon Lagoon,* the signature wave pool that offers waves every 90 seconds; and *Humunga Kowabunga,* a snaking water slide area. You can spend all day here.

☎ *407-560-4141. To get there: Located west of Downtown Disney and south of Lake Buena Vista Dr., between the Disney Village Marketplace and Disney-MGM Studios. Admission: $30 adults, $24 kids 3–9. Open: 10 a.m.–5 p.m. daily, extended to 9 a.m.–8 p.m. during peak periods.*

Beyond Disney

Believe it or not, some folks escape the theme parks *and* Disney. (Skip ahead to see the "Yet More Attractions in Orlando" map.) Here are a few of the options.

Florida Splendid China

Kissimmee

Ancient mysteries are the theme of this 76-acre attraction, which has more than 60 miniature replicas of China's most notable wonders. These attractions include a half-mile replica of the 4,200-mile Great Wall, the Forbidden City's Imperial Palace, Tibet's Potala Palace, the Leshan Buddha originally carved into a mountainside, and the Mongolian mausoleum of Genghis Khan. Live shows (acrobats, martial artists, storytellers, dancers, puppeteers, and The Magical Tiger performers) take place throughout the day. The Mysterious Kingdom of the Orient is a 90-minute dance/acrobatic show performed nightly, except on Monday, in the Golden Peacock Theater.

3000 Splendid China Blvd., off West Irlo Bronson Memorial Hwy./U.S. 192 between Entry Point Blvd. and Black Lake Rd. ☎ *800-244-6226 or 407-396-7111. Internet:* www.floridasplendidchina.com. *To get there: (From I-4 take Exit 25A, stay to your left and follow U.S. 192 west; turn left at the Splendid China dragons.) Parking: Free. Admission: $27.25 adults, $17.25 kids 5–12. Open: Daily 9:30 a.m.; closing time varies seasonally.*

Flying Tigers Warbird Restoration Museum

Kissimmee

Tom Reilly, the founder and owner of this museum, restores vintage warplanes from World War II through Vietnam. His guided tours go through hands-on exhibits and a lab where his restorers perform magic before your eyes. The outdoor showroom includes a B-25 Mitchell, a P-51 Mustang, a B-17, P-38 Lightnings, and three dozen others. Allow 2 to 4 hours to see the museum.

231 N. Hoagland Blvd., south of U.S. 192. ☎ *407-933-1942. Internet:* www. warbirdmuseum.com. *To get there: Take U.S. 192 east of Disney to Kissimmee, turn right on Hoagland Blvd.) Parking: Free. Admission: $8 adults, $6 children 6–12 and seniors 60 and over. Open: 9 a.m.–5 p.m. daily.*

Gatorland

South Orlando

Founded in 1949 with a handful of alligators living in huts and pens, Gatorland, today, is a throwback park that features thousands of alligators and crocodiles on 70 acres. Breeding pens, nurseries, and rearing ponds are scattered throughout the park, which also displays monkeys, snakes, birds, Florida turtles, and a Galápagos tortoise. There are three shows daily: *Gator Wrestlin',* which is more of an environmental awareness program; the *Gator Jumparoo,* in which one of the big reptiles lunges 4 or 5 feet out of the water to snatch a long-dead chicken from a trainer's hand; and *Snakes of Florida.* Allow about 4 to 6 hours to see all the exhibits.

14501 S. Orange Blossom Trail/U.S. 441, between Osceola Pkwy. and Hunter's Creek Blvd. ☎ *800-393-5297 or 407-855-5496. Internet:* www.gatorland.com. *To get there: From I-4, take Exit 26A to U.S. 417 north, and then Exit 11 to U.S. 441 south. Gatorland is 1 one mile on the left. Parking: Free. Admission: $17.95 adults, $7.95 kids 3–12, including tax. Open: 9 a.m.–6 p.m. daily, closing time varies by season.*

Orlando Science Center

North of Orlando

This four-story center has 10 halls that allow visitors to explore everything from the swamps of Florida to the arid plains of Mars. The *Dr. Phillips* CineDome is a 310-seat theater that uses the latest technology to present large-format films, as well as planetarium and laser shows. In *KidsTown,* little folks wander in a miniature version of the world around them. One section has a pint-sized community that includes a construction site, park, and wellness center. *Science City,* located nearby, has a power plant, suspension bridge, and the *Inventor's Workshop,* a garage-like station for creative play. Children stopping by at *123 Math Avenue* work on puzzles and play with math-based toys that teach as they entertain. Plan to spend 3 to 4 hours.

777 E. Princeton St., between Orange Ave. and Mills Ave. in Loch Haven Park. ☎ *888-672-4386 or 407-514-2000 or 888-672-4386. Internet:* www.osc.org. *To get there: Take I-4 east to Princeton St. and cross Orange Ave. Parking: Free. Admission: $9.50 adults, $6.75 kids 3–11; additional charges for the CineDome and planetarium. Open: 9 a.m.–5 p.m. Tues–Thurs, 9 a.m.–9 p.m. Fri–Sat.*

Yet More Attractions in Orlando

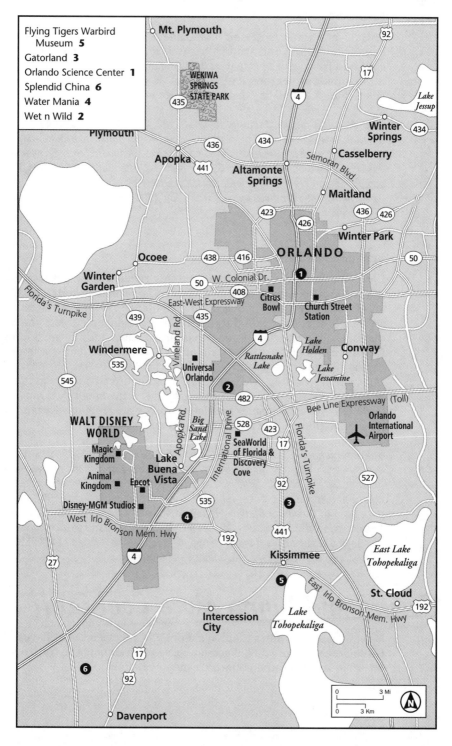

Flying Tigers Warbird Museum **5**
Gatorland **3**
Orlando Science Center **1**
Splendid China **6**
Water Mania **4**
Wet n Wild **2**

Water Mania

Kissimmee

This 36-acre water park isn't on a Disney scale, but it offers a variety of aquatic thrill rides and attractions. You can boogie board or body surf in continuous wave pools, float lazily along an 850-foot river, enjoy a white-water tubing adventure, and plummet down spiraling water slides and steep flumes. A half day makes for a nice stay.

6073 W. Irlo Bronson Memorial Hwy/U.S. 192. ☎ *800-527-3092 or 407-396-2626. Internet:* www.watermania-florida.com. *To get there: Take Exit 25-B/U.S. 192 off of I-4; go west for 2 miles; turn left on Old Lake Wilson Rd./ Hwy. 545; the park is one mile ahead on left. Parking: $5 Admission: $25.95 adults, $18.95 kids 3–9 and seniors 55 and older; half-price admission after 4 p.m. in summer. Open: 11 a.m.– 5 p.m. daily, Oct–Feb; 10:30 a.m.–5:30 p.m. daily, Mar–Sept.*

Wet 'n Wild

International Drive

Here's a 25-acre water park that not only rivals **Disney** but also is part of the **FlexTicket** package that includes **Universal Orlando, SeaWorld,** and **Busch Gardens.** Among the highlights: *Fuji Flyer,* a six-story, four-passenger toboggan ride through 450 feet of banked curves; *The Surge,* one of the longest, fastest multipassenger tube rides in the Southeast (580 feet of banked curves); *Bomb Bay,* where you enter a bomblike casing 76 feet in the air for a speedy vertical flight straight down; *Black Hole,* where you step into a spaceship and board a two-person raft for a 30-second, 500-foot, twisting, turning, space-themed reentry through total darkness; *Raging Rapids,* a simulated white-water tubing adventure with a waterfall plunge; and *Lazy River,* a leisurely float trip.

6200 International Dr., at Universal Blvd. ☎ *800-992-9453 or 407-351-9453. Internet:* www.wetnwild.com. *To get there: Take I-4 east to Exit 30A and follow the signs. Parking: Cars $5, RVs $6. Admission: $30 adults, $24 kids 3–9, $14.48 seniors 55 and older. Tube, towel, and locker rental $9, plus $4 refundable deposit. A 7-day, four-park pass to Universal Studios Florida, Islands of Adventure, Wet 'n Wild, and SeaWorld is $159.95 for adults, $127.95 for kids 3–9. A 10-day, five-park pass, which also includes Busch Gardens in Tampa, is $196.95 for adults and $157.95 for kids. Open: Daily, but hours vary seasonally, call before you go.*

Seeing and Doing More Cool Stuff

Now, we get into things that have more of a special interest flavor. (And, here's where you'll discover we were stretching the truth a wee bit when we suggested you were escaping Disney.)

✔ **Baseball:** The **Atlanta Braves** (☎ 407-939-1500) train at Disney's Wide World of Sports complex (see earlier in this chapter), and if you're a true fan, you know to book in advance. Players begin arriving in mid-February and the Braves play 18 or so games during a 1-month season that begins in early March. Tickets cost $8.50 and $15.50, and can be ordered by calling ☎ 407-828-3267. Walt Disney World, On Victory Way, just north of U.S. 192 (west of I-4).

✔ **Golf:** The Magic Mickey operates five 18-hole, par-72 golf courses and one 9-hole, par-36 walking course. All are open to the public and include pro shops, equipment rentals, and instruction. Rates range from $100 to $125 per 18-hole round for resort guests; the fee is $5 more if you're not staying at a Walt Disney World property. For tee times and information, call ☎ 407-824-2270 up to 7 days in advance (up to 30 days in advance for Disney-resort and official-property guests). Call ☎ 407-934-7639 for information about golf packages.

Additionally, you can get information about other courses on the Internet at www.golf.com and www.floridagolfing.com. If you prefer to call, request course information from the **Florida Sports Foundation** (☎ 850-488-8347) or **Florida Golfing** (☎ 877-222-4653). Popular courses include Cypress Creek, 5353 Vineland Road, Orlando (☎ 407-351-2187; under $25 summer, $40 to $65 winter), which has forgiving fairways but lots of bunkers, and Eastwood Golf Club, 13950 Golfway Boulevard, Orlando (☎ 407-281-4653; under $25 summer, $40 to $65 winter), which blends wildlife habitat with a lot of water.

✔ **Mini Golf:** Normally, we wouldn't list this category, but Diz makes it something special. Both **Winter Summerland,** off Buena Vista Drive, north of Osceola Parkway (☎ 407-939-7639; $9.25 adults, $7.50 kids 3 to 9), and **Fantasia Gardens,** Buena Vista, east of World Drive (☎ 407-560-8760; $9.25 adults, $7.50 kids 3 to 9) have two 18-hole, ton-of-fun courses.

Shopping

In addition to the following listings, Church Street Station (skip ahead to see more under "Universal after dark") has a number of specialty shops, restaurants, and clubs.

Orlando's best shopping areas

Orlando doesn't have a central shopping district or districts. Instead, it has tourist areas that are best avoided, unless you want cheap goods at high prices, as well as neighborhood retail locations, such as malls, where locals shop. The following is a list of some of the more frequented shopping zones.

- **Celebration:** Think *Pleasantville* with a Mickey touch. This Disney-created town of 20,000 is more of a diversion than a shopper's paradise. The downtown area has a dozen shops, a couple of art galleries, and four restaurants. The shops offer some interesting buys, but the real plus is the atmosphere. To get to Celebration from Walt Disney World, take U.S. 192 east 5 miles, past Interstate 4. The entrance to Celebration is on the right. Call ☎ 407-566-2200 for more information.

- **Downtown Disney Marketplace:** This Size XXXL shopping hub on Buena Vista Lagoon is a colorful place to browse, people-watch, have lunch, and maybe buy a trinket. Stores include the *Lego Imagination Center,* where kids can play in a free Lego-building area while their parents browse; *EUROSPAIN,* which sells products that crystal and metal artists make before your eyes; and *World of Disney,* a store that claims that, if it exists and it's Disney, it's on their shelves. Call ☎ 407-828-3800 for more information on Downtown Disney Marketplace.

- **Downtown Disney West Side:** This shopping venue on Buena Vista Drive has many specialty stores where you can find unique gifts and souvenirs. *All Star Gear* offers a wide array of apparel and accessories; *Guitar Gallery* tempts string-strokers and wannabes with custom jobs and rare collectibles; and *Sosa Family Cigars* beckons with sweet smells, as well as a tradition reaching back to yesterday's Cuba. The *Virgin* (as in records) *Megastore* is a movie, music, and multimedia gold mine that also has a cafe and occasional live (rather than dead) performances. Call ☎ 407-828-3800 for more information on Downtown Disney West Side.

- **Kissimmee:** Southeast of the Disney parks, Kissimmee straddles U.S. 192/Irlo Bronson Memorial Highway — a sometimes-tacky strip lined with budget motels, smaller attractions, and every fast-food restaurant known to man. Kissimmee's shopping merit is negligible, unless you're looking for a cheap T-shirt or a white elephant gift. (Seashells, anyone?)

- **International Drive:** This tourist magnet extends 7 to 10 miles north of the Disney parks between Florida 535 and the Florida Turnpike. The southern end has a little elbowroom, but the northern part is a tourist strip crowded with small-time attractions (there's bungee jumping for those who have a death wish), fast fooderies, and souvenir shacks. There are two main shopping draws: *Pointe Orlando* and *The Mercado* (☎ 407-345-9337), which has restaurants, music, and shops (Conch Republic, Designer Gear, Classic Characters) in a complex designed like a Mediterranean village.

✔ **Winter Park:** Just north of downtown Orlando, Winter Park began as a haven for Yankees escaping from the cold. Today, Winter Park's centerpiece is Park Avenue, a collection of upscale shops and restaurants along a cobblestone street. Ann Taylor and Banana Republic are among the dozens of specialty shops. Park Avenue also has some art galleries. For more information on Winter Park, call ☎ **407-644-8281,** or head over to `www.winterpark.org` on the Web.

Searching for shopping hot spots

Orlando has the usual collection of outlets and malls. Except for Disney, Universal, and SeaWorld souvenirs, though, it doesn't have any products to call its own.

Factory outlets

In the last decade, the tourist areas in Orlando have bloomed with places where shoppers can find some name-brand bargains — maybe. To borrow advice from a popular rhyme: Things aren't always what they seem. The smartest outlet shoppers know suggested-retail prices before going to outlet stores. Therefore, they know what is — and *isn't* — a bargain.

✔ **Belz Factory Outlet World,** 5401 W. Oak Ridge Rd., at the north end of International Dr. (☎ **407-354-0126;** Internet: `www.belz.com`), is the granddaddy of all Orlando outlets. It has more than 60 shops that, alone, sell clothing (London Fog, Jonathan Logan, Guess Jeans, Aileen, Danskin, Jordache, Leslie Fay, Carole Little, Harvé Benard, Calvin Klein, and Anne Klein, for example). You can also buy books, toys, electronics, sporting goods, jewelry, and so on.

Don't kill yourself trying to get to every building.

✔ **Orlando Premium Outlets,** 8200 Vineland Ave., just off the southern third of I-Drive (☎ **407-239-6101;** Internet: `www.PremiumOutlets.com`), opened in July 2000. This 440,000-square-foot center houses 110 upscale stores, including Bottega Veneta, Coach, Cole-Haan, Donna Karan, Kenneth Cole, Nike, Polo/Ralph Lauren, Tahari, Theory, Timberland, and Tommy Hilfiger.

Malls

There are several traditional shopping malls in the Orlando area. Like tenants in malls everywhere, these merchants pay a hefty rent, so good buys are elusive. Arguably, a mall's best bargain is people watching, which is free.

✔ **Florida Mall:** Fresh off a $70-million expansion, this mall's anchors include Dillard's, Saks, Burdines, JCPenney, Sears, an Adam's Mark Hotel, and more than 200 specialty stores, restaurants, and entertainment venues. You can find the Florida Mall at 8001 S. Orange

Blossom Trail at Sand Lake Road, 4 miles east of International Drive. Call ☎ **407-851-7234** for details.

✔ **Pointe Orlando:** Although it's set up like a mall, this complex's two levels of stores, restaurants, and a 21-screen IMAX theater aren't under one roof. Headliners among the 80 shops include Banana Republic, Foot Locker, and a 33,000-square-foot FAO Schwarz, whose exterior is adorned with a three-story Raggedy Ann. Pointe Orlando is located at 9101 International Drive, and the phone number is ☎ **407-248-2838.**

Enjoying the Nightlife

If you have the energy to go out after a day in the theme parks, Orlando has plenty for you to do when the sun goes down.

Disney after dark

After Church Street Station (skip ahead for more on this) proved that many visitors possessed enough energy to party all night after a day in the parks, the Disney folks — never the type to pass up a new opportunity to rake in some bucks — promptly built several haunts where night owls could dance, drink, and play to their hearts content. In general, Disney's venues are far more family friendly than Orlando's other evening entertainment zones, but keep in mind that distinction is relative; even some of Disney's clubs lock out the under-21 crowd.

Pleasure Island

This six-acre, sometimes gated, entertainment district is the home of several nightspots. Admission to the island is free from 10 a.m. to 7 p.m. Admission is $21, including tax, after 7 p.m., when the clubs open. The Pleasure Island admission is included if you have a Park Hopper Ticket (see Chapter 19 for information on Disney admission passes). Self-parking is free. For information on **Pleasure Island,** call ☎ **407-934-7781,** or check out Disney's Web site at http://disney.go.com/DisneyWorld/intro.html.

Mannequins Dance Palace, a high-energy club with a big, rotating dance floor, is the main event on Pleasure Island. Being a local favorite makes it hard to get into, so arrive early, especially on weekends. Three levels of bars and mixing space are adorned with elaborately dressed mannequins. The DJ plays contemporary tunes loud enough to wake the dead. You must be 21 to enter.

The *Adventurers Club* is a club that almost defies description — it needs to be experienced. According to Walt Disney World legend, it was designed to be the library and archaeological trophy room for Pleasure Island founder and explorer, Merriweather Adam Pleasure. Pleasure's zany band of globetrotting friends and servants, played by skilled actors, interact with guests, while staying in character. Improvisational comedy and cabaret shows are performed in the library. You can easily hang out here all night.

If you're a fan of the BET Cable Network, you'll probably love *BET Soundstage* (☎ 407-934-7666), which offers traditional R&B and the rhyme of hip-hop. You can dance on an expansive floor or kick back on an outdoor terrace. Cover charge for the *Soundstage* is included in the Pleasure Island pass, except for major concerts.

A very talented troupe, the Who, What and Warehouse Players, are the main event at the *Comedy Warehouse.* The group performs 45-minute improvisational shows based on audience suggestions. They do five shows a night.

Disco and polyester rule at *8Trax,* a 1970s-style club where 50 TV screens air diverse shows and videos over the dance floor. A DJ plays everything from "YMCA" to "The Hustle."

The Wildhorse Saloon attracts country connoisseurs with some of the millennium's best boot-scootin' music. If you don't know how to scoot, the Wildhorse Dancers can show you the moves before you hit the 1,500-square-foot dance floor. The cover charge is included in Pleasure Island admission, except on nights of big concerts. Call ☎ 407-934-7781 to find out if anyone is performing while you're in town.

Disney's West Side

Immediately adjacent to **Pleasure Island, Disney West Side** is a slightly newer district, where you'll find clubs, restaurants, and *DisneyQuest* (see earlier in this chapter).

Singer Gloria Estefan and her husband, Emilio, created *Bongo's Cuban Café* (☎ 407-828-0999; Internet: www.bongoscubancafe.com), which serves up loud salsa music and second-rate Cuban fare. Come for the atmosphere, rather than the food (which will run you about $10 to $26). The *Café* is open daily from 11 a.m. to 2 a.m. and doesn't take reservations. You can also find plenty of free self-parking.

Cirque du Soleil doesn't have any lions, tigers, or bears; but you won't feel cheated. This Circus of the Sun is nonstop energy. Its 64 performers deliver nonstop energy on trampolines, the trapeze, and a high wire, in a five-star show called *La Nouba.* Tickets for the 90-minute show cost $62 for adults and $38 for kids 3 to 9, yet there's rarely an empty seat in the 1,671-seat arena. Show times are at 6 and 9 p.m., Wednesday through Saturday; 3 and 6 p.m. on Sundays. For information, call ☎ 407-939-7600, or go visit its Web site at www.cirquedusoleil.com.

The walls and rafters in the *House of Blues* (☎ 407-934-2583) literally shake with rhythm and blues. The *House* is decorated with colorful folk art and serves up some spicy cuisine. The *House of Blues* is open daily 11 to 2 a.m. and offers free self-parking.

Disney's Boardwalk

The *Boardwalk* is a great place for a quiet stroll or more. Street performers sing, dance, juggle, and make a little magic most evenings. *Atlantic Dance* (☎ 407-539-5100) offers retro-swing and contemporary Latin music ($3 cover charge). The rustic, saloon-style *Jellyrolls* (☎ 407-939-3463) offers dueling pianos (no cover). If you need a game fix, *ESPN Sports* (☎ 407-939-3463; Internet: www.disneyworld.com) has 71 TV screens, a full-service bar, food, and a small arcade, all without a cover charge.

Universal after dark

Universal's answer to **Disney's** nightspots is a two-level collection of clubs and restaurants located between its two theme parks. **CityWalk** (☎ 407-363-8000; Internet: www.uescape.com/citywalk/) is open 11 to 2 a.m. daily. There's no admission, but several clubs have cover charges after 5 or 6 p.m., and some aren't open earlier than that. If you're only planning to see a few clubs, it's cheaper to pay individually. Club hoppers are better off buying the *CityWalk Party Pass,* which for $18, including tax, allows entry to all the clubs. Call ☎ 800-711-0080 for information on the pass. Parking costs $6 in the Universal garage.

Bob Marley — A Tribute to Freedom (☎ 407-224-2262) has architecture said to replicate Marley's home in Kingston. Local and national reggae bands perform. Light Jamaican fare is served under umbrellas. Hours are 5 p.m. to 2 a.m., Monday through Friday, and 11 to 2 a.m. on Saturday and Sunday. There's a cover of $4.25 after 8 p.m.; cover prices increase when there are special concerts.

The collection of memorabilia at the *Downbeat Jazz Hall of Fame* ranges from Buddy Rich to Ella Fitzgerald items. The adjoining *Thelonious Monk Institute of Jazz* is a performance venue that's also the site of workshops. Nationally acclaimed acts perform frequently. *The Institute of Jazz* is open 7:30 p.m. to 2 a.m.

the groove (☎ 407-363-8000) is CityWalk's answer to Pleasure Island's *Mannequins,* though it's not as crowded. The sound system is guaranteed to blow your hair back, and the dance floor is in a room gleaming with chrome. Music-wise, *the groove* features hip-hop, jazz fusion, techno, and alternative music. A DJ plays tunes on nights when recording artists aren't booked. You must be at least 21 to enter, and it will cost you a cover charge of $5.25 for the privilege. The club is open from 9 p.m. to 2 a.m.

CityWalk's *Hard Rock Cafe* (☎ **407-351-5483**) is the largest in the world, and the adjoining *Hard Rock Live* is the first concert hall bearing the name. There's also a free exhibit area in the cafe, where you can browse through displays of rock memorabilia, including the platform heels, leather jumpsuits, and tongue actions of KISS. Cover charge varies by act. It is open daily 11 a.m. to 2 a.m.

Canned music is piped through *Jimmy Buffett's Margaritaville* (☎ **407-224-2155**), with a Jimmy sound-alike strumming on the back porch. Bar-wise, you have three options. *The Volcano* erupts (we're not kidding) margaritas; the *Land Shark* has fins swimming around the ceiling; and the *12 Volt*, is, well, a little electrifying. *Margaritaville* is open from 11 to 2 a.m., and there's a $3.25 cover after 10 p.m.

Guessing the focus of a place that has a one-page food menu and a booklet filled with drinks doesn't take a genius. Just like the French Quarter's version, drinking is the highlight at CityWalk's *Pat O'Brien's* (☎ **407-224-2122**). You can enjoy dueling pianos and a flame-throwing fountain while you suck down the signature drink — the Hurricane. No one under 21 is permitted after 7 p.m. Hours are 4 p.m. to 2 a.m., and there is a $2 cover charge after 9 p.m.

Church Street Station

The success of the first Orlando nightspot, *Church Street Station,* prompted Disney and Universal to enter the night games. The Station is a cobblestone city block with real turn-of-the-century buildings. This club-and-dining complex offers 20 live shows and street performers, and its interiors have a magnificent collection of woodwork, stained glass, and antiques.

Dixieland bands, banjo pickers, and cancan girls keep your blood broiling in *Rosie O'Grady's Good Time Emporium,* an 1890s-style gambling hall and saloon. If you like folk and bluegrass, try *Apple Annie's Courtyard,* a brick-floor building with arched trusses from a nineteenth-century Louisiana church. The *Cheyenne Saloon and Opera House* is a three-level bar that has balconies, a stained-glass skylight, and Western art. It has the best show of the bunch, with a tight country band that really knows how to kick up its heels (and yours). The Orchid Garden Ballroom, decorated in Victorian doodads, has an oldies dance club where a DJ plays rock 'n' roll classics. Allow a half-day or full evening.

The district is located at 129 W. Church St., off I-4, between Garland and Orange Avenues, in downtown Orlando (☎ **407-422-2434**; Internet: www.churchstreetstation.com). To get here, take I-4 east to Exit 38 (Anderson St.), stay in the left lane, and follow the signs to Church Street Station. Admission is free before 5 p.m.; after 5 p.m., admission to clubs is $17.95 ($11.95 for kids 4 to 12). Entry to the restaurants, the *Exchange Shopping Emporium,* and the Midway game area is free. The shops stay open from 11 a.m. to 11 p.m., clubs are open from 7:15 p.m. to 2 a.m. Metered parking costs $1 per hour, or you can use valet parking for $7.

Other nighttime venues

The **Laughing Kookaburra Good Time Bar** in the Wyndham Palace, Lake Buena Vista (☎ 407-827-3722), is open from 7 p.m. until 2 a.m., with live music and a DJ most nights. The piano bar in **Arthur's 27** (☎ 800-327-2990 or 407-827-2727), also in Wyndham Palace, has a great view of Disney's fireworks. **Baskerville's** (☎ 407–827-6500), in the Grosvenor Resort Hotel, Lake Buena Vista, features jazz nights Wednesday through Friday, 7 to 9 p.m., and a solve-it-yourself mystery show on Saturday at 6 and 9 p.m. The **Lobby Bar** (☎ 407-352-4000), at the Peabody Orlando, is a popular gathering spot with piano music.

Side-Tripping to John F. Kennedy Space Center

Explore the history of manned flights at the **Kennedy Space Center,** beginning with the wild ride of Alan Shepard (1961) and Neil Armstrong's 1969 moonwalk. (Lunar Theater's re-creation of Apollo 11 and Firing Room Theater's look at the Apollo 1 fire are gripping.) There are also three 5½-story, 3-D IMAX theaters that literally shake, rattle, and rock 'n roll with special effects. We think the best two movies are *L5,* a fictional look at the first space colony, and *The Dream Is Alive,* a rousing past-and-present focus on the space shuttle program.

The *Kennedy Space Center Visitor Complex* has real NASA rockets and exhibits that look at space exploration into this millennium. There are also hands-on activities aimed at kids, a daily encounter with a real astronaut, several dining venues, and a shop selling a variety of space memorabilia and souvenirs.

Bus tours (rent the audiotape for $5) run continuously. The bus makes stops at the *Vehicle Assembly Building,* where shuttles are prepared for launch; the *LC-39 Observation Gantry,* which has a 360-degree view of shuttle launch pads; and the *Apollo/Saturn V Center,* which includes artifacts, photos, interactive exhibits, and the 363-foot-tall Saturn V rocket.

If you want to go out on the launch pads, take the *Cape Canaveral Then and Now* guided tour. This once daily, 2-hour excursion focuses more on the history of the space program, and it stops at sites where the shuttle buses don't. You explore *Hangar S,* where the Mercury astronauts lived; the launch pads for the Mercury, Gemini, and Apollo missions; the *U.S. Air Force Space and Missile Museum;* and historic *Cape Canaveral Lighthouse.*

On launch day, the Kennedy Space Center is closed until after early shuttle launches, or, for later ones, it closes 6 hours before the scheduled liftoff. Launch days aren't good days to tour the facility, which deserves a 6- to 8-hour stay. However, launch days are great for seeing history in the present tense. *NASA Parkway,* one of the better launch-viewing areas for spectators, is no longer open to public traffic on launch days. (That's a blessing, because it used to get so crowded that there was a 2- to 4-hour traffic jam.) But for $10, the Kennedy Space Center will take you on a 2-hour (longer if there's a launch delay) excursion to the parkway to see the launch, and you won't have to fight traffic. You must pick up tickets, available 5 days prior to the launch, onsite. For information, call ☎ **321-449-4444.**

Despite 2.8 million visitors a year, the Kennedy Space Center feels far less crowded than the Orlando parks or **Busch Gardens.** If you're not driving your own sedan or coming on some other prepaid tour, you can arrange the trip through Mears Transportation (☎ **407-423-5566**).

We recommend this attraction for anyone who's ever dreamed about the final frontier. The Kennedy Space Center is also a great day trip for visitors 6 and older. Those ages 3 to 5 will enjoy some play areas but may be bored by the exhibits and even scared by the explosive movies.

To get to the Kennedy Space Center from Orlando, take the BeeLine Expressway east to Fla. 407, turn left, and then turn right at Fla. 405. Directions to the center are well marked along the roadside. The Space Center is located at NASA Parkway/Fla. 405, 6 miles east of Titusville, about ½ mile west of Fla. 3. Admission is free; bus tours $14 adults, $10 kids 3 to 11; IMAX movies $7.50 adults, $5.50 kids; bus tour and one movie $19 adults, $15 kids; bus tour and two IMAX movies $26 adults, $20 kids; *Then and Now* guided tour (bus and launch pad tours, see more information earlier in this section) $35 per person. Wheelchairs and strollers are free. Hours are 9 a.m. to dusk daily. Call ☎ **321-452-2121** for general information and 321-449-4444 for guided bus tours and launch reservations. Visit www.kennedyspacecenter.com online.

Side-Tripping to Cypress Gardens

Franklin D. Roosevelt was in his first term when this park opened in 1936. Water-ski shows and flowers are still its bread and butter. **Cypress Gardens** offers 200 acres of ponds, lagoons, waterfalls, classic Italian fountains, topiaries, bronze sculptures, manicured lawns, and ancient cypress trees shrouded in Spanish moss. Southern belles in Scarlett O'Hara costumes stroll the grounds or sit on benches under parasols. In late winter and early spring, more than 20 kinds of bougainvilleas, 40 types of azaleas, and hundreds of varieties of roses burst into bloom. Crape myrtles, magnolias, and gardenias perfume the late-spring air, while brilliant birds of paradise, hibiscuses, and jasmines brighten the summer. And in winter, the golden rain trees, floss silk trees, and camellias of autumn give way to millions of colorful chrysanthemums and red, white, and pink poinsettias.

Cypress Gardens has rides too. *Carousel Cove* has eight old-fashioned kids' rides, ponies, and arcade games centering on an ornate turn-of-the-twentieth-century-style carousel. It adjoins another kid pleaser, *Cypress Junction,* an elaborately landscaped model railroad that travels 1,100 feet of track and visits miniature landmarks including New Orleans and Mount Rushmore. *Electric boats* navigate a maze of lushly landscaped canals in the original botanical gardens. *Island in the Sky* gives you a panoramic view from 153 feet up. *Cypress Roots,* a museum of park memorabilia, displays photographs of famous visitors (Elvis on water skis) and airs ongoing showings of *Easy to Love* starring Esther Williams, which was filmed here.

Raptors and Reptiles features a show-and-tell with anacondas, rattlesnakes, Gila monsters, iguanas, gators, crocodiles, and a 15-foot albino python that answers to the name Banana Boy. This audience- and learning-friendly show also features hawks, owls, and falcons, with a trainer explaining their predatory habits.

On the water, the celebrated skiers of Cyprus Gardens keep tradition alive with such standards as ramp jumping, the aqua-maid ballet line, human pyramid, flag line, and slapstick comedy.

On ice, there's a wonderful European-style ice-skating show called *Hot Nouveau Ice,* while on stage, *Variete Internationale* features clowns Zaripov and Gratchik, who weave magic acts into their zany antics. The show also includes jugglers, fire-eaters, and gymnasts.

Wings of Wonder is a Cypress Gardens conservatory with more than 1,000 brilliant butterflies in a Victorian-style, climate-controlled, free flight aviary. This man-made rain forest also has a hatching display that shows the various stages of butterfly metamorphosis.

Lories and lorikeets are the stars in the *Birdwalk Aviary.* These birds land on your shoulders to welcome you. The young Australian parrots are brilliantly colored and very inquisitive. They share the sanctuary with pheasants, ducks, and muntjac deer (the smallest deer species in the world).

To get to Cypress Gardens from Orlando, take I-4 West to U.S. 27 South, and proceed to Fla. 540. Cypress Gardens is located off of Fla. 540 at Cypress Gardens Boulevard. (In Winter Haven, 40 miles southwest of Disney World.) Admission costs $31.95 for adults, $27.15 for seniors 55 and older, and $14.95 for kids 6 to 17. Parking is $5. Hours of operation are 9:30 a.m. to 5 p.m. daily. Call ☎ **800-282-2123** or visit www. cypressgardens.com on the Web for more info.

Fast Facts

Area Code

The local area codes are **407** and **321**.

American Express

To locate offices in Orlando, call ☎ **407-843-0004**. There's a **Travel Service** office in Epcot (☎ **407-827-7500**) and another at 7512 Dr. Phillips Blvd. (☎ **407-345-1181**). American Express is the official card of Walt Disney World.

Doctors

If you want a direct feed to a doctor, try **Ask-A-Nurse**. A representative will ask if you have insurance, but that's for information purposes only — so the service can track who uses the system. Ask-A-Nurse is a free service open to everyone. In Kissimmee, call ☎ **407-870-1700**; in Orlando call ☎ **407-897-1700**.

Hospitals

Sand Lake Hospital, 9400 Turkey Lake Rd. (☎ **407-351-8550**) is about 2 miles south of Sand Lake Road. **Celebration Health** (☎ **407-764-4000**), at 400 Celebration Place, is in the Disney-run town of Celebration.

Information

To receive local telephone information, call ☎ **411**. The other most common sources of information **are Walt Disney World,** Box 10000, Lake Buena Vista, FL 32830-1000 (☎ **407-934-7639**; Internet: http://disney.go.com/DisneyWorld/intro.html), and the **Orlando/Orange County Convention & Visitors Bureau,** 8723 International Dr., Suite 101, Orlando, FL 32819 (☎ **407-363-5871**; Internet: www.go2orlando.com).

Internet Access

One local cybercafe is **The Netkaffee,** 22 Broadway, Kissimmee (☎ **407-943-7500**; Internet: www.netkaffee.com). It's open Monday through Saturday from 9 a.m. to 9 p.m. The cafe serves coffee shop fare and offers high-speed Internet access for $10 an hour.

Mail

If you want to receive mail on your vacation, and you aren't sure of your address, you can have your mail sent to you, in your name, in care of General Delivery at the main post office of the city or region where you expect to stay. Orlando's main post office (☎ **800-275-8777**) is located at 1040 Post Office Blvd. Lake Buena Vista's main post office (☎ **800-275-8777**) is at 12133 S. Apopka-Vineland Rd. You must pick up your mail in person and produce proof of identity (driver's license, passport, and so on).

Newspapers

After you land in O-Town, you can find a lot of bargains in the *Orlando Sentinel* (online, check out www.orlandosentinel.com) throughout the week. The paper's Friday "Calendar" section is a literal gold mine for current information on the area's accommodations, restaurants, nightclubs, and attractions.

Pharmacies

Walgreens drugstore, 1003 W. Vine St. (Hwy. 192), just east of Bermuda Avenue (☎ **407-847-5252**), operates a 24-hour pharmacy. There's also **Eckerd** drugstores at 7324 International Dr. (☎ **407-345-0491**) and 1205 W. Vine. (☎ **407-847-5174**) that are open 24 hours a day.

Safety

Don't let the aura of Mickey Mouse allow you to lower your guard. Orlando has a crime rate that's comparable to other major U.S. cities. Stay alert and remain aware of your immediate surroundings. Renting a locker is always preferable to leaving your valuables in the trunk of your car, even in the theme park lots. Be cautious and avoid carrying large amounts of cash in a back-pack or fanny pack, which thieves can easily access while you're standing in line for a ride or show.

Smoking

If you smoke, you most likely know to expect a diminishing playground. Restaurant space and hotel rooms for smokers are evaporat-ing. The Wizard of Diz stopped selling tobacco years ago, but it has also started establishing precious few "you can smoke here" areas in the outside world. Light 'em while and where you can.

Taxes

Expect to add 11 or 12 percent to room rates; and 6 to 7 percent on most everything else — except groceries and health supplies or med-ical services.

Taxis

Yellow Cab (☎ **407-699-9999**) and **Ace Metro** (☎ **407-855-0564**) are among the cabs serv-ing the area. But for day-to-day travel, cabs are expensive unless your group has five or more people. Rates are $2.50 for the first mile, $1.50 per mile thereafter.

Transit Info

Lynx (☎ **407-841-8240**; Internet: www. golynx.com) bus stops are marked with a paw print. The buses serve Disney, Universal, and International Drive ($1 for adults, 25 cents for kids and seniors; $10 for an unlimited weekly pass), but they're not very tourist-oriented.

Weather

Call ☎ **321-255-0212** to get forecasts from the **National Weather Service.** When the phone picks up, punch in **412** from a touch-tone phone, and you'll get the Orlando fore-cast. Also, check with **The Weather Channel,** if you have cable television, or go to its Web site, www.weatherchannel.com.

Part VI
The Great North

The 5th Wave   By Rich Tennant

"We try to offer an alternative to SeaWorld, but we're having trouble pulling people in."

In this part . . .

No Miami Vice. No Orlando Mice.

And in spite of that, Florida's top half has plenty to keep you busy. Daytona Beach is the closest this region gets to glitzy tourism, and you can find plenty of it there. Even historic St. Augustine sports a tourist-trap atmosphere. But when you wander north to Fernandina Beach and then move west across the Panhandle to Pensacola, you find a different Florida. With the exception of such vacation hot spots as Panama City, Destin, and Fort Walton Beach, this part of Florida is wide-open territory, showcasing dune-lined beaches and vast pine forests.

Chapter 21

Daytona Beach

· ·

In This Chapter

▶ Driving with the pros at Daytona International

▶ Biking at Daytona: Biketoberfest

▶ Sunbathing at Daytona, Ormond, and Ponce Inlet Beaches

▶ Dining and staying over in Daytona: Restaurants and hotels

▶ Partying the night away

· ·

Anyone who has ever been a teenager has heard of Daytona Beach. The self-proclaimed "World's Most Famous Beach" still attracts thousands of snowbirds in winter, families in summer, college kids in spring, and bikers during Bike Week and Biketoberfest. But consider three of the more common side effects of driving and parking on this famous stretch of sand and surf:

> ✔ **Carbon monoxide:** *Gasp, choke.* This is fresh air?
>
> ✔ **High tide:** Oops. Maybe you should've parked a little farther from the surf line. But, heck, you rented the car, why worry?
>
> ✔ **Traffic jams:** But with a 10 mph speed limit, who notices?

These minor annoyances are real, but they alone have not caused Daytona's title as the "World's Most Famous Beach" to fall into dispute. Some of Daytona's charm was lost during its spring-break heyday in the '60s and '70s; it also fell victim to competition in the '80s and '90s. Nevertheless, it's pretty affordable for a prime beach destination and visitors continue to flock here.

 If you want less clutter, head north to Ormond Beach or south to New Smyrna Beach. If you decide to pitch your tent on ground zero, well, come expecting one big, noisy party.

Getting There

Air travel is the perennial favorite for getting to Daytona, because it saves time and, in most cases, isn't prohibitively expensive. But since Daytona lies in North Florida, it's a little easier to reach by car or train than most Florida destinations, should you prefer to travel on land.

By plane

Daytona Beach International Airport, on U.S. 92 (☎ **904-248-8069;** Internet: http://flydaytonafirst.com), is served by two major airlines: **Continental** and **Delta. Alamo, Avis, Budget, Dollar, Hertz,** and **National** have rental counters at the airport. **Yellow Cab** (☎ **904-255-5555**) will take you from the airport to most places in the area for $7 to $15.

If you want a greater selection of airlines to choose from, **Orlando International Airport** (☎ **407-825-2001;** Internet: http://fcn.state.fl.us/goaa) is about 90 minutes southwest of Daytona by car or shuttle (see Chapter 18) and is serviced by a number of major carriers.

By car

I-95 is the best route when driving to Daytona from the north or south. U.S. 1 is an option, but plan on stopping and starting as you pass through tiny towns. A1A is the scenic beach route, but it's slower yet. I-4 will get you to Daytona from Orlando. From the west, take I-10 to I-95; from the Midwest, follow I-75 to I-10, and then onward to I-95.

By train

Amtrak (☎ **800-872-7245;** Internet: www.amtrak.com) offers scheduled service to Deland at 2491 Old New York Ave.

Orienting Yourself in Daytona Beach

Center stage is the Daytona Beach Boardwalk and the Main Street Pier, located (appropriately enough) just east of Main Street and U.S. A1A, and just north of the eastern end of Volusia Avenue/U.S. 92. Ormond Beach is north of Daytona; New Smyrna Beach and Port Orange are south. The mainland and the rest of Volusia County are to the west. (See the "Daytona Beach" map coming up in this chapter.)

Daytona Beach

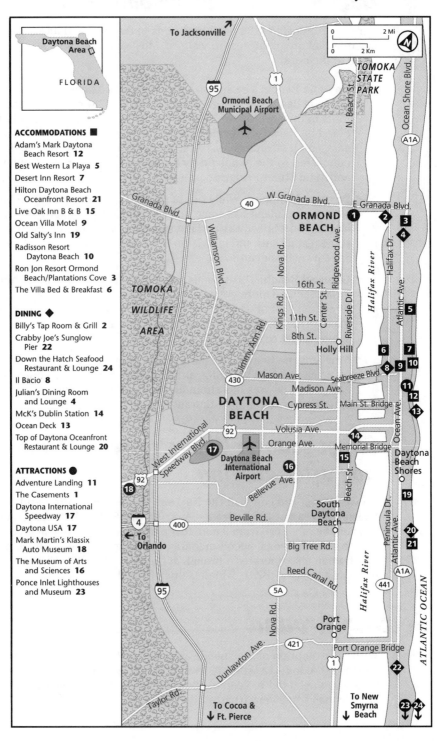

Daytona Beach Area
FLORIDA

ACCOMMODATIONS ■
Adam's Mark Daytona
  Beach Resort **12**
Best Western La Playa **5**
Desert Inn Resort **7**
Hilton Daytona Beach
  Oceanfront Resort **21**
Live Oak Inn B & B **15**
Ocean Villa Motel **9**
Old Salty's Inn **19**
Radisson Resort
  Daytona Beach **10**
Ron Jon Resort Ormond
  Beach/Plantations Cove **3**
The Villa Bed & Breakfast **6**

DINING ◆
Billy's Tap Room & Grill **2**
Crabby Joe's Sunglow
  Pier **22**
Down the Hatch Seafood
  Restaurant & Lounge **24**
Il Bacio **8**
Julian's Dining Room
  and Lounge **4**
McK's Dublin Station **14**
Ocean Deck **13**
Top of Daytona Oceanfront
  Restaurant & Lounge **20**

ATTRACTIONS ●
Adventure Landing **11**
The Casements **1**
Daytona International
  Speedway **17**
Daytona USA **17**
Mark Martin's Klassix
  Auto Museum **18**
The Museum of Arts
  and Sciences **16**
Ponce Inlet Lighthouses
  and Museum **23**

Daytona Beach by neighborhoods

Here is a rundown of the neighborhoods in Daytona and its surrounding area that are of interest to visitors. Most of these spots are pretty close to the coast.

- ✔ **Daytona Beach:** The spot where most tourists come to play, Daytona Beach has the greatest selection of hotels and restaurants in the area, as well as a few attractions. This sector is bordered by Hwy. 400/Beville Road in the south and by A1A in the east, and it stretches northward to within 1 mile of Hwy. 40. It's connected to the mainland by the Memorial, Seabreeze Boulevard, and Main Street Bridges.

- ✔ **Daytona Mainland:** While not as popular with tourists as the beach side, the mainland has some prime attractions, including Daytona International Speedway and Daytona USA. Visitors will also find some restaurants and motels on U.S. 1 and U.S. 92/International Speedway Boulevard.

- ✔ **Ormond Beach:** This town is a step quieter than Daytona, though it has become more congested in the last 10 years. Its beach, centered just east of where Hwy. 40 hits A1A/Atlantic Avenue, is its main attraction. Most of the city's motels and restaurants are strung along A1A.

- ✔ **New Smyrna Beach:** The south coast is quieter still. It has some nice beaches and less glitz, although, like most of the county's east side, this area has shoulder-to-shoulder development, including many motels and restaurants.

Street smarts: Where to get information after arriving

On weekdays, you can visit the **Daytona Beach Convention and Visitors Bureau** at 126 E. Orange Ave. (☎ **800-854-1234;** Internet: www. daytonabeach.com) from 9 a.m. to 5 p.m. Staff members can give you advice on attractions, accommodations, dining, and special events. The bureau also operates a branch at Daytona USA, 1801 W. International Speedway Blvd., which is open from 9 a.m. to 7 p.m.

Getting Around

With the exception of the speedway area, most of the prime tourist zone is set along A1A/Atlantic Avenue, so it's easy to find the places where you need to be. Keep in mind, however, that the highway occasionally has some very frustrating traffic.

By bus

VOLTRAN (☎ 904-761-7700), Volusia County's public transit system, runs a trolley along Atlantic Avenue (A1A) from noon to midnight, Monday through Saturday. The trolley runs only from March to the beginning of September. VOLTRAN also runs buses throughout the beach and mainland daily. Bus and trolley fares are $1 for adults, 50 cents for seniors and kids under 18.

By car

Daytona is primarily a driver's town, so a car is a good idea. The major east-west roads in Daytona are U.S. 92, which is called International Speedway Boulevard inside the city, and Hwy. 430/Mason Avenue, which links the mainland to the beaches. Hwy. 40 is the main east-to-west road in Ormond Beach, while it's Hwy. 44 for New Smyrna Beach. The main north-south roads are U.S. 1/Ridgewood Avenue, Riverside Drive, and Beach Street on the mainland. A1A/Atlantic Avenue and Halifax Avenue are the primary north-south beach routes.

By taxi

Yellow Cab (☎ 904-255-5555) is the main taxi franchise. Fares cost $2.60 for the first mile and $1.40 per additional mile.

Staying in Daytona Beach

Finding a place to lay your head in this area of Florida requires a bit of planning. Most folks who come here want to stay on Daytona Beach, so that's the area we emphasize.

The good news for bargain hunters is that Daytona offers some of the most affordable digs in Florida, provided you don't arrive during a major event or at the height of the spring break season. Rates during those periods skyrocket, hotel rooms become a *very* scarce commodity, and most establishments require minimum stays.

Although a few major chains do operate in the area, hundreds of the hotels lining Atlantic Avenue along the beach are family owned and operated. The **Daytona Beach Convention and Visitors Bureau,** 126 E. Orange Ave. (☎ **800-854-1234;** Internet: www.daytonabeach.com), distributes a list of "Superior Small Lodgings" (75 rooms or fewer) in the area, all of which have passed muster with the bureau.

All of the accommodations listed here offer free parking, air conditioning, and pools.

The following are year-round rates and don't include the county's 10 percent hotel tax.

Daytona Beach's best hotels

Adam's Mark Daytona Beach Resort

$$ Daytona Beach

Right in the middle of all the beach action, this hotel's 437 rooms, cabanas, and suites offer scenic views of the Atlantic Ocean. The standard rooms come with a sofa and coffee table and are equipped with data ports, voice mail, desks, and minibars. Cabanas are decorated in bright flora fabrics and have a sofa, small table, and chairs. Guests can use the health club, complete with a sauna, steam room, whirlpools, and massage and tanning services. There are numerous recreational activities, three restaurants, and a lobby bar.

100 N. Atlantic Ave./A1A. ☎ *800-444-2326 or 904-254-8200. Fax: 904-253-8841. Internet:* www.adamsmark.com. *To get there: From I-95, exit east on International Speedway Blvd./U.S. 92, cross the Intracoastal Waterway to the beaches and A1A/Atlantic Ave., and go north. Rack Rates: $89–$129. AE, DC, DISC, MC, V.*

Best Western La Playa

$$ Daytona Beach

This large, modern high-rise is located right on the beach. The accommodations — ranging from standard rooms to efficiencies and suites — are decorated with tropical prints, and all come with microwaves, refrigerators, coffee makers, and balconies. The hotel has an onsite restaurant, a lounge, and an indoor spa equipped with a heated pool, whirlpool, and sauna.

2500 N. Atlantic Ave./A1A. ☎ *800-874-6996 or 904-672-0990. Fax: 904-677-0982. Internet:* www.staydaytona.com/. *To get there: I-95 to International Speedway Blvd./U.S. 92, head east to A1A, turn north and go 3 miles. Rack rates: $104–$199. AE, CB, DC, DISC, MC, V.*

Desert Inn Resort

$$ Daytona Beach

This property promises guests "a fun and exciting time," and it delivers comfortable rooms, a wide array of recreational activities, and a friendly atmosphere. Most of this oceanfront resort's accommodations sport balconies and views of the beach. The large deluxe rooms come with microwaves; refrigerators and free rollaway beds are available. Efficiencies offer two double beds and a kitchenette. Suites have one or two bedrooms and full kitchens; a few have Jacuzzis.

900 N. Atlantic Ave./A1A (1 mile north of the boardwalk on A1A). ☎ *800-826-1711 or 904-258-6555. Fax: 904-238-1635. Internet:* www.desertinnresort.com. *To get there: From I-95, exit east on International Speedway Blvd./U.S. 92 and head to the beaches and A1A, then go north. Rack rates: $119–$179. AE, DC, DISC, MC, V.*

Hilton Daytona Beach Oceanfront Resort

$$$ Daytona Beach Shores

Arguably the best hotel in Daytona, this 3½-acre resort features an elegant lobby, filled with wicker and tropical prints. The hotel's 271 guest rooms sport a French provincial motif and bright fabrics. All rooms have refrigerators, data ports, and hair dryers; many have balconies or patios. Suites include a sofa bed and wet bar. Amenities include a restaurant, lounge, small fitness center, and a recreation room for kids.

2637 S. Atlantic Ave./A1A. ☎ *800-445-8667 or 904-767-7350. Fax: 904-760-3651. Internet:* www.hilton.com. *To get there: Take I-95, exit east on International Speedway Blvd./U.S. 92 and go to A1A, head south to Daytona Beach Shores. Rack Rates: $229–$279. AE, DC, DISC, MC, V.*

Live Oak Inn B&B

$$ Daytona Beach

This historic property offers ten units in two restored Victorian homes. Its rooms are named after events in Florida history, including such sporting events as auto racing and baseball, and each features memorabilia or furniture from the period. Some rooms have Jacuzzis or Victorian soaking tubs, some offer private balconies, and all have private baths. A continental breakfast is offered daily. Smoking is prohibited on the premises.

444–448 S. Beach St. (between Loomis St. and Orange Ave.). ☎ *800-881-4667 or 904-252-4667. Fax: 904-239-0068. To get there: Take I-95 and exit east on International Speedway Blvd./U.S. 92, and turn north at Beach St. Rack rates: $80–$150. AE, DISC, MC, V.*

Ocean Villa Motel

$$ Daytona Beach

All the rooms, efficiencies, and suites here feature refrigerators and face either the ocean (more expensive) or a courtyard. The property's large suites, equipped with living rooms, balconies, bedrooms, and sofa beds, as well as full baths, kitchens, and vanities, make this a good choice for larger families. Kids flock to the property's 60-foot waterslide. Year-round recreation programs include Florida's state sport (yes — bingo), volleyball, and games for kids.

828 N. Atlantic Ave./A1A. ☎ *800-225-3691 or 904-252-4644. Fax: 904-255-7378. Internet:* www.ocean-villa.com. *To get there: I-95 to International Speedway Blvd./U.S. 92, then go east to A1A, and head north. Rack rates: $45–$299. AE, DC, DISC, MC, V.*

Old Salty's Inn

$ **Daytona Beach Shores**

This nautically themed property offers clean, well-appointed rooms on grounds that feature banana and palm trees, waterfalls, and a bridge over a fishpond. All the brightly decorated rooms and suites have microwaves and refrigerators, while some offer picture-perfect views of the beach. Take a ride on one of the free beach bikes or indulge at a weekly hot dog roast.

1921 S. Atlantic Ave./A1A. ☎ *800-417-1466 or 904-252-8090. Fax: 904-441-5977. Internet:* http://visitdaytona.com/oldsaltys. *To get there: From U.S. 192, head south on A1A for 1.4 miles. Rack rates: $51–$111. AE, DISC, MC, V.*

Radisson Resort Daytona Beach

$$ **Daytona Beach**

This luxurious 11-story resort is close to the Main Street Pier, Ocean Center, the Boardwalk, shopping, and restaurants. All 206 rooms have balconies that overlook the beach, and they are furnished with chairs and sofas, a desk, and data ports. Some have kitchenettes with microwaves, coffee makers, and refrigerators. There's a restaurant and bar on the premises.

640 N. Atlantic Ave./A1A (between Seabreeze and Glenview Blvds.). ☎ *800-333-3333 or 904-239-9800. Fax: 904/253-0735. Internet:* www.radisson.com/RAD/RadissonHome. *To get there: I-95 to International Speedway Boulevard/U.S. 92, east to A1A, north to the Ocean Center. Rack rates: $89–$129. AE, DC, DISC, MC, V.*

Ron Jon Resort Ormond Beach/Plantations Cove

$$ **Ormond Beach**

This six-story beachfront lodge offers studios and one- to two-bedroom units. Studios sleep up to four, with a Murphy bed and sleeper sofa; they also have full kitchens. The two-bedroom units (some with more than 950 square feet of space) have room for six and come with kitchens that include microwaves, dishwashers, icemakers, and blenders. All rooms have balconies that offer a view of the ocean.

145 S. Atlantic Ave./A1A. ☎ *888-475-2626 or 904-677-1446. Fax: 904-677-2834. Internet:* www.islandone.com. *To get there: Take International Speedway Blvd./U.S. 92 to A1A and turn north. Rack rates: $41–$180. AE, DISC, MC, V.*

The Villa Bed & Breakfast

$$ **Daytona Beach**

This clay-tiled Spanish mansion, listed on the National Register of Historic Places, is situated near the Halifax River and is a great spot for a romantic getaway. The Mediterranean-style property features elegant rooms, such as the large King Juan Carlos Room, which has a large four-poster bed, sofa, a separate dressing room, and French doors that open onto a rooftop terrace. Other units come with queen- or king-size beds, and all have private baths. An elaborate continental breakfast is included with your stay.

801 N. Peninsula Dr. (located close to Seabreeze Blvd. and the Halifax River). ☎ ***904-248-2020.*** *Fax: 904-248-2020. Internet:* www.thevillabb.com. *To get there: I-95 to International Speedway Blvd./U.S. 92, east to U.S. 1/Ridgewood Ave., then north on Mason Ave., cross the river to Peninsula Dr., turn north; the inn is just north of Seabreeze Blvd. Rack rates: $90–$190. MC, V.*

Runner-up accommodations

Sometimes the first team doesn't make the earth move for you, or you tried to get a reservation at these locations and did not succeed. If that's the case, here are more options.

Aruba Inn

$ Daytona Beach   This 33-unit, Spanish-style motel has a great location right on the beach. *1254 N. Atlantic Ave./A1A* ☎ ***800-214-1406*** *or 904-253-5643. Fax: 904-248-1279. Internet:* www.daytonabeach.com/daytona/dynaindex.html?DID=164.

Castaways Beach Resort

$ Daytona Beach Shores   This beachfront property offers rooms, efficiencies, and suites south of the big-league noise. *2043 S. Atlantic Ave./A1A* ☎ ***800-407-0342*** *or 904-254-8480. Fax: 904-253-6554. Internet:* www.bsrresorts.com/castaways.htm.

Daytona Inn Beach Resort

$$ Daytona Beach   Smack dab in the heart of the boardwalk-and-pier mayhem, this resort offers comfortable studios and suites. *219 S. Atlantic Ave./A1A* ☎ ***800-874-1822*** *or 904-252-3626. Fax: 904-255-3680. Internet:* www.bsrresorts.com/daytona-inn.htm.

Makai Lodge Beach Resort

$ Ormond Beach   An old-style, high-rise motel, this location offers tropically themed rooms and efficiencies, right off one of the area's more popular beaches. *707 S. Atlantic Ave./A1A* ☎ ***800-799-1112*** *or 904-677-8060. Fax: 904-677-8060. Internet:* www.makailodge.com.

Shore Line All Suites Inn

$$ Daytona Beach Shores   Situated right off the beach, this neat little complex of 30 (very small) cottages dates back to 1927. *2435 S. Atlantic Ave./A1A* ☎ ***800-293-0653*** *or 904-239-0653. Fax: 904-293-7068. Internet:* www.daytonashoreline.com.

Dining out in Daytona Beach

If you like fast food, you'll feel right at home in Daytona Beach, but if you prefer fine dining, this isn't the place for you. Nevertheless, the area does offer a nice mix of cuisine, headlined by seafood, which is one of the blessings of Daytona Beach's coastal location.

Daytona Beach's best restaurants

Billy's Tap Room & Grill

$$ Ormond Beach   SEAFOOD

This 78-year-old restaurant still has a congenial 1920s atmosphere and serves great seafood in a mahogany-paneled dining room filled with historical memorabilia. Notable entrees include Maryland crab cakes, sautéed shrimp, shrimp scampi, and a seafood casserole (shrimp, scallops, white fish, and crabmeat) topped with cheese. Have a drink before dinner at the solid maple bar.

58 East Granada Blvd. ☎ *904-672-1910. Internet:* www.billys-tap.com. *To get there: Located on Granada/Hwy. 40, just west of the beach area. Reservations not required. Main courses: $15–$27. AE, MC, V. Open: 11 a.m.–10 p.m. Mon–Sat, 11:30 a.m.–9 p.m. Sun.*

Crabby Joe's Sunglow Pier

$ Daytona Beach   SEAFOOD

Located on the south end of the beach, this informal restaurant offers indoor/outdoor dining and a fantastic view of the ocean. Joe's serves a respectable grouper, crab legs, and, if you want to get even with Jaws, shark bites. The portions are huge, and the price is certainly right.

3701 S. Atlantic Ave. ☎ *904-788-3364. Internet:* www.sunglowpier.com/grill.htm. *To get there: U.S. 92/International Speedway Blvd. east to A1A, then south. Reservations not accepted. Main courses: $12–$14. Credit cards not accepted. Open: 6 a.m.–10 p.m. daily.*

Down the Hatch Seafood Restaurant & Lounge

$$ Ponce Inlet   SEAFOOD

Watch the world glide by this fish-serving, camp-style eatery on the Halifax River. You can start with oysters (on the half shell, steamed, or raw) and then go on to entrees such as lobster and fried fish. The family-oriented restaurant also offers a kids' menu and a few selections for those counting their calories. There's a cocktail lounge, in case you need a drink after a long day at the beach.

4894 Front St. ☎ *904/761-4831. Internet:* http://visitdaytona.com/ downthehatch/. *To get there: A1A/Atlantic Ave. south to Ponce Inlet, at 4-way stop turn right and go to the river. Reservations not accepted. Main courses: $8–$26. AE, MC, V. Open: 7 a.m.–9 p.m. daily.*

Il Bacio

$ Daytona Beach ITALIAN

The food at this restaurant/deli is delightful, but the business hours make a meal here an advance-planning chore. The specials are veal marsala topped with tomatoes, baked grouper simmered in wine and garlic, and, for dessert, *tiramisu*, a delicious cake roll. All the tables at this friendly spot allow you to see the chef at work.

631 N. Grandview Ave. ☎ *904-255-9822. Internet:* www.daytona.net/ilbacio. *To get there: East of A1A; located at Grandview Ave. and Seabreeze Blvd. Reservations required. Main courses: $12–$17. Credit cards not accepted. Open: Lunch 11 a.m.–2 p.m. Tues – Fri; Dinner 5–9 p.m. Wed–Sat only.*

Julian's Dining Room and Lounge

$$ Ormond Beach AMERICAN

This family-owned-and-operated restaurant caters to locals and tourists, offering a casual atmosphere and friendly service. Unlike most restaurants in this area, it specializes in prime Western beef, but the seafood is far from second fiddle. Choices include salmon, Maine lobster, and deviled crab. The chef also makes schnitzels and a black-bean soup that's surprisingly good.

88 S. Atlantic Ave. ☎ *904-677-6767. Internet:* www.juliansrest.com. *To get there: Just south of Hwy. 40, on the west side of A1A. Reservations suggested. Main courses: $10–$30. AE, DC, DISC, MC, V. Open: 4–11 p.m. daily.*

McK's Dublin Station

$ Daytona Beach/Mainland PUB GRUB

The acceptable cuisine at this upscale tavern includes sandwiches, burgers, burritos, and grilled veggies. The only entrée that pays tribute to the pub's name is corned beef and cabbage, and it's only served on Thursdays. To compensate, there is a good selection of ales.

218 S. Beach St. (between Magnolia Street and Orange Lane). ☎ *904-238-3321. To get there: International Speedway Blvd./U.S. 92 east to Beach St. and go right. Reservations not accepted. Main courses: $8–$16; sandwiches and salads, $4–$7. AE, MC, V. Open: 11–3 a.m. Mon–Sat, 11 a.m.–midnight Sun.*

Ocean Deck

$ Daytona Beach   SEAFOOD

If you want a square meal at a square price, you won't be disappointed in this beachfront restaurant near the Main Street Pier. The plates lack those sprigs of this and that for decoration, but the oysters, crabs, clams, and shrimp have been delighting diners since the 1950s. It gets noisy and crowded very fast, so this is a nooner or an ultra early-bird destination only.

127 S. Atlantic Ave./A1A. ☎ *904-253-5224. To get there: Go north from International Speedway Blvd. on A1A to first right (next to the Mayan Inn). Reservations not required. Main courses: $9–$16. AE, DISC, MC, V. Open: 11 a.m.–3 p.m. daily.*

Top of Daytona Oceanfront Restaurant and Lounge

$$ Daytona Beach   AMERICAN/CONTINENTAL

Located 29 floors above sea level in a circular high-rise, this restaurant's view is almost worth the price you pay for a meal. The menu isn't up to the scenery, but the chow is respectable. Pastas are the featured appetizers. Non-pastafarians can ponder chicken, steaks, seafood, and surf-and-turf platters. All kids' meals (pasta, chicken, beef, and shrimp) cost $7. Have a cocktail in the lounge before dinner.

2625 S. Atlantic Ave./A1A. ☎ *904-767-5791. Internet:* www.topofdaytona.com. *To get there: South of International Speedway Blvd. on A1A. Reservations suggested. Main courses: $13–$28. AE, DISC, MC, V. Open: 4–9 p.m. Tues–Sun.*

Runner-up restaurants

Just in case our first offerings weren't enough to satisfy your appetite, here are a few more options.

Aunt Catfish's On the River

**$$ Daytona Beach   **This local landmark has been dishing out first-rate catfish for 22 years. *4009 Halifax Dr.* ☎ *904-767-4768.*

Booth's Bowery

**$$ Port Orange   **This family restaurant offers everything from finger foods, such as Buffalo wings, to ribs, steaks, and shrimp scampi. *3657 S. Nova Rd.* ☎ *904-761-9464. Internet:* www.boothsbowery.com/.

Dancing Avocado Kitchen

**$ Daytona Beach   **This eatery specializes in light fare such as sandwiches, pizzas, and salads and other vegetarian fare. *110 S. Beach St.* ☎ *904-947-2022.*

Exploring Daytona Beach

In the old days, you could drive on most of Daytona's 23-mile beach. Today, only 9 miles are open to cars. Car-pedestrian run-ins — some fatal — have been an issue, but endangered sea turtles were one of the biggest factors in the decision to close most of the beach to vehicles. The turtles nest here, and their young, once hatched and heading for the water, don't stand much of a chance against cars.

Touring the top sights

Adventure Landing

Daytona Beach

This Caribbean-themed amusement park is right across the street from Daytona's Boardwalk. It has three nine-hole miniature golf courses, go-karts, a video arcade, and a water park. The water park's 12 water slides include *Panama Jack's Slideaway,* a 55-foot tower that you descend via an inner tube. The *Twin Vipers* are body slides that twist tornado-style (what a deal: a ride and an anxiety attack in one). There are also wave machines and other tools of mass drenching. Allow 2 to 4 hours for this destination, depending on the depth of your pockets.

601 Earl St. ☎ *904-258-0071. Internet:* www.adventurelanding.com. *To get there: Take I-95 to International Speedway Blvd./U.S. 92 to A1A; it's next to the Boardwalk. Admission: $20 adults, $17 kids (must be 48 inches and over). Open: 11 a.m.–6 p.m. or later daily.*

The Casements

Ormond Beach

Visit the home of the late billionaire, John D. Rockefeller, who built The Casements when he discovered that he was being charged more than the other guests at the nearby Ormond Hotel. After he moved into his new digs, the townies dubbed him "Neighbor John." Today, his restored home is a cultural cave that includes art exhibits, a museum of the city, a Rockefeller-period room, and Boy Scout exhibits. Two-hour tours are conducted Monday through Saturday. Otherwise, allow an hour to see everything.

25 Riverside Dr. ☎ *904-676-3216. Internet:* www.daytonabeach.com/daytona/dynaindex.html?DID=32. *To get there: It's on Hwy. 40 at the Granada Boulevard Bridge (Halifax River). Admission: donations. Open: 10 a.m.–3 p.m. Mon-Fri, 10 a.m.–noon Sat.*

Daytona International Speedway

Daytona Beach Mainland

The speedway and its new adjoining tourist attraction, Daytona USA (see the listing later in this section), are second only to the beach in visitor magnetism. Built in 1959, the speedway is the home of the Daytona 500, Speed Week (February), Biketoberfest (October), and several other excuses to drive fast and get rowdy. Even when there isn't a major event, the visitor center at the World Center of Racing offers 30-minute guided track tours, early films of beach racing, and a Gallery of Legends photograph collection. Allow 1 hour to see the highlights.

1801 W. International Speedway Blvd./U.S. 92. ☎ *904-254-2700. Internet:* www. daytonaintlspeedway.com. *To get there: Take I-95's Exit 87 to International Speedway Blvd., then head east. The huge grandstand is really hard to miss. Admission: Free. (Who pays to look at an empty track and stands?) Open: 9 a.m.–5 p.m. daily.*

Daytona USA

Daytona Beach Mainland

This state-of-the-art, interactive attraction gives you a chance to beat the pros' record at a NASCAR Winston Cup pit stop, design and test your own racecar, compete with other aficionados in a trivia game, and call the final laps of a race from the broadcast booth. You can also see Sir Malcolm Campbell's Bluebird V — the 30-foot, five-ton monster that set the land speed record on the beach back in 1935 and a Jeff Gordon car that comes apart, section by section, to show visitors how a racecar is built. For an extra two bucks, you can tour the speedway in a tram. You can spend 3 to 4 hours here; more if you're a hard-core fan.

While you're at Daytona USA, you can take three laps on the storied speedway in a real racecar. The bad news: It costs $105 and you have to leave the driving to a pro. Blame the lawyers, the insurance companies, and your mother (who always was too protective).

2909 W. International Speedway Blvd./U.S. 92. ☎ *904-947-6800. Internet:* www.daytonausa.com. *To get there: It's next to the speedway, 4 miles west of A1A. Admission: $12 adults, $10 seniors, $6 kids 6–12; $16 adults, $14 seniors, $11 kids 6–12 for combined Daytona USA and tram tour. Open: 10 a.m.–11 p.m. Sun-Thurs, 10 a.m.–midnight Fri-Sat.*

Mark Martin's Klassix Auto Museum

Daytona Beach Mainland

This modest museum displays vintage cars, including a Corvette collection that has every model manufactured since 1953. You can see retired racecars and discover the history of beach racing. An old-fashioned ice cream parlor is also inside. This stop takes 1 to 2 hours, max.

2909 W. International Speedway Blvd./U.S. 92. ☎ ***800-881-8975*** *or 904-252-3800. Internet:* www.klassixauto.com. *To get there: I-95 to exit 87, head east on International Speedway Blvd. Admission: $8.50 adults, $4.25 children 7–12. Open: 9 a.m.–6 p.m. daily.*

The Museum of Arts and Sciences

Daytona Beach

Trace Florida's history from prehistoric times to the present. Exhibits include the skeleton of a 13-foot-tall, 130,000-year-old giant ground sloth that was found near the museum in 1974. The museum also features changing art exhibits and a planetarium with a computer-animated program that shows the early Earth from space and multiple star systems. Allow 1 to 2 hours to take in everything.

1040 Museum Blvd. ☎ ***904-255-0285.*** *Internet:* www.moas.org. *To get there: Take International Speedway Blvd./U.S. 92 to Nova Road, go south, then west on Museum Boulevard. Admission: $5 adults, $1 kids and students; planetarium shows, $3. Showtimes: 2 p.m. Tues-Fri, 1 and 3 p.m. Sat-Sun. Open: 9 a.m.–2 p.m. Tues-Fri, 1–3 p.m. Sat-Sun.*

Ponce Inlet Lighthouse and Museum

Ponce Inlet

This structure is one of only a handful of Florida lighthouses that has managed to keep its brick torso. Built in 1887, it stayed in service for 83 years and then was reactivated by the Coast Guard in 1982. If you're up for the 203-step climb, the 175-foot sentinel offers a panoramic view of this tiny town and the ocean. The keeper's house is the museum; the assistant's house is maintained as it would have appeared around 1890. The site has a lens exhibit, a display of lights from around the world, and a 46-foot tugboat that was built in 1938 and served until a few years ago. Allow 1 hour and then hit the bar across the street.

4931 S. Peninsula Dr. ☎ ***904-761-1821.*** *Internet:* www.poncelinlet.org. *To get there: Located at the southern end of the county, off A1A/Atlantic Blvd. Admission: $4 adults, $1 kids 11 and under. Open: 10 a.m.–4 p.m. daily.*

Seeing and doing more cool things

Here's where we give visitors with varied interests a few more specialized options for their Daytona vacation:

 ✔ **Beaches: Ormond Beach,** Hwy. 40 at A1A, is a quieter version (sans boardwalk and odd characters) of its Daytona counterpart. **Ponce Inlet,** south of Port Orange off A1A, is almost as peaceful. **Daytona Beach,** Seabreeze Boulevard to Volusia Avenue east of A1A, is where the nerve-jarring action is. The **Daytona Beach**

Boardwalk, just east of where U.S. 92 crosses A1A and dives into the ocean, is arguably one of the top five people-watching places in Florida, and it offers a cheesy, midway-style arcade to sweeten (or sour) the pot.

✔ **Fishing:** More than 25 vessels offer half- and full-day charters into the Atlantic Ocean, where you might hook a tuna, wahoo, or grouper. **Charters by Cindy** (☎ **904-761-0680;** Internet: www. daytonabeachfishing.com) charges $450 half-day and $650 full-day rates, for up to six people. **Cookie Cutter Sport Fishing** (☎ **904-304-0006;** Internet: www.charternet.com/fishers/ cookiecutter) offers the same charter options for $400 and $800, respectively.

✔ **Golf:** In addition to the following options, you can find more local golf information on the Web at www.golf.com and www. floridagolfing.com. If you like surfing the old-fashioned way, request course information from the **Florida Sports Foundation** (☎ **850-488-8347**) or **Florida Golfing** (☎ **877-222-4653**). Here's a list of some of the better local courses:

- **Deltona Hills Golf and Country Club,** 1120 Elkcam Blvd., Daytona (☎ **904-789-4911**), has rolling hills and fairways. Greens fees are $25 to $40 in the winter and under $25 in the summer.

- **Daytona Beach Municipal Golf Course,** 600 Wilder Blvd. (☎ **904-258-3119**), has twin courses — the south course has fairways with palm trees and lakes, the north course offers rolling fairways with lush vegetation. Greens fees are $25 to $40 in the winter and under $25 in the summer.

- **Halifax Plantation,** 4000 Old Dixie Hwy., Ormond Beach (☎ **800-676-9600**), offers a canopy of oaks, combined with a terrain featuring rolling hills. Greens fees are $40 to $65 in the winter and under $25 in the summer.

✔ **Parks: Washington Oaks State Park,** 6400 Oceanshore Blvd./A1A, Palm Coast (☎ **904-446-6780**), is a nineteenth-century plantation turned 400-acre park that stretches from the Atlantic to the Matanzas River. You can take guided tours, but exploring the ornamental gardens, tidal pools, and dunes on your own is much more fun. The park is 14 miles north of Flagler Beach (about 35 miles north of Daytona Beach) on A1A. Admission is $3.75 per car.

Seeing Daytona Beach in 3 Days

To prevent you from running yourself ragged, we include the following sample itinerary for Daytona Beach. It will get you to the must-see-and-do places in Daytona, but if your plans or interests don't match our suggestions, feel free to tailor it to your own needs.

You're off to the races on **Day 1.** Start with a combined visit to **Daytona International Speedway** and **Daytona USA,** grab a late lunch at **McK's Dublin Station,** and then catch **Mark Martin's Klassix Auto Museum.** If you still have gas in your tank, see the **Museum of Arts and Sciences,** before heading north to **Julian's Dining Room & Lounge** for dinner. If you're in the mood for a nightcap, visit the **River Deck Nite Club and Restaurant** (skip ahead to "Enjoying the Nightlife" and look under "Bars").

We take things slower on **Day 2.** Rise and shine at **Washington Oaks State Park,** grab lunch on the fly, and then spend the afternoon soaking in the sun and surf at **Ormond Beach. Billy's Tap Room & Grill** is a good spot for your evening meal.

On **Day 3,** head south for a casual morning at the **Ponce Inlet Lighthouse and Museum,** have lunch at **Down the Hatch Seafood Restaurant,** and then spend the afternoon strolling and people-watching along the **Daytona Beach Boardwalk.** Continue your sight-seeing from the twenty-ninth-floor view at the **Top of Daytona Oceanfront Restaurant & Lounge.**

Shopping

There are some shopping "districts" in and around Daytona, but remember that this is a tourist zone and has all the related trappings — over-priced antiques shops on one side, and trinket shacks on the other. Look for the tackiest souvenirs along Atlantic Avenue/A1A, especially near the boardwalk (where U.S. 92 connects with A1A). Most shops sell barely-there bathing suits, seashells, and T-shirts decorated with some of the world's most forgettable expressions.

Main St. Inc., 512 Canal St. (☎ **904-423-3131**), in the New Smyrna Beach Downtown Historic District, has several places to hunt for antiques. There are also a number of restaurants, an Indian River Bazaar, jewelry shops, and on the weekends, a Farmers' Market.

Volusia Mall, 1700 International Speedway Blvd. (☎ **904-253-6785**), has 120 stores anchored by Belks, Burdines, Maison Blanche, Dillard's, and Sears. Some smaller nearby strip centers feature stores such as T.J. Maxx.

Adventure Landing (see "Touring the top sights," earlier in this chapter) will soon become part of a new $200 million renovation project known as **Ocean Walk Village.** The complex will include entertainment venues, condos, shopping, and the Ocean Center Convention and Civic Center. The facility will open in stages; the first phase includes $45 million in renovations to the **Adam's Mark Hotel** (see "Daytona Beach's best hotels," earlier in this chapter) and a new 350-room tower. The 300-room Beachfront Condominium Resort is set to open in the fall of 2001. The Seaside Shopping and Entertainment complex will open in the fall of 2002.

Enjoying the Nightlife

In addition to the following, you can find a lot of action along the main beach strip, A1A/Atlantic Avenue. You should also check the Daytona Beach *News-Journal* for its Friday "Go-Do" and Sunday "Master Calendar" sections.

Bars

None of the following bars charge a cover.

Coach's, 200 Beach St., Daytona Beach (☎ 904-258-8468), has slot-car racing, darts, video games, and live music. There's also a restaurant and Friday-night boxing. The **River Deck Nite Club & Restaurant,** 2739 S. Ridgewood, Ormond Beach (☎ 904-761-0022), features classic dance tunes, and Wednesday is ladies' night. **Frank's Front Row,** 308 Seabreeze, Daytona Beach (☎ 904-255-9221), has a dart room and pool tables. Saturday night is jam night, where amateurs can get into the act. **New Marker 32,** 849 Ballough Rd., Daytona (☎ 904-257-3989), offers live music on Friday and Saturday nights.

Clubs

Billy Bob's Bar and Grill, 2801 S. Ridgewood, South Daytona (☎ 904-756-0448), features karaoke on Wednesdays and live music on Fridays and Saturdays. There's a $5 cover. **The Rockin' Ranch,** 801 S. Nova Rd., Ormond Beach (☎ 904-673-0904), is pure country. Mondays are for karaoke and line dancing, Wednesdays are ladies' nights, and live bands play on Fridays and Saturdays. There's a $6 cover.

Performing arts

The **Peabody Auditorium,** 600 Auditorium Blvd., Daytona Beach (☎ 904-258-3169 or 904-255-1314, box office), is home to the Daytona Beach Symphony Society, the Civic Ballet of Volusia County, and the Concert Showcase of Florida. It also hosts touring companies.

The **Seaside Music Theater,** 176 N. Beach St., Daytona Beach (☎ 800-854-5592 or 904-252-6200; Internet: http://volusia.org/echotourism/cultural/seaside.htm), stages musicals, opera, and Broadway-style entertainment. Summer offers the larger of two production schedules, with a full orchestra playing Tuesday through Sunday and a children's theater each weekend. The winter schedule features dramas, musicals, and classical works.

Fast Facts

Area Code

The local area code is **904**.

American Express

There are two local offices: **New Smyrna Travel,** 301 Flagler Ave., New Smyrna Beach (☎ **904-427-3444**), and **Odyssey Travel,** 1474 W. Granada Blvd., Ormond Beach (☎ **904-672-8113**).

Hospitals

The region's major hospital is **Halifax Medical Center,** 303 N. Clyde Morris Blvd., Daytona Beach (☎ **904-254-4000**).

Information Sources

You can contact the **Daytona Beach Convention and Visitors Bureau,** 126 E. Orange Ave. (☎ **800-854-1234**; Internet: www.daytonabeach.com), from 9 a.m. to 5 p.m. on weekdays.

Mail

There are post offices at 220 N. Beach St., Daytona Beach, and 260 Williamson Blvd., Ormond Beach. For other local branches, call ☎ **800-275-8777**.

Maps

The visitors bureau (see "Information Sources," earlier in this section) is a great place to get maps, before or after you land. You can also find good maps at your rental-car agency and inside convenience stores, which sell them for $3 to $5.

Newspapers

The *News Journal* (☎ **904-252-1511**) is the local paper and publishes an informative Friday entertainment section.

Pharmacies

There's a 24-hour **Walgreens** at 1420 Beville Rd., Daytona Beach (☎ 904-257-5773), and another at 790 W. Granada Blvd., Ormond Beach (☎ **904-672-7107**).

Taxes

The sales tax is 6 percent; hotels tack on an additional 4 percent.

Taxis

The main taxi company is **Yellow Cab** (☎ **904-255-5555**). Its rates are $2.60 to start the meter and $1.40 per additional mile.

Transit Info

Volusia County's public system, **VOLTRAN** (☎ **904-761-7700**), runs the Jolly Trolley along Atlantic Avenue (A1A), from noon to midnight Monday through Saturday. VOLTRAN also runs buses throughout the beaches and mainland daily. Fares for both run $1 for adults, 50 cents for seniors and kids under 18.

Weather Updates

For a recording of current conditions and forecast reports, call the local office of the **National Weather Service** at ☎ **321-255-0212** or check out its Web site at www.srh.noaa.gov/mlb. You can also get information by watching **The Weather Channel** or checking out its Web site at www.weatherchannel.com.

Chapter 22

Northeast Florida

. . . .

In This Chapter

▶ Drinking from the fountain of youth in our oldest city

▶ Touring a good Navy town: Jacksonville

▶ Riding an uphill water coaster: Adventure Landing

▶ Seeing a nineteenth-century sugar plantation

. . . .

*R*emember Ponce de Leon from your high-school history class?
Well, it turns out he was a better dreamer than an astronomer. He
was supposed to land at Bimini and find the "fountain of youth" that
would keep Jolly Ol' King Ferdinand and his daughter, Joanna the Mad
(we're not making that up), on their thrones forever. But Ponce bounced
his azimuth off the wrong star and wound up near present-day Cape
Canaveral. Instead of eternal life and the hand of Joanna, he got snakes,
angry natives, and alligators that were more than happy to sample a
little Spanish take-out.

As for the fabled fountain, well, St. Augustine has one, complete with a
gift shop. But at the risk of bursting your bubble, it goes downhill after
you buy your glow-in-the-dark key chain. Here's the post-mortem on
the whole fountain-of-youth saga:

✔ Because no one has seen Ponce or King Ferdinand in quite a few
years, it's a safe bet that the everlasting-life theory, at least in this
dimension, is a wash.

✔ Legend says you have to sip from the fountain to reap its rewards.
If you do, you're making a *BIG* mistake. The water in St. Augustine's
fountain contains sulfur, which, as anyone who's ever been held
captive in chemistry class knows, smells like rotten eggs.

✔ The fountain is indoors. It even has a dome.

More on that domed scandal later in this chapter, but for now, here's
our 3-minute thumbnail on this region.

After you drive away from the coast, the Great Northeast is about as rural as Florida gets. The St. Johns River is the interior's biggest attraction. The river is a magnet for anglers, boaters, and other river rats, but for most tourists it's little more than a reference point or a backdrop for some other activity, closer to the coast.

Due to the lack of action away from the coast, this chapter's tour bus stays near the Atlantic. We divide this region into two general areas, south to north. St. Augustine is the oldest city in the United States, and this city has a lot to do, if you like to live history. Jacksonville is the largest city in Northeast Florida, but it's not necessarily where you can find the most to do, and its neighbors, Fernandina Beach and Amelia Island, have colorful histories but, again, not much in the way of attractions.

Now, if some of you will hum a few bars of traveling music, we can get started on the road to Northeast Florida.

Visiting Northeast Florida and Its Attractions

Established in 1565, **St. Augustine** is the oldest continuously settled city in the United States. Few things worth mentioning can be found west of the San Sebastian River and the Intracoastal Waterway. But the downtown coastal area has a ton of history, including the **Bridge of Lions, Castillo de San Marcos,** and the century-old **St. Augustine Alligator Farm.** Most of the points of interest are on the water, including **Vilano Beach** and **Anastasia Island State Recreation Area,** which are great places to get wet.

The best of **Jacksonville** is along the Atlantic Ocean and St. Johns River. The highpoints include the **Jacksonville Zoo, Little and Big Talbot Island State Parks, Kingsley Plantation,** and **Neptune, Atlantic,** and **Jacksonville Beaches.**

Fernandina Beach and Amelia Island are more laid-back. Centre Street and Fort Clinch State Park are the main stops in these two areas.

St. Augustine

As we said, this is the oldest city in the United States, and you can find a bounty of history in its architecture, attractions, and accommodations. At least a half dozen places in town claim to be the oldest something or other. A few of them actually are. (Skip ahead to see a map of St. Augustine.)

St. Augustine

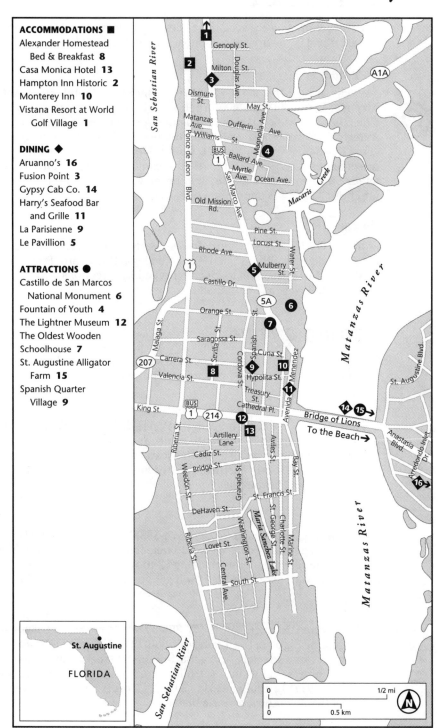

ACCOMMODATIONS ■
Alexander Homestead
  Bed & Breakfast **8**
Casa Monica Hotel **13**
Hampton Inn Historic **2**
Monterey Inn **10**
Vistana Resort at World
  Golf Village **1**

DINING ◆
Aruanno's **16**
Fusion Point **3**
Gypsy Cab Co. **14**
Harry's Seafood Bar
  and Grille **11**
La Parisienne **9**
Le Pavillion **5**

ATTRACTIONS ●
Castillo de San Marcos
  National Monument **6**
Fountain of Youth **4**
The Lightner Museum **12**
The Oldest Wooden
  Schoolhouse **7**
St. Augustine Alligator
  Farm **15**
Spanish Quarter
  Village **9**

St. Augustine

FLORIDA

0   1/2 mi

0   0.5 km

Getting there

The further north we travel, the easier it is to leave the driving to you, but air travel is the arrival-and-departure method of choice.

By plane

The only airport that serves this area is **Jacksonville International Airport** (☎ **904-741-2000;** Internet: www.jaxport.com/jai.cfm), which is 43 miles north of St. Augustine. A dozen major lines, including **American, Continental, Delta, Northwest, TWA,** and **US Airways,** serve it. There are **Avis, Budget, Dollar, Hertz,** and **National** rental-car desks on the airport's lower level. You can also get a ride into town on **Super Shuttle** (☎ **800-258-3826;** Internet: www.supershuttle.com), for about $30 to $45 per person one-way.

By car

From the North, take I-95 south to Exit 94/Hwy.16, and then go east into the city, and go south on U.S. 1/Ponce de Leon Boulevard. From the west, take I-10 to I-95 and follow the preceding directions. From the Midwest, follow I-75 to I-10, then I-95.

Getting around

The city's historic downtown is user-friendly enough to allow visitors to get around on foot, but here are some other options.

By car

In addition to U.S. 1 (which becomes Ponce de Leon Boulevard in the city), A1A is the main north-south route, and it stays pretty close to the water. In town, you may also use Cordova and St. George Streets to travel north and south. East-west routes include Hwys. 16 and 312, King Street, and May Street.

By taxi

For a taxi, call **Yellow Cab** (☎ **904-824-6888**). St. Augustine taxis use a complicated zone system that would take half this book to explain, but you can generally figure on spending $2 to $8 for one person and $1.50 for each extra body. Those rates will get you to most parts of the city.

By tour

St. Augustine Historical Tours (☎ **800-397-4071** or 904-829-3800) and **St. Augustine Sightseeing Trains** (☎ **800-226-6545** or 904-829-6545) offer two-for-one specials. You get a 1-hour sightseeing tour, plus you can use their respective buses, trolleys, and trains to get around town for three days ($12 adults, $5 kids 6 to 12). This is an inexpensive way to travel the downtown historic district.

Staying in St. Augustine

St. Augustine has plenty of moderate and inexpensive hotels. If you want a unique experience, however, stay in one of the city's bed-and-breakfasts, many of which occupy restored historic homes. Note, however, that kids aren't usually welcome, and smokers are definitely not. The **Historic Inns of St. Augustine,** P.O. Box 5268, St. Augustine, FL 33085-5268 (www.staugustineinns.com), provides visitors with a list describing its member properties.

Hotel rates increase significantly on weekends, when the city is usually inundated with visitors, so try coming during the week to lower your costs. Also, don't forget to add the hotel tax of 9 percent to your budget.

St. Augustine's best hotels

Alexander Homestead Bed and Breakfast

$$ St. Augustine

This historic, two-story, Victorian inn was built in 1888 and now offers four cozy rooms decorated with antiques (two have fireplaces). Rates include gourmet breakfasts that might include country French apple casserole, French toast, homemade muffins, granola, and orange juice and fruit. Picnic lunches are available ($25 to $35), but forget about a pool.

14 Sevilla St. ☎ **888-292-4147** *or 904-826-4147. Internet:* www.alexanderhomestead.com. *To get there: Located east of U.S. 1, just south of Orange St. Parking: Free. Rack rates: $125–$175 year-round. AE, DISC, MC, V.*

Casa Monica Hotel

$$ St. Augustine

This stately downtown hotel was built in 1888 and, for three decades, served as the county courthouse. Reborn in 1997 as a luxury hotel, the Casa Monica has roomy quarters outfitted with cushy beds, large baths, and armoires. This hotel is situated in the heart of the historic district near the Lightner Museum and is within walking distance of many attractions.

95 Cordova St. (at King St.). ☎ **800-648-1888** *or 904-827-1888. Fax: 904-827-0426. Internet:* www.casamonica.com. *To get there: Take U.S. 1/Ponce de Leon Blvd. south to King St., and then left to Cordova. Parking: $8 valet. Rack rates: standard rooms $149–$209 Jan–Feb and June–Aug, $159–$229 Mar–May and Sept–Dec; suites to $599. AE, DC, DISC, MC, V.*

Hampton Inn Historic

$ St. Augustine

This 52-room chain motel is 6 blocks north of the historic district. This motel is neither luxurious nor in the heart of the action, but the privately run city trolleys (see "Getting around," earlier in this chapter) stop here. It presents a clean option, for those on tighter budgets. Rates include continental breakfast.

2050 N. Ponce de Leon Blvd./U.S. 1. ☎ **800-426-7866** *or 904-829-1996. Fax: 904-829-1988. Internet:* www.hamptoninn.com. *To get there: On U.S. 1, just north of downtown. Parking: Free. Rack rates: $95–$115 Feb–Apr, $85–$105 May–Sept, $75–$85 Oct–Nov. AE, CB, DC, DISC, MC, V.*

Monterey Inn

$ St. Augustine

This 59-unit, family-owned motel overlooks Matanzas Bay, and you can't beat the price. The guest rooms are tight on space but clean and comfortable. Free morning coffee is offered.

16 Avenida Menendez (between Cuna St. and Hypolita St.). ☎ **904-824-4481.** *Fax: 904-829-8854. Internet:* www.themontereyinn.com. *To get there: Located at U.S. 1 Business Rt. and A1A. Parking: Free. Rack rates: $59–$99 year-round, though weekday rates are as low as $39. AE, DC, DISC, MC, V.*

Vistana Resort at World Golf Village

$$ St. Augustine

This beautifully landscaped property's large one- and two-bedroom villas can hold anywhere from six to ten people. All accommodations overlook the 17th and 18th holes of the resort's championship golf course. The villas have full kitchens, living and dining rooms, whirlpools, and washers and dryers. This is golfers' heaven, but the property also has a fitness center, tennis, volleyball, and a pool.

100 Front Nine Dr. ☎ **800-477-3340** *or 904-940-2000. Fax: 904-940-2092. Internet:* http://vistanainc.com/resorts/WGV. *To get there: Take I-95 to Exit 95A, just west to the resort. Parking: Free. Rack rates: $219–$259 Jan–Mar, $179–$219 Dec–Jan and Apr–May, $159–$189 Jun–Sept. AE, DC, DISC, MC, V.*

Runner-up accommodations

If you can't find something already listed that suits you, consider this four-pack of choices on our second tier.

Bayfront Inn

$$ St. Augustine   This modest, but comfortable motel offers 39 rooms in the heart of the historic district. *138 Avenida Menendez, just south of A1A and the Bridge of Lions* ☎ *800-558-3455 or 904-824-1681. Fax: 904-829-8721. Internet:* www.bayfrontinn.com.

Casablanca Inn on the Bay

$$ St. Augustine   This 1914 Mediterranean-style house faces the bay and offers beautifully decorated rooms, plus free beer, wine, soft drinks, and cookies. There isn't a pool. *24 Avenida Menendez, between Hypolita St. and Treasury St.* ☎ *800-826-2626 or 904-829-0928. Fax: 904-826-1892. Internet:* www.casablancainn.com.

Coquina Gables Oceanfront Bed & Breakfast

$ St. Augustine Beach   This oceanfront inn has a great room with a fireplace, luxurious suites named for famous authors, a gourmet breakfast, and a nice beach. *1 F St.* ☎ *904-461-8727. Fax: 904-461-4346. Internet:* www.coquinagables.com.

La Fiesta Oceanside Inn & Suites

$$ St. Augustine Beach   This modest property offers comfortable motel-style rooms, large suites, and a nice beach. *810 A1A/Beach Blvd.* ☎ *800-852-6390 or 904-471-2220. Fax: 904-471-0186. Internet:* www.lafiestaoceanside.com.

Dining Out in St. Augustine

When one considers St. Augustine's popularity with the tourist crowd, it isn't surprising that the city is loaded with tourist-trap restaurants and fast-food joints. That said, the dining in town is, on the whole, pretty good and fairly priced. The local cuisine is (surprise!) seafood mixed with a variety of other ethnic dishes.

Don't forget to add the 6 percent sales tax to your meal budget.

St. Augustine's best restaurants

Aruanno's

$$ St. Augustine Beach   ITALIAN

Open since 1982, this upscale eatery specializes in traditional pasta dishes, a nice selection of steaks, and house favorites, such as herb-crusted rack of lamb, roast duck, potato-crusted salmon in horseradish sauce, and scallops sautéed in garlic, onions, hot peppers, tomatoes, black olives, and Italian sausage.

Corner of A1A/Beach Blvd. and D St. ☎ *904-471-9373. Internet:* www.oldcity.com/aruannos. *To get there: Follow A1A from the mainland south to D Street. Reservations accepted. Main courses: $8–$20. AE, MC, V. Open: 5–10 p.m. Tues–Sun.*

Fusion Point

$ St. Augustine   ORIENTAL/SUSHI

This eatery offers a mix of cuisines from the Far East. As with most tapas bars, a hearty appetite at this restaurant can turn a $ eatery into a $$ or $$$ one. Specialties include tilapia served with black-bean sauce and yum-yum rolls (smoked salmon, cream cheese, avocado, and fish flake). The food is fresh and tasty.

237 San Marco Ave. ☎ *904-823-1444. Internet:* www.fusioncuisine.com. *To get there: Located on San Marco/U.S. 41 Business Rt., just north of the heart of town. Reservations not accepted. Main courses: $1.25–$3.00 per item; $2.50–$6.00 per roll. MC, V. Open: 5–10 p.m. daily.*

Gypsy Cab Co.

$$ St. Augustine   NEW AMERICAN

The menu changes frequently in this restaurant that looks like a gaudy house built in the '40s or '50s (it was). The "urban cuisine" here is among the city's most interesting and is expertly prepared by the owner himself, Chef Ned Pollack. Try the black bean soup and the veal with bacon-horseradish cream. As a capper, try the chocolate-raspberry cheesecake or Key lime pie. The Gypsy Bar & Grill (next door) serves lunch from 11 a.m. to 3 p.m. daily.

830 Anastasia Blvd./A1A. ☎ *904-824-8244. Internet:* www.gypsycab.com. *To get there: Located on A1A, 1 mile south of the Bridge of Lions. Reservations accepted. Main courses: $10–$18, with many in the $16–$18 range. AE, DC, DISC, MC, V. Open: 5:30–10 p.m. daily.*

Harry's Seafood, Bar, and Grille

$$ St. Augustine   NEW ORLEANS/SEAFOOD

Come to this Cajun restaurant hankering for crawdad etouffee, spicy gumbo, chicken-and-andouille-sausage jambalaya, and other treats straight out of *Naw'lins*. We love the shrimp en brochette (large wraps stuffed with shrimp and Monterey Jack, wrapped in bacon, and grilled). There are almost enough under-$15 entrees to make this a $ restaurant.

46 Avenida Menendez. ☎ *904-824-7765. Internet:* www.hookedonharrys.com. *To get there: On Avenida Menendez near Hypolita. Reservations accepted. Main courses: $10–$23. AE, MC, V. Open: 11 a.m.–10 p.m. daily.*

La Parisienne

$$ St. Augustine   CONTEMPORARY FRENCH

This charming French restaurant serves up fine and elegant cuisine in the heart of the historic district. Begin with escargot in puff pastry and then dive into an elegant entree from the rotating menu that includes roast rack of lamb Provençal or steak au poivre. Along the way, add something from the extensive wine list.

60 Hypolita St. ☎ *904-829-0055. Internet:* www.laparisienne.net. *To get there: Located between Spanish St. and Cordova St. Reservations suggested. Main courses: $14–$27. AE, DISC, MC, V. Open: 11 a.m.–3 p.m. and 5–10 p.m. Thurs–Tues.*

Le Pavillon

$$ St. Augustine   CONTINENTAL

This romantic restaurant in the historic district has been dishing out first-class food since 1977. Swiss Chef Claude Sinatsch and his wife, Giselle, let the menu range from crepes to seafood (shrimp, scallops, and snapper in cream sauce) to duck (in glazed apricots and cherries) to schnitzel Viennese.

45 San Marco Blvd. ☎ *904-824-6202. Internet:* www.lepav.com. *To get there: Just north of Mulberry St. on San Marco. Reservations suggested. Main courses: $14–$27. AE, CB, DC, DISC, MC, V. Open: 11:30 a.m.–2 p.m. and 5–10 p.m. daily.*

Runner-up restaurants

Sometimes, your stay exceeds the number of restaurants on our list. Other times, you just run into some that don't suit your palate. So here are a few other good dining choices to consider.

Columbia Restaurant

$$ St. Augustine   It isn't as good as the original Columbia in Tampa's Ybor City, but it has some of the same Cuban fare, including boliche, paella, and ropa vieja. *98 St. George St. (at Hypolita St.)* ☎ *904-824-3341. Internet:* www.columbiarestaurant.com.

Cortesse's Bistro

$$ St. Augustine   This bistro offers a wide-ranging menu that includes burgers, jerk chicken, pasta, peppered salmon, Minorcan fish stew, and herb-crusted lamb chops. *172 San Marco Ave.* ☎ *904-825-6775.*

O.C. Whites Seafood & Spirits

$$ **St. Augustine**   This restaurant serves fresh seafood and steaks in a mansion, built in 1791, that overlooks Matanzas Bay and the Bridge of Lions. *118 Avenida Menendez* ☎ *904-824-0808.* *Internet:* www.oldcity.com/ocwhite.

Salt Water Cowboy's

$ **St. Augustine Beach**   It looks like a turn-of-the-century fish camp, but it's a modern restaurant that serves barbecue (ribs and chicken), seafood, and steaks. *299 Dondanville Rd.* ☎ *904-471-2332.*

Exploring St. Augustine

As you already know, history is the highlight in St. Augustine, and the special effects are pretty overwhelming. This city contains 144 blocks of houses and buildings that are on the National Register of Historic Places. The center of the district is St. George Street, a few blocks east of U.S. 1. Much of the action takes place on St. George, the Avenida Menendez, King Street, San Marco Avenue, Castillo Drive, or across the Bridge of Lions, which leads to Anastasia Island. Speaking of which . . .

Touring the top sights

Bridge of Lions

St. Augustine

An Italian sculptor carved the two kings of beasts on the historic Bridge of Lions, which goes from the mainland to Anastasia Island. Alas, the artist left a few physical attributes off his lions, and legend has it that he was subjected to such ridicule by townies that he stabbed himself with a blunt sculpting knife. The Bridge, located where U.S. 1/San Marco turns into Anastasia Boulevard and crosses the Intracoastal Waterway, is one of the most photographed (and congested) sights in town.

Castillo de San Marcos National Monument

St. Augustine

First off, the fort is closed for one year, at least through October 2001, while the National Parks Service makes repairs to damage done by years of harsh weather, including hurricanes. That said, this Spanish fortress was built in the eighteenth century and includes plenty of bastions, dungeons, and artillery positions to explore. While the site is closed, the park service plans to beef up free activities on the outside grounds. When open, most folks can see it all in 1 to 2 hours.

1 E. Castillo Dr. (at San Marco Ave.). ☎ *904-824-2806. Admission: $4 adults, kids under 16 Free. Open: 8:45 a.m.–4:45 p.m. daily.*

Fountain of Youth

St. Augustine

We promised to get back to (drum roll, please) Ponce's Fountain of Youth. So, here you are. This fountain's for you, if you're the kind who flushes, er, spends money on anything, or you want to be the only one on your block with an "I-Drank-Sulfur-Water" bumper sticker. If you go, we hope you remember our warning about this foul-tasting liquid. There is also a planetarium where you can stargaze at the dome, old excavations, a 45-minute tour that gets downright silly, and the Ponce de Leon Gift Shop. Allow 90 minutes to see everything.

11 Magnolia Ave. ☎ *800-356-8222 (yes, an everlasting phone line) or 904-829-3168. Admission: $6 adults, $3 kids 6–12. Open: 9 a.m.–5 p.m. daily.*

The Lightner Museum

St. Augustine

This cutie began life in 1888 as Henry Flagler's elaborate, Spanish Renaissance-style resort spa. These days it makes a gorgeous museum that has substantial collections of cut glass, vases, wood-jointed dolls, and a music room that provides automated concerts at 11 a.m. and 2 p.m. daily. The first floor has a row of shops. You can also meet a mummy, equally dead birds, samples of Victorian glassblowing, and a collection of rocks, minerals, and Native American artifacts in period cases. There are 1-hour guided tours (call in advance for schedule). Allow 1 to 2 hours to see the highlights.

75 King St. ☎ *904-824-2874. To get there: Located at King and Cordova. Admission: $6 adults, $2 kids 12–18. Open: 9 a.m.–5 p.m. daily.*

The Oldest Wooden Schoolhouse

St. Augustine

This is one of many "oldests" in this city (others include a house, store, jail, and so on). The schoolhouse dates to 1763, and the red-cedar building is held together by wooden pegs and nails that were made by hand. Today, the last class — held in 1864 — is re-created for visitors. You'll be ready to leave after 45 minutes.

14 George St. ☎ *904-829-9729. Admission: $2.50 adults, $2.00 seniors, $1.50 kids 6–12. Open: 9 a.m.–5 p.m. daily.*

St. Augustine Alligator Farm

St. Augustine

It's not as old as some landmarks, but it is the oldest, continuously running reptile retreat in Florida. This throwback opened in 1893 and features *Land of Crocodiles,* which has all 23 species of crocodiles. Until 1999, its biggest star was Gomek, an 18-foot, 1,800-pound Porosus crocodile that, in his native New Guinea, munched on water buffaloes and slow-moving humans. Alas, Gomek has gone to that big swamp in the sky, but his skin has been stuffed so you can sit on him and get your picture taken. The park also has alligator, snake, and bird shows. Figure on staying 4 to 5 hours.

999 Anastasia Blvd. ☎ *904-824-3337. Internet:* www.alligatorfarm.com. *To get there: Located across the Bridge of Lions on A1A. Admission: $12 adults, $11 seniors, $8 kids 3–10. Open: 10 a.m.–6 p.m. daily (closes 1 hour earlier in winter).*

Spanish Quarter Village

St. Augustine

This living-history village dates to 1740 and features blacksmiths, weavers, and woodworkers, among other trades people. The **City Gate,** on San Marco near Orange, was erected in 1808 as a defensive wall to keep vacuum-cleaner salesmen and religious-tract distributors out of the city. **Mission of Nombre de Dios,** west of San Marco Avenue on Old Mission Road at the Intracoastal, goes way back to 1565 and has a 208-foot cross that's visible from 25 miles at sea. It's where the first Catholic Mass in the United States was said, but mass is no longer offered there. Allow 2 to 3 hours to see it all.

29 St. George St. ☎ *904-825-6830. To get there: Located between Cuna St. and Orange St. Admission: $6.00 adults, $5.00 seniors, $3.50 kids 6 and older. Open: 9 a.m.–5 p.m. daily.*

Doing more cool stuff

If you need a break from sightseeing and want to get a catch a ray on the beach or snag a grouper that could feed an army, you can choose from several outdoor recreational activities. And when you're ready to hit the touring trail again, you may want to try one of the tour companies that offer specialized programs for visitors.

✔ **Beaches: Vilano Beach,** on the north side of St. Augustine Inlet on A1A, is a public beach with restrooms, volleyball courts, and picnic areas. After you cross the Bridge of Lions, **Yankee Beach** is the first stop on Anastasia Island. It earned its name because many tourists never venture beyond it. Those that do discover **Anastasia Island State Recreation Area** (☎ 904-461-2033). This

1,700-acre bird sanctuary has 5 miles of beaches, lagoons, sabal palms, and sea oats, growing wild from 20-foot dunes. Admission costs $3.25 per car.

✔ **Fishing:** Snapper, grouper, amberjack, and other species are common catches in the Atlantic Ocean. You can charter a fishing boat from **Sea Love Marina,** 250 Vilano Rd./A1A N. (☎ **904-824-3328**). Half-day trips are $35; full days cost $50.

✔ **Golf:** The popular-but-pricey **World Golf Village** (☎ 904-940-6000) offers 54 holes, including The Slammer and The Squire, a fairly open course with kind greens. Greens fees are $110 and up in winter, $86 to $110 in summer. **St. Johns County Golf Course,** 4900 Cypress Links Blvd., St. Augustine (☎ **904-825-4900**), is forgiving on the average player and his or her wallet — fees here are $25 to $40 year-round.

You can find more places to play golf in the area on the Internet at `www.golf.com` and `www.floridagolfing.com`, or you can call the **Florida Sports Foundation** (☎ **850-488-8347**), or **Florida Golfing** (☎ **877-222-4653**).

✔ **Land Cruising:** The **St. Augustine Electric Car Company,** 125 King Street (☎ **904-829-9255**), rents futuristic electric cars that go 24 mph and can travel up to 50 miles before you need a recharge. Hourly rates are $24.50 for two-seaters and $39.50 for four-seaters.

Seeing St. Augustine by guided tour

St. Augustine Historical Tours (☎ 800-397-4071 or 904-829-3800) and **St. Augustine Sigthseeing Trains** (☎ 800-226-6545 or 904-829-6545) offer a 1-hour sightseeing tour, and then you get to use their respective buses and trains to get around town for 3 days. The tour costs $12 for adults, $5 for kids 6 to 12.

Colee's Carriage Tours (☎ 904-829-2818) offers 45-minute to 1-hour horse-drawn carriage tours through the city's historic district. Tours cost $15 for adults, and $7 for kids 6 to 12; add $3 to the price if you take a tour after dark.

Ancient City Tours (☎ 800-597-7177 or 904-797-5604) has several guided tours, including an evening ghost walk. Prices begin at $5.

Shopping

There are no special shopping areas, but you will find an assortment of shops, scattered throughout the historic district, that sell everything from antiques to local hot sauces. The heart of the district is a pedestrians-only area on **St. George Street**, between Cuna Street and Cathedral Place. The trolleys and trains make frequent stops here.

There are two outlet malls on Hwy. 16, near I-95. **Belz Factory Outlet World** (☎ **904-826-1311**; Internet: www.belz.com) has 65 shops, including Polo Ralph Lauren, Tom Hilfiger, Liz Claiborne, Timberland, Royal Doulton, and Black and Decker. The **St. Augustine Outlet Center** (☎ **904-825-1555**) houses 95 stores, including Coach, Jones of New York, Ann Taylor, Calvin Klein, and Brooks Brothers.

Enjoying the nightlife

St. Augustine has dozens of small bars scattered along the beach and inside the historic district. **Murphy's Pour House,** 72 Spanish Street (☎ **904- 826-3533**; Internet: www.murphyspourhouse.com), features live music and a DJ on Friday and Saturday nights. **Ann O'Malley's,** 23 Orange St. (☎ **904-825-4000**), is another friendly Irish pub that has a good selection of ales, stouts, and drafts. **A1A Ale Works,** 1 King St. (☎ **904-829-2977**) is a microbrewery that attracts a young-to-middle-age crowd.

Seeing St. Augustine in 2 Days

Day 1 is a getting-to-know-the-area day. Hitch a ride with **St. Augustine Historical Tours** or **St. Augustine Sightseeing Trains** and get an overview of the city. Along the way, make pit stops at **Castillo de San Marcos, The Lightner Museum,** the **Bridge of Lions,** the shops in the St. George pedestrian area, and **Spanish Quarter Village.** Grab lunch in between stops and then have dinner at **Le Pavillon,** after you've worn yourself out.

Start **Day 2** at **St. Augustine Alligator Farm.** Get a burger in the park and, when you've had your fill, go for a swim or catch some sun at **Anastasia Island State Recreation Area.** Have dinner at **Harry's Seafood, Bar, and Grille,** and then lift a pint at **Murphy's Pour House.**

Jacksonville, Amelia Island, and Fernandina Beach

Jacksonville is part Navy town and part business destination, though it has some decent attractions and nice beaches. (See maps for Jacksonville, Amelia Island, and Fernandina Beach later in this chapter.) To its north, you'll find Amelia Island, a natural, upscale resort area, and Fernandina Beach, which has much of the area's history (but is nothing, in scope, like St. Augustine).

Getting there

Here, we go back to the usual three transportation modes to get here: planes, trains, and automobiles.

Jacksonville

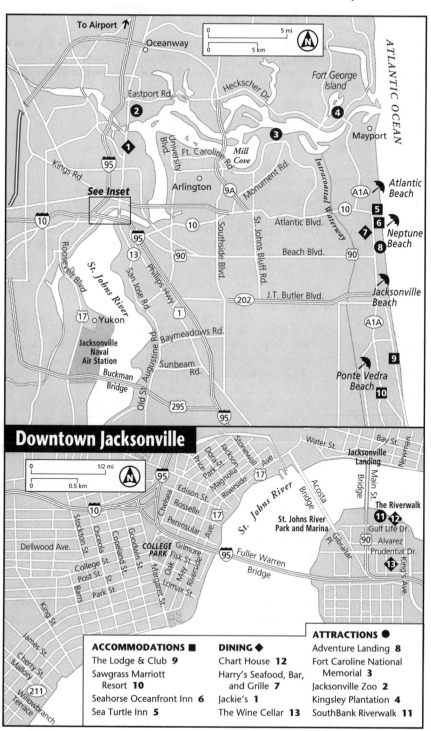

To Airport ↑

Oceanway

ATLANTIC OCEAN

0   5 mi
0   5 km

Eastport Rd.

Heckscher Dr.

Fort George
Island

2

University Blvd.

1

Ft. Caroline Rd.

Mill
Cove

3

Mayport

4

95

Kings Rd.

See Inset

Arlington

9A

Monument Rd.

Atlantic
Beach

A1A

10

5

Atlantic Blvd.

6

Neptune
Beach

7

8

10

95

90

Southside Blvd.

St. Johns Bluff Rd.

Beach Blvd.

90

Roosevelt Blvd.

13

San Jose Rd.

Phillips Hwy.

St. Johns River

90

Intracoastal Waterway

J.T. Butler Blvd.

202

Jacksonville
Beach

1

17 Yukon

Baymeadows Rd.

A1A

Jacksonville
Naval
Air Station

Old St. Augustine Rd.

Sunbeam
Rd.

Ponte Vedra
Beach

9

Buckman
Bridge

10

295

95

Downtown Jacksonville

0   1/2 mi
0   0.5 km

Water St.

Bay St.

Newnan

Jacksonville
Landing

Stonewall

Jackson

Dora

Price

Magnolia

Riverside

17

95

Main St.

Acosta Bridge

Edison St.

Chelsea

Rosselle

Peninsular

17

St. Johns River

St. Johns River
Park and Marina

Fuller Warren
Bridge

The Riverwalk

11 12

Gulf Life Dr.

90

Alvarez

Prudential Dr.

Dellwood Ave.

Stockton St.

Osceola

Copeland St.

Goodwin St.

**COLLEGE
PARK**

Gilmore

Fisk St.

Oak

May

Riverside

95

Fuller Warren
Bridge

Gibraltar Pl.

13

King's Ave.

College St.

Post St.

Barrs

Park St.

Margaret St.

Lomax St.

King St.

James St.

Cherry St.

Mallory

211

Willowbranch
Terrace

ACCOMMODATIONS ■
The Lodge & Club **9**
Sawgrass Marriott
  Resort **10**
Seahorse Oceanfront Inn **6**
Sea Turtle Inn **5**

DINING ◆
Chart House **12**
Harry's Seafood, Bar,
  and Grille **7**
Jackie's **1**
The Wine Cellar **13**

ATTRACTIONS ●
Adventure Landing **8**
Fort Caroline National
  Memorial **3**
Jacksonville Zoo **2**
Kingsley Plantation **4**
SouthBank Riverwalk **11**

By plane

Jacksonville International Airport (☎ **904-741-2000;** Internet: www.
jaxport.com/jai.cfm) has a dozen major carriers, including
American, Continental, Delta, Northwest, TWA, and **US Airways.**
There are **Avis, Budget, Dollar, Hertz,** and **National** rental-car desks
on the lower level. You can also get a ride on **Super Shuttle** (☎ **800-
258-3826;** Internet: www.supershuttle.com) for $10 to $30 per person
one-way. Or, you can hail a **Gator City Taxi** (☎ **904-355-8294**). It's $1.25
to start the meter, plus $1.25 per mile.

By car

From the North, take I-95 south. From the West, take I-10 to I-95. From
the Midwest, follow I-75 to I-10, then I-95.

By train

Amtrak (☎ **800-872-7245;** Internet: www.amtrak.com) has a terminal in
downtown Jacksonville at 3570 Clifford Lane, off U.S. 1 and just north of
45th Street.

Getting around

Jacksonville is a large city and Fernandina Beach is about 30 miles
north of town. Unless you're going to stick close to a base camp, you're
going to need wheels of one sort or another. We recommend a rental
car as your best mode of transportation, although your feet will more
than suffice in downtown Jacksonville.

By car

I-10 and I-95 enter the heart of the city. I-295, with help from Highways
9A and 115, creates a loop that will help you avoid the traffic-laden
downtown business district.

Bay Street divides the north and south. Main Street divides the east
and west. But be wary of any address that has east, west, north, or
south attached to it. Compass directions don't always correspond to
addresses and street signs. The best thing to do is ask someone at your
destination for exact directions from your starting point.

By bus

Fares on **Jacksonville Transportation Authority** buses (☎ **904-
630-3100**) run from 70 cents to $1.50. Remember, though, that public
bus routes are the worst mode of transportation for tourists — they're
slow and designed primarily for commuters and locals heading to business and shopping venues.

By taxi

Gator City Taxi (☎ **904-355-8294**) charges $1.25 to get in and $1.25 for
each mile thereafter.

Amelia Island and Fernandina Beach

ACCOMMODATIONS ■
Amelia Island Plantation **5**
Fairbanks House **3**

ATTRACTIONS ●
BEAKS **6**
Fort Clinch State Park **1**
Little & Big Talbot Island
    State Parks **6**
Centre Street **2**

DINING ◆
Beech Street Grill **4**
Le Clos **2**

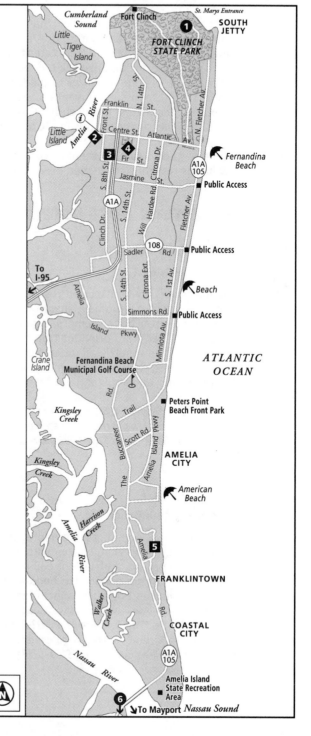

Staying in the Jacksonville Area

Jacksonville offers a variety of accommodations, from upscale resorts to business hotels to chain motels. A number of chains are represented along I-95. The downtown hotels cater to the business crowd, and rates there are higher during the week but can drop quite a bit on weekends. The beach hotels tend to be less expensive from December through March. The Jacksonville Convention and Visitors Bureau (see "Information" in "Fast Facts" at the end of this chapter) provides visitors with a list of accommodations in the area.

Hotel taxes add 9 to 12 percent to your bill, depending on where you stay in this region, so ask when making a reservation.

The area's best hotels

Amelia Island Plantation

$$ **Amelia Island**

This magnificently landscaped resort offers accommodations ranging from standard motel rooms to luxurious condos, villas, and penthouses. Many of the latter have washers, dryers, and full kitchens; some have two baths. A free tram provides transportation throughout the resort's 1,250 acres. The resort's all-inclusive rates allow unlimited use of the property's three championship golf courses, 23 clay tennis courts, health club privileges, and substantial kids' and teens' programs.

3000 First Coast Hwy. ☎ *888-261-6161 or 904-261-6161. Fax: 904-277-5945. Internet: www.aipfl.com. To get there: Located on A1A, on the south end of the island. Parking: Free. Rack rates: $130–$705 year-round; $189–$790 all inclusive. AE, DC, DISC, MC, V.*

Fairbanks House

$$ **Fernandina Beach**

This smoke-free (including the grounds) bed-and-breakfast delivers turn-of-the-century Victorian charm with heart-pine floors, a wonderful mahogany staircase, and 12-foot ceilings. Its 12 rooms, suites, and cottages have king- or queen-size beds and a Jacuzzi, claw-foot tub, or shower. A gourmet breakfast is included.

227 South 7th St. ☎ *888-891-9882 or 902-277-0500. Fax: 904-277-3103. Internet: www.fairbankshouse.com. To get there: Located south of Centre St., just west of A1A. Parking: Free. Rack rates: $150–$250 year-round. AE, DISC, MC, V.*

The Lodge & Club

$$$ Ponte Vedra Beach

This is one of two romantic resorts under the same umbrella. The second is **The Ponte Vedra Inn & Club** (☎ 800-234-7842). All 66 of the large and comfortable units at The Lodge & Club offer an ocean view from their balconies or patios. They also have garden tubs or Jacuzzis, refrigerators, window seats, and coffee makers with coffee. Privileges include use of the two golf courses and 15 tennis courts at the Inn & Club.

607 Ponte Vedra Blvd. (at Corona Rd.). ☎ 800-243-4304 or 904-273-9500. Fax: 904-273-0210. Internet: www.pvresorts.com. *To get there: Located off A1A, 20 miles south of Jacksonville. Parking: Free. Rack rates: rooms $185–$300 year-round, suites $250–$370. AE, DC, DISC, MC, V.*

Sawgrass Marriott Resort

$$ Ponte Vedra Beach

One of the largest golf resorts in the United States, the options at the Sawgrass Marriott range from standard hotel rooms to comfortable villas, suites, and condos. Some suites have full kitchens, minibars, and coffee makers. Sawgrass, home of the PGA's annual Players Championship in March, offers 99 holes of golf. The resort also features a steak-and-seafood restaurant, two health clubs, eight tennis courts, and several kids' programs.

1000 PGA Tour Blvd. ☎ 800-457-4653 or 904-285-7777. Fax: 904-285-0906. Internet: www.marriotthotels.com/jaxsw/. *To get there: Located south of Jacksonville, off A1A between Hwy. 210 and Butler Blvd. Parking: Free self-service, $9 valet. Rack rates: rooms $120–$320 year-round, suites and condos $190–$625. AE, DC, DISC, MC, V.*

Seahorse Oceanfront Inn

$ Neptune Beach

The Seahorse is a 1950s-style motel with clean rooms that offer a grand view of the Atlantic Ocean from balconies or patios. Some accommodations have kitchenettes, and several restaurants are nearby.

120 Atlantic Blvd. ☎ 800-881-2330 or 904-246-2175. Fax: 904-246-4256. Internet: www.seahorseresort.com. *To get there: Go to Atlantic Blvd. and 1st St. Parking: Free. Rack rates: motel rooms $79–$119 year-round, penthouse suite (sleeps 6) $200–$250. AE, DC, DISC, MC, V.*

Sea Turtle Inn

$$ Atlantic Beach

Completely renovated in 1999, this eight-story hotel offers 193 spacious rooms with ocean views, data ports, and coffee makers. Some rooms have balconies and refrigerators. Free coffee and newspapers are available on weekdays. A lounge and restaurant are on the premises.

1 Ocean Blvd. ☎ *800-874-6000 or 904-249-7402. Fax: 904-249-1119. Internet:* www. seaturtle.com. *To get there: Located at the ocean and Atlantic Boulevard. Parking: Free. Rack rates: $125–$239 year-round. AE, DC, DISC, MC, V.*

Runner-up accommodations

Here's a quartet of other lodging choices, in case we haven't lit a spark yet.

Florida House Inn

$$ Fernandina Beach   Open since 1857, this bed-and-breakfast's 11 rooms boast quilted beds, antique armoires, heart-pine floors, and private baths. Breakfast is included, but a pool isn't. *20 South 3rd St.* ☎ *800-258-3301 or 904-261-3300. Fax: 904-277-3831. Internet:* www.floridahouseinn. com.

Plantation Manor Inn

$$ Jacksonville   This nine-unit bed-and-breakfast has a lap pool, and its location is near the St. Johns River, in the downtown historic district. *1600 Copeland St.* ☎ *904-384-4630. Fax: 904-387-0960. Internet:* www. plantationmanorinn.com.

Ritz Carlton

$$$ Amelia Island   This posh golf-and-tennis resort has 450 oceanview and oceanfront rooms. *4750 Amelia Island Pkwy.* ☎ *800-241-3333 or 904-277-1100. Fax: 904-277-1145. Internet:* www.ritzcarlton.com.

Sabal Palm Inn B&B

$$ Jacksonville Beach   This small property offers four ocean-view rooms, with private baths, and a free continental breakfast. *115 5th Ave. South* ☎ *904-241-4545. Fax: 904-241-2407. Internet:* http://hometown.aol. com/sabalpalmin.

Dining Out in the Jacksonville Area

As in the rest of Florida, seafood rules in Jacksonville and its surrounding towns, although you will be able to find a variety of cuisine available in a decent range of prices.

Sales tax varies from 6 to 7 percent in this region.

The area's best restaurants

Beech Street Grill

$$ Fernandina Beach   NEW AMERICAN

Housed in an historic two-story home, this perennial award-winner is one of our favorite restaurants in North Florida. The upscale cuisine is fantastic, the service is professional, and the atmosphere is grand. Portuguese fish stew (lobster, mussels, clams, and whitefish in tomato broth, served over linguine), and roasted loin of venison in blackcurrant sauce are just two of the treats on the menu. Beech Street also has an extensive wine list.

801 Beech St. ☎ *904-277-3662. Internet:* www.beechstreetgrill.com. *To get there: On A1A at 8th St. Reservations recommended. Main courses: $13–$26. AE, DC, DISC, MC, V. Open: 6–10 p.m. nightly.*

Chart House

$$ Jacksonville   AMERICAN

This 40-year-old, 40-restaurant chain's menu is a cut above standard chain cuisine. And the atmosphere isn't bad either — this branch offers great views of the city skyline. Regulars on the menu include grilled mahi-mahi in a teriyaki glaze, pan-seared scallops, peppercorn chicken, and prime rib.

1501 River Place Blvd. ☎ *904-398-3353. Internet:* www.chart-house.com. *To get there: Take Prudential Dr./U.S. 1 to Hendricks Ave., go north and then left on River Place. Reservations suggested. Main courses: $16–$28. AE, MC, V. Open: 5–10 p.m. Sun–Thurs, 5–11 p.m. Fri–Sat.*

Harry's Seafood, Bar, and Grille

$$ Jacksonville   NEW ORLEANS/SEAFOOD

Déjà vu. This is a branch of the same six-restaurant chain that we list under St. Augustine, and it's worth repeating. The Cajun-inspired cuisine is worth sampling and the atmosphere is friendly. Try the shrimp en brochette (jumbos stuffed with Monterey Jack cheese and wrapped in bacon, and grilled), or the Cajun popcorn (crawdad tails lightly breaded, fried, and served with a remoulade.)

1018 N. 3rd St. ☎ *904-247-8855. Internet:* www.hookedonharrys.com. *To get there: Go south from Atlantic Beach on 3rd St., the main beach road. Main courses: $10–$23. AE, MC, V. Open: 11 a.m.–10 p.m. daily.*

Jackie's

$ Jacksonville   SEAFOOD

Almost all the entrees at this nautically themed restaurant cost under $15, including fried or broiled shrimp, oysters, catfish, grouper, and

scallops. The menu also features a number of combination seafood platters, including a couple dishes that serve two people. You can dine inside
or eat on the outdoor deck, which has view of the Trout River.

8132 Trout River Dr. ☎ *904-764-0120. Internet:* www.wecook4u.com/jackies. *To
get there: Just south of St. Johns River off Main St./U.S. 1. Reservations accepted.
Main courses: $9–$29. AE, MC, V. Open: 11 a.m.–10 p.m. daily.*

Le Clos

$$ Fernandina Beach   FRENCH

Situated in Fernandina's historic district, this charming restaurant serves
first-rate Provençal cuisine in an historic 1906 cottage. Feast on *Coquelles
St. Jacques a la Provençal* (scallops sautéed with shallots, tomatoes, and
herbs) in the candle-lit dining room. There's an extensive wine list (Le
Clos means "the vineyard" in French), and the desserts are fabulous.

20 S. 2nd St. ☎ *904-261-8100. Internet:* www.leclos.com. *To get there: From A1A,
take Ash St. west to 2nd St. Reservations accepted. Main courses: $15–$22. MC, V.
Open: 5:30–9 p.m. Mon–Thurs, until 9:30 p.m. Fri–Sat.*

The Wine Cellar

$$$ Jacksonville   CONTINENTAL

This exclusive restaurant offers fine dining in an intimate, Old World setting. You can dine inside or on the outdoor brick terrace. Blackened
breast of duck with brandied mushrooms, rack of lamb in a pecan crust,
and a bouillabaisse of lobster, mussels, shrimp, clams, and scallops lift
the menu two cuts above the norm. There's a long wine list, and some
servers have been here since the restaurant rang its opening bell in 1974.

1314 Prudential Dr. ☎ *904-398-8989. Internet:* www.winecellarjax.com. *To get
there: Located on the east side of the St. Johns River, near the Riverwalk.
Reservations recommended. Main courses: $23–$29. AE, MC, V. Open: 11 a.m.–
2 p.m. Mon–Fri, 5:30–10 p.m. Mon–Sat.*

Runner-up restaurants

As is the *For Dummies* custom, here are a few more opportunities to
work your appetite into a frenzy.

Island Grille

$$ Jacksonville Beach   This popular spot on the beach offers fun
food, such as conch fritters with spicy pink remoulade and escargots in
mushroom caps, in addition to steaks, seafood, and pasta. *981 1st St. North.*
☎ *904-241-1881.*

Manatee Ray's

$$ **Jacksonville Beach** This casual restaurant uses local seafood and Key lime pie as its headline acts. *314 1st St. North.* ☎ *904-241-3138.*

Singleton's Seafood Shack

$ **Mayport** A rustic fish house, this restaurant offers specials, including shrimp, clams, oysters, and a variety of fish. *4728 Ocean St.* ☎ *904-246-4442.*

Venny's Italian Restaurant

$ **Jacksonville** This eatery has a nice selection of Italian standards, including pasta, veal, chicken, and shrimp entrees, as well as pizzas. *9862 Old Baymeadows Rd.* ☎ *904-642-1161. Internet:* www.welcometo.com/venny. htm.

Exploring the Jacksonville Area

Jacksonville may cater more to business travelers than tourists, but there are still a number of excellent attractions, ranging from charming historic districts to adrenaline-boosting water rides, in the area.

Touring the top sights

Adventure Landing

Jacksonville Beach

Kids and hot (or energetic) adults have a ball at this water park, where you can splash around Shipwreck Island or challenge the Rage, an uphill water coaster. The park (open May through September) also has a wave pool, miniature golf, go-carts, video games, and batting cages.

1944 Beach Blvd. (at 20th St.). ☎ *904-246-4386. To get there: Take Atlantic Blvd. east to St. Johns Bluff Rd., make a right, and go left on Beach Blvd. Admission: $22 adults, $17 kids 3–12. Open: 10–1 a.m. Sun–Thurs, 10–2 a.m. Fri–Sat, water park closes at dusk.*

BEAKS

Big Talbot Island

It's an acronym for Bird Emergency Aid and Kare Sanctuary, and it's a neat eco stop, where staffers raise and care for thousands of injured or deformed birds, including bald eagles, ospreys, pelicans, and owls. BEAKS also cares for deer, but birds come first. In addition to the 1-hour round-trip from Jacksonville, plan to spend 1 to 2 hours visiting.

12084 Houston Ave. ☎ *904-251-2473 (expect a message about how to care for an injured bird but leave a message of your own, and they'll call back). Internet:* http://users.choice.net/~matschca/beaks.html. *To get there: It's complicated; ask for directions when you call. Admission: You'll feel guilty without leaving a donation. Open: noon–4 p.m. Tues–Sun.*

Centre Street

Fernandina Beach

Centre Street and Historic Fernandina Beach offer a self-charted walking tour that costs nothing but calories. The 50-block downtown historic district is loaded with Victorian and Queen Anne homes that date to the town's birth as a port in the mid-nineteenth century. Grab a tour map from the chamber of commerce, located in the old depot, 102 Centre Street (☎ **800-226-3542** or 904-261-3248). It's open between 9 a.m. and 5 p.m. Monday through Friday. If you have strong legs, good shoes, and a desire to shop, this is worth 3 to 4 hours of your time.

Fort Caroline National Memorial

Jacksonville

This is a shrine to the short-lived French Huguenot settlement founded here in 1564. The park has a replica of the fort, a museum of French and Native American artifacts, and a trail.

12713 Fort Caroline Rd. ☎ *904-641-7155. To get there: Take Atlantic Blvd east, head past Southside Expressway, turn on Monument Blvd, and follow the signs. Admission: Free. Open: 9 a.m.–5 p.m. daily.*

Fort Clinch State Park

Fernandina Beach

The sign is small, and most passersby don't have a clue that this treasure is just over the dunes. After you slap through the mosquitoes, there's a small museum and store, and then a crushed-shell trail through coastal scrub to the fort. A small museum-style interpretive center is on the grounds, but the rangers set this site apart from other state parks. Dressed in wool uniforms (even in summer), they give a stark but frequently humorous look at a soldier's life in the 1860s. In addition to living-history lessons, the fort offers candlelight tours on Friday and Saturday evenings. On the first weekend of the month, some 40 volunteers stage a larger demonstration of the daily routines in a surgeon's office, carpentry shop, forge, and kitchen. An hour or two should be plenty.

2601 Atlantic Ave. ☎ *904-261-4212. To get there: Located 1 mile from the ocean on A1A. Admission: $3.25 per car. Open: 8 a.m.–dusk daily.*

Jacksonville Zoo

Jacksonville

Lions, tigers, white rhinos, cheetahs, jaguars, wart hogs, anteaters, and lowland gorillas. Wow! This city zoo has grown up in recent years and is one of the top five in Florida. Pay attention to the thatched roof when you enter — Zulu craftsmen built it. Allow 2 to 4 hours to see it all.

8605 Zoo Rd. ☎ *904-757-4463. Internet:* www.jaxzoo.org. *To get there: Take I-95 exit 124A and go east on Heckscher Dr. Admission: $8.00 adults, $6.50 seniors, $5.00 kids 3–12. Open: 9 a.m.–5 p.m. daily.*

Kingsley Plantation

Jacksonville

Here's a lesson on nineteenth-century Florida plantation life and slavery. This plantation, built in 1817 by Zephaniah Kingsley, grew sugarcane and Sea Island cotton. The site has a well-preserved plantation house, as well as the ruins of 23 slave quarters that were built from oyster shell and sand. There are ranger-guided tours, but scheduling is a bit inconsistent, so call to check on times. Allow 1 to 2 hours to catch the highlights.

On the Avenue of Palms. ☎ *904-251-3537. To get there: Located north of Mayport U.S. Naval Station on A1A; follow the signs west on Palmetto Ave. (a gravel road). Admission: Free. Open: 9 a.m.–5 p.m. daily.*

Little and Big Talbot Island State Parks

Mayport

Little Talbot is a 2,500-acre preserve with salt marshes, hammocks, and Atlantic dunes (these are the tall puppies), along with 4 miles of gorgeous beaches. You might see some of the park's river otters; you will see a rocky beach carved by erosion and decorated by driftwood. Big Talbot Island State Park, which is on the same stretch of coastline, has some spectacular bluffs carved by erosion, the ruins of two plantations, and five marked trails that wind through dunes, salt marshes, tidal creeks, and prairie. If you're a park or beach buff, allow 3 to 4 hours.

20 miles northeast of downtown Jacksonville. ☎ *904-251-2323. To get there: Little and Big Talbot islands are off A1A, north of the Mayport Naval Station. Admission: $3.25 per carload. Open: 8 a.m.–dusk daily.*

SouthBank Riverwalk

Jacksonville

Walkers, joggers, tourists, and people-watchers frequent this 1.2-mile boardwalk on the south side of the St. Johns River. At night, it's colorfully illuminated. By day, the biggest attraction is the **Museum of Science and**

History, located at Museum Circle and San Marco Boulevard (☎ 904-396-7062), which has some interactive exhibits for kids. The Riverwalk also has occasional seafood and arts festivals.

On riverbank, beside Main Street Bridge (between San Marco and Ferry St.). ☎ 904-396-4900. To get there: Take I-95 to Prudential Dr., exit right, and follow the signs. Museum admission: $6.00 adults, $4.50 seniors, $4.00 kids 3–12. Museum hours: 10 a.m.–5 p.m. Mon–Sat, 1–6 p.m. Sun.

Seeing and doing more cool stuff

This section offers a few additional things to do, including a few for folks with special tastes.

✔ **Baseball:** The **Jacksonville Suns,** a Class AA minor-league affiliate of the Detroit Tigers, play 70 home games from early April to early September at **Wolfson Park,** 1201 E. Duval St. (☎ 904-358-2846; Internet: www.jaxsuns.com). Tickets run $5 to $8.

✔ **Beaches:** The four most popular bathing spots are **Atlantic Beach** (east end of Hwy. 10), **Neptune Beach** (on A1A, 1 mile south of Hwy. 10), **Jacksonville Beach** (east end of U.S. 90), and **Ponte Vedra Beach** (Hwy. 203, 2 miles south of Butler Boulevard).

✔ **Fishing: Capt. Dave Sipler's Sportfishing** (☎ 904-642-9546; Internet: www.charters@captdaves.com) is one of several guide services offering charters for small groups. Rates for 2 to 4 people are $185 to $300 for a half day and $250 to $400 for all day.

✔ **Football:** The National Football League's **Jacksonville Jaguars** play their preseason and regular season home games at **Alltel Stadium,** One Alltel Stadium Place (☎ 904-633-6000; Internet: www.jaguarsnfl.com). Prices start at about $25, but single-game tickets are hard to come by.

✔ **Golf:** The **Golf Club of Jacksonville,** 10440 Tournament Lane (☎ 904-779-2100), has rolling, tree-lined fairways and, with fees under $25 year-round, affordable prices. **Baymeadows Golf Club,** 7981 Baymeadows Circle West, Jacksonville (☎ 904-731-5701), offers water hazards on ten holes and plenty of doglegs. Greens fees run between $41 and $65 year-round.

You can find more courses on the Internet at www.golf.com and www.floridagolfing.com, or call the **Florida Sports Foundation** (☎ 850-488-8347) or **Florida Golfing** (☎ 877-222-4653).

Shopping

The **Avenues Mall,** 10300 Southside Blvd., Jacksonville (☎ 904-363-3060), has 150 stores, including such anchors as Dillard's and Sears. **Jacksonville Landing,** 2 Independent Dr., on the St. Johns River (☎ 904-353-1188), has about 65 shops, plus a number of restaurants.

Enjoying the nightlife

Jacksonville Landing, 2 Independent Dr., on the St. Johns River
(☎ 904-353-1188), stages periodic festivals and outdoor rock, jazz,
blues, and country concerts. Check the "Weekend" section in the *Florida
Times-Union* on Fridays for up-to-the-minute entertainment news.

Bars

None of the following bars mentioned charge a cover.

Fernandina Beach's **Palace Saloon,** at Centre and 2nd Streets (☎ 904-
261-6320), was Florida's oldest, continuously run watering hole (dating
to the Rockefellers' and Carnegies' days), until a fire turned the lights
out in February 1999. It reopened a month later, though renovations
continue to be made. The bar offers rock and blues on Thursday,
Friday, and Saturday nights. As an added bonus, you'll hear haunting
stories about a lovable former bartender called "Uncle Charlie."

Ragtime Tavern and Seafood Grill, 207 Atlantic Blvd., Atlantic Beach
(☎ 904-241-7877), presents local blues and jazz bands Thursdays
through the weekend. **Sloppy Joe's,** 200 1st St., Jacksonville Beach
(☎ 904-270-1767), features blues, rock, and reggae outside on the
patio. **Manatee Ray's,** 314 1st St. North, also on Jacksonville Beach
(☎ 904-241-3138), offers live music on Friday and Saturday nights,
reggae on Sunday, and a DJ on Tuesday.

Performing arts

The **Florida Times Union Center for the Performing Arts,** 300 Water
St., Jacksonville (☎ 904-630-3900), hosts Broadway shows, big-name
concerts, and dance companies. Its Robert E. Jacoby Hall is home to
the **Jacksonville Symphony Orchestra,** which performs from early fall
through spring.

Seeing Jacksonville and Fernandina in 2 Days

Day 1 has you launching north of Jacksonville to visit the winged
things at **BEAKS,** before you continue northward to Fernandina Beach
for a self-guided walking tour of historic **Centre Street,** where you can
grab lunch. Catch the rangers' act at **Fort Clinch State Park,** stuff yourself to the gills at the **Beech Street Grill,** and then call it a night at the
Palace Saloon.

On **Day 2,** spend your morning talking to the animals at the **Jacksonville
Zoo,** enjoy lunch at **Harry's Seafood, Bar, and Grille,** and then finish the
afternoon off at **SouthBank Riverwalk,** making sure to include a stop at

Jacksonville's **Museum of Science and History.** Dine at **The Wine Cellar** and then have a little after-hours fun at **Ragtime Tavern and Seafood Grill.**

Fast Facts

Area Code

The local area code is **904.**

American Express

There is an American Express Travel Service office at 9908 Baymeadows Rd., Jacksonville (☎ **904-642-1701**).

Hospitals

The following hospitals are in the immediate area: **Baptist Medical Center,** 800 Prudential Dr., Jacksonville (☎ **904-202-4000**); **Baptist Medical Center/Nassau,** 1250 S. 18th St., Fernandina Beach (☎ **904-321-3501**); **Flagler Hospital,** 400 Heath Park Blvd., St. Augustine (☎ **904-829-5155**); **Memorial Hospital Jacksonville,** 3525 University Blvd. South (☎ **904-399-6111**); **St. Vincent's Medical Center,** 1800 Barrs St., Jacksonville (☎ **904-308-7300**).

Information

Good sources of information include the **St. Johns County Visitors & Convention Bureau,** 88 Riberia St. (☎ **800-418-7529**; Internet: www.visitoldcity.com); the **Jacksonville & the Beaches Convention & Visitors Bureau,** 201 E. Adams St. (☎ **800-733-2668**; Internet: www.jaxcvb.com); and the **Amelia Island Tourist Development Council,** 102 Centre St. (☎ **800-226-3542**; Internet: www.ameliaisland.org).

Mail

There are U.S. post offices at 3000 Spring Park Rd., in downtown Jacksonville, and at 99 King St., in St. Augustine. To find a branch near your hotel, call ☎ **800-275-8777.**

Maps

Ask the information sources listed earlier in this section. Rental-car agencies (including those at the airport) are another good source of maps, as are convenience stores, which sell them for $3 to $5.

Newspapers

The **Florida Times-Union** (☎ **904-359-4111**; Internet: http://jacksonville.com), in Jacksonville, and **the St. Augustine Record** (☎ 904-829-6562) are the two major papers in this region.

Pharmacies

Look for a 24-hour **Walgreens** drugstore at 406 Atlantic Blvd., Neptune Beach (☎ **904-247-1953**).

Safety

Always stick to well-lit, populated tourist areas and even then be careful.

Taxes

Florida assesses a 6 percent sales tax on everything except groceries and medicine. St. Augustine hotels raise the total to 9 percent, while those in other parts of the region kick it as high as 12 percent.

Taxis

Yellow Cab (☎ **904-824-6888**) of St. Augustine has a complex zone system, but generally figure on spending $2 to $8 for 1 person and $1.50 for each additional body. **Gator City Taxi** (☎ **904-355-8294**), in Jacksonville, charges $1.25 to start the meter and $1.25 for each mile thereafter.

Weather Updates

Check the Web site for the **National Weather Service** at www.nws.noaa.gov or try **The Weather Channel** (Internet: www.weatherchannel.com).

Chapter 23

The Panhandle

In This Chapter

▶ Exploring the land of the two-way sun

▶ Looking for UFOs in Gulf Breeze

▶ Pacing yourself in Pensacola

▶ Hitting the Panhandle's beach towns

*B*efore we get into the nitty-gritty details on vacationing in the Panhandle, here are a few memorable monologues uttered after a UFO encounter:

✔ "Lord, I'll never touch another drop."

✔ "I didn't see it if you didn't see it."

✔ "Johnny Mack, I think I'm having a hot flash."

No, we haven't lost our marbles. Some of you may be wondering what UFOs have to do with a *For Dummies* guide to Florida. The answer is plenty, if you land in Gulf Breeze, a splinter of sand sticking out of the Gulf of Mexico. It may not be another Roswell, but this little burgh has more UFO "sightings" than anywhere east of the Mississippi, and the visuals are just part of the mix. Folks here say they've been beamed aboard starships, forced to enter alien wedlock, and probed by the unfriendly end of a light saber.

Whether they're real or imagined, these extra-dimensional encounters are one of the factors that set Gulf Breeze and the Panhandle apart from the Florida peninsula. The culture of the Panhandle offers the same disparity. This region remains Southern, a rarity in a state that serves as a haven for transplanted northerners.

The coastal side of the Panhandle has some of America's prettiest, least discovered beaches, which boast sunrises *and* sunsets (thanks to beaches that run from east to west), water as blue as the Caribbean, and thousands of acres of preserves. (See the map ahead of "The Panhandle.") We don't know why all of you haven't invaded yet (maybe it's the UFOs).

The Panhandle

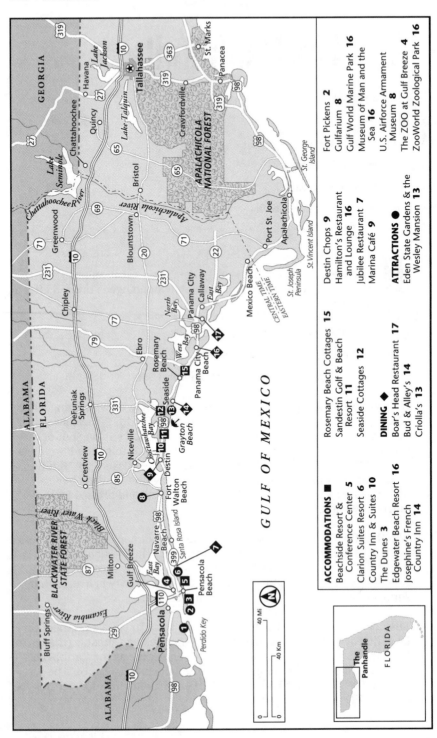

ACCOMMODATIONS ■
Beachside Resort & Conference Center **5**
Clarion Suites Resort **6**
Country Inn & Suites **10**
The Dunes **3**
Edgewater Beach Resort **16**
Josephine's French Country Inn **14**
Rosemary Beach Cottages **15**
Sandestin Golf & Beach Resort **11**
Seaside Cottages **12**

DINING ◆
Boar's Head Restaurant **17**
Bud & Alley's **14**
Criolla's **13**
Destin Chops **9**
Hamilton's Restaurant and Lounge **16**
Jubilee Restaurant **7**
Marina Café **9**

ATTRACTIONS ●
Eden State Gardens & the Wesley Mansion **13**
Fort Pickens **2**
Gulfarium **8**
Gulf World Marine Park **16**
Museum of Man and the Sea **16**
U.S. Airforce Armament Museum **8**
The ZOO at Gulf Breeze **4**
ZooWorld Zoological Park **16**

Visiting the Panhandle and Its Attractions

The western Panhandle kisses Alabama at Perdido Bay; then stretches east through UFO-ville, Navarre Beach, and Santa Rosa Island. Next comes Fort Walton Beach and Destin, which, with nearby Panama City, are known locally as the **Redneck Riviera,** thanks to their popularity with tourists from Louisiana, Alabama, and Georgia. This part of Florida's horizontal coast also has several villages that still retain an old-fashioned look, including Laguna Beach, Seagrove Beach, Seaside, and Grayton Beach. As the Panhandle stretches east, you encounter the state's capital, Tallahassee, which is a dud when it comes to excitement (unless you're a presidential lawyer seeking vote recounts), so this mention is about all you hear of Tallahassee from us.

 One final note before we dive into the destinations. Most of Florida is on Eastern Time. But, some of the places we discuss in the first two sections of this chapter are on Central Time, which is 1 hour earlier. These include Pensacola, Fort Walton Beach, Destin, and Panama City.

Pensacola

Florida's westernmost big-little city isn't known as a tourist hot spot, but visitors will find some pleasant surprises, including dandy beaches and public preserves. (Skip ahead to the "Pensacola" map.)

Getting there

The Panhandle tends to be more of a regional destination than a national one. The area draws a lot of visitors from the lower Southeast — Louisiana, Mississippi, Alabama, and Georgia. Therefore, land travel is just as popular a method for getting here as flying.

By plane

This region lacks a big-league airport, so flying usually means that you have to make an extra connection. **Pensacola Regional Airport** (☎ 850-435-1746; Internet: www.flypensacola.com) offers service by **Continental, Delta, Northwest, US Airways,** and some commuter airlines. **Avis, Budget, Dollar, Hertz,** and **National** have rental desks at the airport. (Look for more airline and rental-car information in the Appendix in the back of the book.) Taxis line up outside the airport terminal, and a trip to Gulf Breeze will run you about $15; a ride to Pensacola Beach will cost about $20.

Pensacola

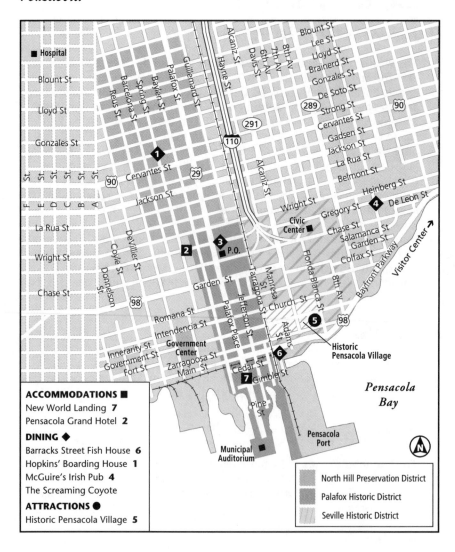

ACCOMMODATIONS ■
New World Landing 7
Pensacola Grand Hotel 2

DINING ◆
Barracks Street Fish House 6
Hopkins' Boarding House 1
McGuire's Irish Pub 4
The Screaming Coyote

ATTRACTIONS ●
Historic Pensacola Village 5

North Hill Preservation District
Palafox Historic District
Seville Historic District

By car

I-10 is the primary east-west route across the Panhandle, although it hardly makes for an exciting ride. U.S. 98 is an often-scenic, often-slow choice that runs along the Gulf coast. If you're coming from the North-east, take I-95 to Jacksonville; then go west on I-10. From the Great Lakes region and the Midwest, I-75, I-65, and I-55 will lead you into I-10 and the Panhandle.

By train

Amtrak (☎ 800-872-7245; Internet: www.amtrak.com) offers service into Pensacola. The train station is at 980 E. Heinberg Street.

Getting around

Unless you're going to stick close to a single zone for the duration of your trip, which we don't recommend for smaller and more scattered destinations such as the ones in the Panhandle, you're going to need a set of wheels to get around.

By car

The highways that get you here (see "Getting there," earlier in this chapter) are also the primary routes for getting from town to town. If you have time, take a scenic spin along U.S. 98. This route is congested in and around Pensacola, but along the coastline it offers wonderful scenery in the "tweener" areas.

In Pensacola, Fairfield Drive runs east and west, while 9th Avenue and I-110 are the north-south traffic movers. Pensacola has avenues, drives, lanes, and boulevards that run every which way but an understandable one. *Get a map!* (For map sources, see "Fast Facts" at the end of this chapter.)

On Perdido Key, adjacent to the Pensacola mainland, the chief east-west routes are Johnson Beach Road and Perdido Key Drive. On Pensacola Beach, the main east-wester is Highway 399.

By bus

The **Escambia County Area Transit System** or ECAT (call ☎ 850-463-9383, for schedule information) runs buses and trolleys in the Pensacola area. Bus fares are $1 for adults, 75 cents for kids, and 50 cents for seniors. Buses do not run to the beach. Downtown trolley service costs 25 cents. A free Pensacola Beach trolley runs daily from 10 a.m. to 3 p.m., May through September.

By taxi

Cabs are usually never a cost-efficient option and they're even less so in this region. **Yellow Cab** (☎ 850-433-3333) and **Crosstown Cab** (☎ 850-456-8294) are two of the major taxi companies in Pensacola. The rate is $1.50 when the flag drops and $1.40 per mile, thereafter.

Staying in Pensacola

Unlike most of Florida, the peak tourist season in the Panhandle runs from mid-May to mid-August. Room rates also soar during spring and summer holiday periods and during spring break. If you decide to come here during a peak period, make sure to reserve a hotel room well in advance. You can leave the reservation work to others by contacting the **Florida Hotel Network** (☎ **800-538-3616;** Internet: www. floridahotels.com), a hotel-booking service.

Don't forget to budget for Pensacola's 11.5 percent hotel tax.

Pensacola's best hotels

Beachside Resort & Conference Center

$ **Pensacola Beach**

Rooms at this beachfront resort aren't fancy, but they have dandy views of the Gulf, microwaves, refrigerators, coffee makers, and balconies on the upper floors. There's also an onsite restaurant.

14 Via De Luna. ☎ *800-232-2416. Internet:* www.innisfree.com/bsr. *To get there: Cross Pensacola Bay Bridge, go through Gulf Breeze, and it's just east on Hwy. 399. Parking: Free. Rack rates: $110–$140 Mar–Aug, $85–$110 Sept–Oct, $50–$70 Nov–Dec, $60–$80 Jan–Feb. AE, MC, V.*

Clarion Suites Resort

$$ **Pensacola Beach**

This gulf-side resort was designed to resemble a village of cozy cottages. It has 86 comfortable one-bedroom suites, furnished in wicker and wood, each with a bedroom, living area with sofa sleeper, and full kitchen with microwave and coffee maker. A free continental breakfast is served.

20 Via De Luna. ☎ *800-874-5303 or 850-932-4300. Fax: 850-934-9112. Internet:* www. clarionsuitesresort.com. *To get there: Cross Pensacola Bay Bridge through Gulf Breeze and it's just east on Hwy. 399. Parking: Free. Rack rates: $143–$173 May–Aug, $95–$135 Mar–Apr and Sept–Oct, $79–$109 Nov–Feb. AE, DC, DISC, MC, V.*

The Dunes

$$ **Pensacola Beach**

Fully renovated in 1998-99 (thanks to hurricane damage), The Dunes offers great views of the Gulf and spacious rooms that have balconies and coffee makers. The penthouse suites feature whirlpools. An onsite restaurant and supervised summer programs for children round out the amenities here.

333 Fort Pickens Rd. ☎ *800-833-8637 or 850-932-3536. Fax: 850-932-7088. Internet:* www.theduneshotel.com. *To get there: Cross the Pensacola Bay Bridge, go through Gulf Breeze, and it's west on Fort Pickens Rd. Parking: Free. Rack rates: $150–$310 June–Aug, $130–$285 Apr–May, $115–$265 Mar and Sept–Nov, $79–$255 Dec–Feb. AE, DISC, MC, V.*

New World Landing

$$ Pensacola

Each of the 14 rooms and one suite at this inn are named for someone in Pensacola's past, such as Andrew Jackson and Geronimo. The stylish rooms are decorated to reflect the city's British, French, Spanish, and colonial American roots, and all of them feature antiques. Rates include a continental breakfast. The inn doesn't have a pool.

600 S. Palafox St. ☎ ***850-432-4111.*** *Fax: 850-432-6836. Internet:* www. newworldlanding.com. *To get there: At the corner of Pine St., 2 blocks from the bay. Parking: Free. Rack rates: $85–$125 year-round ($20 higher for holidays). AE, MC, V.*

Pensacola Grand Hotel

$$ Pensacola

If you *really* want to treat yourself, take the plunge at this member of the Crowne Plaza chain. The Grand's entrance is inside the historic, 1912 L&N Train Depot; the ultra-modern, glass-and-block hotel sits behind it. Standards rooms are at the lower end of the price range; mini and three-bedroom suites are at the other end. The hotel has, among other treats, a gym, an onsite restaurant, a bar, and a library.

200 E. Gregory St. ☎ ***800-348-3336*** *or 850-433-3336. Fax: 850-432-7572. Internet:* www.pensacolagrandhotel.com. *To get there: It's at I-110 and U.S. 98. Parking: Free. Rack rates: $100–$140 standard, $250–$408 suites, year-round. AE, DC, DISC, MC, V.*

Runner-up accommodations

Here are some more choices in case our first-tier lodgings didn't hook you, or they were booked solid.

Five Flags Inn

$ Pensacola Beach This old-style motel has small rooms, but it offers a great view and great prices. *299 Fort Pickens Rd.* ☎ ***850-932-3586.*** *Fax: 850-934-0257. Internet:* www.fiveflagsinn.com.

Hampton Inn Pensacola Beach

$$ Pensacola Beach Located directly on the Gulf, half of this hotel's spacious rooms have private balconies. *2 Via De Luna* ☎ ***800-320-8108*** *or 850-932-6800. Fax: 850-932-6833. Internet:* www.hampton-inn.com.

Yacht House Bed & Breakfast Inn

$ Pensacola This bed-and-breakfast offers 6 beautifully decorated rooms and suites with Amazon and mariner themes, among others. There isn't a pool. *1820 Cypress St.* ☎ ***850-433-3634.*** *Internet:* www.yachthouse.com.

Dining out in Pensacola

Although it's not a hotbed of fine cuisine, Pensacola does have some decent places to eat. Southern cooking and seafood rule, but there is a nice mix of ethnic restaurants as well.

Don't forget to allow for the 6.5 percent sales tax.

Pensacola's best restaurants

Barracks Street Fish House

$$ Pensacola   SEAFOOD

The friendly staff at this bayfront restaurant serves up Southern-style seafood in a casual setting. If you're looking for something a little out of the ordinary, try the cashew-crusted soft-shell crab. The fish of the day (snapper, grouper, amberjack, scamp, or others) is served in a pineapple glaze or with a ginger or pecan crust. Live music entertains nighttime diners from Wednesday through Sunday.

600 S. Barracks St. ☎ *850-470-0003. Internet:* www.goodgrits.com. *To get there: Take Palafox St./Hwy. 29 south to East Main, left to Barracks, and then right. Reservations accepted. Main courses: $9–$20. AE, MC, V. Open: 11–1 a.m. daily.*

Hopkins' Boarding House

$ Pensacola   SOUTHERN

Located in the downtown historic district, this Victorian boarding house serves Southern-style vegetables, grits, chicken, and fish, depending on the day of week. And, in keeping with the boarding house theme, you get to clear your own dishes.

900 N. Spring St. ☎ *850-438-3979. To get there: Palafox St./U.S. 29 south to Strong St., then west to Spring. Reservations not accepted. Main courses: $7–$9. No credit cards. Open: 7–9:30 a.m., 11:15 a.m.–2 p.m., and 5:15–7:30 p.m. Tues–Sat; 11 a.m.– 2 p.m. Sun.*

Jubilee Restaurant

$$ Pensacola Beach   SEAFOOD/CAJUN

In its Top Side restaurant, you can enjoy a bird's-eye view of the waterfront while feasting on dozens of Louisiana-style fish and shellfish creations. Downstairs, the Beachside Café serves fish, shellfish, pasta, sandwiches, and barbecued pork.

400 Quietwater Beach Rd. ☎ 850-934-3108. To get there: Located on U.S. 98 at Quietwater Beach Boardwalk. Reservations recommended in the Top Side restaurant. Main courses: Beachside Café $11–$18; Top Side restaurant $17–$40. AE, DC, DISC, MC, V. Open: Beachside Café 11 a.m.–10 p.m.; Top Side restaurant 6–10 p.m. daily.

McGuire's Irish Pub

$$ Pensacola   IRISH/AMERICAN

It's not often that you can find an award-winning Irish pub in Florida, but this 24-year-old eatery has won a ton of kudos for its savory seafood (red snapper and bouillabaisse), as well as standards, such as lamb stew and corned beef and cabbage.

600 E. Gregory St. ☎ 850-433-6789. Internet: www.mcguiresirishgifts.com. *To get there: It's on Hwy. 29/Palafox St. at Gregory St. Reservations not accepted. Main courses: $16–$25. AE, DC, DISC, MC, V. Open: 11–2 a.m. Mon–Sat, 11–1 a.m. Sun.*

The Screaming Coyote

$ Pensacola   MEXICAN

Here's a gut-filling stop you can save for a low-budget night. Come hungry for burritos (beef, pork, chicken, and fish) and quesadillas (cheese, crawfish, and blackened chicken). The menu also has tacos, salads, and side dishes.

196 N. Palafox St. ☎ 850-435-9002. Internet: www.goodgrits.com. *To get there: On Palafox St./Hwy. 29, just north of Gregory St. Reservations not required. Main courses: $6–$8, MC, V. Open: 11 a.m.–9:30 p.m. Mon–Thurs, 11 a.m.–11 p.m. Fri–Sat.*

Runner-up restaurants

Our second team of eateries is almost as good as the first:

Chan's Market Café

$ Pensacola Beach   This small cafe and bakery offers low-cost ribstickers, such as meat loaf, pot roast, grilled fish, and barbecued chicken. *16 Via De Luna ☎ 850-932-8454.*

Jamie's Wine Bar & Restaurant

$$ Pensacola   This romantic restaurant features a Cajun-influenced menu and a great wine list. *424 E. Zaragossa St. ☎ 850-434-2911.*

Peg Leg Pete's Oyster Bar

$$ **Pensacola Beach** This informal restaurant offers a varied menu of seafood served fried, steamed, or Cajun style. *1010 Fort Pickens Rd.* ☎ *850-932-4139. Internet:* www.peglegpetes.com.

Yamato

$$ **Pensacola** You can find a variety of oriental cuisine — hibachi, tempura, Sushi, and more — at this stylish Japanese restaurant. *131 New Warrington Rd.* ☎ *850-453-3461. Internet:* www.yamato.pen.net.

Exploring Pensacola

Beautiful beaches are, arguably, the biggest tourist attractions in the Panhandle, and we list some of them in this chapter and provide even more details in Chapter 24. Nevertheless, even the most diehard sun worshipper needs a break once in a while, so here are some other diversions to feast your eyes on.

Touring Pensacola's top sights

Fort Pickens

Pensacola Beach

Held by Union troops during the Civil War, this brick fort opened in the 1880s and counted Apache Chief Geronimo as one of its prisoners. Today, it's part of the **Gulf Islands National Seashore** on Santa Rosa Island. The fort includes cannon casements and bulwarks where shooters would have been stationed, had they had a fight — they didn't. Public tours are available, and the site has a visitors center. Most folks can see it all in 1 to 1½ hours.

☎ *800-874-1234 or 850-934-2600. To get there: Located at the western end of Pensacola Beach on Fort Pickens Rd. Admission: $6 per carload. (The admission receipt is good for seven days.) Open: 8 a.m.–sunset daily.*

Historic Pensacola Village

Pensacola

This collection of several small museums traces the 200-something-year history of Pensacola. The wonders include **Christ Church** (founded in 1823), the **Pensacola City of Five Flags, St. Michael's Cemetery,** the **Museums of Industry and Commerce,** the **T.T. Wentworth Jr. Florida State Museum,** and the **Julee Cottage Black History Museum.** This historic area encompasses two districts. **North Hill Preservation District** is an upper-class neighborhood that was plotted from the 1870s through the 1930s. The **Seville Historic District** dates from the 1780s to the early 1800s and includes Creole and Victorian homes. Depending on your tolerance for yesteryear's items, plan to spend 2 to 4 hours here.

205 E. Zaragossa St. ☎ *850-595-5985. Internet:* www.dos.state.fl.us/ dhr/pensacola. *To get there: Located in downtown Pensacola, 2 blocks east of Tarragona St. Admission: $6.00 adults, $5.00 seniors, $2.50 kids 4–16. Open: 10 a.m.–4 p.m. Tues–Sat.*

The National Museum of Naval Aviation

Pensacola

The Blue Angels fly their homecoming air show here in November, but you can catch the act on tape year-round at the museum. In addition to in-flight videos, you can watch a display at the top of a seven-story atrium that shows members cutting a diamond in their A-4 Skyhawks. The 250,000-square-foot museum contains exhibits featuring early wood biplanes, blimps, and space-age aircraft, such as the Skylab Command Module. If you want to try your hand at barnstorming, strap your buns into a simulator for a test flight. Over 100 vintage Marine Corps, Navy, and Coast Guard aircraft are parked outside of the building. Many of the guides are retired aviators who brighten the tours with amusing recollections of their experiences. The museum also features two IMAX movies. If all this isn't enough to hook you, check out the admission price that follows. Unless you're a diehard naval aviation nut, you can see this in about 2 hours.

1750 Radford Dr. ☎ *800-327-5002 or 850-452-3604. Internet:* www.naval-air. org. *To get there: Located off Hwy. 295, 12 miles south of downtown at the Pensacola Naval Air Station. Admission: Free. IMAX movies: $5.50 adults, $5.00 seniors over 61 and kids 4–12. Open: 9 a.m.–5 p.m. daily.*

UFOs

Gulf Breeze

By now, some of you are wondering if we provide more details about the UFOs that we discuss in the introduction to this chapter. Well, now that you ask, welcome to Gulf Breeze. Some locals swear this is the best place in two time zones to see an alien craft. If you want to see for yourself, take U.S. 98 south from Pensacola, cross the Bay Bridge, go through what there is of Gulf Breeze, and then make a decision: a) turn right (west) on Shoreline Drive or b) go left (east) on U.S. 98. Then, turn out the lights, listen to a little Pink Floyd, be patient, and, if you remembered to bring it, unscrew the cap on a bottle of Mad Dog. Sooner or later, you're going to see something.

The ZOO

Gulf Breeze

Approximately 700 critters call this 50-acre, forestlike zoo home. Headliners, such as white tigers, rhinos, and gorillas, live in specially landscaped habitats. You can visit Japanese gardens, a giraffe feeding tower, and a petting zoo. A safari train lurches through much of the park and the zoo's merry-go-round sports exotic animals, instead of horses. Allow 4 to 5 hours to see everything.

5701 Gulf Breeze Pkwy. ☎ *850-932-2229. Internet:* www.the-zoo.com. *To get there: Cross the bay bridge south from the mainland, and then go east on U.S. 98. Admission: $16 adults, $15 seniors 65 and older, $12 kids 3–11. Open: 9 a.m.–5 p.m. daily.*

Doing more cool stuff

Like the rest of Florida, Pensacola has some special-interest activities and attractions that may help fill your days.

- **Beaches: Perdido Key State Recreation Area,** which is part of the **Gulf Islands National Seashore,** is a great beach that's among our favorites (see Chapter 24). The barrier island, stretching 1.4 miles along the coast, has some spectacular sunsets and a white-quartz beach, dotted with sea oat-covered dunes.

  The rip currents here are strong enough to drown even the best of swimmers, if they panic. If you're caught in a tide or current that you can't beat, relax and join it (floating or swimming with it) until it weakens; then try for shore. *DO NOT* fight the current. It will weaken you and put you at greater risk for drowning.

- **Canoeing:** A few years back, the Florida Legislature designated Milton, a small town just 20 miles north of Pensacola, as "The Canoe Capital of Florida." It offers five river trails — four of them rated for beginners, and most with multiple entry and exit points, so you don't have to make like a marathoner and do the whole length. The trails include the **Perdido River Trail** (24 miles), **Coldwater Creek Trail** (18 miles), and **Blackwater River Trail** (up to 31 miles). The trails are inland, and some go by limestone formations, bluffs, cypress and cedar stands, caves, sandbars, and occasional critters, such as otters, deer, turkeys, and wading birds. Before you leave home, get maps from the **Office of Greenways and Trails,** 325 John Knox Rd., Building 500, Tallahassee, FL 32303-4124 (☎ **850-487-4784**). You can get information on outfitters from the **Florida Professional Paddle Sports Association**, P.O. Box 1764, Arcadia, FL 34265 (☎ **800-268-0083**).

- **Fishing:** Some of the best fishing in Florida is available off the Panhandle. Six-hour rates for party boats average $50 for adults and $35 for kids under 12. Six-hour small-charter rates fall in the vicinity of $750 to $1,200 for 1 to 10 people. Charter captains include **Chuck Nicholson, Ed Lively,** and **John Fetzer** (☎ 877-650-3474 or 850-932-0304; Internet: www.fishpensacola.com).

Dedicated anglers may be better off heading for **Destin** (which we cover later in this chapter), where charter and party boat rates tend to be a bit cheaper.

✔ **Golf:** For course information online, surf over to www.golf.com and www.floridagolfing.com, or call the **Florida Sports Foundation** (☎ 850-488-8347) or **Florida Golfing** (☎ 877-222-4653). Locally, **Lost Key Golf Club,** 625 Lost Key Dr., Pensacola (☎ 888-256-7853), has enough water hazards to empty your ball stash. Greens fees here will set you back $41 to $65, year-round. Another favorite is **Marcus Pointe Golf Club,** 2500 Oak Pointe Dr., Pensacola (☎ 850-484-9770). This club has large greens and fairways lined with trees. Greens fees run under $25 in the summer and between $45 and $65 in the winter.

Shopping

There are no prime shopping districts in or around Pensacola, but there are some places to whittle down your bank account, if you feel the urge.

The **Ninth Avenue Antique Mall,** 380 N. 9th Ave. (☎ 850-438-3961), sells pieces of yesterday. **Quayside Art Gallery,** 17 E. Zaragossa (☎ 850-438-2363), displays paintings and other artworks of local artists.

Alvin's Island Tropical Department Store, 934 Quietwater Beach Rd., Pensacola Beach (☎ 850-934-3711), gifts and souvenirs.

Living the nightlife

In addition to the following listings, you can get up-to-the-minute entertainment information in the Friday edition of the *Pensacola News Journal* (☎ 850-435-8500; Internet: www.gulfcoastgateway.com).

Bars

Loosen your arm, grab a mullet by the tail, and get ready to serve a clammy curve right into the "Interstate Mullet Toss" Book of Records. Welcome to The Wide World of Bar Sports, Southern edition, and the **Flora-Bama Lounge** — also known as the Last Great American Roadhouse — on Perdido Key. This hotspot has a beach, a bar, a bathroom, and plenty of bikinis. It's also the home field for a number of country music events during the year. But the wackiest shindig held here certainly has to be April's Interstate Mullet Toss and Beach Party, which defies more in-depth description. The lounge is at 17401 Perdido Key Dr. (☎ 850-492-3048; Internet: www.florabama.com). There's no cover.

McGuire's Irish Pub, 600 E. Gregory St. (☎ **850-433-6789;** Internet:
www.mcguiresirishgifts.com), features Irish bands on Saturday and
Sunday nights throughout the year, and every night during summer.
This one's also a freebie.

Clubs

Pensacola's major entertainment complex, **Seville Quarter,** 130 E.
Government St. (☎ **850-434-6211;** Internet: www.rosies.com), houses
a collection of clubs and pubs, including Rosie O'Grady's Goodtime
Emporium, Apple Annie's Courtyard, End o' the Alley Bar, and Phineas
Phogg's Balloon Works. Admission charge varies at each club. The
complex is open daily from 11 to 2 a.m.

Seeing Pensacola in 2 Days

We get you out of the blocks early on **Day 1** for a morning tour of
Historic Pensacola Village. Eat lunch at **Hopkins' Boarding House,**
before spending the afternoon at **The ZOO.** Do dinner at **McGuire's
Irish Pub** and top off your day at **Seville Quarter.**

On **Day 2,** spend your morning at **Fort Pickens** and then grab lunch on
the fly. Enjoy your afternoon, and the natural wonders of the Gulf of
Mexico, at **Perdido Key State Recreation Area.** Then, relax over dinner
at the **Jubilee Restaurant.** If you have the energy, head to the **Flora-
Bama Lounge** and toss down a few beers, if not a mullet.

Panama City, Fort Walton Beach, Destin, and Seaside

As we mentioned earlier, all these destinations, except Seaside, have
earned the title of the Redneck Riviera. And, while things do get a
shade rowdy from time to time, it's more of a local reference to the
clientele; this region is a beloved escape for folks who live in Louisiana,
Alabama, and Georgia.

Getting there

Because this is mainly a regional vacation spot, many visitors drive
here. But there are other options if you're coming from farther afield.

By plane
Panama City-Bay County International Airport (☎ 850-763-6751;
Internet: www.pcairport.com) is serviced by **Northwest Airlink** and
US Airways Express, but most travelers who rent a car use **Pensacola
Regional Airport** (earlier in this chapter) because they have more

car-rental options. If you do decide to fly into Panama City, several car rental agencies maintain desks in the airport, and you can also find taxis that will get you from the airport to the beach for about $25.

By car

I-10 is the primary east-west route across the Panhandle, although U.S. 98 offers a more scenic, if somewhat slower route along the Gulf coast. If you're coming from the Northeast, take I-95 to Jacksonville, and then go west on I-10. From the Great Lakes region and the Midwest, I-75, I-65, and I-55 will lead you to I-10 and the Panhandle.

By train

Amtrak (☎ **800-872-7245;** Internet: www.amtrak.com) offers transcontinental service to Crestview (26 miles northeast of Panama City) and Chipley (46 miles north of Panama City).

Getting around

There is no public transit system serving this region, so you're pretty much stuck with one self-propelled and one guided system.

By car

The highways that get you here (see "Getting there," earlier in this chapter) are the primary routes for getting from town to town. If you have the time and transportation, take a scenic spin along U.S. 98.

The street address system used in Destin and Fort Walton Beach is so bizarre that it would require two chapters of this book to explain. To save yourself an anxiety attack, get yourself a map (see "Information," in the "Fast Facts" at the end of this chapter) and call for exact directions to your desired destination.

By taxi

Yellow Cab serves Panama City (☎ **850-763-0211**) and Fort Walton Beach (☎ **850-244-3600**). **AAA Taxi** (☎ **850-785-0533**) operates in Panama City, and **Charter Taxis** (☎ **850-863-5466**) serves Fort Walton Beach. Rates vary, and in some cases are based on a complicated zone system, but expect to pay as much as $2.50 to climb aboard and $1.50 per mile thereafter.

Staying in the beach communities

Condominiums and cottage rentals rule the lodging scene in Destin, Fort Walton Beach, and Seaside, although you will find a decent selection of chain hotels along U.S. 98. Scores of inexpensive and moderately-priced chain motels are strung along the beach in Panama City, and the city's visitors bureau (see "Information" in the "Fast Facts" at the end of this chapter) publishes an annual list of lodging choices in the area. One reservation service that can book you into local properties is the **Florida Hotel Network** (☎ **800-538-3616;** Internet: www.floridahotels.com).

Panama City is the most seasonally oriented of Northwest Florida's destinations, and many hotels close between October and the spring break season in March.

Don't forget to add the area's 9 to 9.5 percent hotel tax.

The area's best hotels

Country Inn & Suites

$$ Destin

This facility's 83 rooms are set inside a three-story, colonial-style building located 1 block from the beach. All the comfortable rooms come with complimentary coffee and a coffee maker, and local phone calls are free. Guests also get a free continental breakfast and weekday newspaper.

4415 Commons Dr. East. ☎ *800-456-4000 or 850-650-9191. Fax: 850-654-1802. Internet:* www.countryinndestin.com. *To get there: Located at the east end of U.S. 98 in Destin, near Midbay Bridge Rd. Parking: Free. Rack rates: $105–$135 May–Aug, $70–$95 Sept–Apr. AE, DC, DISC, MC, V.*

Edgewater Beach Resort

$$ Panama City Beach

This sports-minded resort's 110 acres and five towers make it one of the Panhandle's biggest resorts. All of its condominium units have balconies and views of the Gulf. You can play the nearby Hombre Golf Club course or the resort's own nine-hole course. There are also 12 tennis courts, 6 of which are lighted, and three swimming pools.

11212 Front Beach Rd. ☎ *800-874-8686 or 850-235-4044. Fax: 850-235-6899. Internet:* www.edgewaterbeachresort.com. *To get there: From the east, take U.S. 98 west through the fork where it joins Back Beach Rd. and follow the signs to the resort. Parking: Free. Rack rates: $195@$395 May–Aug, $99–$155 Sept–Apr. AE, DC, DISC, MC, V.*

Josephine's French Country Inn

$$ Seaside

All the accommodations in this Georgian-style plantation home are elegantly decorated with antiques, and each bears the name of a noted figure in French history. Rooms also come with baths, microwaves, coffee makers, and refrigerators. Most units have fireplaces, and the suites have living rooms and full kitchens; two suites sport Gulf views. A full breakfast is included. The inn doesn't have a pool and smoking is strictly prohibited.

101 Seaside Ave. ☎ ***800-848-1840*** *or 850-231-1940. Fax: 850-231-2446. Internet:* www.josephinesfl.com. *To get there: U.S. 98 east from Destin to Hwy. 283, go south to Hwy. 30A, then east to Seaside Ave. Parking: Free. Rack rates: $140–$225 year-round. AE, MC, V.*

Rosemary Beach Cottages

$$$ **Rosemary Beach**

Designed by the same architects as Seaside Cottages (see it listed later in this section), the residences in this complex, just west of Seaside, are meant to mimic those you might find in exclusive waterfront areas in the Tropics or Southeastern United States. Also, like Seaside, this is a pedestrian-friendly community (almost everything is within a 5-minute walk), and most of the homes are owned by people who live here part-time and lease to tourists during the rest of the year. There are two styles of lodgings: Carriage houses have beds for two to four guests; cottages have two to five bedrooms that can accommodate six and more people.

County Road 30-A. ☎ ***888-855-1551*** *or 850-78-2100. Fax: 850-231-1900. Internet:* www.rosemarybeach.com. *To get there: It's at the east end of County Road 30-A. Parking: Free. Rack rates: $200–$640 carriage houses, $405–$1,450 cottages. AE, DISC, MC, V.*

Sandestin Golf and Beach Resort

$$ **Destin**

Units at this luxurious 2,300-acre development range from hotel rooms at the Inn at Sandestin to junior suites and condos — complete with full kitchens, living rooms, and patios or balconies — scattered throughout the property. All accommodations offer coffee makers, Internet access, kitchenettes, and irons and ironing boards. The luxurious townhouses offer two to four bedrooms and glorious views of the property's lakes and golf courses. Sandestin offers 73 holes of golf, 14 tennis courts, a health club, and children's programs. Rates include the use of the facility's health club, bicycles, canoes, and kayaks.

9300 U.S. 98 West. ☎ ***800-622-1922*** *or 850-267-8000. Fax: 850-267-8222. Internet:* www.sandestin.com. *To get there: Located 10 miles east of Destin. Parking: Free. Rack rates: $67–$504 year-round. AE, DC, DISC, MC, V.*

Seaside Cottages

$$$ **Seaside**

If you saw the Jim Carrey movie *The Truman Show,* you saw glimpses of this fu-fu, half-Disney/half-Gatsby creation that could have been designed by Martha Stewart in a psychedelic funk. This is gingerbread at its best (or worst, depending on your perspective). Developer Robert Davis's goal of creating a quiet Utopia was blind-sided by its own popularity, but if you're a fan of cramped and often oddly designed Victorian homes, you will likely love this place. Some of the 275 or so owned-but-leased properties even come with butler service.

County Road 30-A. ☎ *800-277-8696 or 850-231-1320. Fax: 850-231-2293. Internet:* www.seasidefl.com. *To get there: U.S. 98 east from Destin to Hwy. 283, go south to 30-A, and then east to Seaside. Parking: Free. Rack rates: $190 and up. AE, MC, V.*

Runner-up accommodations

Here are a few more perfectly good options, in case our previous selections haven't made the earth move for you — or you waited too long and there's no room at the inn.

Hampton Inn

$$ Destin   This pink two-story motel is planted firmly on the beach. *1625 U.S. 98 East* ☎ *800-426-7866 or 850-654-2577. Fax: 850-654-0745. Internet:* www.hampton-inn.com.

Hibiscus Coffee & Guesthouse

$$ Grayton Beach   A funky, little, four-room bed-and-breakfast, this facility offers private baths and breakfast. It doesn't have a pool. *85 Defuniak St.* ☎ *850-231-2733. Internet:* www.hibiscusflorida.com.

Leeside Inn

$$ Fort Walton Beach   This property has standard motel-style rooms, some with kitchenettes. *1350 Miracle Strip Pkwy. SE* ☎ *800-824-2747 or 850-243-7359. Internet:* www.leesideinn.com.

Marriott Bay Point Resort Village

$$ Panama City Beach   The only knock against this golf and tennis resort is that it's not on the Gulf. *4200 Marriott Dr.* ☎ *800-228-9290 or 850-236-6000. Fax: 850-233-1308. Internet:* www.marriottbaypoint.com.

Dining out at the beaches

Seafood rules in this region, as it does in most of Florida. You won't find much gourmet dining outside of the resorts in Destin, but you won't go hungry either. A seemingly endless supply of national chain restaurants line U.S. 98. Panama City has numerous fast-food joints along 15th and 23rd streets.

The beaches' best restaurants

Boar's Head Restaurant

$$ **Panama City**   STEAKS/SEAFOOD

A local institution, this 22-year-old restaurant sports an English-tavern atmosphere and an award-winning wine list. House specialties include prime rib, steaks, and baby-back ribs, but the menu also includes a nice selection of seafood (stuffed shrimp and lobster tails) and game (venison and quail in winter).

17290 Front Beach Rd. ☎ *850-234-6628. Internet:* www.boarsheadrestaurant. com. *To get there: Located on U.S. 98-A, .3 mile from Hwy. 79. Reservations accepted. Main courses: $15–$22. AE, DC, DISC, MC, V. Open: 4:30– 9 p.m. daily; until 10 p.m. summer.*

Bud & Alley's

$$ **Seaside**   SEAFOOD/MEDITERRANEAN

In this cracked-crab- and champagne-loving community, this trendy eatery features spectacular sunsets and a menu that changes frequently but always has pleasant surprises. You may run into pan-seared catfish in tomato tarragon sauce, apple-and-walnut stuffed quail, or none of the above. So, call if you want to lock in on your options. The menu also has tapas for starters and an exhaustive wine list.

County Rd. 30-A. ☎ *850-231-5900. Internet:* www.budandalleys.com. *To get there: Located between Grayton Beach and Seagrove Beach. Reservations recommended. Main courses: $16–$31. MC, V. Open: 11:30 a.m.–3 p.m., 5:30–9 p.m. Wed–Mon.*

Criolla's

$$ **Grayton Beach**   CARIBBEAN

Johnny Earle's popular eatery delivers a blessing of flavors, inspired by cuisine found along the equator. His grouper is bathed in lime and olive oil, before it's charred and served with shrimp, littleneck clams, and calamari, in a spicy broth. And the swordfish is wrapped in bacon and grilled. In addition to the regular menu, there's a four-course *prix-fixe* menu ($42 per person).

170 E. County Road 30-A. ☎ *850-267-1267. Internet:* www.criollas.com. *To get there: U.S. 98 east to Hwy. 283, turn right, and then left on 30-A. Reservations recommended. Main courses: $19–$29. DISC, MC, V. Open: 5:30–10 p.m. daily, May–Aug; Tues–Sat, Jan–Feb and Oct–Dec; Mon–Sat, Mar–Apr and Sept.*

Destin Chops

$$ Destin   STEAKS/SEAFOOD

This wood-and-glass beauty offers contemporary cuisine and a sparkling view of Destin Harbor. Hang out with Destin's "beautiful people," and scarf down such house specialties as steaks and veal chops, served in unique sauces. If don't like to do as the Romans do, the menu also features lobster, grilled grouper, and yellowfin tuna.

320 E. U.S. 98. ☎ *850-654-4944. Internet:* www.marinacafe.com. *To get there: It's on the main drag, on the west side of town. Reservations recommended. Main courses: $14–$33. AE, DC, DISC, MC, V. Open: 5–9:30 p.m. daily.*

Hamilton's Restaurant and Lounge

$$ Panama City Beach   SEAFOOD

The Angus steaks, chicken, ribs, and many seafood entrees at this waterfront restaurant are cooked over a mesquite grill. Other specialties include snapper etouffee, crabmeat-stuffed shrimp, and crab cakes. In case you're in the mood, Hamilton's features an upper level deck out back for al fresco dining. A good wine list and an oak bar, where you can have a pre-dinner cocktail, can also add to your dining experience.

5711 N. Lagoon Dr. ☎ *850-234-1255. Internet:* www.hamiltonspcbeach.com. *To get there: It's off of Thomas Dr., overlooking Grand Lagoon. Reservations recommended. Main courses: $12–$20. AE, DISC, MC, V. Open: 5–9 p.m. daily, sometimes later.*

Marina Café

$$ Destin   NEW AMERICAN

A progressive menu and an incredible view of Destin Harbor have kept this cafe around since the mid-1980s. The cafe has an indoor dining room, but it's a shame to waste the deck and the view of the marina on nice days. The offerings here include pizza, pasta, and seafood. The latter includes pan-seared redfish, yellowfin tuna, and almond-crusted mahi-mahi.

404 E. U.S. 98. ☎ *850-837-7960. Internet:* www.marinacafe.com. *To get there: Located at Destin Harbor on E. U.S. 98. Reservations recommended. Main courses: $15–$29. AE, DC, DISC, MC, V. Open: 5–9:30 p.m. daily.*

Runner-up restaurants

Here are another half-dozen entries for you to choose from, if our first-tier selections didn't tickle your taste buds.

Beach Walk Café

$$ Destin   This elegant restaurant has a constantly changing menu that usually includes well-prepared steaks and seafood. *2996 Scenic Hwy. 98,* ☎ *850-650-7100. Internet:* www.beachwalkcafe.com.

Café Thirty-A

$$ **Seagrove Beach** This funky little pit stop has won awards for a menu that includes grouper and salmon cooked in a wood-fired oven. *Scenic Hwy. 98* ☎ *850-231-2166. Internet:* www.cafethirtya.com.

Capt. Anderson's Restaurant

$$ **Panama City Beach** This local legend offers the usual seafood suspects, including grilled fish, stuffed shrimp, and several platters. *5551 N. Lagoon Dr.* ☎ *850-234-2225. Internet:* www.captanderson.com.

Chef Paul's

$$ **Panama City** Here, you can dine on high-class cuisine, with an emphasis on seafood and game — including a venison-ostrich-duck trifecta — in a cozy indoor or a romantic outdoor setting. *102 Market St.* ☎ *850-235-2811. Internet:* www.chef-paul.com.

Lake Place Restaurant

$$ **Santa Rosa Beach** You can feast on jumbo shrimp, scallops, steaks, or lamb chops at this cozy eatery (just 14 tables). *5960 W. County Road 30-A* ☎ *850-267-2871. Internet:* www.lakeplacerestaurant.com.

Pandora's Steakhouse

$$ **Fort Walton Beach** This family-owned restaurant offers fresh steaks and seafood, seared on a wood-burning grill. *1120 Santa Rosa Blvd.* ☎ *850-244-8669. Internet:* www.pandoras-steakhouse.com.

Exploring Panama City, Fort Walton Beach, Destin, and Seaside

From end to end, this region is about 60 miles long, which means that, with sedan in hand, you can explore it from a single base camp. The beaches are obviously a big attraction, but there are other things to occupy your interests as well.

Touring the top sights

Eden State Gardens and the Wesley Mansion

Grayton Beach

William Henry Wesley, founder of the Wesley Lumber Company, built this estate in 1898. The Greek-Revival mansion, its French provincial furnishings, and the lush gardens were restored in the 1960s and given to the park service. Self-guided and 45-minute ranger-led tours (on the hour) show off heirloom furnishings and gardens, scented by thousands of azaleas. That said, this isn't the kind of place you want to visit with kids or restless adults. But if you're into yesterday's treasures, allow 1½ to 2 hours.

181 Eden Gardens Rd. ☎ *850-231-4214. Internet:* www.dep.state.fl.us/parks/edengardens. *To get there: Go south of U.S. 98 on Hwy. 395. Admission: $2 per carload; tours $1.50 adults and 50 cents kids 12 and under. Open: 8 a.m.– 5 p.m. daily.*

Gulfarium

Fort Walton Beach

Welcome to one of the country's longest-running marine shows, dating back to 1955. In addition to the requisite dolphin show, its residents and performers include California sea lions, Peruvian penguins, Ridley sea turtles, moray eels, American alligators, and dozens of fish that the gators would love to wrap their lips around. Shows run at 10 a.m., noon, 2, and 4 p.m. daily. Figure on spending 3 to 4 hours here.

1010 Miracle Strip Pkwy./U.S. 98. ☎ *850-244-5169 or 850-243-9046. Internet:* www.gulfarium.com. *To get there: Located northwest of the Brooks Bridge on Okaloosa Island. Admission: $16 adults, $14 seniors, $10 kids 4–11. Open: 9 a.m.– 5:30 p.m. daily.*

Gulf World Marine Park

Panama City Beach

Cut from the same cloth as Gulfarium, in the preceding listing, Gulf World is an old-style marine park with trained dolphins, sea lions, penguins, sea turtles, alligators, sharks, and more. If you've seen one of these marine parks, you've seen them all; if not, allow 3 to 4 hours for this excursion.

15412 Front Beach Rd. ☎ *850-234-5271. To get there: Located on U.S. 98-A at Hall Ave. Admission: $17.00 adults, $10.50 kids 5–12. Open: 9 a.m.–3 p.m. daily; until 7 p.m. summer.*

Museum of Man and the Sea

Panama City Beach

Relics of the earliest days of scuba diving join treasures from shipwrecked Spanish galleons in this museum. You can climb through a submarine, see live sea critters, or try on a diving helmet. The museum also features an aquarium, housing sea life from the nearby bay. Allow 2 hours to hit the highlights.

17314 Panama City Pkwy./U.S. 98. ☎ *850-235-4101. To get there: It's just west of Hwy. 79 on U.S. 98. Admission: $5.00 adults, $2.50 kids 5–15. Open: 9 a.m.–5 p.m. daily.*

U.S. Air Force Armament Museum

Fort Walton Beach/Eglin Air Force Base

Take a gander at several vintage flying machines, including an SR-71 Blackbird spy plane and vintage craft that flew through four wars. Speaking of vintage, Jimmy Doolittle's Raiders trained here. The museum, part of the world's largest air base, also has an exhibit on guns, bombs, rockets, lasers, radar, and "smart" bombs. Allow 2 to 3 hours, if you're into military aviation.

100 Museum Dr. (off Eglin Pkwy). ☎ *850-882-4062. To get there: Located at Eglin Air Force Base, 5 miles north of downtown Fort Walton Beach on Hwy. 85. Admission: Free. Open: 9:30 a.m.–4:30 p.m. daily.*

ZooWorld Zoological Park

Panama City Beach

The zoo offers a look at orangutans, snow leopards, lemurs, otters, bats, and an 8-foot albino python named Sunny. The park also has a kids' petting zoo. Expect to spend 2 to 3 hours here.

9008 Front Beach Rd./U.S. 98-A. ☎ *850-230-1243 or, if you want a live person, 850-230-4839. To get there: It's west of Thomas Dr. Admission: $11.00 adults, $7.50 kids 3–11. Open: 9 a.m.–dusk daily.*

Doing more cool stuff

Before we offer a suggested itinerary for seeing the region, here are a few more activities that might appeal to some of you.

✔ **Amusement Parks:** There are two popular amusement parks in this neck of the woods. **Miracle Strip Amusement Park**, 12000 Front Beach Rd., Panama City Beach (☎ 850-234-5810; Internet: www.miraclestrippark.com), has a 105-foot high roller coaster, a carousel, and several other kids' rides. It's open from mid-March to Labor Day and costs $15 for unlimited rides. The adjoining **Shipwreck Island Water Park** (☎ 850-234-0368) has water slides and tubing runs, among other aquatic amusements. It's open from June to mid-August. Admission costs $20 for folks over 50 inches, $17 for those between 35 and 50 inches.

✔ **Beaches:** A string of wonderful, old Florida-style beaches are along County Road 30-A and U.S. 98 in South Walton County, beginning with Seaside and extending east to Seagrove, Hollywood, Sunnyside, and Laguna Beaches. Additionally, the **Grayton Beach State Recreation Area**, on U.S. 98 west of Seaside (☎ 850-231-4210), is a quartz beauty and a reasonably safe beach for swimmers. The area features dunes and lots of native critters. Admission is $3.25 per carload.

✔ **Fishing:** The **Destin Fishing Rodeo,** in October, is a month-long fishing extravaganza held in an area billed as the "World's Luckiest Fishing Village." That may be a stretch, but Destin is a hot spot for anglers. Call ☎ **850-837-6734,** if you want more information about the event. Day-to-day trips are easy to arrange, if you just stop along the waterfront at Destin Harbor. Large boat trips run about $25 to $30 for a half day; private charters run about $100 per hour for up to six people. One of the best sources for charter information is **FishDestin.com** (☎ **850-837-9401** or 850-585-0049; Internet: www.fishdestin.com).

✔ **Golf:** You can obtain local course information online at www.golf.com and www.floridagolfing.com, or you can call the **Florida Sports Foundation** (☎ **850-488-8347**) or **Florida Golfing** (☎ **877-222-4653**). **Bay Dunes Golf Club,** 5304 Majette Tower Rd., Panama City (☎ **850-872-1667**), and a par-71 course with water hazards on eight holes is very popular. Greens fees run between $41 and $65 year-round. Another good choice is **Bluewater Bay Resort,** 1950 Bluewater Blvd., Niceville (☎ **800-874-2128**), which offers 36 holes, north of Destin. Greens fees run $65 to $84.

And last but not least, a trip to the Panhandle can't be considered complete without a visit to **Seaside,** County Road 30-A (☎ **800-277-8696;** Internet: www.seasidefl.com), the whimsical, Disney-like community featured in the Jim Carrey movie, *The Truman Show.* The town square has a charming, Greek revival-style post office, a scattering of shops where you'll pay too much for everything, and a market with fun foods and sauces. Architecture is the big draw. This place is dripping in gingerbread, including a lot of Victorian replicas.

Shopping

Like the rest Panhandle, this area has no shopping districts, but there are a few places for browsers. **Grayton Beach** has a collection of shops, restaurants, and century-old architecture on Highway 283. Ditto for **The Market at Sandestin,** which is in the Sandestin Resort on U.S. 98 in Destin. **Silver Sands Factory Stores,** 5021 U.S. 98, Destin (☎ **850-865-9780**), features outlets for Ann Taylor, Cole Haan, Donna Karan, Laura Ashley, Timberland, and 85 other shops in three buildings.

Living the Nightlife

In addition to the following listings, you can get up-to-the-minute details on where to party in the Friday editions of the *Northwest Florida Daily News* in Fort Walton Beach (☎ **850-863-1111;** Internet: www.nwfdailynews.com) and the *News Herald* in Panama City (☎ **850-747-5000;** Internet: www.newsherald.com).

None of these clubs charges a cover.

AJ's Seafood & Oyster Bar, 116 U.S. 98 East, Destin (☎ **850-837-1913;** Internet: www.ajs-destin.com), attracts a young crowd with reggae. The **Blue Moon Saloon,** 1030 Miracle Strip Pkwy., Fort Walton Beach (☎ **850-796-0260;** Internet: www.ftwaltonpier.com), offers live entertainment above Angler's Beach Side Grill. The **Blues Jazz Bar & Restaurant,** 327 U.S. 98, in Destin (☎ **850-269-2583;** Internet: www.bluedestin.com), features live jazz and other music nightly. **Fudpucker's Beachside Bar & Grill,** Emerald Coast Pkwy., Destin (☎ **850-654-4200;** Internet: www.fudpucker.com), has twin stages and classic rock, if you come in summer. Mellow rock floats from the lounge at **Harry T's,** 320 U.S. 98 East, Destin (☎ **850-650-4800;** Internet: www.harryts.com), Wednesday through Saturday. In the Marriott Bay Point Resort Village, **Teddy Tucker's,** 4200 Marriott Dr., Panama City Beach (☎ **850-236-6000;** Internet: www.marriottbaypoint.com), offers nightly Jimmy Buffett tunes.

Seeing Panama City, Fort Walton Beach, and Destin in 2 days

On **Day 1,** head for Panama City Beach. Fill your morning with a visit to **Gulf World Marine Park.** Then, after grabbing lunch on the fly, visit **ZooWorld Zoological Park** and, if you still have gas in the tank, the **Museum of Man and the Sea.** Have dinner at the **Boar's Head Restaurant** and call it a night at **Teddy Tucker's.**

Start **Day 2** at **Eden State Gardens** and the **Wesley Mansion** in Grayton Beach and then have a leisurely lunch at **Bud & Alley's.** Afterward, spend your afternoon taking the self-guided tour of **Seaside,** where you can ogle the architecture and explore the shops. Enjoy your dinner at **Destin Chops** or the **Marina Cafe** and then unwind a little more at the **Blues Jazz Bar & Restaurant.**

Fast Facts

Area Code
The local area code is **850.**

American Express
There are travel service offices at **Cordova Travel Services,** 4400 Bayou Blvd., Pensacola (☎ **850-477-6560**) and **Travel Adventures Unlimited,** 15 Yacht Club Dr., Fort Walton Beach (☎ **850-244-4186**).

Hospitals
The major hospitals in the area are **Baptist Hospital,** 1000 W. Moreno St., Pensacola (☎ **850-469-2313**) and **West Florida Regional Medical Center,** 8383 N. Davis Hwy., Pensacola (☎ **850-494-4000**).

Information
The following are good sources of tourist information and maps:

The **Pensacola Convention and Visitor Bureau,** 1401 E. Gregory St. (☎ 800-874-1234 or 850-434-1234; Internet: www.visitpensacola.com); the **Emerald Coast Convention and Visitors Bureau,** 1540 Miracle Strip Pkwy., Fort Walton Beach (☎ 800-322-3319 or 850-651-7122; Internet: www.destin-fwb.com); the **Destin Area Chamber of Commerce,** P.O. Box 8, Destin, FL 32541 (☎ 850-837-6241; Internet: www.destinchamber.com); and the **Panama City Beach Convention and Visitors Bureau,** P.O. Box 9473 Panama City Beach, FL 32407 (☎ 800-PCB-EACH; Internet: www.pcbeach.com).

Mail

There are U.S. post offices at 3001 N. Davis Hwy., Pensacola; 51 Walter Martin Rd. NE, Fort Walton Beach; and 2800 S. Adams St., Tallahassee. Call ☎ 800-275-8777 to find a post office near your hotel.

Maps

The information sources listed earlier in this section are good places to ask about maps. So are auto clubs, if you're a member, and rental-car agencies. You can buy them at most local convenience stores for $3 to $5.

Newspapers

The region's major papers include **The Pensacola News Journal** (☎ 850-435-8500; Internet: www.gulfcoastgateway.com); **Northwest Florida Daily News,** Fort Walton Beach (☎ 850-863-1111; Internet: www.nwfdailynews.com); and the **News Herald,** Panama City (☎ 850-747-5000; Internet: www.newsherald.com).

Pharmacies

There are 24-hour **Walgreens** stores at 6314 N. 9th Ave., Pensacola (☎ 850-479-2544) and 825 Beal Pkwy., Fort Walton Beach (☎ 850-314-0851).

Taxes

A 6 percent state sales tax is added to most purchases, except groceries and medicine. Hotels tack on an additional 3 to 5.5 percent.

Taxis

Yellow Cab (☎ 850-433-3333) and **Crosstown Cab** (☎ 850-456-8294) serve Pensacola. The rate is $1.50 when the flag drops and $1.40 per mile. **Yellow Cab** serves Panama City (☎ 850-763-0211) and Fort Walton Beach (☎ 850-244-3600). **AAA Taxi** (☎ 850-785-0533) operates in Panama City, and **Charter Taxis** (☎ 850-863-5466) serves Fort Walton Beach. Rates vary, but expect to pay as much as $2.50 to climb in and $1.50 per mile thereafter.

Weather Updates

For a recording of current conditions and forecast reports, call the local office of the **National Weather Service** at ☎ 850-942-8999 or check out its Web site at www.nws.noaa.gov. You can also get information by watching **The Weather Channel** or visiting its Web site at www.weatherchannel.com.

Part VII
The Part of Tens

The 5th Wave   By Rich Tennant

"You're sure you don't want to drive a little further to find an orange grove stand?"

In this part . . .

Ah, tradition. "Parts of Ten" are to *For Dummies* guides what hangovers are to New Year's Day. This area of the book is where you can find plenty of useful and fun information that we couldn't fit somewhere else in the book.

Chapter 24

The Top Ten Florida Beaches

•••

In This Chapter

▶ South Florida

▶ Central Florida

▶ The Northeast

▶ The Panhandle

•••

There are two kinds of beaches in Florida: those that the TV ads trumpet and the less-discovered gems. The former includes some of the places we visited in earlier chapters, such as Miami Beach, Daytona Beach, Clearwater Beach, Panama City Beach, and so on. The latter are off the beaten path. In many cases they're in state parks or preserves.

These off-the-path beaches are also less crowded, and vacationers who walk the extra mile are rewarded with features that are often extraordinary — towering sand dunes, wind-bent sea oats, powder-fine sand, crystal-clear water, solitude, good shelling, or a combination of these features.

One of the founders of the Real Florida Beach Club is Dr. Stephen Leatherman, a professor and geologist at Florida International University. Several years ago, he earned the nickname "Dr. Beach" for his annual ranking of the best stretches of sand in the world. He uses more than 50 criteria (like width, sand softness, safety, water temperature, wave size, bugs, trash, and amenities) to come up with his top-ten list of beaches. Our method, based on plain old creature comforts, is much less scientific. But in many cases, we agree with Dr. B. Here are our favorites, listed from south to north:

Bill Baggs Cape Florida State Recreation Area

Miami/Key Biscayne

This park is certainly the most secluded beach in Miami. With its historic lighthouse (originally built in 1825) and native flora, the park provides a welcome respite from the hustle and bustle of this international city. But watch out for the raccoons and other critters that are more than happy to walk off with your picnic basket, among other things.

1200 Crandon Blvd., Key Biscayne. ☎ *305-361-5811. To get there: From the mainland, take U.S. 1 south to Rickenbacker Causeway and cross to Key Biscayne, and then follow the signs. Admission: $4 per car (up to eight people).*

Bahia Honda State Park

Big Pine Key

Bahia Honda (that's *deep bay* in Spanish) is the only state park in the lower Keys and one of the rare beaches in this area. Fact is, this is the only natural beach in the Keys. Can it get any better than brilliant white sand, turquoise water, and a brisk breeze? The park's 524 acres include dunes, coastal mangroves, and hammocks. The white-sand beach has deep water close to the shore, making it a good snorkeling venue. (You may find lobster and starfish in 3 feet of water.) While you're here, climb aboard what's left of the old Henry Flagler rail line and treat yourself to an awesome panorama of the surrounding Keys.

36850 Overseas Hwy., Big Pine Key. ☎ *305-872-2353. To get there: Located 12 miles south of Marathon on Overseas Hwy. (Mile Marker 37.5). Admission: $4 per vehicle.*

Delnor-Wiggins Pass State Recreation Area

Naples

If you crave the natural wonders that used to be everywhere on Florida's coasts (sea oats, sea grapes, cabbage palms, and mangroves), you'll love Delnor-Wiggins. Its resident birds wade among mollusks and soft coral. **Manatees** find sanctuary in the warm waters during the winter, and loggerhead sea turtles come ashore on summer nights to lay their eggs. Parking is plentiful, and boardwalks lead into the nature areas.

 While the swimming at Delnor-Wiggins Pass is good, be careful to stay out of the pass (the narrow space between the shore lines) to avoid the dangerous undertow.

Entrance at 11100 Gulf Shore Dr., Naples. ☎ *941-597-6196. Admission: $4 per car.*

Siesta Beach

Sarasota

This beach is short, just a quarter of a mile long, but it's also 500 feet wide. The tide has pounded the sand granules for so long that they feel like fine flour beneath your toes. (This is the kind of sand that squeaks when you walk on it.) By Gulf of Mexico standards, it has good swimming (the water is a little on the warm side and very tame by Atlantic standards, but there's virtually no undertow). You'll have a hard time finding a better place to chill out. Just sit at the water's edge and let the small waves lap at your legs. Lifeguards add to the safety level. Siesta Beach gets a little crowded with families at times (it's Sarasota's most popular beach), but there's a 700-car parking lot, and the price is right.

☎ *941-346-3310. To get there: Heading west on State Road 72, cross U.S. 41 and the Intracoastal Waterway. At the road's end, turn right at Midnight Pass and follow the signs. Admission: Free.*

Caladesi Island State Park

Dunedin

This 3-mile island (our apologies to the nuclear power industry) is among the best shelling locations in Florida. The no-vehicles policy means that you don't need to worry about noise or air pollution. It's secluded with soft sand, sea grass, small dunes, and a variety of birds, including blue herons. You may have the opportunity to see the resident dolphins performing off the beach, and in summer, you'll probably see the crawl marks left by nesting loggerhead turtles. To get there, use the ferry ($7 adults, $3.50 kids 3 to 12) at Honeymoon Island State Recreation Area (see Chapter 16), where there's also a $4-per-vehicle admission fee.

3 Causeway Blvd., Dunedin. ☎ *727-469-5918. To get there: From Clearwater, go north on U.S. 19, and then west on Curlew Road, which leads to Honeymoon Island and the ferry.*

Washington Oaks State Park

Palm Coast

This park gets lost in the tourist shuffle between Daytona Beach to the south and St. Augustine to the north. All the better for those who visit. Originally part of an early nineteenth-century plantation, the 400-acre park reaches from the Atlantic Ocean to the Matanzas River. A hammock and marsh are on one side, but a beautifully rocky beach across the way presents our favorite picture. The waves' constant pounding on the coquina rocks gives the beach a ghostly, out-of-this-world, orange appearance.

The depressions in the rock are neat places to search for mussels, limpets, and barnacles, among other critters. The rocks make swimming a little hazardous, but a short walk to either side gets you clear of them.

6400 Oceanshore Blvd., Palm Coast (about 20 miles south of St. Augustine). ☎ *904-446-6780. Admission: $3.75 per car.*

Little Talbot Island State Park

Jacksonville

Actually, this 2,500-acre park is on Little *and* Big Talbot Islands. Salt marshes, hammocks, and Atlantic dunes (these are tall puppies) complement more than 4 miles of gorgeous beaches, marshes, and centuries-old live oaks. Fiddler crabs scurry about the beach, and lucky visitors get a glimpse of the park's river otters.

This is another place to see a rocky beach carved by erosion, as well as plenty of driftwood formations. On the trails and observation platform, you'll see some of the nearly 200 species of land, wading, and sea birds that come to the island. Despite the major city just south of the park and a large Navy base, this is one of Florida's least spoiled beaches.

☎ *904-251-2320. To get there: From Jacksonville, follow Highway A1A 20 miles northeast. Admission: $3.25 per car.*

St. George Island State Park

Eastpoint

Located near the fishing village of Apalachicola, this park is a great place to see dolphins offshore and wading birds on the island. The park has 9 miles of unspoiled beaches, hiking trails, and an observation platform to give you a close view of the scenery. Bald eagles and other rare birds nest in the park. Loggerhead turtles nest on the beach in the summer. One of the dandiest things about St. George is location — virtually in the middle of nowhere. Franklin County has just 9,000 residents. Heck, you have to drive 90 minutes if you want to shop at one of Sam Walton's finest. The park reaches across 9 of the island's 27 miles.

☎ *850-927-2111. To get there: From Apalachicola, go east on U.S. 98 to the bay bridge (Highway 300), turn left, and follow Highway 300 to the island. Admission: $4 per vehicle.*

St. Joseph Peninsula State Park

Port St. Joe

Getting to this park is part of the fun. The highway takes you through Cape San Blas, a nostalgic settlement of summer homes and bungalows. St. Joseph's has a long beach nuzzled by saw palmettos, pines, and dunes that are 60 feet tall, 200 feet wide, and stretch shoulder to shoulder for 9 miles. This also is one of the best places along the Gulf Coast to see broad-winged hawks, peregrine falcons, and during the fall, Monarch butterflies.

☎ *850-227-1327. To get there: From downtown Port St. Joe (what there is of it), take U.S. 98 two miles to County Road 30 and follow it south to the peninsula, and then take Highway 30-E to the park. Admission: $4 per car.*

Perdido Key State Recreation Area

Near Pensacola

This barrier island stretches along 1.4 miles of the coast. It has some spectacular sunsets and an equally spectacular white quartz beach. The Johnson Beach Area on the eastern third of the island is undeveloped, except for a bathhouse. Perdido means *lost island* in Spanish.

☎ *850-492-1575. To get there: Located 15 miles SW of Pensacola off S.R. 292. Admission: $2 per vehicle.*

Chapter 25

Ten or More of Florida's Favorite Foods

. . . .

In This Chapter

▶ Sampling the seafood

▶ Dining the Latin way

▶ Eating your pie

. . . .

*1*n this chapter, we cheat — twice.

First, we list more than ten items here.

Second, while some of these dishes are true Florida specialties, we remind you that this state is a melting pot. So most of the food that you find on restaurant menus or in the supermarket is someone else's recipe. Most of what's presented as Cracker cuisine (think grits, and so on) has roots in Alabama, Georgia, or another Southern state that ends in a vowel. Our food also shows a substantial (and delightful) Cuban influence, as well as a Caribbean flair.

The local cuisine is sometimes called *Floribbean.* We don't think any self-respecting Cracker, Cuban, or Caribbean islander would ever con-coct a name like that. The likely culprit is a chef with too much time on his hands. He probably drew three columns on a sheet of paper. He listed meat, poultry, and seafood in one; his favorite fruits and veggies in another; and condiments and spices in the third. Then, he paired a food from each group and — voilà! — Floribbean was born.

We steer clear of Floribbean in this part and instead deal with some older and more conventional staples because they give you a far better feel for the foods that you'll see on menus throughout the state.

Ambrosia

There's something whimsical about the name and this salad. It blends mandarin oranges, pineapple strings, coconut, marshmallows, and sour cream into a mouth-watering explosion of taste.

Citrus Fruits

Sticking with fruit a moment more, winter is the big season for Florida oranges, grapefruit, and tangerines. Nevertheless, you'll find them, or their imported cousins, sold pretty much year-round at roadside stands or grocery stores and supermarkets. While they're not citrus, strawberries are another popular wintertime fruit.

Conch

These critters live in those shells that some of you will buy in souvenir shops, take back home, and (after a carafe of wine) put to your ear and swear that you can hear the ocean.

Conch can be pretty tough, so cooks have to whack the heck out of it with a tenderizing mallet before serving it. That's if you want it in chowder or fried, the two most common ways conch is prepared. Also served in salads, conch tends to be grainy and not real sweet, unless you have the courage to try it raw.

Cuban Cuisine

Florida had a sizable Hispanic population even before Fidel's fiasco, and since 1959, the population has increased dramatically. The Tampa and Miami areas have large Latin bases — the reason for such a strong Cuban/Spanish influence in our food.

To sample a day's worth of Cuban delights, begin at breakfast with a wedge of hot, buttered Cuban bread dunked in a cup of *café con leche* — strong coffee cut with milk. Things get downright funky after that. Specialties include *frijoles negros* (black beans), *arroz con pollo* (chicken and yellow rice), *boliche* (tender, sausage-stuffed beef), Cuban mojo-roast pork, *salteado* (chorizo, onion, and pepper stew), and deviled crab with hot sauce. Arguably, though, it doesn't get any better than a heaping dish of *paella* — rice buried under a blanket of treats that may include mussels, clams, shrimp, scallops, lobster, oysters, stone-crab claws, chicken, and/or pork. If you survive, try your luck with *flan*, egg custard dripping in caramel sauce.

Divinity

 Divinity should be called dentists' delight. It's instant tooth decay (but, oh, what fun you're going to have getting there). This chewy candy is composed of a ton of sugar, corn syrup, egg whites, vanilla, and pecans.

Florida Lobster

Like conch, Florida lobster tends to be grainy and not sweet, especially in inland restaurants. It's also commonly served broiled with butter. Many places cheat and give you margarine.

 Our advice: Leave the lobsters to the Mainers.

Grits

Like other Southerners, real backwoods Floridians know "gree-its" is a two-syllable word. Grits are corn, coarsely ground to a slurry. The trick is to eat them before they congeal into something that resembles a hockey puck. Salt, pepper, and butter are allowed. Some folks like to add cheese, but in a real Cracker diner adding cheese will get you almost as many disapproving stares as using sugar — a common mistake made by northerners who mistake grits for Cream O' Wheat.

Key Lime Pie

 If it's green, send it back to the kitchen. The real stuff is yellow, thanks to the backyard fruit grown throughout much of South Florida. Pretenders use the wrong limes or — and this is true sacrilege — green food coloring. Key lime pie usually comes with a graham cracker or regular crust and is made with condensed milk (not low-fat). This dessert is tangy and tart and sometimes has a dollop of whipped cream on top. One variation uses meringue.

Mullet

This local fish has dark, fatty meat and a pretty strong flavor when compared to white-meat fish. Mullet is more common in down-home, shorts-are-welcome restaurants than in the fancier establishments. It's usually served smoked or fried with a light cornmeal wrapping. The roe (fish eggs) is often sent to the Orient, where it's considered a delicacy.

Seafood

Florida's Gulf and Atlantic coasts and its inland waters cough up a delightful menu of marine cuisine. Depending on the time of year and your location, you can feast on Apalachicola oysters, Fernandina Beach shrimp, St. Johns River blue crabs, Florida Bay lobsters, and Cedar Key clams. Grouper, mahi-mahi, largemouth bass, speckled perch, and trout are also menu regulars.

Stone Crab Claws

In season from mid-October until May, this catch is the crab world's answer to Maine lobster, a sweet treat that results in a heck of a lot more meat and a lot less work than blue crabs. Steamed or boiled, these claws are close to heaven when dipped in butter. They're also at the top of the price chart.

Appendix

Quick Concierge

● ●

*T*his handy section is where we condense all the practical and pertinent information — from airline phone numbers to mailbox locations — you need to make sure that you have a successful and stress-free vacation. And for those of you who believe there is no such thing as too much preparation, we give you some additional resources to check out.

Florida A to Z: Facts at Your Fingertips

AAA

If you belong to the American Automobile Association, you can contact your local office for maps and optimum driving directions or call ☎ 800-222-4357 and ask to be transferred to the office nearest your location. Some other auto clubs also have service agreements with AAA, so ask your club whether this is the case before you leave. You can get information online at www. aaa.com.

American Express

You can reach the card company's Travel Service offices nationally by calling ☎ 800-297-3429. We list local branch offices under "Fast Facts" in some of the destination chapters (Chapters 11 to 23).

Banks

Banks are generally open Monday through Friday from 9 a.m. to 3–4 p.m. ATMs honoring Cirrus, Honor, Plus, and other systems are commonly found in most malls, banks, and convenience stores, such as 7-Eleven and Circle K, as well as at larger tourist attractions and shopping venues. To locate an ATM near your hotel in Florida, contact either of the two most popular networks: **Cirrus** (☎ 800-424-7787; www.mastercard. com/atm/) and **Plus** (☎ 800-843-7587; www.visa.com/atms).

Credit Cards

American Express, MasterCard, and Visa are universally accepted in all but a few places. Carte Blanche, Diner's Club, and Discover are also accepted in many locations. We list the accepted credit cards under hotel and restaurant entries.

Customs

Every visitor over 21 years of age may bring into the United States, free of duty: 1 liter of wine or liquor; 200 cigarettes, 100 cigars (but no cigars from Cuba) or 3 pounds of smoking tobacco; and $100 worth of gifts. These exemptions are offered to travelers who spend at least 72 hours in the United States and who haven't claimed the exemptions within the preceding 6 months. It's forbidden to bring food (particularly cheese, fruit, cooked meats, and canned goods) and plants (vegetables, seeds, tropical plants, and so on) into the country. Foreign tourists may bring in or take out up to $10,000 in U.S. or foreign currency with no formalities; larger sums must be declared to Customs on departure.

Doctors

You don't need fools like us to tell you to go to the ER in an emergency. We list local hospitals and pharmacies in the various regions of Florida under "Fast Facts" in Chapters 11 to 17, and Chapters 20 to 23.

Emergencies

All of Florida uses **911** as the emergency number for police, fire departments, ambulances, and other critical needs. There's also a 24-hour, toll-free number for the **Poison Control Center** (☎ 800-282-3171).

For less urgent requests, call ☎ 800-647-9284, a number sponsored by the **Florida Tourism Industry Marketing Corporation**, the state's tourism promotion board. Its operators speak more than 100 languages and can provide general directions, as well as help with lost travel papers and credit cards, medical emergencies, accidents, money transfers, airline confirmations, and much more.

Information

Visit Florida (661 E. Jefferson St., Suite 300, Tallahassee, FL 32301; ☎ 888-735-2872; www.flausa.com) is the state's official tourism office. You can order a copy of the *Florida Vacation Guide* as well as brochures on golf, fishing, camping, and biking.

See "Fast Facts" in Chapters 11 through 17, and Chapters 20 to 23 for local tourist information sources. Also, see "Where to Get More Information," later in this chapter.

Information II

To get local telephone information, dial ☎ 411.

Liquor Laws

We're pretty straightforward in Florida. Florida law requires you to be 21-years-old or older before you can buy or consume alcohol. And they're very strict about enforcing the law. You can get into parimutuels and bars where food is served at an earlier age (don't worry if you're coming in diapers). **Note:** Depending on the region, liquor stores in Florida either stay open all week, or close on Sundays.

Mail

If you want to receive mail on your vacation and you aren't sure of your address, your mail can be sent to you, in your name, care of General Delivery at the main post office of the city or region where you expect to be (see "Fast Facts" in Chapters 11 to 17, and 20 to 23). You can get the address and phone number of any post office in the area that you visit by calling ☎ 800-275-8777.

Maps

AAA and other auto clubs offer good Florida maps to members. You can also find maps in bookstores and libraries in your hometown. Most Florida convenience stores sell local maps for $3 to $5. If you rent a car, ask the rental agent for a map — many of the agencies carry pretty thorough ones. You can also request maps from many of the local tourist information bureaus listed in the "Fast Facts" sections of some destination chapters (Chapters 11 through 23).

Newspapers/Magazines

Check out the Sunday travel section in your hometown paper (or the one in the biggest city nearby) for travel bargains, ideas, and tips. We list local newspapers in the "Fast Facts" sections of Chapters 11 to 17, and 20 to 23, and we also mention when they publish an entertainment section. Also, don't overlook all of those handout (free) coupon books and throwaway magazines that you find in restaurant and hotel lobbies. Everyone wants to give you a coupon — some of them are actually worth the paper they're printed on, and more.

Police

In any emergency, call **911**. If you have a cellular phone and need help, dial ***FHP** for the Florida Highway Patrol.

Restrooms

Foreign visitors often complain that public toilets are hard to find, but Florida is no worse than most U.S. destinations. True, there are no restrooms on the streets, but you can usually find one in a bar, restaurant, hotel, museum, department store, convenience store, attraction, fast food barn, or service station — and it will probably be clean. In particular, Mobil service stations have made a public pledge to provide exceptionally clean bathrooms, most decorated with homey touches. Note, however, that restaurants and bars in resorts or heavily visited areas may reserve their restrooms for the use of their patrons. Some establishments display a notice that toilets are for the use of patrons only. You can ignore this sign or, better yet, avoid arguments by paying for a cup of coffee or a soft drink, which will qualify you as a patron. Within the theme parks, restrooms will be clearly marked on the park maps. Don't panic if you find the flushing handle is missing; many new toilets are installed with lasers that trigger the flush automatically when you leave the stall.

Safety

Stay alert and remain aware of your immediate surroundings. Keeping your valuables in a safe-deposit box (inquire at your hotel's front desk) is a good idea, although nowadays many hotels are equipped with in-room safes. Keep a close eye on your valuables when you're in a public place — restaurant, theater, and even an airport terminal. Renting a locker is always preferable to leaving your valuables in the trunk of your car, even in the theme park lots. Be cautious, even in the parks, and avoid carrying large amounts of cash in a backpack or fanny pack. If you rent a car, carefully read the safety instructions that the rental company provides. Never stop in a dark area, and remember that children should never ride in the front seat of a car equipped with air bags.

Smoking

Smokers should expect a diminishing playground in Florida. Restaurant space and hotel rooms for smokers are evaporating; the same goes for many public areas, such as stadiums. Many bars and some restaurants still allow you to light up, and some of the major attractions do provide an area for smokers (although it may be outdoors).

Taxes

How we love to nail you! Florida's state sales tax is 6 percent, and many municipalities add an additional 1 percent or more to that. In general, you can expect to add 11 to 13 percent to your hotel bill; and 6 to 7 percent to most everything else — except groceries and health supplies or medical services. If you rent a car be prepared to fork over an additional 20 percent or more in taxes.

Time Zone

Florida, for the most part, is on Eastern Standard Time from late fall until mid-spring and then on Eastern Daylight Time (one hour later) for the rest of the year. That means, when it's noon here, it's 7 a.m. in Honolulu, 8 a.m. in Anchorage, 9 a.m. in Vancouver and Los Angeles, 11 a.m. in Winnipeg and New Orleans, and 6 p.m. in London. The Panhandle, however, operates on Central Standard Time, which is one hour behind the rest of the state. So when it's noon in Miami, it's 11 a.m. in Pensacola.

Weather

To check weather forecasts online, go to www.weather.com or surf over to the National Weather Service's site at www.nws.noaa.gov. You also can get information by watching the Weather Channel (www.weatherchannel.com). Local forecast contacts are listed under "Fast Facts" in Chapters 11 to 17, and 21 to 23.

Toll-Free Numbers and Web Sites

Airlines

Air Canada
☎ 888-247-2262
www.aircanada.ca

America West Airlines
☎ 800-235-9292
www.americawest.com

American Airlines
☎ 800-433-7300
www.americanair.com

British Airways
☎ 800-247-9297
☎ 0345-222-111 in Britain
www.british-airways.com

Canadian Airlines International
☎ 800-426-7000
www.cdair.ca

Continental Airlines
☎ 800-525-0280
www.continental.com

Delta Air Lines
☎ 800-221-1212
www.delta-air.com

JetBlue Airways
☎ 800-JETBLUE
www.jetblue.com

Northwest Airlines
☎ 800-225-2525
www.nwa.com

Southwest Airlines
☎ 800-435-9792
www.iflyswa.com

Trans World Airlines (TWA)
☎ 800-221-2000
www2.twa.com

United Airlines
☎ 800-241-6522
www.ual.com

US Airways
☎ 800-428-4322
www.usairways.com

Virgin Atlantic Airways
☎ 800-862-8621 in the continental
United States
☎ 0293-747-747 in Britain
www.fly.virgin.com

Car-rental agencies

Advantage
☎ 800-777-5500
www.arac.com

Alamo
☎ 800-327-9633
www.goalamo.com

Avis
☎ 800-331-1212 in the continental
United States
☎ 800-879-3847 in Canada
www.avis.com

Budget
☎ 800-527-0700
www.budgetrentacar.com

Dollar
☎ 800-800-4000
www.dollar.com

Enterprise
☎ 800-325-8007
www.enterprise.com

Hertz
☎ 800-654-3131
www.hertz.com

National
☎ 800-227-7368
www.nationalcar.com

Payless
☎ 800-729-5377
www.paylesscar.com

Rent-A-Wreck
☎ 800-535-1391
www.rent-a-wreck.com

Thrifty
☎ 800-367-2277
www.thrifty.com

Major hotel and motel chains

Best Western International
☎ 800-528-1234
www.bestwestern.com

Clarion Hotels
☎ 800-252-7466
www.hotelchoice.com

Comfort Inns
☎ 800-228-5150
www.hotelchoice.com

Courtyard by Marriott
☎ 800-321-2211
www.courtyard.com

Days Inn
☎ 800-325-2525
www.daysinn.com

Doubletree Hotels
☎ 800-222-8733
www.doubletreehotels.com

Econo Lodge
☎ 800-553-2666
www.hotelchoice.com

Fairfield Inn by Marriott
☎ 800-228-2800
www.fairfieldinn.com

Hampton Inn
☎ 800-426-7866
www.hampton-inn.com

Hilton Hotels
☎ 800-445-8667
www.hilton.com

Holiday Inn
☎ 800-465-4329
www.holiday-inn.com

Howard Johnson
☎ 800-654-2000
www.hojo.com/hojo.html

Hyatt Hotels & Resorts
☎ 800-228-9000
www.hyatt.com

ITT Sheraton
☎ 800-325-3535
www.sheraton.com

Marriott Hotels
☎ 800-228-9290
www.marriott.com

Quality Inns
☎ 800-228-5151
www.hotelchoice.com

Radisson Hotels International
☎ 800-333-3333
www.radisson.com

Ramada Inns
☎ 800-272-6232
www.ramada.com

Red Roof Inns
☎ 800-843-7663
www.redroof.com

Residence Inn by Marriott
☎ 800-331-3131
www.residenceinn.com

Rodeway Inns
☎ 800-228-2000
www.hotelchoice.com

Super 8 Motels
☎ 800-800-8000
www.super8motels.com

Wyndham Hotels and Resorts
☎ 800-822-4200
www.wyndham.com

Where to Get More Information

If you want some more information on accommodations, dining, attractions, or just about anything else involving Florida, you won't find it difficult to come by. In the upcoming sections we list a host of places that offer tourist information, maps, and brochures.

Online sources

Florida Association of Convention and Visitor Bureaus

This Internet-only source provides contact information and links to the tourist bureaus of many of the cities in Florida that we cover in this book.

Web site: www.facvb.com

Absolutely Florida

It's more of an unofficial line, but this excellent Web site is overflowing with Florida information on topics ranging from lodging and restaurants to nightspots and nude beaches.

Web site: www.funandsun.com

Beach Directory

This virtual guide to the beaches along Florida's Gulf Coast includes a tour, maps, beach recommendations and information on lodging and dining near the coast.

Web site: www.beachdirectory.com

Official state welcome centers

You can get information on the go by stopping in at the official state welcome center at these locations.

- ✔ **I-10:** To find this welcome center, travel 16 miles west of Pensacola, Florida.

- ✔ **I-75:** This location is about 1.5 miles south of the Florida-Georgia border and 4 miles north of Jennings, Florida.

- ✔ **I-95:** This center is located 7 miles north of Yulee, Florida.

- ✔ **State Road 231:** You can visit this branch right after you cross into Florida from Georgia. It's 3 miles north of Campbellton, Florida.

Other sources of information

Here are contacts on a few other statewide fronts:

- ✔ **Accommodations:** Information on accommodations throughout the state is available from the **Florida Motel and Hotel Association,** P.O. Box 1529, Tallahassee, FL 32302 (☎ **850-224-2888;** www.flausa.com).

- ✔ **Attractions:** Contact the **Florida Attractions Association,** P.O. Box 10295, Tallahassee, FL 32302 (☎ **850-222-2885**) for information on special things to see and do in Florida.

- ✔ **Campgrounds:** If you are interested in camping while you're in the Sunshine State, get in touch with the **Florida Association of RV Parks and Campgrounds,** 1340 Vickers Dr., Tallahassee, FL 32303-3041 (☎ **850-562-7151;** www. florida-camping.com).

- ✔ **Historical Sites:** History buffs can get a line on cool places to visit from the **Division of Historic Resources,** Department of State, R.A. Gray Building, 500 S. Bronough St., Tallahassee, FL 32399-0250 (☎ **850-488-1480;** www.dos.state.fl.us).

- ✔ **Sports:** Active travelers and sports nuts can contact the **Florida Sports Foundation,** 2964 Wellington Circle No., Tallahassee, FL 32308 (☎ **850-488-8347;** www.flasports.com).

- ✔ **State Forests:** Nature lovers should contact the **Department of Agriculture and Consumer Services,** Division of Forestry, 3125 Conner Blvd., Tallahassee, FL 32399-1650 (☎ **850-488-6611;** www.doacs.state.fl.us).

- ✔ **State Parks:** If a trip to a state park is on your agenda, contact the **Department of Environmental Protection,** Office of Recreation and Parks, Mail Station 535, 3900 Commonwealth Blvd., Tallahassee, FL 32399-3000 (☎ **850-488-9872;** www.dep.state.fl.us/parks).

- ✔ **Tourist Assistance:** For 24-hour assistance regarding things such as lost credit cards, wallets, traveler's checks, and passports, or to get travel directions, call ☎ **800-656-8777.**

Making Dollars and Sense of It

Expense	Amount
Airfare	
Car Rental	
Lodging	
Parking	
Breakfast	
Lunch	
Dinner	
Babysitting	
Attractions	
Transportation	
Souvenirs	
Tips	
Grand Total	

Notes

Fare Game: Choosing an Airline

Travel Agency:_____ Phone:_____

Agent's Name:_____ Quoted Fare:_____

Departure Schedule & Flight Information

Airline:_____ Airport:_____

Flight #:_____ Date:_____ Time:_____ a.m./p.m.

Arrives in:_____ Time:_____ a.m./p.m.

Connecting Flight (if any)

Amount of time between flights:_____ hours/mins

Airline:_____ Airport:_____

Flight #:_____ Date:_____ Time:_____ a.m./p.m.

Arrives in:_____ Time:_____ a.m./p.m.

Return Trip Schedule & Flight Information

Airline:_____ Airport:_____

Flight #:_____ Date:_____ Time:_____ a.m./p.m.

Arrives in:_____ Time:_____ a.m./p.m.

Connecting Flight (if any)

Amount of time between flights:_____ hours/mins

Airline:_____ Airport:_____

Flight #:_____ Date:_____ Time:_____ a.m./p.m.

Arrives in:_____ Time:_____ a.m./p.m.

Notes

Sweet Dreams: Choosing Your Hotel

Enter the hotels where you'd prefer to stay based on location and price. Then use the worksheet below to plan your itinerary.

Hotel	Location	Price per night

Menus & Venues

Enter the restaurants where you'd most like to dine. Then use the worksheet below to plan your itinerary.

Name	Address/Phone	Cuisine/Price

Places to Go, People to See, Things to Do

Enter the attractions you would most like to see. Then use the worksheet below to plan your itinerary.

Attractions	Amount of time you expect to spend there	Best day and time to go

Going "My" Way

Itinerary #1

- ☐ _____
- ☐ _____
- ☐ _____
- ☐ _____

Itinerary #2

- ☐ _____
- ☐ _____
- ☐ _____
- ☐ _____

Itinerary #3

- ☐ _____
- ☐ _____
- ☐ _____
- ☐ _____

Itinerary #4

- ☐ _____
- ☐ _____
- ☐ _____
- ☐ _____

Itinerary #5

- ☐ _____
- ☐ _____
- ☐ _____
- ☐ _____

Itinerary #6

- ☐ _____
- ☐ _____
- ☐ _____
- ☐ _____

Itinerary #7

- ☐ _____
- ☐ _____
- ☐ _____
- ☐ _____

Itinerary #8

- ☐ _____
- ☐ _____
- ☐ _____
- ☐ _____

Itinerary #9

- ☐ _____
- ☐ _____
- ☐ _____
- ☐ _____

Itinerary #10

- ☐ _____
- ☐ _____
- ☐ _____
- ☐ _____

Notes

Index

• A •

AAA, 64, 491
AARP, 45
The Abbey Hotel (Miami), 108
Above and Beyond Tours, 49
Absolutely Florida, 82, 496
Access-Able Travel Source, 46
accommodations
  Accommodation Search Engine
    Network, 82
  with bars, 80
  bed-and-breakfasts, 77
  best room rates, 76–77
  budget, 36–37
  and children, 43
  Clearwater, 275–277
  condominiums, 78
  corner rooms, 80
  Daytona Beach, 411–415
  with discos, 80
  discounts, 76
  Everglades, 189–190
  Fort Lauderdale, 205–209
  Fort Myers, Sanibel, and Naples,
    302–305
  hotel and motel chains, list of, 495–496
  hotels, 77
  Islamorada, 159–160
  Jacksonville, 444–446
  Key Largo, 154–155
  Key West, 171–174
  Lower Keys, 167–168
  Marathon, 163–164
  Miami, 107–119
  motels, 77
  online reservation services, 80–82
  Orlando, 326–339
  Palm Beach County, 219–223
  Panama City, Fort Walton Beach,
    Destin, and Seaside, 469–472
  Pensacola, 459–461
  price categories, 78–79
  rack rates, 75
  renovations, 80
  reservations, arriving without, 82
  resorts, 77
  restaurants, 80
  room rates, 75–77
  Sarasota and Bradenton, 291–293
  smoking preference, 80
  St. Augustine, 431–433
  St. Petersburg, 265–268
  Tampa, 238–244
  taxes, 77
  travel agents, 80
  vacation rentals, 78
  views, 79–80
  Walt Disney World, 326–339
Accommodation Search Engine
    Network, 82
Action Sportfishing, 214
Adam's Mark Daytona Beach Resort
    (Daytona Beach), 412
Adventure Island (Tampa), 252
Adventure Landing (Daytona Beach), 419
Adventure Landing (Jacksonville
    Beach), 449
Adventureland (Magic Kingdom), 357
airfare coupons, 46
airfares, 60–61
airline packages, 58
airlines, 494
airports. *See specific airports*
Akershus (World Showcase at Epcot), 344
Alden Beach Resort (St. Pete Beach),
    265–266
Alexander All-Suite Luxury Hotel
    (Miami), 116
Alexander Homestead Bed and Breakfast
    (St. Augustine), 431
Alexander's Guest House (Key West), 182
All Hotels on the Web, 81
Amazing Adventures of Spider-Man (Walt
    Disney World), 14
ambrosia, 488
Amelia Island Plantation (Amelia
    Island), 444
American Express, 85, 86, 491

American Express Vacations, 58
American Foundation for the Blind, 47
American Police Hall of Fame and
    Museum (Miami), 129
American Veterinary Medical
    Association, 95
AmeriSuites Airport West (Miami), 108
AmeriSuites Tampa Airport (Tampa), 239
Amtrak
    disabled travelers, 47
    senior travelers, 46
    travel to Florida, 64
    travel within Florida, 73
Animal Kingdom, 367–371
Anna Maria Oyster Bar (Bradenton), 295
Antique Row (Dania), 215
Arabian Nights (Orlando), 347
Art-Deco Cycling Tour (Miami), 140
Art Deco Weekend (South Beach), 28
Arthur's 27 (Lake Buena Vista), 339
Arts and Sciences, Museum of (Daytona
    Beach), 421
Aruanno's (St. Augustine Beach),
    433–434
Aruba Inn (Daytona Beach), 415
Asolo Theatre (Sarasota), 298–299
Astor Place Bar & Grill (Miami), 126
Atlanta Braves, spring training, 393
Atlantic's Edge (Islamorada), 12, 160
ATMs, 84–85, 86
At The Water's Edge (Key West), 179
attractions
    Clearwater, 279–281
    Daytona Beach, 419–422
    Disney-MGM Studios, 364–367
    Everglades, 191–198
    Florida Attractions Association, 497
    Fort Lauderdale, 211–214
    Fort Myers, Sanibel, and Naples,
        307–310
    Islamorada, 161–162
    Jacksonville, 449–452
    Key West, 176–180
    Lower Keys, 169–171
    Marathon, 165–167
    Miami, 129–139
    Orlando, 386–393
    Palm Beach County, 225–228
    Panama City, Fort Walton Beach,
        Destin, and Seaside, 475–478
    Pensacola, 464–467

Sarasota and Bradenton, 295–298
St. Augustine, 436–439
St. Petersburg, 270–272
Tampa, 247–255
Walt Disney World, 386–389
Audobon House & Tropical Gardens
    (Key West), 176
Aunt Catfish's On the River (Daytona
    Beach), 418
Auto Train, 64–65
Autumn, visiting during, 22–23
Aventura, 142
Aventura Mall (Miami), 143
A World of Options, 46

• *B* •

Babcock Wilderness Adventures (Punta
    Gorda), 307
babysitting, 45
Back Porch (Destin), 13
Bahama Breeze (International Drive),
    344
Bahama Hotel (Fort Lauderdale),
    208–209
Bahia Honda State Park (Big Pine Key),
    484
Bahia Honda State Recreation Area
    (Lower Keys), 167, 170
Balans (Miami), 126
Baltimore Orioles, spring training, 213
Banana Bay Resort & Marina
    (Marathon), 163
Banana Cafe (Key West), 175
banks, 491
Barnacle Bed & Breakfast (Big Pine Key),
    167–168
Barnacle State Historic Site (Miami), 135
Barracks Street Fish House
    (Pensacola), 462
Barracuda Grill (Marathon), 164–165
bars. *See also specific bars*
    best, list of, 15
    in hotels, 80
Bash (Miami), 145
Bass Pro Shops Outdoor World (Dania
    Beach), 213
Basta's (St. Petersburg), 270
Bayfront Center (St. Petersburg), 273
Bayfront Inn (St. Augustine), 433

Baymont Inn & Suites (Tampa), 244
Bayside Marketplace (Miami), 143
Beach Bistro (Holmes Beach), 12, 293
Beach Directory, 496
Beached Whale (Fort Myers Beach), 312
beaches. *See also specific beaches*
  best, list of, 483–486
  Clearwater, 280–281
  Daytona Beach, 421–422
  Fort Lauderdale, 213
  Fort Myers, Sanibel, and Naples,
    309–310
  Jacksonville, 452
  Palm Beach County, 227
  Panama City, Fort Walton Beach,
    Destin, and Seaside, 477
  Pensacola, 466
  Sarasota and Bradenton, 297
  St. Augustine, 438–439
  St. Petersburg, 262, 271
Beach Haven (St. Pete Beach), 266
Beach Inn (Holmes Beach), 293
The Beachouse (Clearwater Beach),
  275–276
Beach Pierside Grill (Fort Myers
  Beach), 307
Beach Retreat on Casey Key
  (Nokomis), 291
Beachside Resort & Conference Center
  (Pensacola Beach), 460
Beach Trolley (Fort Lauderdale),
  204, 214
Beach Walk Cafe (Destin), 474
BEAKS (Big Talbot Island), 449–450
Beau Rivage Beach Resort (Fort
  Lauderdale), 209
bed-and-breakfasts, 77
Beech Street Grill (Fernandina
  Beach), 447
Beech Street Grill (Jacksonville), 13
Belleview Biltmore Golf Club
  (Clearwater), 281
Belleview Biltmore Resort and Spa
  (Clearwater), 277
Bergamo's (International Drive), 340
Bermuda Bar (Miami), 145
Bern's Steak House (Tampa), 244–245
Best Western All Suites (Tampa), 239
Best Western Florida City (Everglades),
  189–190
Best Western Key Largo (Key Largo), 154

Best Western Lake Buena Vista, 327
Best Western La Playa (Daytona Beach),
  412
Best Western on the Bay Inn & Marina
  (Miami), 116
Best Western Pelican Beach Resort
  (Fort Lauderdale), 205
Best Western Sea Spray (Palm
  Beach), 221
Best Western Siesta Beach Resort
  (Siesta Key), 291
Big Ben Pub (Clearwater Beach), 279
Big Cypress National Preserve, 194–195
Biketoberfest (Daytona Beach), 28
bike tours (Miami), 140
Bike Week (Daytona Beach), 27–28
Bill Baggs Cape Florida State Recreation
  Area (Miami), 135, 483–484
Billie Swamp Safari (Everglades), 198
Billy's Tap Room & Grill (Ormond
  Beach), 416
The Biltmore Hotel (Miami), 108–109
Biscayne National Park (Miami), 132
B-Line Diner (International Drive), 344
Blizzard Beach (Disney-MGM Studios),
  386–387
Blue Moon Fish Co. (Lauderdale-by-the-
  Sea), 209
Boar's Head Restaurant (Panama
  City), 473
Bobby Jones Golf Complex
  (Sarasota), 297
Bob Marley — A Tribute to Freedom
  (Universal Orlando), 345
Boca Raton, 19. *See also* Palm Beach
  County
Booth's Bowery (Port Orange), 418
Boston Red Sox, spring training, 309
Botticelli Trattoria (Miami), 119
Brass Key (Key West), 183
The Breakers (Palm Beach), 221
Bridge of Lions (St. Augustine), 436
British Night Watch and Grand
  Illumination (St. Augustine), 33
Britt's Beachside Cafe (Clearwater
  Beach), 277–278
Bubbaloo's Bodacious BBQ, 340
Buccaneer Beach Resort (Treasure
  Island), 267–268
Bud & Alley's (Seaside), 473

budget
  accommodations, 36–37
  children, sharing room with, 42
  cutting costs, methods of, 41–42
  Discount Guide to Florida, 42
  discounts, 42
  entertainment, 37–38
  following a, 35
  free magazines with coupons, 42
  including everything in, 35
  kitchen, staying in room with, 42
  minibar charges, 40–41
  Naples, sample costs for, 39–40
  nightlife, 38–39
  off-season travel, 41
  Orlando, sample costs for, 39
  package tours, 41–42
  phone calls from hotel rooms, 40
  rental cars, 36, 40
  restaurants, 37
  room rates, average, 36–37
  sales tax, 40
  shopping, 38
  souvenirs, 42
  theme park food, 41
  tipping, 41
  views, not staying in rooms with, 42
bulkhead seats, 62
Burt & Jack's Restaurant (Fort
    Lauderdale), 12, 209–210
Busch Gardens (Tampa), 13–14, 250–251
bus travel within Florida, 73
Butterfly World (Coconut Creek), 212

• *C* •

Cadillac Jack's (Treasure Island),
    272–273
Café L'Europe (Palm Beach), 223, 229
Café L'Europe (St. Armands Key), 295
Cafe Marquesa (Key West), 175
Cafe Maxx (Pompano Beach), 210
Cafe on the Bay (Longboat Key), 295
Café Thirty-A (Seagrove Beach), 475
Cafe Tu Tu Tango (International Drive),
    340
Caffe Abbracci (Miami), 121
Caladesi Island State Park (Dunedin) 279,
    485
Calder Race Course (Miami), 139

calendar of events, 27–34
Calle Ocho, 142
campgrounds, 497
Candlelight Procession (Walt Disney
    World), 34
Capriccio (International Drive), 341
Capri Restaurant (Everglades), 190
Capt. Anderson's Restaurant (Panama
    City Beach), 475
Capt. Hook's Marina & Dive Centers
    (Marathon), 166
Capt. Tony's (Key West), 15, 181
Captain Nemo's Pirate Cruise
    (Clearwater Beach), 281
Caribbean Gardens (Naples), 308
Carlin Park (Jupiter), 227
Carmine's Restaurant & Bar
    (Tampa), 245
Carnival Miami/Calle Ocho, 30
car rental
  advertised rates, 70
  age limits, 71
  budget, 36, 40
  collision damage waiver, 70
  disabled travelers, 47
  drop-off fees, 70
  insurance, 70
  online booking, 71
  optional charges, 70–71
  pricing, 69
  rates, 69, 70
  refueling packages, 70
  taxes, 71
car-rental agencies, 494–495
Casablanca Inn on the Bay
    (St. Augustine), 433
Casa Grande Suite Hotel (Miami), 109
Casa Juancho (Miami), 121
Casa Monica Hotel (St. Augustine), 13,
    431
The Casements (Ormond Beach), 419
cash, carrying, 83
Castaways Beach Resort (Daytona Beach
    Shores), 415
Castillo del Mar Resort (Miami), 116
Castillo de San Marcos National
    Monument (St. Augustine), 436–437
Cavalier (Miami), 109
Celebration, 322–323, 394
Celebration Hotel (Kissimmee), 328

Central Florida, 19–20
Ceviche Tapas Bar (Tampa), 247
Cha Cha Coconuts (Sarasota), 298
Channel Mark (Fort Myers Beach), 305
Channelside (Tampa), 256
Chan's Market Cafe (Pensacola Beach), 463
Chart House (Jacksonville), 447
Cheeca Lodge (Islamorada), 13, 159
Chef Allen's (Miami Beach), 12, 121
Chef Mickey's (Disney's Contemporary Resort), 346
Chef Paul's (Panama City), 475
Chekika (Everglades National Park), 194
Chez Porky's (Pompano Beach), 211
children, 42–45, 63
Choice Hotels group, 46
Christini's Ristorante (International Drive), 341
Christmas in the Park (Winter Park), 34
Chrysanthemum Festival (Cypress Gardens), 33
Chrysanthemum (Miami), 122
Church Street Station (Orlando), 15, 399–400
Cincinnati Reds, spring training, 297
Cinderella's Royal Table (Magic Kingdom), 346
Citricos (Walt Disney World), 341
citrus fruits, 488
City Walk (Walt Disney World), 15
Clarion Hotel-Miami Airport (Miami), 116
Clarion Suites Resort (Pensacola Beach), 460
Clearwater
  accommodations, 275–277
  arrival in, 273
  attractions, 279–281
  baseball and spring training, 281
  beaches, 280–281
  day trips, 283–284
  described, 273
  facts on, 284–285
  golf, 281
  guided tours, 281
  itineraries, sightseeing, 282–283
  map of, 274
  nightlife, 282
  restaurants, 277–279
  shopping, 281
  travel within, 273–275

Clearwater Beach, 280–281
Clearwater Marine Aquarium (Clearwater Beach), 279–280
Clematis Street (West Palm Beach), 229–230
Clevelander Hotel (Miami), 144
Club Liquid Blue (Clearwater), 282
Coconut Grove, 102–103, 142
Coconut Grove Chamber of Commerce, 148
Coconut Grove Goombay Festival, 31
Coconuts Dolphin Tournament (Key Largo), 31
Coco's Kitchen (Big Pine Key), 169
CocoWalk (Miami), 143
Collier-Seminole State Park, 196–197
Colony Beach & Tennis Resort (Longboat Key), 292
The Colony Palm Beach (Palm Beach), 222
Columbia (Tampa), 245
Columbia Restaurant (Ybor City), 12, 435
Comfort Inn Airport (Miami), 116
conch, 488
Conch Train (Key West), 178
condominiums, 78
consolidators, 61
Continental Airlines Vacations, 58
Coquina Gables Oceanfront Bed & Breakfast (St. Augustine Beach), 433
Coral Castle (Miami), 132
Coral Gables, 103, 142
Coral Gables Chamber of Commerce, 148
Coral Grill (Islamorada), 160
Coral Reef (Epcot), 345
Corkscrew Swamp Sanctuary (Naples), 309
corner rooms, 80
Cortesse's Bistro (St. Augustine), 435
Council Travel, 61
Country Inn & Suites (Destin), 470
Courtyard by Marriott (Lake Buena Vista), 328
Courtyard by Marriott Miami Airport West (Miami), 111
Crabby Jack's (Deerfield Beach), 216
Crabby Joe's Sunglow Pier (Daytona Beach), 416
Crab Shack (St. Petersburg), 270
credit cards, 84, 491
crime prevention, 85–86

Criolla's (Grayton Beach), 473
Crystal River, 284
Cuban cuisine, 488
cuisine, 9–13
customs, 491–492
cutting costs, methods of, 41–42
Cypress Gardens, 401–402
Cypress Glen at Lake Buena Vista
      (Lake Buena Vista), 337
Cypress Woods (Naples), 310

• D •

Dancing Avocado Kitchen (Daytona
      Beach), 418
Days Inn Art Deco/Convention Center
      (Miami), 116–117
Days Inn Oceanfront Resort
      (Islamorada), 159
Days in Spain (St. Augustine), 32
Daytona Beach
   accommodations, 411–415
   arrival in, 408
   attractions, 419–422
   beaches, 421–422
   described, 20, 407
   facts on, 425
   fishing, 422
   golf, 422
   itinerary, sightseeing, 422–423
   neighborhoods, 410
   nightlife, 424
   orientation, 408–410
   parks, 422
   restaurants, 416–418
   shopping, 423
   travel within, 410–411
Daytona Beach Municipal Golf Course
      (Daytona Beach), 422
Daytona Inn Beach Resort (Daytona
      Beach), 415
Daytona International Speedway
      (Daytona Beach Mainland), 420
Daytona USA (Daytona Beach Mainland),
      14, 420
Delfino Riviera (Universal Orlando), 342
Delnor-Wiggins Pass State Recreation
      Area (Naples), 309, 484
Delray Beach Golf Club, 228
Delray Beach Marriott (Delray Beach),
      221–222

Delta Dream Vacations, 58
Deltona Hills Golf and Country Club
      (Daytona Beach), 422
Desert Inn Resort (Daytona Beach),
      412–413
Destin. *See* Panama City, Fort Walton
      Beach, Destin, and Seaside
Destin Chops (Destin), 474
Destin Fishing Rodeo, 32
Destin Mayfest, 31
The Dining Room at Little Palm Island
      (Little Palm Island), 169
disabled travelers, 46–47
discos in hotels, 80
discount coupons, 43
Discount Guide to Florida, 42
discounts, 42
Discovery and Science, Museum of
      (Fort Lauderdale), 212
Discovery Cove, 37, 383–384
Disney. *See* Walt Disney World
Disney All-Star Movie Resort (Walt
      Disney World), 329
Disney Christmas, 33–34
Disney-MGM Studios, 14, 364–367
DisneyQuest (Downtown Disney),
      387–388
Disney's All-Star Music Resort (Walt
      Disney World), 337
Disney's Beach Club Resort (Walt Disney
      World), 329
Disney's Boardwalk (Walt Disney World),
      329–332, 398
Disney's Coronado Springs Resort (Walt
      Disney World), 337
Disney's Grand Floridian Resort & Spa
      (Walt Disney World), 332
Disney's Port Orleans Resort (Walt
      Disney World), 332
Disney's Wide World of Sports (Disney-
      MGM Studios), 388
Disney's Wilderness Lodge (Walt Disney
      World), 337
divinity, 489
Dock at Crayton Cove (Olde Naples),
      305–306
doctors, 492
Dolphin Research Center (Marathon),
      13, 165
Dolphin Resort & Marina (Little Torch
      Key), 168
Dolphins Plus (Key Largo), 156

Don CeSar Beach Resort and Spa
(St. Pete Beach), 266
Don Shula's Golf Club (Miami), 137
Doral Golf Resort and Spa (Miami), 111
Doral Resort Gold Course (Miami), 138
Doral Resort Silver Course (Miami), 137
Doubletree Grand Hotel Biscayne Bay
(Miami), 111–112
Doubletree Guest Suites (Lake Buena
Vista), 333
Doubletree Guest Suites/Busch Gardens
(Tampa), 239–242
Doubletree Hotel Oceanfront (Fort
Lauderdale), 207
Down the Hatch Seafood Restaurant &
Lounge (Ponce Inlet), 416–417
downtime, 43
Downtown Disney Marketplace, 394
Downtown Disney West Side, 394,
397–398
driving
  in Florida, 67–69
  to Florida, 63–64
Dry Tortugas National Park (Key West),
178–179
Dueling Dragons (Walt Disney World), 14
The Dunes (Pensacola Beach), 460
Durty Harry's (Pompano Beach), 216
Duval Street (Key West), 15
Dux (Orlando), 12, 342

• E •

The Eagle (Islamorada), 162
Eagle Ridge (Fort Myers), 310
Eden State Gardens and the Wesley
Mansion (Grayton Beach), 475–476
Edgewater Beach Hotel (Naples), 304
Edgewater Beach Resort (Panama City
Beach), 470
Edison and Ford Winter Homes
(Fort Myers), 308
801 Bourbon Bar (Key West), 182
Embassy Suites (Boca Raton), 223
emergencies, 492
emergency-exit-row seats, 62
Emeril's (Universal Orlando), 12, 343
Epcot, 358–364
Epiphany (Tarpon Springs), 28
Epoch (Key West), 182

Ernest F. Coe Visitor Center (Everglades
National Park), 192
Ernest Hemingway Home and Museum
(Key West), 177
escorted tours. *See* guided tours
Euphemia Haye (Longboat Key), 12,
293–294
Everglades
  accommodations, 189–190
  arrival in, 188
  attractions, 191–198
  Big Cypress National Preserve, 194–195
  canoeing, 197
  car travel within, 188
  cell phones, need for, 188
  Collier-Seminole State Park, 196–197
  cycling, 197
  described, 185–188
  Everglades National Park, 185–188,
  192–194
  Fakahatchee Strand State Park, 195–196
  fishing, 197–198
  restaurants, 190–191
Everglades Alligator Farm (Miami), 132
Everglades National Park, 185–188,
192–194
Everglades Seafood Festival (Everglades
City), 29

• F •

Fairbanks House (Fernandina Beach),
444
Fairfield Inn Miami Airport (Miami), 117
Fakahatchee Strand State Park, 195–196
The Falls (Miami), 143
Family Abroad, 49
family travel, 43–45
Family Travel Times, 43
Fandango Grill Restaurant (West Palm
Beach), 225
Fantasy Fest (Key West), 176
Fantasyland (Magic Kingdom), 354–355
FEDCAP Rehabilitation Services, 47
Fernandina Beach Shrimp Festival, 31
Festival of States (St. Petersburg), 30
15th Street Fisheries (Fort Lauderdale),
210
fireworks, 358, 364, 367
The Fish House (Key Largo), 155

fishing
  best places for, 16
  Boca Grande, 16
  Daytona Beach, 422
  Everglades, 197–198
  Fort Lauderdale, 16, 213–214
  Fort Myers, Sanibel, and Naples, 310
  Islamorada, 162
  Jacksonville, 452
  Key Largo, 158
  The Keys, 16
  Key West, 180
  Lower Keys, 170–171
  Marathon, 166–167
  Miami, 16, 139
  Palm Beach County, 228
  Panama City, Fort Walton Beach,
    Destin, and Seaside, 16, 478
  Pensacola, 466–467
  Sarasota and Bradenton, 297
  St. Augustine, 439
  St. Petersburg, 271–272
  Tampa, 255
Five Flags Inn (Pensacola Beach), 460
Flagler Greyhound Track (Miami), 139
Flamingo Campground (Everglades
    National Park), 194
Flamingo Lodge, Marina & Outpost
    Resort (Everglades), 190, 198
Flamingo Lodge Restaurant
    (Everglades), 191
Flamingo Visitor Center (Everglades
    National Park), 193
Fleming: A Taste of Denmark
    (Miami), 122
Flora-Bama Lounge (Perdido Key),
    15, 467
Floribbean cuisine, 487
Florida Aquarium (Tampa), 252
Florida Association of Convention and
    Visitor Bureaus, 496
Florida Grand Opera (Miami), 145
Florida Hotel Network, 81, 221
Florida House Inn (Fernandina Beach),
    446
Florida International Museum
    (St. Petersburg), 270
Florida Keys Fly Fishing (Marathon), 167
Florida Keys Land & Sea Trust at Crane
    Point Hammock (Marathon), 166

Florida Keys Wild Bird Rehabilitation
    Center (Key Largo), 157
Florida lobster, 489
Florida Marlins, 138
Florida Museum of Hispanic and Latin
    American Art (Miami), 135
Florida Panthers, 138
Florida Philharmonic Orchestra (Miami),
    145
Florida Splendid China (Kissimmee), 389
Florida State Fair (Tampa), 29
Florida Strawberry Festival (Plant City),
    29
Florida Times Union Center for the
    Performing Arts (Jacksonville), 453
Florida Travel Online, 81
Flying Fish Fleet (Sarasota), 297
Flying Tigers Warbird Restoration
    Museum (Kissimmee), 389–390
flying to Florida, 60–63
Flying Wheels Travel, 47
flying within Florida, 71–72
foods
  ambrosia, 488
  citrus fruits, 488
  conch, 488
  Cuban cuisine, 488
  divinity, 489
  Floribbean cuisine, 487
  Florida lobster, 489
  grits, 489
  Key lime pie, 489
  local cuisine, 487
  mullet, 489
  seafood, 490
  stone crab claws, 490
  theme park food, 41
The Forge (Miami), 122, 144
Fort Caroline National Memorial
    (Jacksonville), 450
Fort Clinch State Park (Fernandina
    Beach), 450
Fort DeSoto Park, 272
Fort Jefferson (Key West), 178–179
Fort Lauderdale
  accommodations, 205–209
  arrival in, 202–203
  attractions, 211–214
  baseball and spring training, 213
  beaches, 213

cars, 203–204
described, 19
facts on, 217
fishing, 213–214
golf, 214
guided tours, 214
itinerary, sightseeing, 216
map of, 206
nightlife, 215–216
restaurants, 209–211
shopping, 215
trains, 204
trolley, 204
water taxi, 204–205
Fort Lauderdale Beach, 213
Fort Lauderdale-Hollywood International
    Airport, 100, 202, 218
Fort Lauderdale Marina Marriott, 207
Fort Myers, Sanibel, and Naples
accommodations, 302–305
arrival in, 300
attractions, 307–310
baseball and spring training, 309
beaches, 309–310
described, 299–300
driving in, 300
facts on, 313–315
fishing, 310
golf, 310
guided tours, 310–311
itineraries, sightseeing, 313
map of, 301
nightlife, 312
parks, 309–310
restaurants, 305–307
sample costs for, 39–40
shopping, 311–312
souvenirs, 312
travel within, 300–302
Fort Pickens (Pensacola Beach), 464
Fort Walton Beach. *See* Panama City,
    Fort Walton Beach, Destin, and
    Seaside
Fountainebleau Hilton Resort & Towers
    (Miami), 112
Fountain of Youth (St. Augustine),
    427, 437
Four Green Fields (Tampa), 247, 257
Frankie's Patio (Tampa), 257
free magazines with coupons, 42

Frenchy's Cafe (Clearwater Beach), 279
Frontierland (Magic Kingdom), 356–357
FSU Center for the Performing Arts
    (Sarasota), 298
Fulton's Crab House (Downtown
    Disney), 12, 343
Fusion Point (St. Augustine), 434
Future World (Epcot), 359–361

• *G* •

Gale Force Charters (Lower Keys), 171
gambling in Miami, 139
Gasparilla (Tampa), 27
Gator Club (Sarasota), 298
Gatorland (South Orlando), 390
Gator's Cafe (Treasure Island), 273
gay and lesbian travelers, 48–49
Gay Guide to Florida, 48
Gay Travel A to Z, 48
Gay Weekend, 31, 48
Ghost Walk (Key West), 178
Globus, 59
Gold Coast Railroad Museum (Miami),
    135–136
golf
Clearwater, 281
Daytona Beach, 422
Fort Lauderdale, 214
Fort Myers, Sanibel, and Naples, 310
Golfpac, 91
Jacksonville, 452
Key West, 180
Miami, 136–138
package tours, 58
Palm Beach County, 228
Panama City, Fort Walton Beach,
    Destin, and Seaside, 478
Pensacola, 467
Sarasota and Bradenton, 297–298
St. Augustine, 439
Tampa, 255
Tee Times USA, 91
Walt Disney World, 393
Golf Club of Miami (Miami), 138
Golfpac, 91
Goodland Mullet Festival, 28
Grandview All-Suite Resort (Fort Myers
    Beach), 303

Grayton Beach State Recreation Area, 477
Greater Miami, 103
Greater Miami Chamber of Commerce, 148
Greater Miami Convention and Visitors Bureau, 105, 147
Great Explorations Hands-On Museum (St. Petersburg), 271
Great North, 20–21
green flash, 287
Green Flash Restaurant (Captiva Island), 312
Green Iguana Bar & Grill (Tampa), 257
Green Turtle Inn (Islamorada), 163
Greyhound, 73
Grillfish (Miami), 124
grits, 489
Grosvenor Resort (Lake Buena Vista), 333
Grouch Charters (Lower Keys), 171
Guavaween (Ybor City), 28
guided tours
  cancellation policy, 56
  Clearwater, 281
  described, 56
  Fort Lauderdale, 214
  Fort Myers, Sanibel, and Naples, 310–311
  Key West, 178–179
  Miami, 140
  Palm Beach County, 228
  price, what is included in, 57
  schedule, 56
  size of group, 56
  St. Augustine, 430, 439
  St. Petersburg, 272
  Tampa, 255
Gulfarium (Fort Walton Beach), 476
Gulf Coast, 19
Gulf Coast Visitor Center (Everglades National Park), 193
Gulf World Marine Park (Panama City Beach), 476
Gypsy Cab Co. (St. Augustine), 434

• *H* •

Half Moon Beach Club (Lido Beach), 292
Halifax Plantation (Ormond Beach), 422

Hallandale Beach Boulevard (Fort Lauderdale), 215
Halloween Horror Nights (Universal Studios), 32–33
Hamilton's Restaurant and Lounge (Panama City Beach), 474
Hampton Inn (Destin), 472
Hampton Inn (Miami), 112
Hampton Inn & Suites (Marathon), 164
Hampton Inn at Universal Studios (International Drive), 337
Hampton Inn Historic (St. Augustine), 432
Hampton Inn Pensacola Beach (Pensacola Beach), 461
Harbourside Grill (Madeira Beach), 270
Harrington House Bed & Breakfast (Holmes Beach), 293
Harry's Seafood, Bar, and Grille (Jacksonville), 447
Harry's Seafood, Bar, and Grille (St. Augustine), 434
Haslam's Book Store (St. Petersburg), 272
Havana Music Fest, 30
Hawk's Cay Resort (Marathon), 164
The HayeLoft (Longboat Key), 298
Hemingway Days (Key West), 31–32, 176
Henry B. Plant Museum (Tampa), 253–254
Henry Morrison Flagler Museum (Palm Beach), 225
Hialeah Park (Miami), 139
Hibiscus Coffee & Guesthouse (Grayton Beach), 472
Hillsboro Inlet Marina, 214
Hilton Clearwater Beach (Clearwater), 277
Hilton Daytona Beach Oceanfront Resort (Daytona Beach Shores), 413
Hilton Senior Honors Program, 46
Hilton St. Petersburg (St. Petersburg), 266–267
historical sites, 497
Historic Pensacola Village (Pensacola), 464–465
Hog's Breath Saloon (Key West), 181
Holiday Inn Indian Creek (Miami), 117
Holiday Inn Nikki Bird Resort (Kissimmee), 339
Holiday Inn Sunspree Resort Lake Buena Vista (Lake Buena Vista), 339

Holiday Inn Tampa City-Centre
(Tampa), 242
Hollywood Beach, 213
Hollywood Beach Resort Hotel
(Hollywood), 207
Holocaust Memorial (Miami), 136
Homewood Suites Maingate (Lake Buena
Vista), 339
Homosassa Springs State Wildlife
Park, 283
Honeymoon Island State Recreation Area
(Dunedin), 280
Hoop-Dee-Doo Musical Revue (Fort
Wilderness Resort), 347–348
Hopkin's Boarding House
(Pensacola), 462
hoteldiscount!com, 81
hotels, 77. *See also* accommodations
Hotel Sofitel Miami, 112–113
Hubbard's Marina, 271–272
Hugh Jorgan's (Delray Beach), 230
Hungry Heron (Sanibel), 306
hurricanes, 25
Hurricane Seafood Restaurant (St. Pete
Beach), 268
Hyatt Regency (Tampa), 242
Hyatt Regency Grand Cypress (Lake
Buena Vista), 333
Hyatt Regency Miami, 113, 117
Hyatt Regency Pier Sixty-Six (Fort
Lauderdale), 209

• I •

iCan online, 46
Il Bacio (Daytona Beach), 417
Imaginarium (Fort Myers), 308
Incredible Hulk Coaster (Walt Disney
World), 14
information, 492
The Inn on Fifth (Old Naples), 303
Inns of Florida, 78
International Drive, 323, 394
International Gay & Lesbian Travel
Association, 49
International Hemingway Festival
(Sanibel Island), 31
International Museum of Cartoon Art
(Boca Raton), 225–226

International Swimming Hall of Fame
(Fort Lauderdale), 212
Islamorada
accommodations, 159–160
arrival in, 158–159
attractions, 161–162
boating, 162
described, 158
diving, 162
fishing, 162
nightlife, 162–163
restaurants, 160–161
Island City House Hotel (Key West), 172
Island Grille (Jacksonville Beach), 448
Island's End Resort (St. Pete Beach), 267
Islands of Adventure, 14, 376–380
Ivey House (Everglades), 190, 197

• J •

Jackie's (Jacksonville), 447–448
Jacksonville
accommodations, 444–446
arrival in, 440–442
attractions, 449–452
baseball, 452
beaches, 452
described, 20–21, 440
facts on, 454
fishing, 452
football, 452
golf, 452
itinerary, sightseeing, 453–454
nightlife, 453
restaurants, 446–449
shopping, 452
temperatures, chart of average, 25
travel within, 442
Jacksonville International Airport, 442
Jacksonville Symphony Orchestra, 453
Jacksonville Zoo, 451
Jamie's Wine Bar & Restaurant
(Pensacola), 463
Jammers Grill & Pub (Islamorada), 161
jellyfish, 261
jet lag, 63
Jimmy Buffett's Margaritaville (Key
West), 181
J.N. "Ding" Darling National Wildlife
Refuge (Sanibel), 309–310

Joe Allen (Miami), 126
Joe's Stone Crab Restaurant (Miami), 128
John D. MacArthur Beach State Park
    (Palm Beach), 227
John F. Kennedy Space Center, 400–401
Johnny Leverock's Seafood House
    (Clearwater Beach), 278
John Pennekamp Coral Reef State Park
    (Key Largo), 157
John's Pass Seafood Festival (Madeira
    Beach), 33
John's Pass Village and Boardwalk
    (Madeira Beach), 272
Josephine's French Country Inn
    (Seaside), 470–471
Jubilee Restaurant (Pensacola Beach),
    462–463
Jules' Undersea Lodge (Key Largo), 154
Julian's Dining Room and Lounge
    (Ormond Beach), 417
Jungle Queen (Fort Lauderdale), 214
Juno Beach, 227

• K •

Kennedy Space Center, 14
Key Largo
    accommodations, 154–155
    arrival in, 153–154
    boating, 157
    described, 153
    diving, 157
    fishing, 158
    nightlife, 158
    restaurants, 155–156
    shopping, 158
Key Largo National Marine Sanctuary,
    157
Key lime pie, 489
Key Lime Products (Key Largo), 158
The Keys
    arrival in, 150–152
    described, 18, 149
    facts on, 183
    5-day itinerary, 153
    Islamorada. See Islamorada
    itinerary, sightseeing, 153
    Key Largo. See Key Largo
    Key West. See Key West
    Lower Keys. See Lower Keys
    map of, 151

Marathon. See Marathon
    Mile Marker system, 152
    orientation, 149–150
Keystone Steak and Chop House (St.
    Petersburg), 270
Key West
    accommodations, 171–174
    attractions, 176–180
    bike rental, 171
    currency exchange, 183
    described, 171
    diving, 179–180
    festivals, 176
    fishing, 180
    gay and lesbian travelers, 182–183
    golf, 180
    guided tours, 178–179
    itinerary, sightseeing, 180–181
    nightlife, 181–182
    restaurants, 174–176
    scooter rental, 171
    souvenirs, 181
    3-day sightseeing itinerary, 180–181
Key West Aquarium, 177
Key West Cemetery, 177
Key West Flats Fishing, 180
Key West Golf Club, 180
Key West International Airport, 150
Key West Seafood, 181
Kingsley Plantation (Jacksonville), 451
Kissimmee, 323, 394
kitchen, staying in room with, 42

• L •

Lady Cyana Divers (Islamorada), 162
La Fiesta Oceanside Inn & Suites
    (St. Augustine Beach), 433
Lago Mar Resort and Club (Fort
    Lauderdale), 207–208
Lake Buena Vista, 322
Lake Place Restaurant (Santa Rosa
    Beach), 475
Lansbrook Golf Club (Palm Harbor), 281
Lantana Park, 227
La Parisienne (St. Augustine), 435
La Pensione (Key West), 172
La Quinta Inn & Suites (Tampa), 242–243
Largo Lodge (Key Largo), 155
Las Olas Boulevard (Fort Lauderdale),
    15, 215

last-minute details
  golf course, reserving, 91
  illness away from home, 88–90
  International Association of
      Convention & Visitor Bureaus, 91
  packing, 91–94
  table, reserving a, 90
  Ticketmaster, 90–91
  travel insurance, 87–88
Latigo Yacht Charters (Marathon), 165
Lauro Ristorante (Tampa), 245–246
La Vigna Ristorante (Redington Shores),
    268–269
Le Bordeaux (Tampa), 247
Le Clos (Fernandina Beach), 448
Le Coq Au Vin (Orlando), 343–344
Leeside Inn (Fort Walton Beach), 472
The Left Bank (Fort Lauderdale), 211
Legacy Golf Club (Bradenton), 297–298
Le Pavillon (St. Augustine), 435
Lethal Weapon Charters (Key West), 180
Liberty Square (Magic Kingdom),
    355–356
Liberty Travel, 58
Liberty Tree Tavern (Magic
    Kingdom), 346
Lighter Museum (St. Augustine), 437
lightning, 26
Lignumvitae Key State Botanical Site
    (Islamorada), 161
Lime House Inn (Key West), 182
Lion Country Safari (Loxahatchee),
    13, 226
liquor laws, 492
Little and Big Talbot Island State Parks
    (Mayport), 451
Little Havana, 104
Little Palm Island (Little Torch Key), 13
Little Palm Island Resort & Spa (Little
    Torch Key), 168
Little Talbot Island State Park
    (Jacksonville), 485–486
Live Oak Inn B & B (Daytona Beach), 413
The Living Room (Clearwater), 282
Living Room at the Strand (Miami), 145
local cuisine, 487
The Lodge & Club (Ponte Vedra
    Beach), 445
Loews Miami Beach Hotel (Miami), 113
Long Pine Key Campground (Everglades
    National Park), 194

Looe Key National Marine Sanctuary
    (Lower Keys), 170
Looe Key Reef Resort and Dive Center
    (Lower Keys), 170
Lorelei Restaurant (Islamorada), 163
lost, when children get, 43
Louie's Backyard (Key West), 12, 175
Lower Keys
  accommodations, 167–168
  attractions, 169–171
  described, 167
  diving, 170
  fishing, 170–171
  restaurants, 168–169
  tours, 171
Lowry Park Zoo (Tampa), 252
Loxahatchee Everglades Airboat Tours
    (Boca Raton), 228

• *M* •

Magic Kingdom
  Adventureland, 357
  described, 14, 352
  Fantasyland, 354–355
  fireworks, 358
  Frontierland, 356–357
  Liberty Square, 355–356
  Main Street, U.S.A., 352
  Mickey's Toontown Fair, 354
  parades, 358
  Tomorrowland, 352–354
Mahaffey Theater (St. Petersburg), 273
mail, 492
Main Street, U.S.A. (Magic Kingdom), 352
Makai Lodge Beach Resort (Ormond
    Beach), 415
Man and the Sea, Museum of (Panama
    City Beach), 476
Manatee Ray's (Jacksonville Beach), 449
manatees, 284
Mangia Mangia (Key West), 175–176
Mango's (Miami), 145
maps, 492
Marathon
  accommodations, 163–164
  attractions, 165–167
  boating, 166
  described, 163
  diving, 166

Marathon *(continued)*
  fishing, 166–167
  restaurants, 164–165
Marathon Divers (Marathon), 166
Mardi Gras at Universal Studios, 29
Marek's Collier House Restaurant (Marco
    Island), 306
Marina Cafe (Destin), 13, 474
Mark Martin's Klassix Auto Museum
    (Daytona Beach Mainland), 420–421
Marquesa Hotel (Key West), 13, 173–174
Marriot Bay Beach Resort (Key
    Largo), 155
Marriott Bay Point Resort Village
    (Panama City Beach), 472
Marriott's Golf Club (Marco Island), 310
Martha's on the Intracoastal
    (Hollywood), 210–211
MasterCard, 85, 86
Mature Outlook, 45
The Mature Traveler, 45
McGuire's Irish Pub (Pensacola), 463
McK's Dublin Station (Daytona
    Beach), 417
Mel Fisher Maritime Heritage Museum
    (Key West), 177–178
Melreese International Links
    (Miami), 138
Mel's Hot Dogs (Tampa), 246
Mezzanotte (Miami), 128
Miami
  accommodations, 107–119
  airports, 100
  arrival in, 99–101
  Art-Deco Cycling Tour, 140
  attractions, 129–139
  bars, 144
  bike tours, 140
  Biltmore Hotel Tour, 140
  bus tours, 140
  clubs, 144–145
  Coconut Grove Chamber of Commerce,
    148
  Coral Gables Chamber of Commerce,
    148
  cultural attractions, 145–146
  described, 18, 99
  Downtown, 103, 142
  driving in, 106
  facts on, 146–147
  fishing, 139

Florida Charter Captains, 139
Florida Charter Fishing Guide, 139
Florida Marlins, 138
Florida Panthers, 138
4-day itinerary, 141
gambling, 139
golf, 136–138
guided tours, 140
itineraries, sightseeing, 140–141
neighborhoods, 102–105
nightlife, 143–145
orientation, 101–102
restaurants, 119–128
shopping, 141–143
sightseeing itineraries, 140–141
sports, professional, 138–139
temperatures, chart of average, 24
3-day itinerary, 141
trains, 107
walking tours, 140
Miami Beach, 105
Miami Beach Rod & Reel Club, 139
Miami Chamber Symphony, 145
Miami City Ballet, 146
Miami Design Preservation League,
    105–106, 140
Miami Dolphins, 138
Miami Heat, 139
Miami International Airport, 100, 202
Miami International Boat Show, 29
Miami Jai Alai Fronton, 139
Miami MetroZoo, 13, 133
Miami Museum of Science & Space
    Transit Planetarium, 133
Miami Nice Excursions, 140
Miami Seaquarium, 133
Miccosukee Indian Village & Airboat
    Tours (Miami), 136
Michael's on East (Sarasota), 294
Mickey's Toontown Fair (Magic
    Kingdom), 354
Mickey's Very Merry Christmas Party
    (Walt Disney World), 33
Mile Marker system, 152
Ming Court (International Drive), 345
minibar charges, 40–41
Minnesota Twins, spring training, 309
Miracle Strip Amusement Park (Panama
    City Beach), 477
Molly Malone's (Miami), 144
Moment's Notice, 61

money
American Express, 85, 86
ATMs, 84–85, 86
cash, carrying, 83
credit cards, 84
crime prevention, 85–86
MasterCard, 85, 86
payment options, 83–85
safes, hotel, 86
theft, what to do after a, 86
traveler's checks, 85, 86
Visa, 85, 86
Monkey Jungle (Miami), 134
Monterey Inn (St. Augustine), 432
Monte's Restaurant & Fish Market
(Summerland Key), 169
Montreal Expos, spring training, 227
Montreal Inn Motel (Hollywood), 208
Monty's Stone Crab & Seafood House
(Miami), 12, 124
The Moon Under Water
(St. Petersburg), 269
Morgan's Forest (Sanibel), 307
Morikami Museum and Japanese
Gardens (Delray Beach), 226
Moss Rehab Hospital, 47
motels, 77
Mote Marine Laboratory (Longboat
Key), 295
mullet, 489
Murphy's Law Irish Pub (Miami), 144
Mutineer Restaurant (Everglades), 191
My Martini Grille (West Palm Beach),
223–224

New World Symphony (Miami), 145
New York, New York (Clearwater), 282
New York Yankees, spring training, 254
nightlife
budget, 38–39
Clearwater, 282
Daytona Beach, 424
Downtown Disney West Side, 397–398
Fort Lauderdale, 215–216
Fort Myers, Sanibel, and Naples, 312
Islamorada, 162–163
Jacksonville, 453
Key Largo, 158
Key West, 181–182
Miami, 143–145
Orlando, 396–400
Palm Beach County, 229–230
Panama City, Fort Walton Beach,
Destin, and Seaside, 478–479
Pensacola, 467–468
St. Augustine, 440
St. Petersburg, 272–273
Tampa, 256–257
Universal Orlando, 398–399
Walt Disney World, 396–398
Night of Joy (Walt Disney World), 32
1900 Park Fare (Disney's Grand Floridian
Beach Resort), 347
No Anchovies Pastaria (Palm Beach
Gardens), 225
non–ocean view rooms, 80
Norman's (Coral Gables), 12, 124–125
North Miami Beach, 105
No Wake Charters (Key West), 179

• N •

Naples. *See* Fort Myers, Sanibel, and
Naples
Naples Beach Hotel & Golf Club
(Naples), 303
naps, 43
National Council of Senior Citizens, 45
National Key Deer Refuge (Big Pine Key),
170
National Museum of Naval Aviation
(Pensacola), 465
Nellie & Joe's (Key West), 181
New Smyrna Beach, 410
newspapers/magazines, 492
New World Landing (Pensacola), 461

• O •

Oar House Restaurant (Everglades), 191
O.C. Whites Seafood & Spirits
(St. Augustine), 436
Ocean Deck (Daytona Beach), 418
oceanfront rooms, 79
ocean-view rooms, 79
Ocean Villa Motel (Daytona Beach), 413
Odysseus, 48
Off-Center Theater (Tampa), 257
official state welcome centers, 497
off-season travel, 41
Olde Naples, 308–309, 311
Oldest Wooden Schoolhouse (St.
Augustine), 437

Old Hyde Park Village (Tampa), 256
Old Naples Inn & Suites (Naples), 304
Old Salty's Inn (Daytona Beach
    Shores), 414
Old Town Trolley (Key West), 178
Omni Colonnade Hotel (Miami), 115
1-800-FLY-CHEAP, 61
One Saloon (Key West), 182
online, booking trip, 61–63
online reservation services, 80–82
Ophelia's on the Bay (Siesta Key), 294
Orlando
    accommodations, 326–339
    arrival in, 319–321
    attractions, 386–393
    Cypress Gardens, side trip to, 401–402
    described, 19–20
    Disney transportation system, 324
    Downtown Orlando, 323
    driving in, 324
    facts on, 403–404
    John F. Kennedy Space Center,
        side trip to, 400–401
    mileage to, 64
    nightlife, 396–400
    orientation, 322–323
    restaurants, 339–348
    sample costs for, 39
    shopping, 393–396
    shuttles, 326
    temperatures, chart of average, 25
    travel within, 324–326
    trolleys, 326
Orlando International Airport, 320–321
Orlando International Fringe Festival, 30
Orlando Science Center (North of
    Orlando), 390
Orlando Visitors Center, 323
Ormond Beach, 410
Osborne Family Christmas Lights (Walt
    Disney World), 34
Out and About, 48
Ovo Cafe (Tampa), 246

• P •

Pacific Time (Miami), 125
Pacino's Italian Ristorante
    (Kissimmee), 344

package tours
    airline packages, 58
    American Express Vacations, 58
    budget, 41–42
    buying, 55–56
    choosing, 56
    comparing, 55
    Continental Airlines Vacations, 58
    Delta Dream Vacations, 58
    desribed, 55
    finding, 57–59
    Globus, 59
    golf theme, 58
    Liberty Travel, 58
    options, 55–56
    price, what is included in, 55
    researching, 55
    SeaWorld, 57
    SunStyle, 59
    Tauck Tours, 59
    Touraine Travel, 59
    Universal Studios, 57
    Walt Disney World, 57
packing
    bug repellent, 94
    carry-on luggage, 93
    described, 91–92
    essentials, 92
    sun tan lotion, 94
    tips for, 92–94
Palm Beach, 18
Palm Beach accommodations, 221
Palm Beach County
    accommodations, 219–223
    arrival in, 218
    attractions, 225–228
    baseball and spring training, 227
    beaches, 227
    cars, 219
    diving, 227
    fishing, 228
    golf, 228
    guided tours, 228
    itinerary, sightseeing, 230
    map of, 220
    nightlife, 229–230
    polo, 228
    restaurants, 223–225
    shopping, 228–229
    trains, 219

Palm Beach County Cultural Council, 229
Palm Beach Hawaiian Ocean Inn, 222
Palm Beach International Airport, 218
Palm Beach Opera, 229
Palm Beach Zoo at Dreher Park (West
    Palm Beach), 226
Panama City, Fort Walton Beach, Destin,
    and Seaside
  accommodations, 469–472
  amusement parks, 477
  arrival in, 468–469
  attractions, 475–478
  beaches, 477
  facts on, 479–480
  fishing, 478
  golf, 478
  itinerary, sightseeing, 479
  nightlife, 478–479
  restaurants, 472–475
  shopping, 478
  temperatures, chart of average, 25
  travel within, 469
Panama City-Bay County International
    Airport, 468–469
Pandora's Steakhouse (Fort Walton
    Beach), 475
The Panhandle, 21, 455–457
Park Inn & Suites (Bradenton), 292
Parrot Jungle and Gardens (Miami), 134
partial ocean-view rooms, 79–80
party, best places to, 15
Peabody Auditorium (Daytona
    Beach), 424
Peabody Orlando (International
    Drive), 13, 334
Peg Leg Pete's Oyster Bar (Pensacola
    Beach), 464
Pelican Cove Resort (Islamorada), 159
Pelican Man's Bird Sanctuary (Sarasota),
    296
Pensacola
  accommodations, 459–461
  arrival in, 457–459
  attractions, 464–467
  beaches, 466
  canoeing, 466
  described, 21
  fishing, 466–467
  golf, 467
  itinerary, sightseeing, 468
  nightlife, 467–468

restaurants, 462–464
  shopping, 467
  travel within, 459
Pensacola Grand Hotel, 461
Pensacola Regional Airport, 457
Peppers of Key West (Key West), 181
Perdido Key State Recreation Area (near
    Pensacola), 486
pets, traveling with, 94–95
PGA National Resort & Spa (Palm Beach
    Gardens), 222, 228
Philadelphia Phillies, spring training, 281
Philharmonic Center for the Arts
    (Naples), 312
phone calls from hotel rooms, 40
Pier Top Lounge (Fort Lauderdale),
    215–216
Pittsburgh Pirates, spring training, 297
Places to Stay, 81
*Planning Guide for Travelers with
    Disability,* 46
Plantation Manor Inn (Jacksonville), 446
Pleasure Island (Walt Disney World), 15,
    396–397
police, 493
Polly Esther's (Boca Raton), 230
Polynesian Luau Dinner Show (Disney's
    Polynesian Resort), 348
Ponce Inlet Lighthouse and Museum
    (Ponce Inlet), 421
Portofino Bay Resort (International
    Drive), 334

Qixo, 62
The Quay (Key Largo), 156
The Quay Marathon (Marathon), 165

Race Rock (International Drive), 345
rack rates, 75
Radisson Deauville Resort (Miami), 115
Radisson Resort Daytona Beach
    (Daytona Beach), 414
Radisson Riverwalk Hotel (Tampa), 243
Radisson Suite Resort on Sand Key
    (Clearwater), 277

rain, 27
Rainbow House (Key West), 182
Rainforest Cafe (Downtown Disney
    Marketplace and Animal Kingdom),
    345
Raymond F. Kravis Center for the
    Performing Arts (West Palm
    Beach), 229
Redneck Riviera, 21. *See also* Panama
    City, Fort Walton Beach, Destin, and
    Seaside
red tide, 262
Renaissance Vinoy Resort
    (St. Petersburg), 13, 267
renovations in hotels, 80
reservations, arriving without, 82
Resort at Longboat Key Club (Longboat
    Key), 293
resorts, 77. *See also* accommodations
restaurants
    best, list of, 12–13
    budget, 37
    Clearwater, 277–279
    Daytona Beach, 416–418
    Everglades, 190–191
    Fort Lauderdale, 209–211
    Fort Myers, Sanibel, and Naples,
        305–307
    in hotels, 80
    Islamorada, 160–161
    Jacksonville, 446–449
    Key Largo, 155–156
    Key West, 174–176
    Lower Keys, 168–169
    Marathon, 164–165
    Miami, 119–128
    Orlando, 339–348
    Palm Beach County, 223–225
    Panama City, Fort Walton Beach,
        Destin, and Seaside, 472–475
    Pensacola, 462–464
    Sarasota and Bradenton, 293–295
    St. Augustine, 433–436
    St. Petersburg, 268–270
    Tampa, 244–247
    Walt Disney World, 339–348
restrooms, 493
Riande Continental Bayside (Miami), 117
Richard Petty Driving Experience (Walt
    Disney World Speedway), 388
Ringling Museums (Sarasota), 296
Ringside Cafe (St. Petersburg), 273

Ritz Carlton (Amelia Island), 446
River Country (near Magic
    Kingdom), 388
Riverfront Cruises (Fort Lauderdale), 214
River Rock Cafe (Fort Lauderdale), 216
Riviera Court Motel (Miami), 117
Robbie's Pier (Islamorada), 161
Rock 'n Roller Coaster (Walt Disney
    World), 14
rollercoasters (best), 14
Romano's Macaroni Grill (Tampa), 246
romantic hideaways (best), 13
Ron Jon Resort Ormond Beach/
    Plantations Cove (Ormond
    Beach), 414
room rates, 36–37, 75–77
Rose Bar at the Delano (Miami), 144
Rosemary Beach Cottages (Rosemary
    Beach), 471
Royal Palm Visitor Center (Everglades
    National Park), 193
rules for children to follow, 43
The Rusty Pelican (Miami), 128
Ruth Eckerd Hall (Clearwater), 282

• *S* •

Sabal Palm Inn B & B (Jacksonville
    Beach), 446
Saddlebrook Resort (Tampa), 243
safes, hotel, 86
safety, 43, 493
Safety Harbor Resort & Spa (Safety
    Harbor), 276
sales tax, 40
Salt Rock Grill (Indian Shores), 278
Saltwater Angler (Key West), 181
Salt Water Cowboy's (St. Augustine
    Beach), 436
Salvador Dali Museum (St. Petersburg),
    271
Samba Room (Fort Lauderdale), 211
sand, irritation from, 262
Sandestin Golf and Beach Resort
    (Destin), 471
Sandpiper Gulf Resort (Fort Myers
    Beach), 305
Sanibel. *See* Fort Myers, Sanibel,
    and Naples
Sanibel Inn (Sanibel), 13, 304

Sarasota and Bradenton
  accommodations, 291–293
  arrival in, 288–289
  attractions, 295–298
  baseball and spring training, 297
  beaches, 297
  described, 19, 288
  driving in, 289
  fishing, 297
  gardens, 297
  golf, 297–298
  itinerary, sightseeing, 299
  map of, 290
  restaurants, 293–295
  shopping, 298
  travel within, 289–290
Sarasota Ballet, 299
Sarasota-Bradenton International
  Airport, 288–289
Sarasota Jungle Gardens, 296
Sarasota Medieval Fair, 29
Sawgrass Marriott Resort (Ponte Vedra
  Beach), 445
Sawgrass Mills (Fort Lauderdale), 215
Schooner Motel (Madeira Beach), 268
Science and Industry, Museum of
  (Tampa), 252–253
The Screaming Coyote (Pensacola), 463
seafood, 490
Seafood & Sunsets at Julie's (Clearwater
  Beach), 12, 278
Seahorse Oceanfront Inn (Neptune
  Beach), 445
Seaplanes of Key West (Key West), 179
Sea Raven Dive Boat (Islamorada), 162
Sears Discount Travel Club, 61
Seaside, 13, 478. *See also* Panama City,
  Fort Walton Beach, Destin, and
  Seaside
Seaside Cottages (Seaside), 471–472
Seaside Music Theater (Daytona
  Beach), 424
seasons, 21–24
Sea Turtle Inn (Atlantic Beach), 445–446
SeaWorld, 37, 57, 380–383
Selby Botanical Gardens (Sarasota), 297
senior travelers
  AARP, 45
  airfare coupons, 46
  Amtrak, 46
  Choice Hotels group, 46

Hilton Senior Honors Program, 46
Mature Outlook, 45
The Mature Traveler, 45
National Council of Senior Citizens, 45
Seven-Mile Bridge (Marathon), 166
Shark's Tooth & Seafood Festival
  (Venice), 32
Shark Valley Tram Tours (Everglades
  National Park), 197
Shark Valley Visitor Center (Everglades
  National Park), 193
Sharon Wells' Biking & Walking Guide to
  Key West, 178
Sheldon's Drugs (Miami), 128
Sheraton Biscayne Bay Hotel
  (Miami), 117
Sheraton Sand Key Resort (Clearwater
  Beach), 276
Sheraton Suites Tampa Airport
  (Tampa), 244
Sheraton Yankee Clipper Resort (Fort
  Lauderdale), 208
Shipwreck Island Water Park (Panama
  City Beach), 477
shopping
  budget, 38
  Celebration, 394
  Clearwater, 281
  Coconut Grove, 142
  Coral Gables, 142
  Daytona Beach, 423
  Downtown Disney Marketplace, 394
  Downtown Disney West Side, 394
  Downtown Miami, 142
  Fort Lauderdale, 215
  Fort Myers, Sanibel, and Naples,
    311–312
  International Drive, 394
  Jacksonville, 452
  Key Largo, 158
  Kissimmee, 394
  Miami, 141–143
  Orlando, 393–396
  Palm Beach County, 228–229
  Panama City, Fort Walton Beach,
    Destin, and Seaside, 478
  Pensacola, 467
  Sarasota and Bradenton, 298
  South Beach, 142
  St. Augustine, 439–440
  St. Petersburg, 272

shopping *(continued)*
Tampa, 255–256
Walt Disney World, 393–396
Winter Park, 395
Shore Line All Suites Inn (Daytona Beach Shores), 415
Shula's Steak House (Miami), 128
Siam Orchid Restaurant (Sarasota), 294–295
SideBerns (Tampa), 247
Siesta Beach (Sarasota), 484–485
Silver Sands Beach Resort (Miami), 117
Silver Spurs Rodeo (Kissimmee), 29
Singleton's Seafood Shack (Mayport), 449
Sloppy Joe's (Key West), 181
Smart Traveler, 61
smoking, 80, 493
snacks, 43
Snappers Seafood & Pasta (Boynton Beach), 224
Snapper's Waterfront Saloon & Raw Bar (Key Largo), 158
Snook's Bayside (Key Largo), 156, 158
SouthBank Riverwalk (Jacksonville), 451–452
South Beach
described, 15, 105
map, 110
shopping, 142
South Beach Oceanfront Motel (Key West), 174
South Florida, 18–19
South Florida Museum, Bishop Planetarium, and Parker Manatee Aquarium (Bradenton), 297
South Florida Science Museum (West Palm Beach), 227
Southpoint Divers (Key West), 180
South Seas Resort (Captiva), 304
Southwest Airlines, 61
Southwest Florida International Airport (Everglades), 188, 300
souvenirs
budget, 42
Fort Myers, Sanibel, and Naples, 312
Key West, 181
Spanish Monastery Cloisters (Miami), 136
Spanish Quarter Village (St. Augustine), 438
Spanish River Park (Boca Raton), 227

Spartacus International Gay Guide, 48
sports, 138–139, 497
spring, visiting during, 22
Spring Break, 28
Spring Flower Festival (Cypress Gardens), 30
Spring Training (baseball), 29–30. *See also specific teams*
St. Armands Circle (St. Armands Key), 298
St. Augustine
accommodations, 431–433
arrival in, 430
attractions, 436–439
beaches, 438–439
described, 20, 427–428
fishing, 439
golf, 439
guided tours, 430, 439
itinerary, sightseeing, 440
map of, 429
nightlife, 440
restaurants, 433–436
shopping, 439–440
travel within, 430
St. Augustine Alligator Farm, 438
St. George Island State Park (Eastpoint), 486
St. Josephine Peninsula State Park (Port St. Joe), 486
St. Louis Cardinals, spring training, 227
St. Petersburg
accommodations, 265–268
arrival in, 264
attractions, 270–272
beaches, 262, 271
described, 19
driving in, 264–265
fishing, 271–272
guided tours, 272
map of, 263
nightlife, 272–273
parks, 272
restaurants, 268–270
shopping, 272
St. Petersburg-Clearwater International Airport, 236, 264
St. Petersburg Fall Boat Show, 33
Stan's Idle Hour Seafood Restaurant (Goodland), 15, 307, 312
Starlite Cruises (Clearwater Beach), 281

state forests, 497
state parks, 498
STA Travel, 61
stingrays, 261
stone crab claws, 490
Stranahan House (Fort Lauderdale),
212–213
Suez Ocean Front Resort (Miami), 119
Summer, visiting during, 22–23
Summerfield Suites (International
Drive), 336
Summit Plummet (Walt Disney World), 14
sun, effects of the, 26–27
sunburn, 26, 261
Suncoast, 262
Sunfest, 31
Sun 'N Fun Fly-In (Lakeland), 30
Sunny Days (Key West), 179
sun poisoning, 26, 261
sun prevention, 27
Sunset Celebration at Mallory Square
(Key West), 182
sunstroke, 26
SunStyle, 59
Sushi Blues Cafe (Hollywood), 211
Suwannee River Jam (Live Oak), 30
Sweetwater's (Clearwater), 279

• T •

Tallahassee, 21
Tampa
accommodations, 238–244
arrival in, 235, 236
attractions, 247–255
baseball, 254–255
cars, 238
described, 19, 235
facts on, 258–259
fishing, 255
football, 255
golf, 255
guided tours, 255
itineraries, sightseeing, 257–258
map of, 236–237, 248–249
neighborhoods, 237
nightlife, 256–257
orientation, 237
restaurants, 244–247
shopping, 255–256

temperatures, chart of average, 24
travel within, 237–238
Tampa Bay Buccaneers, 255
Tampa Bay Devil Rays, 271
Tampa Bay Performing Arts Center, 257
Tampa Bay Visitor Information Center,
237
Tampa/Hillsborough Convention &
Visitors Association, 237
Tampa International Airport, 236, 289
Tampa Museum of Art, 254
Tampa Theatre, 254
Tarpon Springs, 280
Tatum Ridge Golf Links (Sarasota), 297
Tauck Tours, 59
taxes, 77, 493
Teddy Bear Museum (Naples), 309
Ted Peters' Famous Smoked Fish (South
Pasadena), 12, 269
Tee Times USA, 91
temperatures, chart of average, 24–25
Testa's (Palm Beach), 12, 224
Texas Rangers, spring training, 309
TFI Tours International, 61
Theatre of the Sea (Islamorada), 162
theft, what to do after a, 86
The Guided Tour, Inc., 47
32 East (Delray Beach), 224
Thunderbird Beach Resort (Treasure
Island), 268
time zone, 493
tipping, 41
Tiramesu (Miami), 125
toiletries to bring during flight, 63
Tomorrowland (Magic Kingdom),
352–354
Toni's Sushi Bar/Japanese Restaurant
(Miami), 128
Top of Daytona Oceanfront Restaurant
and Lounge (Daytona Beach), 418
tornadoes, 26
Toronto Blue Jays, spring training, 281
Touraine Travel, 59
tourist assistance, 498
Tradewinds Sandpiper Hotel and Suites
(St. Pete Beach), 267
train travel to Florida
Amtrak, 64
Auto Train, 64–65
discounts, 65
train travel within Florida, 72–73

travel agents
  accommodations, 80
  deciding to use, 53
  homework to do before using, 54
Travel Avenue, 61
Travel Bargains, 61
travel clubs, 61
Travel Dog, 95
traveler's checks, 85, 86
travel insurance
  Access America, 88
  with credit cards, 88
  described, 87
  issuers, 88
  lost luggage insurance, 88
  medical insurance, 88
  Travelex Insurance Services, 88
  Travel Guard International, 88
  Travel Insured International, Inc., 88
  trip cancellation insurance, 87–88
TravelWeb, 82
travel within Florida
  airlines, 71
  airports, 72
  Amtrak, 73
  bus travel, 73
  Cape Air, 71
  driving in Florida, 67–71
  flying in Florida, 71–72
  Greyhound, 73
  train travel, 72–73
Triangle, 48
Turnberry Isle Resort & Club (Miami),
    115–116, 138
Turtle Kraals (Key West), 176
Twilight Zone Tower of Terror (Walt
    Disney World), 14
Typhoon Lagoon (near Downtown
    Disney), 389

nightlife, 398–399
  Universal Studios Florida, 372–376
Universal Studios Florida
  described, 14, 57, 372
  Hollywood, 372
  New York, 373
  Production Central, 373–374
  San Francisco, 374
  Woody Woodpecker's KidZone, 374–375
  World Expo, 375–376
U.S. Air Force Armament Museum (Fort
    Walton Beach), 477

• V •

vacation rentals, 78
Van Dyke Cafe & Upstairs
    at the Van Dyke (Miami), 128
Van Wezel Performing Arts Center
    (Sarasota), 299
Venetian Pool (Miami), 136
Venny's Italian Restaurant
    (Jacksonville), 449
Victorian Seaside Christmas (Amelia
    Island), 34
views, not staying in rooms with, 42
views, room, 79–80
The Villa Bed & Breakfast (Daytona
    Beach), 414–415
Villa Vizcaya Museum & Gardens
    (Miami), 134–135
Visa, 85, 86
Visit Florida, 82
Vistana Resort at World Golf Village
    (St. Augustine), 432
Viva (Captiva), 306

• W •

Walt Disney World
  accommodations, 326–339
  Animal Kingdom, 367–371
  attractions, 386–389
  baseball and spring training, 393
  character dining, 345–347
  cost of, 37
  described, 57, 322, 349–351
  dinner shows, 347–348

UFOs (Gulf Breeze), 465
Underwater Music Festival (Big Pine
    Key), 32
Universal Orlando
  cost of, 37
  described, 371–372
  Islands of Adventure, 376–383

• U •